1979
Yearbook of Science and the Future

1979 Yearbook of Science and the Future

Encyclopædia
Britannica, Inc.

Chicago Toronto London
Geneva Sydney Tokyo
Manila Seoul

THE UNIVERSITY OF CHICAGO
The Yearbook of Science and the Future
is published with the editorial advice of the faculties of
the University of Chicago.

 # Yearbook of Science and the Future

EDITOR-IN-CHIEF, YEARBOOKS
James Ertel

EDITOR
David Calhoun

EDITORIAL CONSULTANT
Howard J. Lewis, Director, Office of Information,
National Academy of Sciences—National Academy
of Engineering—National Research Council

EDITORIAL STAFF
Charles Cegielski, Daphne Daume, Karen Justin,
Arthur Latham

ART DIRECTOR
Cynthia Peterson

DESIGN SUPERVISOR
Ron Villani

PICTURE EDITOR
Julie A. Kunkler

PICTURE STAFF
Kathryn Creech, Holly Harrington

LAYOUT ARTIST
Richard Batchelor

ILLUSTRATOR
John L. Draves

ART PRODUCTION
Richard Heinke

CARTOGRAPHERS
Gerzilla Leszczynski, *supervisor;* William Karpa

ART STAFF
Paul Rios

COMPUTER TYPESETTING SERVICES
Robert Dehmer, *supervisor;* Ronald J. Laugeman,
Marie Lawrence, Arnell Reed, Melvin E. Stagner,
Gilberto Vaile, Elaine Yost

EDITORIAL PRODUCTION MANAGER
J. Thomas Beatty

PRODUCTION SUPERVISOR
Ruth Passin

PRODUCTION STAFF
Mary Peterson Berry, Kathryn Blatt, James Carnes,
Maria Dolores del Valle, Terry Geesken,
Cheryl A. Johnson, Juanita L. Murphy, John Park,
Julian Ronning, Harry Sharp, Melinda Shepherd,
James G. Stewart, Susan Tarcov, Joyce P. Walker,
Sylvia Wallace, Coleen Withgott

COPY CONTROL
Mary Srodon, *supervisor;* Mayme Cussen

INDEX
Frances E. Latham, *supervisor;* Mary Reynolds

LIBRARIAN
Terry Miller
Shantha Channabasappa, *assistant librarian*

SECRETARY
Ines Baptist

Editorial Administration

MANAGING EDITOR
ENCYCLOPÆDIA BRITANNICA, INC.
Margaret Sutton

DIRECTOR OF BUDGETS
Verne Pore

Contents

248

431

The New Museum of Flight

by Edwards Park

Opened in July 1976, the U.S. National Air
and Space Museum provides a showcase
for America's achievements in flight.

U.S. National Air and Space Museum (above) extends for three city blocks along the Independence Avenue side of the Mall between the U.S. Capitol (background) and the Washington Monument. Rockets (opposite page) are among the attractions in the museum's Space Hall.

EDWARDS PARK *is a member of the Board of Editors of* Smithsonian *magazine.*

Several of the world's greatest museums line the famous Mall in Washington, D.C., between the U.S. Capitol and the Washington Monument. They display achievements in arts and sciences, today and in the past, and they form the nucleus of the Smithsonian Institution. Largest and most spectacular of these is the National Air and Space Museum. Stretching for three city blocks along the Independence Avenue side of the Mall, it is a vast celebration of the U.S. involvement with flight.

This huge but relatively simple rectangle with its bays of tinted glass and pinkish marble is as modern as space science, yet conforms to the classical look of the nation's capital. Inside, one is struck by its openness. No columns or other obtrusive roof supports interrupt the expanse and soaring height of its three great exhibition halls, so that together they seem to have captured a sizable piece of the sky itself.

The great halls and the broad galleries that fringe them house the Smithsonian collection of air- and spacecraft, one that is probably unmatched in the world. It includes the Wright brothers' "Flyer I," the plane that carried man on his first heavier-than-air flight in 1903; Charles Lindbergh's "Spirit of St. Louis," the plane that crossed the Atlantic from New York to Paris in 1927; and the Apollo 11 spacecraft, the command module that took astronauts to the Moon in 1969. The collection ranges in age from Otto Lilien-

10

public dining room

offices

flight technology

Apollo to the Moon

World War I aviation

rocketry and space flight

space hall

theater

milestones of flight ⟶

offices

special exhibits

spacearium

life in the universe

balloons and airships

air transportation

library reading room

World War II aviation

sea-air operations

vertical flight

Cross section of the museum reveals the diversity of its exhibits and facilities.

Illustration by John Craig

thal's hang glider of 1894 to the latest satellites and space probes and in size from the Skylab Orbital Workshop to a record-breaking Frisbee.

Many of the exhibits hang from the ceiling and seem caught in mid-flight. This impression is enhanced by the use of glass. One can look up at, for example, the gleaming DC-3 transport and see, through the glass-bubbled roof 62 feet above, the clouds sweep by. Or one can look out toward the Mall and see grass, trees, and distant buildings. Thus the open environment of flight is maintained.

Origins

The Smithsonian's interest in flight can be said to date from 1861 when Joseph Henry, the institution's first secretary, discussed with aeronaut Thaddeus Lowe the feasibility of a transatlantic balloon flight. Secretary Henry, incidentally, voted firmly against it. Real involvement with flight started when Samuel Langley became secretary in 1887. Fascinated with manned, heavier-than-air devices, Langley built successful steam- and gasoline-powered models. He tested a full-size "aerodrome" in 1903, but it failed to fly. Nine days after his last attempt, the Wright brothers flew successfully at Kitty Hawk, North Carolina.

Langley sought a department of aeronautics for the institution. Gradually a collection of aircraft grew, but it lacked a place for shelter and display, making do with space in the old Arts and Industries Building. In 1946, however, a public law was passed by the U.S. Congress to "memorialize the national development of aviation; collect, preserve, and display aeronautical equipment of historical interest and significance; serve as a repository for scientific equipment and data pertaining to the development of aviation; and provide educational material for the historical study of aviation." The National Air and Space Museum is the result of that law.

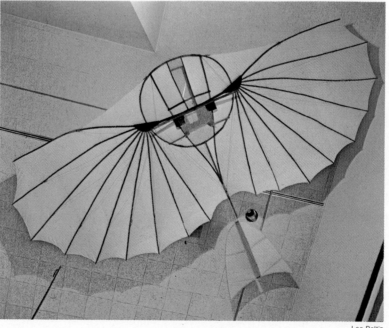

Glider built by Otto Lilienthal in 1894 (right) is in the Flight Testing gallery. It achieved flights as long as 375 feet at altitudes up to 50 feet. "Flyer I" (opposite page), with which Orville and Wilbur Wright made the first powered, sustained, and controlled airplane flight, hangs in the Milestones of Flight hall.

Structural design and engineering

The building opened on July 1, 1976, three days ahead of schedule and some half a million dollars under its $42 million appropriation. It had taken four years to build, and its design won an award for architect Gyo Obata of Hellmuth, Obata and Kassabaum. During the last few months before its completion, the Smithsonian's treasure trove of historic aircraft was gently lowered from positions under the roof of the Arts and Industries Building and carefully "serviced" and cleaned. The planes were then eased through a removable glass wall at the west end of the new structure, and hoisted to renewed prominence.

The seemingly unsupported ceiling takes the weight of hanging planes and spacecraft because of a grid of tubular steel trusses, triangular in section, which span the great halls between pylons of similar construction. This engineering device was adapted, fittingly enough, from a technique used in aircraft construction. Many loads, then, can be hung high up, under the ceiling, yet the open effect of the glass roof remains unimpaired. The heaviest load is the DC-3 of Eastern Air Lines' "Great Silver Fleet" of the 1930s, about eight tons.

Dominated by a DC-3 from Eastern Air Lines' "Great Silver Fleet" of the 1930s suspended from its ceiling, the Air Transportation hall (following pages) also contains many other types of transport planes.

Alex Webb—Magnum

Milestones of Flight

The main entrance to the museum is from the Mall. Visitors enter through the glass wall of the central hall, called Milestones of Flight, and immediately face the Wright "Flyer I" apparently soaring straight at them some 12 feet off the carpeted floor—about the same height that it achieved on that momentous December day in 1903. Well above it and to the right, Lindbergh's "Spirit of St. Louis" looks much the way it must have appeared on a May evening in 1927 as it flared out for its landing at Le Bourget Field, Paris. And close under the tail of the Wright plane stands the Apollo 11 spacecraft, its blunt end discolored by the blazing heat of reentry after its flight to the Moon in July 1969. The close juxtaposition of these three craft, each marking an extraordinary human plateau, is of course quite deliberate, for it dramatizes the rapid progress of manned flight after centuries of dreaming.

The Milestones of Flight include other epochal craft. Visitors can inspect the capsules of Alan Shepard, first American in space, and of John Glenn, first American in orbit. Looking up, they can see the orange X-1 "Glamorous Glennis," first plane to fly faster than the speed of sound, and the X-15, which flew more than six times the speed of sound and provided an experimental "bridge" between atmospheric and space flight. One of Langley's steam-powered models hangs beside a backup Mariner 2 spacecraft (the

FIRST EARTH SATELLITES

THE RYAN NYP SPIRIT OF ST. LOUIS

This airplane was flown by Charles A. Lindbergh on the first solo, nonstop, transatlantic flight in history, May 20-21, 1927. The flight covered 5058 kilometers (3610 miles) between New York and Paris in 33 hours, 30 minutes. A fuel tank made it impossible for Lindbergh to see forward except by using a periscope or by turning the airplane. He flew without a radio or a parachute and with only sandwiches for food. The two openings on the underside are for emergency flares.

original is in orbit around the Sun). The two small craft look strangely alike, both awkward and unstreamlined, yet are eons apart in sophistication. But they shared a common purpose. Both flew as unmanned probes, one of the Earth's atmosphere and the other of space, and both flew within a not unusually long human life span.

The rapid step from air to space was made possible in large part by the rocket experiments of Robert Goddard, a farsighted scientist who braved ridicule and worked on rocketry even before World War I. In March 1926, on a snowy meadow in Auburn, Massachusetts, Goddard touched off the combustion chamber of a simple little rocket that carried tanks of gasoline and liquid oxygen and mixed their vapors in a highly volatile gas. The primitive device rose slowly from its frame and shot up about 40 feet before arching over and returning to the ground. It was a small flight but mighty in its consequences, for it constituted the first use of a liquid propellant. The little rocket that made this vastly significant hop is memorialized in the Milestones of Flight by a full-scale model.

Air Transportation and Space halls

From the central hall one can move toward the west end of the building, and quickly become involved in Air Transportation. The DC-3 and its predecessor, the Ford Trimotor, dominate the hanging exhibits there because of their size, but other splendid old transports join the formation that seems to soar overhead. There is a Pitcairn Mailwing, designed to carry airmail in the late 1920s. Sacks were stowed forward of this biplane's open cockpit, where the pilot, goggled and scarfed, peered down at the railroad lines beneath to guide him from town to town. The Northrop Alpha, a gleaming monoplane, carried a handful of passengers inside, behind its single Pratt & Whitney engine, while its pilot braved the elements in an open cockpit aft of the cabin. The Alpha was all-metal with many features of modern construction, and performed well until supplanted by such newer transports as the Boeing 247.

Command module of Apollo 11, the first manned spacecraft to land on the Moon, is featured in the Milestones of Flight hall. It is joined there by "Glamorous Glennis" (opposite page, top), the first plane to fly faster than the speed of sound, and "Spirit of St. Louis," in which Charles Lindbergh in 1927 made the first solo, nonstop, transatlantic flight.

Grumman F8F "Bearcat," a World War II fighter plane, stands in the World War II Aviation gallery.

The latter introduced retractable landing gear for added speed, a soundproof cabin for greater comfort, and two engines for greater safety.

The other great hall, east of the Milestones of Flight, is Space Hall. There the exhibits are so large that many visitors take the escalator to the balcony to gain a better perspective. Four rockets—Jupiter C, Vanguard, Minuteman, and Scout—rise from a 15-foot pit that was sunk in the floor of the hall to allow them to fit under the roof. These historic devices mark steps into space made by the U.S. Large as they are, they would be dwarfed by the Saturn V rocket that was used for the Apollo moonshots. The building would have to be four or five times higher in order to accommodate it. Small World War II rockets, hanging near the edge of the balcony, as well as Goddard's little device in the Milestones of Flight show the progression of rocketry.

The museum's largest object stands in Space Hall: the Skylab Orbital Workshop with one of its rectangular solar panels, which holds about 150,-000 solar cells, extending outward from it. The Skylab is a huge cylinder through which visitors can walk, circling its inside core past workrooms where astronauts lived while in orbit.

Another huge exhibit is the Apollo-Soyuz linkup. An Apollo and a Soviet Soyuz spacecraft are displayed joined as they were while in orbit in 1975 when U.S. and Soviet astronauts met in space. These, of course, are backup models of the original spacecraft, but are identical to them.

An experimental lifting body also hangs in Space Hall. It was one of the test craft that resulted finally in the development of the space shuttle. This one, the M2-F3, is simply a flattened, delta-shaped fuselage designed to maneuver in space and then reenter the atmosphere and glide to a landing. This particular test vehicle cracked up on one landing, and the film of it breaking up was used in the opening sequence of the television show "The Six Million Dollar Man." Unlike the fictional pilot, who was made into a "bionic man," the actual test pilot suffered only minor injuries. The plane, moreover, was rebuilt from its wreckage, modified, and, after serving its purpose, was donated to the Smithsonian.

M2-F3 lifting body, a test vehicle used in the development of the space shuttle, cracked up during one landing. Film of the accident was used in the opening sequence of the television series "The Six Million Dollar Man." The rebuilt craft is displayed in Space Hall.

21

Displays in Space Hall include Gemini 4 (above), from which Edward White II in 1965 made the first space walk by a U.S. astronaut, and the linkup of the Soviet Soyuz (left) and U.S. Apollo (right), achieved in 1975.

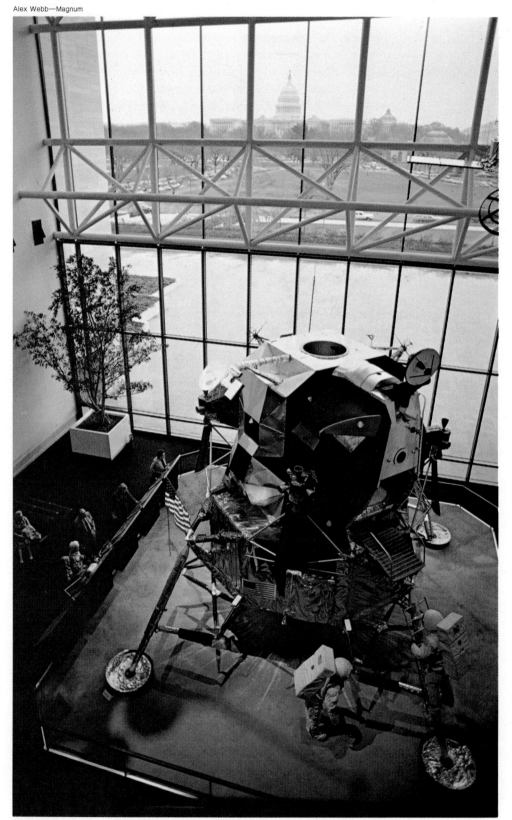

*Apollo landing module, a backup to those that actually landed on the Moon,
dominates the museum's East Gallery.*

Special galleries

The ends of the museum contain exhibits that may be changed after periods of display. But it seems doubtful that the dominating feature of the East Gallery, lit by the glass wall that faces the Capitol, will ever be replaced. For this awkward looking device, partially wrapped in gold foil and standing on angular legs like some huge insect, is an Apollo landing module—a backup to those that have deposited a number of U.S. astronauts on the Moon's surface. (In the case of an actual landing module, the legs were left behind when the vehicle blasted off the Moon to return to the orbiting spacecraft.) The West Gallery of the museum does undergo periodic change. Generally, its exhibits are keyed to aeronautics, since that is the theme of most of the galleries around it.

The remaining galleries are dedicated to particular aspects of flight. On the ground floor, the Exhibition Flight gallery evokes barnstorming days with displays of acrobatic planes and films of the daredevil stunts at county fairs when the Curtiss "Jenny," originally designed to train World War I pilots, came into its own as the ticket to a livelihood for hundreds of unneeded fliers. A small film theater shows spectacular acrobatic footage, including a flight with the famed U.S. Navy team the Blue Angels.

The adjacent gallery, Life in the Universe, is devoted to a sophisticated look at space and all that it may mean to us in the future. The old question of extraterrestrial life is examined and subjected to theoretical answers through imaginative and thoughtful films and devices.

World War I Aviation gallery depicts a U.S. airstrip near Verdun, France. A French SPAD VII flies overhead in a victory roll to celebrate the capture of the German Fokker D.VII at the lower right.

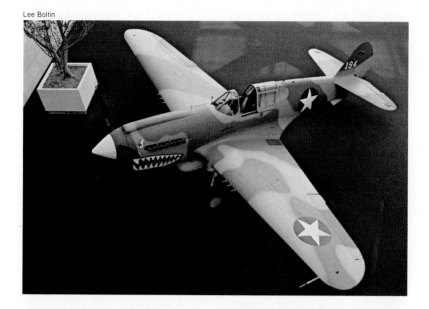

General Aviation, covering the broad field of private flying, occupies a corner gallery. Hanging there are familiar light planes and sailplanes that offer aviation to everyone. One of the old dreams of the private flier, the car that turns into an aircraft and soars over congested traffic, is recalled across the West Gallery in the Vertical Flight gallery. Displayed there are autogiros and helicopters that range downward in size from large transport models to the Pentecost Hoppicopter, which was designed to be strapped on the shoulders of a paratrooper. A couple of the "car-to-aircraft" machines are displayed, but neither of them achieved much success despite the dreams of their inventors.

The Flight Testing gallery contains "Winnie Mae," the Lockheed Vega in which Wiley Post set a transcontinental record, flew around the world solo, and tested altitude flying. He wore a self-designed "space suit" with a cylindrical helmet, the progenitor of today's space equipment. A figure representing Post, laced up and helmeted, sits beside his plane. On the ground floor, too, are galleries of rocketry in 13th-century China and 19th-century Britain and of satellites that hang from the ceiling in a galaxy.

Upstairs, military and naval aviation are spectacularly described in three halls. One, devoted to World War I, takes a moment at the Western Front, when a German Fokker D.VII landed either by accident or as a means of surrender, at a U.S. air base near Verdun just before the Armistice in 1918. This true incident is dramatized by speaking voices and sound effects, and the actual German plane, beautifully restored, perches in front of a shell-shattered ready room while two French SPAD's hang overhead, one inverted as though in the midst of a victory roll.

The World War II gallery contains a fine collection of fighters from all parts of the world, including the only remaining Italian Macchi, and features a mural of an actual attack on a B-17 formation over Germany. World War II action in the Pacific is strikingly portrayed as from the bridge of an aircraft carrier in the Sea-Air Operations exhibit. This entire gallery re-creates the below-decks and bridge area on the carrier "CVM-76."

U.S. "Flying Tiger" fighter plane is displayed in the World War II Aviation gallery.

25

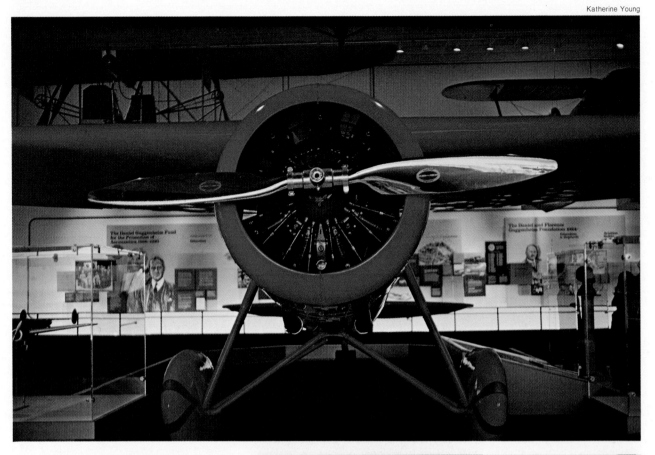

Plane used by Amelia Earhart during her solo transatlantic flight in 1932 (above) is in museum area devoted to air traffic control. In the Flight Testing gallery a figure representing Wiley Post (right), wearing a self-designed "space suit," sits in front of the "Winnie Mae," the Lockheed Vega in which Post set a transcontinental speed record and flew solo around the world in the 1930s.

Model of the balloon in which the Montgolfier brothers rose above the Paris rooftops in 1783 hangs in the balloon gallery.

Model of German dirigible "Hindenburg," which crashed in 1937, hangs in the gallery devoted to balloons and airships.

Balloons, man's first aeronautical vehicles, are housed in a gallery that includes representations of that first fragile envelope of the Montgolfier brothers, which rose on hot air and hung above the rooftops of Paris in 1783. The gallery catches some of the elegance of the balloon age, when art and decor made full use of the new and exciting motif of flight with balloon-shaped lamps, vases, and other ornaments. There, too, are a table setting from the "Graf Zeppelin," one of Germany's luxury liners of the sky after World War I, and a model of the other great German dirigible, the "Hindenburg," which crashed in 1937 when its hydrogen exploded.

In the Apollo to the Moon gallery, the taped voices of U.S. astronauts Neil Armstrong and Edwin Aldrin, Jr., are heard as they bring the landing module within feet of the unknown lunar surface and then report, momentously, that "The 'Eagle' has landed." Also displayed is an electric-powered lunar roving vehicle of the kind used on three later Apollo missions.

The gallery of Flight Technology is perhaps the most revealing and entertaining of all the areas. There, with the help of films, sound tracks, self-manipulated exhibits, and especially a set of puppets who "age" as the visitor progresses, the whole story of flight unfolds, from the sea gull to a glimpse of what the future holds in space exploration. Aircraft design is revealed as a series of compromises between speed, range, capacity, purpose, and other factors. As the visitor learns this lesson, stage by stage, a central display, half-hidden by panels, yields glimpses of an exceptionally beautiful plane, seemingly a sort of ideal toward which designers can only strive. At last it is introduced to the viewer—Howard Hughes's H-1 racer. A wonder in its day (the mid-1930s), it set many speed records and its design features were reflected in such World War II fighters as the German Fw 190, the Japanese Zero, and the U.S. Navy's Grumman Hellcat.

Presentation areas

The museum contains two general presentation areas. One is a theater with a screen, some four stories high, built for extra-large film so that viewers become enveloped in their visual experience. The other is the Albert Einstein Spacearium, where a West German planetarium instrument projects space programs on the dome overhead. The instrument was a Bicentennial gift from West Germany to the people of the United States.

The South Lobby, off the Independence Avenue entrance, is walled by two murals, one by Robert McCall depicting space exploration and the other by Eric Sloane titled "Earth Flight Environment." Above the South Lobby, on the second floor, is a gallery used for short-term displays.

Acquisition of exhibits

Acquisition is made easy by the prestige of the Smithsonian Institution and the superb use to which the museum puts its exhibits. It was not always so. The Wright plane took a long time to acquire. After the Wright brothers were through with it, they donated it to the Massachusetts Institute of Technology in 1916. In 1928 it went to the South Kensington Science Museum in London, where it was sheltered in a subway during World War II. In 1948 negotiations were completed to bring it back to the U.S., and it arrived, with

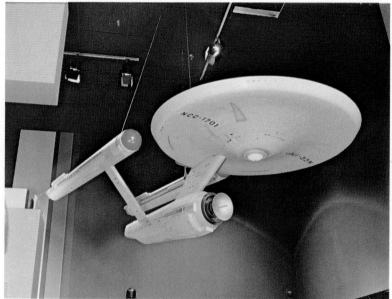

the help of the Navy, in time to be accepted by the institution on December 17, the 45th anniversary of its first flight at Kitty Hawk.

Most famous pilots have arranged to have their notable aircraft sent to the Smithsonian because they realize that millions of people will be able to see a carefully preserved and presented exhibit. Charles Lindbergh took the "Spirit of St. Louis" on a tour of Latin America at the end of 1927, acquiring, on the engine cowling, the flags of countries he visited. On April 30, 1928, just under a year after his flight to Paris, Lindbergh flew the plane from St. Louis to Washington and presented it to the Smithsonian. Those flags remain on the cowling.

As the years passed, Lindbergh occasionally visited the Arts and Industries Building, where the plane hung. One evening after closing time he asked for a ladder—and permission to climb inside. Both were granted, and the flier sat quietly in his old cockpit, checking the pencil marks he had made on the gasoline gauge to show fuel consumption during his famous flight. The marks have never been removed.

Facilities for visitors

The museum welcomed its millionth visitor less than a month after its opening, its second millionth 25 days after that, and continued at that pace during the Bicentennial year. There is basement parking for 500 cars, a museum shop on the ground floor, a cafeteria on the third floor, and facilities for the handicapped. Researchers have at their disposal a library containing more than 20,000 volumes, half a million microfilmed reports, and some 600,000 photographs and drawings. A rare book room is available for qualified scholars. Admission to the National Air and Space Museum, like that to other museums under the Smithsonian aegis, is free.

Displayed in the Life in the Universe gallery is the spaceship model "Enterprise" used in the "Star Trek" television series.

Bias in Scientific Research
by Ian St. James-Roberts

Intentional bias is a common feature of scientific research. The danger is that fallacious results of such studies might be inflicted on the public.

IAN ST. JAMES-ROBERTS is Lecturer in Psychology at the University of London Institute of Education.

In his studies of twins Sir Cyril Burt faked his research findings by falsifying some of his data.

On Oct. 24, 1976, *The Sunday Times* of London published dramatic allegations that Sir Cyril Burt (1883–1971), considered by many the father of British psychology, had faked some of his research findings. The importance of the allegations derived not only from the preeminence of Burt's reputation but also from the wide application of his research in British educational practice; both the adoption of grouping for ability in schools by the 1944 Education Act and the 1929 Wood Report's sexual segregation of mental retardates were based on Burt's finding that intellectual capacity is largely inherited. Thus, the case illustrated the existence of a real danger that the consequences of biased research could be inflicted on society. The exposé also had two other results. First, it emphasized how difficult the demonstration of deliberate malpractice is; the ensuing debate in *The Times* and elsewhere was sharply divided according to whether Burt's misrepresentation was regarded as deliberate or unintentional. Second, the case clearly demonstrated the impossibility of rational discussion of such issues. In mid-1977 the *Bulletin* of the British Psychological Society was still receiving vitriolic and often abusive letters from members of factions both critical and supportive of Burt's position.

30

The mysterious N-ray, supposedly discovered by René Blondlot, was believed to be able to penetrate metals.

Paintings by Warren Linn

Intentional and unintentional bias

By way of coincidence, the Burt disclosure came at a time when an attempt to quantify the extent and importance of bias in scientific research was already underway. On Sept. 2, 1976, *New Scientist* had published an article arguing that what could be called "intentional bias" in research required investigation. The argument was based on the premise that the inducements to deliberately bias research were considerable, whereas the constraints operating to detect or punish miscreants were paltry. Perhaps more important, the article proposed that science's uncritical attitude and the consequent lack of information on intentional bias in research were inimical to a discipline whose way of life is based on skepticism. The September 2 article was accompanied by a questionnaire which invited readers to provide information concerning their experiences of intentional bias. Analyses of the questionnaire replies, 204 of which were received, amply justified the view that intentional bias in science was more prevalent than many would allow.

Like beauty, intentional bias is in the eye of the beholder, or rather in this case the experimenter, since only he can know whether an "error" is intentional or unintentional. The subtlety of this distinction should not be underemphasized. One colleague, for example, communicated that when he had completed an analysis of results he sometimes had a "niggling feeling" that all was not well. It was his experience that if the result of the analysis contradicted his hypothesis, he would check it. If, however, the analysis confirmed his hypothesis, he found that, although never making a deliberate decision not to check, he didn't quite get around to doing it.

32

The subject of unintentional bias has received considerable attention in scientific literature, and the common use in research of control groups and double-blind procedures is one consequence of the realization of its importance. Perhaps the best-known example of bias presumed to be of this sort is the N-ray scandal of 1903. The case concerned a mysterious ray, analogous to the X-ray but with the considerable advantage of being able to penetrate metals. This ray, initially isolated by René Blondlot, was soon also identified by dozens of other respectable laboratories, and its characteristics and properties quickly became well known. In 1904, however, Robert W. Wood was able to demonstrate conclusively that the rays did not exist. Given the reputations of those concerned, it seems most likely that the rays were the result of unintentionally biased observation resulting from excessive experimental zeal. In any event, they provide a perfect example of the extent to which fashionability and expectation can overrule the effects of common sense and scientific training.

Science has undoubtedly made considerable progress in developing controls to minimize unintentional bias, and it seems unlikely that an N-ray-like affair could occur today. In the process, however, the idea of intentional bias has been more or less swept under the carpet and the thin and indistinct nature of the line separating the two has been ignored. In this context, it is worthwhile to examine in some detail the cause célèbre of scientific fraud—Paul Kammerer's experiments on the midwife toad—since it provides an excellent demonstration of how difficult absolute proof of deliberate deception can be.

33

The midwife toad

The case of the midwife toad (to borrow the title of Arthur Koestler's excellent book on the subject) concerns a species of toad that, unlike most others, normally mates on land. In the years up to 1909, Kammerer had managed to persuade several generations of the toad to mate instead in water. This was no mean feat—from both Kammerer's and the toad's point of view—and the technical difficulty of these breeding experiments may be one reason why they do not appear to have been repeated. The difficulty the toad faced was to remain attached, during the long time required for fertilization, to the slippery back of the female. In toads that habitually mate in water, this behavior is facilitated by the existence on the male's hands and feet of "nuptial pads," which assist in clinging. Kammerer's claim was that he had caused these nuptial pads to appear on the limbs of the land-mating toad after only a few generations of forced mating in water. The importance of such a finding would be that it would be contrary to orthodox Darwinism, favoring instead Jean-Baptiste de Lamarck's theory of inheritance. According to Darwinian theory, the effects of the environment can be incorporated into the genetic makeup of a species only indirectly, as a result of the "survival of the fittest" dictum. Kammerer's findings suggested that such effects had been incorporated directly into the genetic material and thereafter were passed on as an inherited characteristic to subsequent generations.

Kammerer's results were greeted with hostility because of their controversial nature. Initially, there was no consideration of fraud, Kammerer's reputation in general being excellent. Some years after the original work, however, the only laboratory specimen of midwife toad that Kammerer had preserved was found to have been tampered with: the nuptial pads were merely judiciously applied india ink. Kammerer subsequently committed suicide and so implicitly accepted the blame for the tampering. However, as Koestler emphasized, it is by no means certain that Kammerer's suicide is attributable solely to the faked specimen and a possibility also exists that he did not himself apply the ink. One interpretation of the evidence is that, when the midwife toad specimen began to deteriorate, a technician attempted to restore the essential characteristics with ink so that they might be better seen. This kind of refurbishment is by no means uncommon in biology. The existence of the nuptial pads was not, however, ever verified by any other scientific observer.

A significant aspect of the case is that no attempt to repeat Kammerer's results appears to have been made. This is not just because the experiments are so difficult to perform. Scientists are as sensitive to impropriety and stigma as any other group, and one scandal of this sort can make a complete area of inquiry disreputable.

The Kammerer case raises a number of questions. The ethical issues involved in intentional bias are too complex to receive attention here. However, since the subject of the gray area between intentional and unintentional bias is under consideration, it is appropriate to point out that a similarly indistinct area exists for moral perspectives. Two famous examples may even be seen as evidence that bias in some instances may be to the ultimate good. The best-known concerns statistical reanalysis by R. A. Fisher of

The "nuptial pads" that Paul Kammerer claimed to have induced on the midwife toad were found on the only preserved specimen to be india ink.

Gregor Mendel's data, which form the basis of modern views on heredity. Fisher showed that Mendel's results were just too good to be true—the chances of his getting them, given his research techniques, were something like 1 in 10,000.

Nobody knows whether Mendel deliberately misrepresented his data or not, but it is clear that, whatever the means, the results of his work are of inestimable importance for modern society. A more controversial and recent instance concerns the alleged publication of misleading data on wheat radiation mutation by the influential Indian agriculturalist M. S. Swaminathan. Swaminathan claimed that he had increased the protein and lysine content of a strain of wheat by subjecting seeds of a parent strain to a combination of gamma radiation and ultraviolet light. In this case, the issue is not so much whether Swaminathan deliberately fabricated his experiments but rather whether he was less than vigilant in his attitude to the data after it had been discredited. Swaminathan's supporters argued that any carelessness on his part was more than justified by the contribution he had made to the Green Revolution that brought about increased agricultural yields in India. His detractors maintained that such calculated unscrupulousness was contrary to the ideals of science and completely inappropriate for a man in such a prestigious position.

Pressures of competition

In trying to understand the reasons for the existence of intentional bias one must think of the scientist as an individual under considerable pressure to obtain particular results. The pressure comes from a number of sources. Research funding from industry, for example from pharmaceutical firms, is normally assigned to groups producing results that look promising from the funder's point of view. The temptation to produce experiments that yield such results is, consequently, a strong one. At a different level, the postgraduate scientist, working strenuously for his Ph.D., is all too aware that his research is funded for a very limited period. If, toward the end of that time, he is failing to get "good" results, the temptation to "improve" the data a little so as to get the Ph.D. must be extraordinary. And also, at all levels, advancement in science depends primarily on publication of impressive research findings. All journals receive far more material for publication than they can possibly handle, so they have to be selective. Selection relates to the importance of findings, and consequently "failed" experiments—those where hypotheses have not been confirmed and so no "positive" results have been obtained—are seldom published. Once again, therefore, the emphasis is on obtaining clear-cut experimental evidence in favor of predicted phenomena.

Two recent examples of fraud were generated in large part by such pressures. The first concerned the work of William T. Summerlin at the Memorial Sloan-Kettering Cancer Center in New York City. In 1974 it was discovered that Summerlin had altered the results of experiments so that it appeared that skin and organs maintained for a time in tissue culture could be grafted onto recipient animals without provoking the immune-system reaction that causes transplant rejection. Also in 1974 Walter J. Levy, Jr., the director of

Though Gregor Mendel probably misrepresented his research findings, they still provide the foundation for many contemporary views of heredity.

37

the Institute for Parapsychology at Durham, N.C., confessed to falsifying results of his experiments to indicate that rats could anticipate events by means of extrasensory perception and could achieve physical changes by sheer willpower. Both Summerlin and Levy claimed that they had been under considerable pressure to produce positive results.

Every scientist is likely at some time in his career to have to face a choice between morally acceptable and expedient choices of action. While the ethical standards of science are no doubt keenly felt on such occasions, the individual's need to survive must also be taken into account. When ambition and career, to say nothing of more mundane considerations like holding down a job and salary, depend on getting results of a particular sort, it is obvious that expediency must sometimes win.

Sanctions against intentional bias

In contrast to the considerable pressures working in favor of intentional bias, the sanctions operating to prevent it are negligible. The most significant is replication, and it can be argued that intentional bias may safely be ignored because important experiments are always replicated independently by other researchers before their findings are accepted or applied.

For some major advances, there is undoubtedly something in this viewpoint. For less celebrated work, though, exact replication is seldom carried out and is published even less often; journals are understandably not sympathetic to repetitious material. Moreover, the increasing expense and complexity of research is making replication even less common. Many experiments involve extremely sophisticated and costly apparatus, which, consequently, exist only in a few laboratories. Access to such apparatus is keenly sought, and it is unlikely that precious apparatus time will be allowed to be used simply for repeating experiments. In other cases, experiments are simply not reproducible, either for technical reasons (as in the Kammerer case) or because of some peculiarity in the design or subject matter. A notorious example of the sort of problem associated with the latter is the Piltdown man, a fraudulent skull specimen that led archaeology astray for more than 40 years before it was discredited.

It could even be argued that the increasing complexity of modern experimentation provides a ready cloak for the would-be charlatan, since discrepant results may be explained away as the consequences of equipment or sample idiosyncrasies. Indeed, for obvious and laudable reasons, researchers normally go to great trouble to detect possible reasons for discrepancies between their own results and those of others. If replication of the experiment, involving systematic testing of each idiosyncrasy, is then attempted, the cost in time and resources is likely to be considerable; a recent disclosure itemized one case in which four man-years had been wasted in this way on a faked original result.

M. S. Swaminathan claimed that he increased the protein and lysine content of a strain of wheat by subjecting seeds of a parent strain to a combination of gamma radiation and ultraviolet light.

Perhaps the most important reason why detection of intentional bias is unlikely, though, is that experimenters neither want to keep checks on one another nor do they have the time to do so. As indicated earlier, research is an extraordinarily competitive business and time spent overseeing someone else's work is time deducted from one's own.

New Scientist questionnaire

The questions that made up the *New Scientist* questionnaire were written with the sort of issues thus far considered very much in mind. The researchers hoped to obtain information about the circumstances most likely to give rise to intentional bias, about the sort of individual most likely to succumb, and about the likelihood and consequences of detection. In addition, it was hoped that recommendations could be made with respect to the development of safeguards to minimize intentional bias if they proved to be needed.

Five of the 204 questionnaires received were spoiled, and so analysis involved 199. The questionnaire consisted largely of multiple-choice answers, where one or more of several alternatives had to be selected, but in some cases respondents were encouraged to provide additional information. Some did this, to the extent of sending in letters and complete documented case histories of fraud they had encountered. An important qualification of the survey's data is that respondents were a self-selected (rather than randomly selected) group. In the vast majority of cases (92%) they were individuals who had had some experience of intentional bias, and almost all of them (90%) were in favor of investigation of fraud in science. Although no figures exist, it seems unlikely that such high proportions would be obtained if scientists were selected at random. Hence, the group of respondents must be regarded as "unrepresentative" in the formal statistical sense in that they almost all shared an attitude not necessarily characteristic of all scientists. Of course, this kind of selectivity does not imply dishonesty or even that respondents were necessarily people with a personal ax to grind. Indeed, the reasoned and dispassionate nature of most of their reponses and the certainty of their evidence suggest that their information is reliable (75% were reporting unequivocal evidence, and in 52% of cases the evidence was based on direct personal experience).

There are other good reasons for assuming respondents to be reasonable, responsible, and mature individuals. Nearly two-thirds were over 30 years of age and one-third were over 40. Their job backgrounds and status varied considerably, but 23% were tenured academic staff and an additional 12% were senior industrial officials.

How, then, is intentional bias detected (question 5) and what is its nature (question 6)? Nearly a fifth of the detections resulted from catching the suspect in the act and nearly as many from confessions, but the principal detection technique involved encountering suspicious data (33%) or replication difficulties (26%). Some respondents rated more than one category, suggesting that encountering one suspicious piece of information sometimes leads to a search for others. At first sight, it is reassuring to learn that so many cases of intentional bias are detected through formal scientific procedures of data checking and replication and through rigorous detective work. Since these data concern only those cases actually encountered, however, they may reflect only the ineptitude of the most inefficent and unskilled malpractitioners.

The most common kind of intentional bias detected was data "massage" (74% of total), a category that included deliberate interference with data to make it appear more acceptable. As expected, this area provoked the most

Responses to a questionnaire in New Scientist *magazine reveal that intentional bias is a too frequent feature of research.*

CHEATING IN SCIENCE

1. **In your opinion, does intentional bias warrant investigation?**
   Yes—90%
   No—10%

2. **Is your knowledge of intentional bias based principally upon**
   direct personal contact—52%
   information obtained from colleague with a direct contact—17%
   the scientific grapevine—11%
   the media—12%
   article in *New Scientist*—6%
   other—2%

3. **Do you know of or suspect intentional bias?**
   No—8%
   Yes—92%
   Yes, more than one incident—66%

4. **Was the intentional bias**
   suspected—25%
   demonstrated unequivocally—75%

5. **How was the intentional bias detected?**
   individual(s) caught in the act—17%
   individual(s) confessed—14%
   suspicious data obtained—33%
   replication difficulties—26%
   other—10%

6. **Nature of malpractice**
   Area of research—five with the largest number of occurrences were physics (20), psychology (14), biochemistry (13), chemistry (12), and biology (11). All others had 6 or fewer.
   Nature of intentional bias—altering data (74%), experiment rigging (17%), complete fabrication of experiment and data, sometimes involving plagiarism (7%), deliberate misinterpretation (2%).
   Where did it take place?—university laboratories (58%), industrial laboratories (17%), field location (9%), local government (9%), hospitals (4%), school laboratories (2%), observatories (less than 1%).
   How often did it occur?—once (32%), 1–5 times (32%), more than 5 times (36%).

7. **How many people were involved?**
   one—55%
   more than one, unspecified—21%
   two—9%
   three–five—11%
   six–ten—1%
   more than ten—3%

8. **Nature of suspects**
   age—under 20 (4%), 20–29 (37%), 30–39 (26%), 40–49 (19%), 50–59 (13%), over 60 (1%)
   sex—male (89%), female (11%)
   status—largest categories were industrial scientists (19%), postgraduate students (15%), research associates and assistants (15%), undergraduate students (11%), professors (10%), lecturers and senior lecturers (9%). All other categories had 5% or less.

9. **What happened to suspects?**
   dismissed—10%
   nothing—80%
   reprimand—3%
   don't know—2%
   other—5%

10. **What is your own field of research?**
    Largest categories were physics (12%), chemistry (10%), biochemistry (10%), and biology (8.5%).

11. **What is your own status?**
    Largest categories were tenured academic staff (23%) and senior industrial officials (12%).

12. **Please ring the appropriate category for your age and sex**
    under 20 (3%), 20–29 (33%), 30–39 (28%), 40–49 (15%), 50–59 (12%), over 60 (9%)
    male (86%), female (14%)

Adapted from Ian St. James-Roberts, *New Scientist*, Sept. 2, 1976, pp. 481–483, and *New Scientist*, Nov. 25, 1976, pp. 466–469. London, The Weekly Review of Science and Technology

controversy. Not all respondents were happy, for example, that omitting to report results that did not conform to overall trends was considered a sin of the same magnitude as relocating decimal points. Others noted that some less than heinous crimes, such as pretending to have run 50 control animals in a biological experiment when only 5 were really run, were commonplace and unimportant. The need to consider each case of intentional bias within its particular context was frequently alluded to. Other types of intentional bias encountered were experiment rigging (17% of total), complete fabrication or plagiarization of an experiment and data (7%), and deliberate misinterpretation of results (2%).

Part 1 of question 6 yielded 75 research areas and 184 instances of intentionally biased research. Since, however, part 4 of this question indicated that intentional bias was twice as likely to occur often as it was to occur once, it may be assumed that the actual number of cases being reported by respondents was considerably higher. Because of the statistically unrepresentative nature of the respondents, referred to earlier, it is difficult to know whether the quantitative trends revealed by the answers to question 6 apply to scientific research in general. A reasonable overall conclusion, bearing in mind the heterogeneity of the responses, is that almost every area of research appears to be represented. The more obscure areas, such as extrasensory perception, did not attract an excessively large number of responses. An additional point is that, although the quantity of intentional bias detected is of interest, both the status of the biaser and the area of research are also important. A music undergraduate's faking, for example, is unlikely to affect others, whereas a single fraud by an eminent medical researcher may prove far more serious.

Although the largest number of intentional biasers were those "junior" in age (20–29) and status (research assistants and associates, postgraduates), they by no means dominated the response. A third of the biasers were over 40 at the time of bias, and nearly 60% were over 30. Those in particularly prestigious positions (professors, senior lecturers, lecturers, readers, research fellows, and industrial staff) among them perpetrated a third of all biased research reported.

Perhaps the most important question concerned what happened to those individuals whose intentional bias had been detected (question 9). In the vast majority of cases (80% of total) the answer was "nothing." A qualification frequently included was "promoted." Dismissal occurred in 10% of cases and reprimand in 3%. Because these figures concern only those cases actually detected, the low dismissal rates and high likelihood that nothing will happen even if the culprit is detected bear out the study's prior misgivings about the adequacy of existing sanctions against fraud.

Conclusions

Taken as a whole, the results of the survey suggest that intentional bias of one sort or another is a common feature of scientific research and that existing controls are incapable of preventing it. One question that was included with the subject of controls specifically in mind asked how many scientists were involved in each case of bias because it was anticipated that

William T. Summerlin altered his experimental results to make it appear that grafting of skin and organs could be achieved without transplant rejection.

42

fraud would be less likely to occur where a number of individuals were working together. Data on this issue were difficult to evaluate because the relative amounts of research done by groups of different sizes were unknown. It seemed reasonable to assume, however, that most research is done by one or two workers, with decreasing amounts as the size of the group increases. With this proviso taken into account, the responses to the question offer less support than suspected for the effectiveness of multiple experimenters as controls of intentional bias. Although the proportion of fraudulent experimentation diminishes as the number of experimenters increases, nearly half of the intentional bias reported involved more than one experimenter and approximately 15% involved three or more. The informal comments of respondents suggested that an important consideration may be whether they collaborate only afterward, as often happens in multidisciplinary research.

Insistence on multiple authors for papers and joint running of experiments might, therefore, provide at least some measure of control of intentional bias. What other constraints are possible? Perhaps the simplest would be for journals to insist that experimenters oversee one another's research and retain "open" data books so that anyone can have ready access to their entire data. Such controls are unlikely to be wholly effective, but they may reduce at least some kinds of intentional bias.

Whatever methods are used, the cost of controls must be evaluated in terms of inconvenience and loss of time and personal liberty to the researcher. Implementation of tight controls will inevitably involve considerable red tape, and few researchers are likely to welcome this. On the other hand, scientists can no longer ignore their responsibility to the community they serve. Perhaps the most disturbing aspect of the survey has been the scientific establishment's continuing failure to consider the matter or to take any action. Recent revelations of research fraudulence in *Nature* magazine suggest that the problem is not going to go away by itself.

By falsifying his experimental results, Walter J. Levy, Jr., indicated that rats were able to use extrasensory perception to anticipate events. The rats actually succeeded about as well as most horse players.

Research Submersibles: Explorers of the Ocean Depths

by Robert D. Ballard

The deep waters of the world's oceans can now be visited and studied by man thanks to the development of small, maneuverable, undersea craft.

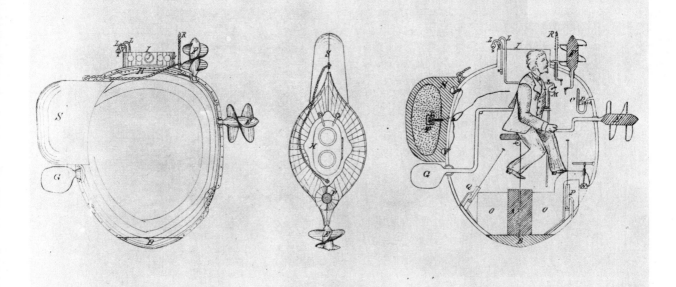

*Drawings of the "American Turtle,"
the first submersible used in combat,
are based on descriptions of the craft
by its inventor, David Bushnell.
Constructed of wood during the
American Revolutionary War, the craft
boasted a conning tower, glass
windows, snorkels, valves operated by
foot pedals to pump water for
ballasting, a rudder, and
hand-operated propellers.*

ROBERT D. BALLARD *is an Associate
Scientist in the Department of
Geology and Geophysics at the
Woods Hole Oceanographic
Institution, Woods Hole,
Massachusetts.*

(Overleaf) Illustration by John Rush

The great oceans of the Earth make it truly unique among the planets of the solar system. Their vast water volume provides this planet with a moderate climate capable of supporting advanced life. Although man owes his existence to and is dependent upon these oceans, which cover more than 70% of the Earth's surface, his air-breathing and land-loving ways have led to a fear of the sea and its unknown depths. He has filled it with monsters and angry gods and has written of its violent moods. Content to remain on solid ground, he has ventured to sea only when necessary and then only as a means to another end: to wage war, to transport goods, to travel to distant lands, and to obtain food.

As the world's population has grown, however, and the resources on land have become ever more depleted, man has begun to focus more attention on the vast region of the Earth beneath the sea. As a result, a greater need has developed to explore the depths of the ocean and to probe its floor. Initially, such oceanographic explorations were conducted in surface ships from which instruments were lowered. Beginning with the "Challenger" Expedition in 1873–76 and continuing to the present, vast amounts of information about the biology, chemistry, geology, and physics of the world's oceans have been collected from these ships. Scientists have learned, for example, that the floor of the ocean is as complex as the land masses. It contains the largest mountains, the deepest valleys, and the greatest plains on the surface of the Earth. Its waters contain vast living resources and its sediments tremendous oil and gas reserves.

This information has led to fundamental changes in concepts of the oceans' origin, as well as of the Earth itself. With these changes has come a growing need for new data, some of which cannot be obtained by using conventional surface-ship techniques. This information is of a nature requiring the presence of man himself on the floor of the ocean where he can use his mind to react to what he is seeing and so continually modify his ex-

perimentation. This requirement brought about the development of the small, maneuverable undersea craft called research submersibles.

Early explorations

The technology that has provided the scientific community with research submersibles evolved as a result of other needs. Tracing this technology back in time, one finds that it began for military and commercial reasons. Historical accounts of underwater activities date back to the 16th century with the use of divers, snorkels, and diving bells. Leonardo da Vinci was known to have designed underwater diving instruments for war and salvage purposes and is said to have made a descent himself within a diving bell. During the 17th century several attempts were made to construct crude submarines. Cornelius van Drebel, a Dutch inventor, constructed a submarine made of wood, covered by leather, and driven by oars for King James I in 1620. It was built presumably for military purposes, as were other submarines during that century, but no record exists of any of them ever being used in combat. The first record of such an occurrence is attributed to David Bushnell during the American Revolution. A patriot from Connecticut, Bushnell constructed his submarine from wood. It resembled two turtle shells joined together, and Bushnell named it the "American Turtle." The

Alexander the Great used diving bells to send men below the water's surface during his siege of Tyre, according to an account by Aristotle. The painting above, from a 13th-century manuscript, depicts Alexander himself in a diving bell.

49

craft was complete with conning tower, glass windows, snorkels, valves operated by foot pedals to pump water for ballasting purposes, a rudder, and hand-operated propellers. When the time came to use his invention in combat, Bushnell's nervousness proved too much, and an army sergeant named Ezra Lee volunteered to man the submarine. Lee maneuvered the "Turtle" under the British flagship "Eagle," commanded by Admiral Howe. Submerged beneath the stern of the "Eagle," Lee attempted to screw the torpedo into the hull. The torpedo was a hollowed-out timber filled with 150 pounds of gunpowder. Once the torpedo was screwed into the hull, it was fired using a clock-timing device. Fortunately for the British, and perhaps for Lee himself, the screw struck copper sheathing around the rudder and Lee broke off his attack without firing.

Following the Revolutionary War and continuing until the Civil War, inventors designed and built a wide variety of submarines. The first to sink a ship was the "H. L. Hunley." Built by the Navy of the Confederate States of America, it was about 50 feet in length and had a hand-operated propeller. In 1864 the "Hunley" sank the 1,240-ton, 13-gun "Housatonic." Upon exploding, the torpedo also sank the "Hunley" and the era of submarine warfare had begun.

Piccard's bathyscaph

Despite this long history of submarine development, all the devices designed and built were only capable of diving to shallow depths. It was not until World War II that the first truly deep-diving research submersible was built. The bathyscaph "FNRS 2" was the first in its class of deep-diving vehicles. Designed by the Swiss physicist Auguste Piccard, the bathyscaph was in essence a high-altitude balloon in reverse. Applying his experience in stratospheric balloon flights, Piccard designed his bathyscaph by using many of the same principles. Seven years after ascending to a world altitude record of 72,177 feet in his balloon "FNRS," named for his sponsor, Fonds National de la Recherche Scientifique, Piccard was given a $25,000 grant by the same organization to construct his first bathyscaph. The outbreak of World War II, however, postponed his efforts. At the war's end Piccard rekindled his deep-diving interests, and at that time began the construction of the "FNRS 2."

This vehicle and other bathyscaphs built later were the simplest of deep-diving submersibles. Their principal components included a gasoline-filled float, a cast-steel sphere, iron-shot ballast, small motors for propulsion, and batteries for power. The float was divided into six compartments holding approximately 7,000 gallons of gasoline. When the pilot released gasoline from one of the compartments, seawater replaced it. As a result the bathyscaph's displacement did not change, but its weight increased and the craft started sinking toward the ocean floor.

Suspended beneath the float was a small pressure capsule (a container capable of withstanding great pressures) called a gondola, borrowing the term from ballooning. A sphere was used for this purpose because that geometric form provides the smallest surface area for its volume and allows the pressure on it to be equally distributed. The sphere was made of two

French undersea explorer Jacques-Yves Cousteau (opposite page, top) peers out from the minisub "PUCE" (Perry Underwater Submersible). "Tektite II" (opposite page, bottom) provided living quarters for marine scientists 50 feet below the surface of the Caribbean Sea in 1970.

50

Photos, Flip Schulke—Black Star

cast-steel hemispheres held together by clamps. Two people would enter the sphere while it was out of the water and remain there until the dive was over and the bathyscaph was lifted clear of the water once again. The sphere had conical-shaped viewports made of acrylic plastic, and the life-support system consisted of a carbon-dioxide removal unit and oxygen released from a high-pressure bottle. For ballast the "FNRS 2" carried several tons of iron shot, which was held in steel tanks with the assistance of electromagnets. When the electromagnetic field was applied, the iron shot acted as a single object. When the electromagnets were turned off, the shot would begin coming out as a small stream of pellets. Should the bathyscaph experience a power failure, the electromagnetic doors would open, all the shot would be dropped, and the bathyscaph would rise rapidly back toward the surface.

An additional form of buoyancy control was obtained by hanging a cable beneath the craft. As the bathyscaph approached the bottom this cable would touch first, resulting in a weight loss to the vehicle. With such an arrangement it was possible to adjust the bathyscaph's buoyancy in such a manner that the craft would hang suspended over the floor with just a portion of the cable touching the bottom. Once on the bottom, the "FNRS 2" had small electric motors and external lights that made it possible to traverse the floor and make visual observations.

The "FNRS 2" made its first dive Oct. 26, 1948, with Piccard aboard accompanied by Theodore Monod, to a depth of 84 feet. This initial test dive was followed in early November by an unmanned dive of 4,544 feet. Severely damaged by heavy seas shortly thereafter, the craft never made another dive. Although other bathyscaphs followed ("FNRS 3," "Trieste I" and "II," and "Archimède"), the basic principles remained the same. The bathyscaph reached its peak of achievement in 1960 when the "Trieste I" made a record-setting plunge 35,800 feet to the floor of the Challenger Deep in the Mariana Trench. Although the bathyscaph is still the deepest-diving manned submersible, it is no longer competitive with the new vehicles.

Modern craft

It is difficult to determine which vehicle was the forerunner of today's deep submersibles. If "deep" is considered to be 1,000 feet or greater, the first "free-swimming," small submersible to reach that depth was the "SP-350" ("La Soucoupe Plongeante"), designed by Jacques-Yves Cousteau. Retaining some of the principles of Piccard's bathyscaph, Cousteau changed others. Instead of a heavy, negatively buoyant steel pressure sphere, he built a lightweight, disk-shaped hull having positive buoyancy, thus lessening his flotation problem; instead of an iron-shot ballasting system, the "Soucoupe" adjusted its buoyancy by flooding or pumping seawater in and out of a ballast tank much like a military submarine.

The greatest advantages of such a submersible over the bathyscaph are its small size and its ability to operate on much less gasoline. Sacrificing depth for mobility, the "Soucoupe" could be transported easily, undergo maintenance aboard ship, and avoid the risk of a gasoline explosion. In the water it was highly maneuverable and provided excellent visibility.

Robert D. Ballard

These small submersibles thus supplanted the bathyscaphs. As newer ones were designed to dive to greater and greater depths, various methods were devised to keep them small. Lightweight metals such as aluminum and titanium were used for the pressure spheres to maintain their positive buoyancy. If heavier spheres had to be used, the innovation of syntactic foam eliminated the need for gasoline flotation. This foam, which consists of microspheres of glass embedded in an epoxy resin, is now a critically important part of deep-submergence technology. Lighter than seawater and undamaged by continuous recycling to great depths, the foam can be poured into forms to harden or cut into blocks like wood.

Other developments took place after the early "Soucoupe" which greatly improved the new smaller submersibles. The use of iron shot as a ballasting technique was replaced by the development of new variable ballast systems. These were of two basic designs. One involves the pumping of oil or similar fluid from a reservoir such as a metal sphere into a rubber bladder. The weight of the submersible does not change but its volume or displacement does, resulting in an increase in the vehicle's buoyancy. In the other case, seawater is pumped into a metal sphere, resulting in a change in weight but not in volume. This would cause a decrease in buoyancy. Both systems can be used in either direction, making it possible to change the submersible's ballast continuously. Other advances included the use of sophisticated obstacle-avoidance sonars, the development of precision acoustical navigation systems, and the introduction of extended life-support units.

The bathyscaph "Trieste II," shown above at its shore base in San Diego, California, has dived more than 20,000 feet to explore the depths of the world's oceans.

53

Scientific explorations

Paralleling the technological development of the submersibles by marine engineers was the development of the science of the sea itself. At first these efforts were intertwined, as scientists initiated the early diving programs; later science lagged behind, as military and potential industrial needs accelerated the development efforts. Recently, however, scientific programs again began to advance the technology.

The first scientific efforts in deep diving were not carried out in free-swimming submersibles. In the same year (1948) that Piccard lowered the "FNRS 2" on its deep unmanned dive to 4,544 feet, Otis Barton took his tethered diving bell, the "Benthoscope," to a depth of 4,488 feet off Santa

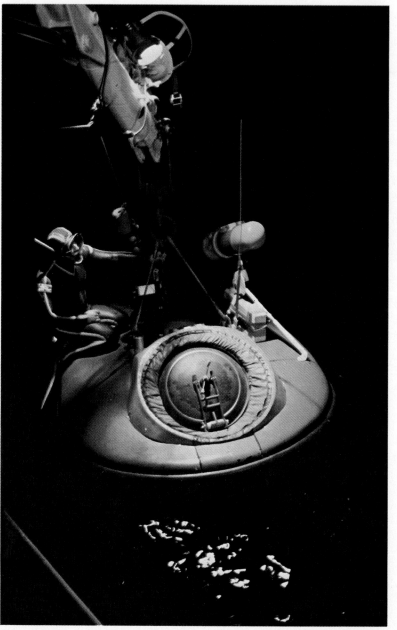

The "Sea Flea," a minisub developed by Jacques-Yves Cousteau, is lowered into the water. The craft was used in several research expeditions during the early 1970s.

Cruz Island, Calif. Originally built in 1929 and called the "Bathysphere," the diving bell was used by naturalist William Beebe to study deep-sea organisms off Bermuda. Beebe's diving program in the "Bathysphere" from 1930 to 1934 represented the first scientific investigation in the deep sea conducted by man in a pressure capsule. Despite this early beginning and interesting scientific results, the diving bell proved too dangerous and limited for scientific studies, and a period of inactivity followed until Piccard's bathyscaph program began in the late 1940s.

In the early stages of deep diving, the submersible was basically an elevator capable of taking scientists to the floor of the ocean and providing them with a viewport and lights. Its horizontal range was severely limited. On the way to the seafloor scientists studied material suspended in the water column, visibility, the nature of light penetration, acoustical properties of sea water, ambient noise, and the composition of the deep-scattering layer. Upon reaching the floor, biologists described and photographed new animal species, studied their behavioral traits, and investigated their habitats; geologists studied erosional features cut into the floor.

Despite the interesting observations made during the 1950s and 1960s, the results of those programs lacked major scientific significance. For that reason many scientists criticized the usefulness of the submersibles and referred to them as toys too expensive for their potential value. The investigations continued, however, because the funding of deep submersibles in the 1960s came primarily from private industry, which was interested in their potential commercial use, and from the U.S. Navy for deep-sea rescue and salvage operations.

Although the many private aerospace companies that built sophisticated submersibles during the 1960s did not find deep submergence a profitable venture and quickly discontinued their efforts, their entrance into the field brought with it modern space-age technology. Many improvements were made in propulsion systems, ballast systems, manipulators, power supplies, navigational tracking systems, and surface support. For example, the aerospace industry introduced lightweight hydraulic systems originally developed for aircraft and space vehicles. They significantly improved underwater propulsion and mechanical-arm manipulators. The space firms also brought with them microminiaturization, which greatly improved deep-submersible technology. Despite this sudden influx of talent and money, the now-large family of subs slowly dwindled in size in the late 1960s and early 1970s as one after another was deactivated because of a lack of governmental and commercial funding.

Project FAMOUS and later studies

The first truly significant scientific use of manned submersibles took place in 1973. Called Project FAMOUS, for French-American Mid-Ocean Undersea Study, this program consisted of an investigation of the Mid-Atlantic Ridge rift valley using three deep-diving vehicles, "Alvin," "Cyana," and the bathyscaph "Archimède." The initial phases of the study began in 1970 with a series of cruises conducted by surface ships using a wide variety of instrument systems. These included sophisticated mapping techniques, deep-tow

"Nemo" was built by the U.S. Navy in 1970 to test the feasibility of acrylic plastic as a material for use in deep submergence. Operating at a depth of about 600 feet with limited lateral capability, it had a length and beam of 7.5 feet and a height of 9.2 feet.

French bathyscaph "Archimède" (right) and submersible "Cyana" (above) operated at depths of approximately 9,000 feet during Project FAMOUS to study the processes of plate tectonics in the rift valley of the Mid-Atlantic Ridge.

Dive of the bathyscaph "Archimède" begins on the surface (opposite page, a) with ballast tanks filled with air. Opening the tank valves causes the air to escape and be replaced by water, making the bathyscaph heavy enough to begin its dive (b). During the descent (c) water rises in the ballast tanks; at this time, the "Archimède" is communicating with its surface escort ship by ultrasonics. As the bathyscaph nears the bottom (d), iron shot is released from silos to slow its descent. On the bottom (e) the "Archimède" conducts its experiments. By releasing more iron shot, the crew allows the craft to become light enough to rise to the surface (f, g, and h).

sonars, and large-area photography systems precisely navigated. These extensive pre-dive preparations were able to pinpoint target areas where significant scientific problems might be better understood by using manned submersibles.

During the summers of 1973 and 1974, the "Alvin," "Cyana," and "Archimède" logged more than 40 dives, with the majority being conducted in the narrow rift valley, some two miles in width. Working at a depth of 9,000 feet, scientists within their tiny pressure capsules drove across a young complex volcanic terrain. While the majority of deep dives until that time had been made on old ocean floor commonly covered by thick accumulations of deep-sea ooze or mud, these dives were made on some of the youngest rock floor in the world's oceans. The rift valley is a region on the surface of the Earth where the solid crust has cracked and is separating, with one segment traveling west and the other east. The region is, therefore, the site of renewed volcanic activity, and the scientists in the deep submersibles were able to locate the freshest volcanoes in the study area, sample their glassy pillow-shaped lavas, and learn firsthand about how the Earth's crust is initially formed and how it cracks and later transports itself horizontally away from its site of formation.

During the years following Project FAMOUS, studies were conducted in other regions of the ocean floor where active volcanism is taking place as new crust is formed. In 1976 and 1977 a program was conducted in the Cayman Trench using "Alvin" and the bathyscaph "Trieste II." There, dives were made ranging in depth from 12,000 to 20,250 feet in a steep rocky valley four times deeper than the Grand Canyon of Arizona. While a portion of the dives concentrated on the deepest volcanoes in the world and their fresh, glassy lava flows, the majority focused on the steep vertical fault scarps. There, the deeper layers of the Earth that form in rift valleys below the thin volcanic cover were exposed. In early 1976 scientists were able to see and sample in place, for the first time, layer three of the Earth's oceanic crust, which is the foundation of the world's oceans.

(Top, left and right) Courtesy, Woods Hole Oceanographic Institution; photos, John Porteous

U.S. submersible "Alvin" (right and opposite page) explored deep into the Cayman Trench of the Caribbean Sea, where the octopus (below right) was only one of many sea creatures sighted by the crew. Arm of the "Alvin" (above) grasps T-bar and uses it to inject underwater samples with chemicals or nutrients. As the craft nears the seafloor, its pilot peers from porthole (below).

(Bottom, left and right) Photos, Robert D. Ballard

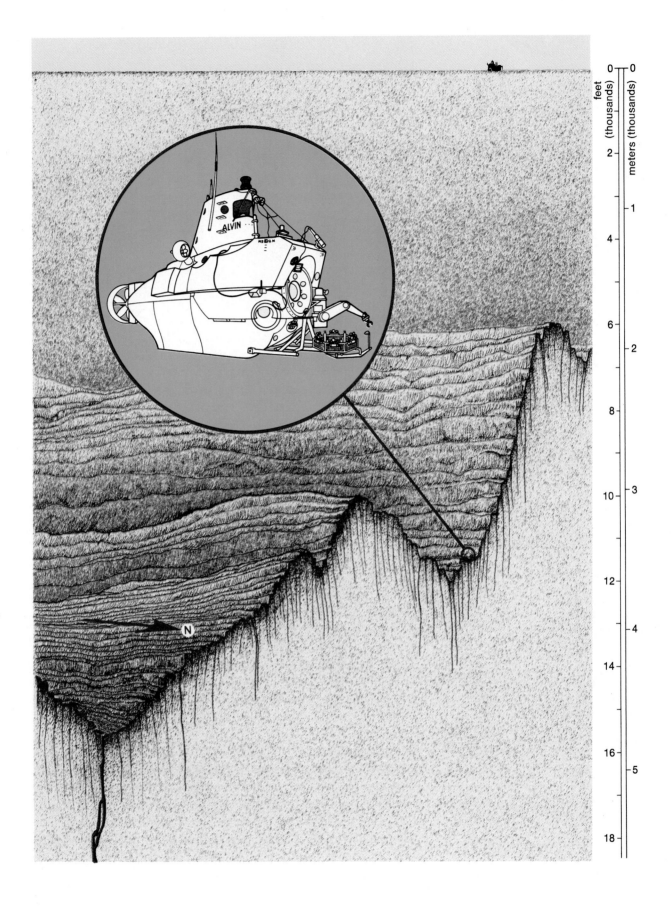

"Alvin" is tethered to "Lulu," its floating garage. The twin hulls of the motor-driven catamaran are giant floats that contain sleeping and working space for its crew of 20.

In 1977 a major scientific discovery was made by the submersible "Alvin," diving in the Galápagos Rift off the Pacific coast of South America. Because it is similar to the Mid-Atlantic Ridge, scientists had come to the rift to investigate its fresh lava terrain. Earlier surface-ship studies of the rift, located some 220 miles north and east of the Galápagos Islands, suggested that warm water might be flowing out of the young crust into the overlying seawater. Scientists inside "Alvin" hoped to locate these warm-water springs and sample their unusual water to learn more about the hydrothermal circulation of seawater within young, hot, fractured crust. Aided by cameras lowered from the surface and a precision tracking system, they found a warm spring on the first dive. They were surprised to find highly developed and dense accumulations of large animals living in and around the warm-spring vents. The vent areas were approximately 80 meters in diameter and contained several openings from which warm water was flowing. The water coming out of the vents had a temperature of up to 17° C (63° F) compared with the near-freezing bottom waters of 2° C (36° F). Not only was it warm, the water was also laden with hydrogen sulfide, carbon dioxide, and oxygen, upon which bacteria thrived. These bacteria formed the base of the food chain that led up to the many observed large animals.

In all, the submersibles succeeded in finding five separate vent regions; four were thriving, but in one the warm springs had stopped flowing and all the organisms were dead. In addition, each vent area had its own ecology, consisting in many cases of totally different organisms.

Future prospects

With the recent success of manned deep submersibles in the above mentioned programs, the future for such craft looks promising. How the submersibles will be employed is difficult to predict. It is clear that for the next three to five years they will be used in science programs similar to those previously discussed. The nature of oceanographic research is such that the next two years of field work have already been scheduled.

Although submersibles have now become reliable and are outfitted with advanced scientific instrumentation, their surface-support ships continue to be severely limited in their operating range. Therefore, large areas of the world's oceans at present are logistically inaccessible. In addition, present-day research submersibles can only dive to 12,000 feet, thus reaching only 50% of the ocean floor. In the mid- to late 1980s, a submersible capable of reaching 20,000 feet, carried on a surface-support ship having a worldwide range, will probably be developed and available to scientific research. One of the programs at that time may be a study of the deep-sea trenches as possible sites for nuclear waste disposal. By the beginning of the 21st century small nuclear submarines able to reach great ocean depths may be available. With such craft all parts of the world's oceans will become readily accessible to man.

The U.S. Navy's nuclear submarine "NR-1" explores the Straits of Florida on a scientific expedition. The deep-diving craft may be the prototype of future research submersibles.

Animal
Guidance Systems
by Robert T. Orr

The biological systems upon which animals depend for such essential tasks as finding food, avoiding danger, and locating mates achieve a sophistication that in many cases outstrips the best efforts of human ingenuity.

Below the surface of a turbid, mud-laden river, a silvery streamlined object makes its way confidently among the rocks and debris; surrounded by a self-generated electric field, it possesses sensors that respond to distortions in the field introduced by nearby objects. Airborne, a tiny sleek flying device equipped with a computer no larger than a pea checks its heading against the pattern of stars in the night sky. A well-armored observer, patrolling the desert on multiple sticklike appendages, detects movement ahead from vibrations conducted through the loose sand; within seconds it locates and intercepts its target.

   The above descriptions may well be glimpses of the bizarre technology of a distant future, when sophisticated electronic navigation and detection systems will have far surpassed and supplanted the human senses—but they are not. They portray a tropical fish, a migrating songbird, and a desert scorpion on the hunt, three denizens of the 20th century that nature has provided with incredible tools for survival. Animal life could not have evolved were it not for the development of various kinds of sensory systems that make communication possible between the individual and its environment as well as among individuals themselves. These systems, which may use chemical, visual, auditory, tactile, or even electric cues, serve many purposes. They are involved in such fundamental activities as the securing of food, protection and defense, reproduction, and migration.

(Overleaf) Ants on a trail between a source of food and their colony are a common sight. The trail consists of minute amounts of chemicals, called pheromones, laid down by a successful foraging worker on its return to the nest. Attracted by natural chemical secretions from a newt, two water beetles locate and attack their prey (opposite page, top left). Freshwater eels of the genus Anguilla (top right) mature in streams and ponds; assisted by an acute sense of smell they migrate great distances to and from the ocean, where they breed and spend their larval stages. Malodorous secretions of the stinkpot turtle, Sternotherus odoratus, from glands under the edge of its carapace (bottom) seem to act as feeding deterrents and may serve to warn predators of the turtle's general undesirability as food.

ROBERT T. ORR *is Senior Scientist at the California Academy of Sciences, San Francisco.*

Illustrations by John Youssi

Chemoreception

The most basic and widespread types of sensory systems are chemoreceptors. Organisms as primitive as single-celled bacteria and protozoans can react to chemical stimuli; a protozoan that encounters a chemical change in its liquid environment may be either repelled or attracted. From this relatively simple protoplasmic response to chemical irritation, chemoreceptors have evolved to such complicated organ systems as the olfactory apparatus found in vertebrates. A bloodhound, for instance, can follow the trail of a specific human being and readily distinguish the odor of that individual from all others, so sensitive is its sense of smell to minute chemical differences. Among fish it was recently demonstrated that the olfactory organs of freshwater eels are capable of detecting a concentration of 2-phenylethanol equivalent to half a teaspoonful in a volume of water as large as Lake Constance in Switzerland, which has a surface area of 209 square miles and a maximum depth of 827 feet. Such sensitivity implies that their olfactory epithelium must react to as little as two or three molecules of the chemical.

The term pheromone, once limited to chemicals that served as intraspecies sex attractants, has broadened to include any substance secreted by animals that elicits a specific reaction from other individuals of the same species. The production of certain chemical signals in honeybees, for example, results in the aggregation of large numbers of the species for defense; other pheromones serve to indicate the location of food. The males of some moths have highly specialized olfactory organs that react only to the scent of females of the same species. Although the male silkworm moth can detect a female more than a mile away, he does not react to any other odor. His only function as an adult is to mate with a female of the species.

Monarch butterflies breeding in regions of northern North America where milkweed is plentiful have definite migratory routes leading southward to their various wintering grounds. The male monarchs possess scent pockets on the hind wings, and it is believed that they leave a trail of odor for females to follow. Certain "butterfly trees," on which thousands of individuals congregate in the wintering areas, are visited year after year; in some places they have become a major tourist attraction.

Scent glands are highly developed in mammals and serve a number of purposes. Many large herbivores have glands on the feet and lower legs. Their secretion is deposited along trails, either on the ground or on adjacent vegetation. These chemical signals may be of temporary use in keeping members of a herd together or on the same route, or they may have a more extended use in marking a migratory trail that may not be used again for many months. Scent glands also play a role in reproductive behavior. The males of many kinds of mammals possess glands in the foreskin of the penis (preputial glands) whose exudate is deposited with urine at specific locations. The chemical messages at such scent posts may indicate presence, territory, or sex to others of the same species. Coyotes, wolves, and other members of the dog family regularly engage in this type of marking behavior. During the breeding season male beavers deposit castoreum, a secretion from their preputial glands, at certain places along the shores of streams and lakes as a means of attracting a mate. Likewise, in most mammals the time

Udo Hirsch

Jane Burton—Bruce Coleman Inc.

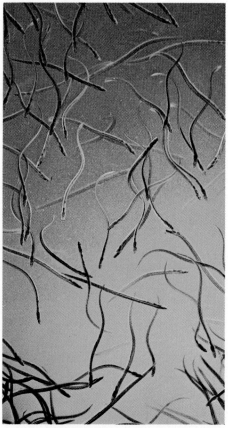

of estrus in the female, when she is capable of conceiving, is signaled by a specific scent that she produces.

During the past several years studies made on Pacific salmon of the genus *Oncorhynchus* showed that the young at a very early age somehow learn, or "imprint" to, the odor of the freshwater stream in which they hatch. Later they move to sea, where they remain for one to three years until they have attained sexual maturity. They then return, sometimes over a distance of more than a thousand miles, to the exact home stream in which they were hatched. There they spawn and die.

In one set of such experiments, conducted in Wisconsin during the mid–1970s, large groups of hatchery-raised and tagged juvenile coho salmon (*O. kisutch*) were exposed for six weeks to concentrations of either morpholine or 2-phenylethanol, two chemicals foreign to natural waters. At about 16 months of age (the time of normal downstream migration) the fish were released into Lake Michigan (*see* map on p. 67). During their spawning migration 18 months later, morpholine and 2-phenylethanol were metered into two separate streams that fed into the lake, and monitoring efforts were established to determine the number of chemically treated fish captured in these streams. In addition, 17 nonscented locations in the vicinity were monitored for tagged fish. Of all captured morpholine-treated fish (M), about 95% were taken in the morpholine-treated stream. Likewise, more than 90% of captured fish that were imprinted to 2-phenylethanol (PA) were

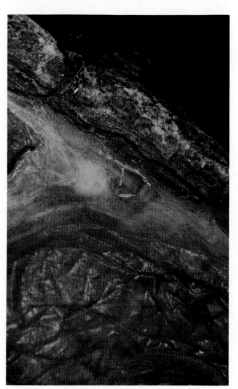

Thomas Eisner, Cornell University

found in the correspondingly scented stream. By contrast, many fish from a control group (C) that had been tagged and released without exposure to these chemicals were captured in nonscented streams.

To prove that the salmon's sense of smell is the main guiding factor, experiments were made in the state of Washington on coho salmon returning upstream to spawn. A number of individuals were captured above a fork in a watercourse. All were marked and half had their olfactory pits occluded. Following this they were all released below the fork. Those with unoccluded olfactory pits ascended to the junction and took the proper branch to the spawning bed, whereas the others were unable to differentiate between the two forks and were randomly distributed. One concludes, therefore, that every stream has a slightly different smell, being the result of differences in minerals, soil, plant life, and other factors in each drainage, and that the memory of this odor of the parental stream is a major guiding factor in homeward migration.

Experiments performed on newts of the genus *Taricha* also demonstrated that olfaction plays a very significant part in their orientation. These small caudate (tailed) amphibians emerge from their underground dens after the fall rains in western North America. Later they move to nearby ponds or streams to breed. In one study in coastal California, 692 such newts were captured, marked, and removed from their home stream to another watercourse two miles away. In the following three years, 77% of the displaced individuals were found to have returned to the original point of capture. Even newts whose eyesight was impaired were able to return home successfully.

Photoreception

In some one-celled animals such as *Amoeba*, the entire body exhibits definite sensitivity to light, reacting either positively or negatively. Further along the evolutionary scale, specialized clusters of photoreceptive cells are found in many multicellular organisms. In certain marine animals, for instance, these may function in relation to circadian movements (movements geared to a 24-hour cycle) toward the ocean surface at night and to deeper water during daylight hours.

In addition to photoreceptors, some invertebrates as well as certain vertebrates have bioluminescent structures that seemingly function for species recognition or for sexual recognition. To cite one instance, the Bermudan polychaete *Odontosyllis enopla*, a marine worm, swarms at certain seasons with the females resting in a glowing mass on the surface of the sea at night. This display attracts the males who then rise to the surface to mate. Cessation of glowing by the females causes the males to flash signals that apparently induce the females to resume glowing. Similarly among fireflies, which are beetles of the family Lampyridae, males are attracted at night to the flashing of females. Bioluminescent organs also occur in many species of fish, especially those living at abyssal depths or those active mainly at night. These structures are either self-luminous photophores or organs in which symbiotic luminous bacteria are cultured. The light intensity of these organs may be controlled or even completely shut off by a movable lid.

Eyelike structures for true optical communication reach their greatest

monitoring stations

1. Stony Creek area (3)
2. Ahnapee River
3. Three Mile Creek
4. Kewaunee River
5. Point Beach area (2)
6. Molash Creek
7. Two Rivers breakwater
8. East and West Twin rivers
9. release site
10. Little Manitowoc River
11. Manitowoc River
12. Fisher Creek area (2)
13. Pigeon River
14. Sheyboygan area (3)
15. Port Washington
16. Milwaukee area (3)
17. Oak Creek
18. Racine
19. Kenosha area (2)

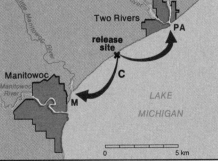

Imprinting of juvenile coho salmon to molecules of characteristic odor allows their later return to their home stream to spawn (opposite page). Map above details the experimental plan discussed on p. 65. Scenting was carried out in the Little Manitowoc River and Two Rivers breakwater area. Figures in parentheses represent the number of streams monitored by the stations in question.

67

Photos, Courtesy, P. J. Herring, Institute of Oceanographic Sciences, UK

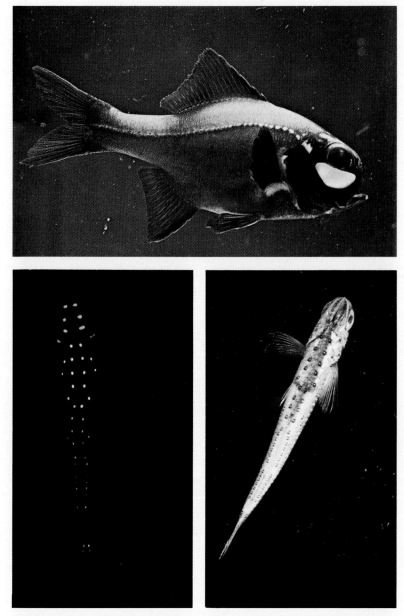

Symbiotic light-emitting bacteria populate the luminous organ beneath the eye of Photoblepharon palpebratus *(top), popularly called a flashlight fish. Photographed both in darkness and by reflected light (bottom left and right), the ventral surface of a lantern fish (*Myctophum species) *appears studded with rows of jewels, which are actually self-luminous photophores.*

development in mollusks, arthropods, and vertebrates. Although the eyes of such widely divergent organisms as cephalopods, insects, and vertebrates vary anatomically, they are all capable of producing a visual image. During the past several decades studies showed that sight plays a vital role in the migration of many kinds of vertebrates ranging from fish to mammals. Some freshwater fish were discovered to depend upon the Sun as a compass for orientation to locate breeding areas. For example, white bass (*Roccus chrysops*) removed from a spawning area along a lake shore, marked, and then released several miles away with visible floats attached to their backs returned directly to the breeding site on sunny days. If the day was overcast or if their eyes were covered, they moved at random after being displaced.

Studies on migratory orientation in certain frogs and toads also demon-

68

strated that celestial cues are important to some species. Young frogs and toads were found to imprint to a celestial pattern in relation to the shoreline about the time they are ready to metamorphose from the tadpole stage and emerge onto land. If they are removed at this time from the breeding pond and maintained elsewhere in a pen where they can only see the sky, they will continue to orient in the same direction in relation to the sky as they did in the pond in which they were hatched. This orientation is lost if the sky is obscured. For species active during the day (diurnal species) the position of the Sun is important, whereas nocturnal species must see the night sky.

The phenomenon of bird migration is a semiannual feat of amazing precision. Birds of many species repeatedly travel hundreds and even thousands of miles through disruptive weather and over unfamiliar country, yet somehow succeed in finding the same few square miles of ground that comprise either their winter or summer quarters. Only in the past 20 years have biologists made significant progress in unraveling the mysteries of this navigational ability, which apparently involves use of a variety of environmental cues that rely heavily on the sense of sight. Celestial patterns, water-wave action, ocean currents, and the position of the Sun have all been demonstrated or implicated as factors.

Numerous experiments have been made on the homing ability of migratory birds that were captured and then displaced great distances. In one of these, 18 adult Laysan albatrosses (*Diomedea immutabilis*) were captured during the nesting season on Midway Atoll in the Pacific Ocean. Each bird was marked and numbered and then transported by plane to one of six release localities in the North Pacific, ranging from Guam to the coast of the state of Washington. Fourteen of the 18 birds eventually returned to their nests. One bird released in the Philippine Islands returned to Midway Atoll 4,120 miles away in 32 days. Two birds released along the Washington coast returned the 3,200 miles in 10 and 12 days, respectively. Migratory land birds exhibit similar homing ability. Wintering sparrows of the genus *Zonotrichia* captured in central California and flown to Maryland for release were recaptured in subsequent winters back in the same region in California. Because these birds nest in Canada and Alaska, it was presumed that they migrated north in the spring following their displacement and then returned south in the fall to their regular wintering grounds.

For many years it had been observed that many small songbirds which are diurnal throughout most of the year seem to migrate between their summer and winter homes at night. This was evident from the fact that during the migratory season large numbers of migrants might be present in the morning where there was none the previous evening. Those who maintained migratory songbirds also observed a nocturnal restlessness in their captives during the spring and fall migratory period. The significance of these facts remained obscure until Gustav Kramer, a German ornithologist, showed in 1959 that these nocturnal movements of captive birds were directionally oriented if they could see the night sky. Kramer maintained Old World warblers of the genus *Sylvia* in circular cages where they could see the sky but not the horizon or any landmarks. These birds nest throughout most of Europe and winter in tropical Africa. In the fall of the year on clear nights the captive

Photos, Courtesy, John R. Meyer, North Carolina State University

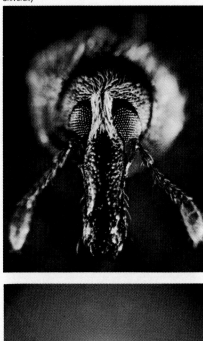

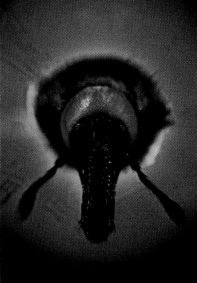

Head capsule of the alfalfa weevil contains regions recently discovered to transmit far-red and near-infrared light. Although the head seems completely opaque when viewed by reflected light (top), when lit from behind with a spot of white light its translucent portion takes on a deep red hue (bottom). This filter may assist the insect's compound eyes in locating its host plant, which strongly reflects infrared light.

no sky

North Star

Betelgeuse

warblers all faced toward the south, whereas in the spring they directed their nocturnal efforts toward the north.

To further verify this reliance on celestial cueing, similar experiments were carried out by Franz and Eleanore Sauer on the same kinds of warblers. The Sauers, however, transferred their birds during migration time to the Olbers Planetarium in Bremen, West Germany. There, when the dome overhead was illuminated with a diffused light, the nocturnal movements of the birds were of a random nature. But when an artificial spring sky was produced by the projector during the period of spring migration, the birds immediately oriented in a northerly direction. When the sky was rotated 180°, the birds turned with it. Subsequent experiments of a similar nature in Europe and America proved conclusively that celestial clues are used by many avian migrants. Some of these studies also suggested that at least some bird species orient specifically with reference to certain prominent groupings of stars within about 35° of the North Star and that juveniles learn to distinguish the north-south axis from other directions by observing the rotation of stars around the celestial pole.

Phonoreception

Among some vertebrates sound is used for orientation as well as communication. Scientific knowledge of this started with the work of Lazzaro Spallanzani near the end of the 18th century. This Italian physiologist noted that bats could fly around in a dark room at night without colliding with objects. In a series of experiments he blinded some of these animals and found that loss of vision did not impair their ability to avoid objects while they were in flight. When the bats' ears or mouths were covered, however, they lacked this avoidance ability. Spallanzani's observations went overlooked for a century and a half, and it was not until 1938 that U.S. biophysicist Donald R. Griffin, using high-frequency pulse-detecting equipment, showed conclusively that bats in flight emit sound pulses above the range of human audibility. Griffin, in collaboration with U.S. physiologist Robert Galambos, repeated Spallanzani's experiments by covering bats' eyes with darkened collodion plates, which could later be removed, and then releasing them in rooms strung with wire. The bats, although unable to see, easily avoided the wires, but they could not do so when their ears were plugged.

It is now known that small insectivorous bats emit high-frequency sounds (often in excess of 100,000 hertz) as they fly about at night. These pulses are produced with great rapidity, and although they do not travel far they are reflected from small nearby objects such as flying insects that are sought for food. The returning echoes apprise the animals not only of the presence of objects but also of their size and shape. Bats are not the only aerial animals to make use of echolocation. Bursts of rapid clicks within the range of human hearing are utilized by the oilbird (*Steatornis caripensis*), a nocturnal species that lives in caves in northern South America and on the island of Trinidad. Certain species of cave-inhabiting swiftlets also make use of echolocation.

After the discovery of the use of echolocation by bats it was found that many kinds of marine mammals produce underwater sounds of a wide range

Georg Quedens

Among birds of prey the owl (above) enjoys a popular reputation for unrivaled nocturnal visual acuity. A special membrane, or "second eyelid," offers its eyes increased protection. Exposure of young indigo buntings to the starry night sky (opposite page) is believed to figure prominently in their learning of the north-south axis. In one experiment three groups of laboratory-reared nestlings were given differing nocturnal stimuli: one group was kept indoors and isolated from all point sources of light; a second group was exposed on alternate nights for two months to a planetarium-simulated sky, which rotated like the true sky about the North Star; and a third group was similarly exposed to a sky that rotated about Betelgeuse, a star in the constellation Orion. In the fall when the birds began to display restlessness, all were exposed in the planetarium to a normal night sky. The group raised in relative isolation could not choose a preferred migration orientation; the second group oriented to the south; and the third group behaved as if Betelgeuse were the polestar and oriented their activity 180° from it.

71

bone

eardrum

ear canal

bone

bone

eardrum

foam-filled
sacs

ear canal

CURTAIN

FLOATS

BANK

of frequency, which may be as high as 300,000 hertz. Underwater sound reception by dolphins, porpoises, and whales presents problems that terrestrial or aerial animals do not face. Sound travels four times as rapidly in water as in air; hence echoes of sounds emitted by an underwater animal return more rapidly. Furthermore, sound waves do not pass readily from a lighter to a denser medium; in fact, the greater the density difference between two substances, the greater the amount of reflectance at their interface. In a bat, sound waves penetrate the body only at the eardrum, where they are transformed into waves that are transmitted mechanically across the three auditory ossicles of the middle ear to the inner ear. Essentially opaque to sound, the bat's head serves as an insulator, separating the ears. This assists in directional hearing because a given sound will be received with equal intensity by both ears only if the animal is facing directly toward or away from the source. If not, the sound will be more intense in the ear nearer the source. In water this type of directional orientation is lost because the body tissues of marine mammals are of nearly the same density as the surrounding water. Underwater sounds, therefore, can penetrate any part of the body with ease.

Cetaceans have seemingly solved the problem of sound penetration by developing an insulated inner ear. This is housed in the tympanic bone, which is suspended from the skull by ligaments and surrounded by a low-density foam- or air-filled cavity. This arrangement allows sound to penetrate only through the opening in the skull leading into the tympanic bone.

The underwater sounds of cetaceans are thought to serve as a means of communication between members of a group and probably as one means of sexual recognition at a distance. Such sounds also are believed to be an aid in locating food and determining water depth. It is likely that certain migrating cetaceans use echolocation as a means of orientation in relation to adjacent land masses. More recently it was demonstrated that certain species of seals and sea lions produce underwater sounds and that their echoes from objects in the environment provide a guiding system when visibility is reduced. Experiments by U.S. scientist and polar explorer Thomas C. Poulter showed that sea lions in total darkness not only can detect objects under water when they are swimming but also, by means of their sonar system, are able to determine composition, size, and shape of unseen objects with great rapidity.

Infrasonic waves, or sound frequencies below about ten hertz (the lower limit of human hearing), are commonly produced by weather fronts and storms, auroras, seismic disturbances, and various man-made devices. It has been suggested that some migratory and homing bird species may orient themselves with respect to cues provided from infrasound sources. In the mid–1970s studies of restrained homing pigeons (*Columba livia*) demonstrated that they could be conditioned to anticipate the onset of a mild electric shock when it was immediately preceded by a brief exposure to infrasound. These birds seemed able to detect frequencies below one hertz and to respond to intensity levels within the range of naturally produced infrasound. Because sound attenuation is proportional to the square of the frequency, atmospheric infrasounds can travel hundreds of miles with relatively little loss of intensity, and thus could provide birds with information

concerning distant storms and even with landmarks for triangulation of their destinations. Whether homing pigeons actually exploit such clues, however, is not known.

Mechanoreception

There exists another group of guidance systems that are associated with touch or contact, pressure changes, vibrations, and balance. These are called mechanoreceptors and are important in one way or another in all forms of animal life. Small free-floating or moving organisms may retreat when a solid object is contacted. This reaction is effected by the sudden pressure of contact. By contrast, many other small water-dwelling animals are positively thigmotactic; that is, they always orient to keep in contact with their substratum.

Gravity is important in the orientation of most living organisms, and the animal world has evolved various methods of detecting the direction of gravitational attraction. In multicellular animals, gravitational detectors are sensory cells that react to pressure. Some invertebrates, for example, have hollow pits called statocysts lined with sensory hairs. The movement of grains of sand or tiny calcareous concretions within these pits enables the organism to orient itself in relation to gravitational pull. This principle is also

Lobsters and crayfish detect the direction of gravitational attraction by means of hollow pits called statocysts at the base of each of their two smaller antennas. Developed from an inward folding of surface tissue, each statocyst is lined with sensory-cell hairs and contains trapped grains of sand that push or pull the hairs in various parts of the statocyst in relation to the animal's movement or body position. An inverted position, for example, will cause the sand grains to fall toward what is normally the top of the hollow organ, stimulating a peculiar combination of sensory nerves. The normal response of the animal would be to use its legs to right itself.

surface waves

walking legs

compressional waves

found in vertebrates, in which it reaches a peak of development in the semicircular canals of the inner ear, the organs of balance and orientation.

A different type of sensory organ that responds to changes in pressure is found in fish and aquatic amphibians. Called the lateral line system, it consists of a row of small nipple-like protuberances called neuromasts on each side of the body that branches into three parts on the side of the head. The sensory organs are in covered canals that open to the outside by means of pores. The tips of these structures flex in response to pressure changes and currents caused by displacement of the surrounding water. Proper orientation, close approach of objects, and even migratory movements depend in part on the proper functioning of the lateral line system. Studies reported in 1976 also implicated the lateral line system in the schooling activities of at least one species of fish under laboratory conditions.

Other organisms make use of surface wave action in the water for orientation. Some fish depend upon surface waves to locate prey. It is interesting that such fish possess modified lateral line organs on the surface of the head. The neuromasts are arranged in various directions so as to detect the source of surface waves. A similar system is found in whirligig beetles of the genus *Gyrinus*. These insects occur in aggregations and swirl about on the surface of the water without colliding even though they mass very closely together. Each beetle as it swirls produces a tiny wave that bounces off nearby objects and returns, somewhat like sound echoes, as smaller waves. The beetle producing the wave detects the echoes through a modified antennal segment. Part of the segment consists of a set of fine brushes that rest upon the surface of the water.

Some animals are known to use vibrations propagated through solid media to locate prey. The nocturnal sand scorpion (*Paruroctonus mesaensis*), for instance, can sense disturbances as far as 50 centimeters (20 inches) away that are due to small insects moving across or burrowing into loose sand, and can determine the direction of and the distance from the source of the disturbance with great accuracy. Recent experiments involving seismic modeling of the desert surface defined two major components to vibrations arising from such insect movements: higher frequency, higher velocity compressional waves that are quickly attenuated as they pass through the sand; and lower frequency, lower velocity surface waves that are more slowly attenuated. One set of mechanoreceptors called slit sensilla, which are located at the end of each walking leg of the scorpion, were found to be sensitive to surface waves, whereas a second, similarly located set, the tarsal sensory hairs, were shown to respond primarily to compressional waves. It was suggested that sand scorpions detect direction by sensing the pattern of leg stimulation as the wave front passes, with the leg nearest the source of the vibrations being stimulated first. Judgment of distance might result from an ability to sense the magnitude of the time delay between the higher velocity, and hence earlier arriving, compressional component and the later arriving surface component; the greater the distance to the source of the waves, the longer will be the time delay between components.

Electric and magnetic reception

Several different groups of fish have developed organs that can generate electric currents. In the electric eel (*Electrophorus electricus*), the electric catfish (*Malapterurus electricus*), and the electric ray (*Torpedo nobiliana*), the electrical discharge is strong, ranging from about 220 to 550 volts and as much as one ampere. Organs of such fish produce a powerful shock and serve both for defense and for stunning prey. There are two other unrelated families of fish that have electric organs capable of producing only a weak discharge. One of these, the Mormyridae, lives in the turbid rivers of Africa. The other is the Gymnotidae, inhabiting the muddy waters of South America. Both groups of fish show a reduction in size of the tail fin and the development of a single long fin which is dorsal in the mormyrids and ventral in the gymnotids. Undulatory movement of these single fins is used for both forward and backward propulsion. Both groups of fish also tend to develop long snouts and to possess weak electric organs in the tail region. During electric discharge the tail becomes negative relative to the anterior end; it is kept straight since it is not used in swimming.

The weak electric fields so established are thought to serve as a means of orientation. If there is a nearby object in the water that differs in electrical conductivity from the surrounding water, it will distort the pattern of the electric field. The fact that objects of the same size and shape but differing in electrical conductivity can be distinguished is highly useful to fish living in turbid water. Detection of electric impulses appears to be associated with special cells located along the lateral line system. In some species these electroreceptors can detect very weak electric fields. In captivity it also has been shown that both *Gymnarchus niloticus* of the family Mormyridae and

Insects burrowing invisibly beneath loose sand still find it difficult to elude the nocturnal sand scorpion, which can detect disturbances propagated through the sand as seismic waves. See illustration on opposite page and text above.

77

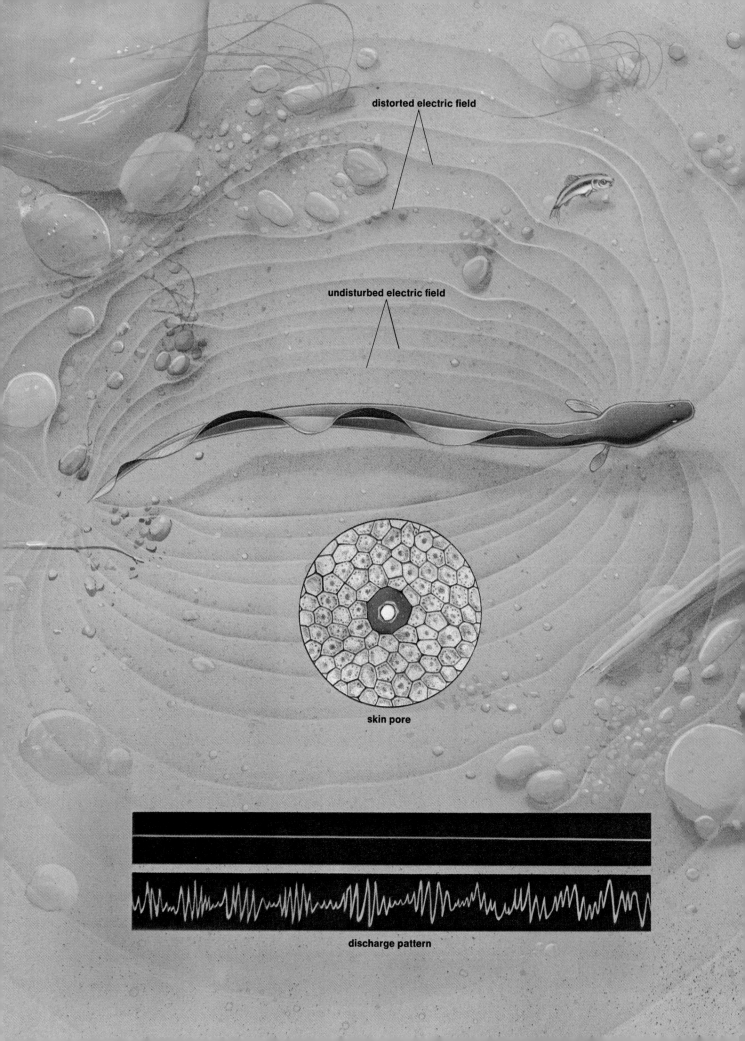

distorted electric field

undisturbed electric field

skin pore

discharge pattern

Gymnotus carapo of the family Gymnotidae are able to detect the presence of a magnet on the outside of an aquarium and can even be conditioned to come for food when a magnet is placed near a side of the container.

For nearly a hundred years there have been recurring arguments regarding the possibility that birds have a special sense enabling them to detect the Earth's magnetic field. Early experiments failed to demonstrate that a bird's homing or migratory ability could be disrupted, for instance, by attaching a permanent magnet to its body. Several recent studies, however, have presented some positive, though as yet inconclusive, evidence. In one type of experiment, homing pigeons with bar magnets or battery-powered wire coils affixed to their heads appeared disoriented when they were released from unfamiliar locations on overcast days; on clear days the pigeons oriented toward home, presumably taking their compass direction from the Sun. Similar experiments with permanent magnets on juvenile ring-billed gulls (*Larus delawarensis*) inexperienced in migration produced disorientation in the birds on both clear and overcast days. Studies of caged migratory European robins (*Erithacus rubecula*) and indigo buntings (*Passerina cyanea*) deprived of visual cues revealed that orientation of the birds' nocturnal movements could be shifted predictably when an artificial magnetic field surrounding the cages was altered. Some evidence also was cited to suggest that natural geomagnetic disturbances and even man-made radio emission from the antennas of low-frequency communications systems may affect migratory activity.

The human element

There is still much to be learned about the various mechanisms involved in animal orientation, especially among the more than one million known invertebrates (including insects), very few of which have been studied in any depth. Most of mankind's present knowledge has been acquired within the past three or four decades as a result of technological advances. Such basic discoveries as the use of celestial navigation by migratory species,

The electric ray (left) and the electric catfish (above) have developed organs that can generate electric currents sufficiently powerful to stun both attackers and prey. The African fish Gymnarchus niloticus of the family Mormyridae is capable of weak electric discharges that are thought to serve guidance functions (opposite page). Its electric field is generated from organs in the tail region, which during discharge becomes momentarily negative with respect to the head. Detection of this electric field seems to be associated with specialized pores in the skin on and near the head, which lead to spherical capsules of cells called mormyromasts that are believed to be the actual sense organs. Mormyromasts detect variations in the electric field caused by nearby objects that are either better or poorer conductors of electricity than the surrounding water. Whereas Gymnarchus is difficult to locate visually in its turbid native waters, its movements between feeding and rest areas can be inferred from the absence or presence in the water of its characteristic discharges, which are generated continuously at a rate of about 300 times per second.

sunny

overcast

counterclockwise current

sunny

overcast

clockwise current

See caption on opposite page. In the circular diagrams above, placement of
each dot represents the observed vanishing bearing of a released pigeon,
and up is the true direction of home. The direction of each arrow represents
the mean bearing of each test group of birds. The length of each arrow is
directly proportional to the degree of agreement among birds of a group in
selecting the mean bearing.

Courtesy, L. R. Nault, Ohio Agricultural Research and Development Center, Wooster; photo by G. L. Berkey

echolocation by animals in air and in water, the sensory use of electric impulses by some fish, and many others beyond the scope of this article represent merely the beginning of research into the vast, fascinating field of animal guidance systems.

Knowledge of this subject already has proved to be of practical importance to man in a number of ways. The use of pheromones is currently under study as a possible means of controlling certain insects injurious to cultivated crops. Traps using the odor of females of such species may capture large numbers of males and thereby reduce the reproductive potential. Recently it was discovered that males of a parasitic intestinal nematode, when maintained in an environment permeated with a pheromone produced by the female, temporarily lost their ability to orient to a gradient of the same pheromone coming from living females. It was suggested that this knowledge could lead to a new anthelmintic technique that would disrupt the mating communication of parasitic worms.

The discovery that young salmon imprint to the smell of the home stream has been very useful to fishery biologists. In one application spawning fish are captured and removed to new streams suitable but not previously used for salmon culture. There eggs are removed from the females, fertilized with milt from the males, and left to hatch and grow. After descending to the sea and maturing, the new generation of salmon return to the stream in which they hatched, not to the stream of their parents.

For many years sonar has been employed by ships to determine water depth at sea and to locate submerged objects. Man's use of instruments for echolocation, however, is very new compared with its probable use for millions of years by bats in their nocturnal search for insects, and by marine mammals in their movements through the ocean. Undoubtedly further studies on animal guidance systems will lead to new techniques in solving human problems as well as to a better understanding of the delicate environment in which man lives.

In typical experiments that tested the navigational dependence of birds on the Earth's magnetic field, homing pigeons were fitted with battery-powered wire coils in which current could be made to flow in either direction (opposite page). When released at a distance from home on both sunny and cloudy days, pigeons whose brains were subjected to magnetic fields from counterclockwise current were seen to fly almost directly homeward. When current flow was clockwise, released pigeons still tended to orient homeward when they could see the Sun, but on cloudy days their direction averaged almost 180° from home, suggesting that induced magnetic fields could interfere with some natural magnetic sense. (Above) Under attack by a predator, a plant-eating aphid (smaller insect at right) signals the presence of danger to nearby aphids by means of an "alarm" pheromone, which can be seen as a tiny droplet adhering to one of the insect's extremities. Treatment of crop plants with synthetic alarm pheromones may prevent insect infestations in the future by frightening potential pests.

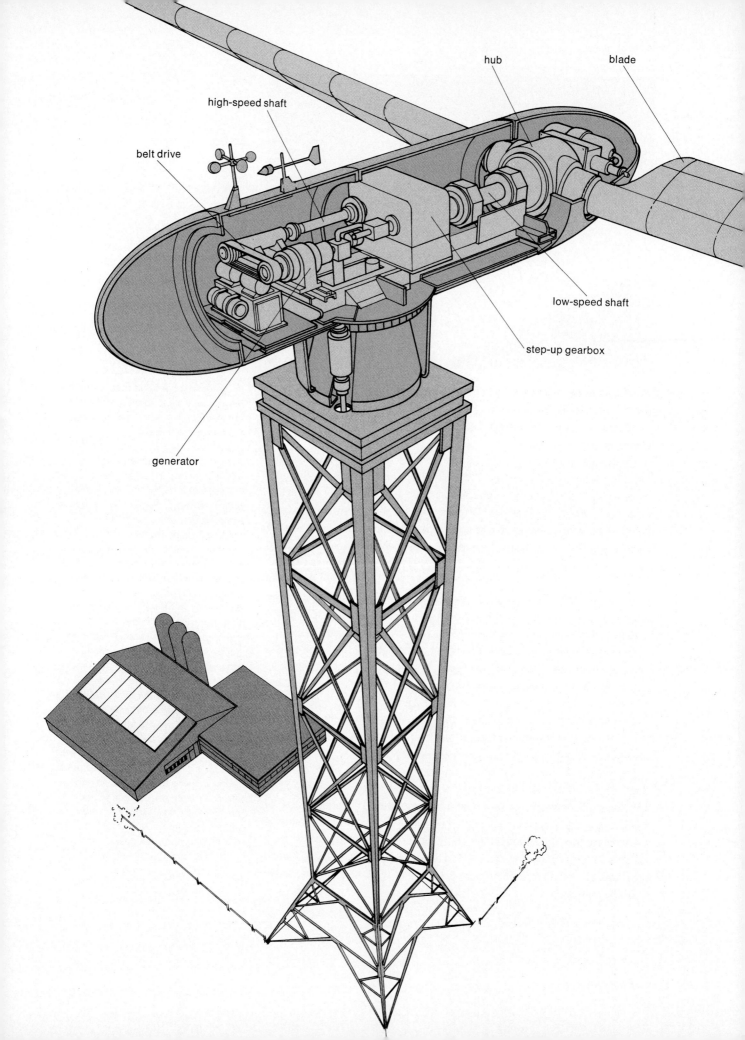

belt drive

high-speed shaft

hub

blade

generator

low-speed shaft

step-up gearbox

Renewable Energy: The Other Answer

by C. Sharp Cook

Low-technology energy systems using only renewable resources offer attractive alternatives to nuclear power and the burning of fossil fuels.

The United States currently consumes energy resources at a rate amounting to about one-third of the world total. During recent decades it has obtained more than three-quarters of its energy from petroleum and natural gas, both of which have become very limited in supply. Domestic extraction of crude oil and of natural gas peaked in 1971 and, except for a one-time increase because of the availability of Alaskan oil, has shown a continued decline since that time. To offset the loss of these domestic resources, an ever increasing amount of foreign oil has been imported, at a cost of about $100 million a day in 1976 and about $125 million a day in 1977, an expenditure that has caused large trade deficits and has hurt the U.S. dollar.

The U.S. is not alone with this dilemma. Other industrialized nations such as Japan and the countries of Western Europe are currently very dependent on oil and natural gas for the continuation of their economic strength. Some of these countries import an even larger percentage of their oil supplies than the U.S., but most have found ways to avoid huge trade deficits. Foreign oil suppliers cannot continue indefinitely to supply the demands of the industrialized world because their deposits are also finite. Experts differ in their opinions as to when a world oil catastrophe will arise if mankind continues its present patterns of energy use, but even the most optimistic predictions foresee serious problems within a few decades. Although the time for oil exhaustion cannot yet be pinpointed, world leaders generally agree that an urgent need exists to develop alternative energy systems.

Experimental U.S.-built wind turbine produces enough electricity in 19-mph winds to power 30 homes. Its blades span 125 feet. A more powerful version recently went into commercial use in New Mexico.

Ben Kocivar

The growing worldwide scarcity of petroleum and natural gas has driven exploratory and extraction efforts to remote locations in the Arctic Circle (right) and at the ocean floor. The increased expense of such operations is reflected in higher costs to consumers. Strip mining of coal (opposite page, top) destroys the Earth's surface, which if not restored becomes a useless wasteland. Use of coal as an energy source also pollutes the air with fly ash and sulfur; its conversion to an environmentally acceptable fuel taxes the best efforts of modern technology. Effectiveness of an experimental solvent-refining process is shown in color-enhanced photomicrographs of raw, high-sulfur coal (center) and solvent-refined coal from which sulfur and fly ash have been removed (bottom).

C. SHARP COOK *is Professor of Physics at the University of Texas, El Paso.*

Illustrations by Ben Kozak

Problems with current planning

The governments of many nations have formulated at least a tentative plan for coping with the energy crisis. They think in terms of an increased use of coal and nuclear fission and the development of nuclear fusion as ways to keep the wheels of industry turning. Each of these replacement fuels, however, has its own unique problems, some of which are of such serious nature that many people are concerned that implementation of a plan to use these resources could destroy present-day civilization.

One drawback of coal is that it must be mined. Deep deposits require underground mining, one of the most dangerous occupations that a person can enter, both because of safety problems in the mines and because of potential long-term health hazards. Currently, an average of more than 100 people are killed annually in mine accidents in the U.S. If the use of oil and natural gas were to be replaced with that of coal and the number of miners increased proportionally without making any change in mining procedures, the projected death rate from mining accidents would be in excess of 500 per year. Whereas shallow deposits can be extracted more easily and more safely, they require strip mining, the tearing away of the Earth's surface. If the surface is not restored, a barren wasteland results that often can no

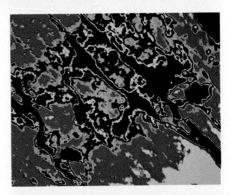

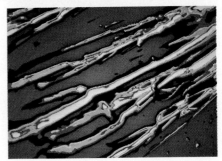

longer serve any useful purpose. Restoration is possible using methods that rely on the availability of large amounts of water, as exemplified by regions that have been restored west of Cologne, West Germany. Most of the shallow coal deposits in the U.S., however, are in the drier western states where surface restoration would be considerably more difficult, perhaps impossible, unless precious water is diverted from other uses.

Burning of coal creates a pollution problem. Fly ash and numerous chemicals, such as sulfur, escape into the atmosphere unless expensive equipment is added to remove them. Furthermore, burning of coal adds carbon dioxide to the Earth's atmosphere. It has been shown that the carbon dioxide content of the air is increasing rapidly, by about 5% during the past 20 years and about 10% during the last century. Some scientists and nonscientists have expressed concern that this buildup of carbon dioxide will slow the escape of solar infrared radiation through the Earth's atmosphere and cause a temperature increase at the surface. A change in climatic conditions at the surface of the Earth, even a small one, could have disastrous effects on such life-supporting processes as the growing of food crops. Although in the late 1970s it was not clear whether this change really had been taking place, waiting for evidence could undermine mankind's ability to avert disaster, for it is impossible to effect a rapid removal of carbon dioxide from the air.

85

Continued proliferation of nuclear fission reactors increases the health-threatening hazards of radioactive waste and exacerbates problems of waste disposal. In addition, breeder reactors produce large quantities of fissionable material that can be diverted to production of nuclear weapons.

Nuclear fission, which is used currently for the production of some electrical energy in several nations of the world, also has its problems. All fissioning elements produce radioactive atoms that can threaten health or even life unless special precautions are taken to prevent their escape into the biosphere. Of special importance are two long-lived radioactive products of nuclear fission, strontium-90 and cesium-137, both of which have half-lives of about 30 years. Wastes removed from a fission reactor contain sufficient quantities of these two radioactive substances to produce hazardous radiation for hundreds of years. Use of nuclear fission as a source of power means committing future generations to the maintenance of a vigil over radioactive wastes for several centuries. (See *1978 Yearbook of Science and the Future* Feature Article: NUCLEAR WASTE DISPOSAL.)

Another controversy centers on the use of breeder reactors. All commercially operated power reactors in the U.S. presently use the rare isotope uranium-235 as fuel. Of every 1,000 tons of mined uranium, only seven tons are uranium-235, the remainder being uranium-238, which cannot be burned as fuel in a nuclear reactor. Because uranium, like coal, oil, and natural gas, is also finite in quantity, a time limit exists on the availability of uranium-235 as reactor fuel, perhaps a few decades beyond the era of available oil and natural gas. To make nuclear fission a truly long-term source of energy, one must turn to breeder reactors. In these, uranium-238 is transformed into plutonium-239, which can then be burned in reactors to fuel the needs of the industrialized world for as much as 1,000 years. In addition, if breeder reactors are used to transform thorium-232 into uranium-233, another fission fuel, the amount of time that nuclear fission can be used for energy is further extended. A few countries, including France, Great Britain, and the Soviet Union, already have working breeder reactors supplying some of their electrical power needs.

Breeder reactors produce large quantities of uranium-233 or plutonium-239 and of such purity that this material can be used to make nuclear explosives. Present-day nonbreeder reactors already produce smaller but significant quantities of plutonium-239. Indeed, India demonstrated with its nuclear detonation in early 1974 that plutonium can be extracted from a nonbreeder reactor and made into an explosive. It was estimated that the total cost of making India's explosive device was only about $400,000, financially within the reach of the poorest of governments, provided they can find the scientists, engineers, and laboratory facilities to do the work. Scattered throughout the world, power reactors would provide possible access to nuclear explosives to a growing number of people and would greatly increase the chances for nuclear war.

Nuclear fusion, the merging of two hydrogen atoms to form helium, is the process believed to provide the energy of the Sun. Using the heavy isotopes of hydrogen (deuterium and tritium), such a thermonuclear fusion reaction has been adapted to explosives, the so-called hydrogen bomb as well as the neutron bomb, but has not been developed as a commercial source of energy, although its advocates continue to praise it highly. Furthermore, to use nuclear fusion as a controlled source of energy requires some of the most advanced technological procedures yet developed. Any system found-

Technicians service nuclear fission reactor in France (left). Cooling towers from immense power reactors (above) dissipate a large fraction of unexploited energy into the air. Carried by air currents, this heat can affect climate many miles downwind of the generating station.

ed on this process can never be made very simple. If it can ever be put to practical use, however, enough deuterium exists in the oceans to supply the energy needs of the world for more than a million years.

The most basic problem with controlled nuclear fusion is that it is still in the research stage; until a prototype reactor is built and operated, no one will know whether it offers a viable source of energy for the industrialized world. To demonstrate the nature of the problem, one need only recall statements by experts in the field of nuclear fusion. In 1955, at the first Geneva Conference on Peaceful Uses of Atomic Energy, experts predicted that a prototype fusion reactor would be built and in operation in about 20 years. At a hearing on nuclear fusion held by the U.S. Congress in 1971, experts again predicted that a prototype fusion reactor would be built and in operation in about 20 years. Most recently, when experts speculated on the time required for a prototype fusion reactor to be built and in operation, the average answer was about 20 years.

Courtesy, Argonne National Laboratory

Depicted in model form is an ion-beam fusion device conceived by scientists at Argonne National Laboratory in Illinois. Pellets containing heavy isotopes of hydrogen would be introduced into the central chamber of the device at a governed rate and bombarded from multiple directions by high-energy ions channeled from a peripheral storage ring. Each intense pulse of energy would cause the isotopes in a pellet to fuse, inducing a miniature thermonuclear explosion. Such a concept makes use of some of the most sophisticated technology yet developed.

All three of the proposed schemes for solving the energy crisis suffer from a common problem, that of scale. In order to be used efficiently or in some cases even used at all, the power station must be very large. In such a case the most effective way to use the energy is to generate electricity or some other transportable form of energy and to distribute it to customers in a large region surrounding the power station. With each transformation from one type of energy to another, a loss occurs. For example, the most efficient electric power stations presently in operation deliver only about 40% of the energy of the fuel that they consume to the outgoing power lines. Furthermore, additional losses of energy occur along the transmission route from station to final destination, so that the customer seldom receives more than one-third of the energy initially consumed at the power station. The energy from this unexploited fuel is usually dissipated as waste heat, generally into the atmosphere near ground level through a cooling tower. This release of heat can sometimes modify the local climate downwind from the power station for as much as 100 miles.

The alternative scheme

Many people feel that civilization is racing madly into a nuclear and coal-burning age without giving adequate consideration to a strategy that would require neither the priesthood of specialists to operate the proposed high-technology systems nor the potentially extreme risks of these systems. The basic imperatives of this alternative scheme are as follows: (1) Use only renewable energy resources; completely stop using depletable resources after a transition period of about 50 years. (2) Use only energy resources that will allow maintenance of an essentially pollution-free environment. (3) Keep operations as simple as possible; high technology adds to cost, to the chance of system breakdown, and to other problems. (4) Eliminate waste;

a viable economy does not require present-day wastage of approximately half the energy resources consumed.

George Dodge—D.P.I.

Solar energy—an abundance beyond belief

The largest and most important of the Earth's renewable energy resources is solar energy. Every 22 minutes as much energy strikes the Earth in the form of solar radiation as is currently used in a year by all consumers of energy resources. In two weeks this solar energy exceeds the energy content of all known coal deposits of the world. Primary deterrents to effective use of solar energy are nighttime extinction of the source and intermittent daytime reductions caused by cloud cover. The amount of radiation reaching the Earth's surface can also be greatly reduced by haze and other atmospheric interference. Nevertheless, solar energy has found considerable use in the past and could be harnessed for many more applications. Furthermore, additional use of solar energy would eliminate both environmental difficulties and the potential health hazards associated with nuclear fission and the burning of coal.

Of the solar energy intercepted by the Earth, 30% is reflected back into space, in large amounts from clouds and polar ice. About 47% is absorbed at or near the Earth's surface and is transformed into heat, which is vital to the support of life. A third major portion of the Sun's radiation, 23%, goes into the evaporation of water, both from seawater and through transpiration from the leaves of green plants. This water ultimately returns to the Earth as rain or snow. Although these three categories account virtually for 100% of the Sun's radiant energy, two other categories are very important, even though fractionally small. About 0.2% is used to produce winds, ocean waves, and other phenomena resulting from atmospheric motions. An even smaller amount, 0.02%, is absorbed by plants in the process of photosynthesis, a chemical transformation that must take place for living things to exist on the Earth.

Why is solar energy not used more extensively? Primary among many reasons is that over the past century the use of oil and natural gas has been much more convenient and more economical than the use of solar energy. Furthermore, in view of the awesome potential of the first nuclear reactors and nuclear weapons developed during World War II, the U.S. Congress decreed in the late 1940s, with the support and advice of the experts of that period, that nuclear fission would be the replacement for oil and natural gas when these resources approach depletion. Congress then established the Atomic Energy Commission (AEC) to oversee this transfer to nuclear power. Thirty years later, however, nuclear fission was supplying only 3% of the energy used in the U.S. Had a solar energy commission been established at the same time as the AEC, it seems likely that the U.S. would currently be much closer to energy self-sufficiency.

Most of the basic science and engineering needed to make use of solar energy is already known, and equipment capable of accomplishing much of this task has been demonstrated. The most basic problem is the establishment of an economic climate that will put solar energy on the same footing with other energy resources. Essentially all energy industries presently sell

Fixed-mirror device developed by Sandia Laboratories in New Mexico is a product of research aimed at improving the efficiency of solar collectors.

89

Experimental array of 135 silicon cells and concentrating lenses (above) at Sandia Laboratories produces one kilowatt of electricity directly from sunlight. Excess heat piped from the cells by liquid coolant also can be put to useful work. The U.S. Department of Energy's Solar Thermal Test Facility at Sandia (opposite page) comprises more than 220 heliostat arrays, each of which contains 25 four-foot-square mirrors. As much as five megawatts of solar thermal energy can be concentrated upon any desired test location on the 200-foot "power tower."

an energy resource, as demonstrated by the oil and gas companies or the electric utilities. Because solar energy is diffusely scattered over the Earth, it cannot easily be collected and sold but is available to almost everyone. What appears to be needed is a type of company that supplies expertise and equipment to install a system for the collection and utilization of solar energy and the maintenance needed to make the system operate smoothly. No centralized energy source would be required. On the other hand, use of coal, nuclear fission, or nuclear fusion would continue to require current marketing techniques and to allow energy companies to sell energy to consumers from a centralized energy plant. To move to the entirely different solar energy system would require a relatively drastic change from current operating procedures and perhaps even the abandonment of some existing facilities. However, if mankind could obviously benefit from such a change, the reward would be worth the effort.

90

Prototype electrical generating plant uses about 135 square meters of mirror surface to focus sunlight on a solar boiler suspended above the reflector array. Superheated steam produced in the boiler can be made to drive a conventional turbogenerator.

Applications of solar energy

Technology for the generation of heat using solar radiation has long been available. The simplest solar energy system is a flat-plate collector used either for hot-water heating or for space heating of buildings. A flat-plate collector absorbs both incident sunlight and scattered radiation that strike it. Water, air, or other fluids circulate through the collector, transferring the collected heat to a location where it can be used. In the U.S. as of late 1977 the economic competitiveness of this type of system depended largely on the climatic conditions of the region in which construction was to take place. In much of the country solar energy was already competitive with all-electric heating, sometimes competitive with fuel-oil heating, but generally not competitive with natural-gas heating, especially in those regions where federally controlled pricing applied.

A large part of the cost of installation of a solar energy system is the heat storage subsystem, required because heating is especially needed at night. Three basic storage systems have been developed: one stores heat in a liquid (usually water) in an insulated tank; the second stores heat in a bed of pebbles; and a third transfers heat to a salt that changes phase, using the heat of fusion as the basic storage mechanism with only a minimal change of temperature. Currently the first system is most commonly used, but commercial installations are also available using the second system, based on a design by U.S. solar engineer George Löf. A potentially useful salt for the

92

third system is a hydrated form of sodium sulfate, $Na_2SO_4 \cdot 10H_2O$, which melts at 32° C (90° F).

An important step in reducing the use of fossil fuels should occur if residential space heating is transferred to solar energy, because home heating represents about 50% of residential energy use and about 13% of all energy use in the U.S. Heating of commercial buildings by solar energy is also technically feasible, and appropriate systems have already been installed on a number of such buildings. For example, the New Mexico Department of Agriculture Building in Las Cruces has derived all hot water and space heating from solar energy since it was completed in 1975. Several buildings in more northerly climates have also been fitted with solar energy equipment that provides a large fraction of their winter heating requirements.

Air conditioning in summer is not quite as easy as space heating in winter, but techniques already exist to accomplish this task, based on principles used in early refrigerators that used natural gas as their energy source. For example, the New Mexico Department of Agriculture Building receives between one-third and one-half of its summer cooling in this way, using a lithium bromide and water absorption system. The system produces chilled water that in turn is used to cool the air circulated throughout the building.

A very basic problem with solar energy air-conditioning systems is that flat-plate collectors do not heat their circulating fluids to a temperature sufficiently high to make the system very efficient. Higher temperatures can be attained through the use of focusing collectors, most of which are constructed as a trough with parabolic cross section, which focuses solar radiation onto a fluid-filled tube along the focal line of the reflector. Such systems are quite effective if they are rotated to follow the Sun and can heat the fluid to as much as a few hundred degrees Celsius rather than to a temperature usually just below the boiling point of water.

Solar radiation can be used for many purposes other than simple heating of air or water. Solar energy water pumps, for instance, have already been built and operated. Whereas the pioneer work in this field was concentrated in West Africa, in the late 1970s it was also becoming important elsewhere.

Solar reflector constructed as a trough with parabolic cross section (below) focuses sunlight onto a fluid-filled tube suspended along the focal line of the reflector. Applications of this low-technology device include installation in the individual home (above), where solar energy can supplement or supplant conventional space heating and hot-water systems.

The Mexican government has constructed solar energy water pumps using a flat-plate collecting system and is planning a whole series of such pumps to supply water to remote villages that do not have electric power and to which the hauling of fossil fuels is both difficult and expensive. Calculations indicate that such a system can be amortized in 20–25 years. The U.S. has also constructed an experimental water pump for agricultural purposes, using a concentrating collector, at Willard, New Mexico. All these systems appear to be working in a very satisfactory manner.

Where electric power is needed in reasonable quantities, it can often be generated using photovoltaic cells, the ultimate in technologically oriented, renewable-resource schemes. These cells have been used extensively in the U.S. and Soviet space programs to power orbiting space stations and satellites. The reasons usually offered for minimal use of these cells in ground-based applications are cost and efficiency, since cost per kilowatt using solar cells is presently about 20 times the cost of power from central generating stations. Technological developments, however, continue to lower the cost of solar cells and, if the trend continues, probably will make them economically competitive near the end of the 20th century. Even though cells now commercially available convert only about 10% of the incident sunlight to electrical energy, experimental cells have been constructed with much higher efficiencies, silicon cells at 19% and gallium arsenide cells at 24%. Because solar-cell output is directly related to incident light intensity, use of a light concentrator reduces the cost per kilowatt for a single cell. Furthermore, heat generated by the 90% of the unconverted solar energy can be carried away by a circulating fluid to perform other tasks of the types already mentioned.

One of the greatest difficulties in making effective use of solar energy is simply inducing people to "think solar." When a city plans a new subdivision or an architect designs a building, neither usually considers orienting lots or buildings to maximize use of solar energy. Yet, placing buildings to allow maximum entry of the Sun's rays in winter and minimum entry in summer undoubtedly can lower fuel bills. Systems have also been proposed for illuminating the interior of buildings with channeled, reflected sunlight as a sensible alternative to the completely enclosed building that requires artificial lighting throughout.

Wind power, waterpower, and ocean thermal energy

As mentioned above, wind also derives its energy from the Sun. It is somewhat fickle, however, blowing one day and not the next, or blowing predominantly in one season of the year. Nevertheless, some regions of the U.S. are blessed with relatively large amounts of wind energy, sometimes as much as a few hundred watts per square meter, which is greater than the average direct insolation on many parts of the country. Specific regions with high wind energy include those just off the northwest and northeast coasts, the Great Lakes region, and a large expanse just east of the Rocky Mountains. In these regions, wind energy can easily supplement existing energy resources and in some instances can supply a large fraction of energy needs.

Use of wind power is not new. It has been used throughout recorded

Farmhouses with their wind pumps for drawing water from the ground have been a common rustic sight in many countries for generations.

Hiroji Kubota—Magnum

94

history by technically primitive people. From the mid–19th century until 1940 more than six million windmills were built and sold in the U.S., primarily to farmers and ranchers. A somewhat larger, 1.25-megawatt wind generator was constructed and operated during the early 1940s at Grandpa's Knob, Vermont. At the time the builder had intended to sell these energy sources to farmers and other people in isolated positions but was put out of business by the rural electrification program of the federal government, with which he could not compete. Like other solar systems, a single windmill requires an energy storage system to provide energy when the wind is not blowing. However, windmills producing electrical power can be interconnected. As

George Dodge—D.P.I.

Seven-story-high vertical-axis wind turbine undergoes testing at Sandia Laboratories as part of the U.S. federal wind energy program. The eggbeater-shaped device is designed to produce 60 kilowatts of electricity in a 28-mph wind.

early as 1945, U.S. engineer Percy Thomas pointed out that such an inter-connecting system in a favorable wind region would almost always find some windmills working and would considerably reduce the required storage capacity relative to that needed for a system operating from a single windmill or a small group of windmills.

With the ever increasing costs of conventional electric power, wind systems in some parts of the U.S. are rapidly approaching competitive positions. Furthermore, engineering knowledge needed for optimized windmill design is relatively mature, so that large-scale cost-beneficial manufacture of windmills could be initiated almost any time.

Waterpower is a solar energy derivative that for years has been supplying energy on a reasonably large scale. About 4% of the energy consumed in the U.S. presently comes from the generation of electricity by hydroelectric power stations. A few countries, such as Iceland, derive most of their electric energy from this source. Unfortunately, most U.S. hydroelectric installations are built to supplement other sources of electric power and are considered effective only when they are reasonably large. Smaller installations, however, can often be quite effective. By the late 1970s some communities and a few individuals had already made use of these possibilities or were planning small-scale waterpower projects. One such community is Springfield, Vermont, which had obtained its electric power from the Black River at the turn of the century but later abandoned this source to convert to commercially supplied electric power. In 1977 a new dam and turbine to generate at least part of the electrical needs of the town were being planned.

In 1977 the U.S. Army Corps of Engineers estimated that about 49,000 dams presently existing on rivers and streams throughout the U.S. do not have turbines to generate electric power. A sufficient number of these dams could be so equipped to provide an estimated power output equivalent to more than 30 commercial-size nuclear power stations.

Throughout the aeons of history the Earth's oceans have been extremely efficient collectors of solar energy. Radiation from the Sun penetrates the water and is trapped, with the result that the ocean surface temperatures in tropical latitudes are maintained at about 25° C (77° F) throughout the year, both day and night. By contrast, the temperature in the ocean depths constantly remains only a few degrees above the freezing point of water. In some areas ocean currents such as the Gulf Stream carry the warm surface waters into the temperate zones, creating a thermal gradient of as much as 20° C (36° F) between water at the ocean's surface and layers only a few hundred meters in depth.

Even though such temperature differences are not large, heat engines can be built that use this small thermal gradient; this was demonstrated as early as 1929 by French engineer Georges Claude, who built and operated a small (22-kilowatt) thermal gradient power plant off the coast of Cuba. The efficiency of such a system will never be more than 5%, but the total available energy is tremendous. For example, the total thermal gradient energy passing the coast of Florida each day in the Gulf Stream is about 10,000 times the average daily use of electrical energy in the U.S. Systems of reasonable size are being considered to tap this source of energy.

Modern wind turbine in operation in New Hampshire.

H. Wendler—The Image Bank

96

Use of biological systems

Another large reservoir of solar energy is the biomass material that traces its origin to photosynthesis, a process in which green plants change carbon dioxide, water, and nutrients into oxygen and various organic compounds. Only a century ago one type of biomass material, wood, was the primary fuel used in the U.S., and in many parts of the world wood is still the primary source of heat. Biomass also offers a natural and convenient energy storage system in which energy can be held for relatively long periods of time. Dried plant matter has an energy content by weight which is less than (but usually more than half) that of bituminous coal.

Many uses of biomass as a source of energy have been either proposed or tried, usually on a small scale. One suggestion is tree farms on which fast-growing pines, sycamores, poplars, and other high-yield species are produced for firewood. Other possibilities include fast-growing annuals, such as sugarcane and sunflowers. Another suggestion, the growing of kelp in the open ocean on huge rafts, would not require use of productive land surfaces. Another interesting photosynthesis system in water is exemplified by the water hyacinth plantation at Bay St. Louis, Mississippi, which obtains its nutrients from raw sewage, thereby providing sewage disposal as well as energy. These water hyacinths can produce up to ten tons of wet biomass per acre per day, which reduces to about a half ton when dried. Unlike the burning of fossil fuels, burning of dried plant material should not increase the carbon dioxide content of the air since it is only returning carbon dioxide that was taken from the air a relatively short time earlier during the growth of the plant. However, a significant factor that limits the growth of plant life in much of the U.S. and that must be considered in land-based biomass systems is lack of adequate water supplies.

In addition to direct burning, energy can be extracted from biomass materials as methanol, ethanol, and various hydrocarbons that are more easily transported than solid material and are often more convenient fuels for some specific uses, such as the operation of moving vehicles. Engineers at the University of Santa Clara, California, demonstrated that automobiles can be modified to operate with alcohol as a fuel, and the state of Nebraska successfully tested a mixture of gasoline and ethanol in state-owned vehicles. The basic idea of the Nebraska project was to look for other markets for the grain they grow. To use agricultural crops as a commercial energy source, however, is not yet economically feasible because the price per calorie received by the farmer for wheat or corn to be used as food is between two and four times the price per calorie received by exporters of oil. On the other hand, several hundred million tons (dry weight) of organic wastes are produced each year in the agriculture, forest, and other photosynthesis-dependent industries. Many of these wastes are recoverable at a cost per calorie that is less than the equivalent cost of imported oil.

Some types of desert plants appear to be very good biomass energy converters. For example, during World War II a desert shrub called guayule was used extensively in the U.S. as a source of rubber. Another desert plant, jojoba, can produce an oxidation-resistant oil with many industrial and consumer applications. (See 1977 *Yearbook of Science and the Future*

Biomass, which has its origin in plant photosynthesis, offers a natural and convenient system for storing energy from the Sun. Certain marine species of brown algae called kelp (top left) could be cultivated on large floating "farms" in the ocean and harvested for fuel and other purposes (right and above).

Feature Article: THE JOJOBA: CINDERELLA CROP FOR THE '70s?) Claims have been made that a substance resembling gasoline can be obtained from at least some species of the genus *Euphorbia*. All these plants can be grown in regions of the southwestern U.S. where production of other crops often is not feasible. (*See* Year in Review: LIFE SCIENCES: *Botany*.)

In a well-known bacterial process known as anaerobic digestion, which is presently in use on a small scale on a number of farms throughout the world, animal manure is turned into methane. Methane from the breakdown of urban sewage has also provided the energy requirements for many sewage-disposal plants. Yet it is not known exactly what fraction of existing animal wastes can be collected and used. Effective use of this resource appears to depend on scale. If a large number of small units are put into operation on individual farms, the amount of energy that can be produced will be much

98

larger than that from large units built to convert large quantities of animal wastes (such as from feed lots) to methane.

Many other ways also exist for the conversion of biomass to useful energy sources. At present the extent to which such sources can replace conventional fuels is not known, but the possibilities appear to be very large. Another uncertainty is cost but, as with all other new developments, initial costs are usually not indicative of final costs; after a product is more widely used, mass production of equipment and supplies becomes possible. Even in the late 1970s some uses of biomass as energy sources appeared to be reasonably cost effective.

Tidal and geothermal energy

Although they are generally very localized, either tidal energy or geothermal energy can play a significant role in the proposed alternative energy strategy. Both of these energy resources usually fit the specified criteria enumerated above. The feasibility of tidal energy has already been shown by the La Rance energy station on the coast of France. A region of North America where tidal action can supply a relatively large percentage of local energy needs is the Bay of Fundy, on the Atlantic coast between Nova Scotia and New Brunswick.

That geothermal sources can be used successfully has been demonstrated in Iceland and in a few other volcanically active locations around the world. A considerable amount of ingenuity but no complex technology was

La Rance hydroelectric plant at the seaport city of Saint-Malo, France, derives its energy from tidal power. During high tides the dam is opened to allow water to fill the artificial basin behind it; at low tides, when the water level in the ocean drops below that of the basin, water is allowed through the dam in the opposite direction. Water flowing in either direction is used to drive reversible turbines.

Michelangelo Durazzo—Magnum

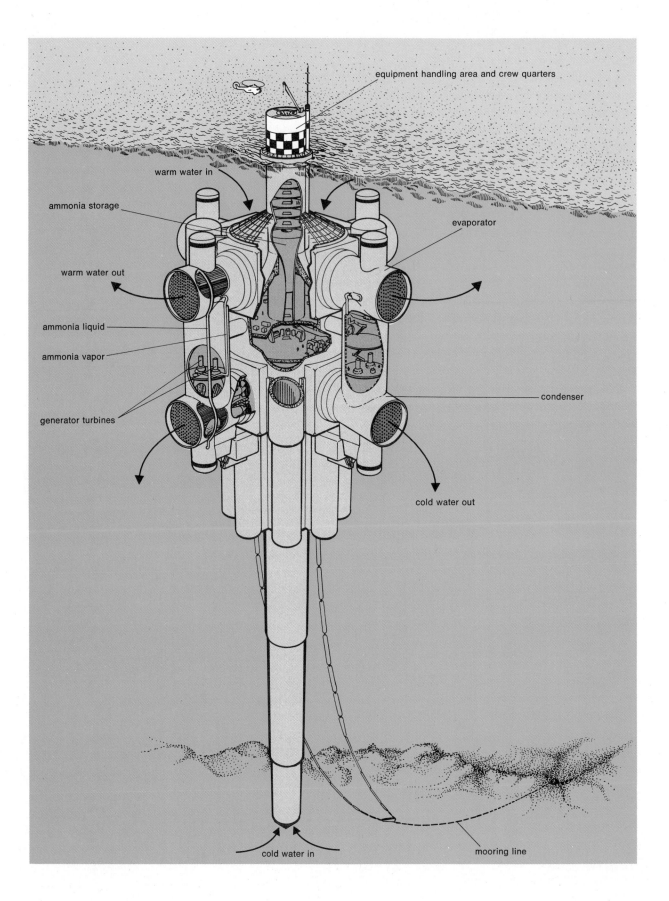

equipment handling area and crew quarters

warm water in

ammonia storage

evaporator

warm water out

ammonia liquid

ammonia vapor

generator turbines

condenser

cold water out

cold water in

mooring line

needed to develop the systems used by the city of Reykjavik and the town of Husavik to obtain hot water and space heating from geothermal wells. Geothermally heated greenhouses at Hveragerdi allow Icelandic people to grow vegetables and fruits that otherwise would not be possible. In the rural areas of Iceland, people often pipe water from nearby hot springs to provide hot water and space heating for single buildings or a small group of buildings.

Needed: a change in attitude

Modern civilization appears to have both the energy resources and the expertise to derive all of its energy needs from renewable resources in a manner that does not require complex technological developments. Many systems that use these resources have already been built and tested. If such a course of action is followed, the potential hazards and uncertainties associated with the use of coal and nuclear fuel can be avoided. An additional reason for using renewable resources is that the associated equipment will be distributed throughout the country and therefore will be much less vulnerable to natural disasters and to military and terrorist attack than large electric generating stations and long transmission lines. On the economic side, current costs associated with the use of renewable resources will certainly be reduced, especially as these resources are used in sufficient quantities to realize a savings through mass-production techniques.

One of the primary obstacles impeding implementation of the overall scheme discussed above appears to be the present tremendous financial investment in systems that use nonrenewable energy resources and the inability of many energy professionals to think of any type of operation other than the direct sale of energy to the public. Yet these huge investments are in no immediate danger of being lost because a change to renewable resources cannot be made instantaneously. It is impossible to avoid an intermediate period during which fossil and nuclear fuels continue to be used. On the other hand, if serious attention is given to the use of renewable resources as the sole source of energy, this goal should be attainable within 50–100 years. A persuasive effort by its advocates will be required to create the attitudes needed to accomplish the change of direction.

FOR ADDITIONAL READING

Barry Commoner, *The Poverty of Power: Energy and the Economic Crisis* (Knopf, 1976).

T. J. Gray and O. K. Gashus (eds.), *Tidal Power* (Plenum Press, 1972).

P. Kruger and C. Otte (eds.), *Geothermal Energy* (Stanford University Press, 1973).

Ralph E. Lapp, *The Logarithmic Century* (Prentice-Hall, Inc., 1973).

Amory B. Lovins, *Soft Energy Paths: Toward a Durable Peace* (Ballinger, 1977).

A series of articles in the *Bulletin of the Atomic Scientists* between November 1975 and October 1976 provides an excellent overview of the current situation regarding solar energy.

Thermal gradient power plants, such as the model shown on the opposite page, could exploit temperature differences in the ocean to supply large amounts of power. The tubular base of the floating plant is designed to extend some 450 meters (1,500 feet) below the sea surface, where the water temperature is only a few degrees above freezing. Cold water from this level is raised by pumps to chill condensers, through which is passed a low-boiling working fluid such as ammonia. Warm surface water of about 25° C (77° F) is brought into near contact with this fluid in an evaporator, where the fluid is vaporized by the heat of the water, absorbing energy in the process. The expanding vapor is passed through a turbine, which drives a generator, and then returned to the condenser to be chilled to a liquid and begin another cycle. The plant is tethered to the seafloor by a mooring line, which also serves to support power cables carrying electricity from the plant.

The Body's Natural Opiates
by Solomon H. Snyder

**The human body is now known to manufacture
chemical substances that, like the opiate narcotics,
act on the central nervous system to relieve pain.**

Raw opium, a powerful narcotic drug obtained from the unripe fruits of the opium poppy, can be found listed among the physician's most effective pharmaceuticals at least since classical Greek times. It relieves pain, even in severe, intractable cases, and gives rise to feelings of well-being and elation. Unfortunately, continued use of opium and its several component and derived alkaloids, including morphine, codeine, and heroin, produces physiological addiction with consequent physical and mental deterioration. Thus the discovery of a nonaddictive opiate drug has become an important goal of modern medicine.

During the past few years medical investigators from several nations have isolated and identified a new class of substances that occur naturally in the human brain. Collectively called natural opiates, these chemicals have been found to function almost exactly like the addictive opiate narcotics, regulating the same body functions that are the most strongly influenced by opiate drugs. Understanding how these compounds act could help clarify basic functions of the brain and could assist in developing powerful pain relievers that are not addicting. Unlike many fundamental scientific breakthroughs whose practical implications were not realized for decades or centuries, the payoff from the discovery of natural opiates in the brain has emerged rapidly and could result in clinical application by the early 1980s.

How were the natural opiates discovered? Even more fundamentally, why would anyone suspect that the brain contained its own opiatelike

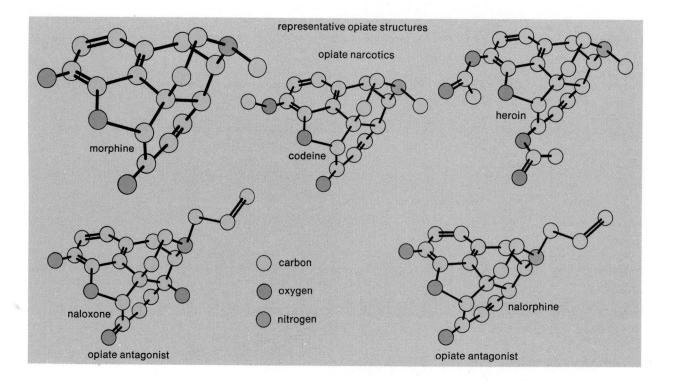

representative opiate structures

opiate narcotics

morphine

codeine

heroin

○ carbon

● oxygen

● nitrogen

naloxone

opiate antagonist

nalorphine

opiate antagonist

Comparison of the molecular structures of the addictive opiate narcotic morphine and its derivatives codeine and heroin reveals a common base structure with small differences in certain side groups. Ironically, heroin, with two added acetyl groups $(COCH_3)$, was developed as a nonaddictive pain reliever. Other minor modifications to the basic opiate structure can produce opiate antagonists like naloxone and nalorphine, which block the effects of opiate narcotics apparently by competing successfully for the body's opiate receptors. (For clarity, hydrogen atoms on the structures are not shown.)

SOLOMON H. SNYDER is Distinguished Service Professor of Psychiatry and Pharmacology at Johns Hopkins University School of Medicine, Baltimore, Maryland.

(Overleaf) Painting by Ron Villani. Illustrations by Leon Bishop

chemicals? There has never been a comparable search for substances of human origin that mimic the effects of such drugs as aspirin or penicillin. Nevertheless, discovery of the natural opiates was not an accident. It was the result of a well designed, systematic research program that began in 1973 with the identification of specific opiate receptors in the human brain.

The search for opiate receptors

Although some drugs such as the anesthetic gas diethyl ether produce their typical effects by acting nonspecifically on the surfaces, or membranes, of many nerve cells (neurons), scientists had several good reasons to believe that opiate narcotics must act at discrete sites on the cell membrane that are specifically receptive to certain molecular structures. For instance, the human body has been shown capable of recognizing extremely subtle differences in chemical structures of opiates, differences that only a site constructed to accept the drugs could distinguish. Opiates usually exist in either of two forms (enantiomers) that are identical in chemical structure except that one is the mirror image of the other. The body differentiates between these two forms and responds to only one of them.

Another reason to suspect that opiate drugs act at specific receptors is the fact that some of them are extraordinarily potent. One opiate, etorphine, relieves pain in doses only 1/5,000 of the effective dose of morphine. Such a potent drug would not be expected to act in a general, nonspecific fashion over the entire surface of many cells; there simply are not enough molecules of etorphine in the body after a typical therapeutic dose.

The existence of a class of compounds structurally related to the opiates, called opiate antagonists, also favors the notion of specific opiate receptors.

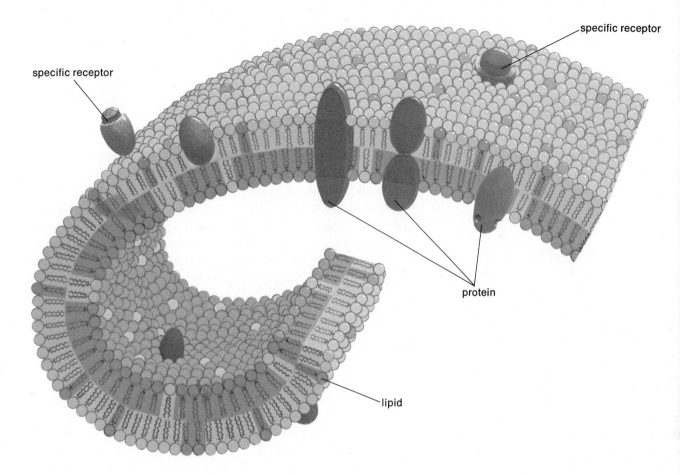

specific receptor

specific receptor

protein

lipid

Pure opiate antagonists, such as the drug naloxone, do not relieve pain or cause euphoria themselves, but prevent or abolish the effects of other opiate drugs. Apparently these antagonists successfully compete for and bind to opiate receptors without inducing the biochemical changes normally associated with opiate narcotics. Somehow the antagonists prevent the access of morphinelike drugs to the opiate receptor.

For these reasons scientists devoted many years to detecting by biochemical means the specific opiate receptors in the brain. The simplest approach would be to measure the binding of radioactively labeled opiates to membranes of neurons. Unfortunately, like most chemicals the opiates also bind nonspecifically and without narcotic effect to many kinds of molecular groups on the surface of nerve membranes. Almost any portion of a protein, lipid, or carbohydrate will bind to an opiate drug. The number of such nonspecific binding sites is quite large compared with the minuscule number of true opiate receptors.

The successful biochemical detection of opiate interactions with opiate receptors required some fairly straightforward technical developments. At Johns Hopkins University School of Medicine, Candace B. Pert and Solomon H. Snyder used the radioactive form of an opiate drug containing such a high amount of radioactivity per molecule that very low concentrations could be measured. They also developed procedures for washing away the nonspecific binding rapidly and thoroughly while preserving specific

The biological membrane that encloses each living cell is composed mainly of lipid and protein molecules held together by forces in a dynamic state characterized by considerable fluidlike motion. The lipids are thought to be arranged in the form of a bilayer, their head regions (small spheres) oriented toward the watery media inside and outside the cell and their hydrocarbon tails turned inward and away from the water. Proteins are distributed unevenly within this bilayer; some are found near the inside or outside surface, whereas others partially or completely span the membrane. Any carbohydrates present are chemically bound to the lipids and proteins. Some drugs, including the opiate narcotics, and many of the body's active substances produce their effects by binding to certain proteins on the membrane surface that act as specific receptor sites.

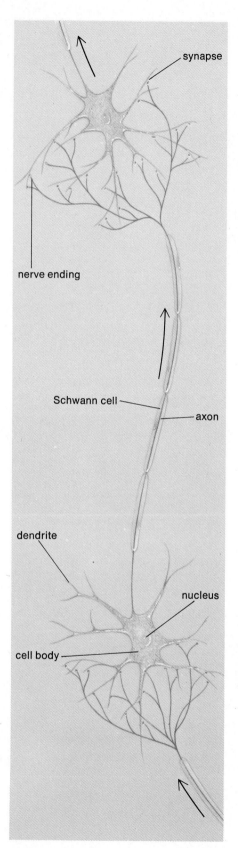

synapse

nerve ending

Schwann cell

axon

dendrite

nucleus

cell body

interactions with the opiate receptor. To prove that the remaining binding involved the biologically meaningful opiate receptors, it was shown that the relative potencies of many opiate drugs in competing for those binding sites closely paralleled the effects of the drugs in relieving pain in animals and humans. Independently, Lars Terenius at the University of Uppsala in Sweden and Eric Simon at New York University obtained similar results.

These binding techniques provided a simple and sensitive way of measuring opiate receptors and of learning a great deal about their normal functioning in the body. It was found that the number of opiate receptors varies in different parts of neurons. Each neuron consists of a cell body containing the nucleus and a long component called the axon. The axon terminates in a number of nerve endings that contact other neurons. Receptors are highly localized to a portion of the neuron called the synaptic membrane. This membrane occurs at the synapse, the site at which the nerve ending of one neuron contacts the cell body of another neuron. Neurons communicate by the release of a chemical, called a neurotransmitter, from their nerve endings. Neurotransmitter molecules diffuse across the synapse to act at the synaptic membrane on the cell body of the next neuron, on one of the branchlike extensions (dendrites) of the neuron, and sometimes on the nerve ending of the next neuron. Hence, receptors for the neurotransmitters are likewise concentrated in the synaptic membrane of a cell body, its dendrites, or the nerve ending. The fact that opiate receptors were contained in synaptic membranes suggested that they might be receptors for some normal neurotransmitter.

Photos, courtesy, John E. Heuser, University of California, Davis

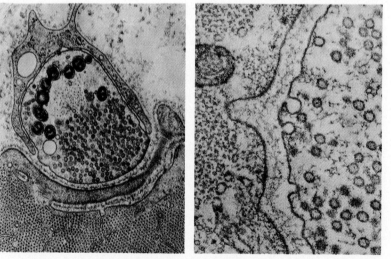

General features of a neuron constituting part of a nervous pathway are shown at left. Neurons communicate impulses by means of a chemical neurotransmitter that diffuses from the nerve endings of one neuron to receptors on the synaptic membranes of the next neuron. The nerve ending, shown highly magnified (above left), is filled with saclike vesicles containing neurotransmitter molecules. On arrival of an impulse these vesicles fuse with the membrane of the nerve ending and empty their contents into the synaptic space between the cells (above right).

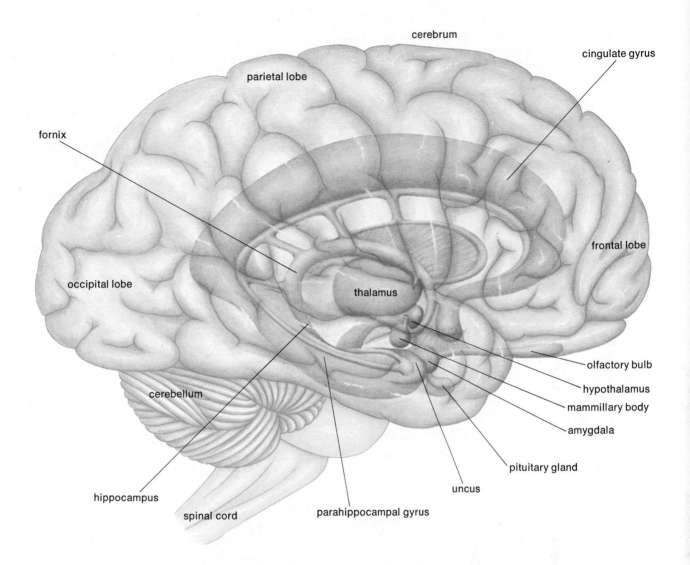

cerebrum

cingulate gyrus

parietal lobe

fornix

frontal lobe

occipital lobe

thalamus

olfactory bulb

hypothalamus

mammillary body

amygdala

cerebellum

pituitary gland

hippocampus

uncus

spinal cord

parahippocampal gyrus

Opiate receptors and the brain

In other experiments Michael Kuhar, Pert, and Snyder attempted to determine whether different parts of the brain varied in their content of opiate receptors. They simply dissected many regions of the brain and measured the binding of radioactively labeled opiate drugs to each region. There were striking differences. For instance, the medial portion of the thalamus contains a high concentration of opiate receptors whereas the lateral thalamus has few. Located deep within the cerebral hemispheres, the thalamus receives input from nearly all the body's sensory systems and functions as a major brain center for integrating information about what a person perceives in his environment. The lateral thalamus deals with information relating to light pressure, touch, and sharp, prickly pain, which are not influenced by opiates. The medial thalamus, on the other hand, deals with deep, chronic,

Regions of the brain that contain high concentrations of opiate receptors include portions of the thalamus, which serves as a sensory integration center, and the amygdala, hypothalamus, and other parts of the limbic system (shown in pink), a group of evolutionarily primitive structures that regulate emotional behavior. Natural opiatelike materials that bind to these receptors have been found both in brain tissue and in the pituitary gland.

107

Signals from peripheral pain receptors in the body appear to follow two major pathways in the central nervous system. Sharp, localized pain—the kind little affected by opiate drugs—is carried by the neospinothalamic system, a pathway of comparatively recent evolution that connects with cells on each side of the thalamus (lateral thalamus). Deep, burning pain—the kind strongly affected by opiates—seems to be carried by a second, more primitive paleospinothalamic system which connects with the central (medial) thalamus and with parts of the limbic system that may be involved with the emotional content of pain. The substantia gelatinosa, a dense band of gray matter in the spinal cord, is an important sensory integration station contributing to the paleospinothalamic system. High concentrations of opiate receptors have been found on cells of both the medial thalamus and the substantia gelatinosa, offering strong evidence that the opiate drugs exert their effects at both locations.

burning pain, the type that opiates are most successful in relieving. Presumably the abundance of opiate receptors in the medial thalamus accounts, at least in part, for the ability of these drugs to relieve pain.

By developing techniques to visualize radioactively labeled opiate molecules under the microscope, Kuhar was able to extend these experiments to a microscopic level. He found that opiate receptors are very highly concentrated in a number of small, discrete regions of the brain. In the spinal cord, for instance, opiate receptors are localized along a narrow, dense vertical band of central gray matter referred to as layers one and two, or the substantia gelatinosa. Nerve physiologists have known for many years that layers one and two of the spinal cord represent the first place in the central nervous system where information about pain is integrated to allow a response from the individual involved. Scientists had debated whether opiate drugs relieve pain by acting only in the brain or whether part of the pain relief may occur at a lower level, in the spinal cord. The very dense band of opiate receptors discovered in the spinal cord, together with the large number of opiate receptors in the medial thalamus, offers strong evidence that the drugs act in both the brain and spinal cord.

Scientists also wondered where in the brain the opiate narcotics might act to produce their characteristic euphoric effects. In addition to creating a physical dependency, these drugs are also psychologically addicting; injection of an opiate such as heroin is soon followed by a "rush" of warm, joyous feeling, likened by many to a whole-body orgasm. The collection of structures of the brain that together regulate emotions is known as the limbic system. It was found that one component, the amygdala, had virtually the highest concentration of opiate receptors in the brain. Perhaps the opiate receptors in the amygdala mediate the euphoric effects of these drugs.

Enkephalins—opiates "in the head"

The remarkably selective localizations of opiate receptors in different regions of the brain as well as the existence of the receptors at synaptic membranes suggest that they are not mere vestiges of evolution. Such specialized structures must serve some normal function. The human body was not born with morphine in it. Instead, opiate receptors presumably must exist in order to interact with some naturally occurring opiatelike substance. But how might one search for such a chemical?

In Scotland at the University of Aberdeen, John Hughes and Hans Kosterlitz took advantage of the fact that opiates can inhibit electrically induced contractions of certain smooth muscles in proportion to their ability to relieve pain. This suggested that these muscle systems possess opiate receptors very much like those that occur in the brain. Hughes and Kosterlitz tested whether the brain contained opiatelike chemicals by determining if brain extracts would mimic the effects of morphine upon these muscles. To check that each effect they observed was a specific opiate action, they showed that it could be blocked by opiate antagonist drugs. Using this system, these scientists identified an opiatelike material and proceeded to purify and isolate it. At Johns Hopkins, Gavril Pasternak and Snyder showed that brain extracts contained something which competed with radioactively labeled

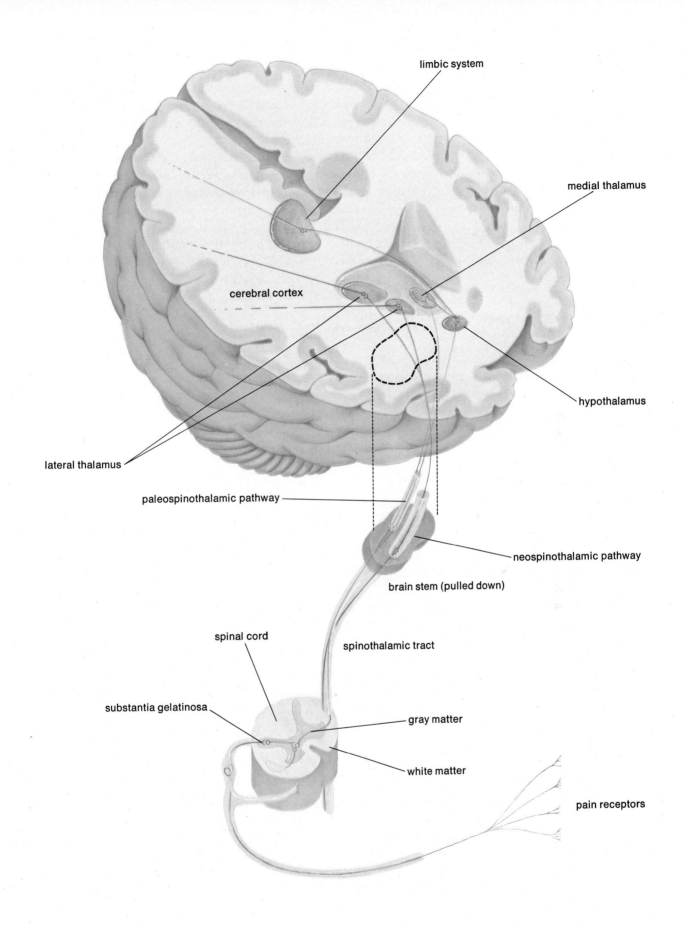

limbic system

medial thalamus

cerebral cortex

hypothalamus

lateral thalamus

paleospinothalamic pathway

neospinothalamic pathway

brain stem (pulled down)

spinal cord

spinothalamic tract

substantia gelatinosa

gray matter

white matter

pain receptors

opiate drugs in binding to the opiate receptors. The relative amounts of this material in different regions of the brain varied in close parallel with regional variations in the number of opiate receptors. At the University of Uppsala, Terenius also noted that brain extracts could inhibit the binding of opiate drugs to the opiate receptors.

In late 1975 Hughes, Kosterlitz, and their collaborators published the chemical structure of the morphinelike material isolated from the brain. It was found to consist of two chemicals, both pentapeptides; that is, a chain of five amino acids. Referred to as enkephalins (from the Greek word for "in the head"), these two molecules differ only in one terminal amino acid, which for one of them is leucine and for the other is methionine. Thus these two chemicals are referred to as methionine-enkephalin and leucine-enkephalin. Working independently, Rabi Simantov and Snyder also isolated the enkephalins, arriving at the same two peptide structures a few months later.

Endorphins—the pituitary's mystery molecules

The enkephalins are not the only opiatelike peptides in the body. Even before their structures were determined, Avram Goldstein of Stanford University had shown that the pituitary gland, a small endocrine organ situated on the lower surface of the brain, possesses opiatelike materials. Once the structures of the enkephalins were known, the pituitary story became most intriguing, because the sequence of the five amino acids of methionine-enkephalin is also contained within a 91–amino-acid peptide that had been

The structure of human β-lipotropin found in the pituitary consists of 91 amino acids linked in a chainlike sequence by peptide bonds. Essentially all of the opiatelike activity of pituitary extracts was discovered to derive from the presence of a 31–amino-acid portion of this peptide called β-endorphin. The first five amino acids (positions 61–65) of β-endorphin have the same sequence as the natural opiate methionine-enkephalin found in the brain.

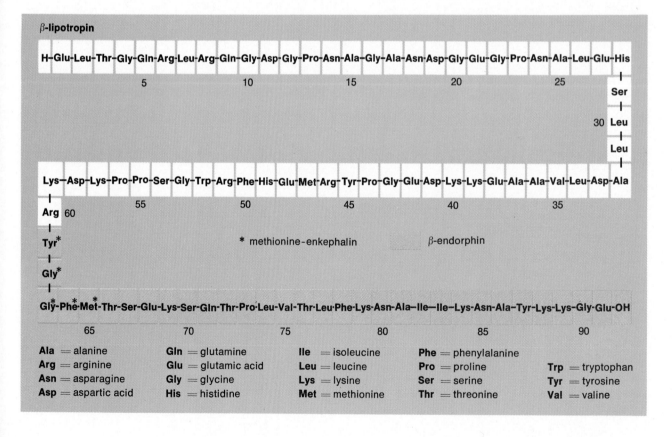

β-lipotropin

H-Glu-Leu-Thr-Gly-Gln-Arg-Leu-Arg-Gln-Gly-Asp-Gly-Pro-Asn-Ala-Gly-Ala-Asn-Asp-Gly-Glu-Gly-Pro-Asn-Ala-Leu-Glu-His
5 10 15 20 25

Ser
30 Leu
Leu

Lys—Asp-Lys-Pro-Pro-Ser-Gly-Trp-Arg-Phe-His-Glu-Met-Arg-Tyr-Pro-Gly-Glu-Asp-Lys-Lys-Glu-Ala-Ala-Val-Leu-Asp-Ala
Arg 60 55 50 45 40 35

Tyr* * methionine-enkephalin   β-endorphin

Gly*

Gly*-Phe*-Met*-Thr-Ser-Glu-Lys-Ser-Gln-Thr-Pro-Leu-Val-Thr-Leu-Phe-Lys-Asn-Ala—Ile—Ile—Lys-Asn-Ala-Tyr-Lys-Lys-Gly-Glu-OH
65 70 75 80 85 90

Ala = alanine   Gln = glutamine   Ile = isoleucine   Phe = phenylalanine
Arg = arginine   Glu = glutamic acid   Leu = leucine   Pro = proline   Trp = tryptophan
Asn = asparagine   Gly = glycine   Lys = lysine   Ser = serine   Tyr = tyrosine
Asp = aspartic acid His = histidine   Met = methionine   Thr = threonine   Val = valine

Methionine- and leucine-enkephalin share identical amino-acid sequences except for their terminal units. Considered spatially, the benzene ring and attached hydroxyl group (OH) of the tyrosine component strongly resemble their counterparts in morphine (compare, p. 104), suggesting that this subunit interacts with the opiate receptor in both cases.

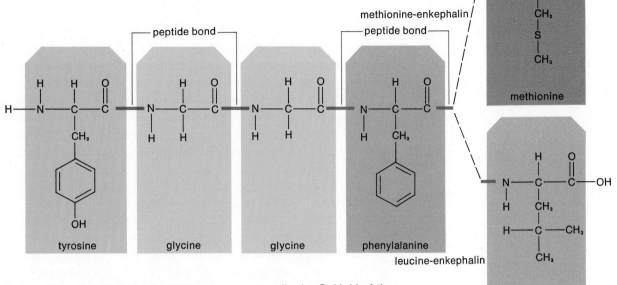

isolated from the pituitary gland about ten years earlier by C. H. Li of the University of California in San Francisco. This large peptide was called β-lipotropin because it had some effects on body fats or lipids, but its true function had been a mystery.

As soon as the chemical structures of the enkephalins were unraveled, several research groups including those of Li, Roger Guillemin at the Salk Institute in La Jolla, California, and Derek Smyth at the National Institute for Medical Research in London attempted to discover whether the pituitary gland contained opiatelike peptides. They assumed that β-lipotropin might serve as a precursor to such peptides, being broken down within the pituitary into smaller peptides that would have opiatelike functions. They quickly found that there is no enkephalin in the pituitary gland. However, they did find an opiatelike peptide in the pituitary. It consists of a 31–amino-acid portion of β-lipotropin, about a third the total size of β-lipotropin, and its first five amino acids have the same sequence as methionine-enkephalin. This material, christened β-endorphin (from the words "endogenous morphine"), accounts for essentially all the opiatelike activity of pituitary extracts.

With the identification of β-endorphin in the pituitary, scientists wondered what a pain-relieving chemical was doing outside of the brain. Surely, pain perception does not take place in the pituitary. Might β-endorphin be transported from the pituitary to the brain, where it is then converted to enkephalin? Several groups of investigators removed the pituitary glands of rats and after varying periods of time measured the enkephalin content of the brain. Even four months after removal of the pituitary, the enkephalin content of the brain did not decline. Thus it appeared that enkephalins are made within the brain and not transported there from the pituitary. To date, the function of β-endorphin in the pituitary remains unclear. It might have a hormonal role, like most pituitary secretions. Its hormonal role presumably would be unrelated to typical morphine actions. Two chemically related peptides, called α-endorphin and γ-endorphin, also have been found in the pituitary, but in much lower concentrations. Both consist of shorter segments of β-endorphin and both begin with the same sequence of five amino acids that constitute methionine-enkephalin.

Locating natural opiates in the brain

What might be the role of such natural opiates as enkephalin in brain function? Are the enkephalins merely nourishment to be processed by brain cells as a source of energy? Do they have a structural role; for instance, in holding up the walls of neurons? Or are they neurotransmitters, released from nerve endings in order to communicate information to other nerve cells? Scientists realized that such questions could be answered if one could literally visualize enkephalin molecules microscopically within cells of the brain. Tomas Hökfelt at the Karolinska Institute in Stockholm, Sweden, as well as Simantov, Kuhar, and Snyder at Johns Hopkins accomplished this task by a technique called immunohistochemistry. In this procedure regions of high concentrations of enkephalin molecules in brain tissue are made fluorescent by the use of special, fluorescent-labeled antibodies that bind selectively to enkephalin-containing structures. First it was observed that enkephalins are highly concentrated in nerve endings, where neurotransmitters tend to congregate. This finding correlates with the notion that the enkephalins indeed function in some way as neurotransmitters. In general those neurons containing high concentrations of enkephalins parallel closely the distribution of opiate receptors throughout the brain. Thus in the spinal cord enkephalin-containing neurons are highly concentrated in layers one and two. In the brain itself the medial thalamus contains high concentrations of enkephalins, as does the amygdala.

Bright areas in the photomicrograph of brain tissue at lower right pinpoint regions of high concentrations of enkephalin molecules, which have been made visible by means of special, fluorescent-labeled antibodies.

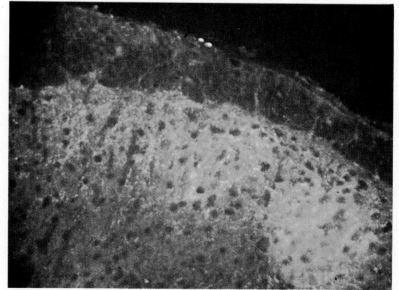

Courtesy, Solomon H. Snyder, Johns Hopkins University

Knowing in detail the microscopic localization of enkephalin neurons and opiate receptors in the central nervous system subsequently enabled investigators to understand more clearly how the body processes information about pain. For instance, when the skin of a fingertip is burned, free nerve endings of the sensory nerves are stimulated, causing a nerve impulse to proceed up the arm and into the spinal cord. In layers one and two of the spinal cord the sensory nerve endings release an excitatory neurotransmitter that causes other neurons in the spinal cord to fire, provoking a sequence of events resulting in pain perception. Carol LaMotte, Pert, and Snyder showed that a major portion of the opiate receptors in the spinal cord are located on the nerve endings of the sensory nerves. This was proved simply by cutting the sensory nerves in the necks of monkeys, which induced degeneration of the nerve endings in layers one and two of their spinal cords. Coincident with the loss of sensory nerve endings was a detectable loss of opiate receptors in that part of the spinal cord. Since opiate receptors are, in fact, receptors for enkephalins, it was inferred that enkephalin-containing neurons make synaptic contact with the sensory nerve endings of the spinal cord. This arrangement suggests that enkephalins act on the endings of the sensory nerves to inhibit the release of their excitatory transmitter, resulting in a lessening of pain.

Whereas investigators have developed a fair understanding of how enkephalin neurons act to relieve pain, how these structures affect pain perception at higher levels of the brain, such as the medial thalamus, is not yet clear. Moreover, it is not known how enkephalin neurons influence mood in such regions of the brain as the amygdala. In the amygdala, one might expect that the normal release of enkephalin acts as the body's own "tonic" against losses and other disappointments. Such a supposition is supported by the known fact that opiates, which mimic the effects of enkephalin at opiate receptors, do produce "good" feelings. One might speculate then that enkephalins normally regulate mood, and perhaps their deficiency in certain regions of the brain results in emotional pain and depression. It is possible that many heroin addicts begin use of the drug to counteract psychic pain, analogous to physical pain that is also relieved by opiates.

Enkephalin is not the only natural opiate in the brain. Using immunohistochemical techniques that had enabled investigators to visualize enkephalin-containing neurons, Floyd Bloom at the Salk Institute was able to localize β-endorphin in the brain. Whereas the pituitary gland contains enormous concentrations of β-endorphin, the brain contains very low levels, in fact only about one-tenth the amount of enkephalins. Because the amino-acid sequence for methionine-enkephalin is contained within that of β-endorphin, one wonders whether β-endorphin might be a precursor of the enkephalins, to which it is converted by some chemical process that breaks larger peptides into smaller fragments.

Bloom's findings argue against this possibility. If β-endorphin were converted to enkephalins, one would expect to find both kinds of chemicals in the same regions of the brain. However, this proved not to be the case. For instance, layers one and two of the spinal cord and the amygdala, which have among the highest concentrations of enkephalins in the central

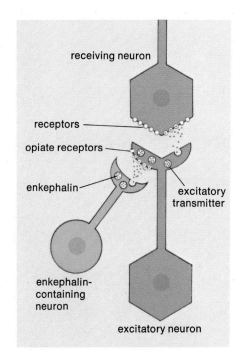

A large proportion of opiate receptors in the spinal cord are known to be located on the endings of excitatory (sensory) nerves. When a pain impulse enters the spinal cord, enkephalin released from specialized neurons nearby may bind to these receptors. This action could inhibit the release of excitatory neurotransmitter to the next neuron in line, thus suppressing pain perception.

113

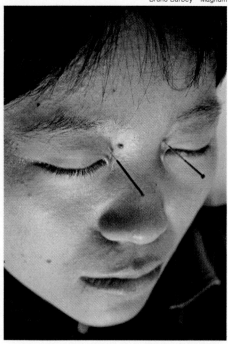

Acupuncture, an oriental medical practice involving insertion of thin needles into the body, may produce its analgesic effects by stimulating the release of the body's natural opiates.

nervous system, are essentially devoid of β-endorphin. On the other hand, β-endorphin is most concentrated in the hypothalamus, the part of the brain that is connected to the pituitary and that regulates pituitary secretions. This evidence suggests a role for β-endorphin in regulating hormone formation and secretion by the pituitary.

Future prospects

Opiates are among the oldest drugs in clinical medicine. Despite massive efforts by drug companies through the years, no pain killers have emerged that are more effective. Yet, because opiates are addicting, they cannot be used in vast numbers of patients with the chronic pain of such maladies as backaches and migraine headaches. Prior to the advent of modern tranquilizers, morphine and related drugs were widely used to ease anxiety, induce sleep, and relieve depression. A nonaddicting opiate drug would be of miraculous benefit in treating both severe, chronic pain and a variety of emotional problems.

Soon after their discovery, it became apparent that the enkephalins themselves could not be used as drugs. Being peptides, they are rapidly destroyed in the body by enzymes that are adept at breaking peptides into their component amino acids. In addition, like most peptides enkephalins are multiply charged molecules, which have difficulty in entering the brain from the general circulation because of the body's natural blood-brain barrier, a system of structures that presumably protects the brain from toxic, electrically charged substances. Thus numerous pharmaceutical companies have embarked on research programs to synthesize and test hundreds of enkephalin derivatives. Replacement of specific component amino acids within the enkephalins has enabled them to better resist enzyme degradation. Other structural modifications have facilitated their penetration into the brain. After extensive efforts several companies have developed potent enkephalin analogues that relieve pain in animals when injected or even when taken by mouth. Although there were some suggestions that certain of these may be less addicting than conventional opiates, in early 1978 research on humans was just beginning.

Should some enkephalin analogues be found nonaddicting, they would rank among the most important breakthroughs in recent medical history. Is there any reason to expect that such chemicals would not be addicting? One could argue that enkephalins should lack addictive properties, simply because the human body presumably is not addicted to itself. However, limited studies in which enkephalins were administered directly into the brains of rats suggest otherwise. After repeated administration of enkephalins, the rats became drug tolerant; in other words, progressively higher doses of enkephalin were required to relieve pain. Moreover, such "withdrawal" symptoms as shaking and diarrhea took place when chronic administration of high doses was terminated abruptly. However, one cannot adequately compare the extent of "addictability" of a drug in rats with its effects in humans. Also, even though enkephalin itself may have addictive potential, it is possible that some derivatives will be found to be much less addicting.

What does continued investigation of the natural opiates hold for the future? As already mentioned, it is likely that useful drugs will derive from innovative chemical tinkering with the natural enkephalins. As more is discovered about the location of enkephalin and β-endorphin neurons in the brain and about the regulation of their firing rates, mankind's understanding of emotional processes and pain perception will be greatly advanced. Finally, it is possible that disorders ranging from depression and schizophrenia to inborn hypersensitivity or undersensitivity to pain are related to abnormal functioning or regulation of the natural opiates. Scientists are presently developing techniques to measure levels of these substances in spinal fluid and blood. Perhaps detection and correction of specific abnormalities will one day alleviate a variety of diseases.

One of the newest perspectives raised by the concept of natural opiates relates to an aspect of medicine whose history probably antedates opiate drugs and perhaps all drugs. This oriental practice, called acupuncture, involves insertion of thin needles into the body to treat illness and relieve pain. Although Western physicians for many years were skeptical about the analgesic effects of acupuncture, recent cultural exchanges between the U.S. and the People's Republic of China have provided U.S. scientists with an opportunity to evaluate the technique. In many documented cases it clearly has produced impressive analgesia.

Might the effects of acupuncture relate to a release of enkephalin in the brain or spinal cord? If acupuncture were to act through enkephalin release, its effects should be blocked by opiate antagonists such as naloxone. David Mayer at the Medical College of Virginia explored this question in human subjects. Applying electrical stimulation to produce experimental pain in their teeth, he found that acupuncture indeed was effective in elevating the threshold for pain. Naloxone or a placebo was then administered in an experimental design in which neither the investigator nor the subjects knew what was being given. Naloxone definitely lessened the pain-relieving effects of acupuncture, strongly suggesting that acupuncture may act by causing a release of enkephalin within the central nervous system.

Whatever additional research may bring, it is clear that the discovery of natural opiates has already rewarded the medical sciences with a vast amount of information. New findings continue to place investigation of the opiate receptors and natural opiates among the most rapidly burgeoning fields of medicine. It is likely that advances in coming years will bear out the great expectations of the present.

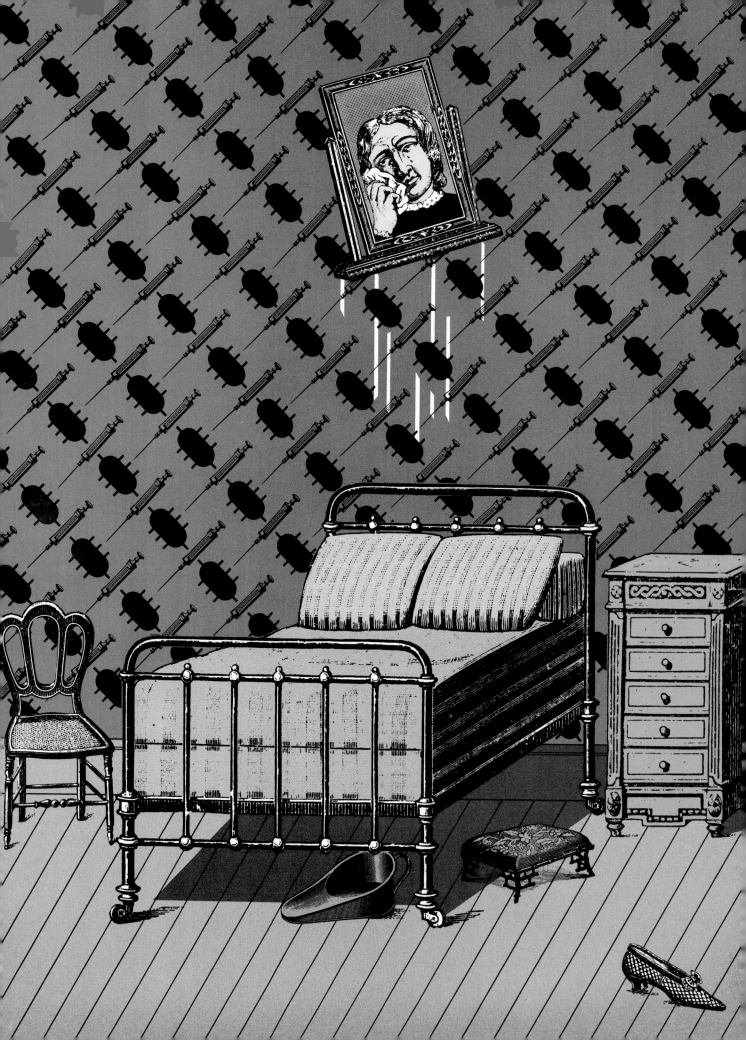

The Microbes Fight Back
by Stanley Falkow

In mankind's war with infectious disease, antibiotics were the first "nuclear weapons." Their imprudent use, however, has allowed microbes to repopulate their decimated legions with a new breed of warrior.

One of the major practical miracles of modern medicine has been the development of antibiotics for the treatment of many infectious diseases. Less than a half century ago bacterial infections that are now considered almost trivial inconveniences were common causes of death. For many people it is difficult even to imagine the ravages caused by typhoid, dysentery, plague, cholera, and other infections now treatable with antimicrobial agents. Only through the historian's eye can one appreciate the dramatic impact of infectious diseases on the rise and fall of civilizations. Indirectly, epidemic diseases must have had remarkable effects on cultural, religious, economic, and political developments. How different might the present be if antibiotics had been available to treat the Black Death of the 14th century, the cholera epidemics of the 19th century, or the fatal bacterial pneumonia attending the great influenza pandemic of 1918–19. Years into the future historians undoubtedly will be analyzing the effects on their civilization of the extension and maintenance of human life, caused in great measure by the antibiotic era of the past 40 years.

Although mankind owes antibiotics the debt of reducing the high mortality rate of many bacterial infections, chemotherapy has created difficulties of its own, among them the emergence of antibiotic-resistant microorganisms. In recent years delayed recognition that previously treatable disease was caused by an antibiotic-resistant organism on several occasions has resulted in unnecessary suffering and loss of life. A serious corollary has been the emergence within the hospital environment of antibiotic-resistant microorganisms that can opportunistically attack patients whose normal defenses have been weakened by disease, surgery, or other causes. Microbic resistance represents a constant threat to the usefulness of existing antibiotics and of therapeutic agents of the future. The problem is a global one and has its roots in the wide, often indiscriminate, use of antibiotics in man and animals. To understand this situation, and more importantly to do something about it, one must consider how antibiotics work on microorganisms and the genetic basis of how microorganisms develop resistance.

117

Entitled "Le Choléra," a French newspaper illustration of the pre-antibiotic 20th century depicts the disease as a merciless reaper of human flesh.

Development and use of antibiotics

Chemotherapy, the administration of a chemical agent that destroys microbes within the body, does not have a long history. To be sure, the annals of folk medicine describe "cures" of skin infection by the application of moldy cheese to wounds. Moreover, it is said that in the early 1600s malaria, a protozoan infection, was first successfully treated in the wife of the Spanish viceroy of Peru with an extract of cinchona bark. A bit later ipecacuanha root was used for another protozoan-caused illness, amebic dysentery. It was only at the turn of the 19th century, however, that the active alkaloid ingredients, quinine and emetine, were actually isolated from these natural plant products. Little more than these were available until 1910 when German medical scientist Paul Ehrlich and his co-workers discovered Salvarsan (also called compound 606), an arsenic-containing compound that was nontoxic yet effective against syphilis and relapsing fever, both of which result from microorganisms called spirochetes.

Ehrlich viewed a useful chemotherapeutic drug as a "magic bullet," which selectively attacked disease organisms without appreciable harm to the patient. He also investigated the unusual notion that certain organic dyes might be toxic to parasitic protoplasm but not to the protoplasm of human cells. Following this same idea, the German dye industry was eventually

STANLEY FALKOW is Professor of Microbiology and Medicine at the University of Washington School of Medicine, Seattle.

Illustrations by William Biderbost

118

rewarded by bacteriologist Gerhard Domagk's discovery in the early 1930s of Prontosil, the forerunner of the sulfa, or sulfonamide, drugs. The sulfonamides were the first really effective treatment for bacterial infections. These drugs could be used against streptococcal sore throat, common bacterial pneumonia, gonorrhea, and some forms of meningitis. Yet, even as this revolution in the clinical treatment of infectious disease took effect, the antibiotic era was ushered in by the development of penicillin.

Salvarsan and the sulfonamides were products of the chemist's bench. Penicillin, on the other hand, was the natural product of a microorganism, the mold *Penicillium notatum*. Although penicillin had been discovered by the British bacteriologist Alexander Fleming in 1928, ten years passed before Howard Florey, Ernst Chain, and their associates in the U.K. were able to isolate it in relatively pure form and to confirm it as a chemotherapeutic agent of unparalleled potency. The success of penicillin spurred the search for other such substances. The term antibiotic was first used in its modern context by U.S. biochemist Selman Waksman, who confined the definition to chemical substances produced by microorganisms that have the property, even in minute concentrations, of inhibiting the growth of other microorganisms. In 1944 Waksman and his colleagues reported the isolation of streptomycin, an antibiotic produced by moldlike soil bacteria called actinomycetes. Streptomycin was active against a number of microorganisms untouched by penicillin, most notably *Mycobacterium tuberculosis*, the causative agent of human tuberculosis.

The systematic search for antagonistic organisms among natural microbial populations of the soil and elsewhere has been repaid by the isolation of hundreds of antibiotics. Before 1950 tetracycline and chloramphenicol were added to the physician's armamentarium of therapeutic weapons. Over the long term, only a small handful of the known antibiotics have proved to possess real or potential clinical application; most are too toxic. Yet, successive discoveries have added to the list of infectious agents amenable to chemotherapy.

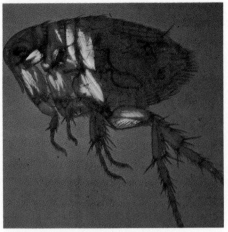

Plague is primarily a bacterial disease of rodents, transmitted by infected rat fleas such as Xenopsylla cheopis (above). The great plagues of the 14th, 17th, and 19th centuries were perpetuated by human contact with the flea, whose bite introduces the causative agent, Pasteurella pestis. Exploitation of the antibiotic activity of penicillin, a natural product of the mold Penicillium notatum (below), heralded the start of the antibiotic era.

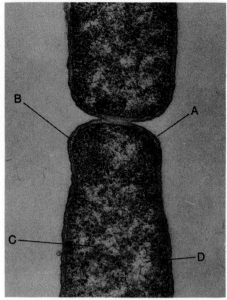

Photomicrograph of the bacterium Escherichia coli *(above) reveals sites at which some antibacterial agents exert their selective effects. Synthesis of the cell wall (A) is inhibited by the penicillins, vancomycin, and the cephalosporins; the cell membrane (B) is affected by the polymyxins; function of the ribosomes (C) is disrupted by a range of antibiotics including streptomycin, neomycin, chloramphenicol, and the tetracyclines; and the bacterial chromosome (D) is attacked by nalidixic acid and mitomycin c. In nature bacteria transfer genetic material, including plasmids that mediate drug resistance, by means of three general mechanisms (opposite page). In conjugation, a type of mating, R plasmids can pass from cell to cell through a hollow tube called a pilus. Transduction involves infection of a resistant bacterium by a bacterial virus, whose DNA enters the cell and takes over the cell's synthesis machinery to produce new viral copies; an R plasmid may be incorporated inside a new virus and carried to another bacterial cell. In transformation a plasmid from a resistant cell may be absorbed directly into a recipient cell from the surrounding medium.*

Some investigators have said it is unlikely that any new antibiotic remains to be discovered. But to offset this assertion, if indeed it is true, what must be recognized is the outstanding success in manipulating antibiotic molecules in the chemical laboratory to produce tailor-made substances with less toxicity and better efficacy. The design of drugs and the modification of existing antibiotics to perform specific chemotherapeutic functions have been aided in no small measure by knowledge obtained in the past few decades about the mode of action of antibiotics.

How antibiotics work

The ideal antibacterial agent is bactericidal; it kills the offending microorganism. Many antibiotics are only bacteriostatic; they inhibit bacterial growth without actual destruction. Treatment with a bacteriostatic agent depends upon normal body defense mechanisms to bring about final eradication of the infecting organism.

The selective toxicity of antibacterial agents has been traced in most cases to specific metabolic or structural differences between microorganisms and mammalian cells. For example, the bacteriostatic sulfonamides interfere with the bacterial conversion of the organic compound para-aminobenzoic acid to the essential vitamin folic acid. Because man does not carry out this particular reaction but rather requires the presence of folic acid in the diet, bacteria that depend on the pathway are inhibited by sulfonamides whereas human cells remain unaffected. The bactericidal action of penicillin offers another example of selective toxicity. Bacteria possess a rigid cell wall, the synthesis of which is inhibited by penicillin. Mammalian cells lack an analogous structure and are thus unaffected.

In a similar vein, the effects of the antibiotics chloramphenicol, streptomycin, and tetracycline on bacterial protein synthesis can be traced to the fact that the ribosomes, the bacterial workbench of protein synthesis, are significantly different from those found in mammalian cells. These antibiotics, which interfere with protein synthesis, may be either bactericidal or bacteriostatic depending upon which step in the complex series of synthesis reactions is directly affected by the antibiotic. Moreover, some microbial agents have more than one primary site of attack or mechanism of action.

As demonstrated by the above examples, an antimicrobial agent may affect either the function or a structure of a microorganism. In theory, bacterial cells could be inhibited or killed by antibiotics in an almost infinite number of ways. However, one of the major factors contributing to the persistence of infectious disease is the tremendous capacity of microorganisms for circumventing the action of antibiotics. Aside from the obvious medical importance, the genetic mechanisms by which microorganisms have managed to develop antibiotic resistance provides one of the most important, unexpected, and exciting avenues of biological research.

How bacteria resist antibiotics

Antibiotic resistance is a relative term, valid only for a specific microorganism and clinical setting. In general, however, when a microorganism is said to be resistant, the implication is that it is not killed or inhibited by antibiotic con-

120

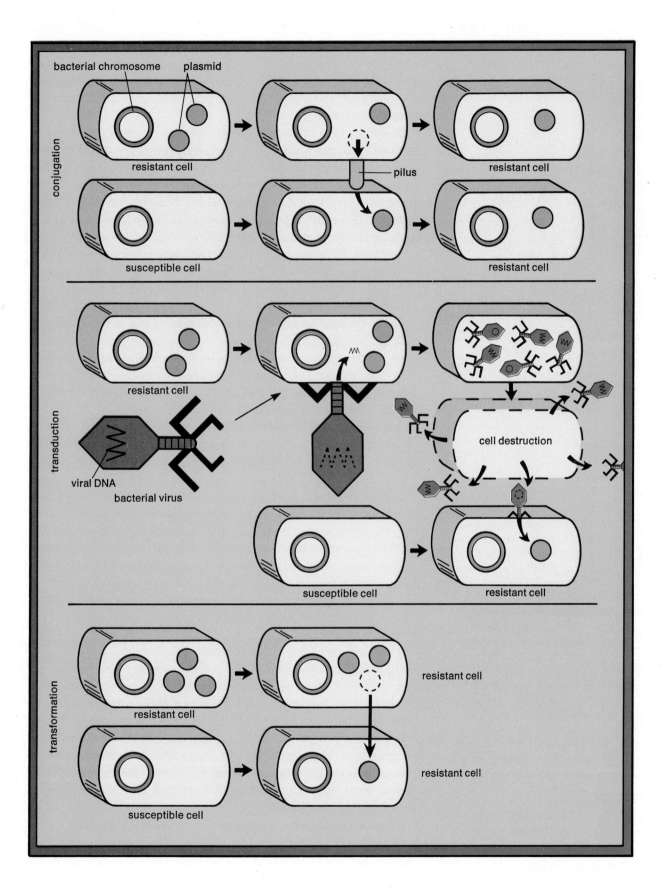

centrations attainable in blood or other appropriate body fluids. The emergence of resistant microorganisms has been recognized since the beginning of chemotherapy. Ehrlich found organisms resistant to his "magic bullets"; even in the early days of penicillin it was clear that some bacteria were not killed by this substance.

Until about 1960 it was generally assumed that the major mechanism of antibiotic resistance was mutation. In this light, resistance was viewed as a consequence of the presence within a large susceptible population of a few (perhaps one in a hundred million) resistant cells that could grow in the presence of an antibiotic. A resistant cell was thought to arise from a subtle change in one of its genes that rendered it indifferent to antibiotic attack. Sometimes a single mutation made a cell highly resistant to an antibiotic. In other cases, the effect of the mutation was only indirectly related to the major biochemical action of the antibiotic so that a number of sequential mutations were required before a sensitive microorganism showed significant resistance.

During the past decade it has become evident that medically relevant antibiotic resistance is not due primarily to chromosomal mutation. Rather, most resistant microorganisms emerge during treatment because they possess or have acquired an accessory genetic element called an R plasmid. Actually, there are many types of plasmids; the term R plasmid is simply a catchall for those that determine antibiotic resistance.

In the basic biological sense a plasmid is nothing more than a molecule of DNA that resides in the cellular protoplasm where it replicates, or reproduces, independently of the bacterial chromosome. Plasmids often carry genes, including those for antibiotic resistance, that permit their host bacteria to better compete with other microorganisms or to survive in an adverse environment. Yet, plasmids may be lost from a bacterial cell without ill effect; they are not necessary for bacterial survival. Of course, a bacterial cell that loses an R plasmid subsequently may be somewhat restricted as to the type of environment that it can populate. By the same token, if a microorganism can gain an R plasmid it may have a marked advantage, for it can then occupy environments in which antibiotics are prevalent; for example, a hospital ward, a patient undergoing therapy, or a farm animal receiving antibiotics to stimulate its growth.

R plasmids vary in the number of resistance genes they carry. In some cases they confer resistance to only a single antibiotic. Others are known that can protect their host against as many as ten distinct antimicrobial agents. The mechanisms by which R plasmids mediate their resistance to antibiotics is rather unique. Antibiotic resistance that develops through mutation is generally associated with a change in the structure of some cellular component; for instance, the cell wall or ribosome. By contrast, R plasmid resistance is usually mediated by reactive protein molecules called enzymes, which either directly destroy the antibiotic or modify its chemical structure to an innocuous form.

Plasmids that mediate antibiotic resistance might never have attained the importance they now have if they were trapped within their host bacteria. But bacteria can share their plasmids—and sometimes in a most promiscuous

The R plasmids found in penicillin-resistant strains of the bacterium Staphylococcus aureus contain a gene, or stretch of DNA, that carries instructions for the synthesis of the enzyme β lactamase (opposite page, a). The gene consists of a specific sequence of nucleotide building blocks that functions as a code for the instructions. By means of an enzyme called RNA polymerase, this code is transcribed into a similar code of nucleotides called messenger RNA, or mRNA (b). In this form the instructions are transported to the bacterial ribosomes, the sites of protein synthesis (c), where the nucleotide sequence in mRNA is translated into a sequence of amino acids that eventually forms β lactamase (d). In an encounter between β lactamase and penicillin (e), the antibiotic activity of the latter is effectively destroyed (f), thereby preventing damage to the bacterial cell.

122

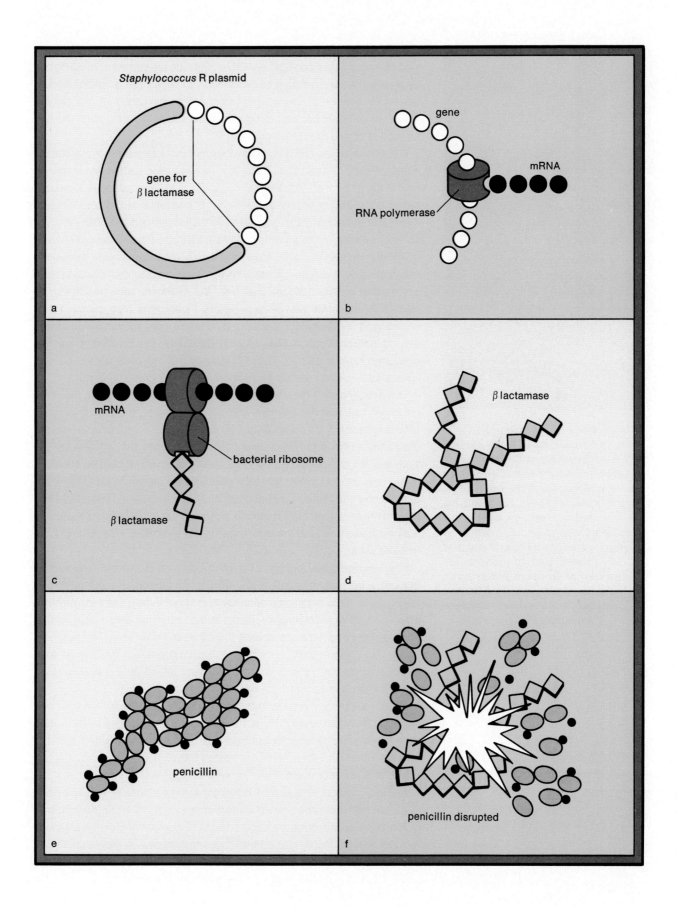

a *Staphylococcus* R plasmid

gene for β lactamase

b gene

RNA polymerase

mRNA

c mRNA

bacterial ribosome

β lactamase

d β lactamase

e penicillin

f penicillin disrupted

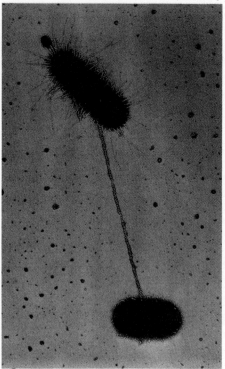

Two bacteria conjugating by means of a pilus are shown in the electron micrograph above. On the opposite page are microscopic views of three microbial agents of human disease: (top to bottom) Bacillus anthracis, *the cause of anthrax and the first microorganism definitely shown to be responsible for a disease of man and animals;* Neisseria gonorrhoeae *(apparent as groups of smaller cells), the cause of gonorrhea; and* Borrelia recurrentis, *a threadlike spirochete responsible for relapsing fever.*

fashion. Some plasmids are transmitted by cell-to-cell contact in a primitive kind of mating called conjugation. Other plasmids are carried from cell to cell by an intermediate vector, a bacterial virus, by a process termed transduction. In rare cases, plasmids in the form of free molecules of DNA are absorbed by recipient bacteria directly from the surrounding medium; this last method is known as transformation.

R plasmids of the microorganism *Staphylococcus aureus* are generally transmitted by transduction. Staph is a very common bacterium, often present in the nose or on the skin. Yet under the right circumstances staph can cause boils, abscesses, or pneumonia, or even invade the bloodstream. About four out of five staph organisms contain R plasmids that carry instructions, or encode, for an enzyme called penicillinase (or β lactamase), which efficiently destroys penicillin. Modern chemical techniques made it possible, however, to develop penicillin derivatives—for example, methicillin and cloxacillin—that are penicillinase resistant. But in recent years resistance to methicillin and other penicillinase-resistant penicillins also started to increase, and an alternative antibiotic, gentamicin, was chosen for treatment of serious staph infection. More recently R plasmids that mediate gentamicin resistance have appeared. Thus R plasmids are not static entities but are constantly evolving, seemingly adding new genes to their repertoire.

The best known R plasmids are molecular parasites of the bacteria that commonly colonize the mammalian bowel. In general, R plasmids in these enteric organisms are disseminated by conjugation. In addition to genes for replication within a host cell, many also carry genes that encode for the synthesis on the bacterial cell surface of a specialized hairlike structure called a pilus. The pilus, together with other proteins of plasmid origin, permits one cell to mate with another and, through a special form of DNA replication, to donate the plasmid to the other cell while keeping a plasmid replica for itself. In turn, the cell receiving the plasmid is able to pass it on to other cells.

In a laboratory and outside of a living body, an R plasmid may spread through a bacterial population like wildfire. Fortunately the gut or throat, where these microorganisms normally live, is not usually the best environment for mating; a multitude of factors in the real world keep conjugation a relatively rare event. The occasions when it does occur, however, may have far-reaching implications, especially if the R plasmid is transferred to a pathogenic microorganism, which by its very infectivity assures its rapid multiplication and spread from person to person.

Despite the rarity of R plasmid transfer in nature, a number of surveys have indicated that more than 50% of healthy adults and children excrete (and therefore harbor) detectable numbers of antibiotic-resistant enterobacterial species. If these healthy people are treated with an appropriate antimicrobial agent for a minor or major illness, several important factors may come into play. First, resistant cells survive in the gut at the expense of sensitive ones and soon multiply to become a dominant component of the total assemblage of species. Second, once this occurs, the likelihood of transfer of R plasmids to other species increases. Both of these factors are an inevitable sequel to the medical, veterinary, and agricultural uses of antibiotics. There is no

124

doubt that future use of antibiotics will continue to exert a considerable selective pressure in favor of antibiotic resistance in both harmless and pathogenic bacteria in man and animals.

Transposons: genes that jump

Plasmid exchange, by whatever means, constitutes a powerful mechanism for the exchange of genetic information among bacteria. Although in most cases there are definite limits to the range of plasmid transfer in nature, the host range of some plasmids is surprisingly broad. Some R plasmids can be transmitted to at least 36 different major species of bacteria. An important variation on the basic theme of extrachromosomal genetic exchange, as well as perhaps a glimmering of the origin of drug-resistance genes, has been recently established with the discovery of transposons. Transposons are segments of DNA within an intact plasmid or bacterial chromosome that have the capacity to excise, or break away, from one DNA molecule and insert themselves into a recipient DNA molecule. What makes this phenomenon so important is that many plasmid genes which confer resistance to antimicrobial agents—including penicillin, sulfonamide, streptomycin, chloramphenicol, and tetracycline—reside upon transposons.

The ability of discrete drug-resistance genes to jump from plasmid to plasmid helps explain the rapid evolution of R plasmids, which possess a variety of such genes. For example, resistance to ampicillin (a form of penicillin) is very common; yet many of the plasmids that specify ampicillin resistance are as unlike in the biological sense as a cat and mouse. However, the one unifying evolutionary thread running through these dissimilar plasmids is the presence of a common transposon, called TnA, carrying a gene for penicillinase.

It has been of considerable interest in recent years to follow the natural history of TnA. *Haemophilus influenzae* is an important bacterial pathogen of young children, causing meningitis, pneumonia, and ear and throat infections. This organism had been exquisitely sensitive to ampicillin since the antibiotic was introduced to clinical therapy. In 1973, however, three infants treated with ampicillin for *Haemophilus* meningitis failed to respond and died. These resistant strains harbored an R plasmid of a type never before seen. But it carried the ubiquitous TnA transposon so common in enteric bacteria. By 1977, only five years later, as many as one in ten of all *H. influenzae* strains in the U.S. were resistant to ampicillin.

In a similar vein, *Neisseria gonorrhoeae* (often called the gonococcus), the organism that causes gonorrhea, had been almost universally susceptible to penicillin. Curing a patient with gonorrhea was so straightforward that it was called the "minute treatment." One shot deftly applied effected a cure 90% of the time. In September 1976 penicillinase-producing gonococci appeared in several places around the world. They contained R plasmids, and the R plasmids contained TnA.

As of mid-1978 the full implications of these extensions of antibiotic resistance were not yet clear. Since 1973 not only has ampicillin resistance appeared in *Haemophilus* but also resistance to tetracycline, kanamycin, and chloramphenicol. In each case, the drug-resistance gene involved is on

Photos, Manfred Kage—Peter Arnold, Inc.

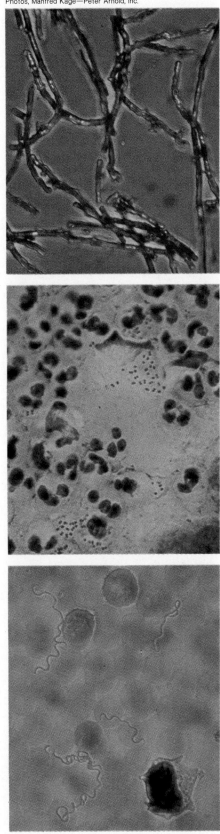

125

a discrete transposon. There is some reason to believe that occurrence of some of the R plasmids in *Haemophilus* represents an instance in which a long-time resident plasmid of *Haemophilus* underwent a metamorphosis —innocuous one moment, the recipient of a transposon the next.

Although it is not known where these "jumping" packets of drug resistance originate, there are some interesting speculations based on a scattering of facts. It can be shown that a very few of the cultures of bacteria that were preserved before the antibiotic era contain R plasmids and that, in rare instances, individuals in primitive societies where antibiotics have never been used harbor microorganisms containing an R plasmid. Plasmids per se are common enough, and it is supposed that antibiotic production in the soil, on moldy bread, and the like provided sufficient selective pressure to make an R plasmid a useful genetic commodity. Given the existence of even a small reservoir of R plasmids, it is not too difficult to visualize how they came so quickly to the fore in the current antibiotic era, when literally tons of antibiotics are used yearly.

Investigators have also noted that some microorganisms possess (and require) antibiotic-inactivating enzymes similar to those found on R plasmids. What is intriguing is that they are the very microorganisms that produce the antibiotics. Experiments are currently under way to examine this question, and it would be a delicious irony of nature to learn one day that the same microorganisms that initiated the antibiotic era may also have been the source of the transposable genes that pathogenic bacteria are using to stage a comeback.

The scope of the resistance problem

Despite the emergence of resistant microorganisms, most common infections remain fully amenable to treatment with antimicrobial agents. In technologically advanced societies, of course, widespread epidemics of typhoid, cholera, and dysentery had taken a downward turn coincident with improvements in sanitation and water quality control—well before the introduction of antimicrobials. Vaccines for diphtheria, tetanus, and a score of viral diseases have been developed. There is no question but that many previously devastating infections caused by pathogenic bacteria are now either prevented or are primarily treated successfully without hospitalization with antimicrobial therapy.

To be sure, the emergence of R plasmids in *H. influenzae* and the gonococcus is an ominous sign. These microorganisms can affect a broad segment of the world's population and can cause serious or even fatal infections. Moreover, it is recognized that the agent of epidemic meningitis, the bacterium *Neisseria meningitidis*, is distributed in the human body in a fashion similar to *H. influenzae*. The occurrence of penicillin-resistant meningococcal meningitis would cause enormous problems in the treatment of disease cases and control of epidemics. Many investigators fear this is an inevitable event.

Early in 1977 there were other unsettling reports, the most serious of which was of the emergence of multiply antibiotic-resistant *Streptococcus pneumoniae* (the common pneumococcus), a major cause of pneumonia.

126

Most of the strains appeared in South Africa and were responsible for several deaths. The organisms are totally resistant to penicillin, an antibiotic to which pneumococci were considered to be universally susceptible. Resistance in the pneumococci does not seem to be plasmid mediated. Rather, resistant organisms appear impermeable to many antimicrobials because of a mutational change affecting the cell wall. Another serious development concerned a classification of streptococci known as group A. Collectively these important pathogens are the most common cause of tonsillitis and are uniquely linked to the development of rheumatic fever and one kind of glomerulonephritis, a peculiar inflammation of the kidney. These streptococci have remained universally susceptible to penicillin; what is worrisome, however, is that their plasmid-mediated resistance to erythromycin, tetracycline, and chloramphenicol has increased markedly. Should the group A streptococci become resistant to penicillin like *Haemophilus*, the gonococcus, and pneumococcus, medical science might well be faced with yet another serious problem.

Nevertheless, it is probably fair to say that antibiotic-resistant microorganisms either have not yet emerged as a significant community problem or have succumbed to antibiotic alternatives in the face of resistance so that the pattern of disease within the community has not changed enough to be alarming. Whereas one might expect fewer patients with infections in hospitals, this has not been the case. The patient population, however, has changed. Hospital beds are now occupied by patients at the age extremes who have underlying chronic disabling disorders. For example, many modern surgical procedures require long periods of hospitalization coupled with the use of therapy that suppresses the body's immune system. Such patients often also receive large amounts of antibiotics. Under these conditions common bacteria that normally inhabit the gut, for example *Escherichia coli* and *Klebsiella pneumoniae*, or organisms that live on inanimate objects in the vicinity of patients, such as *Pseudomonas aeruginosa*, are apt to cause infection because the patient's normal defense mechanisms are diminished. More often than not, these opportunistic invaders harbor R plasmids and seem to have emerged because of the selective pressure of antibiotic use. Thus the killer of many patients is not their malignancy or rejection of transplanted foreign tissue but rather their own bacterial inhabitants. And all too often these infections are difficult to treat because the offending organism is broadly antibiotic resistant.

It is not fully appreciated that a hospitalized individual has a significant risk of acquiring a nosocomial infection; *i.e.*, one that occurs during hospitalization but that was not present or incubating upon admission. During 1975–76 nosocomial infections occurred in the U.S. at a rate of 357 infections per 10,000 patients discharged. In fact, one-third of all infections in hospitalized patients are nosocomial in origin; about 1.5 million people developed a nosocomial infection in 1975–76. The direct cost of providing medical care for this problem exceeded a billion dollars.

More than 50% of all nosocomial infections are caused by multiply antibiotic-resistant *E. coli*, *Klebsiella*, *Pseudomonas*, and staph. These organisms are difficult to control in individual patients, and antibiotic usage is often

Manfred Kage—Peter Arnold, Inc.

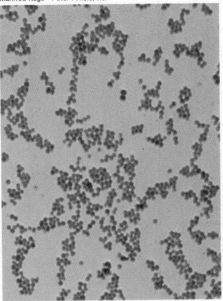

Stained and magnified, common staph (Staphylococcus aureus) has the grape-cluster appearance characteristic of many coccus-type bacteria.

Normally a benign resident of the human gut, rodlike Klebsiella pneumoniae *has significant disease-causing potential. The specimen shown below was taken from the lung of a pneumonia victim.*

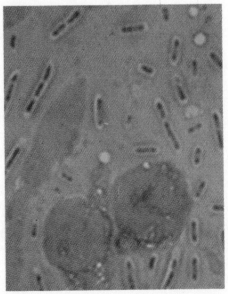

A. W. Rakosy—EB Inc.

Direct application of chemical substances to bacterial cultures is a classic method of evaluating antibiotic effectiveness. Dishes of nutrient are streaked with single bacterial strains; to them are added paper disks that have been saturated with antibiotics of known concentration. The eventual appearance and size of a bacteria-free halo around a disk becomes a measure of the ability of a particular substance to inhibit bacterial growth. Such procedures are used to test new antibiotics and to assess the capabilities of resistant bacterial strains.

high enough to provide ample selective pressure to ensure perpetuation and dissemination of some resistant strains. Thus certain resistant "hospital strains" circulate in-house, colonizing patients and sometimes causing severe infection in those whose normal defense mechanisms have been compromised. If use of antibiotics creates a biological vacuum, it will not go unfilled for long.

In less developed areas, individuals not only must cope with "common" diseases but also must face such epidemic illnesses as typhoid and dysentery. In recent years treatment of epidemic infections with antibiotics has often failed, with tragic results. For example, *Shigella dysenteriae*, a highly infectious, virulent bacterium, caused an extensive outbreak of dysentery throughout Central America from 1968 to 1972, affecting hundreds of thousands of persons and causing tens of thousands of deaths. The disease was initially misdiagnosed as amebic dysentery, partly because patients did not respond to antibacterial drugs in common use. The delay in diagnosis contributed greatly to high mortality. Even when the true offending organism was recognized and was discovered to be multiply resistant to antibiotics, treatment was difficult because effective antibiotics were too expensive for the majority of the affected population.

In a similar vein, during 1972–73 Mexico experienced a typhoid outbreak. The epidemic was unique in its wide distribution and lengthy duration, and cases numbered in the thousands. Its early fatality rate was similar to that experienced before the antibiotic era, even though chloramphenicol, the long-established drug of choice, was employed for treatment. When it was finally learned that the causative typhoid strain was chloramphenicol resistant because it had an R plasmid, subsequent treatment with the antibiotic ampicillin led to a dramatic reduction in mortality. Still later, strains resistant to ampicillin emerged and once again the treatment had to be changed.

Further considerations

It has been amply demonstrated that the emergence of antibiotic-resistant bacteria is closely linked to antibiotic usage, which has been rising on a global scale. In some cases, increased use is due to improved medical care; in other cases it is associated with questionable applications. Dissemination of antibiotics is not limited to the physician's syringe. In most of the developed world antibiotics and other antimicrobial agents—particularly tetracycline, penicillin, and sulfonamides—have been used in the livestock and poultry industries for the past 25 years to "improve feed efficiency and rate of weight gain" and to prevent and treat disease. In the U.S. the amount of antibiotics used in animal production has been estimated to be about 40% of the total consumption.

Not unexpectedly, the vast majority of livestock harbor a predominantly resistant microbial assemblage. This has been the cause for legitimate concern. Some people who live on farms and handle antibiotic-supplemented feeds have inordinately large numbers of antibiotic-resistant bacteria in their intestinal tracts compared with city dwellers. There is also some evidence that drug-resistant bacteria of animal origin are transmitted to people through the food chain. The actual contribution of resistant bacteria or their

R plasmids to the total drug-resistant pool of humans is difficult to assess. It is clear, however, that R plasmids found in pathogenic bacteria from humans are indistinguishable from those found in animal bacteria. In light of these facts, in 1977 the U.S. Food and Drug Administration (FDA) proposed measures to limit (though not abolish) the use of antibiotic-containing feed in the U.S., a step many other countries had already taken. In certain quarters this has been an unpopular decision, the major argument being that any detrimental effect of antibiotics in feeds is small compared with the economic benefits to the farmer and consumer. The World Health Organization and most objective scientific bodies that have studied the question tend to support the FDA's position. Presumably this issue eventually will be solved in a court of law.

Prospects for the future

There is probably no need to fear that medicine's antibiotic armamentarium against disease-producing bacteria will eventually be totally nullified by the development of resistant microorganisms. It is important to understand that most microorganisms isolated from disease victims or the hospital environment still remain susceptible to most antibiotics. Nevertheless, the antibiotic era illustrates a well-known principle concerning the balance of nature. Whenever a biological system is perturbed—in this case by antimicrobials— the system will respond in an attempt to return to a tolerable equilibrium. The final effects of antibiotics on human society are not yet known, nor are their effects on the biology and capabilities of microorganisms.

Obviously, outbreaks of antibiotic-resistant disease-producing microorganisms will continue to be a public health problem and will exact a toll in death, suffering, and increased costs of medical care. Moreover, the reservoir of antibiotic-resistant bacteria will continue to increase in the hospital setting and the community unless a concerted effort is made to bring about a more rational and coordinated use of antibiotics. The past decade in particular has dramatized an important lesson for the future: uncontrolled and excessive use of antibiotics in man and animals results in an alarming increase in resistance, which compromises and in some cases destroys their utility. The problem is man-made; presumably man can reverse the trend, at least in part. Continued understanding of how microorganisms develop resistance and the cooperative efforts of clinicians, veterinarians, commercial interests, and the general public are essential steps toward this goal.

FOR ADDITIONAL READING

S. Falkow, *Infectious Multiple Drug Resistance* (Pion, Ltd., 1975).

E. F. Gale, E. Cundliffe, P. E. Reynolds *et al.*, *The Molecular Basis of Antibiotic Action* (John Wiley & Sons, 1972).

L. P. Garrod, H. P. Lambert, and F. O'Grady, *Antibiotic and Chemotherapy* (Churchill Livingstone, 1973).

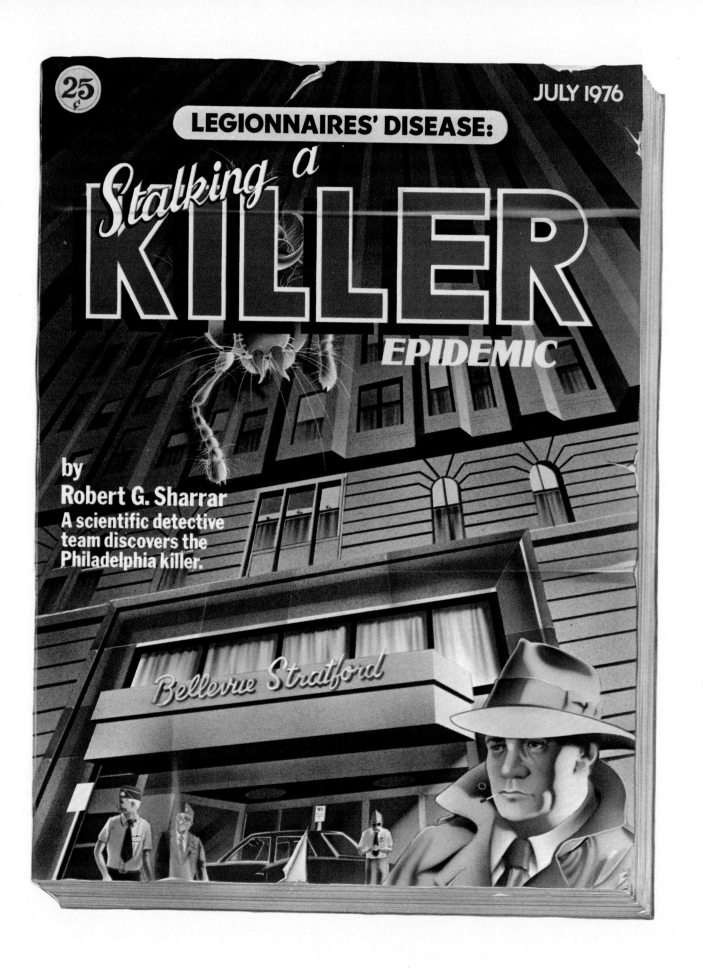

Near the end of a Pennsylvania state American Legion convention that had run from July 21 to 24, 1976, mainly at the Bellevue Stratford Hotel in Philadelphia, some of the participants began to feel ill. Most of them blamed the tiring convention routine of banquets, a parade, and late hours. Back in their hometowns, however, some continued to complain of headache, high fever, chills, dry cough, and muscle aches—symptoms of acute infectious disease. On July 27 an elderly Legionnaire died in Athens, Pennsylvania, but little attention was paid because the man had a history of heart trouble. But by Friday, July 30, five more Legionnaires were dead, and others were hospitalized across the state. Over the weekend five more died.

On the morning of Monday, August 2, William Parkin, acting epidemiologist for the state of Pennsylvania, called the writer, who was then chief of the Communicable Disease Control Section of the health department of Philadelphia. Parkin said that a statewide health alert had been declared. "We've had 11 deaths from pneumonia, and every case attended an American Legion convention last week in Philadelphia."

At that time, the U.S. was braced for a possible epidemic of swine influenza, and public health officials throughout the nation were making plans to administer a massive federal flu inoculation program. Both of us immediately thought "Swine flu!" and began following the epidemic investigative procedures recommended by the federal Center for Disease Control at Atlanta, Georgia. This search eventually involved hundreds of people of various professions, including epidemiologists, physicians, statisticians, sanitarians, laboratory workers, and police officers, and soon grew into the most intensive epidemiologic pursuit in modern medical history.

131

The hunt begins

Epidemics, like the activities of criminals, do not occur by chance. They are caused by a unique combination of events, which include susceptible victims coming into contact with a harmful biological or chemical agent in the proper environment. The disease itself need not be unusual; in fact, an epidemic exists only when the number of cases of disease that occur are unusual in terms of their distribution in the population. This normally refers to a clustering of cases during a short period of time, in a definite geographic region, and in a defined population.

The first two steps in conducting any epidemic investigation are to verify the diagnosis and to establish that an epidemic really exists. Due largely to the extensive news media coverage, which variously named the respiratory illness "Legionnaires' disease," "Legion fever," and the "Philadelphia killer," every suspected case was reported and investigated. The existence of an epidemic, *i.e.*, an unusual number of cases of illness in a defined population—the American Legion—had been readily established. It was impossible, however, to verify the diagnosis by any known laboratory test. This was initially one of the major problems facing investigators. Many cases of pneumonia were reported to health officials, and it was important to sort out those that were part of the epidemic from those that were part of the normal incidence of the disease.

Consequently, the investigators were forced to develop a special definition for a case of the disease, which consisted of a clinical portion and an epidemiologic portion. The clinical portion stated that a case must have had an onset of illness between July 1 and Aug. 18, 1976, and either (1) a temperature of 102° F or higher and a cough or (2) any fever and chest X-ray evidence of pneumonia. This clinical definition is very broad and lists symptoms that could be attributed to a virus, a bacterium, a rickettsia (one of a group of organisms intermediate between viruses and bacteria), a fungus, or a chemical toxin. Epidemiologic criteria were added to the case definition to further define and restrict cases under study. To be counted as a case, a person must either have attended the American Legion convention or have entered the Bellevue Stratford Hotel, the convention headquarters and primary meeting site, on or after July 1. Based on these criteria, three groups of pneumonias were identified. Those that fit the case definition exactly were called cases of Legionnaires' disease. Patients with pneumonia who were within one block of the hotel on Broad Street, the hotel's main access route, were called Broad Street pneumonia cases, and all other Philadelphia cases were referred to as citywide pneumonias.

The scene of the crime

In proceeding with an investigation, be it criminal or epidemic, it is important to have an understanding of the events involved and the place of occurrence. Conventioneers at the Legion gathering in July came from all parts of Pennsylvania. Attendees could be classified into four subgroups: delegates with voting privileges, nondelegates, family members, and members of the women's auxiliary. The women's auxiliary, a companion organization similar to the American Legion, was having its 56th annual convention at the

ROBERT G. SHARRAR is Assistant Professor of Epidemiology at Thomas Jefferson University, Philadelphia, Pennsylvania, and formerly Chief, Communicable Disease Control Section, Division of Epidemiology, Philadelphia Department of Public Health.

(Overleaf) Painting by John Youssi. Illustrations by Ron Villani

132

same time. Participants stayed at five major mid-city hotels and at many other smaller places. Most activities of the American Legion convention took place at the Bellevue Stratford, whereas the women's auxiliary conducted its business meetings at the Benjamin Franklin Hotel, seven blocks away. During the four-day convention 40 official meetings and gatherings took place in 13 different rooms of the Bellevue Stratford, the ballroom of the Benjamin Franklin, a luncheon held at Poor Richard's Club, less than two blocks from the Bellevue Stratford, and a parade on Broad Street.

In addition to these official events, there occurred a number of unofficial gatherings in hotel lobbies and private rooms and of parties in several hospitality suites sponsored by candidates who were running for state office. Legionnaires rarely ate in the hotel restaurants or drank at the hotel bars. Instead, they frequented restaurants that surrounded the hotel and drank at their private gatherings. Hence, attempts to trace the four-day activities of both the disease victims and the unafflicted were difficult.

The Bellevue Stratford was not just any old hotel but a political and historical landmark of Philadelphia that was justifiably called the "Grand Old Lady of Broad Street." (The hotel was forced to close in late 1976 because of a severe decline in business following the epidemic.) The building contained the standard lobby and mezzanine floors, which housed numerous shops, restaurants, bars, offices, a ballroom, and meeting rooms. There were 725 guest rooms located on floors 2 through 16. The 18th floor contained additional conference rooms and a banquet room. Below the lobby floor were three more floors: the kitchen floor; the basement, which included a number of lockers and other storage rooms; and the subbasement, which contained the incinerator and an engine room that housed air-conditioning water chillers, an electric power distribution area, sewage pumps, and water

pumps. On the roof of the hotel were an incinerator stack, air exhaust fans, and an air-conditioning cooling tower.

The hotel had a central, chilled-water air-conditioning system that was installed in 1954. It consisted of two chillers in the subbasement that used a chlorofluorocarbon refrigerant to cool water. This cold water was then pumped to the top of the hotel, and as it descended it passed through 60 separate air cooling and circulating units. Each such unit, with the exception of one in the lobby and one in the subbasement, used approximately 75% recirculated air and 25% outside air. Located over the registration desk, the lobby unit recirculated 100% of its air.

During the investigation careful attention was paid to the air-conditioning system because it represented an efficient, pervasive mode of transportation for a potential airborne disease agent. A boy confessed that he had thrown magician's smoke powder into an air-conditioning vent in the hotel a week before the convention; the powder was checked and found harmless. For analogous reasons drinking water, a centrally supplied commodity in the hotel, was also suspect; its source of supply was the municipal system of Philadelphia. In addition, there were detailed inspections and environmental sampling of other parts of the hotel, including kitchens, elevators, and waste-disposal and sanitation equipment. Local restaurants and bars outside the hotel were also thoroughly examined.

By August 6, 22 were dead and 130 others hospitalized throughout the state. More than 300 health workers were investigating the case, and they were able to draw some conclusions on the basis of laboratory tests. The disease was not the suspected swine flu nor was it bubonic plague, typhoid, parrot fever, tularemia, ornithosis, or any miscellaneous enteric bacteria. Toxicologists then tested for metal poisoning and soon ruled it out as a source of the disease.

Questioning witnesses, examining victims

The next step for the investigators was to characterize the distribution of cases by the variables of person, place, and time. In order to do this they had to collect data on the cases and on the number of people who attended the convention; *i.e.,* the population at risk of contracting the disease. This task offered the second major obstacle. Neither the American Legion nor the hotels knew the exact number of persons who had attended the convention. Therefore, a census survey was conducted to determine not only the number of attendees but also their activities at the convention. Questions included: "Were you sick before you went to the convention? When did you start feeling ill? What hotel rooms did you stay in? What restaurants did you eat in? Did you put ice in your drink in one of the hotel ballrooms? Have you had any recent contact with pigs?"

Ten-thousand two-page questionnaires were delivered by police car and helicopter to the 1,002 American Legion posts throughout the state. Post commanders were instructed to have everyone who had attended the convention complete and return the questionnaires.

While this information was being collected, two additional important questions were studied. Was Legionnaires' disease part of a citywide pneumonia

134

problem, and was it an ongoing problem? To investigate the first question, records of admissions in three mid-city hospitals and emergency-room visits in 11 hospitals were examined for other cases of illness resembling Legionnaires' disease. Next, a comparison of pneumonia and influenza deaths by week of report was examined for the preceding three years. None of these surveys showed any significant increase of pneumonias in the city of Philadelphia. Thus, Legionnaires' disease did not appear to be citywide.

Several other studies were conducted to determine if Legionnaires' disease was an ongoing problem. The investigators were under considerable pressure in this area because nearly one million Roman Catholics were due in Philadelphia the next week for the International Eucharistic Congress. Case investigations failed to document any secondary cases in family members who were not in Philadelphia or in hospital personnel caring for victims of the disease. Fortunately the disease did not appear to be transmissible from person to person. A random telephone survey of guests who had stayed in four different hotels from July 6 to August 7 was conducted to determine if additional cases were occurring. This survey failed to identify any new cases occurring in hotel guests exposed after the week of July 18–24, the week of the Legion convention. These results suggested that Legionnaires' disease was no longer a significant problem and that whatever had happened had been restricted to a short time period surrounding the dates of the convention.

From various surveys and a continual inflow of information from medical reports and hospital records, a clinical picture of Legionnaires' disease gradually took form. A typical case of the disease began two to ten days after exposure—its incubation period—and most victims had already returned home before they became ill. The earliest symptoms consisted of malaise,

135

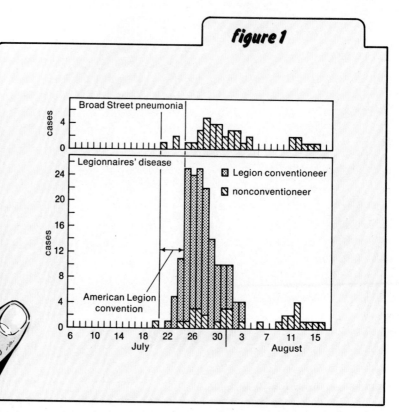

figure 1

muscle aches, headache, and a dry cough. Shortly thereafter, the patient developed a high fever of 102°–105° F and chills. Shortness of breath, chest pain, and gastrointestinal symptoms occurred in many. On the average the patient first consulted a physician two to three days after onset. At this time physical examination of the chest revealed abnormal sounds during breathing but as yet no evidence of consolidation; *i.e.,* that normal spongy, air-filled lung tissue was filling with fluids and cellular matter, as is found in pneumonia. The rest of the examination was unremarkable. Over 80% of the cases eventually required hospitalization and 29 died, for a case fatality ratio of 16%. Death was most likely to occur in elderly patients with chronic underlying illnesses and in those with short incubation periods. Patients treated with the antibiotics erythromycin and tetracycline had an improved chance of survival.

Laboratory findings on disease victims were not helpful in establishing a diagnosis. Most had abnormalities suggesting a recent infection, but these were nonspecific. Those patients who had arterial blood-gas determinations were found to have a low concentration of oxygen in their blood. Chest X-rays were abnormal in 90% of the patients; most showed patchy, fluid-permeated areas of tissue in one lung, a condition that usually progressed to widespread consolidation. In nearly one-half of the most advanced cases, chest X-ray abnormalities remained confined to one lung. Examination of the lungs of deceased victims revealed inflamed and consolidated areas indicative of pneumonia. No other body organ or system was consistently involved.

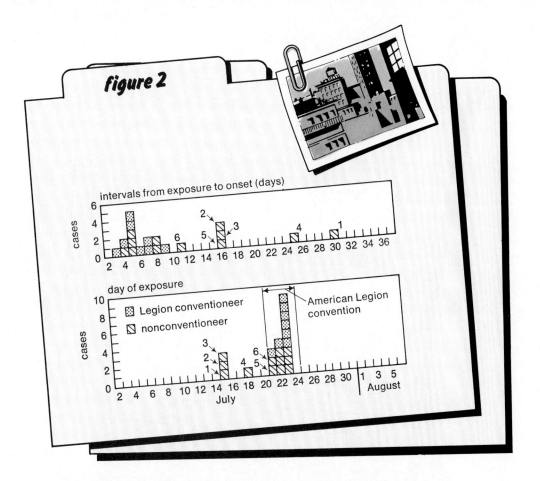

figure 2

intervals from exposure to onset (days)

day of exposure

An analysis of the distribution of cases by time is shown in figures 1 and 2. Figure 1 reveals the epidemic curve for the 182 cases that fit the case criteria for Legionnaires' disease and for the 39 cases of Broad Street pneumonia. The cases of Legionnaires' disease included 149 convention-eers and 33 nonconventioneers. The similarity of the two curves suggests that both groups are part of the same outbreak. Persistence of the disease in nonconventioneers during the first part of August also suggests a continu-ing source but at decreased intensity. Figure 2 illustrates the method of determining the incubation period of Legionnaires' disease by analyzing data concerning those victims who were present only one day at the Bellevue Stratford. The incubation period of conventioneers' cases ranged from three to nine days with a mean of about six days. The incubation period of some nonconventioneers (numbered 1 through 6) extended over a longer period of time, suggesting that their disease was different or that exposure took place elsewhere.

Tables I and II on p. 138 show the results of the Legionnaires' census survey. Table I delineates the attack rate by convention status and hotel of residence. The 3,683 questionnaires returned included those of 1,849 dele-gates. Based upon the number of delegates known to have voted at the convention, the questionnaire had an estimated return rate of 80–85%. The table also reveals that the attack rates were highest for delegates and family members and lowest for nondelegates and members of the women's auxili-ary. The women's auxiliary held its meetings seven blocks from the

Table I.	Legionnaires' Disease Attack Rates by Convention Status and Hotel of Residence		
convention status	number of respondents	number of cases	attack rate (%)
delegate	1,849	125	6.8
auxiliary	701	4	0.6
family member	268	17	6.3
nondelegate	762	3	0.4
unknown	103	0	0
	3,683	149	4.0
hotel	number of all respondents	number of cases	% ill
A	1,161	75	6.5
D	1,046	21	2.0
E	403	19	4.7
F	312	12	3.8
G	104	4	3.8
other	210	7	3.3
home	294	8	2.7
unknown	153	3	2.0
	3,683	149	4.0

Table II.	Legionnaires' Disease Attack Rate by Age and Sex		
age (years)	number of respondents	number of cases	attack rate (%)
less than 40	610	11	1.8
40–49	805	25	3.1
50–59	1,428	58	4.1
60–69	538	36	6.7
70 and older	254	19	7.5
unknown	48	0	0
	3,683	149	4.0
sex			
male	2,292	123	5.4
female	1,380	26	1.9
unknown	11	0	0
	3,683	149	4.0

Bellevue Stratford. Residents of hotel A, the Bellevue Stratford, had the highest attack rate. Table II shows the attack rate by age and sex for all conventioneers. The attack rate increased with increasing age, and it was higher in males than in females. The overall attack rate was 4%.

Investigators also undertook a case-control or retrospective study, which was designed to identify factors that were common to the ill group but not to the well group. All surviving male conventioneer cases and a random sample of 202 completely well men who had answered the census survey were queried to determine their activities while they were in Philadelphia at the convention. The study identified three factors that were statistically significant. First, ill delegates spent an average of four or five more hours in the Bellevue Stratford than did well delegates, and considerably more time in the lobby. However, none of the more than 30 full-time lobby employees became ill. Second, ill delegates visited an average of 2.8 hospitality rooms, compared with 1.8 visits for well delegates. Yet, no one hospitality room had been visited by more than one-third of the cases. Finally, cases were more likely to drink water at the Bellevue Stratford than noncases. Only 62% of the cases, however, admitted to drinking water in any form. Thus, none of these associations could be linked with all of the cases.

The missing modus operandi

The next series of steps in an epidemic investigation can be likened to the task of reducing a criminal's record of activities to a predictable pattern or method of operation. In epidemiologic terms a hypothesis must be established as to the source of infection and its mode of transmission. The hypothesis should then be tested, conclusions drawn, and control measures instituted. As of early 1978, however, no satisfactory hypothesis had been developed. The source of the disease was not known, nor was the reason for its sudden outbreak and swift disappearance.

As mentioned above, investigations of post-convention family contacts failed to demonstrate the likelihood of person-to-person transmission. Likewise, there was no clustering of cases in certain hotel rooms, as would be expected for this mode of spread. Studies of 28 restaurants and bars in the vicinity of the Bellevue Stratford yielded no significant relationship between the disease and food, nor did a check of two convention events that featured common meals. Whereas case-control studies demonstrated a relatively greater risk of illness for cigarette smokers, this correlation holds true generally for respiratory diseases because smokers provide a more susceptible

respiratory tract. No connection was found between the disease and drinking alcoholic beverages in any form, and drinking water at the Bellevue Stratford could not account for nearly 40% of disease cases. Investigators also could develop no relationship between the disease and insect bites or exposure to animals or souvenirs.

Because of the inability to explain what had happened, speculators filled the vacuum with their own pet theories, which included sabotage, germ warfare, various toxins, and even paranormal and occult phenomena. Some of these received a considerable amount of attention in the news media. Unfortunately all of them ignored certain epidemiologic, clinical, or laboratory facts that had been established. And none of the theories could account for the distribution of cases that was observed.

Unmasking the killer

The search for the cause of Legionnaires' disease consisted of collecting and analyzing hundreds of specimens from patients with the disease. The hunt for a microbiologic agent included 9 methods of visualizing the organism, 14 different culture media to isolate bacteria and fungi, and 13 host systems to isolate a virus. In addition, blood serums were processed against 77 known infectious agents to look for the presence of antibodies. Tissue and urine samples were examined for abnormal concentrations of more than 30 metallic substances and a number of different toxic organic compounds. All of the tests failed to identify the cause of Legionnaires' disease. Every conceivable agent known to medical science had been systematically eliminated, one by one.

During late December 1976 a major development occurred when Joseph E. McDade and Charles C. Shepard, microbiologists in the Leprosy and Rickettsia Branch at the Center for Disease Control, began a review of some microscopic specimens prepared at the time of the epidemic. The results of

their laboratory findings were published in January 1977, when the center officially announced that it had isolated the agent believed responsible for Legionnaires' disease.

The organism was isolated using standard techniques for isolating a rickettsial agent. Lung tissue specimens from a deceased victim were homogenized and injected into guinea pigs. After an incubation period of one to two days, the guinea pigs developed an illness that was characterized by fever, watery eyes, and prostration. Suspensions of their spleens were then used to inoculate the yolk sacs of developing chick embryos. The embryos died after four to six days, and microscopic examination of stained smears of the yolk sacs revealed clusters of rod-shaped microorganisms. Although as of early 1978 this organism had yet to be identified, various characteristics eventually led to its classification as a bacterium. With the causative agent in hand, the laboratory was able to develop a test for detecting the presence of substances (antibodies) antagonistic to the invading organism in the blood serums of suspected cases. The immune system of a true victim of Legionnaires' disease would likely have mustered its defenses upon exposure to produce such proteins, which remain in the bloodstream long after an attack has passed. Thus, five and one-half months after the outbreak occurred, epidemiologists finally had a laboratory test that could be used to "verify the diagnosis," which is the first step in conducting an epidemic investigation and which had been the first major problem encountered after the outbreak.

These findings and subsequent studies during 1977 uncovered several important facts:

1. The bacterium was isolated separately from five pneumonia cases in Philadelphia. Four of these had fit the case definition of Legionnaires' disease, and one had been classified a Broad Street pneumonia victim.

2. The antibody test showed that more than 90% of conventioneer cases and more than 64% of Broad Street pneumonia cases from whom adequate specimens of blood serum had been obtained had evidence of a recent infection with the newly isolated bacterium.

3. Blood serums from patients with single-day exposures on July 21, 22, and 23, and from two of the nine disease victims who had attended the Eucharistic Congress in Philadelphia August 1–8 revealed evidence of recent infections, suggesting that the source of infection was present at least during a two-week period.

4. Blood specimens were collected from more than 500 people who lived or worked in mid-city Philadelphia to determine the prevalence in the general population of individuals who possessed antibodies directed against this bacterium. These surveys demonstrated that less than 5% of the general population had any significant concentration of such antibodies. Tested serums from patients from throughout the United States with pneumonias that had been classified as nonbacterial in nature suggested that 1–2% of these cases could in fact be Legionnaires' disease.

5. The organism can be grown in vitro, or outside the body, on several culture media. In vitro studies revealed that the organism is susceptible to a large number of antimicrobial agents, and studies in guinea pigs and chick embryos showed that rifampin, gentamicin, streptomycin, and erythromycin

are effective. Erythromycin appears to be an especially potent antibiotic in treating patients with Legionnaires' disease.

These observations demonstrate that Legionnaires' disease is caused by a biological agent and not a toxin, and that Broad Street pneumonia victims, who were never inside the Bellevue Stratford, were part of the epidemic. Furthermore, exposure took place at least during a two-week period. Whereas this organism is capable of causing a major epidemic, it appears to have only a low level of endemic activity; *i.e.*, the ability to produce disease continually in a geographic region.

A long criminal record

In 1965 an outbreak of acute pneumonia occurred at St. Elizabeths Hospital in Washington, D.C. The outbreak was similar to the Legionnaires' disease epidemic of 1976 with respect to clinical symptoms and time of year of occurrence. There were 81 cases including 14 deaths, for a case fatality ratio of 17%. Whereas the overall attack rate was only 1.5%, it was higher among people whose beds were near windows and among people who had been given the privilege of access to the grounds and surrounding community. Aware of parallels between the two outbreaks, investigators examined 23 samples of blood serum that had been preserved in frozen state from victims of the earlier outbreak. Twenty-one of these showed evidence of antibodies directed against the bacterium of Legionnaires' disease.

In July 1968 an outbreak of an acute illness characterized by malaise, muscle pain, fever, chills, and headache spread through county health department employees and visitors in Pontiac, Michigan. The event occurred when an air-conditioning unit that supplied the department was first turned on for the summer. This group of cases differs from that of Legionnaires' disease in that there were no cases of pneumonia, no deaths, and an extraordinarily high attack rate among employees of 95%. The incubation period was also considerably shorter, ranging from 5 to more than 60 hours with a mean of about 36 hours. Again serologic specimens had been preserved, and of 37 samples examined, 32 had evidence of infection with an organism similar to the bacterium of Legionnaires' disease.

It is of interest to note that these two outbreaks were preceded by construction activity in the immediate locale. Although the significance of this observation is not known, it has caused some speculation that the soil might be the source of the organism.

Since the epidemic in Philadelphia, outbreaks of Legionnaires' disease occurred in 1977 in Ohio, Tennessee, Vermont, and California. By March 1978, 232 endemic or isolated cases of Legionnaires' disease also had been documented in 38 states and the District of Columbia. The patients ranged in age from 16 to 83 years with a mean age of 54. Endemic cases were 2.4 times more common in males than in females, but the case fatality ratio of 19% was approximately the same for both sexes. Although the epidemic form of the disease has occurred only in the summer months, the endemic form can occur throughout the year. The distribution of cases roughly corresponds to the population density of the country. No single occupation or type of work appears to be a significant factor. Cases included individuals who worked indoors as well as outdoors and people who lived in urban and rural settings. Many of these cases had no known underlying illness. Such data portray an endemic pattern of Legionnaires' disease characterized by wide geographical distribution, occurrence throughout the year, and a higher case fatality rate than in the epidemic form of the disease. From such information it seems highly likely that the milder forms of the disease—and in some instances the severe form—go undiagnosed.

Protecting the public

The investigation that began in August 1976 ultimately led to the discovery of a previously unknown biological agent that can produce disease in man. Subsequent studies revealed that this organism has caused epidemics in the past and that it has a low level of endemic activity throughout the year and in a wide geographical distribution. To date epidemiologic investigators have failed to identify those factors that enable this organism to assume epidemic proportions. They also have failed to identify the source of infection, although its probable mode of transmission is airborne.

In early laboratory work with the bacterium, when little was known of its capabilities and limitations, biological containment procedures were necessarily strict and experimentation proceeded slowly and cautiously. In light of recently gained knowledge that the epidemic form of Legionnaires' disease is relatively uncommon, continued investigations are expected to move rapidly. Unlike a criminal, who can be caught and isolated from society, a disease microorganism exists in untold and unconfinable numbers. It remains at large as an ever present threat until its potential victims can be defended against it. It is these defenses—better public health control measures, improved treatment of infections, and perhaps ultimately a protective vaccine—that constitute the important work of the future.

Climate and the Changing Sun

by John A. Eddy

**The long-established belief that the Sun's energy
output has remained constant for thousands of years
has been overturned by discoveries linking solar
variability with changes in the Earth's climate.**

Do changes on the Sun affect the daily weather? Or the long-term trends
in weather, known as climate? Most scientists today are skeptical of any
important, immediate effects of the Sun on local weather conditions; the
structure and dynamics of the Earth's atmosphere are too complex and the
known fluctuations in the flow of solar energy are too small. Scientists are
far less certain, however, when considering the same question of climatic
changes that take place over the decades, centuries, or millennia. Even
small changes in the flow of heat and in other outputs of the Sun, if they
prevail long enough, could alter climate.

There are now indications that this indeed has happened on repeated
occasions in the past. But to be certain, scientists need to know the history
of the Sun and the history of climate far better than they do now. Until
recently both the Sun and climate had been assumed to be either constant
or regular in their variation. It is now known that both have changed significantly, and perhaps in erratic or irregular ways in the time of modern man.

Long-term changes, short-term lives

The most recent of the major ice ages, called the Late Wisconsin on the
North American Continent, gripped the Earth for at least 20,000 years and
ended less than 10,000 years ago. Like uncounted others that had happened before it, the Wisconsin Glaciation was a disabling blow for much of
the Earth, marked by prolonged drops in temperature and humidity, shrink-
age of oceans and surface water everywhere, revisions of coasts and shore-
lines, and a massive spread of permanent, polar ice. Almost all that humanity
knows of its existence on the Earth was played out in the milder interlude
that followed, which many scientists think is slowly drawing to its close. "The
whole of human history," warned historian Norman Pounds, "has been lived
in the shadow of the Ice Age." And oblivious to it, one could add.

It was not until the work of Swiss-born naturalist and geologist Louis
Agassiz, little more than a century ago, that the awful reality of the ice ages
was at last recognized. Thinking man was here, in the Old World and perhaps the New, to witness the slow advance of cold and creaking ice from
the north. Man was here while deep glaciers lingered, through summer and

145

During bitterly cold periods in the Earth's history massive movements of polar ice crept southward down mountain slopes, flowed through former river valleys, and buried vast areas of land for many thousands of years. The impressive Monte Rosa Glacier in the Pennine Alps offers only a hint of that awesome past.

JOHN A. EDDY *is Senior Scientist at the High Altitude Observatory, National Center for Atmospheric Research, Boulder, Colorado.*

(Overleaf) Dan Morrill

winter, for thousands of generations, hiding the soil of Northern Europe and all of present Canada and the northeastern United States under a crushing blanket of permanent ice more than a mile thick. And he was here when at last the ice retreated, exposing again a new and fresh terrain.

But no part of this great drama apparently had been recognized as it happened, or remembered in the oral history of mankind. As with most known climatic changes, it remained for the patient and more objective hand of nature—in rocks and sediments, trees, and ocean cores—to write the history that man had missed.

It is important to understand why this was so and why subsequent, shorter climatic changes also eluded detection for so long. Instrumented weather records have existed for less than 300 years, which constitutes but an instant in the history of life on Earth, and they describe only a tiny fraction of its surface. In interpreting weather accounts of earlier times science must rely in part on human memory and recollection, yet people are poor detectors of long-term changes of any sort: they do not live long enough, and by beneficent design they adjust, adapt, and soon forget. Slow changes in the

(Top) Carleton Ray—Photo Researchers; (bottom) Jerome Wyckoff

environment, even massive ones, that take place over more than a single lifetime can easily go unnoticed, and those accomplished over centuries are probably imperceptible to transient or preliterate people.

Thus it is no surprise that the ice ages, and possibly other significant changes in climate, escape unrecorded. The climate of the Earth seems to shift in subtle ways, marked by gradual, long-term trends that in any month or year are masked by more noticeable weather excursions and by distracting, random spikes of unusual storms, rain and drought, or heat and cold. There may be no way to sense climatic change in real time, while it is happening. Like other history, an accurate history of climate probably can be written with certainty only in retrospect.

The Sun in its place

It is hard to exaggerate man's dependence on the Sun, or its enormous potential for effecting changes in weather and climate. The succession of day and night and of the seasons are all direct manifestations of changes in the amount of sunlight the Earth receives. The Sun is the engine that

A gradual increase in the severity of winters and the encroachment of desert into once-fertile land are comparatively long-term processes that can easily elude the notice of a single generation. It is not surprising that records of such climatic changes are rare, even in the well-documented histories of cultured peoples.

147

drives the weather machine and the force responsible for most weather phenomena: pressure systems, jet streams, clouds, wind, rain, and snow. Scientists have only recently come to learn how very sensitive the Earth is to small changes in the flow of heat and other radiation from the Sun, particularly if these fluctuations persist. Recent numerical models of the atmosphere have shown that a drop in solar flux of only 5% may be adequate to bring on a major glaciation like the Wisconsin. Even a drop of 1–2% could initiate a "Little Ice Age" like one that brought extremes of cold to Europe and North America in the 16th and 17th centuries. In fact an enduring change in sunlight of as little as one part in a thousand could produce a noticeable alteration in climate, with social and economically important consequences.

Humanity has no scientific reason, beyond assumption or pious hope, to think that the output of the Sun or any other star should be constant to 0.1% or even 1% over long time scales. Slow drifts of several percent seem wholly possible over hundreds or thousands of years in the long life of the Sun, and knowledge gleaned from other stars suggests that the Sun should slowly change in brightness as it evolves, increasing its brilliance by as much as 30% during the time that life has evolved on Earth.

Before the Sun is too quickly accused, however, it should be recognized that there are many other potential causes of climatic change: changes in the amount of carbon dioxide or ozone in the atmosphere, injections of volcanic debris, periodic changes in the orbit of the Earth, and shifts in the positions of the continents themselves, to list just a few. One may not need the Sun at all to explain changes in climate. Even if the mighty solar furnace were perfectly regulated, the Earth would still experience varied weather and dramatic climate, as a result of forces contained completely within the atmosphere of Earth. To know whether the Sun is an important cause of climatic change, it is first necessary to know whether or not it varies, and in what ways.

The sunspot cycle: an unwanted discovery

First signs of solar variability were found nearly 400 years ago, in the early 1600s, when primitive telescopes were first turned upon the Sun. Early astronomers, among them Galileo, saw on its bright face an irregular pattern of small, dark spots that drifted slowly from left to right across the solar surface. Initially thought to be silhouettes of planets, they were soon shown to be features of the Sun itself; their daily motion demonstrated that the Sun, like the Earth, rotates on a fixed axis. These little dots, each in fact as large as or larger than the Earth, are the sunspots now known to be cooler regions on the surface of the Sun where intense magnetic fields are concentrated.

That the Sun was imperfect, spinning, and ever changing was to Renaissance philosophers a shattering discovery. Immediate theological opposition to a blemished Sun was soon assuaged by the rationalization that sunspots were only clouds that floated above a still perfect luminous surface. Closer examination, however, showed that they were more intrinsic features. How serious a symptom sunspots really were was not revealed until other, more active layers of the Sun's atmosphere were discovered

148

early in the 20th century. Only then was it realized that the visible surface of the Sun, the white photosphere where spots are seen with simple telescopes, is a deceptively quiet layer, a thin veneer of stability that separates raging layers of the solar atmosphere. Hiding in the slowly changing sunspots are concentrated magnetic forces that bring violence and disruption elsewhere on the Sun. Beneath the placid, photospheric surface, and largely hidden from view, lies a deep layer of boiling, churning turbulence. Sunspots and their patterns of coming and going result in part from the action of this deep, convective layer, which can be far from constant.

Interest in sunspots increased sharply when in 1843 a German astronomer discovered what has since become the best-known feature of solar behavior—an 11-year cycle in the number of spots seen on the Sun. Heinrich Schwabe was not a professional astronomer, but a pharmacist who observed the solar surface as a hobby, and his historic finding was based entirely on his own observing records begun in 1826. His discovery has been abundantly confirmed in the regular succession of similar cycles that have since appeared. Moreover, historical searches following Schwabe's announcement demonstrated that the 11-year cycle of sunspots had been in operation for at least a century before he began his patient record keeping, quite probably as early as the time of Galileo, and possibly for thousands of years before that.

Why the cycle had not been found before is an intriguing question. More than 200 years had passed between Galileo and Schwabe, during which time the Sun was intensively observed. Ten generations of astronomers with adequate telescopes had missed a fundamental feature of the most prominent object in the sky. Moreover, in scientific papers during this time the possibility of solar periodicity was specifically and dogmatically denied. A part of the reason may be that for a portion of the time, between the mid-17th and early 18th centuries, the number of sunspots was severely depressed and the cycle, if present at all, was less obvious than now. With this one

Harvard College Observatory

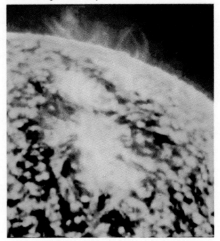

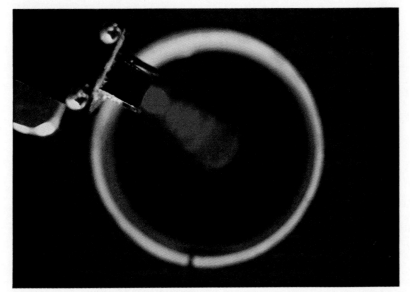

Photos, Clark Dunbar, Lockheed Missiles and Space Company

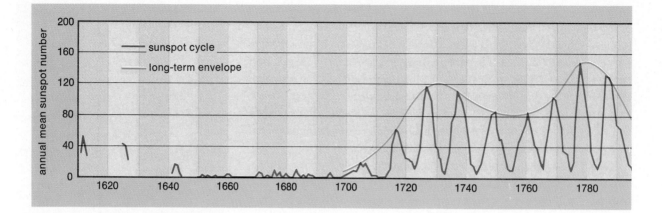

Day-by-day photographic record of an exceptionally large sunspot group reveals its progressive evolution and gives some idea of the period of the Sun's rotation, which varies from about 25 days at the Equator to more than 33 days near the poles.

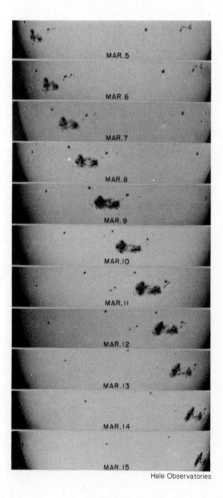

Hale Observatories

might excuse the first half of the error. The 100-year remainder, it now seems, was a clear oversight that can be charged to the conservatism of established science and the tendency to find only what one expects to find.

There are other lessons in the story. The importance of Schwabe's discovery was not initially recognized; it was only following endorsement by the respected German scientist Alexander von Humboldt in 1851 that other action came. Then followed a nearly instantaneous reversal of opinion, from unanimous "no!" to unanimous "yes!" and from "never" to "always." After this turnabout no one seemed to question again the universality of the 11-year sunspot cycle or whether it had always been a dominant feature of the Sun. In fact, it may have occupied too much scientific attention for too long a time. It is now suspected that the 11-year sunspot cycle is merely a ripple in solar behavior compared with longer and perhaps terrestrially more important changes on the Sun.

The spots tell all

When the sunspot cycle was at last recognized, an immediate search was launched for its possible connection with events on Earth. Foremost and most interesting of the possibilities was, of course, the weather. If the Sun's behavior followed a strong pattern of 11 years, it seemed likely that the Earth's atmosphere would follow suit. Indeed, it was soon established that fluctuations in the Earth's magnetic field and appearances of the northern lights, or Aurora Borealis, closely parallel the number of spots on the Sun, and all three phenomena show the same 11-year periodicity. These clear and simple relationships spurred hopes of finding more practical connections, and beginning in the 1870s and 1880s the search received considerable argument and attention.

Success was soon claimed and, for a time, victory followed victory. By the end of the 19th century, relationships had been found linking sunspot numbers and the level of Lake Victoria; the depths of the Nile, the Thames, and the Elbe; monsoons in India; rainfall in Mauritius and Australia; soil temperatures in Scotland; and many other indices of local weather around the globe. "The riddle of the probable times of occurrence of Indian Famines," announced a prominent British astronomer in 1900, "has now been read, and

150

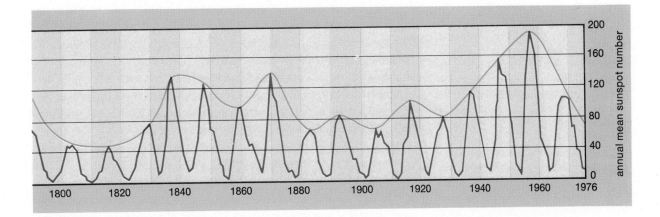

they can be for the future accurately predicted."

And then, with time, the bubble burst. The simple relationships that seemed so obvious to some in limited sets of data could not be found at all by others. Direct measurements of the Sun's light and heat, which were performed to tie down the cause of the purported connections, failed to find any convincing relationships with sunspot numbers, or anything else. One by one, these correlations of Sun and weather faded in the light of longer examination, suggesting that they were no more than chance connections—examples, perhaps, of what chemist and Nobel laureate Irving Langmuir would later call "pathological science": the tendency to find patterns looked for in scientific data whether they are really there or not.

Today the case is still unresolved, and some investigators still search for simple correlations between weather patterns and short-term changes on the Sun. Many others feel that a hundred years of controversial findings is enough to demonstrate that such effects, if present at all, must be of minor importance or subtly connected to many other, interacting influences. Modern knowledge of the complexity of the atmosphere rules against the sort of direct, cause-and-effect relationships sought in the last century and suggests that any mark of the Sun on weather will be tangled in a twisted skein of other atmospheric processes.

The winds of change

It is possible that solar connections have been sought in the wrong places or with the wrong index of solar activity. Most past efforts have looked for connections with visible solar activity, such as solar flares and sunspots. Yet these are only one manifestation of changes on the Sun, and possibly not the most important. Observations of the Sun from space have revealed significant fluctuations in the unseen ultraviolet and X-ray portions of the electromagnetic spectrum that emanates from the Sun. It is also known that the Sun bombards the Earth with a constant and irregular flow of charged atomic particles: electrons, protons, and the nuclei of heavier atoms. The speed and energy of this "solar wind" varies appreciably, but not in any simple relation to the sunspot cycle. Its properties could in some way trigger subtle weather change.

Curve of annual mean sunspot numbers between AD 1610 and 1976 (above) clearly depicts a cyclical variation, which can range from 8 years to 17 years but averages about 11 years. Records of sunspot numbers before 1650 are sparse. The period between 1645 and 1715 has been called the Maunder Minimum, a time of prolonged suppression of the sunspot cycle. The long-term envelope, a curve connecting the cyclical peaks, reveals a modulation that corresponds to 50–100-year stretches of very high or very low solar activity. (Below) Active region near the edge, or limb, of the Sun, as recorded from space in ultraviolet light, shows projecting looplike forms indicative of strong magnetic fields. Hot ionized gases follow these lines of force, which connect regions of opposite magnetic polarity on the solar surface.

Harvard College Observatory

151

A statistical case for such a connection was made by Walter Orr Roberts and Roger Olson at the University of Colorado, and John M. Wilcox and others at Stanford University. They found that subtle changes in the circulation pattern of the upper atmosphere often follow when the magnetic polarity of charged particles in the solar wind switches from predominantly positive to predominantly negative; *i.e.,* when magnetic boundaries separating similarly charged sectors of the solar wind sweep past Earth. The circulation changes that correlate with these sector boundaries may not be of major significance in weather. What seems interesting is that, if real, they correspond to solar-wind changes that make up only a negligible part of the total energy output of the Sun. Moreover, they occur in changing patterns that bear no direct relationship with simple sunspot number, and thus could have been missed in earlier searches for the mark of the Sun on weather.

The case for important Sun-weather connections becomes stronger when one moves from short-term weather to long-term climate. Recently Murray Mitchell of the National Oceanic and Atmospheric Administration (NOAA) and Charles Stockton of the University of Arizona Laboratory of Tree-Ring Research uncovered important new evidence from an extensive regional study of the annual growth rings of trees, whose widths vary with rainfall and thus offer a permanent record of annual moisture at each tree. They found that patterns of drought on the western plains of North America have recurred over the last 300 years in a clearly defined cycle of 20–22 years. These recurrent droughts, which include the "dust-bowl" years of the early 1930s, the Plains drought of the early 1950s, and the Western drought of 1976–77, mesh fairly well with the solar cycle throughout this time, falling at alternate minima of the 11-year sunspot cycle. Magnetic fields on the surface of the Sun are known to reverse their magnetic polarity in the same period of 22 years, or two sunspot cycles, suggesting that the drought connection, if real, involves in some way the magnetic field of the Sun, probably through the solar wind.

Message in an envelope

Evidence of important Sun-climate connections of longer term has come from recent reappraisals of solar history, which, like climate, previously had been presumed constant. Scientists now see evidence of prolonged excursions of very high or very low solar activity, lasting 50–100 years, which may represent a fundamental feature of solar behavior. These major excursions can be seen in modern records of sunspot numbers in the curve, or envelope, that connects the 11-year peaks of annual sunspot numbers. Something fundamental in the Sun may be amplifying, or modulating, a sunspot cycle of otherwise uniform amplitude. In the simplest interpretation, the observed modulation could come about through slow changes in the flow of heat and other radiation through the Sun. When such flow increases, it amplifies the level of sunspot production, and when it gradually falls, it suppresses the level.

At present this is only a guess, but it explains quite well the apparent correlation between the envelope of the sunspot curve and the record of terrestrial climate. When the envelope of solar activity remains low, as it had

152

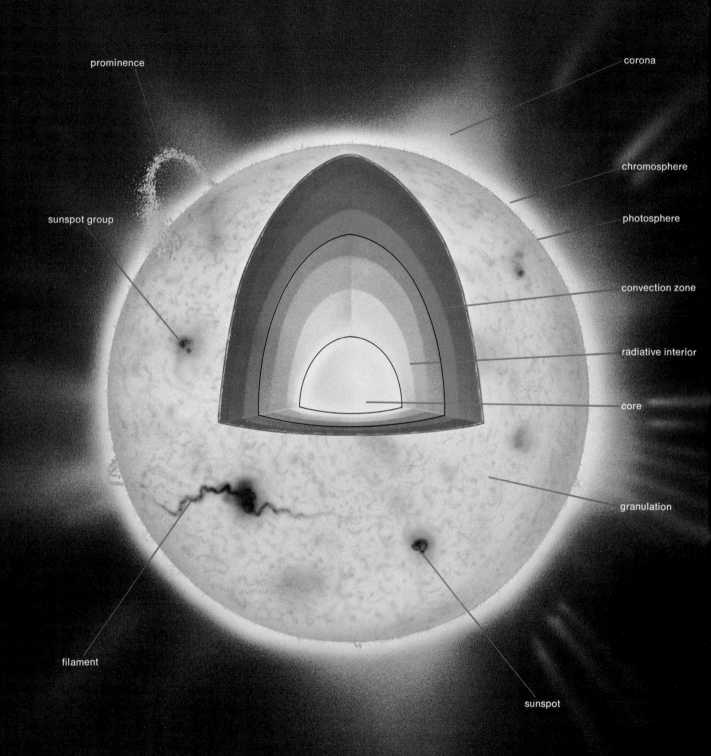

prominence

corona

chromosphere

photosphere

sunspot group

convection zone

radiative interior

core

granulation

filament

sunspot

during several sunspot cycles near the start of the 20th century, climate is generally cooler. When the envelope of solar activity is high, as it was in the last five solar cycles, global temperatures also increase.

Most striking in the historically accessible record of solar activity is a protracted minimum that lasted from about AD 1645 until 1715. Throughout this span of 70 years few sunspots were reported, auroras were infrequent, and the solar corona—the Sun's tenuous outer atmosphere seen during total eclipses—was less visible than it is today. It is not known whether the 11-year solar cycle was in operation during the time or not, but it is certain that the prolonged minimum in solar activity was real, for able astronomers with good telescopes regularly observed the Sun. The remarkable absence

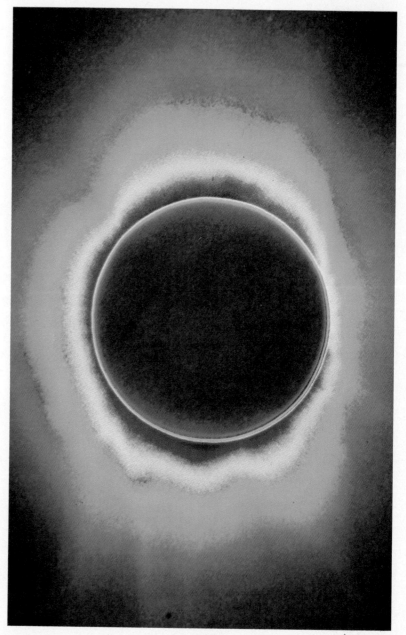

Solar corona, as photographed during a total eclipse in 1973. Special photo processing technique, called isophote mapping, produces zones of false color that identify regions of differing light intensity in the corona.

Fred Espenak

154

of sunspots is well documented in books and journals of the day, and routinely mentioned afterward until the time of Schwabe's discovery of the sunspot cycle. Thereafter, however, it seems to have been largely ignored or lost in the scramble to accept the notion of regular, cyclic behavior on the face of the Sun.

Astronomers Gustav Spörer in Germany and E. Walter Maunder of Great Britain's Greenwich Observatory revived interest in the anomalous period in papers published in the 1890s, but their efforts went largely unnoticed. Only recently, with new historical verification and additional evidence from tree rings, auroras, and other indirect sources, has it finally become accepted as a major feature of solar behavior. Modern scientists also know, as Spörer

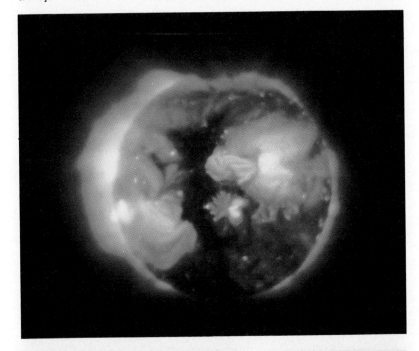

In 1973 the X-ray telescope aboard the Skylab manned space station recorded a "coronal hole" on the Sun (top), a region of reduced coronal temperature and density. The hole is the dark patch cutting across the solar surface; light areas are regions of intense X-ray emission. Coronal holes may be the source of the charged particles that make up the solar wind. (Bottom) Sunlight shining through irregularities along the edge of the Moon combines with the solar corona to produce a dazzling diamond ring effect in the last instants before eclipse totality.

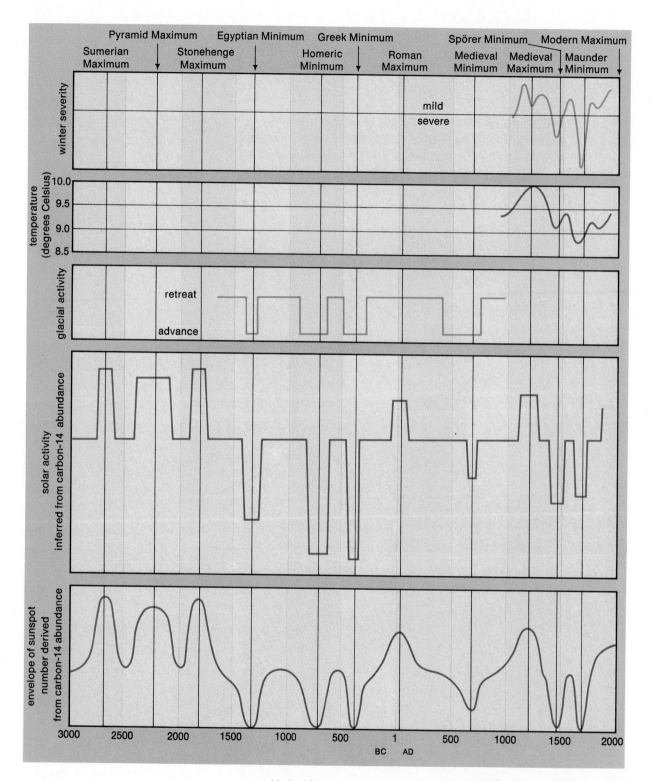

Limited historical records of winter severity (Paris and London), annual mean temperature (England), and Alpine glacial activity correlate well with excursions in the envelope of solar activity as derived from carbon-14 abundance in tree rings. Several highs and lows predating the Maunder Minimum can be traced in the derived envelope.

E. M. Thompson and L. G. Thompson, Institute of Polar Studies, Ohio State University

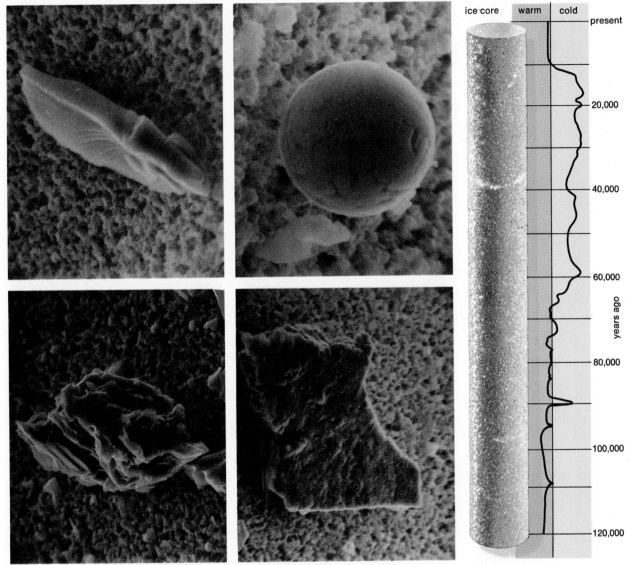

and Maunder did not, that the 70-year period of sunspot absence coincided with a time of remarkable cold, a severe dip in the longer Little Ice Age, when temperatures of the Earth were colder than at any other time in the last 1,000 years. This prolonged period of solar inactivity, now known as the Maunder Minimum, provided the first well-documented case of solar misbehavior and a yardstick for interpreting the longer, indirect record of solar activity that is found in the carbon-14 content of tree rings.

Tell-tale rings

The radioactive isotope carbon-14 is formed continually in the upper atmosphere of Earth by the impact of galactic, or primary, cosmic rays that arrive from all directions in space. Primary cosmic rays are charged atomic particles, like the solar wind, but of significantly higher energies. Measurements of cosmic ray flux show that the Sun in some way modulates the number that

Core drilled from Greenland ice sheet (above) varies in oxygen content along its length according to the temperature that prevailed when snow fell to form the ice. Measurement of the ratio of natural oxygen isotopes throughout the ice core yields a climatic history. Dated microscopic particles taken from a core drilled through Antarctic ice indicate by their origin (volcanic, upper and lower left; meteoric, upper right; from exposed land surface, lower right) something of the climate that existed when they fell.

157

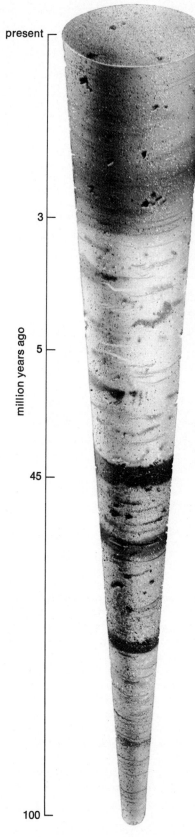

seafloor core

present

3

5

45

100

million years ago

arrive at the Earth, presumably by scattering in the solar wind. This solar shielding is more effective when the Sun is active and less so when sunspot numbers are low. Thus during the Maunder Minimum the Earth should have been much less protected from cosmic rays, and carbon-14 production in its upper atmosphere should have increased markedly.

Tree rings hold the answers to whether and how carbon-14 production varied in the past. Carbon-14 produced in the upper atmosphere eventually finds its way as carbon dioxide into trees, where it enters the leaves through photosynthesis and becomes locked as cellulose in annual growth rings. From a knowledge of the age of a tree and from the chemical analysis of the wood in each of its dated rings scientists can recover carbon-14 variations and hence obtain a precisely dated history of the Sun. It will be slightly ambiguous history, for factors other than the Sun also regulate carbon-14 production; and it will be smeared in time, for there are delays of 10–40 years between production of carbon-14 at the top of the atmosphere and its eventual assimilation into tree leaves at the bottom. The tree-ring record of carbon-14 leaves little doubt, however, about the solar signature of the Maunder Minimum; it is there—a dramatic increase in carbon-14—in the right rings and for the right duration to verify the historical record of sunspot and auroral absences.

The Maunder Minimum, once it was clearly identified in both historical records and tree-ring carbon-14, was the Rosetta Stone that enabled scientists to read the much longer record of solar history found in the wood of long-lived trees like the bristlecone pine. In the long tree-ring carbon-14 record, which presently reaches more than 8,000 years into the past, one can see the marks of repeated solar excursions like the Maunder Minimum. Each of these prolonged lows in solar activity corresponds to a similar period of anomalous cold on Earth, as derived from records of mid-latitude glacier advance, as best these are known. The correlation seems to confirm the more-than-chance connection between the Maunder Minimum and the cold excursion of the Little Ice Age.

Also evident in the tree-ring carbon-14 record are times of anomalously high solar activity, one of which is the present era, and each of these corresponds to times of warm climate and glacier retreat. The first drop in solar activity before the Maunder Minimum appears in both historical data from aurora and solar observations and in tree-ring carbon-14 between about AD 1400 and 1510. Called the Spörer Minimum, it delineates the first of two severe dips of cold temperature during the Little Ice Age. Before that, evidence both in historical records and in tree-ring carbon-14 points to an anomalous high in solar activity that peaked in the 12th and 13th centuries AD, a time known to climatologists as the Medieval Warm Epoch, when temperatures in Europe and America were last as warm as the present.

The future

These remarkable coincidences between solar history and climate suggest that on time scales of 50–100 years changes on the Sun may be a dominant force in altering climate. They also say that for a long time scientists may have missed an important message in the pattern of sunspots and solar activity. Investigators were tuned for too long only to the sunspot cycle, which in the analogy of AM radio may be but the carrier wave. The amplitude modulation now seems to have carried the more important information on solar change and its effects on climate. In this slowly changing modulation there are hints of other cycles: one of about 80 years that has long been noted and a suggestion of a much longer one of about 2,500 years, a period that also appears in records of glacier advance.

The connection seems exciting and important, but so did the false correlations formed in the 1870s. What must be understood is the real nature of the apparent relationship: what it is in the envelope of solar activity that brings about the presumed connection and how it relates to other mechanisms of climatic change. What also needs to be known much better is the history of climate, and that of the Sun. It is expected that trees, ice, and ocean cores soon will yield more complete and more objective histories. One promising new method comes from chemical analysis of ice cores from Antarctica and Greenland, where chemical compounds left in long-fallen snow may register the number of auroras that occurred in the past, and hence, again indirectly, the state of solar activity. If this proves so, it will open up a much longer book of solar history, extending back not 8,000 years but at least 100,000 years, allowing a look at the behavior of the Sun through patterns of repeated major glaciations. Similarly, analyses of longer-lived radioisotopes, such as beryllium-10, in dated ice and ocean cores, could stretch the record of solar history back as far as 20 million years.

In the trees that long outlive mankind and in ice that never melts may lie not only some of the history of climate but old secrets of the Sun as well: fresh clues to what has happened, and perhaps new help in knowing what kind of climate lies ahead.

For related discussions see *1976 Yearbook of Science and the Future* Feature Articles: THE EARTH'S CHANGING CLIMATE; DENDROCHRONOLOGY: HISTORY FROM TREE RINGS.

FOR ADDITIONAL READING

John A. Eddy, "The Case of the Missing Sunspots," *Scientific American* (May 1977, pp. 80–92).

John A. Eddy, *A New Sun (The Solar Results from Skylab)*, NASA SP-XXX (U.S. Government Printing Office, 1978).

Samuel W. Matthews, "What's Happening to Our Climate?," *National Geographic* (November 1976, pp. 576–615).

Oran R. White (ed.), *The Solar Output and Its Variation* (Associated University of Colorado Press, 1977).

Solid core drilled from the North Atlantic seafloor (opposite page) consists of multiple layers of settled debris. The kinds of fossilized life found at various dated levels in the core can be used to derive ocean temperatures that existed when the creatures were alive; from this can be inferred general patterns of current and wind and even the amount of ice cover present on the Earth. For example, certain species of tiny shelled protozoans called foraminiferans flourish only in waters of a certain temperature range; others vary their pattern of shell secretion according to water warmth. Ratios of certain isotopes trapped in such shells during formation also provide clues to past conditions.

Target Earth: Meteorite Craters and Astroblemes

by Robert S. Dietz

Though most of the evidence has been obliterated by the stressful geologic environment, scientists have determined that the Earth has often been struck by meteorites, asteroids, and comet heads.

John S. Shelton

Meteor Crater in northern Arizona (above), approximately 1.2 kilometers (0.75 miles) across and 120 meters (400 feet) deep, was formed some 25,000 years ago by the impact of a large nickel-iron meteorite. The explosion on impact, depicted on the opposite page, destroyed the meteorite except for fragments.

ROBERT S. DIETZ *is Professor of Geology at Arizona State University, Tempe.*

Illustrations by Mark Paternostro

Space exploration over the past two decades has given man a new perspective on his own planet. The deep-space view of Earth as a marbled blue, white, and tan sphere suspended in space must rank among the most remarkable photographs ever taken. Despite the fact that Mars has a valley that dwarfs the Grand Canyon and a volcano three times as high as Mt. Everest, the most striking contrast that impressed scientists is that the neighboring planetary bodies are heavily cratered whereas Earth is not. It is natural to ask why this is so.

Prior to the space program, when only the Moon was known to be cratered, the answer was easy—although wrong: the Moon was peppered with innumerable volcanoes that had seethed up from the lunar interior. Based on his telescopic observations, one astronomer placed the number at 30,000. Much of the Apollo program of the 1960s was devoted to finding with certainty a volcanic crater on the Moon. But although basalts fill the lunar maria, these lavas appear to have flooded quietly through fissures out of the lunar interior. Not a single volcanic explosion crater was positively identified. Instead, the Moon's cratered surface, as well as those of Venus and Mercury, was fashioned largely by the impact of cosmic cannonballs—giant meteorites, asteroids, and comet heads. Only on Mars is there evidence of many craters formed by volcanism.

If the Moon and nearby planets have been bombarded, why has not the Earth? The answer is that it has indeed been struck, but the record of these impacts has been almost entirely lost because of the Earth's stressful environment. When the solar system was born 4.6 billion years ago, the Earth was created of a size such that it evolved into a body with a gravity field that could retain both a hydrosphere and an atmosphere. The subsequent actions of water, wind, and ice made the Earth's exterior highly corrosive so that geomorphic forms such as shallow craters were rapidly erased.

Also, its distance from the Sun caused the Earth to be a silicate-rock sphere rich in radioactive elements that provide an internal heat engine. This causes the Earth's crust to be constantly recycled by the processes of plate tectonics and associated magmatism (flow of molten rock) and volcanism. The planet's outer shell is segmented into a mosaic of about a dozen giant plates that drift across the face of the Earth at rates of some few centimeters each year. New oceanic crust is formed at the mid-ocean ridges, while old crust is carried down and destroyed in oceanic trenches. The entire ocean floor is being repaved with volcanic crust at a rate of about two square kilometers (0.75 square mile) each year so that it is nowhere older than 200 million years. Since the deep ocean floor covers 60% of the world's surface, the Earth is dominantly a volcanic terrain.

Thus, the early Earth was struck by meteorites, but both erosion and recycling of the crust erased most of this evidence. There are few rocks on Earth older than 3.2 billion years, but there are few rocks on the Moon that are younger. The Moon and the other terrestrial planets are museums of ancient rocks and geomorphology. They record an early history of events entirely lost from the Earth. From observations of the lunar surface scientists have concluded that cosmic bombardment was commonplace in early solar system history, reaching a crescendo about four billion years ago. One

G. R. Roberts

Gosse's Bluff in Canada is a circular rim of hills that consist of nearly vertical, intensely deformed sedimentary rocks. The inner rim, shown above, is only part of a 4.5-kilometer-wide central uplift that exhibits much evidence of damage by an impact shock.

planetologist remarked, "The fireworks on the Moon must have been spectacular four billion years ago. It is too bad that there was no one around to watch." This early bombardment ceased 3.8 billion years ago and since that time cosmic impacts have been few and far between and at a uniform rate.

Giant impacts

The Earth may be struck by either comet heads or asteroids on elliptical Earth-crossing orbits, the so-called Apollo asteroids. Of these two, the latter is much more likely. In the solar system about 1,000 Apollo asteroids exist that are of sufficient size, density, and velocity to blast craters on the Earth ten kilometers or more in diameter (1 kilometer = 0.62 mile); such geologic scars would persist for a few hundred millions of years. Statistical studies of known asteroids indicate that the Earth should sustain about three such hits each million years. Only one of these would strike an ice-free continental surface; thus, on an average, one giant crater would be created each million years. Two large craters, Elgygytgyn and Lake Bosumtwi, apparently support this impact flux, although they are not enough to provide a sound statistical sample. The Elgygytgyn crater (discussed in more detail below), in northeastern Siberia, 18 kilometers across, was probably created about 700,000 years ago, while the Lake Bosumtwi crater in Ghana was blasted out 1.3 million years ago.

In historic times the Earth has experienced two sizable cosmic strikes, both in Siberia. The first took place in 1908 and apparently consisted of a small comet head that exploded in the upper atmosphere and released about ten megatons of energy. No craters were formed on the ground, but enough dust remained in the atmosphere to cause eerie twilights that permitted one to read a newspaper at night in parts of Europe for several days. The second strike took place in 1947 when the giant Sikhote Alin nickel-iron meteorite streaked across the sky as a super-fireball and struck the Earth, creating many small percussion craters in the mountains north of Vladivostok. Although these two visitations from space were impressive physical phenomena, they will leave no long-lasting geologic effects.

Only about a dozen certain meteorite craters have been identified on the Earth, nearly all of which are small compared with volcanic craters and calderas. Meteor Crater in northern Arizona, 1.2 kilometers (0.75 miles) across and 120 meters deep, is the prototype. Created 25,000 years ago by the fall of a large nickel-iron meteorite, or small asteroid, this feature is the best-preserved meteorite crater in the world. Although recognized by D. Moreau Barringer in 1903 as an impact crater rather than just another volcanic depression, another 25 years passed before its impact origin was generally recognized. Barringer spent the last years of his life attempting to find and exploit the presumed buried meteorite, a frustrating effort unique in the annals of mining. He did not realize that it had been almost wholly destroyed by the enormous energy of impact.

In a million years Meteor Crater will have been eroded away, and no geologic record will remain to mark this ten-megaton natural explosion. The creation of a new impact crater in Madagascar was widely reported in the summer of 1977, but this turned out to be incorrect.

164

Astroblemes

Although the evidence shows giant impacts to have been rare, it seems reasonable to believe that, over the long sweep of geologic time, the Earth should have sustained many impacts by asteroids and comet heads of sufficient size to create in bedrock deeply embedded scars not readily removed by erosion or tectonism. This is now known to be true, although as recently as 1963 Robert Dietz entered into a lively published debate with a Columbia University professor, who, supported by the scientific consensus at that time, denied the existence of any such structures. The Columbia professor ascribed the circular deformations that some regarded as impact structures to cryptovolcanism, deep-seated muffled steam explosions without the ejection of any lavas. However, recent lunar studies and terrestrial explosion studies have provided numerous criteria for recognizing in these structures the severe shock effects that can be caused only by meteorite impacts. On the basis of these criteria about 100 ancient impact sites on the Earth have been identified with some certainty. They have been named astroblemes (star-wounds) to distinguish them from fresh unaltered craters.

On the basis of the statistical studies the number of sizable astroblemes on the Earth's surface, allowing for some erosional erasure from the rock record, should total a few hundred since the dawn of Phanerozoic time 600 million years ago. But only about 100 astroblemes can be identified at present, and so many presumably remain undiscovered.

The greatest number of known astroblemes are in North America, primarily because of a more intensive search for them on that continent. More than a score have been found in Canada, mostly on the Precambrian rocks of the Canadian Shield, which has provided an ancient undisturbed "counting board" not covered by later sedimentary rocks. The glaciers that moved across this region during the Ice Age effectively bulldozed out the soft sedimentary fillings in many old astroblemes, giving them a freshly etched appearance. Especially impressive is the 65-kilometer-wide Manicouagan astrobleme, which is clearly marked by a down-dropped, ring-shaped, lake-filled margin. The circularity of the structure was greatly enhanced by recently dammed lakes so that it is an especially prominent feature to an observer from near space. The central disk of Manicouagan is filled with a 200-meter-thick sheet of melt rock generated by the heat of the impact. In the center of this melt sheet a mountain mass protrudes, revealing rocks that have been intensely metamorphosed by shock effects.

Undoubtedly the most interesting of the Canadian astroblemes is the giant Sudbury Basin created 1.7 billion years ago. Subsequent folding and tectonism crushed this originally circular basin into a kidney-shaped, filled depression 60 kilometers long and 32 kilometers across, but its formation by the impact of a giant asteroid remains clearly imprinted on the rocks. The basin is filled with layered melt rock created by either the direct fusion of the Earth's crust by shock or the triggering of deep-seated magmatism. A vast layer of crushed and pulverized rock, or breccia, covers this melt rock, similar to the crust on a pie. A sheet of sedimentary rocks, in turn, overlies the breccia. Against the walls of the basin, still another layer of melt rock is plastered like the glaze on a porcelain bowl. This so-called sublayer is of

Photos, courtesy, NASA

Elgygytgyn meteorite crater in Siberia is photographed by Landsat satellite. Snow-covered winter view (top) reveals the circularity of the feature, while the central lake appears during the ice-free summer conditions (bottom). Probably the largest existing meteorite crater on the Earth's continents, Elgygytgyn is 18 kilometers (11 miles) in diameter and was formed about 700,000 years ago in an explosive impact similar to that in the drawing at the left.

special interest because it houses the world's richest deposits of nickel sulfide ores. Whether or not these ores have meteoritic parenthood remains a matter of controversy.

The U.S. also contains several astroblemes, which occur as prominent geologic structures on the little-disturbed flat-lying platform beds of the Middle West. Most of these were discovered in the 1930s but were erroneously ascribed to steam explosions associated with volcanism. The first identified of these is known only from a quarry at Kentland, Ind., because the surrounding terrain is blanketed with glacial drift. Such covering also completely mantles the Manson astrobleme in Iowa so that it is only known from drilling. However, the Wells Creek Basin structure in Tennessee and the Sierra Madera disturbance in Texas are two well-exposed examples. Missouri contains two astroblemes, the Decaturville and the Crooked Creek disturbances.

Most of the U.S. meteorite falls struck limestone, which dissociates rather than melts when heated by shock. Melt sheets are, therefore, absent, but instead there are displays of a curious and unique type of rock fracturing called shatter coning. The outward passage of the shock wave from the target point breaks the limestones into conical fragments that are decorated with packets of horsetail-like striations on their flanks.

Curiously, the ancient astroblemes usually are structurally quite unlike modern meteorite craters. Craters are parabolic bowls, while astroblemes are ring structures with a highly deranged central uplift surrounded by one or more ring-shaped grabens (blocks of the Earth's crust that have dropped relative to the blocks on either side) or ring synclines, layered rocks displaying a wavelike form resembling that created just after rebound when a marble is dropped into water. As a result, these ancient impact sites are not marked by craters but, rather paradoxically, by uplifts, many of which are of mountainous proportions.

Tektites

A fascinating by-product of giant terrestrial impacts is the splashing out of small droplets of natural glass called tektites. In 1844 Charles Darwin described in his book *Geological Observations* the first known Australian specimen, which he understandably regarded as a curious type of obsidian or volcanic glass. Tektites differ from volcanic glass, however, in that they clearly were melted not by slow heating but by instantaneous shock. This is proven by their lack of combined water, the almost complete removal of volatile elements, inclusions of quartz glass (lechatelierite), and the presence of certain minerals generated only by shock such as the shock polymorph of quartz, which has the mineral name of coesite. A simple test to identify a tektite consists of placing an unknown glass in a blowpipe flame. All natural glasses except tektites will froth, indicating the presence of water and other volatiles.

The shock melting of tektites could conceivably be produced by a lightning stroke, but their distribution over extended swaths of terrain, called strewn-fields, rules this out. Tektites occur in four major strewn-fields: in the southern U.S. (32 million years old); in Czechoslovakia (15 million years old); in the Ivory Coast (1.3 million years old); and in Australasia (0.7 million years old). The Czechoslovak tektites were apparently splashed out of the Ries Basin crater in Germany, while those of the Ivory Coast were derived from the Lake Bosumtwi crater in Ghana.

A major unsolved problem has been to find the terrestrial crater responsible for the extensive Australasian field, which stretches from the Philippines across southeast Asia to Australia and which covers 50 million square kilometers, or one-tenth of the Earth's surface. It would seem that there should be an obvious source crater for a tektite field so large and so young and which has yielded millions of specimens. It has been suggested that the missing crater is hidden beneath the oceans or Antarctica ice. A few scientists, however, argue that the Moon must be the likely source, but further research at the site is needed to solve the question.

It appears probable that the Australasian tektites were, in fact, ejected over a long arc of the Earth's circumference. The ballistic path from Elgygytgyn requires that the australites achieved a velocity of about 7.5 kilometers per second, very nearly the minimum orbital velocity (7.9 kilometers per second) necessary for them to be ejected as far as 15,000 kilometers, or nearly one-third of the way around the world. They must have drilled their way through the atmosphere into near space, congealed as marblelike spheres, and then, one-half hour later, reentered the atmosphere over Australasia as minute space capsules. Ablating as they fell to the Earth, they must have created an awe-inspiring pyrotechnic display as literally millions of fireballs streaked across the sky.

FOR ADDITIONAL READING

R. Baldwin, *Measure of the Moon* (University of Chicago Press, 1963).

R. Dietz, "Astroblemes," *Scientific American* (August 1961, pp. 50–58).

B. French and N. M. Short (eds.), *Shock Metamorphism of Natural Material* (Mono Book Corp., 1968).

W. K. Hartmann, *Moon and Planets: An Introduction to Planetary Science* (Wadsworth Publishing Co., 1973).

E. A. King, *Space Geology: An Introduction* (John Wiley, 1976).

Z. Kopal, *The Solar System* (Oxford University Press, 1973).

J. O'Keefe, *Tektites and Their Origin* (American Elsevier Publishing Co., 1976).

N. M. Short, *Planetary Geology* (Prentice-Hall, Inc., 1975).

Stratospheric Ozone: Earth's Fragile Shield

by F. Sherwood Rowland

Twenty miles above the Earth lies the ozone layer, protecting all life from potentially harmful solar radiation. Many scientists believe that its tenuous existence is under attack from man's technological activities.

In 1804 two French scientists, Joseph-Louis Gay-Lussac and Jean-Baptiste Biot, pioneered experimental study of the atmosphere during a balloon ascent of about 2.5 miles (above). Atmospheric samples were collected in flasks in which the air had been evacuated, and the chemical composition of the samples was later analyzed and plotted as a function of height. Laden with sophisticated instruments for sampling and analysis, the modern atmospheric balloon (right) still carries on this experimental tradition.

F. SHERWOOD ROWLAND is Professor of Chemistry at the University of California, Irvine.

(Overleaf) Painting by Eraldo Carugati

Recently and rather suddenly, scientists and the public have become uncomfortably aware of the vital importance of a layer of relatively rare molecules, called ozone, in the Earth's atmosphere. The potential vulnerability of this layer to man's technological activities and the serious consequences of its depletion have been revealed during the past several years through investigation of previously unsuspected chemical reactions occurring more than 20 miles above the Earth's surface. Fortunately such knowledge has come at a time not too late to develop a thorough understanding of the upper air and to take the steps necessary to preserve the ozone layer from inadvertent destruction.

Chemistry of stratospheric ozone

Commonplace observation of rainbows demonstrates that sunlight contains all of the visible colors, from red through violet. In addition, the solar spectrum contains invisible radiation—long-wavelength, low-energy infrared radiation and short-wavelength, high-energy ultraviolet (UV) radiation. Although all incandescent bodies emit radiation over a wide range of wavelengths, scientists have known for a century that UV radiation from the Sun is plentiful only to a wavelength of about 290 nanometers (nm; 10^{-9} meters); it is completely absent at shorter wavelengths. (The limits of human vision range from violet at 400 nm to red at 760 nm.) Numerous observations of light from a variety of stars subsequently were found to show the same sharp UV cutoff at 290 nm that is characteristic of sunlight.

Scientists eventually realized that the existence of this cutoff is not some special property of the Sun and stars but rather a property of the Earth's atmosphere, through which all celestial light must pass to reach the ground. When mountaintop observations showed no change in the UV cutoff point, it became clear that the absorbing material is not evenly spread through the entire atmosphere but is concentrated in its upper reaches far above mountain altitudes. In the 1880s British chemist W. N. Hartley realized that the

172

triatomic form of oxygen, O_3, known as ozone, has exactly the proper light-absorbing characteristics, and he deduced that ozone in the upper atmosphere is indeed the atmospheric material that prevents exceedingly energetic UV radiation at wavelengths shorter than 290 nm from reaching the Earth's surface.

Over the succeeding 90 years, and especially with the advent of rocket and satellite experiments, knowledge of this ozone shield increased enormously. By the late 1970s it was known that the average amount of ozone overhead represents slightly less than one-millionth of the total atmosphere and that ozone concentration varies from day to day, from season to season, and from year to year. On the average, ozone is more plentiful near the poles than at the Equator and more abundant in winter than in summer. Despite its low concentration, however, continuation of the ozone shield in approximately its present form is exceedingly important for mankind.

Almost half a century ago English geophysicist Sydney Chapman outlined a sequence of chemical reactions that were designed to explain not only how ozone was formed in the atmosphere but also how it was destroyed and how much of it was actually there. Known collectively as the "Chapman mechanism," these chemical reactions all involve the various forms of oxygen containing one to three atoms.

The first step in the sequence is the absorption of very-short-wavelength UV radiation by O_2, the ordinary form of molecular oxygen. This molecule accounts for 21% by volume of all atmospheric molecules and is transparent to visible radiation and to UV radiation of wavelengths as short as 242 nm. When O_2 absorbs UV radiation of still shorter wavelength, the molecule is broken into individual, reactive atoms of oxygen (equation 1). Atoms of oxygen then can attach themselves to other molecules of O_2 and form molecules of ozone (equation 2). This formation step creates the ozone

$$O_2 + UV \text{ light} \rightarrow O + O \qquad (1)$$
$$O + O_2 \xrightarrow{(M)} O_3 \qquad (2)$$

Spread like a multihued dome over the land, the rainbow reveals the visible component wavelengths of sunlight. If the color range of man's vision could be further extended, he would perceive other bands of color, the infrared and ultraviolet regions of the spectrum, beyond the rainbow's outer and inner edges.

173

molecule in a highly excited state, and this extra energy is transmitted to other molecules (M) in the surrounding atmosphere. The energy is rapidly converted into heat, which plays an important role in creating that part of the atmosphere known as the stratosphere, as will be discussed below.

Whereas UV radiation at wavelengths longer than 242 nm cannot be absorbed by O_2, it is absorbed by O_3, causing the molecule to split into one atom of oxygen and one molecule of O_2 (equation 3). Again the oxygen

$$O_3 + UV \text{ light} \rightarrow O + O_2 \qquad (3)$$

atom released from ozone can recombine with O_2 (equation 2), making ozone once more. Absorption of UV light by ozone is very strong for wavelengths between 250 and 280 nm but progressively weakens at longer wavelengths. In the vicinity of 290 nm, absorption is no longer strong enough to remove all of the UV radiation, and the ozone cutoff is created.

Ozone is itself a very reactive molecule and occasionally intercepts atomic oxygen, transforming both into molecular oxygen (equation 4).

$$O + O_3 \rightarrow O_2 + O_2 \qquad (4)$$

In summary, ozone is constantly created by the action of solar ultraviolet radiation on the Earth's atmosphere and is constantly removed by reaction with atomic oxygen. Such a steady-state process maintains ozone at a level of one ozone molecule per million molecules of atmosphere. With these chemical reactions involving oxygen, Chapman had presented an explanation for the ozone shield that both qualitatively and quantitatively remained satisfactory until the advent of the space age.

Actually a continuum of energy, the electromagnetic spectrum is conventionally divided at certain wavelengths into various regions. Of interest to chemists studying the upper atmosphere is the output of the Sun in the ultraviolet (UV) region, which plays a pivotal role in the creation of stratospheric ozone. In turn, light-absorbing reactions in the atmosphere affect both the quantity and energy content of solar UV radiation reaching the ground. Changes in this delicate chain of events have serious consequences for all life on Earth. See text.

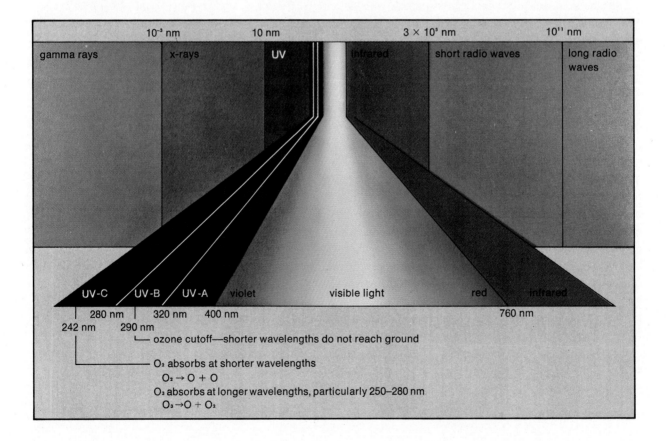

By the early 1960s, however, increasingly precise information on the intensity of solar UV radiation, on the measurements of laboratory chemical reaction rates, and from numerous direct measurements of stratospheric ozone combined to indicate that the Chapman mechanism was incomplete. The heart of the problem was simple: in its natural steady state somewhat less ozone is present than was predicted from the Chapman mechanism. The creation of ozone was not the problem, for the splitting of molecular O_2

Fitted with instrument pods under its wings, the U-2 high-altitude aircraft (top) provides a mobile stratospheric laboratory from which several measurements can be made simultaneously. With a useful ceiling of more than 13 miles, the U-2 has been used to collect data for verifying computer models of the atmosphere, which in turn are employed in evaluating and predicting the effects of human activity. (Bottom) Mounted on the release boom of a carrier trailer, a high-speed interferometer for detecting ozone reactions awaits a balloon ride into the stratosphere.

Courtesy (top) NASA, Ames Research Center, (bottom) Jet Propulsion Laboratory, California Institute of Technology

is clearly the only important process for making new ozone. The problem lay with the removal of ozone. Some as yet unidentified atmospheric reaction (or reactions) was at work in its destruction.

Free radicals and catalytic chain reactions

The largest such removal process was uncovered about 1970 by the work of Dutch meteorologist Paul Crutzen. It involves a reaction of an entirely different kind—a catalytic chain reaction. Whereas the main components of the atmosphere are molecular oxygen and molecular nitrogen, or N_2 (78% by volume), a minuscule fraction of nitrogen and oxygen atoms are combined as nitrogen oxides, chiefly NO and NO_2. While all of the major atmospheric components possess even numbers of electrons, as do almost all of the molecules used in chemical laboratories as well, the two nitrogen oxides belong to the odd-electron class of molecules known as free radicals, with 15 and 23 electrons respectively. Most free radicals are highly reactive chemicals, and NO and NO_2 are typical of the class. The radical NO attacks ozone very efficiently to produce molecular oxygen and NO_2 (equation 5). The radical NO_2 then reacts with atomic oxygen to form NO again, plus another molecule of O_2 (equation 6). After both reactions have occurred, the NO molecule is still present, although one molecule of O_3 and one oxygen

$$NO + O_3 \rightarrow NO_2 + O_2 \qquad (5)$$
$$NO_2 + O \rightarrow NO + O_2 \qquad (6)$$

atom have been removed. The NO-NO_2 catalytic system, often abbreviated as NO_x, can remove hundreds or thousands of ozone molecules before being terminated by reaction with another free radical, as in

$$OH + NO_2 \rightarrow HNO_3 \text{ (nitric acid).}$$

In 1973 atmospheric physicists Ralph Cicerone and Richard Stolarski of the University of Michigan identified another potential free-radical catalytic chain that could occur in the stratosphere, one that involves atomic chlorine and its oxide, ClO. Reactions of the ClO_x chain are very similar to those of the NO_x chain; chlorine oscillates between Cl and ClO, and one O_3 molecule and one oxygen atom are removed per complete cycle (equations 7 and 8). The NO_x catalytic chain is a natural part of the atmospheric cycle, as is

$$Cl + O_3 \rightarrow ClO + O_2 \qquad (7)$$
$$ClO + O \rightarrow Cl + O_2 \qquad (8)$$

a small natural ClO_x contribution to the ozone removal process from the decomposition of methyl chloride, CH_3Cl. With the addition of these free radical chains, and some others involving hydrogen-containing free radicals (HO_x), the basic description of the ozone level in the natural atmosphere is once again satisfactory on a quantitative basis. The NO_x and ClO_x catalytic chains provide a means by which very small concentrations of free radicals can exert a remarkable multiplying effect in removing stratospheric ozone, and concentrations in the atmosphere of as little as one part per billion (10^{-9}) become quite significant.

The existence of these free-radical catalytic chains also brings the activities of man into chemical competition with natural atmospheric processes. About 3.3 billion tons of ozone are in the atmosphere, in a dynamic balance between creation and destruction. On this massive scale the release of one

Profile of the Earth's atmosphere to a height of 200 miles depicts some of the natural phenomena that occur at various levels. The upper boundary of the troposphere, the layer of air nearest the surface, is defined by the region in which the air temperature stops falling with increasing altitude and begins to rise. For tropical latitudes (red curve, latitude 0°) this region, called the tropopause, lies at about ten miles altitude; for polar latitudes (blue curve, latitude 70°), about six miles. About 32 miles up, the stratopause, or top of the stratosphere, is characterized by the beginning of a downward trend in temperature. Similarly, at 50 miles the mesopause, which separates the mesosphere from the ionosphere, is defined by an upward temperature change. The ozone layer, strongly absorbing solar ultraviolet wavelengths between 250 and 280 nanometers at a height of 25–30 miles, actually provides the heat that produces the temperature inversion in the stratosphere.

176

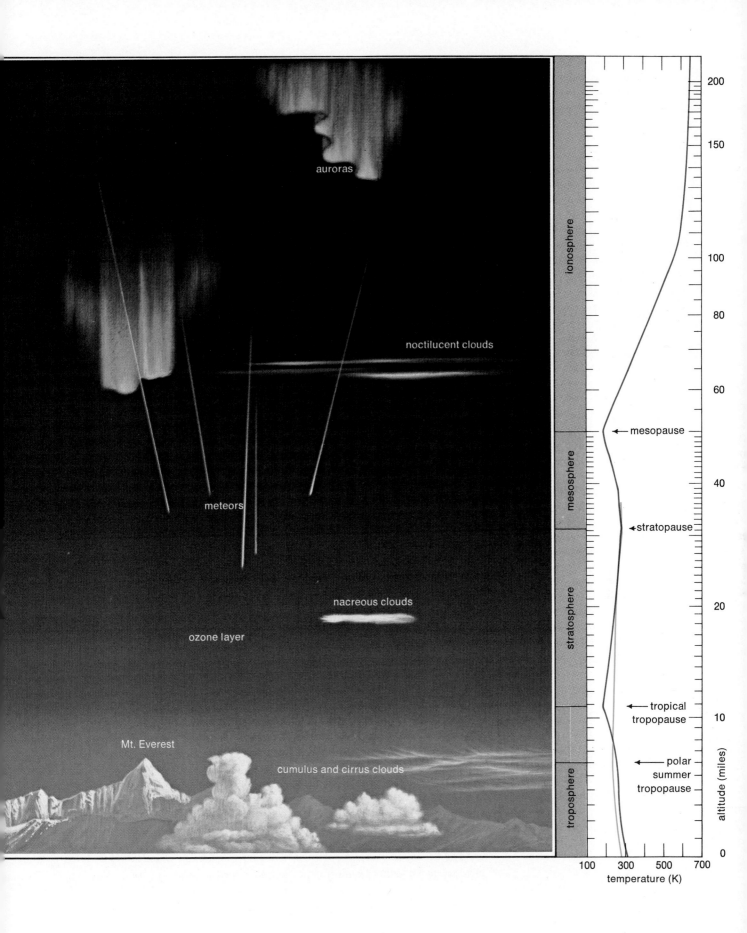

auroras

noctilucent clouds

meteors

nacreous clouds

ozone layer

Mt. Everest

cumulus and cirrus clouds

ionosphere

mesosphere

stratosphere

troposphere

← mesopause

← stratopause

← tropical
tropopause

← polar
summer
tropopause

200

150

100

80

60

40

20

10

0

altitude (miles)

100   300   500   700

temperature (K)

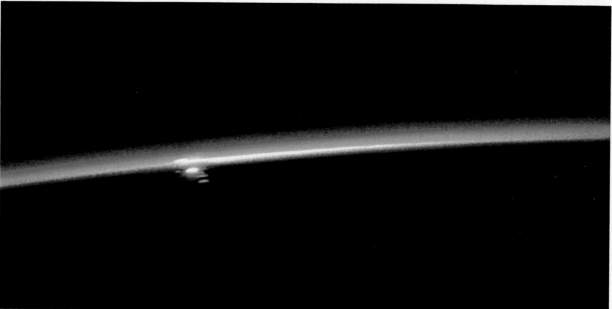

The Greek philosopher Plato wrote: "We are dwelling in a hollow of the Earth, and fancy that we are on the surface. . . . But the fact is that owing to our feebleness and sluggishness we are prevented from reaching the surface of the air." More than 2,300 years later men in spacecraft have finally struggled upward toward that "surface of the air" and have looked down from 100 miles in space to photograph the tropospheric skin of the Earth against the setting Sun. Eggshell thin in relation to the planet to which it clings, the lowest few miles of air nevertheless provide the precious canopy under which all mankind plays out its existence.

million tons of a given man-made material per year may not seem very large, but one million tons multiplied by a factor of 1,000 or more through catalytic chain reactions cannot be ignored.

Natural control of stratospheric ozone

The atmosphere becomes thinner and colder with increasing altitude for the first six to ten miles above the ground. In the lowest regions of the stratosphere, at a height of about ten miles, 90% of the atmosphere lies beneath and the temperature averages about 210 K ($-80°$ F). Furthermore, almost all of the water vapor has been removed at lower altitudes; the atmosphere at this level is practically cloud-free. In the troposphere, that part of the atmosphere between the surface and about six to ten miles altitude, the gases undergo rapid vertical mixing and are cleansed periodically by rainstorms. Consequently, chemicals released in the troposphere can be removed rapidly and long-term pollution is relatively unlikely. The same nitrogen oxides found in the stratospheric NO_x catalytic cycle are also found near the Earth's surface, particularly in urban, automobile-produced smog with its characteristic brown color from NO_2. These compounds formed at the surface, however, do not reach the stratosphere because they are removed by tropospheric weather processes.

Those NO and NO_2 molecules found in the stratosphere are formed there from still another oxide of nitrogen, nitrous oxide or N_2O. Approximately three molecules of every ten million in the atmosphere are N_2O, their presence resulting from natural biochemical reactions. (Molecular N_2 can be "fixed," or converted to forms useful for plant growth, by leguminous plants.) Bacterial denitrification, or the destruction of nitrogen-containing residues in the soil and in the ocean, returns nitrogen compounds to the atmosphere. Whereas most of this nitrogen is in the form of N_2, a small fraction is released as N_2O; this process maintains atmospheric N_2O at its steady level.

N_2O is not a free radical and is chemically not very reactive; neither is it removed from the atmosphere by rainfall. Hence molecules of N_2O can survive unchanged in the atmosphere for decades, long enough to mix upward in the high stratosphere above 20 miles. Here, above 99% of the O_2 in the atmosphere and above most of the ozone as well, the full force of solar UV radiation causes many otherwise inert molecules to become chemically reactive. At this level most of the N_2O is converted to N_2, but about 5% becomes NO, which then can participate in the NO_x catalytic chain.

The ozone concentration of the natural stratosphere is primarily controlled by these two chemical cycles: the solar UV formation of O_3 from O_2, and the biological nitrogen cycle that keeps the atmosphere supplied with N_2O. The formation of ozone by the action of solar UV radiation on atmospheric O_2 represents the expenditure of more energy than that consumed by all of man's activities combined. The possibility of directly interfering with or supplementing solar ozone production is therefore far beyond man's present capabilities.

The reaction of an oxygen atom with O_3, however, releases energy, whether by direct reaction or through one of the catalytic cycles. Maintained through a long chain of reactions, this ozone-removing process does fall within man's current technological reach, either intentionally or inadvertently. The necessary requirement is straightforward—such reactive free radicals as NO or Cl must be introduced into the mid-stratosphere in quantities of about one million tons or more per year.

Stratospheric pollution and the SST

Pollutants can enter the stratosphere through two routes: direct release of free radicals (or molecules easily transformed into them) into the stratosphere and release at the surface of the Earth of compounds that can be converted into free radicals in the stratosphere. Whereas the release of N_2O at the surface forms NO in the stratosphere as a natural process, and will happen in the same manner for N_2O released by man, the relatively recent technology that produced jet aircraft capable of operating at high altitudes has given man the means for direct introduction of free radicals into the stratosphere.

In the late 1960s, as plans took shape for building the Anglo-French Concorde supersonic transport (SST), the Soviet Tupolev-144 SST, and the U.S. Boeing SST, questions were raised about possible environmental effects. The potential stratospheric ozone problems with such aircraft are not a direct result of the supersonic velocities at which they fly but rather of the high altitudes for which their flight is designed. Current subsonic jets generally fly at altitudes of 6–7 miles, and the Concorde and Tu-144 at 10 miles; the Boeing SST, whose production program was abandoned in 1971, was planned to cruise at 12 miles. In general, the higher the aircraft flies, the longer its released pollutants take to drift down through the stratosphere, and thus the more time they have to catalyze the removal of ozone.

When air is heated to high temperatures by passage through a jet engine, some N_2 and O_2 react to form two molecules of NO, ready to participate in the NO_x catalytic chain. In early 1971 physical chemist Harold Johnston of

Through a set of reactions collectively known as the Chapman mechanism, stratospheric ozone is constantly created by the action of solar ultraviolet light on diatomic oxygen (O_2) and destroyed by reaction with atomic oxygen (O). Threats to this steady-state process include natural and man-made activities that add ozone-destroying free-radical catalytic systems like the nitrogen oxides NO and NO_2 and atomic chlorine (Cl) and its oxide ClO. Supersonic transport flights in the lower stratosphere release NO directly, which then makes a slow upward journey into regions of high ozone concentration. The molecule N_2O, released at ground level through bacterial denitrification and to a limited extent in stack gases, is not a free radical and not very reactive; however, it survives to reach altitudes above 20 miles where it is converted by solar UV into the free radical NO. Free chlorine is expected to be exhausted into the stratosphere by space shuttle booster rockets on their way into space. Use of chlorofluorocarbons as aerosol propellants and refrigerants puts hundreds of thousands of tons of these molecules yearly into the lower atmosphere; as with N_2O these normally inert species rise into the stratosphere where the action of solar UV causes their dissociation to release free chlorine. Most urban-produced free radicals are cleansed by rainfall before they can rise above the weather into the stratosphere.

the University of California at Berkeley warned that NO directly released in the stratosphere from SST engines represented a real danger to stratospheric ozone if the proposed fleets of 500 or more Boeing SST's were actually built and flown. In the aftermath of the U.S. Senate decision in 1971, primarily on economic grounds, to halt development of the Boeing SST, the U.S. government funded an intensive, three-year study of the environmental effects from SST's, the Climatic Impact Assessment Program (CIAP) of 1972–74. The examination of the stratosphere carried out during CIAP may well have provided more information about the stratosphere than that acquired from all prior scientific efforts.

During CIAP, high-altitude measurements with balloons and aircraft confirmed that NO and NO_2 are actually present in the stratosphere as expected, and that the NO_x catalytic cycle was indeed the chief ingredient missing from the Chapman mechanism. Stratospheric-model calculations indicated that projected depletion of ozone was strongly dependent upon the altitude of flight of the aircraft, with highest ozone losses for the proposed 500-plane Boeing fleet. Much smaller effects were calculated for the Concorde and Tupolev SST's and smaller still for the current fleets of subsonic aircraft. Present calculations have indicated negligible changes in ozone levels for flight altitudes below about 12 miles, even for large fleets of aircraft.

Although the current phase of SST building has subsided without the construction of 500-aircraft fleets, the potential stratospheric environmental problems have been outlined and will undoubtedly require thorough consideration as the second generation of SST's comes into discussion during the next 10–15 years. The advantages of higher altitude (and higher speed) need to be weighed against the increasing problems accompanying higher release altitudes for such pollutants as NO_x and water vapor.

UV radiation and skin cancer

During the CIAP study, investigators also considered the various environmental consequences of stratospheric ozone loss. Two physical changes to the atmosphere appeared predominant: increased penetration of UV radiation to the Earth's surface, and alteration in the temperature structure of the stratosphere itself. The change in stratospheric structure could have an influence on the world's climate, whereas increased UV radiation at the surface could affect many biological systems.

Solar UV radiation can be conveniently divided into three categories: UV-A, with wavelengths of 320–400 nm; UV-B, with wavelengths of 280–320 nm, which includes the ozone cutoff region; and UV-C, with wavelengths shorter than 280 nm, all of which are absorbed in the stratosphere by either O_3 or O_2 (see illustration on p. 174). Most UV-A radiation currently reaches the surface of the Earth, and its passage through the atmosphere is very little affected by changes in the concentration of ozone. All biological species existing in the sunlight, including humans, evolved under exposure to intense UV-A radiation and would not have survived if they were adversely affected by it. On the other hand, absorption of UV-C by O_3 and O_2 molecules in the stratosphere is so strong that no UV-C would penetrate to the surface even after a major loss of stratospheric ozone.

180

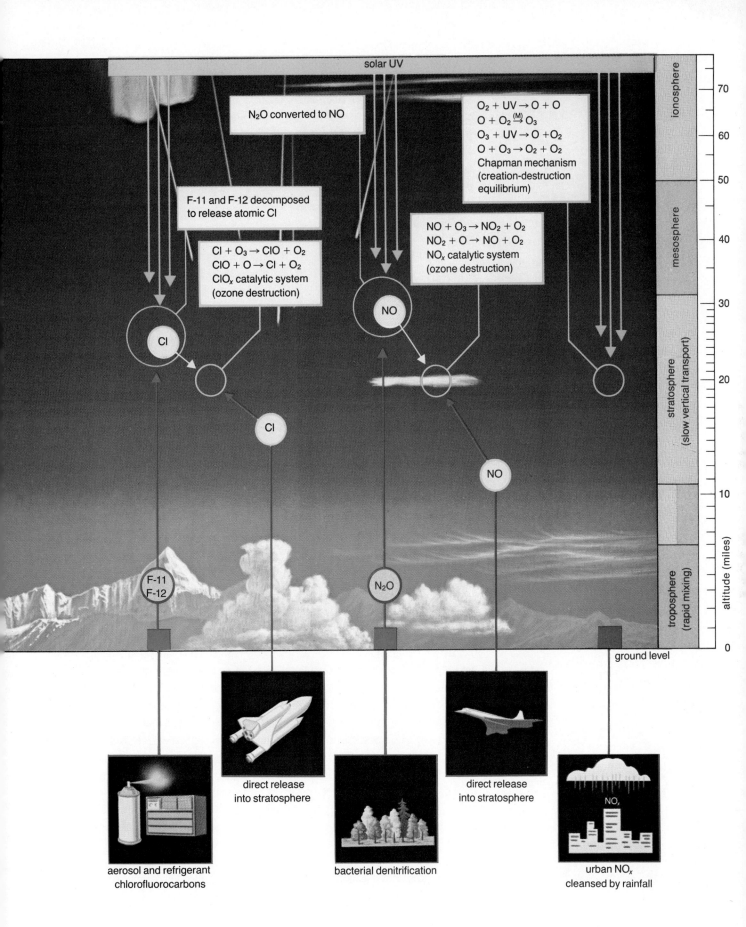

solar UV

N₂O converted to NO

$O_2 + UV \rightarrow O + O$
$O + O_2 \xrightarrow{(M)} O_3$
$O_3 + UV \rightarrow O + O_2$
$O + O_3 \rightarrow O_2 + O_2$
Chapman mechanism
(creation-destruction equilibrium)

F-11 and F-12 decomposed to release atomic Cl

$Cl + O_3 \rightarrow ClO + O_2$
$ClO + O \rightarrow Cl + O_2$
ClO_x catalytic system
(ozone destruction)

$NO + O_3 \rightarrow NO_2 + O_2$
$NO_2 + O \rightarrow NO + O_2$
NO_x catalytic system
(ozone destruction)

Cl

NO

Cl

NO

F-11
F-12

N₂O

ionosphere
mesosphere
stratosphere (slow vertical transport)
troposphere (rapid mixing)

altitude (miles)
70
60
50
40
30
20
10
0

ground level

direct release into stratosphere

direct release into stratosphere

aerosol and refrigerant chlorofluorocarbons

bacterial denitrification

urban NOₓ cleansed by rainfall

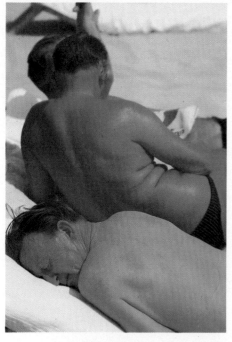

The life-style of many persons involves a seemingly destructive obsession with the Sun; continual overexposure to solar radiation near 290 nanometers (in the UV-B region) often results in premature aging of the skin and increases the risk of acquiring skin cancer. Studies such as that summarized in the chart below, which analyzes incidence of malignant melanoma in the U.S. for white males, have shown the risk of skin cancer to be significantly greater for people living in low latitudes than for those in high latitudes.

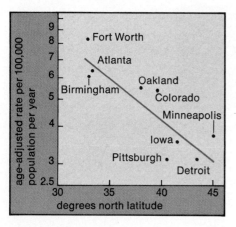

A change in ozone concentration would exert its major effect on the transmission of UV-B radiation near the ozone cutoff. As ozone concentrations in the stratosphere decreased, the fraction of UV-B penetrating to the surface would increase, with consequent increase in biological effects. (Interestingly, most day-to-day measurements of stratospheric ozone are made at ground level with a Dobson spectrophotometer. This instrument simultaneously measures both UV-A and UV-B radiation striking its detector, permitting calculation of atmospheric ozone concentrations from a ratio of the two readings.)

One obvious effect of UV-B radiation on light-skinned humans is reddening of the skin or, when prolonged, sunburn; for this reason, UV-B is sometimes identified as "sunburn UV." Controlled experiments demonstrated that even more prolonged exposure to UV-B induces skin cancer in laboratory animals. Whereas such experiments are not carried out with human beings, natural UV-B exposure varies sufficiently from one geographical location to another so that semicontrolled experiments have occurred by choices of living site. The average ozone concentration is lowest near the Equator. Thus, people living in equatorial latitudes are exposed to more UV-B than those living in temperate or polar regions. In addition, atmospheric absorption of UV-B is also dependent upon the zenith angle of the Sun, with increasing penetration of UV-B as the Sun rises farther above the horizon. The equatorial regions thus also receive increased UV-B exposure because the Sun is more nearly overhead for extended times, whereas in temperate regions primary exposure to UV-B occurs during the four hours around noon. Exposure to UV-B in temperate regions is also much stronger in summer than in winter.

Careful studies by the U.S. National Cancer Institute showed that the incidence of human skin cancer is several times greater in the southern part of the U.S. than in the northern part. For example, the incidence in Dallas, Texas (latitude 32.5° N), is 3.8 cases per 1,000 inhabitants per year, while that in Des Moines, Iowa (latitude 41.5° N), is only 1.2 cases per 1,000 per year. These data refer only to light-skinned people because the sensitivity to skin cancer is substantially reduced for the dark-skinned population through presence in the skin of the light-absorbing pigment melanin. The incidence of human skin cancer is particularly high in Queensland, Australia, with a predominantly white population living in an equatorial region.

Human skin cancer occurs in three principal forms. Two are relatively mild forms identified by the layers of cells in which they grow, basal or squamous. These are slow-growing cancers that can be readily treated medically and are primarily a source of discomfort and disfigurement but only rarely a cause of death. Both result from prolonged, cumulative exposure to UV-B and are consequently much more commonly found among older people. The third form of skin cancer, malignant melanoma, grows rapidly, frequently spreads to other organs, and in the U.S. is fatal in about 40% of diagnosed cases. Malignant melanoma is also often found among younger people. This form of cancer represents only a few percent of the total U.S. cases of skin cancer but accounts for about half of the fatalities. Studies have indicated that exposure to solar UV-B is also a prime contributing factor to its occurrence.

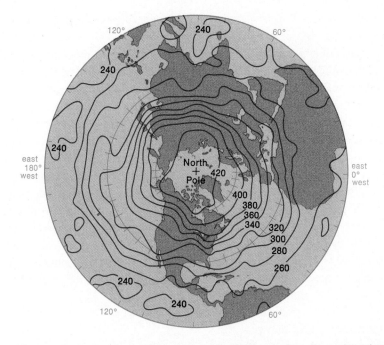

Quite apart from any possible changes in UV-B exposure from alterations in the ozone layer, changes in life-style in recent years have brought about an increased exposure to solar UV-B radiation and consequent increases in the incidence of all forms of skin cancer. Since basal- and squamous-cell skin cancers are often treated somewhat informally without notification of central record-keeping authorities, comparisons over several decades are statistically difficult. Deaths from malignant melanoma, however, are another matter. Records in the Scandinavian countries are particularly comprehensive and clearly show that the incidence of malignant melanoma increased there by a factor of four or five between 1950 and 1975. Undoubtedly this increase is associated with the tendency for these fair-skinned individuals to expose more of the body to direct sunlight for longer amounts of time. Similar increases in malignant melanoma rates are also being observed in the United States. Although a decrease in stratospheric ozone could also cause an increase in the incidence of human skin cancer, the effect would be obscured by the rapid increase accompanying changes in life-style.

Predictions of the increased incidence in skin cancer from loss of atmospheric ozone require evaluation of three separate factors. First, how large will be the average change in ozone concentration? Second, what is the anticipated increase in UV-B radiation resulting from that loss in ozone? Third, how much increase in the rate of skin cancer can be expected for the anticipated increase in solar UV-B radiation? The potential ozone loss, of course, must be estimated for each potential source of stratospheric free radicals. Based on careful calculations, the increase in UV-B has been placed at approximately 20% for a 10% loss in ozone. Finally, the estimate of the increase in skin cancer as a function of the increase in UV-B is basically derived from the record of human skin-cancer rates observed for different latitudes and is somewhat less certain. The best current evaluations postulate that a 20% increase in UV-B (from a 10% loss in ozone)

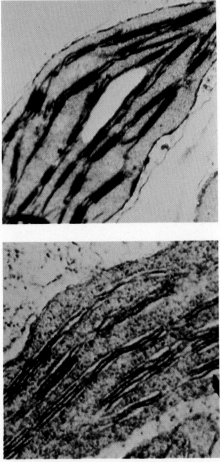

Courtesy, Martyn M. Caldwell, Utah State University, photos by W.F. Campbell

183

Discovery of the chlorofluorocarbon threat to ozone was largely the result of careful experiments in laboratories such as that of F. Sherwood Rowland and Mario Molina (opposite page, bottom), which is equipped for work under the high vacuum necessary for study of the reactions of individual isolated molecules. Such experiments develop a picture of the chemistry occurring in the upper atmosphere; with other data, this information can be used to derive models of future ozone loss. The graph on the opposite page constitutes a recent projection of such a loss if chlorofluorocarbon release were to continue at mid-1970s rates; concentrations of chlorine free radicals are given in parts per billion (ppb).

would result in a 40–50% increase in basal- and squamous-cell skin cancer, and about a 30% increase in malignant melanoma.

Since all biological systems have evolved under the protection of the ozone shield, it is quite unlikely that man is the only species sensitive to an increase in UV-B radiation. Although a very large number of biological experiments have been performed with UV radiation, the most conveniently and widely used artificial UV source, the mercury-vapor lamp, emits chiefly UV-C radiation. While this radiation has strong, deleterious effects on most biological systems, the observations cannot be directly extended to irradiations with UV-B. Biological experiments with 290–320 nm radiation are still scarce, and predictions for effects on species other than man cannot be made. Special concern has been expressed for such very small species as oceanic plankton, for which UV-B irradiates the entire organism and not just the skin. Other possible biological effects of increased UV-B that have been suggested for study include disturbances in aquatic and terrestrial ecosystems; changes in growth characteristics of plants, including agricultural crops; and effects on the behavior of insects.

Ozone loss and climate

The radiation (largely UV-C) absorbed by ozone in the upper stratosphere furnishes a strong heat source at an altitude of 25–30 miles. The temperature of the atmosphere at those altitudes, therefore, is considerably higher than the 210 K found at 10 miles, and peaks near 30 miles altitude at about 275 K (35° F). The stratosphere is actually defined by these temperature variations. The troposphere ends at the tropopause, the altitude (6–10 miles, varying somewhat with latitude and season) at which temperatures cease to fall with increasing altitude. The stratosphere starts at this temperature minimum and ends at the stratopause, the temperature peak. With its steadily rising temperatures with increasing altitude, the stratosphere constitutes a permanent inversion layer. Vertical mixing of the atmosphere is quite slow under these temperature gradients, with time scales measured in years in contrast to the weeks characteristic of tropospheric circulation.

If less ozone is present in the 25–30-mile altitude segment of the stratosphere, then less UV-C radiation will be absorbed there, the heat source will be reduced in intensity, and the temperature at the stratopause will decrease. Although this transmitted UV-C would still be absorbed at lower altitudes, the stratospheric temperature structure would be permanently distorted. Meteorological effects are so complex that in the late 1970s it was not yet possible to predict with any assurance whether general climatic changes would result from such stratospheric alterations.

Chlorofluorocarbons in the atmosphere

As the CIAP study neared the end in its consideration of one possible future stratospheric pollution problem, a separate study uncovered another man-made process of ozone depletion already in progress. For years man has been affecting stratospheric ozone through the release of nearly inert chlorine-containing molecules at the surface, in particular such chlorofluorocarbon compounds as CCl_3F (F-11) and CCl_2F_2 (F-12). Late in 1973 physical chemists Mario Molina and F. S. Rowland of the University of California at Irvine recognized that these compounds, widely utilized as aerosol spray propellants and as refrigerants, are decomposed by solar UV radiation at an altitude of about 20 miles and that their destruction results in the abundant release of atomic chlorine, initiating the ClO_x cycle of ozone destruction.

In 1976 the world usage of F-12 and F-11 was about 500,000 and 300,000 tons, respectively. The largest use of each was in the propellant gas mixtures used in many aerosol sprays, especially in personal products such as hair sprays and deodorants. In addition, F-12 is currently the most widely used refrigerant gas, present in almost all home refrigerators and in larger amounts for automobile air conditioning and for industrial refrigeration. Such applications of chlorofluorocarbons require that the molecules be readily convertible from the liquid to the gaseous state, and almost all of them involve eventual release of the gases to the atmosphere. The aerosol propellants are directly vented into the air during spraying, and, although the refrigerants remain contained during use, they are almost never reclaimed when refrigeration equipment is discarded.

The technological popularity of these gases stems largely from their chemical inertness, as well as their ease of conversion from liquid to gas. The same inertness that is so advantageous inside the aerosol can is also evident in the atmosphere, in which both F-11 and F-12 can survive unchanged for many decades. Both are transparent to visible light and to solar UV-A and UV-B radiation as well. Both are insoluble in water and thus not removed by rainfall. Consequently, their ultimate fate in the Earth's atmosphere is similar to that of natural N_2O. They rise into the stratosphere and are eventually broken up near 20 miles altitude by solar UV radiation, in these cases by wavelengths in the 190–220 nm region.

Photodissociation of the chlorofluorocarbons begins with the ejection of one chlorine atom, with the rest following later. At 20 miles altitude atomic chlorine reacts almost exclusively with ozone. The ClO formed by that reaction (equation 7) can react either with atomic oxygen or with NO and favors the former (equation 8) in the upper stratosphere. The total chlorine cycle also includes time spent as the stable molecule HCl, formed by reaction of a Cl atom with methane, CH_4. However, chlorine can be released from HCl by other reactions in the stratosphere, returning it to the ClO_x cycle. On the average, each chlorine atom passes through the ClO_x cycle more than 10,000 times before eventually disappearing into the tropospheric rainfall as HCl. Both ClO and NO_2 can be tied up in the molecule chlorine nitrate, $ClONO_2$, but it is decomposed rapidly enough by solar radiation to keep its concentration less than that of HCl.

The F-11 and F-12 continually vented at ground level accumulate steadily in the troposphere and randomly diffuse up into the stratosphere. Equilibration into the stratosphere, however, lags behind tropospheric accumulation by about a decade because of the slowness of vertical motion above the tropopause. Furthermore, because at any instant only small fractions of F-11 and F-12 are above 15 miles altitude and exposed to intense 190–220-nm solar UV, the removal of these compounds from the atmosphere will require more than a century. Both the delayed rise and the long residence times are

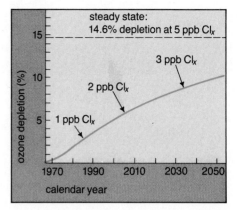

Courtesy, F. Sherwood Rowland

185

Courtesy, James G. Anderson, John Maurer, and Rick
Shetter, Space Physics Research Laboratory, University of
Michigan

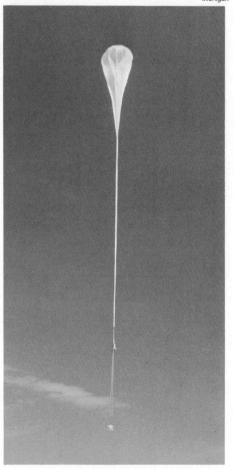

stratospheric gas detector

plasma-discharge photon source

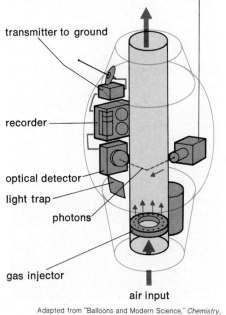

transmitter to ground

recorder

optical detector

light trap

photons

gas injector

air input

Adapted from "Balloons and Modern Science," *Chemistry*,
Vol. 50, No. 8, p. 11, October 1977

independent of the total concentration present at any given time. Even if governmental regulations were to be universally passed against further release of these chlorofluorocarbons to the atmosphere, ozone depletion would continue to worsen for about a decade and would continue for more than a century.

The calculated loss in ozone from chlorofluorocarbons already in the atmosphere is about 1%, and the eventual ozone loss would be more than 10% for long-term yearly release of 800,000 tons of F-12 and F-11. The ClO_x chain preferentially attacks ozone in the upper stratosphere, and the ozone loss near 25 miles altitude could approach 50% as the total ozone loss reaches 10%. This heavier loss from the upper stratosphere was emphasized by the World Meteorological Organization in its 1976 warning of possible meteorological effects from the continued yearly usage of the fluorocarbons in million-ton amounts.

Synthesized more than 40 years ago as a refrigerant, F-12 has been highly successful in this application. Development of the appropriate can and valve technology for F-11/F-12 mixtures in the early 1950s solved the problem of making relatively inexpensive aerosol spray-can packaging, and aerosol usage doubled every 5–7 years thereafter through 1974. Although much of this use originally was confined to the U.S., aerosol packaging has spread throughout the world, and in 1975 U.S. chlorofluorocarbon usage represented about 40% of the world total. With continuation of the exponential rise observed since the 1950s, estimates of eventual ozone loss from the chlorofluororcarbons would have been higher as well. However, world manufacture of F-11 and F-12 peaked in 1974 and was expected to decline in the coming years because of governmental regulatory action throughout the world.

In 1973 there were as yet no measurements of any chlorine-containing molecular species in the stratosphere. Prediction of the chlorofluorocarbon effect on ozone was based instead on general knowledge of the atmosphere plus laboratory experiments. In 1974 and 1975 measurements in the stratosphere confirmed the presence of F-11 and F-12. Their concentrations were found to decrease rapidly with increasing altitude, as expected for destruction by solar UV. Another chlorinated compound, HCl, was also found in agreement with the predictions. In 1976 physicist James Anderson of the University of Michigan detected both ClO and Cl in the stratosphere with an instrument parachuted from a balloon, demonstrating that the ClO_x chain reaction is actually occurring at 15–25 miles altitude.

Governmental regulation

During 1974–77 considerable scientific and public debate took place, mostly within the U.S., over both the general concept and specific details of what came to be called the "fluorocarbon ozone depletion theory." Even as debate continued, the state of Oregon in June 1975 passed a law prohibiting the sale after March 1, 1977, of F-11 and F-12 (and some similar molecules) as aerosol propellants. In 1975, too, a special scientific task force from 14 U.S. federal agencies considered the problem of "Inadvertent Modification of the Stratosphere," concluding that the chlorofluorocarbon threat to stratospheric ozone was "a legitimate cause for concern."

In September 1976 another scientific group, the U.S. National Academy of Sciences Panel on Atmospheric Chemistry, again confirmed the validity of the general scientific description of the potential for ozone destruction, concluding that "selective regulation of CFM [chlorofluorocarbon] uses and releases is almost certain to be necessary at some time and to some degree of completeness." During 1977 three U.S. regulatory agencies jointly announced regulations to control manufacture and use of F-11 and F-12 as aerosol propellants, giving a deadline of April 15, 1979, for their sale for nonessential purposes. The Canadian and Swedish governments also announced plans toward similar ends.

All stratospheric pollution problems are international problems because the pollutants rapidly become distributed globally. Regulation is therefore quite complex because no one country or group of countries can solve a stratospheric problem unilaterally. In the late 1970s the general problem of depletion of stratospheric ozone was taken under consideration by the United Nations Environment Program and other international organizations.

Additional threats

Now that two products of technology, the SST's and the fluorocarbons, have been found to be potential threats to stratospheric ozone concentration, attention has turned to other possible sources for stratospheric free radicals. Although fluorine atoms contained in the chlorofluorocarbons also can initiate a cycle quite analogous to the ClO_x cycle, they are soon diverted into the extremely stable molecule HF, ending the chain process at that point. The fluorine component from these molecules is perhaps 1,000 times less effective than chlorine and is therefore of negligible concern toward ozone removal. Atoms of bromine, another element similar to chlorine, can cause a long BrO_x chain and would be comparable to chlorine in their effect. However, bromine-containing molecules are much less common in technological use, due chiefly to their greater cost, and in the late 1970s none of them seemed to be serious stratospheric threats at their low rates of consumption and release.

Other chlorine-containing molecules also pose stratospheric problems. Carbon tetrachloride, CCl_4, was formerly used in larger quantities, but its atmospheric release has receded in recent decades. The chlorofluorocarbon CCl_2FCClF_2 (F-113) is very similar in atmospheric properties to F-11 and is used as a cleaning solvent, especially in the electronics industry. The total effect on ozone represents the sum of the contributions from these and other chlorine-containing molecules.

Some activities of man could produce increased concentrations of atmospheric N_2O, which would lead in turn to more stratospheric NO and eventually to a reduction in stratospheric ozone. For example, measurements in stack gases from power plants indeed have shown the presence of substantial quantities of N_2O, but far more measurements are needed for quantitative worldwide estimates. Increased fixation of atmospheric nitrogen in the form of fertilizers also has led to the suggestion that the denitrification of such fertilizers could supplement the natural N_2O contribution from natural denitrification. Measurements have suggested a small increase (about 2%)

In 1976 physicist James Anderson demonstrated the stratospheric presence of the ozone-destroying ClO_x catalytic system using an instrument parachuted from a balloon (opposite page and above). During its slow descent the device, a resonance fluorescence spectrometer (opposite page, bottom), permitted entry of a stream of air, which was illuminated by a photon beam. Photons that were absorbed and then reemitted at characteristic frequencies by free chlorine and the chlorine from ClO molecules were received by a detector and recorded. Injection at intervals of certain gases into the airstream was done to purge the system of chlorine for background fluorescence counts or to release chlorine from ClO for detection.

Many of man's activities introduce potential ozone-destroying chemicals into the upper atmosphere, either directly or through upward transport from the troposphere. Under wind-tunnel testing in 1978, solid-fuel booster rockets (above) for the space shuttle orbiter (mounted atop a Boeing-747 jet aircraft at right) are expected to exhaust into the stratosphere many tons of reactive chlorine per weekly flight during the 1980s. Industrial stack gases and increased use of nitrogen fertilizers (opposite page, top left and bottom right) are under study as contributors of destructive nitrous oxide at ground level. Atmospheric atomic testing, which still awaits a universally respected ban, also seriously disrupts the natural chemistry of the atmosphere.

in tropospheric N_2O content between 1964 and 1974, and the atmospheric concentration of this gas will undoubtedly be very closely monitored during the coming years.

Although supersonic aircraft are not the only vehicles penetrating the stratosphere, they are the only ones designed to operate there for long periods of time. Rockets travel through the stratosphere on their way into space, normally leaving behind a small pollutant trail that is soon dispersed. However, plans for the reusable space shuttle in the 1980s and beyond call for weekly flights using very large solid-fuel booster rockets. Currently each flight is expected to exhaust into the stratosphere about 100 tons of chlorine from ammonium perchlorate in the propellant. On a once-a-week basis, the average ozone loss from space-shuttle operation would be about 0.2 to 0.4%. By itself this loss is not particularly large; however, it would be occurring simultaneously with that from chlorofluorocarbons and other stratospheric pollutants. The next decade will certainly bring discussion and possibly regulation of the total loss of stratospheric ozone from man's activities, and not just the control of one or more specific contributors to that loss.

Probing the ozone shield

Direct measurements of ozone loss from man's activities are very difficult because of the natural variability of ozone concentration at any single location. Continual measurement is needed at each monitoring station to gain good averages for the day, month, season, and year, and many stations are needed globally. Measurements at the few stations for which continuous records have been available since the 1930s (for example, at Arosa in the Swiss Alps) show year-to-year natural variations that some investigators have associated with the well-known 11-year cycle of solar activity. With

188

such natural variations, good worldwide measurements over a 40–50 year period at many stations probably would be needed to detect an ozone change of 1–2% introduced by man. Such records do not exist, and probably the best that can be done currently is the detection of an additional man-made change of 3% persisting for at least five years. Because waiting many years for a change of this magnitude would entail severe biological and climatic risks, most scientists prefer to accept the observation of ozone-depleting reactions in the stratosphere as sufficient confirmation of the ozone depletion hypothesis.

U.S. and Canadian records of average ozone concentrations extend back only to about 1960. During the decade of the 1960s the average ozone concentration over North America increased to a maximum in 1970 about 5% higher than the 1960 level. Since 1970 the trend has been downward, and the 1976 U.S. level was approximately equal to the 1960 level. Trends in Western Europe are similar to those in the U.S., with a peak around 1970 and decreases since. The ozone networks elsewhere have fewer stations and are generally less reliable for various reasons. Thus, world ozone estimates have been compiled from good measurements in the North Temperate Zone and fair-to-poor measurements elsewhere.

The increase in ozone levels during the 1960s has not been satisfactorily explained, although both the solar sunspot maximum in 1969 and the almost total cessation of nuclear testing in the atmosphere at the beginning of the decade have been widely discussed as contributing causes. The decrease since 1970 could include a contribution from man's input but is probably chiefly of natural origin. In 1977 the Sun emerged from a solar sunspot minimum and is expected to increase its sunspot activity for the next few years, with a maximum in 1980–81.

189

Continuous ozone monitoring at Arosa in the Swiss Alps provides a rare long-term record of ozone levels (right). The curve in blue plots the deviation of annual mean values from the 50-year mean of 337 Dobson units; the curve in red shows the deviation of five-year running means from the 50-year mean. A change of about 17 Dobson units corresponds to a 5% change in ozone concentration. Such measurements at many stations, plus input from weather outposts (below), laboratories, and other sources, are needed to understand significant fluctuations in ozone levels. Violent eruptions such as that recorded on the Sun in 1972 by satellite (opposite page, left) are thought to have caused severe ozone loss in the past, contributing to the extinction of species of radiolarians (top right). Percentage decrease of ozone, as derived from Nimbus satellite data from the average of seven days before and the seven-day periods centered on 8 and 19 days after the 1972 event, is shown in the graph on the opposite page. The third curve plots a theoretical calculation of ozone reduction for the 28th day after the event, assuming it to be due to event-produced NO.

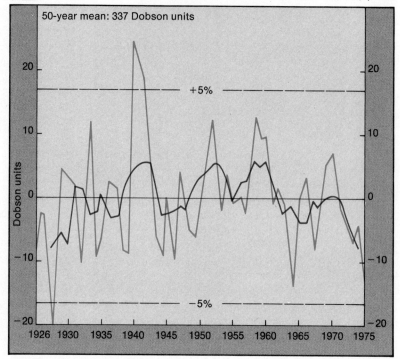

Emil Schulthess—Black Star

190

Continuous ozone measurement by satellite is currently in progress, but the technique requires further refinement. Since no satellite data are available prior to 1970, long-term trends from such instruments will not be available for many years.

Although the basic processes that maintain natural levels of atmospheric ozone are reasonably well understood, the deviations in concentration from year to year require much more precise analysis and, in general, are unexplained. In certain cases, however, short-term changes have been explained successfully. For instance, in August 1972 the Sun erupted violently with long flaming prominences, and its magnetic disturbances were felt on Earth. The cataclysm also spewed out huge numbers of energetic hydrogen nuclei, or protons. This "solar proton event," the largest observed during the two decades in which they have been recorded, caused extensive ionization in the high atmosphere at polar latitudes. The ionized species so created reacted rapidly to form NO, and this sudden appearance of catalytic material caused an ozone reduction that was recorded in satellite ozone measurements. The amount of data returned by such satellites is so voluminous, however, that the immediate atmospheric effects of this solar proton event remained hidden until atmospheric calculations were performed in 1975. A subsequent search in still-unexamined satellite data for 1972 showed a decrease within one day of about 16% in the ozone concentration above an altitude of 25 miles and above latitude 70° N. No effect was observed at lower latitudes where the Earth's magnetic field turned away the solar protons far above the stratosphere, preventing the formation of additional NO. This solar proton event is the best example yet of the actual observation of the removal of stratospheric ozone by the NO_x catalytic effect.

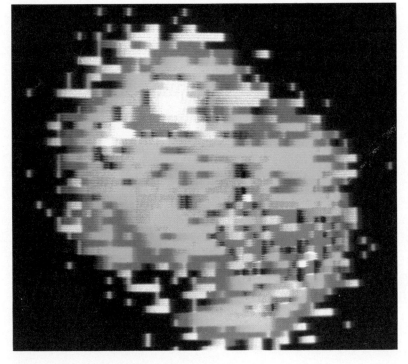

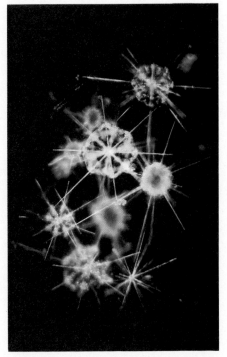

Observation of a sudden ozone decrease coincident with a solar proton outburst has brought forth a possible explanation of some previously unexplained coincidences observed in cores from the deep seafloor. Previous investigations had discovered that, on more than a dozen occasions in the past several million years, certain species of tiny oceanic protozoans called radiolarians had become extinct, and that their disappearances had apparently coincided in most cases with a known reversal of the Earth's magnetic field, also detectable in deep-sea cores. No satisfactory explanation had earlier been offered by which a reduction in the Earth's magnetic field occurring during such magnetic pole reversals was linked to the extinction of these biological species. According to the latest hypothesis, penetration of particularly large solar proton events into most of the atmosphere may have occurred during periods in which the geomagnetic field had been severely weakened by the pole reversal process. Under these conditions, NO could have been produced throughout the stratosphere at all latitudes, resulting in a massive loss of ozone. An increase in solar UV-B at the surface and the extinction of particularly susceptible species are then plausible consequences of such events.

During the 1970s the physical and chemical details of the stratosphere, and particularly of the ozone concentrated there, have been a meeting ground for meteorology, laboratory chemistry, in-flight measurements, and many other fields of science. The quest for understanding will certainly continue unabated into the 1980s as scientists probe the structure of the ozone shield that has played such a central role in shaping and maintaining the current forms of life on Earth.

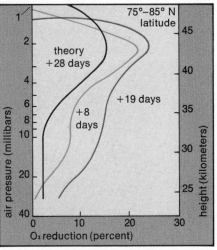

Adapted from *Science*, Vol. 197, p. 888, No. 4306, August 26, 1977, © AAAS

The Cambrian Explosion

by Steven M. Stanley

Nearly 600 million years ago animal life experienced a rapid, almost explosive diversification of species. Explaining this phenomenon has given scientists a new conception of large-scale evolutionary processes.

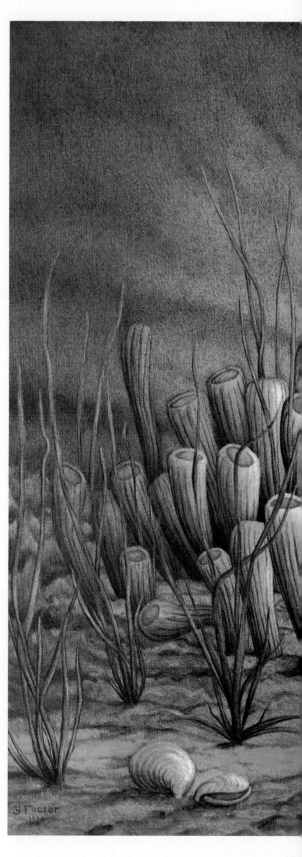

The Earth obey'd, and straight
Op'ning her fertile womb, teem'd at a birth
Innumerous living creatures, perfect forms,
Limb'd and full grown.

—Milton

To scholars of the Middle Ages, life began as a kind of vast multiple birth, an outpouring of the totality of existing species in a few sudden bursts of creation. In line with this belief, fossils were commonly regarded as evidence of preliminary divine tinkering, half-made creatures abandoned in the pursuit of more perfect forms. Although some early observers, including Leonardo da Vinci, understood the true nature of these portraits in rock, general recognition had to await the late 1700s when Scottish naturalist James Hutton laid the foundations of modern geology. In Hutton's scheme, which explained the formation of the Earth's crust in terms of currently observable natural processes, fossils were the remnants of life of the past, entombed within layers of sediment that later hardened into sedimentary rock. In the course of the 19th century, examination of the fossil record over geologic time revealed the broad outlines of the history of life on Earth.

The hand could be that of a sculptor chiseling a marble masterpiece, but it belongs to a paleontologist. And the masterpiece, formed by no human hand, was once a living trilobite, buried in sediment that settled hundreds of millions of years ago. Trilobites are considered important index fossils; where they first appear in the rock record traditionally defines the beginning of the Cambrian Period, about 570 million years in the past.

STEVEN M. STANLEY *is Professor of Paleobiology at the Johns Hopkins University, Baltimore, Maryland.*

(Overleaf) Illustration by Yale Factor

During the first half of the century, owing especially to the influence of the French anatomist and paleontologist Georges Cuvier, it became widely believed that sudden appearances and disappearances of diverse organisms seen in the fossil record represented episodes of divine creation punctuated by mass extinctions. The most striking such discontinuity in the rock record lay between what came to be called the Cambrian System, where fossilized remains of higher life appeared in great abundance, and the Precambrian System, the extensive body of older rocks that seemed entirely barren of fossils. With respect to life the Precambrian interval of time is formally known as the Cryptozoic Eon, or interval of hidden life, whereas the remainder of geologic time forms the Phanerozoic Eon, or interval of well-displayed life. It is now known that the Earth is about 4.6 billion years old and that the Cambrian began slightly less than 600 million years ago.

Cambrian fossils include primitive arthropods called trilobites, creatures with a jointed two-piece shell called brachiopods, snails, and other less conspicuous forms of invertebrate marine life. In fact, the remains of most major phyla of fossil animals are found in rocks of Cambrian age, though many subgroups are known only from younger strata. For example, the phylum Echinodermata is well represented in the Cambrian, but starfish, sea urchins, and sea lilies, which all represent particular classes of the Echinodermata, appear only in younger rocks. Vertebrate animals, including fish, and land plants are absent from the Cambrian. During the first half of the 19th century, the biotic discontinuity between the Precambrian and Cambrian represented no special problem. It was simply taken to demarcate the initial creation of life.

With the rise of evolutionary theory, however, the sudden appearance of diverse fossil remains in the Cambrian posed a major difficulty. If the history of life represented a gradual transformation of organisms, why should the fossil record start abruptly, with the nearly simultaneous appearance of a variety of multicellular invertebrate animals? Darwin despaired of the situation, writing in *On the Origin of Species*, "the case at present must remain inexplicable; and may be truly urged as a valid argument against the views [on natural selection] here entertained." Darwin's rather desperate suggestion was that the history of invertebrate life spanned a considerable period before deposition of rocks of the Cambrian System, but that the early record was unavailable, either because it lay buried beneath the present ocean or because it had been destroyed by metamorphism (alteration of rocks at high temperatures and pressures). Paleontologists of the early 20th century adhered to Darwin's general thesis that a lengthy period of invertebrate evolution was somehow missing from the fossil record. It was suggested that early forms lacked preservable skeletons (hard body parts such as shell or chitinous material) either because they evolved to float in the ocean or because the chemistry of the ocean prevented shell secretion.

Today many of the hypotheses that were advanced to explain the great dilemma seem outlandish. In particular, there is much evidence that when vacant habitats exist in the environment, groups of organisms tend to fill them rapidly by migration of existing species or by evolutionary expansion. It was not until 1948 that U.S. geologist and paleontologist Preston E.

194

(Top, left and right) Riccardo Levi-Setti, University of Chicago; (below) reprinted from *Trilobites: A photographic Atlas*, by Riccardo Levi-Setti, by permission of the University of Chicago Press

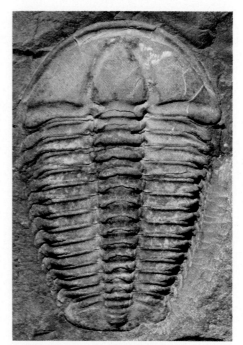

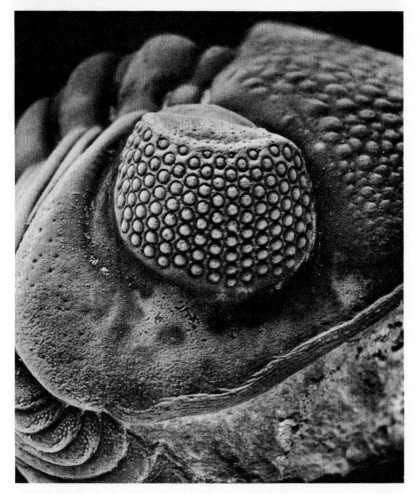

Trilobites make their appearance in the early Cambrian in diverse, fully developed forms. Characteristics shared by all species of these ancient arthropods include a segmented body divided longitudinally into three lobes and an external skeleton of chitinous material. Some trilobites were sightless (above), but most species possessed a pair of compound eyes, the most ancient visual system known, on the cephalon or head region (left, top and bottom). The eyes of many trilobites that evolved later have been shown to comprise arrays of remarkably sophisticated lens pairs that probably served to maximize sensory response to light in a dim marine environment.

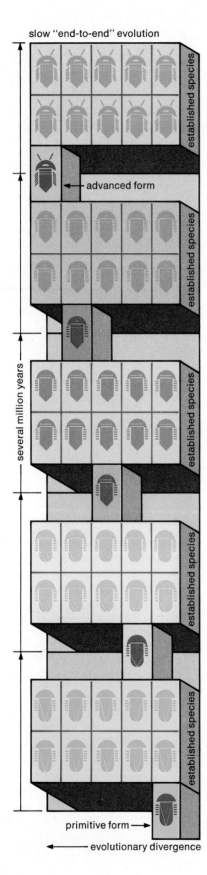

slow "end-to-end" evolution

established species

advanced form

established species

established species

established species

established species

several million years

primitive form →

← evolutionary divergence

Cloud, Jr., suggested that higher organisms of the Cambrian might have originated by what is sometimes referred to as explosive evolution, or very rapid diversification of species. The question that remained was whether the rate of diversification required by fossil evidence was feasible. For many years it seemed that each of the various invertebrate groups of the Cambrian must have had a long Precambrian history. Even by the mid-1960s many paleontologists favored the idea that the development of skeletons after a long interval of Precambrian evolution was what produced a well-displayed fossil record in the Cambrian. Martin Rudwick, a prominent British paleontologist, concluded in 1964 that the accumulation of geological evidence had not alleviated the "Cambrian Problem" but had actually accentuated it.

Since the 1960s, however, the picture has changed dramatically. First, a variety of new fossil evidence has surfaced, documenting not an instantaneous appearance of diverse multicellular organisms at the start of the Cambrian, but a sequential appearance of various groups over several tens of millions of years. Second, it has become apparent that the evolutionary process does not work in quite the way that had traditionally been envisioned. For clarity the second development will be considered first.

Tempo of large-scale evolution

One of the traditional arguments for a long Precambrian history for multicellular life relates to the longevity of species in geologic time. In particular, it has been noted that an average invertebrate species of the Phanerozoic has lasted about six or seven million years. If an advanced form like a trilobite or brachiopod evolved from a primitive ancestor, so the argument goes, a large number of intermediate species, each grading into the next, would have to be positioned end-to-end to accomplish the transition. If an average species existed for six or seven million years, an enormous span of Precambrian time would have been required.

What is now recognized is that the tempo of evolution is highly irregular. Change occurs in fits and starts. There is, in fact, much evidence that species that are well established evolve quite slowly. Most change in the history of life is associated with evolutionary branching, taking place in small populations that diverge rapidly into distinctive new species. These branching events, which occur instantly on a geologic scale of time and in restricted locations, are seldom documented by fossil data. However, there exists evidence of such a process in the recent geologic past. Geographic and geologic data reveal that a number of quite distinctive new animal and plant species arose in local regions as the Earth's climate changed near the end of the last ice age, 10,000–20,000 years ago. In general, having been

Traditional view of evolution (left) postulates the appearance of an advanced form of Cambrian invertebrate life through a long chain of intermediates from a primitive Precambrian ancestor. Recent concepts recognize the role of evolutionary branching (opposite page), in which small populations of established species take advantage of readily available habitats to diversify almost instantly on a geologic scale of time. Though many of these "experiments" prove unsuccessful and become extinct, some expand into distinctive new species.

rapid branching evolution

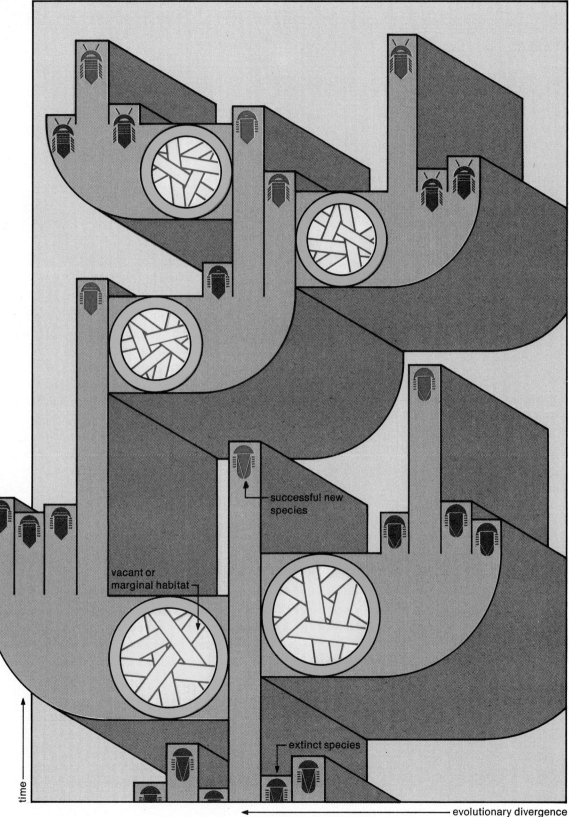

successful new
species

vacant or
marginal habitat

extinct species

time

evolutionary divergence

Cambrian fossils include snails, or gastropod mollusks, such as the specimen from Wisconsin limestone at right. The brown cowrie (above) survives as a modern counterpart.

Burgess Shale deposits in British Columbia provide unique glimpses of many soft-bodied marine animals of the Cambrian Period. The fossil below, a polychaete annelid worm, is preserved as a carbon film on the shale surface.

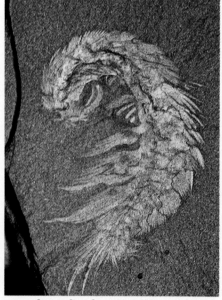

modified through diverse mutations, small populations of established species in nature are constantly "tested" in marginal habitats, but only rarely does one diverge rapidly and expand successfully into a distinctive new species. One would expect the establishment of new species to be especially frequent, and to accomplish especially large adaptive transitions, when there are few predators and competitors to thwart small populations that have the potential to expand. Late in the Cryptozoic, more than at any time during the Phanerozoic, vast habitats lay barren of higher life and available for occupancy. Under such conditions it is not surprising that multicellular forms, when they finally appeared, underwent dramatic diversification. Nothing stood in the way of rapid, stepwise evolutionary branching. Thus, this new view of evolution, which has gained popularity only during the mid-1970s, offers a partial solution to the "Cambrian Problem."

New skeletal fossils

Not only can the pace of large-scale evolution proceed more rapidly than has generally been recognized, but there is now evidence that the proliferation of multicellular groups took place during a substantial period of time. Although it is true that in many local stratigraphic sequences (chronologically successive layers of rock) the earliest fossil occurrence of multicellular life is in assemblages containing members of more than one phylum, careful unraveling has begun to reveal discrete stages of evolution and the sequential appearance of major groups.

Traditionally, trilobites were taken to be the founders of the Cambrian; the level at which the first trilobites were found in a local region was designated as the base of the Cambrian. During the past decade, however, the "trilobites first" idea has been turned into myth. First in the Soviet Union and later in other parts of the world, a new geologic stage, called the Tommotian, has been recognized at the base of the Cambrian. This stage, which spans about ten million years, has yielded a diverse collection of small, shelled animals.

Among its species are snails, sponges, brachiopods, and many forms belonging to extinct groups of uncertain affinity. Many groups of animals represented in the Tommotian have not been found in younger stages of the Cambrian, but those that have include trilobites, echinoderms, new classes of mollusks, and other forms. Thus, the important fossil groups of the Cambrian do not make their appearances concurrently, but in stages spanning an interval of perhaps 70 million years.

One of the general evolutionary trends is toward increase in body size. Few Tommotian species are larger than a few millimeters in maximum dimension. It is partly for this reason that Tommotian animal life remained undiscovered until a few years ago. By contrast, younger Cambrian collections include large fossils along with ones the size of Tommotian species.

Trace fossils

The creatures just described consist of animals with skeletons. As significant as the discovery of these assemblages has been the discovery of even older fossils representing multicellular marine organisms that lacked skeletons. Many of these, called trace fossils, consist of tracks, trails, and burrows formed by the movements of soft-bodied denizens of the seafloor. The kind of animal that created a particular kind of trace fossil is often only generally identifiable, being recognized, for example, as a wormlike animal or an arthropod. Occasionally more specific identification is possible.

A few years ago it was recognized that trace fossils might provide a solution to the debate about the appearance of animals with skeletons in the earlier, or Lower, Cambrian. If trace fossils were found in the later, or Upper, Precambrian, well below the first collections of skeletal fossils, the implication would be that the appearance of skeletal fossils in the Cambrian reflected the sudden evolution of skeletons in groups that had existed in soft-bodied form for some time. On the other hand, if the record of trace fossils was found to originate only slightly earlier than that of skeletal fossils, near the Precambrian-Cambrian boundary, the implication would be that multicellular life in general arose at about this time and that the appearance of skeletons was simply a part of the general proliferation of invertebrates.

The initial search for telltale trace fossils revealed an abundance of trails and burrows in the Lower Cambrian, but none in the Precambrian. It was inferred, therefore, that all early groups of multicellular life—skeletal and nonskeletal—evolved at this time. There seemed to be nothing special about the origin of skeletons. During the past few years more refined studies were undertaken, with a strikingly important result. The general picture has not changed, but the details have. In several parts of the world, sequences of trace fossils have been found slightly below rock strata containing the oldest skeletal fossils. The first trace fossils to appear are small, primitive forms, possibly simple worm tubes. They increase in variety upward into the Cambrian, a trend that seems to represent the initial diversification of life on the seafloor. The appearance of skeletal fossils at the base of the Cambrian simply represents the evolution of skeletons in certain groups of animals a bit later in geologic time. As has already been discussed, the development of skeletons in animals of the Cambrian was spread throughout the Cambri-

Among the commonest of the large variety of mollusks found in Cambrian rock are conical-shelled gastropods called hyolithids (top), which became extinct at the close of the Paleozoic Era about 225 million years ago. (Bottom) A modern shell-less marine gastropod commonly called a sea slug.

199

an, which lasted about 70 million years. Some groups diversified rapidly once they acquired skeletons because skeletons, as sites of muscle attachment and as shields against predation, opened the way to new modes of life.

It is difficult to establish ages for sedimentary rocks of Precambrian and Cambrian age. Whereas it is often assumed that dating methods that exploit the decay of radioactive elements offer accurate dates, this is far from true. One problem is that parent minerals and the decay products of their radioactive components are not preserved perfectly in rocks. Migration and consequent loss of one or both kinds of material often reduce the accuracy of measurement. In addition, measurement of the materials that are present is intrinsically imprecise. Finally, because sedimentary rock derives from rocks of diverse earlier origins, one can ascertain only indirectly when the sediment was laid down, by analyzing associated igneous rocks or rock fragments. Trace fossils cannot be assigned to particular species or genera, so they are of little value in dating rocks. Skeletal fossils are more useful, but are too rare in the lowest Cambrian to be of great value. Another problem is introduced by the tendency for skeletal fossils to occur in limestones and related carbonate rocks, whereas trace fossils are generally visible only in sandstones and mudstones. This situation makes difficult their relative placement in geologic time.

For all of these reasons the establishment of a synchronous Lower Cambrian boundary throughout the world is impossible. Only rough approximations can be made. Still, it seems evident that trace fossils generally precede skeletal fossils, and this relationship is in accord with expectations based on biological inference. Multicellular animals with skeletons generally evolved from other multicellular animals, many of which were soft-bodied. Some of the latter would be expected to have been crawling and burrowing animals of the sort that produce trace fossils.

Fossil imprints

In addition to the kinds of fossils already described, fossils of another variety have played a particularly important role in the recent expansion of information about the origin of multicellular life. These are the imprints of soft-bodied animals. In the late 1940s and 1950s a remarkable collection of imprints was found in sandstone in the Ediacara Hills of Australia. Nearly 30 species were recognized, including a few of uncertain biological relationships. Many of the recognizable forms are jellyfish or other coelenterates related to sea pens. Other members appear to be roughly intermediate in form between annelid worms and arthropods. The Ediacara fossils are of uncertain age but are positioned in the strata well below the oldest trilobites of the region, suggesting that they should be assigned to the latest Precambrian. Similar collections have been found on other continents. Most are less diverse and consist only of jellyfish. A collection discovered in Newfoundland consists of jellyfish and an extraordinary variety of sea pens.

Although the Ediacara collection and its equivalents on other continents seem for the most part to be of Precambrian age, they may span a considerable interval of time, perhaps extending into the earliest Cambrian. The composition of these assemblages is compatible with other fossil evidence.

The feather duster (top), a contemporary polychaete worm, bears some resemblance to its fossil polychaete relative from Burgess Shale (bottom).

(Top) Bob Evans—Peter Arnold; (bottom) National Museum of Natural History, Smithsonian Institution

200

Jellyfish and other coelenterates, which are the dominant elements, are among the most primitive of all invertebrate multicellular animals. Annelid worms, which must have formed many of the late Precambrian trace fossils, clearly gave rise to arthropods before the start of the Cambrian, because Lower Cambrian trilobites are relatively complex arthropods. The discovery of Ediacara fossils having shapes generally intermediate between those of annelid worms and arthropods is hardly surprising.

Adaptive radiation

The general picture that has taken form in the past few years, then, is of what is called adaptive radiation. This pattern, referred to earlier as explosive evolution, amounts to rapid diversification, with one or a few kinds of ancestral organisms evolving into a wide variety of forms. What is unique about the adaptive radiation that began toward the end of the Precambrian is that it represented the initial adaptive radiation of modern multicellular life.

At present it is not possible to establish the sequence of events that this dramatic episode of evolution comprises. As far as is known, the earliest

Wormlike animals of the Precambrian left burrows in the muddy seafloor that later became fossilized (upper left). Sandstone from the Ediacara Hills in Australia carries imprints of nearly 30 species of soft-bodied animals that probably lived during the latest Precambrian. These include coelenterates related to modern sea pens (upper right) and jellyfish (fossil and living counterparts, lower left and right).

201

phase yielded only trace fossils. It is particularly significant that, despite much searching, trace fossils have not been identified with certainty in rocks definitely older than latest Precambrian. One or two possible exceptions have recently been brought to light, but, in the past, similar possible exceptions were always eliminated upon closer inspection. A reasonable estimate would be that the most ancient collections of trace fossils are no older than about 700 million years.

Adaptive radiation continued into the Cambrian, with skeletonization forming but one part of the pattern. Hard skeletons evolved at different times in different groups. Most of the major skeletonized classes of Cambrian animals that are currently recognized probably appeared during an interval of less than 50 million years, beginning at about the start of the Cambrian. Very few skeletal fossils are now recognized in rocks that are regarded as latest Precambrian in age.

The Cambrian explosion of invertebrate life that has been documented during the past decade was no more rapid than subsequent adaptive radiations of the Phanerozoic. A particularly well-documented later radiation is the proliferation of mammals that began at the start of the Cenozoic Era, about 63 million years ago. At this time, the mammals were inheriting the land from the dinosaurs, which had suddenly gone extinct at the close of the preceding era, the Mesozoic. At the beginning of the Cenozoic, only a few groups of small, primitive mammals were in existence. Yet, within only about 12 million years, most of the modern orders of mammals appeared, ranging in form from small flying bats to enormous marine whales. The Cambrian explosion produced perhaps a greater variety of life, but also spanned a much longer interval of time. Neither radiation is difficult to comprehend now that it is recognized that very rapid branching evolution can occur within small populations, as new species rapidly bud off from old ones in the process of occupying new habitats.

A basic difference is that early Cenozoic mammals inherited a world that mass extinction had left vacant for their occupancy. Small mammals had existed for millions of years before their great radiation and had possessed the biological potential to expand, but were thwarted from doing so by the presence of the well-established dinosaurs. Late Precambrian invertebrates, in contrast, took possession of marine habitats never before occupied. It would seem that, for them, simply the attainment of a certain level of biological organization was what triggered explosive evolution. Why it took so long for this level of organization to evolve is the major question that remains.

Timing of invertebrate origins

The Earth existed for nearly four billion years before invertebrate life underwent its great initial adaptive radiation. The explanation for this delay has often been sought in some inhospitability of the physical environment. In particular, it has been hypothesized that until shortly before the Cambrian, the partial pressure of oxygen in the atmosphere was too low to support higher life. This idea is currently favored by some scientists, though it has little factual support. Critics of this idea point to the apparent existence of abundant photosynthetic blue-green algae for a long interval of time before

Living terrestrial onychophoran (bottom) appears remarkably little changed from the image of its Cambrian marine relative (top) captured in Burgess Shale. In evolutionary development onychophorans are considered intermediate between annelid worms and arthropods.

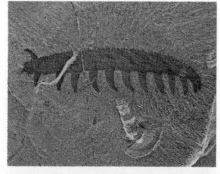

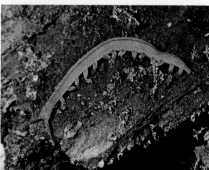

(Top) Charles R. Belinky—Photo Researchers; (center) Manfred Kage—Peter Arnold; (bottom) courtesy, Andrew H. Knoll and Elso S. Barghoorn

the Cambrian. If these organisms had been releasing oxygen into the atmosphere for hundreds of millions of years, it is difficult to imagine how the level of oxygen in the late Precambrian could have been very much lower than that of the present.

The biological characteristics of blue-green algae and bacteria, which constitute a class of especially primitive organisms known as procaryotes, have given rise to another hypothesis that has some current adherents. The procaryotes differ from all higher organisms in their lack of a nucleus and discrete chromosomes. They are basically asexual organisms that exchange genetic material only to a limited degree. In higher organisms, the eucaryotes, sexual reproduction serves the function of shuffling genetic material; this shuffling produces most of the variability upon which natural selection operates. It has been suggested that the evolutionary origin of sexuality triggered the Cambrian explosion.

Clearly, until the eucaryotic cell existed, multicellular organisms could not evolve, for procaryotes never evolved truly multicellular body plans. The question is when the eucaryotic cell actually arose. Identification of fossil remains leaves no doubt that procaryotes were in existence more than three billion years ago. It has been alleged that some cells which left records in fine-grained rocks 1.5 billion–2 billion years old were eucaryotes. The large size and complex wall structures of these cells have led to this suggestion, but the actual identity of the cells is still being debated.

It must be conceded that, even if eucaryotic cells arose long before the Cambrian, it is possible that they did not reproduce sexually until shortly before the Cambrian. However, if the presence of eucaryotic cells long before the Cambrian does come to be recognized, it would seem prudent to consider factors other than the origin of sexuality that might have delayed the explosion of invertebrate life.

The Cropping Principle

One possibility is that the interaction of procaryotic algae and their Precambrian environment was self-limiting in an evolutionary sense. The basis for this suggestion is what can be called the Cropping Principle of ecology. This principle is perhaps best explained through the use of an example. A single kind of grass, if planted in a suitable environment, watered, and fertilized, can virtually exclude weeds. If sheep are introduced to the environment and they proceed to crop the grass, pulling some of it up by the roots and leaving bare patches, then weeds will quickly invade. Continued grazing upon grass and weeds is likely to allow many species to coexist where only one existed in the absence of predation by the sheep.

The Cropping Principle can be formulated more generally by simply stating that predation can increase the number of species coexisting within a habitat. In the absence of a predator (or some other agent of heavy mortality), species having access to a particular habitat tend to compete intensively, with one species often winning out. It has been shown mathematically, in fact, that the number of species able to coexist in the absence of cropping, or some equivalent form of disturbance, is equal to the number of environmental resources, like space or nutrients, that are being used by the poten-

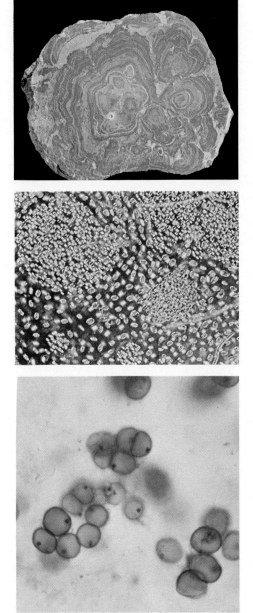

Procaryotic blue-green algae presumably similar to modern varieties (center) carpeted the Precambrian seafloor in vast layered mats, which became fossilized as three-dimensional structures called stromatolites (top). Alga-like bodies from Australian chert nearly a billion years old (bottom) are thought by some scientists to be among the earliest known fossils of eucaryotic cells.

203

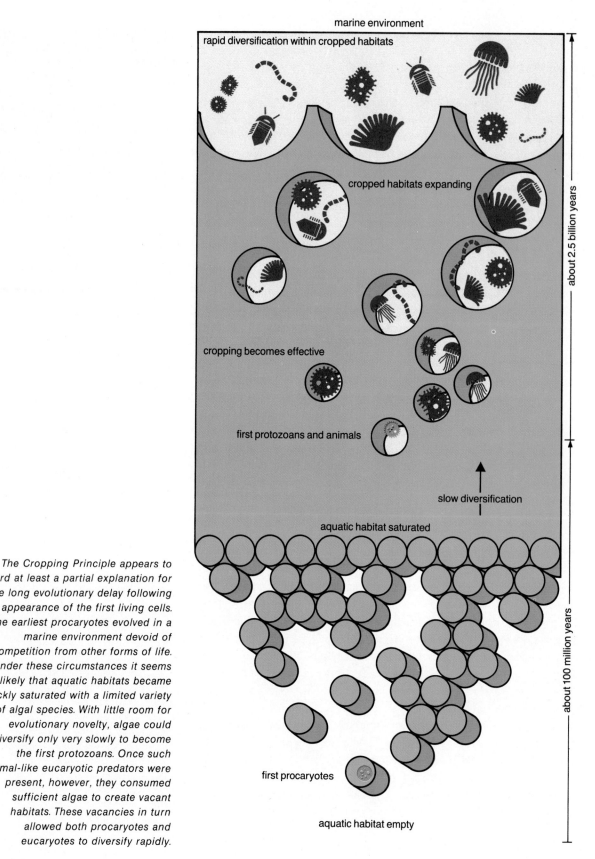

marine environment

rapid diversification within cropped habitats

cropped habitats expanding

about 2.5 billion years

cropping becomes effective

first protozoans and animals

slow diversification

aquatic habitat saturated

first procaryotes

about 100 million years

aquatic habitat empty

The Cropping Principle appears to afford at least a partial explanation for the long evolutionary delay following appearance of the first living cells. The earliest procaryotes evolved in a marine environment devoid of competition from other forms of life. Under these circumstances it seems likely that aquatic habitats became quickly saturated with a limited variety of algal species. With little room for evolutionary novelty, algae could diversify only very slowly to become the first protozoans. Once such animal-like eucaryotic predators were present, however, they consumed sufficient algae to create vacant habitats. These vacancies in turn allowed both procaryotes and eucaryotes to diversify rapidly.

tial competitors. If human beings could transport themselves back to some late Precambrian time when no animal yet existed, they would discover a world devoid of the kind of predation with which they were familiar. Presumably in this world without animals and animal-like protozoans, algae multiplied to limits determined by the supply of resources, like phosphorus and nitrogen. It seems likely, then, that aquatic habitats were saturated by a few kinds of algae, with little room for other varieties. Only occasionally, when a markedly new adaptation arose, would a new kind of organism find a place in the system.

What may have existed was a kind of "catch-22." Protozoans, and ultimately animals, had to evolve from algae, yet algae could diversify only very slowly until protozoans and animals were present to crop them. When after a long delay protozoans and animals finally evolved, they diversified rapidly in the cropped vacancies that awaited them. The Cropping Principle may offer at least a partial explanation for the long delay either in the evolution of eucaryotic cells from procaryotes or in the transition from eucaryotic algae to animal-like creatures.

Unfortunately, as noted above, analysis of Precambrian algae falls short of establishing when eucaryotic cells originated. One thing that the record does reveal is that blue-green algae were extremely abundant on the Precambrian seafloor before the appearance of animal life, which now keeps them in check. If not eaten or disrupted by animals, certain kinds of blue-green algae form mats on the seafloor. They trap and bind sand and mud, grow up through it, and trap and bind more sand and mud, forming three-dimensional layered structures called stromatolites that are readily preserved in the rock record. In Precambrian seas, stromatolites carpeted large tracts of shallow seafloor. Since the Cambrian, however, stromatolites have survived in few places other than supratidal zones, narrow bands of environment between land and sea that are hospitable to few animals of either the terrestrial or the marine realm. It is likely that the first animal-like protozoans arose from floating algae, rather than from algae growing on the seafloor. Even so, the manner in which algae of the seafloor flourished in the absence of cropping by animals provides an idea of the way in which floating algae may have saturated Precambrian lakes and oceans.

The next challenge

Investigations now in progress on many continents continue to shed light on the diversification of the earliest invertebrate animals, but the exciting revelations of the past decade seem to have revealed the basic pattern. Far more uncertain is the evolution of algae during the Precambrian. There is little question that blue-green algae orginated long before the Cambrian. When the eucaryotic cell evolved is currently the subject of heated debate. Here the fossil record is sketchy. Convincing evidence may be available within a decade, or may elude the efforts of science forever.

Manfred Kage—Peter Arnold

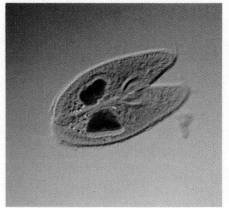

Two protozoans of the genus Paramecium *exchange genetic material by means of a natural sexual process called conjugation. Until such eucaryotic cells existed on Earth truly multicellular organisms could not evolve. When the evolution of eucaryotes occurred is a question currently challenging many scientists.*

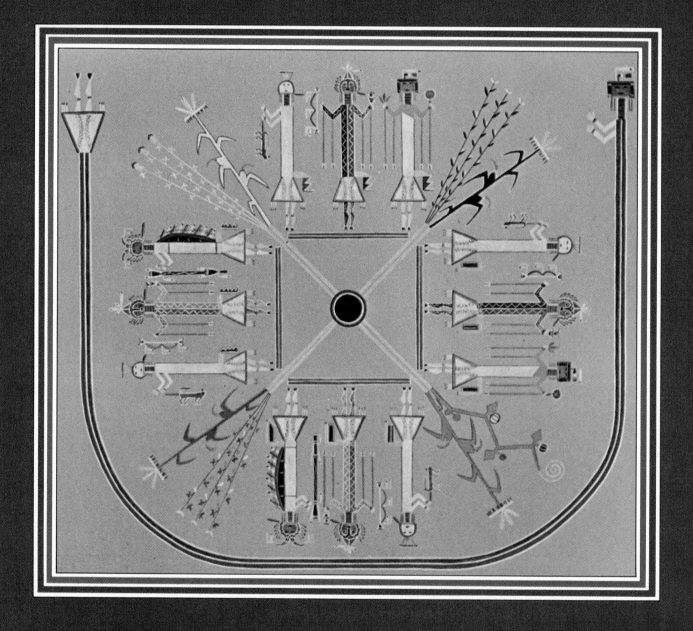

The Science of Native Americans
by Richard I. Ford

To explain the natural phenomena around him, the Native American developed a science which, unlike that of the modern West, envisioned man as an integral part of a harmoniously patterned universe.

Time has erased the commonplace beginnings of Western science. Lost are the disconnected observations of nature by technologically simple cultures that were the genesis of the science we know today. Although Native American traditions are not ancestral to Western culture, their world views are analogous to the European and western Asian folk beliefs that underpin Western thought. From them we can discern the history of science, gain new scientific information, and discover the bases of cultural differences in attitudes toward nature.

Western science and ethnoscience
Broadly defined, science is the description and explanation of natural phenomena. Western science follows conventional procedures for rationalizing empirical observations, postulates general laws for predicting and interpreting results, depends upon institutionalized education and formal communications networks for disseminating conclusions, and pursues a goal of advancing mankind. It is highly organized, dependent upon delicate

Native American in traditional costume. (Overleaf) Navajo sand painting from the Night Way Ceremony. Gods invited to attend the ceremony stand on rainbow bars around the sacred, never-failing lake, from which grow corn, beans, and other plants. Surrounding the painting is the protecting rainbow, represented as wearing a blue dancer's mask.

RICHARD I. FORD *is Director of the Museum of Anthropology and Professor of Anthropology and Botany at the University of Michigan, Ann Arbor.*

(Overleaf) The Wheelwright Museum

instrumentation and precise measurement, and open to alternative explanations. As it evolved, Western science replaced religious dogma as the dominant mode of explaining observed phenomena. It is subdivided into a multitude of specialized fields, and while scientific results are admired by the public, scientific methods are practiced only by trained specialists. In most of these respects, Western science differs from folk science.

Every culture has logical and internally consistent tenets for ordering objects in the universe and for explaining the world around it; each has its own science. The field of study known as ethnoscience attempts to discover the knowledge and metaphysics of different cultures, including the folk beliefs of our own. Casual observations about such beliefs can be found even in ancient manuscripts, but systematic research in the field did not begin until the 19th and early 20th centuries. The first scientific publication with an "ethno" prefix, on ethnoconchology, appeared in 1889, and the first attempts to define and delineate a distinctive subject came in 1895 when John W. Harshberger, a noted botanist, coined and described ethnobotany. Since then, ethnosciences have expanded rapidly in number and scope, primarily in North America where more than 1,500 publications on Indian science are now available.

Despite its brief history, ethnoscience subsumes two different perspectives. The first, which is the oldest and most popular, describes the uses of natural resources by non-Western people. The second, more anthropological and linguistic in orientation, attempts to explain folk ontology and cosmology primarily by ascertaining verbal classifications for ordering natural phenomena, rather than by focusing on actual behavior. Both approaches are essential if Native American scientific contributions are to receive the recognition they deserve.

In traditional societies the way people describe and explain the universe is inseparable from their world view; science is embedded in the culture. Folk science beliefs form a closed system that does not recognize alternative explanations, even those of a neighboring culture. Given their metaphysics, the way in which these peoples solve problems demonstrates that their logical processes and mental faculties are equivalent to those of Western man. At the same time, folk cultures do not approach problems as Westerners do, through cause-and-effect relationships or by experimentation. Instead, they emphasize the recognition and restoration of a pattern of harmony among all elements in the world, as determined through reflection and the human senses. Events in a person's life are explained with reference to personal relations between the observer and physical objects, which are seen as possessing qualities that usually bear little relation to their inherent physical, chemical, or biological properties. In some instances a non-Western science may reach conclusions similar to those of Western science. In other respects, they cannot be compared.

While each native North American culture has its own distinctive science, there are general metaphysical principles that are widely shared throughout the continent. Humans are not separated from nature, and nature is not simply for human manipulation. Instead, humans are products of natural or spiritual forces that created and continue to govern the world. As such,

208

arctic

Greenland
Eskimo

Aleut

subarctic

northwest
coast

Eastern Cree

Sauteau

Nootka

Ojibwa

Malecite

Penobscot

plateau

plateau

Arikara

plains

Cayuga
Seneca
Iroquois

Wyandot

basin

Pawnee

northeast

california

Hopi   Navajo

Kiowa

Pueblo

Cahuilla

Tewa

southeast

southwest

Principal native North American culture areas.

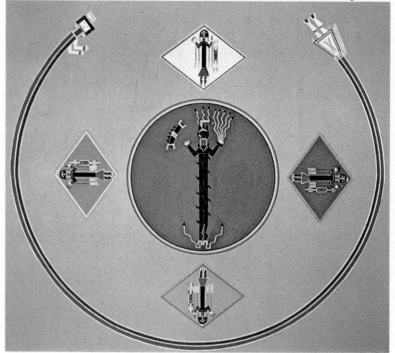

The number four holds considerable significance for the Native American ordering of space and time. In this sand painting from the Navajo Night Way Ceremony, the four directions are indicated by different colored stars, each with a fire god. The Slayer of Enemy Gods appears in the center against a blue Sun.

humans are part of nature and under the influence of these forces. Only thoughts and actions that disrupt the basic harmony of the world order are detrimental. As the most intelligent beings in this world, humans have power, which they learn from various spirits, to influence nature and to restore equilibrium. Abuse of power may invite disaster for the individual, society, or even the world. Spiritual forces will assist humans to survive, but in return humans must be mindful of their responsibility to other forms of life and to the spirits present in nature. Based on these abstract ideas, specific events are explained and universal order is preserved.

The ordering of space

Communication within the international scientific community would be impossible without common standards of measurement for distance, area, and volume. The conceptual importance of space in Western science, however, is relatively recent. Most cultures, and Native Americans are no exception, recognize space in descriptions of their world, but the units of measurement follow local custom, and cross-cultural similarities are infrequent.

The metaphorical meaning of space for Native Americans is more complex than first impressions may indicate. Social relations and ideas have locations within their cultural space. The position a person occupies in a social network or his physical place relative to sacred areas or territorial markers is more significant than a mathematical description. Furthermore, for many Native American cultures, where an object is or where an event occurs has more meaning than what it is or when it happened.

In Native America the axial dimensions of the universe are deduced from the position of a person who stands facing the rising Sun. The four cardinal directions are defined with reference to this person—front, behind, right, left.

210

These directions form the order of space and give significance to the number four. Thus, in contrast to Western thought, space is anthropocentric.

This is illustrated by the Tewa pueblos in the Southwest culture area. As Alfonso Ortiz explains in *The Tewa World*, this world is defined by a sacred mountain and lake, a sacred mesa, and a shrine, each located along a cardinal direction as one moves toward the village. The pueblo, like the universe, is rectangular, with a sacred center opening into the world below. Other ceremonial locations divide the countryside into different types of space. Each of the sacred places designated by a cardinal direction is associated with various spirits and may be approached only by the holders of specific ritual positions.

Moreover, the Tewa world is differentiated into zones based on the resources they contain, and accessibility to these areas is restricted according to age, sex, and social position. Children are limited to land adjacent to the village, and unaccompanied women to farms and fringing prairie. Men range to distant hills and mountainsides, but only male ceremonialists may collect medicinal plants from the four sacred mountain peaks.

Among most groups, the names given to physical features within the tribal territories have cultural significance, serving as a reminder that the physical formations were created during mythological time and remain as enduring embodiments of myth and legend. Equally important, they are material

Far removed from the expanding galaxies and light-year distances of Western science, the Native American orients his universe with reference to a man facing the rising Sun.

Dan Morrill

evidence of the great powers inherent in spiritual forces. Indians travel with reference to the cardinal directions and from one named place to the next. Distance is usually calculated by the number of nights that have elapsed on a long trip or by the position of the Sun on a one-day journey. There are no abstract numerical measures analogous to the mile, kilometer, or other similar standard.

Shorter measurements are based on human body parts or comparison with everyday objects. For example, the finger joint, handbreadth, leg, single and double arm reach, and pace are employed singly or in combination throughout the continent. Other lengths are based upon familiar materials. The Arikara of the upper Missouri River prairie region have standard lengths consisting of dried strips of squash that span the outstretched arms and braids of corncobs that extend from a woman's waist to her foot and back. These criteria of length form the basis for intertribal trade and for appraisals of agricultural productivity.

Area is determined by comparison with familiar objects or places with constant boundaries, such as a tipi or a lake. For some purposes, however, such as deciding where to hunt or collect food, two-dimensional area is not as meaningful as an assessment of the available resources. Thus land or forest may be measured not by area but by an estimate of the yield.

Volume is measured with reference to containers of traditional size. Coiled and wicker baskets of prescribed height and diameter are used throughout the Southwest and California. On the Plains the basic unit is the parfleche or rawhide carrying bag. Yield from farmland is reckoned not in baskets or bushels but according to the fullness of a Pueblo storeroom or of a subterranean storage pit used by Prairie villages.

Quantity is described by counting or by reference to groupings or patterns. On the Northwest Coast the counting system is based on the number 20; elsewhere systems based on 5 or 10 are standard. Although it is possible to count to large numbers, this is rarely done, since terms for groupings, such as a *herd* of bison, are more practical. Indians in the Great Lakes region employ cardinal, ordinal, multiplicative, and distributive terms in their mathematical systems.

The number four is frequently used in estimating long intervals of time or for spatializing time. The Tewa submerge time into space by referring to 4 paces as historical time within their world and 12 paces for distances traveled in mythological time. The number four and multiples of four are essential elements in rituals and sacred formulas. Four plants compose a medicine, which is taken four times a day for four days. A ceremony may require 12 days to prepare, and dances are repeated four times.

A different view of time

Time is the essential organizing principle in the lives of most Westerners. Thus, English expresses time by means of verb tenses, as well as by a rich vocabulary indicating duration, occasion, age, season, and schedules. In contrast, preoccupation with time in thought or action is alien to Native Americans. The expression of time does not figure prominently in their languages, and daily activities are not scheduled by such divisions as hours

212

and minutes. Furthermore, time is not conceptualized as a linear continuum; instead, it is discontinuous from one culturally recognized event to the next.

Two assumptions permit a culture to reckon and to predict time. The first recognizes that certain natural events are repetitious; the rising of the Sun or the arrival of migratory birds are examples of such phenomena. The second acknowledges that the biological growth of plants, animals, and people and the social positions of individuals following rites of passage are irreversible. Consequently, the bodily development of a person or initiation into a secret society is an indicator of age and elapsed time. Obviously, each reference results in a relative time scale.

Past time of any duration is either mythological or historical. Mythological time happened beyond personal memory, the recollections of kinsmen, or the completion of the present world. It was a time when giants and monsters walked the newly formed Earth, when the spirits' acts of heroism were preserved as landforms that are still recognizable, and when the physical forms of plants and animals differed from those of today. For the Ojibwa it was before rose bushes almost became extinct because they lacked thorns for protection. It was then that Nanabush, the culture hero, who aided the defenseless roses, permanently scarred the bark of the white birch for causing him grief.

Historical time is marked by unusual natural events and memorable personal experiences. It is recalled sequentially by reference to a great battle, a pronouncement of a tribal elder, perhaps the birth of a child. Unlike mythological time, which is revealed by reciting myths and legends and by the presence of unusual geologic formations, historical time is sometimes recorded by painting on hides—as with the famous Plains Indian Winter Counts—or, for shorter periods, by marking sticks in some manner. Not

Landforms, plants, and animals whose forms were changed by the spirits in the remote past serve as reminders of mythological time. Thus the black scars on birchbark recall the punishment visited on the tree by the Ojibwa culture hero.

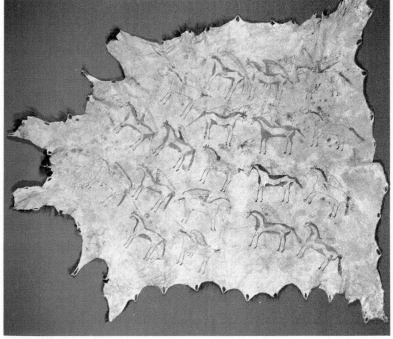

Some Native American groups recorded historic time by such devices as painting on hides. This Cheyenne buffalo robe was executed between 1865 and 1870.

everyone in a culture uses such mnemonics, but all can frame elapsed time with personal stories.

Present time is reckoned by various methods, but all rely on environmental indicators, particularly astronomical and seasonal variations in natural phenomena. Although a few heavenly bodies, such as the Sun and Polaris, are used for directional orientation, the significance of most stars and constellations is to describe mythological events or to reckon present time. Ethnoastronomers are learning that astronomical knowledge varied greatly among Native American groups, depending on the economic pursuits of the society and the settlement pattern of the population.

Days are generally unnamed and are inconsequential. They usually begin with the rising Sun, and any divisions of the day are determined by the Sun's position. Since the Earth is conceptualized as flat and at the center of the universe, the Sun is believed to pass over the Earth in the daytime and under

As in many folk cultures, Native Americans divide time into months, determined by the lunar cycle. Each month is named, usually for a dominant economic activity or seasonal characteristic.

it at night. Nighttime is divided by the presence or position of certain stars. The tabulation of days is actually by nights or "sleeps." The Greenland Eskimos, who for part of the year experience no setting Sun, subdivide the day by tides.

Months are determined by the lunar phases, beginning with either the full or the new Moon. The number of days in each month is unimportant. The months are named, and the names reflect a dominant economic activity or seasonal change. For example, the Ojibwa have, among others, the Wild Goose Moon (April), Strawberry Moon (June), and Wild Rice Moon (September). In the absence of markets or other regularly scheduled communal activities, a seven-day week is generally unknown. If a unit of time approximating a week does occur, it is derived from phases in the lunar cycle. The Wyandots come very close with their four monthly quarters. On the other hand, the Malecites divide the month into nine parts.

As astute observers of their immediate environment, Native Americans quickly relate such signs as the arrival of a migratory bird, the blossoming of a flower, or the appearance of a star with a forthcoming change in weather and in the growth and/or behavior of plants and animals. These sequences of recurrent natural phenomena form the seasons. However, not every tribe has the same number of seasons or relies on the same indicators. Thus the Tewa emphasize two seasons, summer and winter; the Sauteau have five; the Nootka six; and the Eastern Cree eight.

The year is recognized by all Native Americans, but its determination, start, and importance vary enormously. It is almost universally solar, and its length is measured by seasons rather than days or months. In some cases, however, the year may begin with an event such as the winter solstice or the harvest of an important plant that occurs in the middle of a season. The Native Americans recognize the discrepancy between the solar and lunar years and sometimes correct for it. The Malecites, for example, are reported to add a 13th month between July and August when it is needed to bring their months and the seasons into line.

The southward migration of Canada geese heralds the onset of winter. Living close to nature, the Native Americans quickly learned the recurring phenomena that signal the passage of the seasons.

215

A person's chronological age is also relative. A few groups in areas where there are sharp seasonal changes reckon age by the number of winters a person has survived, regardless of the actual birthdate (which more often than not is unknown). In other groups age corresponds with stages of physical growth or social recognition. Old age is related to one's memory of important historical events.

Since formal calendars are unknown in tribal cultures north of Mexico, it is not possible to predict future dates exactly. However, precise predictability is rarely necessary in the small Native American communities. When the need for short-term predictions and scheduling arises, various simple devices serve the purpose. An invitation to a dance in a distant village includes the presentation of a bundle of sticks. The recipient removes one each day until, on the day of the dance, they are exhausted. A traveler leaves a bundle of grass at a designated location. If the next person to come down the trail finds it has wilted, he knows that several days have passed, but if it seems fresh, the interval may be only a few hours.

Plants and animals often serve as scheduling devices. Among the Iroquois, for example, corn is not planted until the white oak leaf is the size of a squirrel's paw. Naturally, this varies from year to year according to the weather, with the result that it reflects actual conditions more accurately than a calendar date. Similarly, Southwest irrigation farmers will not water their

A Tewa elder stands next to a kiva at San Ildefonso, New Mexico. Among groups with no set calendar, a person is reckoned to be old when his memory of past events extends beyond that of most other tribesmen.

Cradoc Bagshaw

fields for four days if the flight of birds and the behavior of horses indicate that rain is imminent.

Nomadic people on the Plains rely on celestial observations to tell them when to gather for ceremonies like the Sun Dance or for cooperative activities. The Pawnee have an elaborate star lore in which each individual and each village is thought to benefit from the powers inherent in certain stars. The earth lodge serves as an observatory for noting the position of the rising Sun and of the stars at night. These determine when the tribe should disband for bison hunting and when the dispersed bands should return to the village. Similarly, isolated Navajo bands assemble for ceremonies according to the position of the stars.

Among farmers in the Southwest and Southeast the Sun is revered as the giver of life and fertility, and observations of the Sun determine the scheduling of agricultural rituals and activities. Special Sun watchers at Hopi and in each Tewa pueblo note the Sun's position as it crosses the horizon. When it reaches specific breaks in the mountains, the signal is given for ceremonies to begin. In the Southeast the Sun is also a calendar for rituals of community well-being. This relationship between the Sun and corn agriculture appears to extend into the distant past. At Cahokia Mounds, an archaeological site near East St. Louis, Illinois, Warren Wittry unearthed a circle of postholes which he interpreted as a woodhenge for observing the Sun.

Rituals serve to remind participants of the essential unity of the universe and at the same time ensure its continued harmony and order. In this Tewa winter dance to awaken the ground, the men dance and chant while the women turn baskets upside down and tell the ground their baskets are empty.

Cradoc Bagshaw

Hundreds of plants known and used by Native Americans have proved valuable to Western man, and others await rediscovery. The jojoba of the arid Southwest, now under intensive study, produces a liquid wax, remarkably similar to sperm oil, which may have a variety of industrial applications.

The classification of being

Every culture, without exception, classifies biological organisms and physical properties into a series of hierarchically ordered categories. Western scientists have formulated inclusive, universal taxonomies which allow for the addition of newly discovered organisms. Folk science taxonomies, on the other hand, are exclusive and concern only those organisms that are known to the local population.

Inquiries into folk beliefs about plants and their uses constitute the oldest branch of ethnoscience. Ethnobotany studies the interrelationships between plant and human populations. It includes the classification of plants, attitudes about them, and how they are used. Although each culture has a separate classification, nomenclature, and identification "key," Native American folk systematics share a fundamental organization.

Brent Berlin and associates of the University of California at Berkeley have established the general principles of folk classification. Plants are recognized as a category of immobile living things distinct from animals and humans, although, curiously, many Indian languages lack a single, collective term for them. Within this category, plants are organized into four hierarchical levels. The most inclusive, which Berlin calls life forms, groups plants according to visually gross morphological characteristics; *e.g.*, trees and grass. At the next level, called generics, plants are subdivided according to differences identifiable by sight, touch, and even taste. The most exclusive levels, specific and varietal, consist of plants that are very important to the culture. Plants that are unimportant, such as fungi in the Southwest, are underdifferentiated, while the most important economic plants have many more names than in Western systematics. In practice, there is a high degree of correspondence between the folk and the Western systems, although, since they are designed to be universal, Western scientific classifications have many more subdivisions.

218

Native Americans also classify plants according to attributes unrelated to their biological properties. The Navajo and Plains tribes assign plants, along with other objects, to male and female categories for conceptual reasons unrelated to actual gender. The Tewa classify plants into "hot" and "cold" categories that relate to rituals, food, and medicine rather than to physical temperature. Some special-purpose classifications bring together plants belonging to different life forms; *e.g.*, "firewood." Behind these classifications lies the belief that all things have spirits or souls, so it is not contradictory to group together plants, animals, minerals, heavenly bodies, cardinal directions, and even colors.

The importance of plants to Native Americans cannot be underestimated, and their knowledge of a vast array of food and medicinal plants has greatly benefited Western man. *American Indian Medicine* by Virgil J. Vogel lists almost 200 plants whose efficacy has warranted their inclusion in the *National Formulary* and the *Pharmacopoeia of the United States of America*. Hundreds more that are recognized as effective by Indians are

Native Americans endowed animals with anthropomorphic traits and believed they had close relationships with humans. The bear, with its seemingly human ways, was thought to be a friend and teacher. To the Kiowa the prairie dog, associated in nature with the rattlesnake, was a source of snakebite medicine.

referenced in Daniel E. Moerman's *American Medical Ethnobotany*. Although still largely untested, many of the indigenous food plants may well have potential for nurturing a hungry world. The edible jojoba also has commercial value for its liquid wax. Even seemingly useless plants may be rendered digestible by using Indian methods of preparation.

The principles of folk classification used for plants also apply to animals. Unlike plants, however, animals are conceived as having anthropomorphic features, behavior, and social organization. Many animals are thought to have personal relationships with people, as friends or as sources of disease and evil. Across much of the northern part of the continent, animals are sought in vision and prayer for the personal protection they can bestow. The comparatively humanlike bear can teach new uses of plants and, through its spirit, can help people be cured. Other animals are linked in a friend-enemy duality. Prairie dogs, which live with rattlesnakes, are thought by the Kiowa to be a source of snakebite medicine. In Navajo thought, morphologically dissimilar but ecologically associated animals, like insects and bats, are classified together in religious contexts.

Lacking scientific methods and instruments, the Indians nevertheless gained considerable knowledge of anatomy and physiology through observation based on a cultural logic. From butchering animals, autopsying dogs, and dissecting sea otters, which are believed to have descended from humans, the Aleuts developed a detailed anatomical terminology and an accurate understanding of bone growth and the circulation of blood. The comprehensive *Navajo Ethno Medical Encyclopaedia* (in process), directed by Carl Gorman, Martha Austin, and Oswald Werner, demonstrates a thorough appreciation for physiological processes within the context of Navajo beliefs about life and the constitution of balance in the world.

At the same time it is inaccurate to bestow a Noble Savage image on the Indian and to ascribe to him unfailing knowledge about nature. The Cayuga, for instance, believe that the song of the spring peeper, a small tree toad, is made by the newt. And the Penobscot reportedly recognize that a frog develops from a tadpole but are ignorant of the life cycle of the toad. Some tribes, such as the Navajo, have a detailed lore about insects, while others ignore all but the most conspicuous or annoying. The role of semen in reproduction is not understood as Western science explains it.

Becoming

The themes discussed so far present a static image of the Native American world; but folk science beliefs are dynamic and can provide an invaluable education in ecology. The origin legend of each Indian culture is a charter for reasoning and living. Each describes the beginnings of the Earth, life, and death. The hierarchical relationships among spirits, humans, animals, and plants suggest the potential for exploitation by man, but higher principles protect all species and result in continuous harmony.

The world does change, mostly as a result of the malevolence and frailty of humans and spiritual beings. Complete disaster is averted because the interrelationship of natural forces and living beings involves mutual causality and the opportunity for correction. Ritual activities replicate the universe, and their performance serves as a constant reminder of its unity. When disharmony and disorder follow inappropriate thoughts or behavior, only the concerted action of intellectuals and ceremonialists can discover the cause, change the course of nature or cure a stricken patient, and restore balance to the world. Beyond communal action, individuals have daily responsibility for the welfare of all beings. Good thoughts and a proper ritual attitude assure good fortune and a long life. If a freak snowfall covers the mountains after a summer dance, Pueblo Indian spectators question what the participants were thinking.

Although no Indian language has a word that means conservation, each culture practices it by following a few basic rules. Need alone does not justify taking another life; how, when, and where this is done are paramount. Thus one takes only the part of the plant one needs. If leaves are sought, the plant is not uprooted. When the Seneca collect a medicinal plant, a gift of tobacco and a prayer are offered to the first plant encountered, the archetype of the species, which is then left to grow while others are picked. Moreover, certain times are considered inappropriate for hunting or collecting. Again the Tewa can serve as an illustration. They do not kill deer during their summer season, with the result that the does and fawns are unmolested and the herd can recover from winter kills. Whenever an animal is killed or a plant taken, a prayer of thanks is given as a respectful reminder that these organisms have a right to life as well.

Some anthropologists and ecologists have asserted that fire has been used indiscriminately by the Indians, though these claims are rarely substantiated. Indians do use fire for cooking, hunting, clearing the land for planting, and encouraging plant growth. These uses, however, are guided by the belief that fire is a deity or the spiritual partner of other beings. Fire is one of the oldest spirits in any Indian pantheon. By means of its smoke, it is the messenger and bearer of gifts from humans to the spirits.

From the Collections of the Oklahoma Historical Society; photo, Fitzgerald and Beals

Depiction of a girls' puberty ceremony was painted on doeskin by an Apache chief, second in command to Geronimo. Each girl, as she dances around the purifying fire, is wrapped in a blanket with an old woman who will be her guardian. Small earth spirits, to the left of the fire, and mountain spirits with tall headdresses attend the ceremony, while other members of the tribe look on.

Fire is closely associated with the Sun. Like the Sun, fire can give and take life, and like the Sun it produces heat and light. Since fertility is partially credited to the Sun, fire is an appropriate tool for use in preparing land for cultivation. Pueblo Indians believe the Sun requires their assistance as it moves from south to north and back each year. The Sun's long journey northward will be successful if people do not insult it by disposing of ashes or by striking fires outdoors at the winter solstice. Thus the misuse of fire is inexcusable; its meaning is culturally defined and its value is understood.

Most groups understand plant succession, and fire is employed by many nonagriculturalists to encourage the growth of valuable plants. Henry T. Lewis, in *Patterns of Indian Burning in California*, shows that fire is used during certain times of the year to stimulate the growth and reproduction of specific plants, and that ritual respect is given to it. Elsewhere in California the Cahuilla burn the fan palm (*Washingtonia filifera*) to rid it of insect pests that are detrimental to the fruit. The available information does not suggest that these uses of fire are wanton, careless, or accidental.

The Indians influence the distribution of North American plants in many ways, and they are responsible for the domestication of several indigenous species. They intervene in the life cycle of economic and ritual plants, in some cases merely tending them, in other cases transplanting them from forest to garden, where they are cultivated and protected. Dispersal does occur accidentally, but mostly it results from deliberate acts. The Hopi, for example, when hoeing their corn, protect the wild tobacco (*Nicotiana attenuata*) which springs up in their fields. This is a pattern that extends back to prehistoric times. Archaeological research in the Midwest by Volney H. Jones and, more recently, by Patty Jo Watson and Richard A. Yarnell verifies that preceramic Archaic farmers domesticated the sunflower (*Helianthus annuus*) and sumpweed (*Iva annua* var. *macrocarpa*), cultivated lamb's-quarter (*Chenopodium bushianum*), and grew maygrass (*Phalaris caroliniana*) in areas well beyond its natural range.

Respect for nature and for life shaped the Native American's interventions in the life cycles of plants. The sunflower was one of the earliest domesticated plants in North America. The Cahuilla of California burned the fan palm to eliminate harmful insects.

Ethnoscience for whom?

Ethnoscience weaves a loose fabric with strands from natural history, ethnology, and linguistics. The research should be scientifically precise, based upon participant observation, and contain folk names and classifications. The majority of ethnoscientific research satisfies this standard. The contradiction is that it is done from the perspective of Western science.

Customarily, folk science publications present utilitarian facts whose distinction is their source in a nonliterate tradition. Such details are interesting for the contrasts with Western science that they provide, the similarities among unlike cultures that they reveal, and the humanitarian potential of new foods or drugs that they offer. Yet they tell us little about the scientific procedures that guide the native people's thoughts and actions.

The ways in which other cultures order the natural world should receive emphasis if ethnoscience is to transcend economic questions and enlighten the dominant culture's understanding of contrasting systems of thought. This requires fluency in a native language, but this is attained only rarely—one reason why Gary Witherspoon's *Language and Art in the Navajo Universe* is so satisfying. At the same time, Native Americans are now attempting to resolve their problems for themselves. By providing new insights into Indian belief systems that order nature and regulate human behavior without sacrificing practical matters, such works as Ortiz' *Tewa World* and Basil Johnson's *Ojibway Heritage* help to build bridges of much-needed understanding.

Each Native American culture has a science, a system of adapting to an environment. The solutions are different from those of Western science, but they are by no means always inferior. If Native Americans are mathematically and technologically unable to send a man to the Moon or to build weapons of mass destruction, neither can they fathom how our culture can ravage the land and life on the continent. Their hope is that when we learn the meaning the world has for Native Americans and respect their philosophy about nature, the more elusive goal of ethnoscience, cultural understanding, will be at hand.

Food, Famine, and Nitrogen Fixation

by Ralph W. F. Hardy

Biological conversion of atmospheric nitrogen into fertilizer is a complex ability shared by a few kinds of primitive organisms. Transfer of this faculty to crop plants could help relieve growing world demands for food.

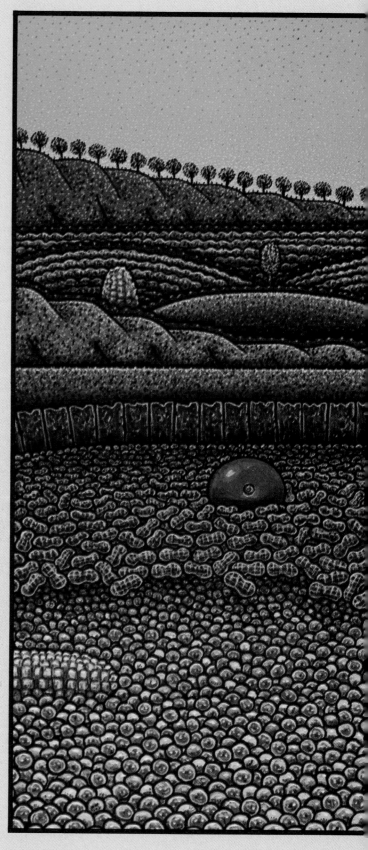

The nitrogen cycle (opposite page) includes conversion of atmospheric nitrogen to ammonia by both symbiotic and free-living microorganisms. Ammonia also enters the soil through the activity of decay organisms on organic compounds. Man's contribution to soil nitrogen takes the form of chemically fixed nitrogen including ammonia and nitrates. Ammonia is removed from the soil by nitrifying bacteria and through assimilation by living plants. Nitrates formed in the nitrification process or added in fertilization may also be taken up by plants or may be returned to gaseous nitrogen through the action of denitrifying bacteria.

RALPH W. F. HARDY *is a Biochemist and Associate Director, Central Research & Development Department, E. I. du Pont de Nemours & Company, Wilmington, Delaware.*

(Overleaf) Painting by Steve Berman. Illustrations by John Draves

The names first given to nitrogen after its discovery in the 18th century were hardly complimentary—"foul air" and "azote," the latter being taken from the Greek, meaning "nonvital" or "without life." These terms seemed appropriate to those early investigators who observed that when oxygen is removed from a sample of air, the gas that remains cannot support the respiration of living organisms. First impressions, however, are often misleading, and scientists eventually realized that this abundant gas was an element in every protein molecule and many other molecules that form living tissues. In fact, so vital is nitrogen in the food of plants and animals that meeting future agricultural demands for nitrogen in fertilizer will most likely mean the difference between enough food for all and a starving world.

It is one of nature's ironies that nitrogen, which in its molecular form (N_2) constitutes nearly 80% of the atmosphere, is yet so scarce in the form of compounds that most living organisms can assimilate. The reason lies in the extreme reluctance of the molecule's two triple-bonded atoms to part company without being forced by the addition of a large quantity of energy. Only after this chemical bond is broken can individual, free nitrogen atoms combine—or be fixed—with atoms of other elements such as hydrogen and oxygen to form compounds, *e.g.*, ammonia (NH_3) and ions of nitrate (NO_3^-), that living organisms can use.

The largest fraction of fixed nitrogen comes from natural, particularly biological, sources. These processes convert less than a ten-millionth of the Earth's atmospheric reserve of 3.5×10^{15} tons of N_2 to fixed nitrogen each year, yet their continuity ensures that plant growth and hence all life is able to continue, because fixed nitrogen is also constantly being depleted by other reactions. Supplementing natural fixation is the high-temperature, high-pressure industrial manufacture of ammonia and related fertilizers, a major world effort that is the largest single agricultural consumer of fossil fuels—0.7% of total fossil fuels in the U.S.—both as starting materials and as a source of heat energy to drive the syntheses reactions.

The cereal grains—such crops as wheat, rice, corn, barley, sorghum, and millet—and the grain legumes—for example, soybeans, peanuts, peas, and beans—are the primary sources of human food and animal feed. Unfortunately, as converters of energy from the Sun, the ultimate source of energy for all life on Earth, these agricultural staples are quite inefficient, with conversion efficiencies of 0.1–0.3%. Nevertheless, these figures represent a near doubling of efficiency during the past 25 years because of various technological advances, probably the most important single factor being a twelve-fold rise in the use of fertilizer nitrogen. To meet the world's needs of AD 2000 it is estimated that cereal grain production must double in the next 20 years while production of grain legumes must quadruple. Improving the energy conversion efficiency of crops through a detailed understanding of nitrogen fixation appears to be a key step toward this goal.

The nitrogen cycle

Atmospheric nitrogen often follows a cycle which includes fixation and two other processes called nitrification and denitrification. There exist many possible ways for nitrogen fixation to occur. These include reactions in which

226

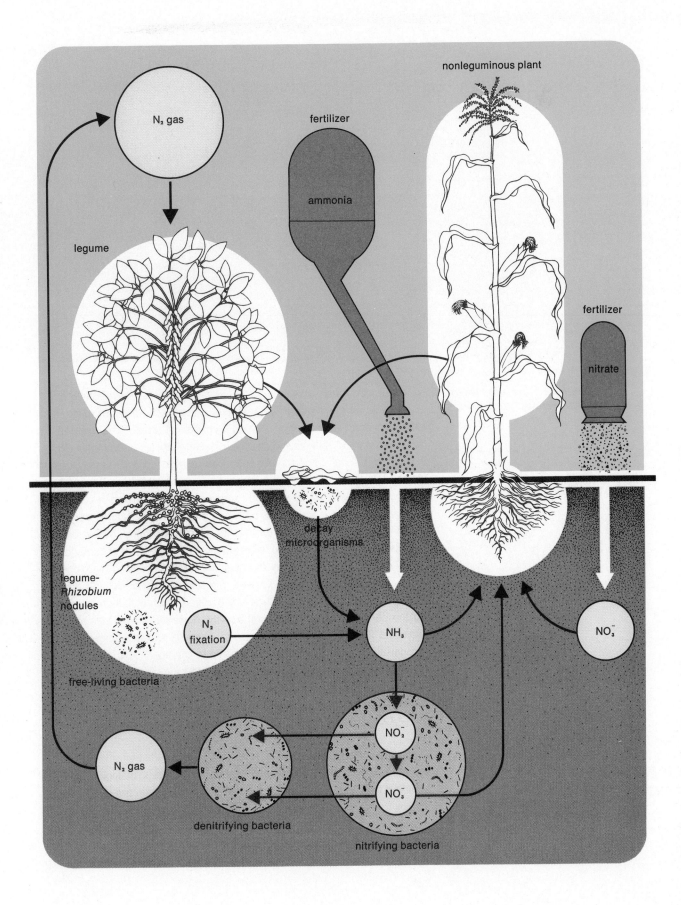

N₂ gas

fertilizer

nonleguminous plant

ammonia

legume

fertilizer

nitrate

legume-
Rhizobium
nodules

decay
microorganisms

free-living bacteria

N₂
fixation

NH₃

NO₃⁻

N₂ gas

NO₂⁻

NO₃⁻

denitrifying bacteria

nitrifying bacteria

nitrogen-fixing organism	free-living organisms				
	 *Clostridium pasteurianum* (bacterium)	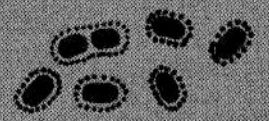 *Klebsiella pneumoniae* (bacterium)	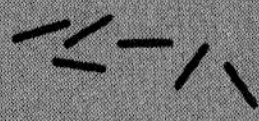 *Azotobacter vinelandii* (bacterium)	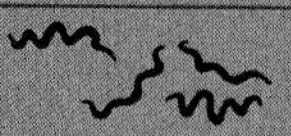 *Rhodospirillum rubrum* (photosynthetic bacterium)	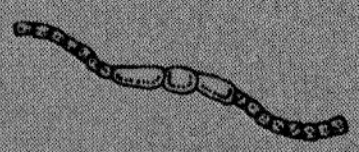 *Anabaena azollae* (photosynthetic blue-green alga)
associated organism	none	lives both free in soils and in association with plants and man	none	none	 *Azolla* (water fern)
significant habitats	anaerobic soils	only under near-anaerobic conditions	aerobic soils, but prefers reduced O_2 concentrations	surface of stagnant, oxygen-deficient pools	in leaf cavities

Nitrogen-fixing organisms include certain forms of bacteria and blue-green algae, some of which are free-living and others symbiotically associated with higher plants. A table of important species appears above.

N_2 loses electrons, or is said to be oxidized, and is converted to such products as nitrate, nitrite (NO_2^-), nitrous oxide (N_2O), or nitric oxide (NO). Other reactions are possible in which N_2 gains electrons, or is reduced, to form such products as diazine (N_2H_2), hydrazine (N_2H_4), or ammonia (NH_3). In practice, the only important nitrogen-fixation reaction and the only known biological one is a reductive process: $N_2 + 6$ electrons $+ 6H^+ \rightarrow 2NH_3$. Through the natural decay of dead organisms and of nitrogen-containing plant and animal wastes, a large portion of fixed nitrogen returns to the soil as ammonia and is eventually assimilated, mostly as nitrate, by the roots of new plant life. Some of it, however, is attacked by other kinds of bacteria that can denitrify it, or reduce it to its molecular form, N_2, and to N_2O, both of which enter the atmosphere. Overall, the natural rate of denitrification is assumed to be equal to the natural rate of nitrogen fixation, thereby balancing the nitrogen cycle. Agricultural activity, however, places demands for additional fixed nitrogen, for harvesting removes with the crop the fixed nitrogen that would otherwise be returned to the soil.

Oxidation of fixed nitrogen in the form of ammonia to nitrate is called nitrification. This reaction occurs rapidly in soils through the action of certain bacteria so that most fertilizer nitrogen applied as ammonia or as urea ($[NH_2]_2CO$) is converted to nitrate prior to uptake by plants.

Biological nitrogen fixers

In nature the major contributor of fixed nitrogen is a single biological process reserved to a few genera of microorganisms that contain the genetic information to synthesize a unique enzyme, called nitrogenase, that catalyzes (speeds up) the conversion of N_2 to ammonia at mild temperatures and normal atmospheric pressure. This group includes certain forms of bacteria and blue-green algae (sometimes called cyanobacteria) that are

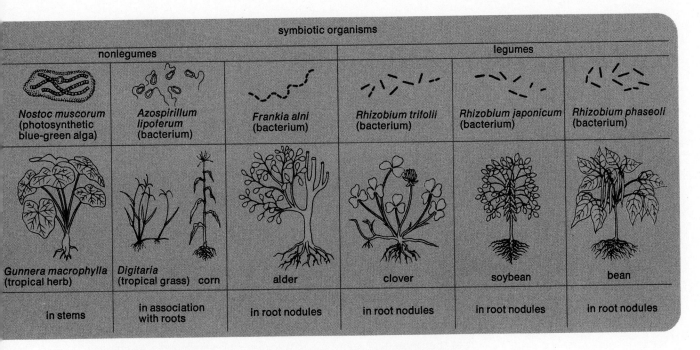

symbiotic organisms					
nonlegumes			**legumes**		
Nostoc muscorum (photosynthetic blue-green alga)	*Azospirillum lipoferum* (bacterium)	*Frankia alni* (bacterium)	*Rhizobium trifolii* (bacterium)	*Rhizobium japonicum* (bacterium)	*Rhizobium phaseoli* (bacterium)
Gunnera macrophylla (tropical herb)	*Digitaria* (tropical grass) corn	alder	clover	soybean	bean
in stems	in association with roots	in root nodules	in root nodules	in root nodules	in root nodules

free-living and others that may form close associations with higher forms of life which are incapable of nitrogen fixation. Some of these microorganisms can function in either mode of existence. Again, some are anaerobes, which can live without oxygen, and a few are photosynthetic, with the ability to manufacture complex organic molecules using energy obtained from light.

There are several important associations between nitrogen-fixing microorganisms and higher plants. The best known is the symbiosis between species of *Rhizobium* bacteria and legumes, resulting in the formation of specialized nodules on the legume roots. This is a most sophisticated relationship, with thousands of bacteria packed within hundreds of membrane-enclosed compartments in each root cell. Another internal association is that of the photosynthetic blue-green alga *Anabaena* within leaf cavities of the water fern *Azolla*. This association is exploited in the Orient as a major natural source of fixed nitrogen for paddy-grown rice by encouraging *Azolla* to flourish in flooded paddies. In each of the above associations, the symbiotic microorganism through its normal metabolic process supplies nitrogen-containing products to its plant partner, enabling it to grow in habitats that are low in fixed nitrogen; in return, it receives nutrients and other essential substances and protection from the plant.

Mainly external associations of nitrogen fixers and nonleguminous plants have been discovered recently in South America. For example, the bacterium *Azospirillum lipoferum* grows on the root surface of the tropical grass *Digitaria* and in association with the roots of corn plants. These findings should be of great importance if future research can encourage reliable symbiotic relationships between nitrogen fixers and nonleguminous cereal grasses like corn and wheat. Another potentially valuable resource, especially for forestry and ecology, is that of a root-nodule association between the bacterium *Frankia* and various trees such as the alder.

229

In general, nitrogen-fixing organisms and the associations that they form have been found to be highly diversified. Hence, the occurrence in all of them of a single biological catalyst, nitrogenase, is somewhat surprising and suggests an early evolution of the gene for nitrogenase and later diversification from a common source by natural genetic engineering. In addition, it is surprising that such an advantageous capability is not more widely distributed unless the drawbacks of nitrogenase, which fixes nitrogen by an inherently energy-wasteful process, made preservation of its genetic information unacceptable in most cases.

Moving toward a golden age

Biologically oriented technologies have been used for centuries to meet the fixed nitrogen needs of world crop production. The plowing of legumes back into the soil (green manuring) and application of such nitrogen-containing wastes as livestock manure date back to biblical times. Use of legumes as green manures is less acceptable today, however, because it takes the land out of cash-crop production for a season. Whereas waste recycling is certainly desirable when economically feasible, it has proved inadequate even in China where it has been maximized.

In the early 20th century inoculation of soil and legume seeds with *Rhizobium* bacterial cultures was begun. It continues to be practiced although in many cases the technology is in need of improvement. One problem to be overcome is the difficulty of introducing a desirable *Rhizobium* strain because of competition from the large number of less favorable strains already present in most agricultural soils.

During the second and third quarters of the 20th century, advances in research included the breeding and selection of crops able to use increased quantities of fixed nitrogen, specifically hybrid corn and dwarf wheats and rices. The more these are fertilized, the greater the yield per acre. Despite continued research efforts, however, legumes in general still show poor response to fertilizer nitrogen, which explains the use of about eight times more fertilizer nitrogen per unit area on U.S. corn than on soybeans.

However useful it has been, the biological process as it presently exists also has limitations. Its extremely high use of energy, as will be described below, makes it at least as energy inefficient as industrial synthesis. In fact, it may be necessary to solve this energy problem before enhancement or extension of the biological process is feasible. In addition, biological fixation provides inadequate fixed nitrogen for high-yield crop productivity in the case of legumes and paddy-grown rice and virtually none in the case of other cereal grains. Biological systems are very diverse and sensitive to many environmental and biological factors so that a large number of nitrogen fixers must be available and preferred ones identified for each site.

The golden age of exploratory research on nitrogen fixation began about 20 years ago with three seminal advances: two associated with chemistry and one with biology. An examination of the consequent advances in chemistry, biochemistry, genetics, biology, and agronomy shows an unusually strong interaction among the different disciplines, a rare event in most scientific fields and a likely reason for progress in nitrogen-fixation research.

Schematic diagrams on opposite page depict a proposed configuration of the protected active site of nitrogenase (top), which is believed to be on its Mo-Fe protein component, and a theoretical reaction sequence for reduction of molecular nitrogen (N_2) to ammonia. In this model the molybdenum (Mo) and iron (Fe) atoms are bridged by a sulfur atom (S); attachment of a nitrogen molecule, first to iron and then to molybdenum, gives the system the stability of a five-membered ring. Reduction proceeds as available electrons (their presence represented by lobe-shaped structures) are first transferred to the nitrogen molecule to begin breaking its triple bond and then to incoming protons (H^+), which become attached to each nitrogen atom to form ammonia (NH_3).

Transition metal chemistry

At the beginning of the 1960s most chemists considered nitrogen to be an almost inert molecule, and there were few attempts to find new N_2-fixing reactions until Soviet scientists M. E. Vol'pin and V. B. Shur used very strong reducing agents (electron donors) in combination with a broad spectrum of transition metal complexes to fix N_2 as ammonia under mild conditions of temperature and pressure. Soon after this important breakthrough Canadian investigators C. V. Senoff and the late A. D. Allen in 1965 found to their surprise that N_2 readily formed a complex with the transition metal ruthenium, and expansion of this second major advance led to the demonstration that many transition metals will form complexes with N_2.

For several years these complexes frustrated inorganic chemists because their main reactivity was simply to release the nitrogen as free N_2, without oxidation or reduction. Then in the early 1970s J. Chatt and colleagues in the U.K. found that some complexes of molybdenum and tungsten which contained more than one molecule of N_2 per atom of transition metal were able under certain conditions to yield either hydrazine or ammonia. Other investigators utilized less well-defined systems to fix small amounts of N_2. In one case G. N. Schrauzer in the U.S. combined molybdenum, thiol, and a strong reducing agent to reduce traces of N_2 to ammonia, a system whose composition crudely mimicked the biological nitrogenase system.

Although scientifically exciting, these processes suffer from their lack of true catalytic activity and their use of impractical reducing agents. The need for an added reducing agent has recently been eliminated by coupling solar energy to N_2 reduction through development of a light-capturing titanium dioxide catalyst. At present, yields are extremely low but the concept is intriguing. Over the longer term, nonbiological systems may be discovered that use catalysts with low or no direct energy input to fix nitrogen from air in irrigation streams at a rate that matches the crops' needs.

Nitrogenase

Enzymes are protein molecules composed of as many as 20 different amino acids linked together by carbon-nitrogen bonds in a chainlike sequence. Cross-links between amino acids at certain places within the enzyme and some other weak interactions help keep the molecule folded in a complex three-dimensional shape. This configuration usually includes a cleft or space that will permit only molecules with highly specific shapes to interact with it; those select molecules that the enzyme accepts for catalysis are called its substrates.

As might be expected for cross-linked chains, enzymes are delicate structures. Certain chemicals or changes in environment can denature them, or disrupt their configuration and consequently destroy their activity. The enzyme that catalyzes the reduction of N_2 to ammonia, nitrogenase, is "poisoned" irreversibly by oxygen, and thus many nitrogen-fixing organisms have evolved special systems to exclude oxygen from the enzyme. Other species such as the free-living bacterium *Klebsiella pneumoniae* can fix nitrogen only anaerobically, presumably because they have no means of preventing their nitrogenase from denaturing.

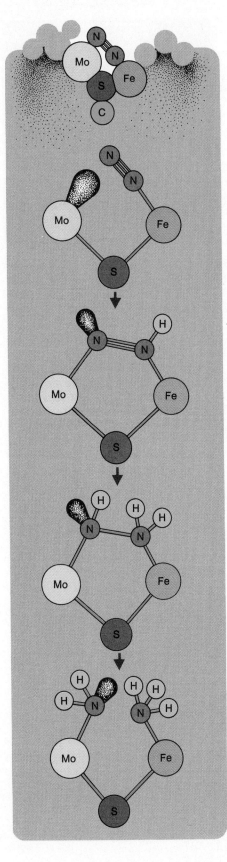

*Roots of the common bean,
Phaseolus vulgaris (above), possess
bulbous nodules that result from
infection with the symbiotic bacterium
Rhizobium phaseoli. Swelling occurs
as root cells become filled with these
nitrogen-fixing organisms. Shown in
the sequence of electron micrographs
on the opposite page are the surface
of a single soybean root nodule (top)
and a nodule cut open to reveal the
interior (center). An enlarged view of
the interior (bottom) shows a dense
mass of Rhizobium spilling from an
opened root cell.*

Nitrogenase resisted all attempts to extract it from bacteria in an active form until 1960 when J. E. Carnahan and associates in the U.S. succeeded. Their trick was to use large amounts of a special substrate called pyruvate and to devise a way to protect the enzyme from oxygen. In the wake of this seminal biological advance, purified nitrogenase has been obtained in recipe fashion from many nitrogen-fixing microorganisms.

Comparison of nitrogenases from different physiological types of biological nitrogen fixers has led to the conclusion that there exists a single basic nitrogenase enzyme with only minor noncritical variations. The enzyme is large, with a molecular weight of more than 300,000, and is composed of two different components, both of which, significantly, contain transition metals. One component contains molybdenum and iron and is called the Mo-Fe protein; the other contains only iron and is called the Fe protein. The Mo-Fe protein has a molecular weight of 200,000–270,000 and includes 24–32 atoms of iron and 2 atoms of molybdenum per molecule. The Fe protein has a molecular weight of about 60,000 and carries 4 atoms of iron per molecule. Both proteins are classed as iron-sulfur proteins and contain some of their iron in iron-sulfur clusters such as Fe_2S_2 and Fe_4S_4.

The Mo-Fe protein was crystallized several years ago by R. C. Burns and R. W. F. Hardy in the U.S., but its three-dimensional structure as determined by X-ray analysis was not known as of early 1978. Both the Fe and Mo-Fe proteins and possible associations of the two as they are assumed to occur in nitrogenase have been photographed with the aid of the electron microscope. The Fe protein contains two identical subunits of 273 amino acids each; their sequence was determined in 1977 by L. E. Mortenson and colleagues in the U.S. Both the Mo-Fe and Fe proteins are essential for the catalytic activity of their parent enzyme. Both proteins are also unusually sensitive to oxygen; only a few seconds exposure to air results in almost complete loss of catalytic activity.

All nitrogenase reactions such as the conversion of N_2 to ammonia are reductions and require electrons. The molecules in nitrogen-fixing organisms that provide these electrons are unique entities, discovered by Hardy, Mortenson, E. Knight, and R. C. Valentine as a by-product of nitrogenase research. One is an iron-sulfur protein called ferredoxin, based on its high iron content and function in reduction-oxidation reactions. The other electron-transferring protein, called flavodoxin, contains a flavin functional group rather than an iron-sulfur cluster. Ferredoxin and flavodoxin have a very strong reduction capability and are quite effective in providing electrons for such tightly bonded molecules as N_2.

In addition to a need for electrons and special electron donors, nitrogenase also requires large amounts of the molecule adenosine triphosphate (ATP), the major energy currency in biological systems. ATP consists of a complex organic structure called a nucleoside to which is attached a tail of three phosphate groups in linear succession. Energy taken up by a living organism (through photosynthesis or from the breakdown of nutrients) appears as a series of electron transfers between donor and acceptor molecules that culminate in the energy-absorbing synthesis of ATP from the two-phosphate molecule adenosine diphosphate (ADP) by addition of a phosphate group. Functioning like a portable rechargable battery, ATP is carried to sites within cells of the organism that require energy, where the terminal phosphate is removed by an energy-releasing reaction to give ADP.

For every molecule of N_2 that nitrogenase reduces to ammonia, 6 electrons are used and 12 ATP molecules are transformed to ADP. The function of at least some of these ATP's is involved with the transfer of electrons from the Fe protein to the Mo-Fe protein, as was recently revealed by W. H. Orme-Johnson and B. E. Smith and colleagues in the U.S. and U.K. This large ATP requirement for nitrogen fixation means that nitrogen fixers must have a high capacity for synthesizing ATP. Moreover, ADP, the product of the ATP interaction with nitrogenase, inhibits the nitrogenase reaction; therefore, nitrogen-fixing organisms must be able to maintain a high ratio of ATP to ADP. Thermodynamically, this massive energy requirement is both unexpected and unnecessary, and is the most significant limitation to more widespread exploitation of the nitrogenase system, such as its transfer to organisms that cannot fix nitrogen.

Nitrogenase is also unusual and energy wasteful in another sense. It interacts catalytically with more types of substrates than perhaps any other known enzyme. It not only reduces N_2 to ammonia but also reduces protons (H^+) to molecular hydrogen (H_2) and many small molecule substrates containing triple or potential triple bonds to a variety of products. These alternate substrates include nitrous oxide, azide (N_3^-), hydrogen cyanide (HCN) and other nitriles (RCN), various isonitriles (RNC), and acetylene (C_2H_2).

This substrate versatility of nitrogenase is both useful and detrimental. Its ability to convert acetylene to ethylene (C_2H_4) has been adapted by R. H. Burris and Hardy and colleagues in the U.S. as a quick and accurate assay for the measurement of nitrogen-fixing activity at all organizational levels, from the isolated enzyme to the biosphere itself. In the acetylene-ethylene assay, acetylene replaces N_2 as a partner for the promiscuous nitrogenase, which reduces the acetylene to ethylene at an electron-addition rate comparable to that for the reduction of N_2 to ammonia. The product, ethylene, is a gas that can be easily sampled and analyzed. This technique, which became available to laboratories in the late 1960s, in large part has been responsible for the rapid advances in nitrogen-fixation research.

On the other hand, the substrate versatility of nitrogenase, which allows protons to be reduced to hydrogen, is detrimental because that reaction occurs in nature even in the presence of atmospheric concentrations of N_2. It represents a complete waste of energy, consuming ATP that could otherwise fix nitrogen. H. J. Evans and colleagues in the U.S. have estimated that the amount of H_2 formed by this reaction in the annual U.S. soybean crop is equivalent to the energy in 300 billion cubic feet of natural gas.

Genetic investigations

A most ambitious and exciting line of research began in 1971 with the discovery by S. L. Streicher and Valentine in the U.S. of the cluster of genes responsible for N_2 fixation, which they called *nif*. With the aid of a virus that can infect bacteria with foreign genetic material, they were able to transfer these genes from an N_2-fixing species of *Klebsiella* bacterium to a mutant

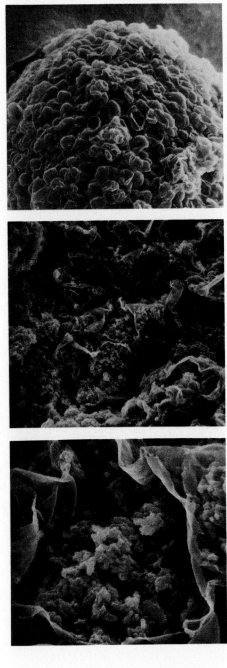

233

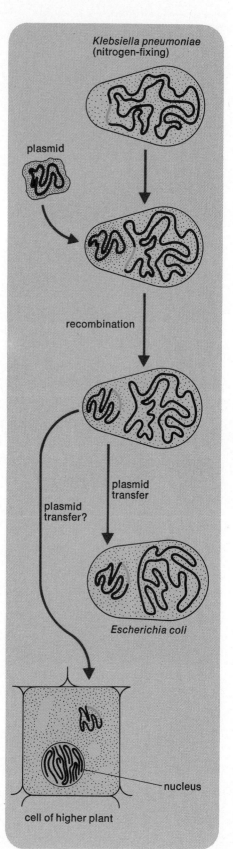

Klebsiella pneumoniae
(nitrogen-fixing)

plasmid

recombination

plasmid
transfer?

plasmid
transfer

Escherichia coli

nucleus

cell of higher plant

of *Klebsiella* that was unable to fix N$_2$. Using a sexual process among bacteria called conjugation, J. R. Postgate and R. A. Dixon in the U.K. subsequently transferred these genes from *Klebsiella* to its close relative *Escherichia coli* and thereby produced the first example of a synthetic nitrogen fixer, because *E. coli* is not known to fix N$_2$ naturally.

Investigators have also incorporated the genes for nitrogen fixation into a freely transmissible plasmid, a circular form of DNA that can exist within a cell but outside its chromosomes. Attempts have been made to move *nif* genes using this plasmid as carrier into a variety of bacteria, with varied success in some cases and unexplained failures in others. In 1977 F. M. Ausubel and colleagues in the U.S. employed recombinant DNA techniques to construct a small plasmid that contained about half of the *nif* genes. Their short-term goal is to make useful quantities of *nif* genes for study by cloning them, or allowing them to be copied, within multiplying populations of host cells. In the more distant future it may be possible to manufacture large numbers of *nif*-containing plasmids in this way for transfer to cells of higher plants and thereby endow them with the ability to fix nitrogen.

In nature *Rhizobium*-legume associations are highly specific; each legume forms a symbiotic relationship with only specific species of *Rhizobium*. During the past two years plasmid-based techniques for transfers of parts of the *Rhizobium* chromosome between species were developed by J. E. Beringer and A. W. B. Johnston in the U.K. This useful new capability should enable the genetic diversity of *Rhizobium* to be increased and should serve as a useful tool in discovering those genes responsible for determining which species of *Rhizobium* will infect which legumes. Among the molecules involved in species discrimination may be plant-produced proteins called lectins. One lectin, trifoliin, was shown by F. B. Dazzo in the U.S. to function as a specific "glue" between *Rhizobium trifolii* and the root surface of clover. Presumably others will also be discovered for other *Rhizobium*-legume associations, and it eventually may be possible to construct a system whereby a single *Rhizobium* would interact with all legumes and perhaps even cereal grains.

Although the activity of nitrogenase is not inhibited directly by its product ammonia, the initial steps in the synthesis of nitrogenase are regulated by ammonia and by some other forms of fixed nitrogen in such a way as to conserve energy. In the presence of adequate quantities of ammonia, the *nif* genes do not direct the synthesis of nitrogenase, and in terms of energy expenditure the plant "coasts," utilizing available fixed nitrogen exclusively. As fixed nitrogen is depleted, the *nif* genes again are permitted to allow manufacture of nitrogenase to enable the organism to meet its needs for fixed nitrogen from N$_2$, but of course at substantial ATP expenditure.

Although the specific details of this regulation are not completely understood, it has been shown that an enzyme, glutamine synthetase, is directly involved in the regulatory process. Using chemical and genetic approaches, W. J. Brill and Valentine and colleagues in the U.S. have isolated mutant nitrogen-fixing bacteria in which the regulatory system has been disrupted, thus enabling N$_2$ fixation in the presence of high concentrations of fixed nitrogen. Whereas some scientists have suggested that such deregulated

234

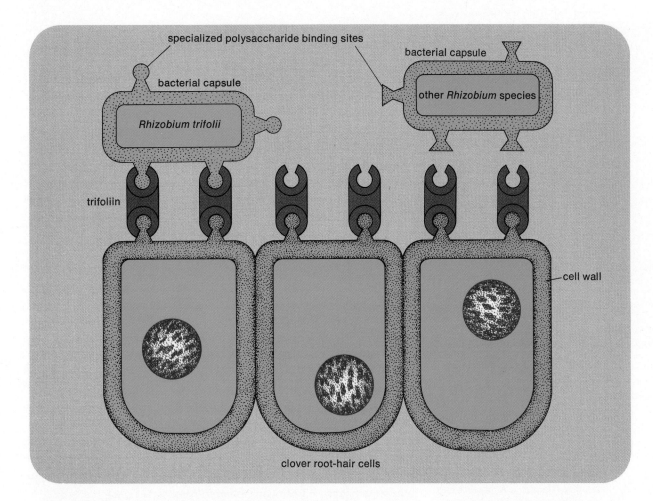

specialized polysaccharide binding sites

bacterial capsule

Rhizobium trifolii

bacterial capsule

other *Rhizobium* species

trifoliin

cell wall

clover root-hair cells

organisms may be put to use as biological fixing factories, *e.g.,* in huge fermentation tanks, it seems doubtful that this will be realized with the possible exception of photosynthetic fixers, which are energy self-sufficient.

Other developments

Oxygen may be another direct or indirect regulator of nitrogenase synthesis. Free-living members of the genus *Klebsiella* live under both aerobic and anaerobic conditions but only produce nitrogenase in the absence of oxygen. A related example may be *Rhizobium*, which for 75 years was thought to fix nitrogen only when symbiotically associated with legumes. Nearly simultaneous reports from five laboratories in three countries in 1975 toppled this accepted phenomenon. A simple combination of a very low oxygen concentration with a source of dicarboxylic acids allowed several *Rhizobium* species to fix nitrogen independent of any legume. This revolutionary advance proved that *Rhizobium* is indeed the source of *nif* genes for the legume-*Rhizobium* symbiosis and provided some support for the concept that the legume-*Rhizobium* association may be extended to cereal grains. The tenet of exclusive *Rhizobium*-legume associations has also been challenged by the chance discovery by M. J. Trinick in Australia of a *Rhizobium* nodular association with a nonlegume shrub, *Trema canabina*. It is reason-

*Success has been achieved in transferring the genes responsible for nitrogen fixation (*nif *genes) between species of bacteria. In one experiment (opposite page)* nif *genes were first moved from the chromosome of* Klebsiella pneumoniae *to a small plasmid of DNA. The plasmid was then introduced into* Escherichia coli *where it provided instructions for the synthesis of nitrogenase. A future possibility is the transfer of* nif *genes directly to the cells of higher plants. (Above)* Rhizobium-legume *recognition may be mediated by plant-produced proteins that bind bacteria to the surfaces of legume root hairs. One such protein called trifoliin, found on clover root hairs, seems to bind only to a specific surface polysaccharide on* Rhizobium trifolii *but not to polysaccharides on other* Rhizobium *species.*

235

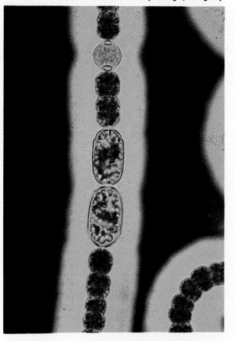

Filament of Anabaena, *a nitrogen-fixing blue-green alga, is composed of small, densely packed vegetative cells that undergo cell division; larger, elongated sporelike akinetes (two cells near center); and spherical heterocysts (transparent cell near top). Heterocysts are sites of nitrogen fixation in* Anabaena *and other filamentous blue-green algae; their special structure and modified photosynthetic system protect the nitrogenase within from the destructive effects of oxygen.*

able to wonder how much more undiscovered diversity exists in nature and if some of this may hold still greater potential for the development of new nitrogen-fixing technologies.

Nitrogen-fixing organisms that require oxygen for their metabolic processes have had to develop a variety of ways to cope with the high sensitivity of nitrogenase to oxygen. In the case of strict anaerobes there is no oxygen and therefore no problem. In some aerobes a high respiration rate depletes oxygen rapidly to protect nitrogenase. In filamentous blue-green algae about 10–20% of the cells in a filament are specialized so as to maintain a low oxygen concentration. Called heterocysts, these large cells have thick walls that slow the inward diffusion of oxygen from the environment and a modified photosynthetic system that eliminates evolution of the oxygen normally formed as a photosynthetic by-product. Nitrogenase is localized and protected in these specialized cells.

Species of *Rhizobium* that form root nodules utilize two oxygen-coping mechanisms. A low oxygen concentration within the nodule is maintained by physical barriers within the nodule architecture. At this low concentration of oxygen, however, aerobic bacteria require a high flux of the gas for proper functioning. This is accomplished by a hemoglobin-like molecule called leghemoglobin that is synthesized by legume nodule cells. As a protein that can bind oxygen reversibly, leghemoglobin facilitates the diffusion of oxygen at low concentration in much the same way that mammalian myoglobin facilitates the diffusion of oxygen in muscle cells. Moreover, this oxygen-coping system can adapt to variations in external oxygen concentrations as they occur in a natural soil environment. These examples demonstrate that any successful man-made biological fixing system will have to incorporate appropriate oxygen-coping systems. Such a requirement will undoubtedly be a major constraint on nitrogenase-based nitrogen-fixing applications.

Of fundamental importance to the optimum activity of nitrogenase is the provision of large amounts of molecules called carbohydrates, which supply ATP, electrons to replenish ferredoxin and flavodoxin, and molecules to carry away the product of the nitrogenase reaction, ammonia. Probably most nitrogen-fixing systems are limited by an inadequate supply of carbohydrates, and recent research has definitively shown this to be the case for several field-grown legumes.

In the nitrogen-fixing legume, more than 30% of the carbohydrates produced by leaf photosynthesis is transported to the nodule, the site of N_2 fixation. Some are used for nodule growth, some to support nitrogenase activity, and some to carry fixed nitrogen back to the leaves and seed. Measurements over the course of plant development revealed that the nitrogen-fixing system slowed down at a critical stage of seed growth when the need for fixed nitrogen was greatest. U. D. Havelka and Hardy added carbon dioxide (CO_2) gas to the air around field-grown legumes to increase their production of carbohydrates, which in turn produced a multifold increase in N_2 fixation. This increase was the result of an immediate rise in nitrogenase activity, a long-term increase in nodule mass and nitrogenase, and a prolonging of fixing activity. These results clearly identify photosynthesis as the most important factor governing N_2 fixation in legumes and proba-

236

bly in almost any biological nitrogen-fixing system. It is impractical, however, to utilize CO_2 directly as a fertilizer to increase photosynthesis. Future research must seek practical chemical or genetic solutions that have the same effect.

Although the legume-*Rhizobium* association has been known for about 100 years, recent recognition of the association of such N_2 fixers as *Azospirillum* with the roots of tropical grasses and corn was quite unexpected and exciting. Scientists moved rapidly to exploit this discovery with the expectation that *Azospirillum* inoculation of the soil in which corn was grown would eliminate at least part of the high requirement for fertilizer nitrogen. Unfortunately, N_2 fixation by *Azospirillum*-inoculated corn proved so small as to be of no practical significance. Scientists are presently trying to understand why root-associated *Azospirillum* fails to fix N_2 well.

The ultimate success

One of the most speculative alternate technologies is the transfer of the genetic information for nitrogen-fixing systems directly to crop plants. This represents an ideal solution: a permanent incorporation of the ability to fix N_2 in plants, transmitted through the seed and eliminating the need for a microorganism and the complexities of putting two living systems together. However, the complexities of the nitrogen-fixing system and the juvenile state of the art of gene transfer indicate that the task is most formidable.

In the somewhat distant future, biology and chemistry in combination may construct an ideal synthetic gene, one that would produce a small, oxygen-insensitive, high-efficiency nitrogen-fixing enzyme with absolute substrate specificity (no proton reduction), no ATP requirements, and appropriate repression by fixed nitrogen. Incorporated in higher plants, such genes would avoid the drawbacks of naturally evolved nitrogenase. Until such a scientific miracle comes to pass, however, opportunities abound for improved technologies—both biological and nonbiological.

FOR ADDITIONAL READING

Richard C. Burns and Ralph W. F. Hardy, *Nitrogen Fixation in Bacteria and Higher Plants* (Springer-Verlag, 1975).

Ralph W. F. Hardy and Ulysses D. Havelka, "Nitrogen Fixation Research: A Key to World Food?" in *Science* (vol. 188, 1975, pp. 633–643).

A Treatise on Dinitrogen Fixation, sections 1 and 2: *Inorganic and Physical Chemistry and Biochemistry*, Ralph W. F. Hardy, Frank Bottomley, and Richard C. Burns (eds.); section 3: *Biology*, Ralph W. F. Hardy and Warren S. Silver (eds.), *Agronomy and Ecology*, Ralph W. F. Hardy and Alan H. Gibson (eds.) (Wiley, 1977, 1978).

Alexander Hollaender, Robert H. Burris, Peter R. Day, Ralph W. F. Hardy, Donald R. Helinski, Marvin R. Lamborg, Lowell Owens, and Raymond C. Valentine (eds.), *Genetic Engineering for Nitrogen Fixation* (Plenum, 1977).

William Newton, John R. Postgate, and Clasius Rodriguez-Barrueco (eds.), *Recent Developments in Nitrogen Fixation*, Proceedings of the Second International Symposium (Academic Press, 1977).

Leucaena
Leucocephala

Leucaena

Leucaena:
New Hope
for the Tropics
by Noel D. Vietmeyer

**A fast-growing tree that flourishes in the highly
leached soil of the tropics, the leucaena is a source
of food, fuel, fertilizer, timber, and paper.**

Long disdained as a nuisance weed, the leguminous tree *Leucaena
leucocephala* now promises to become one of the most valuable
crops for the world's less developed countries.

The humid tropics, where rain falls throughout the year, and the arid and
semiarid lands, where rainfall is highly erratic, both are areas where productive agriculture is difficult to develop. In the humid tropics highly leached soils
retain little water or nutrients, while in the dry lands the curse is unpredictable
drought. In these climatic zones are found the majority of the world's less
developed nations. The populations of these countries are growing at unprecedented rates, thereby creating enormous demands for high agricultural
production.

In 1977 the U.S. National Academy of Sciences reported on a plant that
could make farming productive in the humid and arid tropics and subtropics.
It is *Leucaena leucocephala*, known commonly as leucaena (variously
pronounced loo-*see*-nuh, loo-*kee*-nuh, loo-*kay*-nuh). Depending on variety,
it is either a tall, slender tree or a rounded, many-branched bush. It can
provide forage, fuel, fertilizer, timber, paper, landscaping, soil reclamation,
wind and fire breaks, shading for sun-sensitive crops, dye, gum, jewelry, and
even human food. Moreover, it is one of the fastest growing plants yet
measured, and it seems adaptable to many soils now too barren for conventional crops. It fixes its own nitrogen, resprouts from stumps, survives
drought conditions, tolerates the salt of coastal areas, and has a high resistance to pests and diseases. Today it remains a neglected crop, its potential
largely unrealized, but in the 1980s leucaena could become the wonder plant
of the less developed world.

Although a glimmer of its modern promise has become apparent in the

239

Courtesy, T. H. Stobbs, CSIRO, Australia

Cattle feed on the leaves and stems of the bushy variety of leucaena in Australia.

NOEL D. VIETMEYER *is a Professional Associate at the U.S. National Academy of Sciences.*

(Overleaf) Paintings by Bob Goldstrom

past two decades, leucaena was long ago widely used by the Maya and Zapotec civilizations in Mexico and Central America, where it is native. Indeed, the name Oaxaca (Mexico's fifth largest state and a prominent modern city) derives from a pre-Columbian word meaning the "place where leucaena grows."

Shapes and sizes

Leucaena's versatility stems from the disparity of its three major types. One, called the Hawaiian type, was introduced throughout the tropics by Spanish, British, Dutch, and French colonialists who used it as a "nurse tree" to shade and support plantation crops such as coffee, cocoa, pepper, and vanilla. After World War II the U.S. military used it to reforest bomb-devastated Pacific islands. Unfortunately, it is an aggressive bushy variety that produces its seeds and irrepressible seedlings so prodigiously that it forms dense, impenetrable thickets, which have given leucaena its reputation as a weed.

But in the 1960s two remarkable new non-weedy types were discovered in inland forests of Central America. Mark Hutton and his colleagues from Australia's Commonwealth Scientific and Industrial Research Organisation located bushy genotypes (now known as Peru or Hawaiian types), which produce foliage that is much loved by cattle and has proved almost as good as a feedlot for producing beef and milk.

At about the same time James Brewbaker of the University of Hawaii found tall, virtually branchless, treelike genotypes, called Salvador

240

varieties, that grow with almost incredible rapidity. In both Hawaii and the Philippines these plants, also known as Hawaiian Giants, spurted from seedlings to trees as tall as a six-story building in only six to eight years. Grown in dense plantations, they produce a large volume of wood.

Leucaena is a member of the family Leguminosae and, like most other legumes, it associates with beneficial soil bacteria of the genus *Rhizobium*. These penetrate young rootlets and then multiply, forcing the root wall outward into a nodular swelling. The bacteria then absorb large amounts of nitrogen gas from air trapped in the upper soil layers, and by chemically combining it with hydrogen (obtained from carbohydrate provided by the plant) they produce nitrogen compounds that the plant needs in order to grow and to form protein. Thus, *Rhizobium* bacteria allow leucaena (and most other legumes) to thrive where soil nitrogen is insufficient to sustain other crops. They also ensure that leucaena foliage is rich in protein. (*See* Feature Article: FOOD, FAMINE, AND NITROGEN FIXATION.)

The nodules occur on rootlets in the aerated surface soil, but leucaena's main root is a deep taproot that penetrates far into the soil and exploits water and mineral nutrients below the root zone of most other crops. This enables the plant to reach subterranean water and thus withstand long dry seasons and to tolerate a wide array of surface soil conditions. Furthermore, the root hairs are usually infected with a beneficial mycorrhizal fungus that helps the plant absorb phosphorus and other nutrients from the soil.

Originating in the midlands of Guatemala, Honduras, El Salvador, and southern Mexico, leucaena was spread throughout the coastal lowlands by pre-Columbian Indians. The Hawaiian type is a rapidly flowering, highly seedy shrub, while the Salvador variety is a tree that often reaches 20 meters (more than 60 feet) in height.

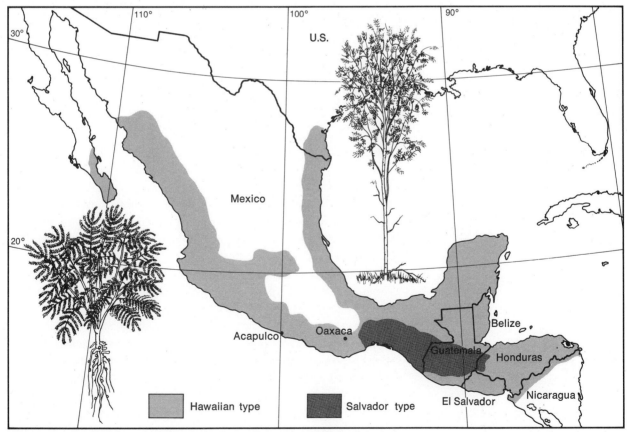

Adapted from *Leucaena: Promising Forage and Tree Crop for the Tropics*, National Academy of Sciences, Washington, D.C., 1977

Livestock

One quickly senses the unusualness of a Peru-type leucaena pasture. It is almost two meters (six feet) high. Cattle are lost among the bushes, only the tops of their heads being visible. But this gives a leucaena pasture an added dimension; cattle find forage from ground level to eye level. Sunlight penetrates through the plant's open feathery leaves, reaching the lowest branches and grasses beneath the bushes so that they too provide healthy, vigorous forage. A field of leucaena is a block of forage rather than a conventional swardlike pasture.

Cattle so relish the leaflets and young stems that they leave the bushes stripped bare. But leucaena quickly regrows new foliage, and within two weeks a "bare" field can be ready for grazing once more. So resilient is the plant that pastures near Brisbane, Australia, have been browsed almost continuously for about 20 years without requiring replanting.

Also, leucaena can be mowed with a forage harvester because, when cut at ground level, many of the tender new shoots regenerate just as though leucaena were an herbaceous plant like alfalfa or a grass. University of Hawaii researchers found that leucaena fields can be mowed this way as often as four times a year. For a plant that is inherently a shrub to withstand such repeated decapitation is astounding. Once harvested, the leaves can be dried and compressed into pellets for easy transportation.

Leucaena leaves, similar to alfalfa in digestibility, protein content, and nutritional value, are particularly palatable to dairy cows, beef cattle, water buffalo, and goats. Under favorable conditions one hectare of leucaena can produce 10–20 metric tons of edible dry matter, compared with 8–9 metric tons for alfalfa. These findings are extremely important as there are acute and chronic shortages of animal feed throughout both the humid tropics and the semiarid lands. Plants that grow well in such areas and that improve the quantity and quality of livestock feed are much needed. Leucaena is thus a remarkable candidate for increasing meat and milk supplies in many less developed nations.

However, leucaena forage has a drawback. Mimosine, an uncommon amino acid, comprises about 5% of the dry weight of the leaflets. If taken in excess, mimosine causes cattle to produce less than normal quantities of thyroxine, a thyroid hormone. Eventually, the cattle lose tail and rump hair and in extreme cases become completely debilitated with goiter. Thus leucaena must always be fed in combination with grass or other feeds and kept to no more than one-third of the diet.

Nonetheless, two decades of research have shown that leucaena complemented with grass can produce extraordinary weight gains in cattle, and can do so over extended periods with little or no adverse effect. Cattle feeding on leucaena near Brisbane gained an average of almost one kilogram (2.2 pounds) each day for more than 200 days. This performance included a winter period when the growth of the leucaena slowed. During warm months weight gains of more than one kilogram a day were recorded. Such growth is about twice what is normally expected from animals grazing in tropical pastures; it approaches the weight increases normally obtained only in feedlots, where animals can stuff themselves with high-energy, concentrated rations. New low-mimosine leucaena varieties, now in advanced development, hold great promise as worry-free tropical feedstuffs of the future.

Leucaena leaf meal contains vitamins and pigments that are vitally important in poultry raising, and chickens thrive on diets containing a little of it. In sheep, mimosine causes the fleece to fall off. Ten days after a sheep has eaten leucaena a stroke of the hand is all that is needed to separate wool from the skin. This could become an extremely cheap way to "shear" sheep. No lasting effects on the animals have been found, and the method would be immediately practical if a means to protect the pink and completely "nude" sheep from sunburn can be discovered.

Wood

The newly discovered Hawaiian Giant varieties, with their tall, thick trunks and light-colored wood, are believed to have much commercial potential for pulp and paper, poles and posts, lumber, and plywood. In equable tropical climates these leucaenas grow so fast that they can be twice the height of a tall man after six months and as high as a three-story building after two years. In only six to eight years they can be over 20 meters (60 feet) tall with a trunk cross-section up to 37 centimeters (15 inches).

Leucaena's productivity is further enhanced by the number of trees that can be packed into a plantation. The vertical taproots of neighboring leucaena trees interfere with each other far less than the spreading roots of most trees. The plant even grows well (though spindly) when planted as densely as corn. This latter method is used to grow poles for agricultural use, and the thickets can be thinned every year or two to provide a continual harvest.

Leucaena wood is a medium hardwood, and is potentially useful for general construction, utility furniture, and other purposes. It is thin-barked and similar in density to oak, ash, birch, or maple. In addition, leucaena pulp, though lacking the exceptional qualities of long-fiber pulp from pine trees, is suited for use in printing and writing paper, which is in short supply in almost all less developed nations.

Courtesy, Kenneth O. Rachie, CIAT, Colombia

Spindly stems of densely planted leucaena trees provide stakes to support climbing bean plants.

Leucaena is prepared for use as firewood in the Philippines.

Fuel and fertilizer

For poor people in less developed countries firewood for cooking and for heating water is as essential as food itself. In vast regions of Asia, Africa, and Latin America each person burns an average of nearly one ton of firewood each year. In some areas a family spends as much money on wood for fuel as it does on food, and often one family member spends full working time collecting firewood from forest areas at ever increasing distances from the village. As supplies diminish, fuel wood prices continually rise. By the late 1970s firewood shortages in many areas constituted what could be described as the "poor man's oil crisis."

Small plantations of the fast-growing leucaena trees could provide fuel wood or charcoal, and thus bring great benefits to rural villages. For a fast-growing tree, the wood has uncommonly high density and provides much heat when it burns. Leucaena is a continuously renewing source of fuel because the stumps readily regrow and thus "defy the woodcutter."

In the late 1970s soaring energy prices were burdening less developed countries with fertilizer prices their farmers could not afford. This occurred because it takes much energy to produce nitrogenous compounds by industrial processes. But *Rhizobium* bacteria in the root nodules of a hectare of leucaena are capable of producing half a metric ton of fixed nitrogen a year, equivalent to providing more than a metric ton of ammonium sulfate fertilizer each year. Most of this is absorbed by the plant and transported to its leaves, and six bags of dried leucaena leaves contain the same nitrogen as one bag of ammonium sulfate. Thus, small farmers, for whom commercial fertilizers may be too expensive or even unobtainable, can grow their own fertilizer. The foliage from a leucaena grove can be cut and used to fertilize adjacent farm fields, or leucaena can be planted between farm crops or under such tree crops as coconuts. The continual fall of the nutrient-rich leucaena leaves provides fertilizer for the main crop.

244

Noel D. Vietmeyer

When nutrient-rich leucaena leaves fall to the ground, they provide fertilizer for adjacent crops. Foliage from one row of leucaena spread over three rows of corn achieved corn yields equal to those obtained by the use of commercial fertilizers.

University of Hawaii researchers found that leucaena foliage laid on the ground decays within ten days in the tropical heat and humidity, releasing the nitrogenous compounds for use by other crops. By spreading leucaena foliage from one row of leucaena over three rows of corn, they were able to achieve corn yields equaling those achieved by commercial fertilizers.

Reforestation

With the unprecedented growth of human populations in all the less developed countries, forests were being cut faster than they could be replenished. By the late 1970s, the expansion of agriculture, the gathering of wood for fuel, and irresponsible commercial timbering had eliminated one-half of Africa's native forests, one-third of South America's, and two-thirds of southeast Asia's. Deforestation leaves the ground unprotected from rain, and one storm can wash away centuries-old accumulations of fertile topsoil. In hilly watersheds destructive erosion increases rapidly; the silt produced by erosion chokes rivers and streams, and each year causes increasingly disastrous floods.

In a tropical forest the bulk of nutrients is in the trees rather than in the soil as in temperate zones, so that deforested land usually ends up denuded and barren or is replaced by almost worthless grasslands unpalatable to livestock. Once these grasses take hold of the land, it is extremely difficult to reestablish a forest.

Leucaena, however, appears to offer a way to do this. The plant survives, indeed often thrives, in nutrient-poor soils. This is largely thanks to its symbiotic *Rhizobium* bacteria and mycorrhizal fungi. These microorganisms together with the deep taproot allow leucaena to exploit atmospheric nitrogen, phosphorus, potassium, and other minerals unavailable to other species. Also, leucaena's vigor usually allows it to outgrow any coarse grasses and other weeds, eventually forming a canopy that shades the grasses to

245

To plant leucaena trees, seeds wrapped in cloth are dipped in a pail of boiled water (above). After a minute in the water they are removed and set aside wrapped in the wet cloth for 48 hours or until germination. The germinating seeds are placed in plastic containers filled with pulverized fertile soil and kept in shade for four weeks (above center). The seedlings are then exposed to sunlight and maintained until the start of the rainy season. At that time holes are dug to accommodate the soil-root balls of the seedlings (above right). The seedlings are removed from their containers (right) and planted in the ground with the root collar on the same level as the soil surface (far right). The leucaena forest in the Philippines (bottom) is only two years old, demonstrating the rapid growth of the trees.

Photos, courtesy, The Philippine National Oil Company, 1978 calendar

a point where they succumb. In the Philippines thousands of hectares of formerly degraded hill land are being reconverted into forest in this way.

Once established, leucaena helps rebuild topsoil. Its foliage shades soil from the baking tropical sun and shelters it from the rain and wind; nutrients from deep strata are gradually deposited on the surface through decay of the leaves; soil organisms increase, topsoil humus rebuilds, and a forest cover is restored. Furthermore, leucaena's aggressive roots help break up compacted surfaces, thus improving moisture absorption and reducing erosion caused by runoff of surface water.

Future prospects

Leucaena may be the forerunner of a whole new world of agriculture in which trees are grown like field crops. Many trees can provide basic foodstuffs, forage, and industrial raw materials, but they have received scant attention from the research community. In the humid tropics and in semiarid lands this combination of agriculture and forestry has particular significance; tree roots penetrate to deep layers of fertility and moisture unavailable to conventional crops, and a tree canopy shelters and shades fragile topsoil from devastating tropical downpours or baking desert heat.

Researchers quickly point out, however, that they still know little about leucaena's limitations. Its best varieties are so newly discovered that none has been tested widely in the field. Nevertheless, some drawbacks have been found. Leucaena grows poorly both at high altitudes and in acid or aluminous soils. Also, some of the bushy varieties may escape cultivation and become nuisance weeds. Much remains to be learned about the plant's value for specific sites.

These limitations notwithstanding, researchers who have worked with the plant are certain that leucaena will soon play a major role in helping fulfill needs for meat, reforestation, wood, paper pulp, and fuel, especially in less developed countries. Pilot projects and adaptability trials are underway throughout the tropics to compare the performance of the best strains. It appears likely that leucaena, yesterday's weed, may become one of the world's major new crops in the near future.

Science
Year in Review
Contents

Contributors to the Science Year in Review

Joseph Ashbrook *Astronomy.* Editor, *Sky and Telescope*, Cambridge, Mass.

Fred Basolo *Chemistry: Inorganic chemistry.* Professor of Chemistry, Northwestern University, Evanston, Ill.

Louis J. Battan *Earth sciences: Atmospheric sciences.* Director, Institute of Atmospheric Physics, University of Arizona, Tucson.

David M. Boore *Earth sciences: Geophysics.* Assistant Professor of Geophysics, Stanford University, Stanford, Calif.

Harold Borko *Information sciences: Information systems and services.* Professor, Graduate School of Library and Information Science, University of California, Los Angeles.

D. Allan Bromley *Physics: Nuclear physics.* Henry Ford II Professor and Director, Wright Nuclear Structure Laboratory, Yale University, New Haven, Conn.

David E. Cane *Chemistry: Organic chemistry.* Assistant Professor of Chemistry, Brown University, Providence, R.I.

F. C. Durant III *Information sciences: Satellite systems.* Assistant Director (Astronautics), National Air and Space Museum, Smithsonian Institution, Washington, D.C.

Robert G. Eagon *Life sciences: Microbiology.* Professor of Microbiology, University of Georgia, Athens.

David R. Gaskell *Materials sciences: Metallurgy.* Associate Professor of Metallurgy, University of Pennsylvania, Philadelphia.

Robert Geddes *Architecture and civil engineering.* Dean of the School of Architecture and Urban Planning, Princeton University, Princeton, N.J.

Robert N. Hamburger *Medical sciences: Allergy research.* Professor of Pediatrics and Head of the Pediatric Immunology and Allergy Division, School of Medicine, University of California, San Diego.

Robert Haselkorn *Life sciences: Molecular biology.* F. L. Pritzker Professor and Chairman of the Department of Biophysics and Theoretical Biology, University of Chicago.

L. A. Heindl *Earth sciences: Hydrology.* Executive Secretary, U.S. National Committee on Scientific Hydrology, U.S. Geological Survey, Reston, Va.

Earl Ingerson *Earth sciences: Geology and geochemistry.* Professor emeritus of Geological Sciences, University of Texas, Austin.

Lawrence W. Jones *Physics: High-energy physics.* Professor of Physics, University of Michigan, Ann Arbor.

John Patrick Jordan *Food and agriculture: Agriculture.* Director, Colorado State University Experiment Station, Fort Collins.

Anthropology

There was continued rapid change in anthropology during the year, away from the earlier concern with describing localized cultures outside the mainstream of world affairs. Among the more apparent reasons for this shift in emphasis were the spread of modernization to all parts of the world and the consequent disappearance of traditional subject matter; a proportionate reduction of funds available to support pure research; and the growing number of individuals entering the discipline, with a corresponding increase in specialization. This was part of a trend that had been apparent for some time, and all the signs indicated that it would persist.

Like other institutions in the last years of the 1970s, anthropology was adapting to a world of cultural, social, environmental, and economic change. For those whose first perception of the discipline came at an earlier time, it was startling to realize just how much had changed over the last decade and to consider the changes that were likely to occur in the next ten years.

In the late 1960s anthropology was undergoing considerable expansion in the U.S., largely under the impetus of government programs and funds aimed at upgrading scientific studies generally. At that time the discipline was dominated by a number of famous "tribal leaders." Ten years later there were fewer great personalities. In part, this was because of the growth in the number of practitioners and increasing specialization, in part, because of the retirement or death of senior anthropologists (John Honigmann and Loren Eiseley both died in 1977). At the same time, the discipline had become more mature and sophisticated. Growing specialization meant that greater depth in research and understanding of particular aspects of the subject could be realized, and the number of named specialties with which anthropologists identified themselves was rising steadily.

Some indication of this trend could be gained from the program of the 1977 annual meeting of the American Anthropological Association, which listed no fewer than 208 different topical and regional entries in the index of sessions. Ranging from agriculture to women, they included such diverse topics as bioarchaeology, class conflict, death, extraterrestrial communities, funding for anthropologists, Gypsies, health care, immigration in Israel, Japanese studies, kin terms, law, Marxist anthropology, network analysis, Oceania, Pentecostalism, reproductive decision-making, Sherpas, urban anthropology, and "The Impact of the Viru Valley Project." Obviously, it had become virtually impossible for any one anthropologist to know his or her discipline from A to Z. In addition, more and more anthropologists were collaborating with colleagues in related disciplines, such as nutrition, biology, geology, economics, or psychology. This often led to results of considerable

sophistication. At the same time, one of the problems facing anthropology in 1977 was how to integrate the diverse specializations and intense loyalties of anthropologists into a unified discipline.

One project that began in 1977 exemplified both growing specialization and the current shift of federal research funds toward applied research. In March 1976 U.S. Pres. Gerald Ford signed into law the Fisheries Conservation and Management Act (PL 94-265), calling for the management of U.S. fisheries for optimum sustained yield. The act divides the country into eight coastal regions, each with a regional council whose task is to manage the fishery, not only for biological ends but with economic and social considerations in mind. Although there are relatively good biological and economic data on U.S. fisheries, there is relatively little social and cultural information of the sort that would help the councils with their task. In an effort to remedy this lack, a social and cultural study of New England fishermen was begun, headed by James

Grandmother Zimza and Savina Maximoff, Gypsies of the Kalderash tribe, live on the outskirts of Paris. Zimza's brother Matéo, a novelist, is an authority on Gypsies.

Patricia Evans

Acheson of the University of Maine and funded by the National Science Foundation.

Acheson and his associates, specialists in the newly identified area of maritime anthropology, designed the project with the aim of obtaining several kinds of social and cultural data in the area under the purview of the New England Region Fishery Management Council. They collected and analyzed baseline sociocultural data on representative fishing communities in New England; information on the core values and social units of importance in the region's fishing population; and data on how fishermen's innovations would affect the application of the new law. They were also working to develop a model for study of the social and cultural aspects of fisheries management that could be used in other regional fisheries-management zones in the U.S. and elsewhere in the world. They hoped to integrate the social information collected through this project with existing economic and biological data in order to obtain a multifaceted analysis of the fishery.

While this study illustrates the trend toward specialization in anthropology, it also has a definite integrative component. Paradoxically, as anthropology grew more specialized, there seemed to be a greater effort to pull the various specialties together into a theoretical whole. This could be seen in many introductory textbooks, which deal with anthropology as a biocultural discipline rather than as a loose amalgam of archaeology, human evolution, social and cultural anthropology, and linguistics. This integrative effort was not entirely

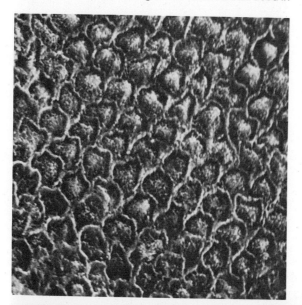
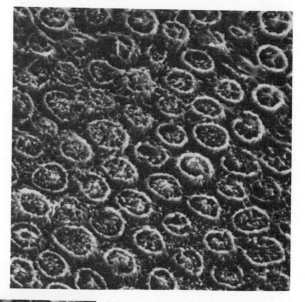
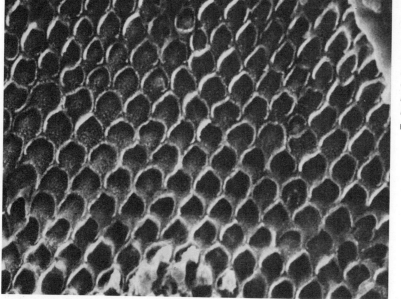

Micrographs reveal the prism pattern of the enamel from the teeth of three hominoids: modern man (top left), orangutan (above), and Ramapithecus punjabicus *(left). The resemblance between the enamels of modern man and* Ramapithecus *lends support to the belief that the latter was an early form of man.*

Photos, courtesy, David G. Gantt, Florida State University

new, but it appeared to be gaining momentum. Instead of just one or two textbooks with this overarching perspective, there were several, and the biocultural integration model of anthropology, set in a framework of evolutionary-ecological theory, appeared not only in introductory textbooks but also in middle-range theoretical and empirical studies and in the efforts of anthropologists to define areas that might be productive for future research.

The integration of biological and sociocultural elements in one theoretical domain of the discipline was noted by Jere Haas and Gail Harrison in their paper on "Nutritional Anthropology and Biological Adaptation" in the 1977 *Annual Review of Anthropology*. Pointing out that several middle-range theoretical papers had appeared in the recent literature dealing with the concept of adaptation and its utilization in sociocultural and biological anthropology, they went on to add that "A significant feature of these discussions is the treatment of population and even individual adaptation as neither solely biological nor social in origin or effect." (It is also worth noting that the label "nutritional anthropology," virtually unheard of just ten years earlier, further illustrates the diverse types of specialization that have emerged in recent years.)

The content of the conference held in November 1977 to plan for the tenth International Congress of Anthropological and Ethnological Sciences, to take place in India in 1978, reflected the dual quest for specialization and integration as well as the strong influence of the biocultural-evolutionary approach. Thus, the conference schedule contained the following topics: The Lessons of Human Evolution and Pre-History; the Bio-Social Interface; System Analysis in Anthropology; Human Ecology-Models for Human Survival; Symbolic Anthropology and the Psycho-Social Interface; and Public Policy and Anthropology.

Perhaps nowhere was the changing focus of anthropology more apparent than in the area of anthropological studies of women's status. The feminist movement of the 1960s was one of several recent social movements that have occurred in those democratic societies furthest along in the complex set of changes unleashed by the Industrial Revolution. In its turn, the feminist movement provided the impetus for the numerous recent studies that are responsible for the creation of new hypotheses and theory concerning the role of women in human society. Naomi Quinn's review of these studies in the 1977 *Annual Review of Anthropology* lists a bibliography with over 90 entries, the vast majority dated after 1970.

Perhaps one of Quinn's most important observations is that there has been a tendency to consider women's status in the extreme. Within any one society women are perceived as having exceptionally low or exceptionally high status, and this status is often explained by a single variable or "key." In reality, however, wom-

en in most human societies occupy a range of statuses in which they may be higher than, equal to, or lower than males, and in most cases the reasons for these statuses are not explained adequately by single "keys," such as greater male physical strength or women's role in child care, but are in fact the result of a combination of interacting variables.

As anthropologists come to conceptualize social and cultural phenomena in their full complexity, as is required in studies of women's status, they must of necessity move toward greater concentration on realistically defined sociocultural research. Although there has been a growing interest in the quantitative methods that accompany a conceptualization of causality that deals with a number of independent variables, anthropologists have been slow to turn sharply toward a strictly quantitative and statistical approach to explanation. In women's studies and in the discipline as a whole, a qualitative-quantitative mix still predominated as the main mode of analysis.

Thus, anthropology in 1977, like other sociocultural institutions, was undergoing considerable change as it

Archaeologist Carl Clausen examines 6,000-year-old human skull that still contains some brain matter. Along with many other remains the skull was found at Little Salt Spring, a 250-foot-deep sinkhole in Florida.

© National Geographic Society, photo by Kerby Smith

grew in maturity and adapted to the changing context in which it operates. Nonetheless, it retained and strengthened its holistic biocultural emphasis, even as it acquired a variety of increasingly sophisticated specialties. The basic aims of the discipline appeared to have remained relatively stable over the past decade. In 1977, as in 1967, anthropology was concerned with the development of theoretical systems for explaining and understanding biological, cultural, and social processes in a holistic framework.

In the years to come, many segments of the world community will need to undergo innovative change. Knowledge of the interrelationships of humans with their biological, sociocultural, and physical environments will be required if new modes of adaptation and new methods of maintaining meaningful lifeways under conditions of rapid sociocultural evolution are to be evolved. It is the philosophy of anthropology that understanding of the human biocultural past and present in the context of a systematic, multifactorial model of human behavior can lead to flexible modes of planning and successful adjustment to the crises and changes of human existence.

—John J. Poggie, Jr.

Archaeology

To anyone observing the long lines of people waiting to see the Tutankhamen exhibition as it toured the U.S., the continuing growth of public interest in the past and in the discoveries of archaeology was impressive. Even more impressive were the massive sales of copies of the treasures from the young pharaoh's tomb and various manufactured items with Egyptian motifs,

reflecting a kind of cult of that ancient world. The discovery of the tomb by Howard Carter and Lord Carnarvon in the 1920s was, of course, one of the most spectacular episodes in the history of archaeology. Such results of archaeological research are very rare, but they still do occur, as was shown by the recent discoveries of several very rich tombs in China and the reported discovery of the tomb of King Philip II of Macedonia. (*See* below.)

As one examined the reported archaeological finds of recent years, however, it was clear that the current trend was toward the unspectacular, systematic excavation of ancient sites threatened by industrial construction. This kind of rescue archaeology had been going on in America and Europe for many years, but it was now becoming an urgent task in the less developed countries of the Middle East, the Far East, and North Africa. Since many of these countries are archaeologically rich and, as a whole, less well-explored than Europe and America, some dramatic finds could be expected. But the principal result of the systematic extensive rescue digging was to extend to the "emerging nations" a new national interest in archaeology and a new approach to research. Current reports were increasingly taken up with analyses of climatic changes, economic developments, settlement patterns, and the evolution of various techniques. What were once primary concerns of prehistoric archaeologists working with primitive cultures were now being applied to the study of the remains of advanced civilizations.

Pakistan. Pakistan appeared to be the main locus of recent important archaeological discoveries in South Asia. More than half the papers presented at the fourth International Conference of South Asian Archaeology in 1977 were concerned with the Indus civilization or its

Archaeologists inspect bones and pottery lying in a recently discovered tomb in Chinghai Province in northwestern China. The age of the tomb is estimated at 4,000 years.

Keystone

antecedents. The most significant reports concerned excavations at two sites in the area.

Mehrgarh, at the head of the Kachi Plain near the Bolan Pass, is a site with two very different levels of occupation. The later settlement, dating from the mid-3rd to the mid-4th millennium BC, contains extremely fine painted pottery and a great many terra-cotta figurines of mother goddesses. Below this, and separated by several meters of deposit, are the remains of a settlement with buildings of mud or mud-brick and a distinctive stone blade and bone tool industry. Significantly, the upper part of this level contains poorly fired or unfired pottery, while the lower part is preceramic with mud-brick buildings, as in the preceramic sites of the Near East. No carbon dates were yet available for this preceramic level, but it was already clear that, for the first time, evidence had been found in Pakistan for preceramic mud-brick settlements comparable to those in western Asia. This eliminated the disparity—so often noted—of several millennia between these developments in the two regions.

Rehman Dheri, on the Indus plains near Dhera Ismail Khan, was occupied for about a millennium and was abandoned before the start of the mature Indus civilization. Excavations there disclosed a town wall and streets, and aerial photographs indicated an oblong town wall and a regular street pattern. The site contains much beautiful painted pottery, many terra-cotta figurines, and many beads, some of lapis lazuli. There are also numerous pots engraved with owners' marks that resemble the signs of the Indus Valley script, although, of course, they are much older. Continued excavation should yield important evidence for the formative stages of the Indus civilization and of an early urbanism previously unknown in South Asia.

One curious discovery at Shaikhan Dheri might well prove that hard liquor was produced some 1,500 years earlier than had been thought. F. R. Allchin analyzed a peculiar type of pottery vessel found throughout the six-century sequence at the site (2nd century BC to 4th century AD) and concluded that one area of the town was used for the manufacture of alcohol.

Middle East. The continuing British excavations at Saqqara, Egypt, resulted in certain identification of the site of the temple town of the jackal-headed embalmer god, Anubis. This was the quarter of the embalmers, and is mentioned by Greek and Egyptian documents of the last six centuries BC. The town was enclosed by a rectangular mud-brick wall within which were three, or possibly four, temple complexes. One of the temples was identified by a wall scene on a sculptured block showing Ptolemy V Epiphanes (king of Egypt from 205 to 180 BC) before Anubis. Another larger temple enclosure may have been that of the cat-headed goddess Bastet.

The excavation at Tell Mardikh (ancient Ebla) in Syria, which produced more than 30,000 clay tablets during 1975 and 1976, was being described as the most important discovery in the Middle East for a generation. The examination of these tablets had reached a stage where their significance was becoming evident, although only a small portion had been thoroughly studied. Paolo Matthiae, chief of the Italian excavators, described the find as "staggering" and believed the content would revolutionize knowledge of the Middle East in the period c. 2500 BC.

It had been assumed that Egypt and Mesopotamia were the chief centers of power and culture in the region during the 3rd millennium, and that Syria was a peripheral area of little importance. However, the Ebla

Life in Great Britain during the Iron Age, more than 2,000 years ago, is reenacted by a group of British men, women, and children. In a rural area near Shaftesbury, not far from Stonehenge, they have simulated an Iron Age environment, building their own huts, firing pottery, weaving clothes, and tending crops and livestock.

Keystone

discovery shows that there was a state in Syria at that time which was a political, economic, and military power rivaling Mesopotamia. It was a great commercial empire doing business from Anatolia to Palestine and from western Iran to the sea.

The hitherto unknown written language, called Eblaite, can be translated without great difficulty since it is one of the Semitic family of languages, similar to Phoenician and Hebrew, and is written in a cuneiform script. Fortunately, there are bilingual texts in Eblaite and Sumerian and actual dictionaries for the two languages. Eblaite is the oldest known Semitic language, dating approximately 1,300 years before the other known forms.

Preliminary studies of the tablets show that they are equivalent to the files of modern ministries of finance and foreign trade. They also contain international treaties, trade agreements, details of taxes, textbooks for teaching, a kind of encyclopedia, and exercise books with students' homework and the teachers' markings. There are also literary and religious texts and calendars. The excavators had uncovered only a small part of the royal palace, and it was likely that many more tablets would be found.

Emerging, though still sketchy, was a picture of a highly centralized state trading in textiles, clothing, and furniture. There was a king, surrounded by a group of about a dozen figures who probably functioned as ministers. Cities in the empire were either ruled directly from Ebla through governors or bound to the capital in a kind of confederation. Although a military power, the country appears to have been less warlike than Mesopotamia. Years are recorded in relation to royal marriages, births, or journeys rather than, as in Mesopotamia, by conquests. Ebla was conquered and finally destroyed by Mesopotamia about 2300 BC.

Turkish and foreign archaeologists, who joined forces for rescue excavations when the first dam on the Euphrates was built at Keban, planned to collaborate again in a rescue operation with the building of the second dam at Karababa. This would flood ancient Samosata, an important Roman outpost on the right bank, set up for defense against the Parthians. The site includes about 445 ac and is known to contain unexplored antiquities dating from early prehistoric to Byzantine periods.

Recent reports of evidence that agriculture was practiced in the Far East as early as 10,000 BC appeared to have inspired a search for evidence in the Near East that would sustain the traditional view that agriculture first evolved there. In any case, excavations in Palestine at Hayonim terrace below the Hayonim cave suggest that plant cultivation originated there 12,000 years ago.

The terrace below the cave has two periods of occupation corresponding to the last two periods in the cave: Geometric Kebaran and the earlier Natufian. The

Natufian, well known from other sites in Palestine, contains many small flint bladelets and worked bone, including sharply barbed harpoons. The animals hunted were deer, gazelle, and boar. Pollen analysis indicates a wooded environment with olive, tabor oak, and carob trees; this was followed by a drier period with few trees, apparently indicated by a decrease in squirrels. Donald Henry, one of the excavators, claimed that the Natufian population was increasing in size while the environment was deteriorating, and observed that "these circumstances placed considerable stress on the economic base of the society and perhaps led to experimentation with, and adoption of, horticultural economy."

Greece. One of those rare discoveries of archaeological treasures that excite great popular interest was first reported in November 1977 and described in detail in February 1978. Moreover, the search and discovery, extending over a period of 40 years, had all the dramatic elements of the Tutankhamen episode. The find was believed to be the tomb of Philip II of Macedonia, father of Alexander the Great, finally discovered at Vergina in northern Greece by Manolis Andronikos. Actually two tombs were found side by side in a single temple-like building 30 ft below the surface of the great burial mound there and nine feet below ground level, but not at the center of the mound. Both held marble sarcophagi within which were solid gold caskets containing partially burnt bones, one belonging to a man and the other to a woman. There were also gold and silver vessels, a royal diadem of gold, magnificent bronze objects, and armor and weapons in both tombs. Other rich Macedonian tombs containing much gold had been found over the years, but these contained what Andronikos considered to be the most important discovery—intact wall paintings representative of the best in Greek painting, an art form only rarely preserved for the modern world. On the facade of the first tomb was an 18-ft-long frieze of a lion hunt, remarkably similar to a mosaic in Pompeii that is a copy of a painting by the great Greek artist Philoxenos of Eretria. The second tomb contained a 12-ft painting of the rape of Persephone by Pluto.

Since there were no inscriptions, it was difficult to prove beyond doubt that this was the tomb of Philip. Presumably much would depend on proving that the present town of Vergina is ancient Aegae, once the capital of Macedonia. The debate over the identity of Vergina began as early as 1861 and continued during the 40 years of Andronikos' work there. In 1968 N. G. L. Hammond proposed that it was ancient Aegae, and by 1976 Andronikos had begun to believe he was right. Now both men were convinced. Five small ivory heads found in the tomb make up one of the best proofs that it is actually that of Philip II. The heads are believed to be representations of Philip (similar to the famous head on his coins); Alexander; Amyntas and Eurydice, Phil-

(Below) Courtesy of the Ny Carlsberg Glyptotek, Copenhagen; (top) Keystone

Tomb of Philip II of Macedonia (above), discovered in Greece in 1977, contained the gold box (top) in which were found what was believed to be Philip's remains. Father of Alexander the Great, Philip died in 336 BC.

ip's father and mother; and Olympias, Philip's first wife. The writer Pausanias (2nd century AD) describes heads of these five people in ivory and gold in a building called the Philipion at Olympia dedicated by King Philip. All pottery in the tomb can be dated between 350 and 320 BC (Philip was murdered in 336 BC). Other clues are two greaves (leg armor) in the tomb of the male, one an inch or so shorter than the other (Philip is known to have been lame), and the remains of a fatty substance on the bones that may be the "aliphar" described in the *Iliad* as used in the burial ritual of Patroclus, indicating that this is the tomb of no common man.

Great Britain. As in many highly populated countries, rescue archaeology in England was commanding the attention of many archaeologists and organizations. An example of this kind of research was the stripping of 40 ac in advance of reservoir construction at Farmoor, Oxfordshire. The excavations uncovered farmsteads and fields that existed between 600 BC and the medieval period. From the standpoint of the kinds of objects found, this was not dramatic archaeology, but the interpretation of living conditions in ancient times made possible by such exploration constitutes an invaluable addition to knowledge.

At Farmoor it was possible to identify 300 species of insects, 125 species of plants, and 50 types of snails for the period under study. Also identified were a type of specialized pastoral farming that existed in the Iron Age and evidence of small-scale ironworking. In the 5th and 4th centuries BC there were farmsteads with small detached enclosures for circular houses and stock pens, fenced yards, and probably workshops. There were also gravel paths to provide firm footing above the surrounding mire. The economy was entirely pastoral, representing an adjustment to grassland on low land subject to flooding by the Thames; the absence of some common perennial plants shows that each farmstead was used no more than about five years. Traditionally, Iron Age farming was thought to be based on mixed farming, but during the Roman period the settlement pattern underwent drastic change. The flood plain was abandoned as an area of occupation, while the gravel terrace above was enclosed for the first time. Thorn and box hedges are indicated by botanical specimens, suggesting a more permanent settlement than in the Iron Age.

Conservation officials clean mortar from a Roman mosaic pavement unearthed in Milk Street in London. After being cleaned the pavement will be relaid in the Museum of London.

Another rescue excavation, at Seamer Carr near Scarborough in Yorkshire, recovered evidence of settlement extending over several thousand years, beginning at the end of the Ice Age. The earliest material so far recovered was of the Mesolithic Age (*c.* 8000–2700 BC). Later flintwork indicates occupation through the Neolithic and early Bronze ages, dating somewhere between 3500 and 1500 BC. Pottery scattered over a large area suggests a late Neolithic or early Bronze Age settlement covering about 2 ac, an unusually large site for that period. Another important result of this excavation was the recovery of a complete sequence of vegetation deposits in the peat, extending from the Mesolithic to the late prehistoric period, which should make it possible to work out the changing environments over those millennia.

The Americas. Continued research at the site of Real Alto, on the Gulf of Guayaquil in Ecuador, resulted in significant conclusions as to the antiquity of large planned communities with public buildings and ceremonial centers in South America. Moreover, there was now good evidence that maize (corn) was cultivated there by 2900 to 2700 BC. The dates were based on

corrected carbon-14 dating and calibrated with the Valdivia site, not far distant, where connections with the Jomon culture of Japan have been claimed. The sequence of dates at Real Alto extends from 3400 to 2300 BC, and the large planned settlement evolved around 3000 BC. Even considering the very early dates now being determined for the Formative Period in Central America, this is remarkably early for such a development in America.

The population of the site in 3000 BC has been estimated at 1,500. Reconstructions by Donald Lathrap and Jorge Marcos indicate a rectangular plaza 400 m long surrounded by groups of houses of elliptical plan, with massive log walls coated with mud, steeply pitched thatched roofs, and interior post supports. Platforms at the end of the plaza are believed to be the bases of a public building for festivals and for a charnel house. Drinking bowls and the remains of deer, lobster, and crab were found in pits around the festival building. Under the threshold of the charnel house was the burial of a woman in a stonelike tomb, and beside the burial were the dismembered bones of a man. Nearby there was a pit containing the bones of seven other men.

Lathrap suggests that the males had been sacrificed to the woman in the tomb. Within the charnel house bundle burials had been placed on shelves.

Corncobs and kernels embedded in pottery provide evidence for domestic maize. The kernels and cobs are much larger than those of Mexican maize, and, though maize was originally domesticated in Mexico, the researchers believe it was first brought to a high level of productivity in northern South America. Discoveries at Real Alto and Valdivia suggest that Mexico and Peru, which reached peaks of civilization in later times, lagged behind the intermediate area from Ecuador through Central America during this early period.

British archaeologists who attended a conference in Vermont in October 1977 were preparing to issue another criticism of Barry Fell's best-selling *America B.C.* (1976). With academic circumspection, they were limiting their comments to his claim that the Celts reached America in the first or second millennium BC and were refraining from any judgments about the other early migrations from the Old World described in the book. They appeared to have no new or devastating arguments, however, but rather fell back on the familiar observation that the supposed Ogham and Proto-ogham Celtic inscriptions said to be found on rocks in New England could just as well be plow marks, natural cracks, or glacial scouring. They also pointed out that the stone structures Fell reported cannot be compared to European Celtic huts and are most probably root cellars of the colonial period. Since there was no infallible way of proving Fell wrong, the argument would undoubtedly continue.

—Froelich Rainey

Architecture and civil engineering

The Centre National d'Art et de Culture Georges-Pompidou in Paris is a celebration of architecture, engineering, and the industrial landscape. It is among the most significant and controversial new buildings of the past decade.

The Pompidou Center is located in the midst of Beaubourg, a Parisian right-bank neighborhood, about 1 km (0.62 mi) from the cathedral of Notre-Dame de Paris. The new building and its plaza are on a site that had been cleared since the 1930s and was used only as a parking lot; therefore, destructive clearance of the neighborhood's 17th-, 18th-, and 19th-century homogeneous buildings is not a factor in the controversy. What are controversial are the design of the building itself and its visual relationships with its surroundings. To some people, the Center is outrageous, a shocking disruption of Paris, a misplaced oil refinery that they call the "Pompidoleum." To others, it is wonderful and courageous.

The public response to the design of the Center recalls the shock caused by the Eiffel Tower when it was constructed as part of the Paris exhibition of 1889. At that time, many artists and writers wrote a letter to the building director "to protest, with all our strength, with all our indignation, in the name of disregarded French taste, in the name of French art and French history presently in danger, against the erection in the very heart of our capital of the useless and monstrous Eiffel Tower." The Pompidou Center shares with the Eiffel Tower many characteristics: both are metal structures, looking more like erector set constructions than conventional buildings; both are open, light, and transparent; both exploit a sense of being advanced industrial products; both have a sense of technological euphoria; and both use their mechanical imagery as a drawing card for the crowds. During its first year of operation, the Center attracted more visitors than the Eiffel Tower and the Louvre Museum.

The Pompidou Center is named for the late French president Georges Pompidou, who took major steps toward its development in 1969. At that time, a bold concept for a multipurpose national center of the arts and culture was embodied in the requirements of an international competition to select the design and architect of the building. The competition called for facilities for four specialized activities: a museum of art; a reference library; a center for industrial design; and a center for music and acoustic research. Other supporting facilities, such as restaurants, administrative offices, staff services, and parking, were required to be planned on the 5-ac (2-ha) site. The design competition was a worldwide event that attracted 681 entries and had an international jury of architects headed by a French master of metal-building design, Jean Prouvé. It eventually was won by a team of two young architects, Renzo Piano and Richard Rogers, from Italy and the United Kingdom, respectively. Their design was immediately a sensation in Paris.

The Piano and Rogers plan for the Pompidou Center featured maximum flexibility so that the uses of all interior spaces could be changed; therefore, their proposal called for large floor areas unbroken by columns, mechanical equipment, elevators, or other fixed elements that might get in the way of change. In their design, Piano and Rogers located all such structures and services on the outside facades of the structure and created (in collaboration with the engineers, Ove Arup and Partners) a building that is like a large warehouse, with six large, clear floors. Each floor measures 550 ft by 157 ft (168 m by 50 m) and is 23 ft (7 m) high. As of early 1978 the building accommodated the National Museum of Modern Art on floors three and four; a reference library on floors one, two, and three; and temporary exhibitions on floor five; however, all those arrangements can readily change. Indeed, the design intention seems to seek an answer to the age-old

question that has fascinated philosophers, painters, and architects: "How can one have a permanent image of change?"

The facades of the Pompidou Center are, indeed, images of change and flow, of people on escalators and walkways, and of air, water, and electricity in pipes and ducts. Therefore, the visual imagery is akin to an oil refinery or processing plant, and the facades cannot be seen without reference to the structural and mechanical systems that are integral parts of the architectural design. The basic structure consists of large truss beams made of steel tubes and rods. These beams do not rest directly on the steel columns but instead are attached to devices known as "gerberettes," developed by a 19th-century German bridge engineer named Heinrich Gerber. At the outside cantilevered end of each "gerberette," vertical and diagonal rods pull down on the structure in order to achieve an axial load on the column. The facade is, therefore, a complex of columns, rods, and struts that are structurally active. Fire protection of the columns is achieved by their being filled with water. The mechanical systems are located in the basement (chilled water, for exam-

Two Paris buildings that generated great controversy when they were opened are (left) the Eiffel Tower, in 1889, and (below) the Centre National d'Art et de Culture Georges-Pompidou, in 1977.

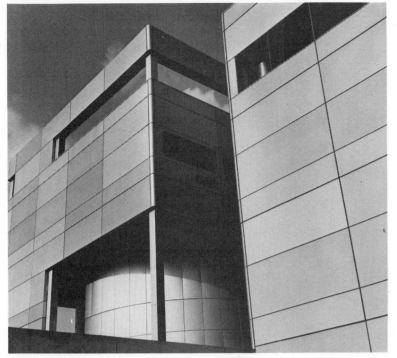

The Bronx Developmental Center in New York City, with its external covering made entirely from aluminum sheet, won the 1977 Bard Award for Excellence in Architecture and Urban Design.

ple), on the roof (heating equipment and exhausts), and on the facades (pipes and ducts for supply and return of air and water).

The result of this design is a highly organized architectural machine. On the back facade, for example, the exposed color-coded mechanical systems are painted red for elevators, blue for heating and air-conditioning ducts, green for water, and yellow for electrical supply. On the front facade, which in historical architecture was embellished with symbols of the stability, permanence, status, and power of authority, the Center consists of a complex collection of glazed galleries and sloping escalators that display the movement of people. The facade expresses the openness of the institution, perhaps the openness and change in society itself.

The Pompidou Center is a striking example of the ability of a building to be a symbol, a cultural image that expresses values. This may be the reason that its design has generated so much controversy. Perhaps the building expresses too clearly the value conflicts and the uncertainties of contemporary society, or perhaps speaks too clearly about restlessness and dynamism without a sense of harmony within itself or with respect to its surroundings, characteristics that could be attributed to contemporary man.

The esthetic roots of the Center are to be found throughout the modern movement in the arts and architecture. It is, probably, the largest achievement of Constructivism, one of the mainstreams of 20th-century thought in architecture and sculpture, which seeks to use modern materials such as metals and glass in welded and bolted constructions that exploit the visual possibilities of lightness, tension, and transparency. The Center is also related to international groups of architects, such as Archigram in the U.K. and Metabolists in Japan, who have sought to embody the changing, dynamic, open-ended aspects of growth in their designs. Thus, though the Center may seem utterly new, it has a clear line of descent from the steel structures for museums and convention halls by Ludwig Mies van der Rohe and from Cedric Price's 1962 "Fun Palace" project for Joan Littlewood. The Center is also a part of the French tradition of metal structures for buildings, including the 19th-century libraries of Henri Labrouste; the market sheds for Les Halles; the Galerie des Machines for the 1889 Paris exhibition; and the metal panels and frame structures of Jean Prouvé. But in spirit the Center is most reminiscent of a British structure that heralded the new age of metal and glass construction, of machine production, of prefabrication and industrialization, and of the esthetic of lightness: the Crystal Palace, built by Joseph Paxton in London in 1851.

In conclusion, it is not possible to give a simple answer to questions such as, "Do you like the Center's design?" or "Is the Center a good design?" In some respects, it is outstanding, courageous, and memorable, as, for example, in the openness of its spirit and in the sense of public participation in its spectacle. But, on the other hand, it can be viewed as awesome, tyrannical, and menacing in its technological arrogance. It does not pay much attention to fundamentals of human comfort, orientation, harmonious repose, and sense of

261

place. In its urban neighborhood, it seems to be a spaceship moored in a clearing of Paris. In its facades and interior spaces, it presents an image that has some of the frantic fascination of the machines in Charlie Chaplin's movie *Modern Times.*

—Robert Geddes

Astronomy

The solar system provided the setting for what were probably the two most surprising discoveries in astronomy during the past year. In March 1977 several groups of astronomers almost simultaneously discovered that the planet Uranus was surrounded by five rings, and in November what appeared to be a tiny planet was detected orbiting the Sun between Saturn and Uranus. Other highlights included the discovery of a dwarf galaxy and of a star that seems to be in the process of forming planets.

Rings of Uranus. No other astronomical discovery in recent months attracted as much public attention as the unexpected finding that the planet Uranus is surrounded by a system of five very faint, narrow rings. Their nearly simultaneous detection by several groups of U.S., Australian, Indian, and South African scientists

was a by-product of observations of the predicted occultation of the 8.8-magnitude star SAO 158687 by Uranus on March 10, 1977. This occultation was important because measurements of the intensity of the light of the star as it faded in going behind Uranus and brightened on reappearing were expected to provide new information concerning the amount, structure, and composition of the Uranian atmosphere. The visibility of the occultation was limited to the Indian Ocean and adjoining parts of South Africa, India, Australia, and Antarctica.

The most important observations of the rings were made by Cornell University astronomer James Elliot and others aboard the Kuiper Airborne Observatory, a modified C-141 aircraft carrying a gyrostabilized 36-in reflecting telescope. At the time of the occultation, this plane was at an altitude of 41,000 ft over the South Indian Ocean, about 1,200 mi southwest of Perth, Australia. Elliot's team was using a high-speed photoelectric photometer to measure the combined light of Uranus and the star, which was recorded on both magnetic tape and a paper strip chart. About 40 minutes before the star was scheduled to pass behind Uranus, it suddenly dimmed and remained much fainter for seven seconds before suddenly regaining its previous full light. During the next nine minutes, the star's light un-

Astronomers aboard the Kuiper Airborne Observatory (above), a modified C-141 aircraft carrying a 36-inch reflecting telescope, discovered that the planet Uranus is surrounded by five very faint, narrow rings (right).

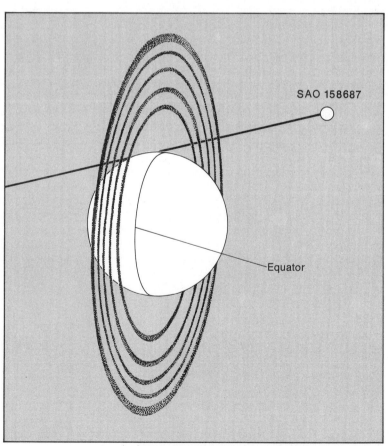

SAO 158687

Equator

(Left) Courtesy, NASA, Ames Research Center; (right) adapted from information obtained from Cornell University, Ithaca, N.Y.

derwent four more dips, each lasting about one second. Then, approximately 30 to 40 minutes after the occultation of the star by the disk of Uranus itself, the same sequence of temporary dimmings occurred in reverse order.

Elliot and his colleagues interpreted this symmetrical pattern of dimmings as due to five very narrow rings around Uranus. Beginning with the innermost and proceeding outward, the rings are called Alpha, Beta, Gamma, Delta, and Epsilon. The distances of the first four from the center of Uranus are 27,860, 28,460, 29,670, and 30,090 mi, respectively. (The radius of Uranus itself is about 16,200 mi.) These dimensions were calculated on the assumptions that the rings are circular and lie in the same plane as the orbits of Uranus' satellites. The radius of the Epsilon ring is about 32,000 mi, but apparently this ring is either slightly elliptical or slightly inclined to the satellite orbit plane.

Less complete observations were made at Perth Observatory in Australia by Robert Millis and others using a photoelectric photometer attached to a 24-in telescope. Before these observations were halted by dawn, five temporary dimmings of the star were recorded, including the initial occultations by the Epsilon, Gamma, and Beta rings. The times of these events were closely consistent with those recorded by Elliot 1,200 mi away, a strong confirmation that the ring interpretation is correct.

Other identifiable dimmings produced by one or more of the rings were recorded photoelectrically at Cape Town, South Africa, and at Naini Tal and Kavalur in India. The combined data indicate that the ring Epsilon is not uniform along its length, since the various timed durations of its dimming are unequal: 7 seconds at the Kuiper Airborne Observatory, 8 seconds at Perth, and 8.9 seconds at Kavalur for its first occultation, and 3 seconds at the Kuiper Airborne Observatory for the final occultation.

The four inner rings, Alpha through Delta, are each only about eight miles wide, while Epsilon is several times broader. This is in marked contrast to the well-known rings of Saturn, each of which is more than 10,000 mi wide. However, J. C. Bhattacharyya and M. K. V. Bappu, after a close inspection of the Kavalur observations, reported 19 other brief dimmings of the star, which they attributed to small bodies in orbit around Uranus. These Indian scientists proposed that the planet is actually surrounded by a set of three very broad but tenuous rings resembling Saturn's, with the features Alpha through Epsilon being local condensations in the outer broad ring. As of early 1978 this interpretation had yet to be confirmed.

After the discovery of the Uranian rings several astronomers sought to observe the rings directly. Using the 74-in reflector at Lowell Observatory in Flagstaff, Ariz., William Baum's group made careful attempts to photograph the rings in infrared light but did not detect them. From this Baum concluded that the rings must be composed of very dark material, reflecting less than 5% of the sunlight falling on them. Other attempts by Bradford Smith and his associates to record the rings with the 61-in and 90-in telescopes of the Steward Observatory at the University of Arizona gave only marginal evidence of the rings' presence and confirmed that the reflectivity of the ring material must be low.

Giuseppe Colombo and William Sinton independently pointed out what may be a prediscovery photograph that reveals the rings. Published in 1972, this picture of the disk of Uranus is a composite of many high-resolution images taken on March 26–27, 1970, by Princeton University astronomers with a 36-in telescope that was carried 80,000 ft aloft by a balloon. On this picture a very faint streak crossing the planet's disk may be the shadow of the rings.

By far the most sensitive method for detecting the rings, however, is the same photoelectric technique that led to their actual discovery in March 1977. Therefore, occultations of stars by the rings will continue as the major source for new observations. The predicted occultation of a 12th-magnitude star on Dec. 23, 1977, was in fact observed at Lowell Observatory but under unfavorable conditions.

The existence and structure of the rings pose interesting problems to celestial mechanicians. All five rings lie well inside Roche's limit for Uranus; this is the distance (about 40,000 mi) from the planet's center within which a large satellite would be torn apart by tidal forces. Peter Goldreich and Philip Nicholson pointed out that the locations of the rings are probably influenced by the orbital motions of the Uranian satellites Ariel and especially Miranda. Colombo noted that the 9½-hour revolution period of the Epsilon ring is approximately 5/4 times the period of the Alpha ring, 6/5 times that of Beta, 9/8 times that of Gamma, and 11/10 times that of Delta.

Chiron. A newly discovered faint, distant object in orbit around the Sun attracted considerable interest because it did not fit into any of the usual categories of solar system objects. Charles Kowal of the California Institute of Technology discovered the object, named Chiron, on Nov. 1, 1977, while comparing two photographs he had taken on October 18 and 19 with the 48-in Schmidt telescope at Palomar Observatory in California. This revealed an 18th-magnitude object moving very slowly among the stars—almost as slowly as Uranus, which implied that it was nearly as distant from the Sun as that planet. From the apparent brightness and distance of the object, Kowal estimated that its diameter was several hundred miles. Because its photographic images were sharp rather than fuzzy, he called his find planetary rather than cometary.

By late November more positions of Chiron had been measured at Palomar, Harvard, and McDonald observatories, and Kowal had identified prediscovery images

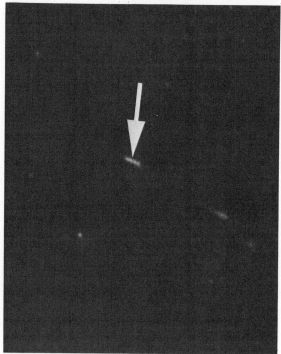

Chiron, an object several hundred miles in diameter that orbits the Sun, was first identified in 1977.

on two photographs he had taken in September 1969, with the 48-in Schmidt telescope. From this material Brian Marsden established that Chiron is traveling around the Sun in a 50.7-year orbit.

With the motion of Chiron thus reliably known, it became possible to identify it on additional old photographs taken with Harvard observatory telescopes in 1895, 1941, 1943, and 1976 and at Palomar in 1952. (Curiously, on the 1941 Harvard plate the short trail of Chiron had been marked by an arrow in ink in the early 1950s, but its nature had not then been recognized.)

With the available observations extending over 1½ revolutions, Marsden could calculate Chiron's orbital elements accurately.

The orbit of Chiron is decidedly elliptical, this object's distance from the Sun ranging from 8.509 to 18.881 astronomical units (791 million to 1,755 million mi). Thus, at perihelion Chiron is a little inside the orbit of Saturn and at aphelion nearly as far as Uranus. However, because of the tilt between the planes of the orbits of Chiron and Saturn, the two orbits do not intersect. When Chiron next returns to perihelion in February 1996, it will become as bright as magnitude 14½. One complete revolution around the Sun at present takes 50.68 years.

Marsden also calculated the changes in the orbit of Chiron over a period of 11½ centuries due to perturbations by the principal planets. He found such changes to be relatively small, though approaches to within 1.1 and 1.3 astronomical units of Saturn had occurred. The average time required for Chiron to complete a revolution around the Sun during this period was about 49 years. Chiron presents an interesting case in celestial mechanics because to a close approximation it completes one revolution for every four of Jupiter, three for every five of Saturn, and two for every one of Uranus.

The classification of Chiron is debatable. In size it is comparable to the largest asteroids, but it moves in a part of the solar system where no known asteroid intrudes except for 1036 Ganymede. The absence of a coma is compatible with a comet at a large distance from the Sun, but Chiron is many times larger than the typical comet nucleus. Possibly it and Pluto are the first discovered members of a new class of small planets in the outer parts of the solar system.

Io's sodium cloud. The second closest satellite to the planet Jupiter is Io, long notorious for its unusual properties. In 1973 Robert Brown at Harvard University discovered that the spectrum of Io shows the yellow

Photograph from Table Mountain Observatory in California reveals sodium vapor surrounding Jupiter's satellite Io. The satellite is indicated by the white dot at the left, and the sodium cloud is both the dark area and the luminescence around it; the dark area is the shadow of the occulting disk used to keep the reflected sunlight from Io out of the spectrograph. Jupiter is at the right.

emission lines of sodium. His observations revealed that the faint luminous glow of sodium vapor comes from a region of space several times larger than Io itself, which is the size of our Moon. In recent months several teams of astronomers succeeded in photographing Io's sodium cloud. Using the 60-in and 100-in telescopes at Mount Wilson Observatory in California, Guido Münch and Jay Bergstralh ascertained that the sodium cloud appears elongated by tens of thousands of miles along Io's orbit, both preceding and following the satellite. The cloud is brightest on the side of Io that always faces Jupiter and is shaped roughly like a banana.

Similar results were obtained by Dennis Matson and his associates with the 24-in reflector at Table Mountain Observatory in southern California. The sodium emission region ahead of Io in its orbit is larger than the region that follows. According to a study made at Wise Observatory in Israel, the luminous sodium vapor extends at least halfway around the orbit of Io.

A widely accepted theory of the origin of the sodium cloud was proposed by Matson, who noted that the surface of Io is an excellent reflector of light and on the basis of spectroscopic investigations appears to be covered largely by salt deposits. Io is bombarded by blasts of high-energy particles from Jupiter's magnetosphere, and this should lead to ejection of sodium ions from the salt surface of Io; these ions later escape from the satellite's weak gravitational field. Sunlight can then cause this sodium ion vapor to fluoresce and emit the characteristic yellow lines of sodium. The asymmetry of the cloud, Matson speculated, may be due either to the distribution of salt across Io's surface, the ejection process, or the ionized gas from Jupiter's magnetosphere. Io and its sodium cloud were to be subjected to close-up scrutiny by the two Voyager spacecraft launched toward Jupiter during the summer of 1977.

Dwarf galaxy in Carina. Many notable new deep-sky objects were discovered in the southern sky by two major coordinated surveys. At Siding Spring Observatory in Australia, British astronomers mapped the heavens in blue light to a very faint limiting magnitude with a 48-in Schmidt telescope, while a similar survey in red light was being conducted with the 39-in Schmidt telescope at the European Southern Observatory in Chile. The goal of this effort was to extend the famous National Geographic Society-Palomar Observatory survey of the northern sky, done about 30 years ago, to the south celestial pole. Owing to great improvements in the sensitivity of photographic emulsions, the new surveys can record considerably fainter objects.

On plates taken with the Siding Spring telescope, R. D. Cannon noticed a peculiar object in the southern constellation Carina. It consists of a loose swarm of thousands of very faint stars covering an area nearly the angular size of the full Moon. He noted that it

Courtesy, Royal Observatory, Edinburgh © 1977

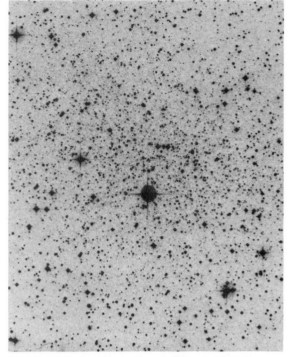

Dwarf elliptical galaxy in the southern constellation Carina is the gray patch in the center of the photograph.

resembles in appearance the two nearby dwarf spheroidal galaxies in Sculptor and Fornax, probably being a less populous system of the same class.

The distance to the Carina dwarf galaxy was provisionally estimated at about 500,000 light-years, or about three times the distance to the Large and Small Magellanic Clouds. Thus, the Carina system is a new member of the approximately two dozen nearby galaxies that comprise the Local Group, which includes the Milky Way, the great Andromeda and Triangulum spiral galaxies, and the Fornax and Sculptor systems.

The Carina system is the seventh dwarf spheroidal galaxy to have been discovered and the first since the completion of the National Geographic-Palomar survey. Presumably, few of these fully resolved nearby galaxies remain undiscovered.

Vela pulsar. In the southern constellation Vela is a large area of radio emission and nebulosity forming the remnant of a supernova explosion that occurred nearly 10,000 years ago, just as the Crab Nebula in Taurus is the remnant of the supernova of AD 1054. Inside the Vela object, Australian radio astronomers in 1968 had discovered a pulsar with a period of 0.089 second. This is the shortest period known for any pulsar, surpassed only by the faint star at the center of the Crab Nebula that emits pulses of radio energy and light each 0.033 second.

The optical counterpart of the Vela pulsar has now been identified with certainty by astronomers at Siding

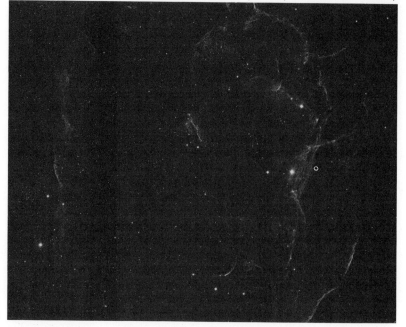

Nebulosity that is associated with the Vela pulsar covers much of the southern sky.

Spring Observatory, by an extraordinary observation with the 154-in telescope. From previous radio studies the position of the pulsar was known to about one second of arc. Very close to that place an extremely faint star of blue (photographic) magnitude about 23.7 had been photographed by Barry Lasker. This was far too faint to be seen in the Siding Spring telescope.

The Australian team used a photoelectric photometer to make a tape recording of the sky brightness of several areas five seconds of arc across, around the radio position. After one or two hours of data were obtained from an area, a computer analysis of the tape was made to search for an 0.089-second cycle. Two overlapping areas did show this periodicity, indicating that light flashes were being emitted by the Vela pulsar. The average brightness of the source corresponds to a yellow (visual) magnitude of 24.2(±0.1), making this one of the faintest celestial objects ever observed optically. The deduced position is within 1.7 seconds of arc of the Lasker star, which thus is identical to the pulsing light and radio source. Optically, the Vela pulsar is about seven magnitudes fainter than the Crab Nebula star, in good agreement with theoretical expectations.

MWC 349. A faint star in the constellation Cygnus, designated MWC 349, has demonstrated remarkable behavior which indicates that it is in the process of forming a family of planets. Our solar system is now generally believed to have originally consisted of a huge, flattened, spinning disk of gas and dust. As mass became concentrated toward the center, the disk eventually became luminous. Then, as glowing material spiraled inward, the disk cooled rapidly, much of its material escaping into space and a small fraction condensing into planets.

MWC 349 seems to be undergoing just this process at the present time. There are three basic pieces of observational evidence. First, at visible wavelengths this object has an abnormally high intrinsic luminosity. Second, it has been fading at the rate of about 1% per month since it was first identified in 1930 as a 13th-magnitude star. Third, the spectrum of the radiated energy is not that of a hot star but that predicted for a glowing disk of dust and gas. The critical observations that established this last fact were infrared measurements, made partly with the 36-in reflector of the Kuiper Airborne Observatory and partly with the 90-in reflector at the Steward Observatory.

In the model proposed to account for the observations of MWC 349, the disk appears to have 20 times the diameter of the central star and to emit 10 times as much light. (The star itself has approximately 30 times the mass of our Sun and is roughly 10,000 light-years distant.)

The disk is cooling from the outer edge inward. Its luminous part is believed to be the inner portion of a surrounding large disk of nonluminous gas and dust from which outer planets may have already formed. Superimposed on our solar system, this nonluminous disk would extend beyond Pluto, while the glowing inner part would reach beyond the Earth's orbit. The observed rate of fading of MWC 349 indicates that the luminosity of the inner portion of the disk will be gone in a century.

HEAO 1. X-ray astronomy continues to be one of the most exciting frontiers of astrophysics. Rocket experiments and satellite missions have revealed several hundred X-ray sources. Perhaps two-thirds of these are inside our galaxy, while the rest are extragalactic,

266

associated with radio galaxies, Seyfert galaxies, quasars, and clusters of galaxies.

Important advances can be expected from the series of three High Energy Astronomy Observatory (HEAO) satellites, of which the first was launched on Aug. 12, 1977 (nearly four months later than originally planned). HEAO 1, weighing more than 2½ tons, is the heaviest unmanned satellite ever flown by the United States. For further information, see SPACE EXPLORATION: *Space probes.*

—Joseph Ashbrook

Chemistry

The search for alternate sources of energy and for chemical reactions that duplicate or, at least, approach some of the incredible biochemical activities found in living creatures remained a dominant concern for chemists during the past year. Two special types of radiant energy, laser light and synchrotron radiation, found new uses, and several novel molecular syntheses were reported. Dioxirane, an unstable molecule whose existence was previously unsuspected, was shown to play a significant part in atmospheric chemistry, particularly in reactions that produce smog.

Inorganic chemistry

Research in inorganic chemistry during the past year remained concerned primarily with the more basic problems of the science. These included investigations of the syntheses and reactions of new compounds, and of the bonding and structures of these and other inorganic molecules. Many of the modern tools of chemistry and physics are made use of in these studies, particularly those that exploit the magnetic and electrical characteristics of electron-nucleus relationships and of electrons participating in the chemical bond. Nevertheless, each succeeding year finds in-

creased research in fields related to practical problems of energy, solid-state electronics, and biology.

Bioinorganic chemistry. A few years ago some inorganic chemists directed their research toward biological systems that contain metals, and toward synthetic models of the natural metal proteins and metal porphyrins, the latter being a class of nitrogen-containing molecules that form an integral part of hemoglobins, chlorophylls, and other biologically important protein complexes. They were able to bring to this interdisciplinary study a new approach that had not been the center of attention of the biologist and the biochemist, an approach that concentrated primarily on the metals in these metal-biological systems.

So successful have the efforts of these scientists been that in the short span of about a decade a division of inorganic chemistry known as bioinorganic chemistry has materialized. Books have been devoted to the subject, a journal entitled *Bioinorganic Chemistry* was founded in 1971, and several national and international symposia have been held to report and discuss scientific accomplishments.

Oxygen carriers and oxygen activation constitute one active area of bioinorganic research, to which James P. Collman and his co-workers at Stanford University have made important contributions. In 1973 they reported the synthesis of a "picket fence" iron (II)-porphyrin complex that mimics the natural iron-porphyrin-protein complex myoglobin in its ability to carry oxygen, or bind it reversibly. (Iron(II) is an iron atom missing two electrons; *i.e.*, the ion Fe^{2+}.) In 1977 they reported the synthesis and characterization of pairs of porphyrins bound "face to face" and speculated about the syntheses and properties of some metal derivatives of these porphyrins.

A schematic representation of a proposed "face-to-face" iron(II)-porphyrin compound and its reaction with oxygen is shown in (1). In this diagram the ovals, each with an iron atom in its center, represent ring-shaped porphyrins, and B is an axial molecular structure that is

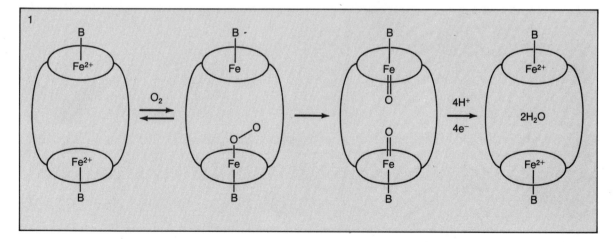

too large to fit in the well-protected "pocket" between the atoms of iron. It was suggested that this arrangement will catalyze, or accelerate, the otherwise difficult four-electron reduction of oxygen to two molecules of water. Such catalysts are essential to the development of fuel cells that generate electricity from the water-forming reaction of hydrogen and air-derived oxygen. The iron compound may also serve as a model for the activation of oxygen by the more complicated natural iron proteins and iron porphyrins. Furthermore, it will be of interest to insert molybdenum into the "face-to-face" porphyrin and determine if it will catalyze the more difficult six-electron reduction of nitrogen to ammonia. In nature this is accomplished by nitrogenase, an iron-molybdenum enzyme employed by nitrogen-fixing microorganisms. Molybdenum is believed to afford the active site for the reduction of nitrogen.

Two of the more important natural oxygen carriers are hemoglobin and myoglobin, both of which are iron (II)-porphyrin complexes combined with the protein globin. The iron family group of the periodic table of elements consists of iron, ruthenium, and osmium, and it has long been of interest to prepare ruthenium(II) and osmium(II) porphyrins and to compare their oxygen-carrying properties with that of the corresponding iron (II) porphyrin. Half of this goal was achieved recently by a research group led by David Dolphin and Brian James at the University of British Columbia. They reported the synthesis of a ruthenium(II)-porphyrin complex and the observation that in certain solvents it acts as an oxygen carrier at room temperature. The corresponding synthetic iron(II) porphyrin reversibly binds oxygen only at temperatures below −50° C (−58° F). The investigators attribute the greater stability of the ruthenium-oxygen complex to its greater tendency to form $Ru(III)O_2^-$, relative to the iron-oxygen system.

Further study of the ruthenium, and later perhaps osmium, system should provide useful indirect information regarding the biologically important iron-porphyrin complexes.

Another biological system of recent interest to inorganic chemists is that of the blue copper proteins. These electron-transfer proteins are components of such natural proteins as azurin, ascorbate oxidase, and stellacyanin, and some of them are involved in plant photosynthesis and the movement of iron within the animal body. Compared with ordinary copper chemical complexes, the blue copper proteins have most unusual spectral properties, one of which is their intense blue color. These proteins have been probed by a variety of techniques, and it has been suggested that copper is surrounded by nitrogen atoms of imidazole (2) and sulfur atoms of a thiolate to give structures of the type CuN_3S, CuN_4S, and CuN_2S_2.

Many attempts have been made to prepare copper complexes with the unusual properties of the blue copper proteins. Modest success was achieved in several cases, but perhaps the most successful model was one (3) reported recently by James A. Ibers, Tobin J. Marks, and co-workers at Northwestern University, Evanston, III. This compound is of the CuN_3S type, but it should be noted that the nitrogens are not from imidazole and, in fact, none of the groups attached to copper has any biological significance, yet the model complex has properties that closely resemble those of the blue copper proteins.

What had been needed was a definitive X-ray structure of one of the natural proteins, but this had not been accomplished because it was not possible to grow crystals suitable for X-ray study. Such an achievement was finally reported by the research group of Hans C. Freeman at the University of Sydney, Australia. A skel-

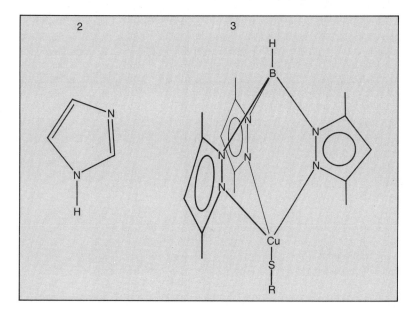

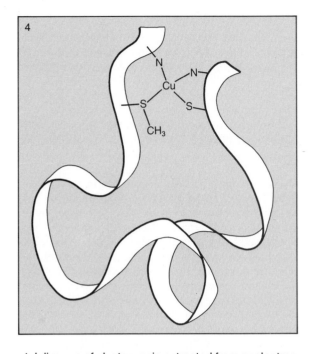

etal diagram of plastocyanin extracted from poplar tree leaves is shown in (4). This protein has a molecular weight of about 10,500, and the copper atom exists in a distorted tetrahedral environment of the type CuN_2S_2 near an opening of the folded protein chain. The two nitrogen atoms are part of imidazole groups, and the $S-CH_3$ sulfur atom and the other sulfur belong to the amino acids methionine and cysteine, respectively. The important feature of the structure of plastocyanin is not that it is of type CuN_2S_2 rather than the model CuN_3S, but that the copper(II) is in a distorted tetrahedral environment. This structure is between that of the stable square planar structure of copper(II) complexes and the stable tetrahedral structure of copper(I) complexes. Such an intermediate structure would readily permit the conversion Cu(II) + 1 electron $\rightleftharpoons$ Cu(I), which is an essential part of the electron-transfer function of the blue copper proteins.

Homogeneous catalysis. Catalysis is an essential part of the chemical and petroleum industry, with about 90% of its production resulting from various catalytic processes. Most of these involve the use of heterogeneous catalysts, which are usually metals or metal oxides, with reactants and products that are either liquids or gases. The first homogeneous catalyst, *i.e.*, one that shares the same state of matter with at least one of the reactants, to be used commercially in the large-scale production of certain organic chemicals was dicobalt octacarbonyl. A few years later a palladium complex was used for the oxidation in air of ethylene to acetaldehyde. These successful industrial processes spurred intensive research activity in the search for other important reactions that make use of homogeneous catalysts, and many inorganic chemists, interested in organometallic chemistry, have made important contributions.

One advantage of homogeneous over heterogeneous catalysis is that the former generally gives reactions of greater selectivity. For example, the present industrial process for the oxidation of hydrocarbons yields a mixture of oxygen-containing products. However, certain metal-containing enzymes catalyze the selective oxidation of alkanes (noncyclic hydrocarbons possessing only single bonds, such as CH_4 and C_3H_8) to alkyl alcohols; for example, $CH_4 + O_2 + 2H^+ + 2e^- \rightarrow CH_3OH + H_2O$. The chemist would like to be able to duplicate this type of reaction, and there is reason to believe that someday this could be done with the use of an appropriate homogeneous catalyst.

Homogeneous catalysis research continued to attack the very important problem of the reduction of carbon monoxide with hydrogen to yield hydrocarbons; *e.g.*, $3H_2 + CO \rightarrow CH_4 + H_2O$. This is presently accomplished by the Fischer-Tropsch process, which uses a heterogeneous catalyst and rather severe conditions of temperature and pressure for the gasification and liquefaction of coal. The goal of research employing homogeneous catalysts was the discovery of a more efficient process to selectively convert coal, by the use of carbon monoxide, to hydrocarbon products that can serve as fuels or feedstocks for other petrochemical processes.

In recent years progress had been reported with such reactions of carbon monoxide using metal-cluster compounds—*i.e.*, molecules containing groups of adjacent metal atoms—as catalysts (see *1978 Yearbook of Science and the Future* Year in Review: CHEMISTRY: *Inorganic chemistry*). Subsequent research showed that such clusters of metal atoms were not required for the reduction of carbon monoxide. For example, Kenneth G. Caulton and his students at Indiana University, Bloomington, Ind., reported the reduction of carbon monoxide by its homogeneous reaction with hydrogen in the presence of a molecule containing a single atom of titanium, $(C_5H_5)_2Ti(CO)_2$. The reaction takes place readily at normal atmospheric pressure and a temperature of 150° C (300° F). Related to this study was work by the research group of John E. Bercaw at the California Institute of Technology, which carried out the hydrogen reduction of carbon monoxide to methyl alcohol, CH_3OH, in the presence of $[C_5(CH_3)_5]_2Zr(CO)_2$, which contains only one atom of zirconium.

Unfortunately, neither the Caulton nor the Bercaw reaction is catalytic; however, they do provide information on the mechanism of the reaction of carbon monoxide with hydrogen on a metal center. Such knowledge may lead ultimately to the discovery of a suitable homogeneous catalyst for the conversion of coal into petroleum products.

—Fred Basolo

Organic chemistry

With its roots in 19th-century medicinal and natural-products chemistry, organic chemistry during the year showed an ever-increasing interest in biological problems. At the same time, a number of fundamental chemical processes were the subject of renewed scrutiny.

Nucleophilicity and electrophilicity. Most theories of chemical reactivity are based on the results of experiments carried out in solution, but the precise influence of the solvent on the structure and stability of transition states and intermediates in organic reactions is poorly understood. Using a technique known as ion cyclotron resonance (ICR), a number of investigators probed fundamental questions of reactivity in the gas phase. John I. Brauman of Stanford University reported a study of bimolecular nucleophilic (electron-donating) substitution reactions and determined the intrinsic nucleophilicity and leaving group abilities of a variety of substrates. (Leaving group ability describes the relative ease with which one atom or group of atoms is displaced by a nucleophilic attacking agent.) While the gas-phase reactions were orders of magnitude faster than the corresponding solution processes, the relative order of nucleophilicity was similar in the gas phase and in dipolar solvents that do not yield or accept a proton; this order was quite different in proton-donating solvents. Also using ICR, Warren J. Hehre and Robert T. McIver, Jr., of the University of California at Irvine found that in the gas phase ring protonation of phenol (acquisition of an additional proton) is favored over protonation of oxygen in contrast to predominant protonation of oxygen in solution.

Chemiluminescence. The mechanisms by which organic reactions generate light, chemiluminescence, were the subjects of a variety of inquiries. Hans Wijnberg of the State University of Groningen in The Netherlands demonstrated that the thermal decomposition of an optically active dioxetane (one that rotates the plane of polarization of plane-polarized light) results in the emission of circularly polarized light (1). As part of a continuing investigation of the mechanism of flavin-dependent enzymatic reactions, Thomas C. Bruice of the University of California at Santa Barbara observed chemiluminescence during the decomposition of 4a-flavin alkyl peroxides, a model for bacterial bioluminescence not involving a dioxetane intermediate.

Synthesis of natural products. The year 1977 marked the 60th birthday of one of the giants in the history of organic chemistry, Robert B. Woodward of Harvard University. The annual Peter Leermakers Symposium at Wesleyan University was dedicated to Woodward, and more than 1,000 faculty, students, and research chemists from universities and chemical companies attended. Gilbert J. Stork of Columbia University described his approach to the synthesis of the physiologically active fungal metabolite, cytochalasin B. The cytochalasins were the subject of intensive investigation, both because of their intriguing biological properties, such as their ability to cause cells to extrude their nuclei, and the chemical challenge of constructing the fused polycyclic (two or more closed atomic rings) skeleton carrying the array of oxygen and nitrogen atoms characteristic of this complex class of natural products.

In recent years a great deal of effort has been directed at the total synthesis of a variety of complex antibiotic and antitumor substances. An important class of such substances is the macrolide antibiotics, represented by erythromycin A. The stereochemical complexity and diverse functionality of this large-ring lactone stimulated a number of imaginative chemical strategies aimed at its synthesis. (Stereochemistry deals with the spatial arrangement of atoms and groups in molecules.) One particularly ingenious approach was described by Woodward in which the various methyl groups are introduced as part of sulfur-containing rings and then unmasked at a later stage by desulfurization. This technique of controlling stereochemistry by the use of rigid ring systems that are opened at an appropriate stage has been a hallmark of

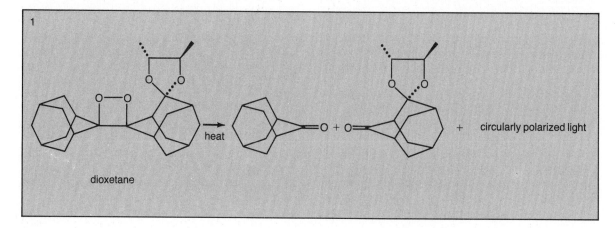

dioxetane   heat   + circularly polarized light

Woodward's work and has had an incalculable impact on the way in which organic chemists design their strategies for synthesis.

Other notable syntheses described during the year included those by Yoshito Kishi of Harvard University, who prepared the redtide nerve poison, saxitoxin, and two members of the mitomycin family of antitumor substances, porfiromycin and deiminomitomycin A. Arthur C. Schultz of Cornell University used a high-yield photochemical cyclization as a key step in the synthesis of the alkaloid lycoramine. (Cyclization is the formation of one or more rings in a chemical compound.)

Renewed interest in prostaglandins (compounds containing 20 carbon atoms and formed from fatty acids occurring in the human body) was stimulated by the discovery of the prostacyclins, potent inhibitors of the aggregation of the disklike platelet components of blood. Such aggregations lead to sometimes lethal clots in diseased blood vessels. Syntheses of prostacyclin were reported by Roy A. Johnson and co-workers at the Upjohn Co. and by Elias J. Corey of Harvard University. A good example of the interaction of synthetic organic chemistry and fundamental studies of chemical structure and reactivity was provided by the preparation of 2,3-dioxabicyclo [2.2.1] heptane independently by two research groups, those of Robert G. and Mary F. Salamon at Case Western Reserve University and of Ned A. Porter at Duke University. These peroxides comprise the nucleus of the prostaglandin endoperoxides, PGG_2 and PGH_2. The latter are key intermediates in the biosynthesis of prostacyclins.

Biosynthesis. Biosynthetic research is the study of the mechanisms by which naturally occurring substances are synthesized by living systems. Working in this area during the year, Robert E. Hill and Ian D. Spenser of McMaster University at Hamilton, Ont., demonstrated intact incorporation of glycerol into all carbon atoms of pyridoxal, vitamin B_6, thereby settling a long-standing controversy. The revision of the stereochemistry of isovincoside, a key precursor of the large family of monoterpene indole alkaloids, by J. Stockigts and Meinhart H. Zenk of the Ruhr University in Bochum, West Germany, also removed a matter of considerable confusion and controversy.

The study of the intricate pathways by which nature synthesizes porphyrins and corrins, the nuclei of heme and vitamin B_{12}, respectively, stimulated a number of ingenious solutions to the problems inherent in the biosynthesis of these complex substances. One debate centered on the precise details of the "switch" mechanism by which a variety of natural porphyrin described as Type III is formed from the monocyclic (single-ring) precursor porphobilinogen. Alan R. Battersby and Edward McDonald and their collaborators at the University of Cambridge presented strong evidence that the rearrangement occurs subsequent to formation of a linear tetrapyrrole (2). The work was made possible by preparation of a highly purified enzyme system from the alga *Euglena gracilis*, development of an efficient high-pressure liquid chromatography system for separation of the various porphyrin isomers, and by the application of carbon magnetic resonance (subjecting a carbon atom to magnetic fields that alternate at frequencies which are in synchronism with the natural frequency of the atom's spin system; this causes the spin system to absorb energy at specific, resonant frequencies).

A second area of intense interest and speculation was the biosynthetic link between porphyrins and corrins. Having previously established the precursor role of uroporphyrinogen (urogen) III, the research groups of Battersby and of A. Ian Scott of Yale and Texas A & M universities independently reported the potential intermediacy of a new class of substances known as sirohydrochlorins. Scott's group also demonstrated that the conversion of urogen III to corrin involves the loss of a single carbon atom at the oxidation state of formaldehyde.

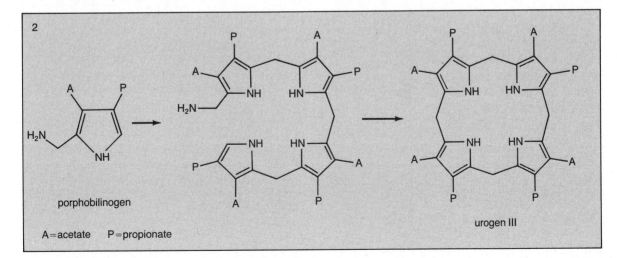

2

porphobilinogen

A = acetate   P = propionate

urogen III

Adapted from *Science News*, Vol. 112, Nov. 19, 1977, p. 340

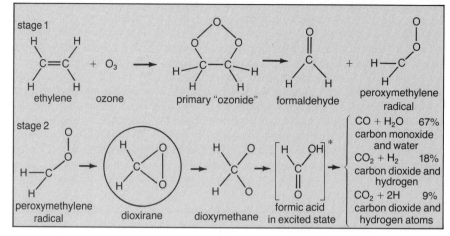

Dioxirane (encircled), a newly discovered product of the reactions of olefins and ozone, plays an important intermediary role in the formation of smog.

Dioxirane. A new organic compound, dioxirane, was detected for the first time during the past year. Consisting of two hydrogen, one carbon, and two oxygen atoms, dioxirane differs from other similar compounds by the ring formed by the carbon and two oxygen atoms. (The two hydrogens are bonded to the carbon outside the ring.) Two teams working at the U.S. National Bureau of Standards at Gaithersburg, Md., discovered the compound. Frank J. Lovas and Richard D. Suenram detected it by microwave spectroscopy during a study of the reaction at low temperatures of olefins, found in automobile exhaust, and ozone. Richard I. Martinez, Robert E. Huie, and John T. Herron discovered it by using mass spectrometry during the ozone-olefin reaction, also at low temperatures.

Because the ozone-olefin reaction had been studied intensively for many years, the discovery of dioxirane was a surprise. The reason that it had not been detected previously seems to be that it is an unstable compound that quickly collapses to its non-ring form, the dioxymethane radical.

The practical significance of the discovery lies in the fact that dioxirane plays an important role in the reactions that generate smog; this role mandates a model of smog chemistry that differs from the commonly accepted one. This difference might affect the future design of emission-control devices.

—David E. Cane

Physical chemistry

There were several notable developments in physical chemistry in 1977. The highlight was the awarding of the Nobel Prize for Chemistry to Ilya Prigogine of the Free University of Brussels and the University of Texas at Austin for his work in irreversible thermodynamics. But just as important was the continuing evolution of the laser, which was fast becoming the dominant instrument in physical chemistry. Topping the list of achievements in laser research was an analytical technique devised by a team at the Oak Ridge (Tenn.) National Laboratory that was able to sense the presence of a single atom against a large background.

Several new experimental techniques were also developed that did not depend on lasers. For example, a special form of radiant energy called synchrotron radiation was applied to the problem of locating atoms and molecules on solid surfaces. And a technique called small-angle X-ray scattering became much more useful in combination with an electronic detector that could record entire scattering patterns very quickly.

Irreversible thermodynamics. The significance of Prigogine's work in irreversible thermodynamics is illustrated in an apparent contradiction. The second law of thermodynamics clearly states that physical systems tend to evolve toward conditions of increasing disorder. This general principle is considered to be one of the basic properties of the universe, as important to scientists as quantum theory and relativity theory. The contradiction arises with the phenomenon of life. Continuing evolution of life on earth and the metabolism of every living organism seem to depend on an increase of organization in the behavior of molecular structures and systems. This is especially apparent in the earliest steps of evolution when complex protein molecules needed for life presumably were formed from simpler, more disorganized entities.

Prigogine concluded that the two seemingly disparate modes of behavior could be encompassed by a single physical description that did not violate thermodynamic principle. It had always been taken for granted that chemical reactions tend to proceed in the direction that produces a system in equilibrium, at which time the relative concentrations of reactants and products no longer change. Prigogine realized that ordered systems could be stable far from chemical equilibrium, so far that the usual laws of equilibrium thermodynamics and near-equilibrium irreversible thermodynamics do not apply. In particular, he and his collaborators showed that it was possible for stable states, which he

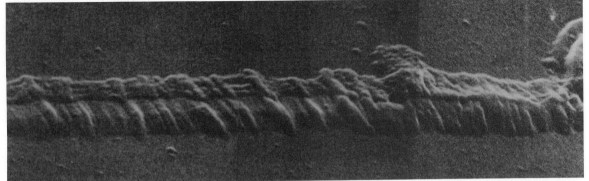

Life-size plastic replica of insect chromosome (shown highly magnified) was made for study by placing a fresh specimen on a thin layer of photosensitive plastic and exposing it to X-rays, which chemically altered the plastic in proportion to the amount of radiation passing through the specimen. Special development of the layer produced a three-dimensional profile much like a relief sculpture.

called dissipative structures, to exist that were spontaneously built up from fluctuations and were actually maintained by a flow of energy and matter from outside the system. Near or at equilibrium, such fluctuations tend to decay rapidly and therefore do not grow into stable structures.

Although the origin of life may be the most engaging application of dissipative structures, the concept is sufficiently general to apply to problems in biology, chemistry, fluid dynamics, meteorology, and even such "soft" sciences as economics and sociology.

Laser chemistry. It would be difficult to single out an instrument that has had as dramatic an effect on physical chemistry as has the laser. Adding to the long list of advances made possible by this remarkable light source was a report in 1977 by G. Samuel Hurst, Munir Hasan Nayfeh, and Jack Young of Oak Ridge National Laboratory that, using a technique called resonance ionization-spectroscopy, they were able to detect a single cesium atom against a background of 10^{19} atoms of another kind. In addition to its analytical potential, the method is also suitable for studies of the kinetics of chemical reactions; that is, the rates at which they proceed.

The Oak Ridge scientists combined two technologies in devising their technique, those of tunable dye lasers and proportional counters that can be filled with gas. The laser is tuned to emit light of a precise frequency, one that will excite only the atoms of a particular species within a gas sample; *e.g.*, cesium, while allowing a predominant, background species such as argon to remain unexcited, or in the ground state. If the laser light is powerful enough, it can further excite the selected atoms so as to ionize or strip them of electrons before they can decay to their ground states. The role of the proportional counter is to detect this ionization process, and the method is extremely precise because even the ionization of a single atom gives rise to a measurable pulse in the counter. By gradually reduc-

ing the density of cesium atoms allowed to pass through the laser beam, the Oak Ridge team was able to detect and identify individual cesium atoms among the 10^{19} argon atoms and the 10^{18} methane molecules in the counter.

The main limitation of the technique stems from the narrow range of frequencies that can be produced by tunable dye lasers, frequencies whose associated photons are not sufficiently energetic to excite most atomic species. With the use of two lasers, it is possible to add the energies of the photons from each and thus reach

High-resolution image of arsenic pentafluoride (AsF_5) molecule was made with a special two-stage holographic microscope. Spherical shell of fluorine atom density surrounding the arsenic is visible at 1.6 Å radius. Magnification is about 120 million power.

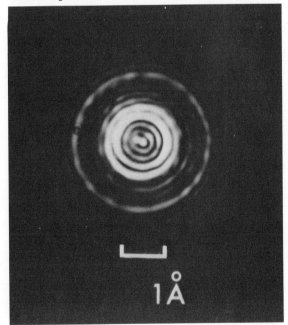

1 Å

about half the elements in the periodic table. For the remainder, however, scientists must await the development of a laser that emits in the more energetic ultraviolet region of the spectrum.

Chemical reactions brought about by the simultaneous absorption by reacting atoms of several photons (multiphoton absorption) from an intense infrared laser have been a topic of intense discussion within recent years. One reason for the interest was the demonstration by Soviet and U.S. scientists that it is possible to separate isotopes (atoms with the same number of protons in the nucleus but different numbers of neutrons) of a given element by irradiating molecules containing a mixture of isotopes with a laser of such intensity that the molecules dissociate. The fragments of the dissociated molecules can then be collected separately. If perfected, such a process could greatly decrease the cost of uranium fuel for nuclear reactors (or weapons). At present, separation of the sparse fissionable uranium isotope ^{235}U from the abundant isotope ^{238}U is an expensive business. It may also be possible to excite molecules into certain quantum states—specific states of energy—forcing them to react and form specific molecules rather than the mixture of molecular species normally produced when reactants are heated in the usual way.

During the past year, a controversy arose that concerned the second possibility more than the first. Experiments with sulfur hexafluoride (SF_6) by Yuan Lee, Yuen-Ron Shen, and their colleagues at the Lawrence Berkeley (Calif.) Laboratory, in which laser beams were focused on beams of SF_6 molecules, seemed to show that the laser-excited molecules occupy a mixture of quantum states rather than just one. Similar results were obtained in experiments of a different nature by

Nicolaas Bloembergen of Harvard University and his associates there and at the Massachusetts Institute of Technology. The two groups disagreed, however, about the degree to which the distribution of filled quantum states is a thermal one; *i.e.*, states filled according to the laws of statistical thermodynamics. Investigators at the Institute of Spectroscopy in Moscow and at the Los Alamos (N.M.) Scientific Laboratory (both groups pioneered the multiphoton technique) disputed the interpretation of the Berkeley and Harvard experiments. The controversy was far from over, but the eventual resolution could have a profound effect on the future of infrared laser chemistry. (See *1977 Yearbook of Science and the Future* Feature Article: LASER-INDUCED ISOTOPE SEPARATION.)

In another area of laser-induced chemistry, a demonstration that could eventually lead to changes in the microelectronics industry was described by John Clark and Robert Anderson of Los Alamos. The silicon used in making integrated circuits is frequently in the form of monosilane (SiH_4) during one stage in the manufacturing process. Parts per billion levels of impurities can adversely affect the end products, so the silane must be exceptionally pure. The Los Alamos investigators used light from an argon fluoride ultraviolet laser to remove phosphorus, arsenic, and boron impurities from silane by selectively dissociating phosphine (PH_3), arsine (AsH_3), and diborane (B_2H_6) molecules mixed with the silane. Upgrading the demonstration into a practical technique awaited, in part, more efficient ultraviolet lasers.

Synchrotron radiation. Once considered merely a nuisance in high-energy physics experiments, synchrotron radiation, the light emitted by high-speed, charged particles moving in curved paths, has become an im-

G. Samuel Hurst, Jack Young, and Munir Hasan Nayfeh (left to right) tend the equipment that enabled them to detect single cesium atoms against a background of 10^{19} atoms of other species.

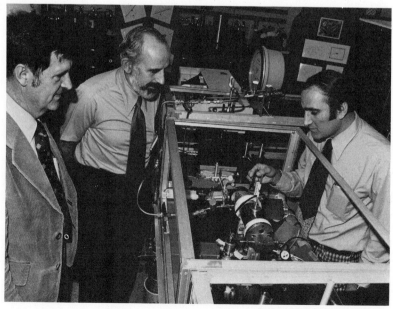

Courtesy, Oak Ridge National Laboratory

Photos, courtesy, Richard A. Muller, Lawrence Berkeley Laboratory

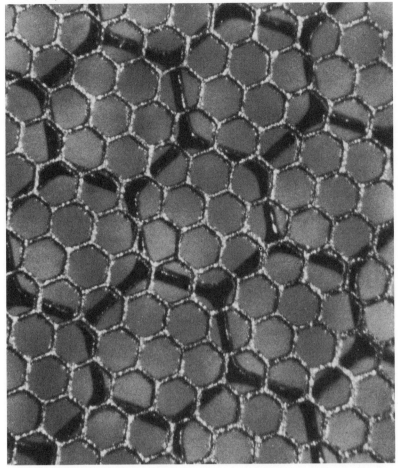

Edward Stephenson (left) and Richard Muller (right) inspect apparatus for determining the age of ancient objects. Ions from material being studied are accelerated through the pipe in the foreground and pass through a honeycombed tungsten screen (left) before entering the cell that separates nitrogen-14 from carbon-14.

portant source of radiant energy, especially in the ultraviolet and X-ray regions of the spectrum. Researchers from several disciplines have made use of synchrotron radiation centers at the University of Wisconsin at Stoughton and at the Stanford Linear Accelerator Center (SLAC) to carry out spectroscopic and X-ray diffraction experiments. Such interest prompted the U.S. National Science Foundation and the Department of Energy to fund two new synchrotron radiation centers and to upgrade the existing ones. Completion of the new facilities was expected between 1980 and 1982.

One exceptionally useful application of synchrotron radiation has been the technique of extended X-ray absorption fine structure (EXAFS), which is used to examine the local atomic arrangement around the species of atom absorbing the X-rays. In the past year, an extension of EXAFS to study the geometry of solid surfaces was reported. Finding exactly where identifiable, single atoms and molecules sit on a surface has long been a frustrating problem. Part of the reason for this is that surface atoms are few in number compared with those in the bulk of a solid, which act as a large "background."

Paul Citrin and Peter Eisenberger of Bell Laboratories, Murray Hill, N.J., showed one way to overcome this problem, using iodine atoms adsorbed on a surface of silver atoms. Rather than measuring the amount of X-rays absorbed, they counted electrons emitted from the surface (Auger electrons) after the X-rays were absorbed. Only electrons from atoms near the surface escape with their characteristic energies, and thus the technique is surface-sensitive. (See *1977 Yearbook of Science and the Future* Year in Review: PHYSICS: *Solid-state physics.*)

Small-angle X-ray scattering. Recent research indicated a bright future for another X-ray technique, known as small-angle X-ray scattering, which is used to examine the size and shape of biological or physical entities with characteristic dimensions from 10 to about 2000 angstroms (an angstrom equals 10^{-8} cm). In 1976 a sophisticated, automated, small-angle X-ray scattering facility with a two-dimensional, position-sensitive proportional counter as the X-ray detector was put into operation at Robert Hendricks' laboratory at Oak Ridge. Combining the sensitivity of electronic detectors with the ability of film to record all scattering angles simultaneously, such area detectors vastly decrease the time needed to carry out experiments.

Hendricks forecast a surge of renewed interest in X-ray experiments.

In a collaborative study, Jerold Schultz of the University of Delaware and Hendricks' group found it possible to obtain a scattering pattern from giant molecules of polyethylene in as little as 30 seconds. This was fast enough to take several successive patterns from the molecule and thereby follow its structural changes as molten polyethylene cooled and crystallized. The area detector also makes possible the use of an experimental geometry that allows anisotropic samples (those not having the same properties in all directions) to be quantitatively examined. For example, Hendricks, Richard Stein of the University of Massachusetts, and their co-workers were able to follow the change in the structure of polyethylene as it was deformed by elongating the sample.

Radioisotope dating. One of the more intriguing developments of the past year was the use of accelerators in radioisotope dating, particularly carbon-14 (^{14}C) dating. A radioactive isotope of an element decays at a fixed rate, which is specific for the isotope and may be any time interval from fractions of a second to billions of years. Thus, the number of undecayed atoms of the isotope relative to the original concentration indicates the time that a radioactive deposit has been localized. Accurate measurement of this number is the key to the technique.

Three groups using accelerators have reported results: Richard Muller and his colleagues at the Lawrence Berkeley Laboratory; Harry Gove of the University of Rochester and his co-workers there, at the University of Toronto, and at the General Ionex Corporation, Ipswich, Mass.; and Earle Nelson of Simon Fraser University in British Columbia and his associates there and at McMaster University in Ontario. Although it was not yet competitive in either accuracy or price with the traditional ^{14}C method developed by U.S. chemist Willard Libby more than 30 years ago, the accelerator technique requires much less sample to be analyzed, is much faster, and may extend the range of ^{14}C dating to 100,000 years from the present maximum of about 60,000 years.

The essence of the technique is the direct counting of the total number of atoms remaining in a sample rather than an indirect assessment based on the rate at which they emit beta rays (electrons) as they decay. The most straightforward way to count ^{14}C atoms would be with a mass spectrometer that separates ^{14}C from stable ^{12}C. But this instrument is not sensitive enough to detect the small concentrations of ^{14}C isotope in most samples, and there is the possibility of confusion with other isotopes, such as the abundant nitrogen-14, which could be present as a contaminant.

Use of an accelerator avoids this difficulty. The sample is vaporized and ionized, and ions of the two isotopes of carbon (positively charged in the cyclotron at Berkeley and negatively charged in the Van de Graaff accelerators at Rochester and at McMaster) are accelerated to several tens of million electron volts. They then are allowed to strike detectors that measure the number and energy of the ions and the rate at which they lose energy in passing through the detectors. It is from all three of these quantities that the identities and concentrations of the two isotopes are computed. Because there is nothing in the technique that limits it to carbon isotopes, there was great interest in extending it to other elements and thereby expanding the range of ages that can be dated.

—Arthur L. Robinson

Applied chemistry

One of the most urgent of world problems, the energy crisis, has accelerated man's search for alternate sources of energy, of which sunlight appears to be the best choice in long-range terms. Several studies detailed below illustrate the potential importance of fundamental chemical research in the critical long-term struggle to develop new energy sources. Other important work of the past year included attempts to combat plant pests by the use of vaccination and of naturally occurring appetite-suppressing chemicals.

Hydrogen from water. Hydrogen, the lightest element and considered by many to be the fuel of the future, is especially plentiful inasmuch as water, its most common compound, covers virtually three-quarters of the Earth's surface. At present, however, the electrical energy needed to split water into hydrogen and oxygen is too expensive to make the process economically feasible. Tapping directly for this purpose, light energy such as occurs in photosynthesis at the cellular level in green plants is an especially attractive route and has been under study in the United States, France, Canada, Israel, Japan, the U.S.S.R., and other countries.

In mid-1977 Harry B. Gray of the California Institute of Technology, Kent R. Mann, a National Science Foundation Energy Fellow, and undergraduate student Nathan Lewis reported a system that uses solar energy to split water molecules. The team synthesized a chemical compound containing the ion [Rh_2(1,3-diisocyanopropane)$_4$]$^{2+}$, composed of two atoms of rhodium (a rare and expensive metal of the platinum group), 20 atoms of carbon, 24 atoms of hydrogen, and 8 atoms of nitrogen, that can convert the energy of sunlight directly into chemical fuel. When a solution of the blue compound is irradiated with sunlight, it reduces (donates electrons to) the hydrogen atoms from water to produce molecules of hydrogen gas and is simultaneously oxidized to a yellow form.

Previously, experimental chemicals used to harness solar energy had been able to activate only a single electron at a time, and pairs of electrons are required

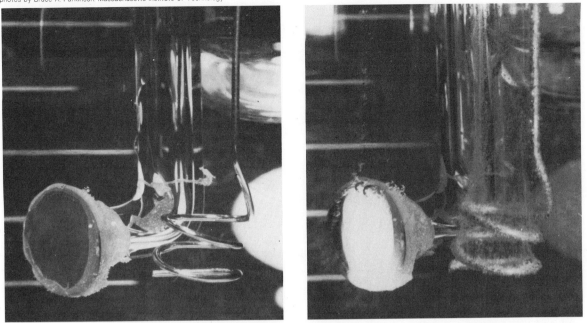

Immersed in water are a strontium titanate ($SrTiO_3$) electrode (left in both photos) and a coiled metal wire. Intense light on the $SrTiO_3$ electrode (photo at the right) causes a current to flow and the water to decompose, freeing hydrogen for energy use and oxygen as a by-product.

to form chemical bonds (*e.g.,* the hydrogen molecule consists of two bonded hydrogen atoms). Because the new compound contains two rhodium atoms, each of which yields an electron upon irradiation, it is a definite improvement over substances previously employed. It also reacts readily with light in the visible region of the spectrum where solar energy is most concentrated. Furthermore, the undesirable "back reaction," in which the yellow form absorbs hydrogen to revert to the blue form, is very slow; thus, free hydrogen will not be absorbed before it can be removed from the system.

The efficiency of the present system is still quite low, however; approximately 100 photons (packets of light energy) are required to produce 4 molecules of hydrogen, whereas an efficiency of 30 molecules of hydrogen per 100 photons would be required to make the process practical. As another limitation the system utilizes only a small portion of the spectrum of sunlight. In order to solve these problems, the Caltech chemists were planning to "fine tune" the molecule by changing its structure to alter the distances between the two rhodium atoms.

Recycling the compound was probably the most important problem to be solved before it could be used commercially. After hydrogen is produced by using the blue form of the compound, the resulting yellow form must regain its lost electrons and revert to its blue form before it can be reused. The Caltech chemists were attempting its reconversion by reacting it with the oxygen atoms in water to produce oxygen gas. In this they collaborated with Mark S. Wrighton of the Massachu-

setts Institute of Technology, who had developed a system to generate oxygen from water and sunlight. If the two reactions can be so linked, the complete solar water-splitting cycle, producing both hydrogen and oxygen, will have been accomplished for the first time by a single light-capturing molecule.

Another such system for producing hydrogen from aqueous solution was devised by Jean-Marie Lehn of the Institut LeBel at the University of Strasbourg in France and Jean-Pierre Sauvage of the Centre National de la Recherche Scientifique. The complex catalytic reaction utilizes four components: (1) triethanolamine (TEA), a mild reducing agent; (2) a photosensitizer, the ruthenium complex $Ru(2,2'\text{-bipyridine})_3Cl_2$ or an acridine dye; (3) an orange complex of rhodium and 2,2'-bipyridine that acts as a storage system for electrons and protons; and (4) potassium hexachloroplatinate(IV), K_2PtCl_6, a platinum catalyst that promotes the release of hydrogen atoms bound as hydrides. The gas evolved from this system consists of more than 80% hydrogen, with the balance comprising argon, nitrogen, and oxygen. Considering the cost of ruthenium and rhodium, the present Strasbourg system was not yet of practical importance, but if the stability and energy economy of the components could be improved considerably, it might be useful for energy storage and photochemical production of fuel.

Ammonia from nitrogen and water. In late 1977 Gerhard N. Schrauzer and T. D. Guth of the University of California, San Diego, reported the first catalytic production of ammonia (NH_3) in a prototype solar cell

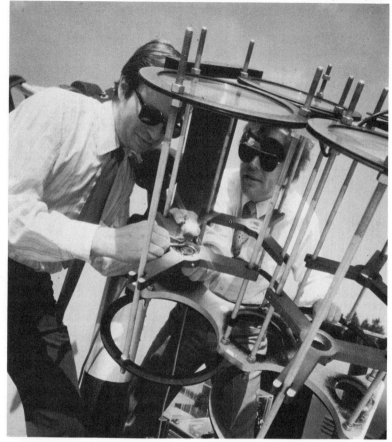

IBM scientists Harold Hovel (left) and Jerry Woodall (right) experiment with a solar cell that they developed. By coating gallium arsenide with a thin layer of gallium aluminum arsenide, they produced a cell that converts 22% of the sunlight falling onto it into electricity. This contrasts with an 18% conversion rate for the best silicon cells.

from nitrogen, water, and sunlight. The potential for developing the new process is enormous because the reaction proceeds at moderate temperatures and at normal atmospheric pressure, whereas the process currently used for meeting the world's ammonia fertilizer needs—the Haber-Bosch process—requires more extreme and more energy-consuming conditions involving temperatures of 500° C (930° F) and pressures of 350 atm. In the new prototype cell a stream of nitrogen gas is passed over a powdered titanium dioxide catalyst, which has been doped, or selectively made impure, with small amounts of iron oxide and saturated with water vapor. Actual or simulated sunlight photochemically reduces the water vapor to oxygen, and the resulting hydrogen atoms simultaneously reduce the nitrogen to ammonia and small amounts of hydrazine (N_2H_4). The catalyst is reactivated by heating to 250° C (480° F) in a partial vacuum.

Before the new process can compete with the Haber-Bosch process to provide a large portion of the 40 million tons of ammonia-based fertilizer now used annually worldwide, the efficiency of the catalyst must be improved 10–100 times and the incoming solar radiation must be concentrated by mirrors or other solar collection devices. Schrauzer suggested that large solar-powered plants might be built in elevated, sunny

regions, and the synthesized ammonia would be absorbed in phosphoric acid solution to yield about five pounds of ammonium phosphate fertilizer per pound of ammonia. The discovery was based on nearly eight years of research by Schrauzer aimed at developing simplified chemical models to explain how certain microorganisms, either free-living or in association with higher plants, convert atmospheric nitrogen to ammonia. This work prompted him to explore what he considered "the ultimate way" of making ammonia, by combining the features of plant photosynthesis with those of biological nitrogen fixation in an abiological solar cell.

Photovoltaics. Solar cells made of highly purified silicon that produce electricity through the direct conversion of solar radiation have been used as efficient, on-board power sources for satellites and space probes since the launching of Sputnik 1 in 1957, but increased efficiency and price reductions by a factor of 20–40 are needed before they can be used on a large scale to produce electricity for large Earth-based power plants. In 1977 Jerry M. Woodall and Harold J. Hovel of IBM's Thomas J. Watson Research Center, Yorktown Heights, N.Y., reported their success in boosting the efficiency of an experimental solar cell. Made of the semiconductor material gallium arsenide coated with a thin layer of gallium aluminum arsenide, the cells convert 22% of the sunlight falling on them into electricity, an efficiency close to the theoretical maximum of 27% predicted for gallium arsenide. Only six years earlier the best efficiency attained with gallium arsenide solar cells was 11%, whereas the best silicon cells are about 18% efficient for terrestrial use.

Although gallium arsenide cells presently are much more expensive than silicon cells, they possess two advantages that could make them competitive: they are more efficient in converting sunlight into electricity at the Earth's surface, and they function well at high temperatures, allowing them to be used under intense concentrations of sunlight. Gallium arsenide cells can operate at concentration levels as high as 1,000 times above the natural level, whereas silicon cells are limited to concentration levels of no more than several hundred, because their efficiency decreases rapidly with rising temperature.

Recently, David E. Carlson and Christopher R. Wronski at RCA's David Sarnoff Research Center, Princeton, N.J., dramatically reduced the cost of solar cells with a new device made of hydrogenated "amorphous" or noncrystalline silicon in place of the single crystals of highly purified silicon used in conventional cells. Scientists and officials at RCA expected amorphous silicon to play a major role in the low-cost conversion of solar energy directly into electricity and believed that such cells would be able to produce electricity at costs competitive with many conventional power sources by the late 1980s.

Amorphous silicon cells are inexpensive because the material (a sand derivative) is plentiful, long lasting, and stable; the fabrication process involves moderate temperatures; and ultrathin films of the material (about 1/20 the thickness of a human hair) can be spread over a large area of inexpensive glass or steel sheets to absorb large amounts of incoming solar energy. Conventional silicon solar cells are more efficient but considerably more costly. Crystalline silicon processing requires temperatures greater than 1,100° C (2,000° F), compared with 300° C (570° F) for the amorphous material. Also, crystalline cells are about 250 times thicker than amorphous ones and are generally limited to relatively small areas because of fabrication problems. Although the new cell presently has an actual efficiency of 6%, compared with a theoretical maximum of about 15%, it is at about the same stage of development as conventional silicon cells were 25 years earlier. The new cells were expected to be used initially for electrification projects in less developed nations that lack the extensive electric power distribution networks of the U.S. and Europe.

Other energy developments. A method for producing hydrogen that does not involve sunlight was developed by scientists at Sandia Laboratories, Albuquerque, N.M., who injected water into magma, the molten material beneath or within the Earth's crust. Hydrogen production is directly proportional to the amount of ferrous iron in the magma, which, on oxidizing, frees the hydrogen. Adding biomass, mainly cellulose, was found to double or triple hydrogen production. For example, at magma temperatures of 1,300° C (2,370° F), injection of water containing 10% biomass

David Carlson, an RCA scientist, operates glow discharge apparatus used in making solar cells out of hydrogenated amorphous silicon. This noncrystalline silicon is much cheaper than the single crystals of highly purified silicon used in conventional cells and thus is expected to play an important role in the low-cost conversion of solar energy into electricity.

Final checkout is performed on an iron-nickel battery system developed by Westinghouse Electric Corp. for powering an underground coal hauler.

into the magma produces steam containing 10% hydrogen, 4% carbon dioxide, 1% carbon monoxide, and a trace of methane. Magma chambers two to three kilometers (1¼ to 1¾ miles) below the ocean floor may be reachable for the process by nominal extension of current technology.

A new type of storage battery using iron and silver for electrodes provided the highest energy capacity presently available in commercial batteries as well as high power capability and long life in heavy-discharge applications. Developed by the Westinghouse Corp., each iron-silver component cell produces a nominal 1.1 volts, and the battery consists of 24 such cells, each weighing 1⅔ kg (3 ⅔ lb) with an energy capacity of about 3.5 kw-hr. The 40-kg (88-lb) battery thus has about five times the energy capacity of lead-acid batteries and twice that of nickel-cadmium batteries of comparable weight. It has the ability to drive a one-horsepower motor continuously for more than four hours on one charge.

With the battery in a charged condition, the anode consists of porous metallic iron, and the cathode of silver oxides. Discharge converts the silver oxides to silver metal and the iron to hydrated magnetic iron oxide. The electrolyte is a solution of 30% potassium hydroxide and 1.5% lithium hydroxide. Described as "commercially available," the batteries must be custom-made at a price of about $10,000 each. (The high price was due largely to the 347 troy oz of silver contained in each battery.) The new batteries have proved successful as emergency power supplies for tethered-balloon telecommunications systems and as power sources for mobile propulsion.

The world's supply of natural gas is expected to be depleted by the beginning of the 21st century. As one alternative, methane, the chief constituent of natural gas, was being produced in a pilot plant at a rate of 20 standard cubic feet per day from about five pounds of cow manure. Developed by Bio-Gas of Colorado, Inc., the Los Alamos Scientific Laboratory, and CH₂M Hill, Inc., the plant was a prototype for a large-scale "bioconversion" plant expected to provide 1,222,450 standard cubic feet of methane daily for the city of Lamar, Colo., from manure from 50,000 feedlot cows. Construction of the $14 million biogasification facility was planned for early 1978.

The Lamar plant was to have four major components: (1) mixing and grit facilities to produce a manure slurry and remove sand particles; (2) a digestion complex heated to 35° C (95° F) in which anaerobic microorganisms act on the wastes to produce methane; (3) a degasification tower and centrifuges to process sludge from the digesters for cattle feed; and (4) algae ponds to purify the effluent from the centrifuges and recycle it to the plant. Much design work was still necessary before a large-scale plant would become commercially feasible.

Applied biochemistry. Because the large-scale application of pesticides destroys not only plant pests but also natural predators that feed on these pests, because many insects have grown resistant to insecticides, and because many insecticides are toxic to man, scientists are currently trying to exploit natural factors in plants and insects to reduce crop losses.

Joseph Kuc and colleagues at the University of Kentucky College of Agriculture at Lexington developed a new technique to increase a crop's resistance to fungi and other plant disease agents. They were able to "immunize" watermelons, cucumbers, muskmelons, and other plants against plant diseases in a manner analogous to vaccination of human beings. For example, injection of one watermelon leaf with the infective organism *Colletotrichum lagenarium* protected the entire plant from the disease. Furthermore, watermelon plants could be protected during the entire growing season by administering a booster shot five weeks after the initial inoculation. The mechanism of immunization was unknown, but the protective action might occur in three different ways. It may block penetration of the disease agent into the plant; it may cause the pathogen to agglutinate into ineffective clumps; or it may inhibit the growth of the pathogen. If immunization switches on a chemical signal allowing the plant to mobilize its defenses, it might be possible to isolate this chemical, apply it to seeds, and protect the plant throughout its entire life cycle.

In recent years farmers have had to make do with fewer pesticides, many of which have been withdrawn from the market either because of toxicity to humans or because they are no longer effective against resist-

Courtesy, The Bancroft Library, University of California, Berkeley

"Plate of Brass," discovered near San Francisco Bay in 1936, was first thought to have been left there by Sir Francis Drake. Recent chemical analyses, however, have cast doubt on the plate's authenticity. An X-ray fluorescence study showed it to contain 34.8% zinc and somewhat over 0.05% lead. But brasses known to have been made about 1600 generally had a zinc content of less than 30% and a much greater proportion of lead than 0.05%.

ant insects. In the search for better pest control agents, Katsura Munakata and his colleagues at the Laboratory of Pesticide Chemistry at Nagoya University in Japan isolated and identified many "antifeedants"—from potatoes, turnips, corn, tomatoes, and other crops. These substances (including alkaloids, sesquiterpenes, coumarins, and diterpenes) probably play a role as resistance factors in protecting the plants against attack, and they appear to be a viable alternative to the use of conventional insecticides for control of many insect pests. When used for insect pest management, antifeedants may be especially advantageous because they control plant-eating insects indirectly through starvation while leaving parasites, predators, and insect pollinators unharmed. If crops were sprayed with efficient, synthetic antifeedants, the pests might turn from crops to weeds.

—George B. Kauffman

Earth sciences

Major developments in the Earth sciences during the past year included investigations of the factors involved in climate change, a study of hydrocarbons in the Mid-Atlantic continental shelf, the installation of accelerometers to help predict the amount of ground shaking produced by earthquakes, and experiments dealing with the effects of water pollutants on plankton. The influence of carbon dioxide on the Earth's climate was the subject of research in several disciplines.

Atmospheric sciences

The subject of climate received a great deal of attention during the past year. Many Earth scientists with various specialized interests have been investigating the factors responsible for climatic changes over periods of time ranging from one year to more than a billion years. Their ultimate goal is to formulate a set of theories to explain the climates of the past and predict climates of the future.

It is clear that no single theory can account for past climatic changes. There is widespread agreement among scientists that climatic alterations over periods from 100,000 to a billion years, which appear in geological records as ice ages separated by warmer episodes, can be explained by the drift of continents. There also is increasing evidence that climatic changes over periods of about 1,000–100,000 years are caused by cyclical changes in the orbit of the Earth around the Sun and in the tilt of the Earth's axis.

Variations of climate over periods from one to 100 years might be caused by a number of factors. Atmospheric scientists were studying the effects of persistent stratospheric dust layers that had resulted from massive volcanic eruptions. Analyses were being made of the effects of atmospheric pollutants, both gaseous and particulate. Geophysicists were giving increasing attention to the degree to which weather is affected by changes in the properties of the Sun.

Climate and the Sun. During the last few years some scientists have reported evidence showing how variations in the solar atmosphere or its emissions are correlated with measured characteristics of the weather and climate. John Wilcox at Stanford University and Colin Hines at the University of Toronto reported a relationship between the interplanetary magnetic fields associated with the Sun's rotation and atmospheric vorticity over the Northern Hemisphere. The vorticity is a measure of the rotational characteristics of the air and is an important quantity in accounting for weather and climate. Researchers claim that the solar influences on vorticity occur over periods of days.

281

Another provocative report issued recently by J. Murray Mitchell of the National Oceanic and Atmospheric Administration (NOAA) and Charles Stockton and David Meko at the University of Arizona reveals a strong correlation between sunspot frequency and the areal extent of droughts over the western United States. Tree-ring data extending back to 1700 indicate that there is an apparent 22-year periodicity in major drought occurrence.

Other investigators also have found correlations between certain elements of solar behavior and weather. Unfortunately, as of early 1978 convincing physical mechanisms for explaining the correlations had not yet been found. Until they are, it is premature to conclude that the weather and climatic effects are caused by the observed solar variations. (*See* Feature Article: CLIMATE AND THE CHANGING SUN.)

Carbon dioxide. Carbon dioxide (CO_2) is one of the variable gases in the Earth's atmosphere. At the start of this century the CO_2 concentration in the atmosphere was about 290 parts per million (ppm), having increased only slightly over the preceding 50 years. Since then there has been an accelerating increase of CO_2 concentration, and in 1978 it reached about 332 ppm. The upward trend of atmospheric CO_2 is shown by measurements at the high-altitude Mauna Loa Observatory in Hawaii. The data also show an annual cycle with highest concentrations in April and lowest in late summer. These changes are ascribed to variations in photosynthetic action by plants. Maximum uptake of CO_2 occurs during the summer.

It is clear that much of the carbon dioxide in the atmosphere has been produced by the burning of fossil fuel. According to Charles Keeling at the University of California at San Diego, since 1973 the increase of

total CO_2 in the atmosphere is about half the amount released into it by fossil fuel combustion. In Keeling's view the biosphere (living things together) may be a small net sink for CO_2; that is, the amount used in photosynthesis exceeds the amount released by decaying plant material.

Some scientists, however, particularly Bert Bolin at the University of Stockholm in Sweden and George Woodwell at Ecosystems Center of the Marine Biological Laboratory at Woods Hole, Mass., and his associates, concluded that a reduced photosynthetic uptake of CO_2 because of the harvesting of forests has caused the biosphere to become a net source of atmospheric CO_2. Woodwell estimates that this biological source of atmospheric CO_2 can be approximately equal to the fossil fuel release. This new research raises serious questions about atmospheric CO_2 concentration in the future.

In 1977 the U.S. National Academy of Sciences released a report entitled *Energy and Climate*, in which estimates are made of atmospheric CO_2 through the next two centuries. On the basis of estimates of future population and energy growth and sources of power (mostly coal) and using a theoretical model of atmospheric CO_2 the report concluded that by the year 2050 the CO_2 concentration might be twice what it was in 1900.

The significance of CO_2 is not that it is a pollutant but rather that it affects radiation transfer in the atmosphere. Specifically, CO_2 is transparent to most incoming radiation but absorbs some wavelengths of infrared radiation emanating from the Earth. According to a mathematical model of the global atmosphere constructed by Syukuro Manabe and Richard Wetherald at the Geophysical Fluid Dynamics Laboratory at Prince-

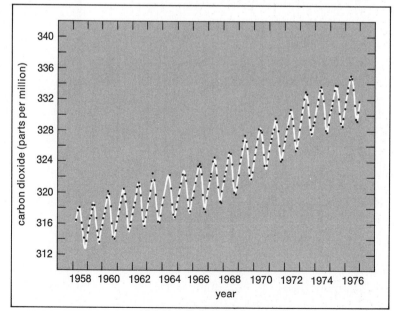

Upward trend in the concentration of carbon dioxide (CO_2) in the Earth's atmosphere is indicated by measurements at the high-altitude Mauna Loa Observatory in Hawaii. The dots represent the observed monthly concentrations based on continuous measurements.

Adapted from Charles Keeling, *Energy and Climate*, U.S. National Academy of Sciences, 1977

ton University, a doubling of atmospheric CO_2 could increase average air temperatures at the Earth's surface by about 2° C. Such an increase would have profound effects on many activities, such as agriculture and ocean shipping.

The National Academy of Sciences report has led to substantial increases in research on atmospheric CO_2 and the consequences of its changes. The Department of Energy was particularly concerned because of the implications for long-range planning for energy sources and supplies.

Ozone and other gases. It is well known that the layer of high ozone concentration at altitudes between 15 and 30 km (1 km = 0.62 mi) is important to life on the Earth. By absorbing ultraviolet radiation from the Sun it reduces the risk of skin cancer among humans and has other biological effects that are difficult to evaluate. Over the last few years a great deal has been learned about the complicated chemistry of the ozone layer. Much of the research was stimulated by concerns that substances such as nitrogen oxides released by supersonic airplanes or chlorofluorocarbons from aerosol spray cans would cause significant decreases in the ozone amounts. Three agencies of the U.S. government, convinced that chlorofluorocar-

bons pose a threat to the ozone layer and human welfare, together set Oct. 15, 1978, as the date after which chemical firms will be prohibited from manufacturing most chlorofluorocarbon aerosol propellants.

Other widely used substances were also being examined as potential ozone destroyers. Methylchloroform, used as a solvent mainly for degreasing metal, has been identified as a stable compound that can serve as a source of chlorine atoms in the stratosphere and react with ozone. Methylchloroform is, however, considered to be less of a threat than the fluorocarbons. There is also concern that widely used nitrogen fertilizers, which release nitrogen compounds, can lead to a reduction of stratospheric ozone. As visualized by some scientists, nitrous oxide produced in soil is released and slowly diffused into the stratosphere, where it reacts with ozone and causes its destruction.

It still is not clear how serious are the manmade threats to the ozone layer, and, if real and substantial, what should be done about them. In view of the need for food throughout the world, it would be more difficult to discontinue the use of nitrogen fertilizers than of aerosol spray cans or even SST airplanes. (*See* Feature Article: STRATOSPHERIC OZONE: EARTH'S FRAGILE SHIELD.)

Technician inspects a Meteosat weather satellite (left); a Meteosat was placed in orbit by the European Space Agency in 1977. Above, the Michelstadt ground station in West Germany serves Meteosat and the Geos weather satellites.

The Global Weather Experiment. A massive international program to observe atmospheric and oceanic conditions over the entire globe moved ahead during the year. The 12-month period ending Dec. 1, 1978, is the "build-up year" during which an imposing array of observational systems was to be put in place. Weather satellites were scheduled to play crucial roles in the program. The Earth was to be circled by four or five geostationary satellites positioned over the Equator, two launched by the U.S. (stationed at longitudes 75° W and 135° W), one by Japan (at longitude 140° E), one by the European Space Agency (longitude 0°), and possibly one by the U.S.S.R. (longitude 70° E). In addition, the plans called for four U.S. and two Soviet polar-orbiting satellites. The global experiment was also designed to employ a wide array of instrumented airplanes, ships, and ocean buoys as well as a greatly augmented network of land-based observing stations.

The Global Weather Experiment, to be carried out during the period December 1978 to December 1979, was designed to provide a data base for many studies. Scientists were awaiting the observations to test ideas on the nature of the general circulation of the atmosphere. In particular, the program of observation and analysis known as the Global Atmospheric Research Program (GARP) was expected to lead to the development of methods for making acceptably accurate weather forecasts for periods as long as one to two weeks. Another major objective of GARP was to develop a better understanding of the factors governing seasonal weather and climate. The global observations were to be used to test and improve physical and mathematical models of regional and global climate.

International Magnetospheric Study. In order to observe the nature of the magnetosphere, two satellites were launched on Oct. 22, 1977. One built by the U.S. and the other by the European Space Agency, they traveled as a pair and followed nearly identical elliptical orbits ranging 280 to 138,000 km from the Earth. The distance between them varied from several hundred to several thousand kilometers. The orbits took the satellites through various parts of the magnetosphere. At the part of the orbit closest to the Earth the satellites moved through the shock wave separating the solar wind from the magnetosphere. As the probes then moved through the distant parts of their orbits, they traveled through the long tail of the magnetosphere extending away from the Sun. In July 1978

Photograph released in 1977 shows radioactive dust venting from the site of an underground nuclear test in Nevada in 1970. The cloud rose 10,000 feet above the surface, but U.S. officials said that the radioactivity levels in the atmosphere posed no hazard to the public.

UPI Compix

a satellite was scheduled to be launched and placed at a distance of about 1,500,000 km from the Earth. It was designed to monitor the perturbations on the Sun.

All three satellites, known as International Sun-Earth Explorers, were instrumented to measure the nature of particles, plasmas, fields, X-rays, cosmic rays, radio waves, and other phenomena associated with the magnetosphere. The system of making measurements by satellites at three places simultaneously should shed light on the mechanisms by which solar emissions affect the properties of the magnetosphere.

Doppler radar observations of storms. Over recent years there has been rapid development of the use of pulsed-Doppler radars for observing storm systems. Such a device can measure the velocity of a particle toward or away from the radar. By means of a zenith-pointing antenna, a radar can measure the vertical velocities of particles such as rain, snow, or hail. Usually it is possible to discriminate between the vertical air velocity and the terminal velocity of the particles. The latter quantity is the vertical velocity the particles would have in still air, and generally it increases with particle diameter. If the air velocity is known, the radar data can be used to calculate the size distribution of the particles, particularly if they are raindrops.

One of the most promising new measurement techniques involves the use of three Doppler radars scanning through the same storm. Since each one gives an independent measurement of velocity, a three-dimensional profile of the velocities of the raindrops or ice particles involved can be made. This technique, pioneered by Roger Lhermitte at the University of Miami, yielded unique, highly detailed observations of the wind structure within showers and thunderstorms. The technique is particularly valuable in observing hailstorms and tornadoes, which generally are too dangerous to be penetrated by scientifically instrumented airplanes.

The capacity of a pulsed-Doppler radar to measure the strong wind velocities associated with tornadoes offers the hope of developing an effective method for tornado detection and tracking. Research at the National Severe Storms Laboratory in Norman, Okla., revealed that identifiable small-scale circulations have been observed as much as 20–30 minutes before a tornado was observed at the ground. Starting in April 1977, the research group in Norman began a cooperative project with the National Weather Service to test the operational value of a Doppler-radar tornado detection procedure. The investigations, scheduled for an 18-month period, were being conducted in Oklahoma, a state that has many tornadoes.

Air pollution. During recent months a new observational program, called Project Da Vinci, was beginning to produce information about sources of air pollution, diffusion of the pollutants after leaving their sources, and the processes of chemical reaction and removal of the pollutants. Manned, instrumented balloons 24 m in

From Voorheeve, Johnson, Gallagher and Remeika, *Science*, Vol. 195, March 4, 1977, p. 828, © AAS

Surface topography of a perovskite oxide is revealed in a photomicrograph. These oxides, structurally similar to the mineral $CaTiO_3$, show promise as stable catalysts for the treatment of automotive exhaust.

diameter were maintained at particular altitudes and carried along by the wind. Two flights originated in St. Louis, Mo., during the spring and summer of 1976. The project represents a Lagrangian approach to the study of atmospheric pollution because it follows a particular volume and measures the changes with time. In the St. Louis launches, special attention was given to ozone and particulate behavior, sulfur chemistry, and the vertical transport of atmospheric pollutants. The observations were expected to be particularly valuable for testing and improving theoretical models for calculating the transport and chemical conversion of pollutants in the atmosphere.

A new study by the Organization for Economic Cooperation and Development calculated the sulfur budget of northwestern Europe. It considered the release of sulfur dioxide into the atmosphere and the deposition of sulfates in various countries. The results showed that the U.K. was the greatest "exporter" of sulfur, with West Germany and France a distant second and third, respectively. The largest involuntary "importer" was Norway, which received almost three times more sulfates than it emitted in the form of sulfur dioxide. Other nations classified as net receivers were Austria, Finland, Sweden, and Switzerland.

The problem is serious in southern Norway because the precipitated sulfates are accumulated in snow dur-

285

Courtesy, Australian Information Service; photo, Don Edwards

Opencut mining in central Queensland, Australia. Conditions for mining in Australia are considered among the best in the world.

ing the winter and are then released in concentrated form when the snow melts in the spring. The resulting acidified water runs down rivers, killing fish and probably having other harmful effects. The magnitude of the problem is difficult to assess, but according to one estimate the loss of fish amounts to about $1 million annually, a small amount when compared with the costs of emission controls that would significantly reduce the quantity of sulfur released by industrial and power plants.

—Louis J. Battan

Geological sciences

Continued investigation of the process of plate tectonics and increasing interest in the geochemistry of health and disease were among the highlights of the past year in the geological sciences.

Geology and geochemistry. There was a continued lag in exploration for metals during the year, with a consequent diminution in the number of new lodes discovered. This was due in part to a lack of funds for extensive exploration, but perhaps the chief cause was uncertainty about the effect of recently enacted tax and environmental laws and the possibility that more such laws would be passed in the future. Economic geologists and government officials expressed concern lest a continuing downward trend reduce the production capacity of mining operations to a point where

the supply of metals would be insufficient to maintain industry at its current level, much less allow for any future growth.

Nevertheless, a number of discoveries of new metal deposits were announced in 1977, as were some plans to reactivate or extend known mining districts. Large copper deposits were found in Poland and Zambia and smaller ones in Arizona and Wisconsin. Significant new porphyry deposits of copper were located in Peru and Papua New Guinea, and a Cyprus-type copper deposit was found in Oman. Amax announced the discovery of a deposit containing some 130 million tons of 0.49% molybdenum disulfide ore in Colorado. Two new Mount Isa-type lead-zinc deposits located northwest of Mount Isa in northern Australia, and Mississippi Valley-type deposits in Ireland were recorded. Aluminum reserves were increased considerably when new deposits of bauxite, the chief aluminum ore, were found in Australia, Brazil, India, and Venezuela. The U.K. announced reactivation and expansion of tungsten and tin mines in England, and a closed tungsten mine in Nevada was reopened. Uranerz revealed plans for a major new mine in the uranium-bearing area of northern Saskatchewan.

The January 1977 issue of *Mining Engineering* pointed out that conditions for mining in Australia had improved to the extent that it was now the best place to mine outside the U.S. If this trend continued, Australia soon could become one of the leading producers

286

of uranium, copper, lead, and zinc; it was already a leader in coal and iron ore. On the other hand, as discussed in the March issue, higher grade deposits in third world countries were not being financed or developed, primarily because of uncertainties about the security of the investments. A committee of some 100 leaders of business, organized labor, agriculture, and the professions from the U.S., the U.K., and Canada was studying the problem. Their preliminary conclusion was that perhaps the barriers to working these deposits could be eliminated by the 1980s. In the U.S. it was feared that current and proposed pollution-control measures might make it almost impossible to institute new production capacity for copper, making the country increasingly dependent on imports.

The relatively new technique of geochemical exploration for metals had already assumed an important place among prospecting methods. Of 29 research papers published in the Proceedings of the sixth International Geochemical Symposium, which was held in Australia in August 1976 in conjunction with the 25th International Geological Congress, 11 dealt with massive sulfide deposits in sedimentary and/or volcanic rocks, and two of these recorded the discovery of new bodies by geochemical means. Only one paper discussed geochemical exploration for petroleum, and none was concerned with prospecting for completely "blind" deposits (with no surface expression or indication). The proceedings appeared as the October 1977 issue of the *Journal of Geochemical Exploration*, the official organ of the new Association of Exploration Geochemists.

Geophysical exploration for oil deposits underwent a comparable development in 1977, but geophysical exploration for ore deposits continued to lag. One of the few significant advances during the year was the possibility of being able to distinguish between the electrical response of a sulfide body and that of a fault zone. Another was the use of induced polarization and resistivity to distinguish between ore and common rock in the south Texas uranium deposits. Presumably this would apply to similar uranium deposits elsewhere, especially in the Wyoming basins.

A process that would make whole shale oil usable by conventional refineries was reported in *Chemical and Engineering News* (June 6, 1977, p. 21). After describing the process in some detail, however, the article concluded that "the problems of operating in locations where water may be insufficient, where the social and economic impacts are unknown, and where the legal entanglements over resource ownership grow ever knottier may continue to stall the development of this energy and chemical resource." Thus, although the technical difficulties apparently had been overcome, the energy crisis would presumably have to get worse before the process became economically and socially feasible.

Adapted from an illustration by Marc Nadel, *Business Week*, Jan. 30, 1978, p. 55

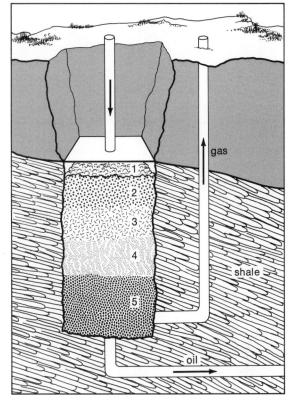

Extracting oil from shale begins by mining out a portion of the shale (1). The rest is blasted with explosives (2), and shale at the top is ignited (3). Separation of the oil from the shale then begins (4). The released oil flows to the bottom (5), where it is pumped into storage.

Persons in the vicinity of major earthquakes have frequently reported the appearance of bright flashing lights, somewhat like heat lightning. Several articles on these earthquake lights appeared during 1977. After noting that "The existence of earthquake lights is well established," the *Earthquake Information Bulletin* suggested that "Two theories have been advanced which are worthy of further investigation: (1) violent low-level air oscillation and (2) piezoelectric effect in quartz-bearing rock. If the latter theory is correct, it may be possible to develop electrical monitoring methods for earthquake prediction. . . ."

Regarding the field of earthquake prediction generally, the report of a conference on Earthquake Prediction on a Global Scale concluded that "the principal results [were] outlining some new areas for research, discussing the requirements for a new generation of seismic instrumentation, and noting how existing data handling procedures could be improved. Many specific suggestions were given to assist the National Earthquake Information Service, Golden, Colo., in improving its service to the seismological community." (See *Geophysics*, below.)

Geochemistry. Studies in the geochemistry of health and disease were appearing in increasing numbers, in publications ranging from the house organs of metal companies and bulletins issued by government bureaus of health to the proceedings of conferences and symposia, and to commercially published books. Major meetings on the subject held during the year included the tenth Annual Conference on Trace Substances in Environmental Health, at Columbia, Mo.; the third International Symposium on Trace Elements and Metabolism in Animals, in Munich, West Germany; and a conference on the effects of nutritional status on response to the environment, Anaheim, Calif.

Although many of the works published in the field, such as Eric J. Underwood's *Trace Elements in Human and Animal Nutrition*, were very general, a notable trend was the appearance of publications dealing with single elements (the bimonthly journals *Zinc Abstracts*, *Lead Abstracts*, and *Cadmium Abstracts*). Still others concentrated on a single disease, as in *Geochemistry and the Environment*, Vol. III, *Certain Cancers*. Despite this vast increase in published material on the subject, however, the closing remark of a review appearing in January 1977 was still appropriate: "One of the biggest problems in the field of trace elements and health is getting the information already available into the hands of the general public and the practitioners of medical and dental services."

Two developments in the field of organic geochemistry were especially noteworthy. The Mid-Atlantic continental shelf region was the subject of a two-year study of the qualitative and quantitative distribution of aliphatic and aromatic hydrocarbons in the surface sediments. The study, conducted by the U.S. Geological Survey as part of a Bureau of Land Management (BLM) environmental assessment of the outer continental shelves, was designed: (1) to provide data points to establish a natural variability curve for the Mid-Atlantic; (2) to differentiate between naturally occurring hydrocarbons and those originating as the result of human activities; and (3) to serve as a basis for determining the environmental impact of petroleum exploration of the continental shelves.

Hydrocarbons were found to total approximately 1 microgram per gram of dry sediment. Seasonal variability and the types of hydrocarbons found generally indicated biological origin, but man-made sediments were recognizable in some samples. Although most of the gas in slope sediments was methane, increasing quantities of ethane and propane in a 1,000-ft core taken from the Baltimore Canyon region seem to indicate a relationship between these gases and a deep gas/liquid hydrocarbon reservoir.

The second development involved studies of oxygen and hydrogen isotopic ratios in plant cellulose made at the California Institute of Technology. It was found that variations in the deuterium/hydrogen and oxygen-18/ oxygen-16 ratios that were derived from analysis of the hydrogen and oxygen content fixed in plant cellulose reveal systematic differences between land- and water-dwelling plant groups. Two models incorporating absorption of carbon dioxide and water from the environment into cellulose precursor molecules were developed to explain the differences. Depending upon the model, data would be provided for either the terrestrial or aquatic origin of a plant or the climatic conditions under which it grew.

A new technique of carbon-14 dating was developed in which the atoms of ^{14}C were literally counted with a mass spectrometer. The great advantage of this method is that it requires only a few milligrams of sample, so that damage to archaeological specimens, old paintings, and other valuable objects is minimal. Moreover, it has the potential for getting good dates as far back as 100,000 years, as opposed to a maximum of about 30,000 years for the commonly used method of measuring the residual radioactivity of samples weighing a few to several grams. The method can probably be applied to other radioactive isotopes produced by cosmic rays, such as tritium, beryllium-10, and aluminum-26. If it works well with all of these isotopes, the geochronologist's dream of being able to determine ages with radioactive isotopes from essentially zero to the age of the universe might become a reality.

Experimental geochemistry continued to be an active field. Among the numerous projects reported, three experimental papers bearing on the origin of kimberlites were presented at the second International Kimberlite Conference. A new and effective technique for determining solubility of salts in aqueous solutions at elevated temperatures was described in the U.S. Geological Survey *Journal of Research*. Also reported in this journal was the determinination of new pressure corrections for fluid inclusion homogenization temperatures, based on the volumetric properties of the system salt (NaCl)-water.

New journals. Although most scientists agreed that there were already too many journals, publications representing a new field or gathering into one journal previously scattered papers in an area of special interest still served a worthwhile purpose. Several new journals had the potential of performing one or both of these functions and therefore deserved a place in the current literature of the Earth sciences.

Organic Geochemistry, the journal of the International Association of Geochemistry and Cosmochemistry (quarterly), was "intended [to] serve as a medium for the publication of reports on *all* phases of geochemistry in which organic substances play a role." *Physics and Chemistry of Minerals*, published quarterly, was "intended to serve as a suitable carrier for scientific results in the regions common to solid state sciences, mineralogy, geochemistry and geophysics." A UN publication, *Natural Resources Forum* (quar-

Specially designed dredgehead is lowered through ship's well. Attached to flexible hose and coupled to 2,700 feet of 9⅝-inch pipe, it is used to mine manganese nodules from the ocean floor.

terly), was "devoted to the economic, scientific, technological, and *policy* aspects of energy, minerals, and water resources development." *Marine Mining* (quarterly) stated that "Papers accepted for publication will be technical in nature and will include, but not be restricted to, such topics as marine minerals exploration and marine mining in general, recovery and processing of ore, sea-floor mineral surveys and assessments—shipboard mining systems—etc."

GeoJournal, published bimonthly by the Akademische Verlagsgesellschaft of Wiesbaden, West Germany, was "focused on careful observation and pressing questions in the wide field of interrelated geo-bio-sciences and their application in environmental planning and ecology." It planned to publish only specialized papers in an interdisciplinary context. In England, *Advances in Water Resources* (quarterly) described itself as "a professional journal designed to act as an international forum for the interchange of scientific and technical information [which] will provide an important alternative to existing journals for those scientists and engineers who are interested in the more quantitative aspects of the water sciences."

Geostandards Newsletter, published by the International Working Group of the Association Nationale de la Recherche Technique, Paris, expected to serve as "a *forum* for exchange of ideas and information on geochemical reference samples (GRS). It also serves as a *medium* for rapid dissemination of analytical data

on GRS of minerals, ores, and rocks." In addition to the establishment of a new journal, *Advances in Organic Geochemistry*, a huge monograph on the subject, the Proceedings of the seventh International Meeting on Organic Geochemistry, was published by Empresa Nacional de Investigaciones Mineras, S.A., in Madrid. Edited by R. Campos and J. Goni, it contained 52 papers under such headings as Geochemical Fossils, Organic Content of Recent Fossils, Environmental Geochemistry, and Origin and Occurrence of Petroleum and Natural Gas.

—Earl Ingerson

Geophysics. The progress of science seems to be a combination of steady growth, occasional rapid advances on several fronts, and infrequent revolutionary breakthroughs. The events that make a particular year memorable might be classified into the occurrence of unusual natural phenomena, the publication of milestone papers, or important developments in technology. Although it is presumptuous to judge the long-term effect of papers published during the last year, for geophysics 1977 seems best characterized as a year of steady, vigorous growth rather than one of major breakthroughs. In two fields, plate tectonics and earthquake hazard reduction, there was considerable progress.

Plate tectonics. It is now generally accepted that the surface of Earth is covered by a number of relatively rigid plates about 100 km (60 mi) thick. New material is being added to these plates at spreading centers such as the Mid-Atlantic Ridge. At the same time, plates are thrust down into the interior of the Earth in a process known as subduction, causing deep trenches on the ocean floor. A dynamic balance between plate creation and subduction assures that the surface area of the Earth is kept constant. In recent months much work in plate tectonics was directed toward the reconstruction of plate movements in the past and the elucidation of the details of plate creation and subduction at present. The latter details can be observed directly at the spreading centers by the use of deep-sea, maneuverable, manned submarines. (*See* Feature Article: RESEARCH SUBMERSIBLES: EXPLORERS OF THE OCEAN DEPTHS.)

During 1971–75 an ambitious program, named the French-American Mid-Ocean Undersea Study (Project FAMOUS), explored the rift valley of the Mid-Atlantic Ridge around latitude 37° N. The preliminary results of this experiment were published in mid-1977. Although a complete synthesis of the data had not yet been made, the results indicated that the evolution of the inner floor of the valley does not take place by a simple spreading from a single rift. Instead, the position of the rift probably switches back and forth laterally in what may be a random pattern.

The success of the FAMOUS project led to the planning of similar experiments on other parts of the sea floor. During early 1977 a series of 24 dives was made to the spreading center east of the Galápagos Islands. One of the objectives was to study at first hand hot springs associated with the volcanism at the spreading center; evidence for these hot springs had been ob-

"I wouldn't worry. With Continental Drift, Africa or South America should come by eventually."

Sidney Harris

tained from previous experiments in which a thermistor was towed just above the bottom. The vents through which the hot water was issuing into the cold ocean water were quite small but were detectable during the manned dives because of the shimmering of the rising plume of warm water. This shimmering is caused by the differences in the refractive index of the warm and cold water.

Many detailed topographic, heat flow, geologic, and geochemical observations were made. Perhaps the most interesting discovery was completely unexpected and had little to do with geophysics: exceptionally large (tens of centimeters in the long dimension) and closely spaced groups of animals such as clams and tube worms were found in productive communities around the vents. The depth of the vents (2.5 km beneath the sea surface) and the numbers of the animals make it unlikely that their food comes from the surface waters. The current speculation is that the organic carbon needed to sustain the animals is obtained from bacteria that use energy obtained by oxidation of the abundant hydrogen sulfide near the vents to produce organic compounds. If true, this is the first instance of such a large number of animals relying on that type of food source.

Precise location of earthquakes occurring at depths of 70–200 km in the Pacific plate as it descends beneath northeastern Japan and the central Aleutian and Kuril islands shows that they occur in two parallel sheetlike zones about 30 km apart. Furthermore, the polarization of the emitted seismic waves has been used to infer that the earthquakes in the upper zone are characterized by an alignment of the direction of principal compressive stress with the direction of the downgoing plate. On the other hand, for earthquakes in the lower zone the direction of least principal compressive stress is aligned with the direction of the downthrust plate. Analogously to a plate being bent upward, with compression on the top and tension on the bottom, the earthquakes may be a response to the unbending of the Pacific plate after its initial sharp downward bending where it starts its descent into the Earth's interior.

Another study of the fine detail of a descending plate was reported by seismologists from Nagoya University in Japan. A fortuitous combination of earthquakes from a plate descending beneath the Ryukyu Islands and an array of seismometers near Yokohama enabled them to see seismic waves reflected off the top of the Pacific plate where it descended below the Philippine Sea just south of Japan. The distances at which these reflections appeared and their amplitudes provided strong evidence for a relatively sharp contrast (over a distance of less than about 10 km) in material properties between the descending plate and the surrounding mantle of the Earth at depths of 200–350 km. The descending plate must eventually warm up and be reassimilated into the mantle. The sharpness of the transition in properties between the plate and the material through which it is descending depends on depth and therefore should provide some constraints on the dynamics of the subduction process.

Earthquake hazard reduction. During 1977 several thousand lives were lost from earthquakes in such widely separated areas as Romania, Iran, and Argentina. This number, which is not unusual, underscores the increasing importance attached to the prediction of the time, place, and size of earthquakes and the amount of ground shaking expected as a result of the earthquakes. This last type of prediction is distinct from the first and is necessary if engineers are to design structures with an adequate level of safety. As might be expected from the global distribution of earthquakes, research on earthquake hazard reduction was being carried out in many countries. This was attested to by the 850 delegates from 38 countries who attended the sixth World Conference on Earthquake Engineering held in New Delhi, India, in January 1977.

Of fundamental importance to the prediction of earthquake shaking are recordings of the ground motion from past events. Most such records have been obtained from California earthquakes, using specially designed seismographs (accelerographs) that record the ground acceleration. In spite of the presence of more than 1,400 such instruments in California alone, the data base is deficient in recordings close to large earthquakes. For example, there are only two useful recordings within 40 km of the faulting associated with magnitude-7 earthquakes and none at all within several hundred km of a truly great earthquake.

Many accelerometers were being installed in countries throughout the world in an attempt to fill this gap. A recent example is the joint U.S.-Soviet strong-motion instrument network in the central Asian republic of Tadzhikistan, one of the most active seismic areas in the Soviet Union. An earthquake on April 8, 1976, in that part of the U.S.S.R. provided one of the two recordings close to a magnitude-7 earthquake referred to above. This record was notable for a large acceleration (1.3 times the acceleration of gravity) in the vertical direction. An acceleration of comparable size was recorded during the 1971 San Fernando earthquake near Los Angeles, Calif., but in keeping with almost all previous recordings its maximum amplitude was in the horizontal direction. This suggests that the existing records, which deal primarily with California earthquakes, may not be representative of earthquake motions from other parts of the world.

Researchers in earthquake prediction continued to grope for reliable early warnings of an impending event. Although the Chinese successfully predicted a shock on Feb. 4, 1975, in Liaoning Province, they did not foresee the greatly destructive earthquake of July 28, 1976, which may have claimed more than 500,000 lives. Crucial to the successful prediction was the occurrence of an unusual swarm of small earthquakes in

A region of about 90,000 square kilometers where the ground level rose as much as 35 centimeters between 1960 and 1974 is visible in a photo from a satellite at an altitude of 920 kilometers above southern California. There has been some subsidence since 1974; however the uplift might be a warning of future earthquake activity, according to some geophysicists. (Los Angeles is in the lower right-hand corner of the photo.)

UPI Compix

the days before the main event. Not all earthquakes are preceded by such foreshocks, however, and in those that are it is necessary to identify the events as foreshocks rather than as randomly occurring small earthquakes. Recent careful studies of several California earthquakes by researchers at the U.S. Geological Survey and the California Institute of Technology suggested that the foreshocks may have subtle but recognizable differences in wave forms as compared with the main earthquake and that a clustering of foreshocks may occur close to the point in the Earth at which the rupture in the main earthquake is initiated. But many more studies of this kind must be accomplished before scientists can be sure that they have developed a reliable means of identifying small seismic events as foreshocks.

During recent years surveys have revealed a rapid uplift of more than 90,000 sq km (originally believed to be 12,000 sq km) in southern California, which might be a forewarning of a major earthquake on a part of the San Andreas Fault that has been relatively quiet since a large earthquake occurred there in 1857. Detailed studies were being made of different aspects of this uplift, which is believed to extend from Point Arguello, Calif., to the Arizona border. Within this region the ground level rose as much as 35 cm between 1960 and 1974. The most recent results of leveling surveys show that the part of the uplift near Palmdale, Calif., has collapsed by about 50% in the last several years. The mechanisms responsible for these large-scale movements of the Earth's crust and the implications for a future large earthquake are not known. A similar pattern of uplift and subsidence may have taken place between 1897 and 1926 in southern California without any noticeable effect on earthquake occurrences.

—David M. Boore

Hydrological sciences

The increasing pressures of actual and projected demands on water resources continued to concentrate attention on research oriented toward solving immediate problems, to some extent at the expense of research aimed at improving understanding of hydrological processes. Priority areas of interest included water supplies, demands for expanded food and energy production, the effect of waste disposal on water quality, and the effect of pollutants on the quality of water sources.

Hydrology. The 1977 drought provided an excellent example of how the demand for immediate solutions influences the pattern of studies. The winter of 1976–77, one of the worst on record in the U.S., sensitized the public to the effects of adverse weather, and when the winter debacle was followed by widespread drought west of the Mississippi River, plans were laid to provide immediate relief. At the same time, some workers, realizing that droughts seem to be repetitive if not cyclic, urged research into the nature of drought, its causes, and its relationship to climatic changes.

The pace of studies accelerated rapidly. Data collected early in the year showed how droughts worsen the quality of water as well as reduce streamflow and recharge to groundwater storage. Concentration of dissolved minerals was at record or near-record highs in many streams. Water quality deterioration was greatest where freezing weather and drought occurred together, because the minerals excluded from frozen stream water were concentrated in the unfrozen portion. Most of the deterioration in water quality occurred because there was less water available to dilute normal discharges of wastes.

Rains fell in the Midwest in the fall, and October was

Workers clear debris from a building in Bucharest, Romania, destroyed by an earthquake that devastated the city in March 1977. Measuring 7.1 on the Richter scale, the quake left 1,500 dead, more than 11,000 injured, and 80,000 homeless in Romania.

Henri Bureau—Sygma

the wettest month in at least a year. In the West only central California continued to experience drought, and even there early winter rains began refilling the reservoirs. The well-structured plan of investigations shrank in scope as the drought shrank in area and intensity, and by year's end the thrust of the proposed hydrological studies was reduced to collecting and recording data and to some studies of ancient droughts.

Nonetheless, the drought provided the opportunity for many experiments as communities and agencies coped with the effects of continuing dry weather. In California these effects were minimized through lowered use of water by municipalities and industries, increased "borrowing" from storage reservoirs, and renewed dependence on groundwater. The groundwater pumpage provided a full-scale test of current theories of subsidence reduction and rebound. In the few years since surface water from northern California had supplanted local groundwater for irrigation, subsidence due to groundwater withdrawals had stabilized and water levels had recovered in most parts of the Central Valley. The renewed pumping lowered some water levels, and although new subsidence had not yet been reported, it was expected, and the effects of pumping were being monitored carefully.

River basin studies. Although research on the application of hydrology to water resources problems tended to overshadow studies of the physical basis of hydrology, applied research often provided valuable insights into the relationships of water regimens to their ecological and social environments and into the nature of the water regimens themselves. A prototype study on the Willamette River Basin in Oregon, undertaken to develop methodologies for assessing the quality of river waters, demonstrated that no single framework of remedial measures can be applied uniformly. Earlier assessments of the pollution potential of industries in the Willamette Basin had suggested the need for many additional water-treatment facilities. However, the Willamette River study showed that existing secondary-treatment measures, combined with summertime additions of water from existing reservoirs, had already raised the dissolved oxygen content of the water considerably, and that further treatment would provide only marginal improvement. This one result alone would lead to great savings, since it eliminated the need to build additional treatment plants.

The study also demonstrated that previously collected data, except for streamflow, were unusable for making quality assessments. Since the Willamette River data base is not fundamentally different from that of most basins, this same shortcoming probably exists elsewhere, indicating that many existing plans for river-basin assessment may have to be changed.

Waste disposal and sedimentation. Waste disposal continued to hold high priority among areas of hydrological research. A few years earlier, disposal of radioactive waste in thick natural salt deposits had been greatly favored, but recent work showed that the heat produced by the stored radioactive materials might affect the concentration of water contained in salt crystals and thus develop avenues of leakage. The Potomac River was studied in an effort to document the extent to which the river can purify itself of organic carbon contamination and the ways in which it adjusts to the higher discharges and increased sediment loads resulting from urban development. It was found that high sediment loads continue even after urban development in a watershed has slowed or ceased. As more and more land is covered with pavement and other impermeable surfaces, stream channels widen to accommodate the increased runoff, and the resulting erosion of stream banks provides a continuing influx of sediment.

Problems of erosion and sedimentation also received attention in other contexts. In Mississippi studies showed that the net area of islands off the coast has been decreasing in the past few decades. The cause appeared to be a deficit in sediment supply, which in some places may result from sediment-control structures along inland rivers. Studies of shoreline erosion of natural and man-made lakes in Illinois resulted in improved design for protective structures. In Oregon studies of logging operations demonstrated that thermal and sediment pollution was minimized where "buffer strips" of timber were retained along stream banks.

Basic research. Although applied research received the most attention during 1977, basic research in the physics of water continued in many centers. Studies at Syracuse (N.Y.) University of transport processes within porous structures resulted in the first rigorous quantitative theory relating to filtration in deep beds and the ability to predict the rate of removal of particles from the fluid stream through the calculation of particle trajectories. The theory explains how entire channels within porous structures can be closed to flow by the accumulation of a cluster of particles in a narrow passage. Major advances also were made in understanding the dispersion of reacting solutes that are in the process of being transported through saturated porous structures.

Of interest to both the U.S. and Canada was the release of the first comprehensive results of the International Field Year on the Great Lakes (IFYGL), a program sponsored jointly by the Canadian and U.S. national committees for the International Hydrological Decade. Billions of bits of data on the hydrology of Lake Ontario and its basin were collected during a massive investigative attack in 1972 by more than 600 scientists. These now are beginning to provide new insights into the physical, chemical, and biological regimes of one of the world's ten largest bodies of fresh water. Perhaps most important, enough data are now

U.S. Coast Guard icebreaker nears a three-quarter-mile-long tabular iceberg off the coast of Greenland. Such icebergs were the subject of a conference in 1977 that tried to determine whether it was feasible to tow them to the coasts of desert countries to serve as sources of fresh water.

available to establish a general synoptic base of lake characteristics to which future local and specialized studies could be referred. In addition, the data permit realistic modeling of large-lake phenomena. The new information clearly demonstrates that the hydrological regimen of Lake Ontario is far more complex than had been previously realized and that the lake is in considerably worse shape biologically than had been previously suspected.

The Field Year confirmed some suspected phenomena and added many heretofore unsuspected perturbations to the hydrological cycle. Studies of the terrestrial water balance demonstrated the reliability of radar for measuring precipitation during summer months, although more measurements of snowfall were needed to evaluate the usefulness of radar in winter. New understanding was obtained regarding the interactions of surface waves, wind profiles, and water at different levels in the lake. When cold air moves in over the lake and strong northerly winds tilt the thermocline and expose cold subsurface waters in the upwind regions, the energy transfer rates in the northern portions can be three to five times greater than those along the southern shore. Evaporation was shown to be unexpectedly sensitive to seasonal temperature shifts, and lakewide evaporation rates in midsummer increase abruptly rather than gradually. Also, one-third of the annual evaporation was found to occur during one-tenth of the year.

The major international event was the UN Water Conference held in Argentina in March. The conference fulfilled one of its aims by drawing world attention to the threat of future water resources crises in many parts of the globe. Although mainly concerned with the development of national policies to improve the management of water resources, its resolutions also stressed the basic fact that adequate information is a necessary prerequisite for rational managerial policies and decisions.

—L. A. Heindl

Oceanography. Oceanographic research during the year continued to cover a broad spectrum of interests. As usual, much of it was focused within the respective disciplines of physical, chemical, biological, and geologic oceanography. However, the field is one of complex interactions in which, for example, living organisms respond to changes within the physicochemical environment driven by the atmosphere, and the sediments retain a record of these responses. As a consequence, truly interdisciplinary investigations were becoming more common, particularly in studies of climate and of the effect of ocean variability on the ecosystems of regions where coastal upwelling takes place.

A perspective on the nature of these cross-disciplinary interactions was provided by a committee of the U.S. National Research Council, which throughout the year was engaged in evaluating the current state of oceanic knowledge and in identifying the scientific opportunities for a possible continuation in the 1980s of the International Decade of Ocean Exploration. Summaries of highlights of the work in 1977 illustrate some of the interdisciplinary characteristics of the field.

Oceanic reservoir for carbon dioxide. The importance of the ocean's storage of heat in modulating climate is well recognized. Another climatic role for the ocean was now becoming apparent, namely, its capacity for isolating the excess of carbon dioxide produced by human activities.

Measurements initiated in 1958 as part of the International Geophysical Year have demonstrated an annual increase of about one part per million (ppm) per year in the atmosphere's content of carbon dioxide, from about 312 ppm in 1958 to approximately 332 ppm in 1978. The pronounced seasonal oscillation in this increase, as measured at the Mauna Loa (Hawaii) Observatory, is related to the annual course of photosynthesis in the Northern Hemisphere forests.

The slow increase of this minor constituent of the atmosphere might be of only academic interest except for the so-called greenhouse effect. Carbon dioxide, along with water vapor and other trace constituents of air, is relatively opaque to the long-wave radiation emitted by the Earth's surface. Thus an increase in atmospheric carbon dioxide should be accompanied by increased surface temperature, and global temperature increases of 2°–3° C or more have been predicted for early in the 21st century. The climatic effect of this warming would be great; for example, the desert regions could be expected to move poleward. Thus it is a matter of some urgency to evaluate—and eventually to predict and, if necessary, to control—the effects of this process.

The increased input of carbon dioxide arises in part from the burning of fossil fuel; this source, together with cement manufacture, is estimated to account for about 5×10^{15} g of carbon per year. A comparable amount comes from reduction in the terrestrial biomass or volume of living matter, from the destruction of forests and the oxidation of humus. Of the total input of 10^{16} of carbon per year, less than half is added to the atmosphere. It is assumed that the rest is stored in the ocean.

The capacity of the ocean surface layer for carbon dioxide is roughly the same as that of the atmosphere (about 700×10^{15} g of carbon). Below the thermocline, which separates the surface layer from the colder, oxygen-poor zones, are the principal oceanic reservoirs: dissolved organic carbon (10^{18} g), the inorganic carbonate-bicarbonate system (10^{19} g of carbon), and the oceanic sediments (10^{22} g of carbon). Although the capacity of the deeper ocean layers appears to be virtually infinite, these layers are protected from exchange with the surface layer by the density barrier across the thermocline.

Oceanographers were attempting to determine the fluxes, interactions, and exchanges between the surface layer and these deeper reservoirs. Are there human activities that increase the ocean's capacity for carbon dioxide or accelerate the exchanges? For example, the fertilization of coastal waters by the runoff of agricultural fertilizer and domestic sewage may increase productivity in the affected area and hence the storage of carbon in plants and debris. The effect is probably small, although it may hasten the deposit of organic matter in sediments.

Data on tritium distribution in the North Atlantic suggest that the physical exchange between surface and deeper waters is probably more rapid than was previously believed. The downward transport of carbon dioxide is probably enhanced by biotic mechanisms,

"Clean Sweep," developed by the Lockheed Missiles and Space Company, is an oil retrieval device that can recover 1,000 gallons of spilled oil per minute in waves as high as 16 feet.

both the passive fallout of dead remains and the dynamic transfer of materials by vertically migrating organisms. Determination of these biotic fluxes is essential if the ocean's capacity to buffer the harmful effects of excess carbon dioxide is to be evaluated.

Antarctic krill. Extensions of national jurisdiction over coastal fisheries and the rising demand for animal protein were causing distant-water fishing fleets to turn to unconventional resources in unfished regions. One possibility was krill, *Euphausia superba*, a small crustacean that is abundant in waters off the Antarctic coast. First observed by Capt. James Cook more than two hundred years ago, these creatures, which reach more than two inches in length, occur in dense swarms, particularly in the South Atlantic sector. They provide the nutritional base for the great Antarctic populations of marine mammals, fish, and birds.

Estimates of the total biomass of krill are crude and uncertain. The distribution is patchy, with concentrations as high as 33 kg per cu m having been observed. The krill migrate vertically over distances of hundreds of meters, and their distribution is controlled by the water circulation. Measurements of primary production by marine phytoplankton suggest that annual krill production is 100 million to 500 million tons per year. It is also possible to calculate the amount of krill eaten by predators, especially whales, seals, penguins and other birds, squid, and fish. The principal consumers are seals (64 million tons per year) and whales (43 million tons). All told, the predators appear to consume more than 200 million tons per year, roughly equivalent to the biomass of the entire human population.

Before whaling operations decimated the stocks, the whale biomass may have been six times larger than at present, and their consumption of krill was probably some 150 million tons greater. Part of this "surplus" is being taken by other predators, such as penguins and seals, whose populations have risen accordingly. The whales have also responded to the increased availability of food by growing and breeding more rapidly. Even if the whale stocks were allowed to recover, there would appear to be sufficient production of krill to permit an annual catch of 50 million–70 million tons for human consumption, roughly the magnitude of the current world catch from all marine fisheries. The current annual catch of krill is less than 20,000 tons.

Plastic enclosures 30 meters deep and with capacities of more than 1,000 cubic meters are installed in Saanich Inlet, British Columbia. They are used to provide a controlled environment for studies of plankton and of the effects of pollutants on plankton and bacteria.

Courtesy, Case Existological Laboratories; photo, Mike Pease

There are some natural impediments to rapid growth of this fishery. During much of the year, the krill is protected against human utilization by rough seas and widespread ice cover. There are also technological difficulties. The meat deteriorates rapidly after the catch and hence must be processed promptly. A more serious problem is that the chitin shell is closely attached to the flesh, and machines for effecting the separation are not yet fully developed.

Because of the central role of krill in the marine ecosystem of the Antarctic, it is essential that far more be learned about the structure and dynamics of this system before the fishery is allowed to grow to the maximum sustainable level. To this end, international plans for a program of Biological Investigations of Marine Antarctic Systems and Stocks (BIOMASS) were being developed. In the meantime, nations interested in the krill resource were being encouraged by the Antarctic Treaty signatories to conduct their fisheries "with proper regard to the Antarctic marine ecosystem as a whole."

Controlled ecosystem experiments. Scientists have always tried to squeeze the world into test tubes so they could observe its behavior at close hand. Unfortunately, the container usually affects the system under study. The problem is to find an ideal size for the microcosm, large enough to behave like the real world and yet small enough to measure and manipulate. In the ocean, the distribution scales of phytoplankton and zooplankton are of the order of kilometers horizontally and tens of meters vertically. Thus a life-size experiment would involve some 10^8 cu m!

In the past, marine plankton ecosystems have been studied in tower tanks ten meters deep and holding about 100 cu m of water. As part of the Controlled Ecosystem Pollution Experiment (CEPEX), plastic enclosures 30 m deep and with capacities of more than 1,000 cu m were installed in Saanich Inlet, British Columbia, where they were being used by U.S. and Canadian scientists to investigate plankton dynamics, natural cycles in plankton ecosystems, and the effects of eutrophication (the result of a detrimental increase in plant nutrients) and pollution. Even such immense "bottles" do not fully reproduce conditions in the ocean. For example, the immigration of new populations transported by ocean currents is prevented by the enclosure. But the similar behavior of plankton populations living within and outside the containers suggests that they provide a useful approximation to natural conditions.

As part of the experiment, bacterial and plankton populations were exposed to low concentrations of copper, mercury, and petroleum hydrocarbons in an attempt to understand the effects of these pollutants. Initially, it was found, the most vulnerable phytoplankton populations collapse while more tolerant bacteria thrive. There is a rapid succession of phytoplankton species, and overall rates of carbon fixation seem to be little changed.

Smaller zooplankton are more likely to be killed by metals than are larger animals. Sublethal pollutant doses appear to reduce the rates of egg production and of ingestion. Pollutants also affect predators, so that an indirect effect of pollution may be to reduce grazing pressure, thus favoring larger standing stocks of some organisms. Where pollutants such as heavy metals and some components of oil are absorbed by particles which then sink to the bottom, benthic (bottom-living) organisms are affected more than pelagic ones.

Although these experiments had just begun, the preliminary results already showed the utility of these super test tubes. The natural populations appeared to adjust to stress by a rapid substitution of tolerant for vulnerable species. In some ways, the succession of events was similar to that occurring over much longer periods of time in the surrounding waters in response to natural environmental changes.

Denitrification, aguaje, and malagua off Peru. The general distribution of dissolved oxygen in the ocean has long been known. At the surface, oxygen exchanges freely with the atmosphere, and the oxygen content of surface waters is close to saturation at the local temperature and salinity. Below the surface layer, dissolved oxygen decreases rapidly to a minimum value, then increases slowly toward the bottom. The minimum reflects the consumption of oxygen by the oxidation of organic matter; the higher values below represent the residual oxygen content of bottom water that sank in the oxygen-rich polar regions. Two immense pools of deoxygenated water lie a few hundred meters below the surface of the eastern tropical Pacific, one off Central America, the other off Peru. The dissolved oxygen content of these pools is a few tenths of a milliliter per liter, a few percent of saturation. High concentrations of nitrite-nitrogen have been observed there, which have been produced from bacterial reduction of nitrate-nitrogen.

Elsewhere in the ocean, nitrite-nitrogen is uncommon except much nearer to the surface. The more highly oxidized nitrate-nitrogen is much more abundant and is the nutrient that commonly limits the magnitude of primary production by phytoplankton. Nitrate-nitrogen is normally low in the surface layer, where it is removed by photosynthetic activity, and increases to a maximum at about the depth of the oxygen minimum. The high concentrations of nitrate in and below the thermocline constitute a reservoir of fertilizer that is returned to the surface layer in the highly productive upwelling regions. Under unusual conditions, massive denitrification can occur. Such an event was observed off central Peru in April 1976. Water samples from the depth of the presumed nitrate maximum were devoid of both nitrate and nitrite. The smell of hydrogen sulfide

Courtesy, Brookhaven National Laboratory; photo, William Marin, Jr.

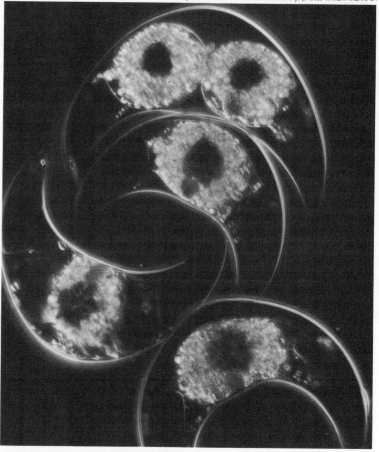

Photomicrograph of phytoplankton is magnified 400 times. Plankton were studied extensively by marine biologists during the year.

was evident, indicating the complete removal of dissolved oxygen. At these depths, concentrations of ammonia, phosphate, and silicate were at a maximum.

This was apparently the first time that complete denitrification and the subsequent production of hydrogen sulfide had been detected in the open ocean. The denitrified layer was contained within the Peru-Chile Undercurrent, the normal source of upwelled water along the Peruvian coast. The event coincided with the presence of the warm El Niño current off Peru, which limited coastal upwelling; that which did occur was supplied with an unusual kind of nitrate-free subsurface water. One consequence was an enormous bloom of the dinoflagellate *Gymnodinium splendens*. This red tide, or *aguaje*, extended all the way from just south of the Galápagos Islands to at least 15° S. It was accompanied by a great abundance of free-swimming jellyfish, a phenomenon known in Peru as *malagua*. In the absence of the usual diatom-zooplankton assemblage, feeding conditions were particularly unfavorable for the already reduced stock of anchovy. Thus the unusual environmental conditions in 1976 dealt a further blow to the anchovy stock, which had never recovered from the El Niño conditions that prevailed in 1972.

—Warren S. Wooster

298

Energy

Energy developments during 1977 were primarily political rather than technological. Among the highlights were the crude oil price actions taken by the Organization of Petroleum Exporting Countries (OPEC); the U.S. National Energy Plan; the energy deliberations of the U.S. Congress; and energy developments in the industrialized countries.

Political and economic developments. Following the OPEC meeting in December 1976, a 10% increase was announced in the price for crude oil. However, Saudi Arabia and the United Arab Emirates refused to go along with the size of the increase. In the United States the weighted price of imported oil acquired by domestic refineries rose from a December 1976 level of $13.71 per bbl to $14.66 by late summer, a 7% increase.

When OPEC met in December 1977 at Caracas, Venez., once again price policy was at the head of the agenda. The meeting adjourned without any agreement to change the prices currently charged by the exporting countries. Continued price stability of imported oil thus seemed to be assured for at least the first half of 1978.

It is significant to realize that for the U.S. price stability for imported oil means, in economic terms, a declining real price for crude petroleum. In 1974 the acquisition cost of crude petroleum from imported sources to domestic refineries stood at $12.52 per bbl. The equivalent figure for 1975 was $13.93; for 1976 it was $13.48, and for the first eight months of 1977 it climbed to $14.48. Thus, over the three-year period, the current dollar price increased by 16%. However, when this price is adjusted to the rate of inflation within the U.S., it translates into an actual decline from $12.52 to $11.64. Thus, the common conception of increasing costs of energy since the imposition of the Arab boycott of 1973 is incorrect. International petroleum prices rose in giant steps to the 1974 level, but since that date they have been declining in real terms. This fact is significant in interpreting the responses of the U.S. and other industrial nations to the OPEC action.

On April 20, 1977, the administration of U.S. Pres. Jimmy Carter presented its National Energy Plan (NEP) to Congress. The philosophy underlying the plan is that the government must take responsibility for energy in the U.S. The major thrust of the NEP was to reduce demand for energy through conservation, largely by increasing the cost of energy to consumers. The distinction was clearly drawn between the NEP and earlier proposals because of the emphasis on conservation rather than on increasing domestic availability of conventional oil and gas resources.

The first of the seven principal elements of the NEP was concerned with crude oil pricing. Existing oil price controls set an average price for crude oil that is between the controlled price of old domestic crude oil and the price of imported oil. This system requires a complex arrangement to equalize the cost of crude oil to all refineries. The NEP would eliminate both the average price standard and the equalization arrangement and would impose a crude-oil equalization tax to be phased in over a three-year period. Certain categories of domestic oil would be allowed to receive prices higher than the import price to encourage exploration and development. Also included in the NEP was a tax on industrial and utility use of oil, which would provide an incentive for such users to convert to other fuels and, thereby, reduce dependence upon imported oil.

The second major component of the NEP dealt with natural gas pricing. The NEP rejected decontrol of the pricing of all new gas. It argued that while such a step would clear the natural gas market it would not increase the available supply of gas. The NEP proposed (1) an increase in the control price of natural gas, to be set equivalent to the price of crude oil acquired by domestic refineries in 1977, estimated to be $1.75 per thousand cu ft; and (2) elimination of the present system of pricing by establishing a single price for all new gas, intrastate as well as interstate. The NEP also proposed to replace consumer pricing based upon the average of all gas delivered to the gas system with a requirement that gas utilities pass on the cost of the most expensive replacement gas to the large industrial users. When coupled with a tax on industrial users of natural gas, this would cause large industries to substitute other fuels for gas.

Coal conversion was a third major aspect of the NEP. Although the major mechanism to encourage coal conversion was the increase in the price of oil and gas to consumers, two other important measures encouraging conversion were recommended. The first proposed a 10% investment tax credit for conversion to coal or other energy source from oil and gas, and the second was a prohibition on the burning of oil and gas in all new utility or industrial boilers.

Conservation was the major feature of the NEP. The plan envisioned it to be achieved by higher prices to consumers, tax incentives, and regulatory requirements. The principal tax measures mentioned above

Forty-ton superconducting magnet system made in the U.S. is transported into the Soviet Academy of Sciences Institute of High Temperatures in Moscow as part of a U.S.-Soviet cooperative experiment aimed at more efficient production of electrical energy.

would raise the cost of oil and gas to the consumer and, therefore, encourage conservation. In addition, a graduated "gas guzzler" tax on new automobiles was proposed to increase greatly the cost of operating low-mileage, high-fuel-consumption cars. Significant tax incentives for home and building insulation and a large tax credit for solar heating were proposed, along with mandatory minimum efficiency standards for major home appliances.

A fifth component of the NEP was a price structure that would confront electricity users with prices that reflect incremental costs of production. This, along with the other proposals, would increase the price of electricity and encourage its conservation.

A sixth aspect of the plan was concerned with nuclear power policy. The NEP envisioned a rapid increase in nuclear power, using current technology. Citing the risk of nuclear proliferation and the environmental hazards of plutonium, the NEP called for cancellation of the construction of the Clinch River (Tenn.) breeder reactor demonstration project and indefinite deferment of the processing of spent nuclear fuel.

Finally, the NEP sought to enlarge the existing plan for a strategic petroleum reserve. The objective was to store 500 million bbl by the end of 1980, enough to cover a four-month interruption of 4 million bbl per day in oil supplies to the U.S., and 1 billion bbl by 1985.

The Carter administration believed that implementation of the NEP would reduce oil imports by approximately 4.5 million bbl per day by 1985. The use of coal was projected to increase to approximately 1.2 billion tons by 1985, and natural gas would be reallocated to high-priority uses.

Aside from the NEP, there were several other administration initiatives during 1977. Under authority granted to the president by the Congress, Carter created the Department of Energy, which brought together the Federal Energy Administration, the Energy Research and Development Administration, the Federal Power Commission, and parts of other agencies. Another significant action was a proposal by the president that Congress establish procedures for building the Alcan natural gas pipeline. This pipeline, which may be operational in 1983, would allow the transportation of more than 800 billion cu ft of Alaskan gas per year to the southern 48 states, representing approximately 5% of total U.S. gas consumption.

The NEP dominated congressional debate for virtually the entire year. Criticism of the NEP began immediately after its submission to Congress in April. Although there was considerable discussion of many aspects of the plan, three issues quickly rose to prominence: natural gas price deregulation, the crude-oil equalization tax, and the per-capita rebate of the crude-oil equalization tax to consumers.

The House of Representatives approved the NEP with minor changes, but in the Senate the plan encountered difficulty. By a close margin the Senate voted for decontrol of new natural gas, rejecting the continuation of price controls and the extension of controls to intrastate gas. In addition, it rejected the crude-oil equalization tax and replaced it with a system of incentive taxation for the development of new energy supplies and for conservation action.

In early 1978 a stalemate still existed over major elements of the NEP within the House-Senate conference committee. Although substantial agreement was reached on loans for coal conversion, for energy conservation, and for solar energy, there was no agreement on other principal elements of the proposal.

Congress did, however, approve the president's request for legislation on the Alcan gas pipeline.

A large number of wildcat strikes took place in the coal fields during the summer of 1977. These strikes were leading up to the expiration of the contract between the Bituminous Coal Operators Association and the United Mine Workers early in December 1977. Negotiations for extension of that contract failed, and early in December a long coal strike began.

Major consumers of coal, recognizing the probability of a strike, had built up large stockpiles of coal during 1977. These were ample to provide a continued flow of energy from coal for a 60-day strike. However, when the strike extended past that time period, coal stocks fell to critical levels, and substantial power curtailments became necessary in several states. It is difficult to evaluate the long-run impact of the strike. It does appear, however, that it will have a significant effect on the NEP philosophy of increasing reliance on coal.

Other industrialized countries were experiencing problems with energy similar to those of the U.S. The deficit in international trade balances between the OPEC countries and the non-Communist industrialized nations rose to about $40 billion in 1977 as compared with $4 billion in 1971–73.

Economic conditions in the major industrial countries outside the U.S. were not good in 1977. Real output in Western Europe increased by only 2% over the year, and even Japan, which has been the notable economic performer over the past two decades, fell short of its projected growth rate. This situation, of course, affected energy developments in those countries. Total energy consumption in most of them declined after 1973 with the exception of Japan, which showed a very moderate increase. All of the major industrialized countries with the exception of the U.S. reduced their imports of crude oil over the 1973–77 period.

Petroleum. Consumption of petroleum in the major non-Communist industrialized countries increased from 33.2 million bbl per day in 1976 to 34.7 million bbl per day in 1977. As can be seen in Table I, this 1.5 million-bbl daily increase was not evenly spread among the countries. The U.S. increase of 1.7 million bbl was by far the largest recorded. Japan's consumption rose 100,000 bbl per day, while most other major nations indicated a continued decline.

Production of petroleum increased in 1977. Of significance was the substantial increase in production by Saudi Arabia, which occurred following the debate over oil prices within the OPEC countries. U.S. production in 1977 increased for the first time since 1971.

A major event of note in 1977 was the opening of the trans-Alaska oil pipeline on June 20, 1977. This pipeline, the construction of which was marked by one of the major environment versus development contests in the 1970s, was among the largest private construction

Members of the United Mine Workers assemble in Cedar Grove, W. Va., to protest the contract agreed upon by the union's leadership. The coal strike lasted a record 109 days.

Michael D. Sullivan

	U.S.	Japan	West Germany	France	United Kingdom	Canada	Italy
Table I. Petroleum Consumption for Major Market Economy Industrialized Countries, 1973–77 (In 000,000 of bbl per day)							
1973	15.1	5.0	2.7	2.2	2.0	1.6	1.5
1974	14.7	4.8	2.4	2.1	1.9	1.6	1.5
1975	14.3	4.6	2.3	1.9	1.6	1.6	1.5
1976	15.2	4.8	2.5	2.1	1.6	1.7	1.5
1977	16.9	5.1	2.4	1.9	1.6	1.6	1.4

Source: U.S. Department of Energy.

projects ever undertaken. The final cost exceeded $8 billion, all of which came from the private sector of the U.S. economy. Although the startup of the pipeline was marked by several accidents, one of which destroyed a pump station, no major oil spills occurred and by the end of 1977 the pipeline was delivering 700,000 bbl of oil per day to the port of Valdez. The commencement of flow through the pipeline was responsible for the year's increase in crude petroleum production in the U.S. Because the pipeline was scheduled to be in operation throughout 1978 and its capacity would be increased upon reconstruction of the destroyed pumping station, crude oil production in the U.S. was expected to continue to increase.

On the world scene, the continued increases in production from the North Sea oil fields and the decision of Saudi Arabia to increase its level of production were the major events in 1977 (Table II). Most of the proved reserves for the North Sea were under the control of the United Kingdom and Norway. In 1977 the U.K. increased its production to 775,000 bbl per day, an increase of 213% over 1976. For Europe as a whole, production increased by 60% over 1976. The Middle East, which accounted for a daily production of 22 million bbl out of a world total of 60 million in 1977, as a region showed little change in 1977; however, Saudi Arabia, by far the largest producer in the area, increased production by more than 7%. This was offset in part by a 4% decline in production by Iran, the second largest producer, and by a general decline in most other Middle Eastern countries. There were substantial increases in production in the Asia-Pacific area, led by a 12% increase in Indonesia, by far the largest producer in that region. Africa's two large producers, Libya and Nigeria, both substantially increased their outputs and the total production from Africa rose by over 7% for the year. In the Western Hemisphere, both Canada and the U.S. increased their production, whereas Venezuela experienced a slight decline. Overall, output from the Western Hemisphere increased by approximately 2.5%.

Several other trends were also discernible during the year. The search for new oil, represented by drilling footage and drilling expenditures, increased substantially. The total footage of wells drilled in the U.S. rose by 12%, as did the number of exploratory wells. Expen-

Supertanker S.S. "New York" (right) is pushed by tugs toward M.V. "British Resolution" (center) and "Washington Trader" (left) near the Pacific terminus of the Panama Canal in August 1977. The "New York" carried Alaskan oil, which it transferred to the "Resolution"; the latter serves as a temporary transfer depot until a mainland terminal can be built. The "Washington Trader" then took some of the oil through the canal, the first Alaskan petroleum to be carried on that route.

Wide World

Table II. World Crude Oil Production (In millions of 42-gallon bbl)		
	1976	1977
U.S.S.R.	3,822	4,000
Saudi Arabia	3,054	3,400
United States	2,976	2,987
Iran	2,168	2,200
Other market economy countries	8,330	8,550
Other central economy countries	794	820
World total	21,144	21,957

Source: U.S. Bureau of Mines.

Table III. World Production of Bituminous Coal and Lignite (In thousands of tons)		
	1976	1977
Australia	100,104	108,000
Canada	27,899	34,000
France	22,328	30,000
Germany, West	239,395	221,000
India	115,586	122,000
South Africa	82,233	82,000
United Kingdom	133,604	140,000
United States	678,685	685,000
Other market economy countries	119,197	122,000
Central economy countries	1,996,019	2,030,000
World total	3,515,050	3,574,000

Source: U.S. Bureau of Mines.

ditures for exploration by all U.S. firms rose 17% to $9.4 billion in 1977. Although data were not available for the rest of the world on a comparable basis, the foreign expenditures planned by major U.S. firms increased 8.4% in 1977 over 1976. This increased exploratory activity resulted in a net increase of more than 1% in the total world crude oil reserves as of Jan. 1, 1978.

Natural gas. The decline in natural gas production in the U.S. leveled off in 1977. On a worldwide basis there was a slight increase in total marketed production in 1977. Though natural gas is expensive to transport by any other means than pipeline, there was a growing trade in liquefied natural gas (LNG); a major U.S. receiving station, at Cove Point, Md., began in 1978 to receive shipments of LNG from Algeria. The development of the natural gas fields in the North Sea sharply reduced the flow of natural gas from Africa to Europe and substantially contributed to Europe's decline in energy imports.

A heat pump using natural gas was under development during the year. Its advantage over electric pumps is that it preheats incoming air with exhaust from its turbine and thereby narrows the temperature differential between heat source and heat sink (the region where heat is absorbed). This allows the pump to operate efficiently at outdoor temperatures as low as 15° F and, less efficiently, at temperatures below 0° F. The electric heat pump, by contrast, does not operate well when the outdoor temperature is below 40° F.

Coal. World production of bituminous coal and lignite rose slightly in 1977. As shown in Table III, these increases were widespread with the notable exception of West Germany, where production declined. Although coal increased substantially in price after the rise in the price of crude oil, it continued to make inroads in competition with other energy supplies. World coal output increased steadily after 1967, with production 28% higher in 1977 than it was ten years earlier. The increase in the United States over the same period was 24%.

The mining and use of coal have been among the major subjects of environmental debate both in the U.S. and in other industrialized countries. The legislation of clean-air standards imposed substantial restrictions on the burning of high-sulfur and high-ash coals, and the land destruction caused by strip mining became a major policy issue. The reaction of the industrialized countries to these issues has varied considerably. For example, West German industry has proceeded under a 1950 law, the Brown Coal Act. This law gave private industry the right of eminent domain, and as a result approximately 18,000 people in an area west of Cologne have been moved out of their homes since 1950 to allow for the mining of lignite there. The importance to West Germany of independence from foreign oil and the fears in that country concerning the development of nuclear power have led to exploitation of coal resources in a manner that sharply contrasts with that of the U.S. In the latter, a strip mine bill enacted into law in 1977 places substantial limitations on the mining of coal in the western states.

Nuclear power. Nuclear-generated electricity continued to increase in importance in the U.S. The percentage of domestic electricity generated by nuclear power increased from 4.5% in 1973 to 11.7% in 1977. As Table IV indicates, the U.S. was by far the most important user of nuclear power among all of the major non-Communist countries, accounting for 47 million of the world's 85 million-kw capacity. The country with the second largest installed capacity was the U.K. with 8 million kw.

The first light-water breeder reactor in the U.S. began undergoing commercial-scale tests late in August. Uranium-233 was used as its fissile material, the fis-

New York City experienced a blackout in July 1977 when a thunderstorm knocked out transmission lines. Below, physicist Joseph Rich prepares to test a new high-power vacuum circuit interrupter designed to protect transmission lines from lightning damage.

Courtesy, General Electric Research and Development Center

sioning atoms ejecting enough neutrons so that a bed of non-fissile thorium is converted into more ^{233}U. The reactor is described as light water because the water that moderates the core contains conventional hydrogen atoms rather than deuterium.

Advantages of this type of reactor are that it utilizes the abundant thorium-^{233}U fuel cycle instead of the increasingly scarce and expensive ^{235}U and that it reduces production of such dangerous by-products as plutonium. Such production of plutonium, which can be made into bombs with comparative ease, is a major drawback of the liquid-metal fast-breeder reactor.

In the rapidly developing field of using lasers to achieve nuclear fusion, Nikolay Basov of the Soviet Union announced that he and his colleagues had reached a plasma density and confinement time necessary for an ongoing fusion reaction. However, Basov and his group lacked by a factor of more than ten the temperature (roughly 10^8 K) necessary to achieve fusion.

Future prospects. In contrast with the volatile period following the 1973 Arab boycott of crude oil production, energy developments both in the producing countries and in the major industrial nations settled down to more normal patterns in recent months. It is this fact, perhaps, that explains both the reluctance of the U.S. Congress to embark on drastic new energy programs and the price constraint being exercised by OPEC.

Without question, the major industrial countries of the world have suffered sharply from the substantial increase in the cost of energy. Paramount among these problems is the continuing balance of trade deficit between oil-importing and oil-exporting nations.

Scientists from Los Alamos (New Mexico) Scientific Laboratory take a water sample from condensing steam shooting from a geothermal well. They had created the well in hot, dry rock by using standard oil-field drilling techniques that did not require explosives, a breakthrough in the effort to tap geothermal energy.

It would be easy, however, to overestimate the impact of energy on world economic development. As indicated above, following the boycott and sharp price rise in 1973–74, energy has been available to the world on a continually increased basis and at prices that are declining moderately in real terms. This is a return to the situation that has generally prevailed since World War I. It has been argued that, once the adjustment is made to the sharp change in level of prices, the world energy economy will move to a normal development based upon adequate supplies and continued real price constancy or decline.

On the other hand, many analysts are warning that the current situation is but a lull before another severe supply crisis occurs about 1985. These analysts indicate that by that year the Soviet Union may need to become a major importer of world petroleum and that productive capacity in the Middle East may begin to decline by 1990. Such developments could generate another severe supply shortage and consequent sharp price increase.

It is this possibility that is causing the industrialized countries to make major investments in alternative energy technologies and in developing new energy supplies. The alternative technologies, including, among others, solar energy, geothermal energy, and wind power, are being supported by increased research and development expenditures. (*See* Feature Article: RENEWABLE ENERGY: THE OTHER ANSWER.)

—William A. Vogely

Table IV. Installed Nuclear Power in Major Non-Communist Countries (September 1977)		
Country	Number of reactors	Capacity
		Thousands of gross electrical kilowatts
Canada	7	3,960
France	11	3,970
Germany, West	10	6,410
Great Britain	31	8,040
India	3	620
Italy	3	630
Japan	13	7,970
Spain	3	1,120
Sweden	6	3,880
Switzerland	3	1,060
United States	64	47,073
Total	154	84,733
Source: U.S. Department of Energy.		

Environment

Two themes seemed to dominate publications and meetings concerning environmental problems during the year. A variety of policies, relationships, and projections were subjected to a more systemic, interdisciplinary analysis than they had received previously, resulting in a series of surprising challenges to the conventional wisdom. In addition, for the first time the point was made frequently that widespread misperceptions, probably of cultural origin, are a central element in the environmental problem.

Results of systemic analysis. U.S. agricultural policies were subjected to a broad reexamination during the year. The United States has about 470 million ac of land that is naturally suitable for crop production. This would appear to be a vast amount, but a study headed by David Pimentel showed that there is a net loss of about 1,250,000 ac each year to highways, urbanization, and other special uses. More alarming, more than 100 million ac have been ruined by erosion, and at least half the topsoil on an additional 100 million ac has been lost.

R. A. Brink, J. W. Densmore, and G. A. Hill raised the question of the price the U.S. is paying in soil erosion for the vast amount of agricultural produce it exports annually. Ordinarily, on slightly sloping arable land with soil suitable for such row crops as corn and soybeans,

Jet airliner flies low over the rooftops of a residential street in Boston, Massachusetts, creating an oppressively high level of noise.

U.S. EPA Documerica

crop rotation would be practiced, with one corn crop being followed by several years of alfalfa. This is necessary for soil-erosion control because, when row crops are grown, the soil under the crop is largely exposed to the direct impact of raindrops during much of the year and is therefore vulnerable to sheet erosion. Recently, however, because of the great demand for U.S. corn and soybeans, this practice has not been followed. In Dane County, Wis., typical of the sloping land at the northern fringes of the Corn Belt, there has been a 57% increase in corn acreage within the past decade, with the result that, of the land parcels sampled, more than half had a rate of soil loss from sheet erosion incompatible with sustained productivity. These figures probably hold true for this type of land nationwide, suggesting a need for intense efforts toward soil conservation, including contour farming, strip cropping, and conservation tillage practices.

The general point of these findings is that the massive export of a small number of crop species to pay for imported crude oil is not necessarily in the national interest, unless there is a major associated effort at soil conservation. Otherwise, the U.S. is in effect exporting its best soils to pay for oil, a policy that, while it may seem to make sense in the short run, appears less advisable when the perspective is broadened to include an understanding of soil processes.

Another, rather curious finding concerning agricultural strategy makes the same point. It seems self-evident that farming should be conducted with tractors, not draft horses. Yet this notion is based on the implicit assumption that the trends that initiated the conversion from horses to tractors will continue. These trends included constantly falling prices for tractor fuel relative to farm wage rates. If that trend should be reversed, so that tractor fuel became progressively more expensive relative to farm labor costs, and if there were a superabundance of food for horses, the indicated strategy would shift. Further considerations are farm size and topography, with horses being more economic on small, hilly farms. Thus, as tractor fuel costs increase relative to farm labor costs, one would expect to find horses replacing tractors first on small, hilly farms, then on somewhat larger, less hilly farms, with very large flat farms being the last to convert. This is the reverse of the horse-to-tractor conversion that occurred between 1925 and 1950.

W. A. Johnson, V. Stoltzfus, and P. Craumer compared Amish farms using horses in various parts of the U.S. with surrounding farms using conventional, tractor-based energy systems. The study showed that where farm country is flat, as in eastern Illinois, the energy efficiency of the Amish (carefully internalizing all inputs and outputs) was only 25% above that of the surrounding farms, but in southwestern Wisconsin, where it is quite hilly, Amish farms were about four times as energy efficient. This finding has an interesting implication. Many procedures have become part of our culture because the entire thought pattern of the society is a response to the ubiquitous presence of extremely cheap fossil fuel energy. To a culture shaped by this factor, a return to horses is unthinkable. But just as the dominant pattern shifted from horses to tractors in response to cheap petroleum, it could shift back if gasoline were to cost $6 a gallon in 1977 dollars. It is worth noting that, while energy prices are expected to rise sharply in the next decade, the U.S. currently has more horse fuel on hand than it knows what to do with. It is also worth noting that the farm sector of the economy is destitute because of its excessively close coupling to and dependence on the rest of the economy— a dependence that would be decreased by a shift from gasoline to horse feed as fuel for farm operations.

Other aspects of the conventional wisdom on linkages between energy consumption and economic factors were also reexamined during the year. For example, it has been widely believed that higher rates of energy consumption are prerequisites for full employment and high rates of economic growth. Denis Hayes questioned this relationship, noting that new energy facilities are among the least labor-intensive investments a society can make. Indeed, capital will produce more employment if it is diverted from investment in energy-generating systems to almost any other type of enterprise.

Continuing this line of argument, K. Watt, L. Molloy, C. Varshney, D. Weeks, and S. Wirosardjono conducted statistical analyses on the relationships between energy and economic variables. They found that, among developed countries, unemployment rates decrease with decreasing energy consumption per capita and increasing energy prices—exactly the opposite of what many people would expect. They also found that, as energy consumption per capita increases, the rate of economic growth increases up to a maximum and then declines, even though energy consumption per capita continues to rise. The maximum rate of economic growth occurs when energy consumption per capita is about 5,500 lb of coal equivalent, the level of consumption in Japan in 1968. This is about two-thirds the per capita level of energy consumption in the U.S. in 1850. Among developed countries there is a clear inverse relationship between energy consumption per capita and rate of growth in gross national product per capita. This is particularly interesting because many people argue that energy consumption per capita must continue to increase if the U.S. is to maintain a healthy, growing economy. The data, on the other hand, suggest that the slow growth of the U.S. economy in recent years relative to many European countries may indeed have been caused, at least in part, by overconsumption of energy.

Many studies appeared in 1977 on the relationships

Horses pull plow on Amish farm in Pennsylvania. Where farmland is hilly, the use of horses for such work is about four times more energy efficient than are conventional tractor-based systems.

between U.S. energy consumption and economic variables, and more and more of them, from a number of disciplines, challenged accepted notions about the role of energy in economic vitality. For example, an investment analyst, Saunders Miller, argued that to rely on nuclear fission as the primary source of stationary energy supplies would constitute economic lunacy on a scale unparalleled in recorded history and might lead to an economic Waterloo. This rather strong language followed an analysis showing that, if the U.S. attempts to build reactors during the rest of the century in accord with Energy Research and Development Administration forecasts, the cost will amount to at least $5.8 trillion by the year 2000, even assuming a conservative estimate of the effects of inflation. In a new book comparing "soft" and "hard" energy paths, Amory Lovins produced a table comparing marginal capital investments for various proposed new energy systems. He forecast that hard paths, such as nuclear-electric, would cost about 100 times as much as fossil fuel energy has cost in the past. Soft paths, such as retrofitted solar heat, would also be more expensive, but would cost only 25 times as much. Quite apart from cost, many new studies, including those of S. M. Dix, Roger Naill, and the Workshop on Alternative Energy Strategies, questioned whether energy would be available to meet projected demand in the mid-1980s or shortly thereafter.

A related matter concerns the ability to predict the role of energy in the economy. Two studies appeared on such planning. One, by William Cundiff, was a Delphi study involving a number of scholars concerned with the future. A major finding was that there was a high probability of large-scale failure in relation to nuclear power facilities and also, surprisingly, a high probability of rapid growth of solar, wind, biomass, and geothermal energy. The other, by Peter House and Edward Williams, made a careful study of forecasts by 17 different agencies. There was remarkably little agreement among them, even over the short term (ten years), but, on the average, the forecasts tended to be much more optimistic if they came from groups with a political stake in an optimistic future. This raised a more general question about the ability of the U.S. government to make credible and useful forecasts. Late in 1977 the government began a study to assess its ability to develop a useful conceptual model for prediction and management of a large number of variables, particularly with respect to the environment.

The Club of Rome also conducted a study to examine discrepancies among various views of the future, including the future of the environment. Herman Kahn and his associates in the Hudson Institute, in *The Next 200 Years*, had presented a remarkably optimistic view of the year 2176, with 15 billion to 30 billion people earning an average of $20,000 each in real 1975 dollars. This, of course, was rather at odds with the picture of the future presented in the Club of Rome's studies *Limits to Growth* and *Mankind at the Turning Point*. Barry Hughes and Mihajlo Mesarovic used a refined and updated version of the *Mankind at the Turning Point* model to explore the possibility of attaining the standard of living projected by Kahn and his associates. This model, the result of an effort by 180 professionals in many countries, may be the most sophisticated computer tool yet developed for consideration of such international, multivariable problems. The researchers found that, around the year 2000, about $140 billion a year would have to be transferred from the developed world to Asia and Africa if those countries were to attain the Kahn projections. The cumulative transfer of funds from North America alone would reach nearly $1 trillion by the year 2000, or the equivalent of 60% of the total current U.S. gross national product. Thus, while it would be possible in principle to attain the world envisioned by Kahn, it would require a degree of altruism never seen in history. Further, this assumes that no overriding difficulties, such as forest and soil depletion, would arise in other sections of the system.

Perceptual malfunction and culture. From many quarters during the year came the observation that a fundamental component of the environmental problem was a widespread misperception of the nature of reality, originating in the interacting system of the human mind and the culture. Polls left no doubt about the magnitude or incidence of misperception. For example, the U.S. Federal Energy Administration discovered that 38% of the people in a sample polled did not believe the U.S. was importing any energy at all. Given that about 3.1 billion bbl of crude oil were imported in 1977, at a cost of about $45 billion, and given the devastating effect this had on the value of the U.S. dollar and the stock market, it was astonishing that this ignorance should exist. Given, further, the constant newspaper attention to massive U.S. oil imports and their relationship to the declining value of the dollar and to Pres. Jimmy Carter's efforts to arouse public interest in this issue, a careful examination of this perceptual defect seems worthwhile.

The phenomenon involved seems to be a cultural inability to hear a message, even though it is being repeated. How could this be? Many writings and analyses in 1977 dealt with this perceptual problem as it related to environmental issues. The previously mentioned study by Watt and others, conducted for the East-West Center, found that the international technoculture has a belief system concerning the availability of resources and the omnipotence of technology that blocks acceptance of the message that we are running out of anything. Further, the beliefs of the technoculture derive from propaganda and a set of historical accidents, not from accurate information about the present situation.

Using a bicycle instead of a car, a cyclist in Washington, D.C., puts into practice the energy conservation message on the billboard she passes.

One constituent of this belief system is the notion that man exists independently of the natural world; hence the rise and fall of civilizations has not been influenced by availability or destruction of resources, such as forests or soil. In fact, there is a huge literature describing the effect of forest and soil destruction on the collapse of civilizations, but this literature is largely unknown to many historians, having originated mainly within such disciplines as soil science. In fairness it should be noted that a few extremely important studies by humanists and social scientists were arguing that environmental factors have had a significant effect on the fall of nations and civilizations. *The Mediterranean and the Mediterranean World in the Age of Philip II* by the geographer Fernand Braudel and *Plagues and Peoples* by the historian William McNeill were recent examples. Nevertheless, the fact remained that these impressive scholarly works had little impact on the culture at large.

The Nobel Prize-winning ethologist Konrad Lorenz argued that the progressive decay of Western civilization "is so obviously pathological in nature, and so obviously shows the symptoms of mental sickness," that it is necessary to utilize the diagnostic tools of medicine to study civilization and the human mind. He concluded that the decline of high cultures may well have resulted from a discrepancy between the development rates of biological behavior and culture. Cultural development becomes too fast for human nature to keep up. And this would be bad enough if culture

evolved in accordance with a rational plan, but it does not. It evolves purely in response to natural selection; that is, at any given time culture develops in response to whatever is being selected for at that particular moment, without regard to its long-term survival value. An additional problem is that many of the artifacts of culture change slowly, because of their size, permanence, or the capital investment they represent, and cannot be adapted easily to changing circumstances. It would be difficult to shift quickly to noncar, nonfreeway transportation or horse-powered agriculture, whereas cheap fossil fuel could disappear suddenly.

A theme that became widespread at meetings and in the literature during the year was that the evolutionary pattern of Western culture, and of mankind's management of the environment, were on a track that could not be followed for more than another decade. Many observers stressed the imminence of change and the inevitability of some type of cultural revolution, involving a transformation from conspicuous consumption to frugality. One of the most effective arguments for both the imminence of change and the necessity of cultural revolution was advanced by Willis Harman, associate director of the Center for the Study of Social Policy at Stanford Research Institute International.

Harman noted that since the Industrial Revolution mankind had operated in accordance with a dominant social paradigm, but this paradigm now confronts mankind with five fundamental, interrelated dilemmas. We need continued economic growth, but we cannot live with the consequences. We need guidance of technological innovation, but we shun centralized control. Ever closer coupling between individuals and organizations appears to lead inexorably to reduced liberties and system fragility. (To illustrate, individual Americans now depend on Arab nations for their gasoline, which was not true ten years ago.) The industrialized nations will find it costly to move to more equitable distribution of the Earth's resources; it may be even more costly not to do so. The less developed nations will sharply increase per capita demand for resources as they develop, but this will only exacerbate present shortages and pose a major threat to world stability. The fifth dilemma is that possession of a societally supported work role is essential to the individual's sense of self-esteem, yet the economy is increasingly unable to provide satisfactory work opportunities.

Harman arrived at a startling conclusion: the industrialized world is simultaneously undergoing a conceptual revolution as thoroughgoing in its effects as the Copernican revolution and an institutional revolution as profound as the Industrial Revolution. Furthermore, this overall transformation is proceeding with such extreme rapidity that the most critical period will be reached within a decade. Whether the social system can withstand the strain is an open question, and the answer will depend on how well mankind understands the nature and necessity of the transformation. The more it is misunderstood, the higher will be the anxiety level and the more inappropriate will be the responses.

Statements of this kind were probably heard more frequently during the year than had been the case for decades, but similar analyses had existed for a long time. The skeptic might ask what it was about the current situation that made them more credible than they had been in the past. One of Harman's five dilemmas, that concerning the ever closer coupling of subsystems within the world, had a definite implied timetable. The U.S. had now genuinely exhausted its supplies of cheap fossil fuel (although it had not exhausted its total supplies of fossil fuel by any means). However, the public simply did not believe this, and hence, Congress did not have a politically safe mandate to increase energy prices significantly. The result was that multinational corporations turned increasingly to foreign sources of crude oil until, by 1977, at least half the oil consumed in the U.S. was imported. All the studies done during the year agreed that this proportion was going to increase.

If this proved correct, within a few years, seven at most, Congress would have lost its temporary control over U.S. energy prices. By 1985 so much of the U.S. energy supplies would be coming from Organization of Petroleum Exporting Countries (OPEC) members that they would be able to determine U.S. domestic energy prices, which would then rise much faster than the overall inflation rate. This would pose a major challenge to the continuance of the present U.S. culture, with its profound dependence on cheap energy.

But another of Harman's dilemmas was lurking in the background: the problem of the equitable distribution of world resources. The extent and magnitude of this problem was elucidated in another report to the Club of Rome, by Ervin Laszlo and associates. This project, *Goals for Mankind*, collected information on the goals of various countries and institutions. Each country was rated in eight different categories of goals and, within each category, the goals of various groups and of the nation at large were rated on a scale from zero to ten. Zero indicated self-centered and short-term goals and ten indicated a full consideration of global goals. Then, for each nation, a national average numerical rating of all eight categories of goals was developed.

For the U.S. the national average was only 3.1, indicating that, on balance, the U.S. is preoccupied with self-centered and short-term goals. By contrast, the rating for Japan was 5.5; for China, 7; and for Ghana, 6.5. Many nations on which the U.S. is critically dependent for imported raw materials showed much more concern with the long term; average goal ratings were 4.2 for Saudi Arabia, 4.2 for Iran, 5.9 for Nigeria, and 4.7 for Indonesia. This suggested a thought-provoking possibility: what if, in order to maintain its chosen lifestyle, the U.S. in 1985 needed to import more raw materials from these countries than their national goals led them to export? This would not be a problem if these nations' financial requirements forced them to export as much as the U.S. desired, but such might not be the case. Even in 1977 there were nations (Kuwait, Saudi Arabia) that could not absorb all the money their exports brought in.

Another perceptual problem was raised implicitly by N. C. Rasmussen and D. J. Rose in connection with fatalities resulting from energy use, expressed in terms of the statistic "fatalities per gigawatt-year." Contrary to most people's beliefs, the risk in fatalities per gigawatt-year for nuclear fuel-cycle employees, with no recycling of nuclear fuel, would be 0.56, while for coal the risk would be in the range 20–200 without emission control and about 4–40 if sulfur and particulate emissions were reduced to meet 1975 standards. Admittedly, these figures are somewhat speculative, because society has not yet made a major effort to replace natural gas and crude oil by coal. Nevertheless, several scenarios published in 1977 indicated that, when and if this happened, air pollution from coal would be a very significant problem.

One of the most devastating discussions of the whole issue of perceptual dysfunction was written in 1977 by Ida Hoos. She points out that any systemic attempt to look into the future is bedeviled with a number of problems. To attain any knowledge about the future, one must have adequate data about the present, but the quality of such data is remarkably bad, even in such environmentally important areas as population size and energy reserves. Further, many of the most important data sets are made available by government or other agencies with a vested interest in making their domain appear trouble-free. Project Independence, which was to ensure U.S. national energy self-sufficiency within a few years, was based on such a set of "facts." But even if statistically reliable data were available, Hoos questions whether the theory and methods of using them to forecast the future are adequate. If not, development of a rational policy for the future will be difficult indeed.

—Kenneth E. F. Watt

Food and agriculture

With the passage of the Food and Agriculture Act of 1977, the U.S. Congress adopted the most important piece of legislation relating to agricultural research since the U.S. Department of Agriculture (USDA) was organized and the land-grant college system established in 1862. Through the 1862 acts, legislators laid the groundwork for a scientific approach to agriculture that provided the basis of the country's food-producing ability. Recently, funding to support that base has eroded, but the 1977 act put the house in order.

Paul Harrison—Camera Press/Photo Trends

Extracts from beans are tested for their chlorophyll content at the International Centre for Tropical Agriculture in Colombia. The Centre is working to develop more nutritious and disease-resistant plants.

In addition to strengthening and adequately funding ongoing research in food and agricultural sciences, the legislation contains authorization for special grants to speed scientific breakthroughs and to address problems of animal health. Small-farm research was to be stimulated, as were special programs encouraging solar energy research and development and research on the extraction of hydrocarbons, especially alcohols, from agricultural products. For the first time, the legislation also clearly defined food and nutrition research as a distinct mission of the USDA and established the USDA as the leading agency in the federal government for research, extension work, and teaching in the food and agricultural sciences.

Agriculture

World agricultural production increased a little more than 1% in 1977. Agricultural output in the developed countries, including those with centrally planned economies, rose almost 1%, but the average was held back by a substantial decline in the U.S.S.R. and by smaller declines in Canada and Oceania. The most notable gains resulted from the recovery in Western Europe and a sizable increase in U.S. output. Among the less developed countries, a sharp increase in Latin-American production and moderate gains in South and East Asia more than offset reduced production in Africa and West Asia, resulting in an overall increase of approximately 2%.

The short-term outlook was for a modest reduction in world grain production and an increase in consumption. The levels of meat production, consumption, and trade in the world's two largest meat-consuming regions—the U.S. and Europe—remained constant in 1976 and 1977, and little change was foreseen in 1978. World milk production rose an estimated 2% in 1977, with the largest gains in the U.S.S.R., the European Economic Community, and the U.S. The rise in world sugar production, forecast at 4%, was expected to outstrip the increase in consumption. World cotton production was expected to increase sharply because of excellent weather in all major producing countries.

Within the U.S., farmers appeared to be facing another year of relatively low prices. Crop output in 1977 was nearly 5% above 1976 and should increase again in 1978, barring poor weather conditions. Livestock numbers would probably rise again in 1978 in response to comparatively low feed costs. Farm milk prices were expected to average a little higher because of higher support prices. It was first anticipated that food prices would continue in the relatively stable pattern exhibited in the second half of 1977, with only small increases well into 1978. However, marketing and distribution costs continued to rise, suggesting that grocery store prices might average at least 4 to 6% above the 1977 average. Prices paid for imported foods, which accounted for most of the food price increase in 1977, were expected to level off in 1978.

The long-term outlook. Over the next decade or two, food production was expected to be influenced both by traditional factors and by some new ones. In the traditional area, the influence of the price structure on the attitudes of farmers and ranchers was a cause for concern. One of the most dramatic developments in 1977 was the rise of the American Agriculture Movement with its demand for parity. In the strict sense, parity is the price that will give a unit of farm produce (bushel, hundredweight, etc.) the same purchasing power as it had in the base period. For most commodities subject to price supports in the U.S., the base period is 1910–14, the period deemed by Congress to represent a balanced relationship between farm and nonfarm prices. More specifically, parity is the ratio of the index of prices received by farmers to the index of prices paid by farmers × 100. Technology and changes in the relative size of farming operations have invalidated some of the components used in calculating parity, and efforts to update the formula have not kept pace with developments. An alternative concept that has been proposed focuses on the cost of production, rather than parity. In 1977 the parity price for

Farmers demonstrate in January 1978 on the steps of the U.S. Capitol in Washington, D.C., in an effort to win legislative backing for higher price supports for their crops.

wheat would have been approximately $2 a bushel higher than the cost of production.

A second factor in the outlook for agriculture was the availability and relative cost of energy required to produce food. Most of the fuels, fertilizers, and chemicals used in agriculture have a petroleum base. Therefore, considerable research was being devoted to the use of alternative energy sources in agricultural production. Such techniques as minimum tillage (tilling the soil a minimum number of times), restricting the use of fertilizer to the least possible amount, and placing limitations on the use of herbicides and pesticides were all being studied. There was also renewed interest in the use of alcohol produced from the fermentation of agricultural products.

A third factor related to the reemergence of basic research. For many years the focus in agricultural research had been on short-term results, and much of the fundamental research required to achieve significant increases in food production was underemphasized and underfunded. However, one of the major thrusts of the Food and Agriculture Act of 1977 was to stimulate and expand research in photosynthesis, biological fixation of nitrogen, and cell culture studies. If photosynthesis, the process by which green plants produce their own food, could be made just 1% more efficient, crop yields could easily double. Research on nitrogen fixation was aimed at reducing the need for synthetic fertilizers, which require extensive energy use; natural nitrogen fixers, such as free-growing blue-green algae in rice paddies, continually fertilize crops,

replenishing nitrogen by biologically producing ammonia. Cell culture studies offer new insights into photosynthesis, nitrogen fixation, and the development of genetically ideal crops. (*See* Feature Article: FOOD, FAMINE, AND NITROGEN FIXATION.)

Energy from agriculture. The technology of producing ethanol and methanol from agricultural products has been known for some time. The starch and sugar-producing crops are the principal substrates used in the production of ethanol. Methanol can be made from wood or wood shavings. During World War II ethanol was used as a motor vehicle fuel in Germany, and it continued to be used in some parts of the world, most notably Brazil. In the U.S. recent increases in the price of oil rekindled interest in gasohol, a mixture of ethanol and gasoline. Perhaps the most extensive research has been done at the University of Nebraska at Lincoln, which carried out basic research and extensive road tests. In the Nebraska experiments, scientists used a mixture of 10% ethanol and 90% gasoline. They were able to increase the octane rating or anti-knock quality of the fuel and obtain 5.3% better mileage than in vehicles run on gasoline. The exhaust emissions also appeared to be somewhat lower. Other items tested included cylinders, valves and valve seats, spark plugs, and the exhaust system. Although ethanol tends to carry water with it, which can be damaging to engine parts, no adverse results were observed during the tests.

If grain is used as the starting material, it is ground to the proper consistency and cooked to gelatinize the starch in the presence of an enzyme called amylase, which is often produced from the growth of a mold on a small quantity of grain. The starch is converted into sugar, which is then converted into ethyl alcohol in the presence of yeast. If sugar-based crops, such as sugar beets, cane sugar, or cane sorghum, are used, a molasses or thick, syrupy solution containing sugar is prepared and used by the yeast as the substrate for conversion to ethyl alcohol. The mixture of solid and liquid is then distilled, and an alcohol-water mixture is separated from the residual grains. The residual grains are dried to yield distiller's dried grains plus solubles, and the alcohol-water mixture is redistilled to produce 95% ethyl alcohol (5% water). A subsequent process will dry out the water to produce essentially 100% ethyl alcohol. Carbon dioxide is one of the other products yielded in the fermentation process, and it may be recovered and sold either as a gas or in solid form as dry ice.

If fossil fuel is used to provide the energy to produce the ethanol from agricultural products, nothing will be gained; in fact, the ethanol will cost more in calories than it will produce. A key factor is that alternative energy sources, such as solar energy, geothermal energy, or even waste heat from a power plant, can be used to provide the energy for the ethanol-producing process. Futhermore, the crop and forest products that can serve as starting materials for ethanol are renewable resources. Based on 1977 fuel prices, gasohol production is economically marginal, but as prices for petroleum products rise the economics should become favorable for gasohol and for the diesel fuel-ethanol combination, called diesohol.

Other current research. One of the major costs of agricultural research involves the screening of millions of plants to find the single plant or group of plants with the desired characteristics for use in developing improved strains. For some years, it has been possible to take a single cell from a tobacco plant and culture it, so that tobacco plants with desirable traits can be selected and the single cell developed into a full plant. More recently, Murray Nabors of Colorado State University showed that this can also be done with major food-crop plants, including corn, oats, and wheat. Therefore, instead of several thousand acres of test plots, a three-foot-square area in a laboratory can be used to select cells responsive to a given environment, and the time required to produce a particular variety may drop from eight or ten years to three or four.

In the Jan. 27, 1978, issue of *Science*, Thomas H. Maugh II described how serendipity and scientific research combined to provide an improvement in cattle fattening. Three Georgia cattle ranchers discovered that cement kiln dust added to cattle feed increased weight, decreased the amount of feed required by the animals, and improved the quality of the meat. When they reported their findings to the USDA Agricultural

Agricultural Research

U.S. agricultural research scientists discuss test results of a laboratory system that simulates field conditions for measuring pesticide residues.

Research Center at Beltsville, Md., the scientists were skeptical, but in three separate tests the farmers' observations were validated. After 112 days, steers fed a diet that included 3.5% cement dust gained 28% more weight than animals fed a control diet and consumed 21% less feed. Laboratory tests showed that the extra weight was all meat and that the animals appeared healthy. Tests with lambs yielded similar results.

The dust is a complex calcium-rich mixture of minerals but does not contain the alkalis and hardeners needed to make the cement set. Scientists suggested that 30% of the effect results from a simple buffering action in the gastrointestinal tract, while the other 70% may arise because the dust contains some element not yet recognized as an essential nutrient for cattle.

—John Patrick Jordan

Nutrition

Probably the most important event concerning nutrition in 1977 was the publication of *Dietary Goals for the United States* in February by the U.S. Senate Select

"It's partly glandular and partly 8,500 calories per day."

Committee on Nutrition and Human Needs. This document created a great deal of controversy among nutritionists. The September/October 1977 issue of *Nutrition Today* carried the entire report and invited "numerous clinicians, nutritionists, and other leaders in the health sciences" to prepare statements on their reaction to the report. Twenty such commentaries were included in the November/December 1977 issue of *Nutrition Today,* of which 13 were from physicians, 4 from dentists, and 3 from chairmen of university departments of food and nutrition.

Briefly, the dietary goals are as follows: (1) Increase carbohydrate consumption to account for 55–60% of the energy (calorie) intake. (2) Reduce overall fat consumption from approximately 40 to 30% of energy intake. (3) Reduce saturated fat consumption to account for about 10% of total energy intake, and balance that with polyunsaturated and monounsaturated fats, which should account for about 10% of the energy intake each. (4) Reduce cholesterol consumption to about 300 milligrams a day. (5) Reduce sugar consumption by about 40% to account for about 15% of total energy intake. (6) Reduce salt consumption by about 50–85% to approximately 3 grams a day.

The predominant criticism of the goals concerned the omission of all nutrients other than carbohydrates, fats, and salt, as though all diseases that lead to death are dependent only on the ratio of these nutrients and all Americans have diets that need these changes. Furthermore, these dietary modifications, even for people who suffer from cardiovascular disorders, cancer, diabetes, and obesity, have not been proved effective in relief of symptoms or survival of the individual. Much more was expected to be said and written about the *Dietary Goals.* An extensive critique was presented in

November 1977 at the 1978 Food and Agriculture Outlook Conference by Gilbert Leveille of Michigan State University.

During the year Mark Hegsted of the Harvard University School of Public Health advocated an "eat less" approach to balance need with intake for people on affluent diets. He encouraged increased consumption of fruits, vegetables, unsaturated fats, and cereal products, especially whole-grain cereals, in exchange for decreased intake of meats, fats, saturated fats, cholesterol, sugar, and salt. The old question is repeated, "What is a nutritious food?" According to Helen Guthrie of Pennsylvania State University, the claims of some foods that only "one serving furnishes all the nutrient needs for the day" actually contribute to "inappropriate diets" that are the basis of many health problems, such as obesity, diabetes, cardiovascular diseases, and anemias.

Repeatedly, numerous research reports stress the urgent need to motivate parents to practice the sound nutrition habits that they want their children to follow. Mary Alice Caliendo and her colleagues at Cornell University concluded that to achieve improved dietary habits of children, special nutrition education of the mother and efforts to achieve an improvement in her attitude toward homemaking would be the most vital approach to use rather than seeking to make changes in the school food service.

Politics of food. Problems of feeding the people of the world persist, in spite of repeated world food or hunger conferences and their clearly stated recommendations. The UN estimated that 400 million–500 million children suffered from malnutrition and starvation in the late 1970s and that an additional 400 million–800 million adults faced hunger or starvation, especially in the older age group. No decrease in those figures is anticipated when one realizes that India, for example, has 25 babies born each minute, an increase in population of one million every 28 days.

Donald Waldern, director of the Research Station of Agriculture Canada, reported that world food production exceeded consumption by 20% in 1977, which raised the world stockpile of cereal grains to a minimum safe level. However, the less developed nations increased their food imports 60% from 1963 to 1975. Even at their annual increase of 2.5% in food production, these countries will have a cereal deficit of 85 million–100 million metric tons per year by 1985. It appears that the best the advanced nations can do for the less developed countries is to provide training and technical skills and assist during disasters.

The waste and suffering of the estimated 400 million to 500 million children who are malnourished and starving must have priority in the solution of world food programs. That 80% of these millions of hungry people live in rural areas of less developed countries leads to the conclusion that only a total effort of the governments and leaders of these areas can solve the nutrition problem in this century. That the less developed countries must undertake such an effort has been one of the recommendations of every world hunger conference during the last decade.

An example of the many considerations involved in relieving hunger in emerging countries is that of the Green Revolution, hailed as a major step in food production. After years of experimentation, varieties of wheat and rice were developed that produced grain in much greater quantity than ever before. Grain-growing regions in certain areas of Asia were given seed to plant, and an abundant crop was produced in due time. Then it became obvious that the available harvesting equipment was inadequate, that storage facilities were limited, and that there was almost no transportation available to take the grain to the other areas where needy people lived in large numbers.

Fiber research. Fiber was discussed in several research reports at the Western Hemisphere Nutrition Congress V in August 1977. The reports stressed that "Each type of plant fiber is itself a heterogeneous entity." Fiber consists of cellulose, hemicellulose, pectins, and gums, which are sugar polymers of various structures. Which ratio of these occurs depends on the plant, its age, and origin. The composition of fiber varies with the food eaten, and the physiological effects also vary with the specific components of fiber present. Thus, it is difficult to answer the questions of how much, which source, and for what purpose fiber should be consumed.

One of the attributes of fiber when it passes through the gastrointestinal tract as a physical entity is its water-holding capacity. The composite fibers of food differ in this aspect. For example, dry bran is 96% fiber and holds only 2–4 grams of water for each gram of fiber, whereas fresh vegetables and fruits will hold 30 grams of water per gram of fiber but contain only 4–15% fiber. A high water-holding capacity is effective in prevention of constipation and for the treatment of diverticular disease.

Fiber also adsorbs bile acids, especially those in the cecum, the first section of the large intestine. This adsorption increases fecal loss and influences cholesterol metabolism but does not alter serum lipids. Research with rats, however, shows that pectin and lignin have an influence on serum lipids, reducing cholesterol levels in the serum as well as in the liver. Perhaps their relatively rapid transit through the gut plus the adsorbing action contribute to this result.

Schoolchildren in Niger eat lunches containing food provided by the World Food Programme. The UN agency supplied the drought-stricken nation with grain, vegetable oil, milk, and beef.

F. Mattioli—F.A.O.

The main fact that is clear about fiber is that the increased fecal bulk attributed to high water-holding capacity and adsorbing bile acids contributes to relief of constipation and diverticular disease. Other assets ascribed to fiber are not clearly established in relation to humans, and the role of special types of fiber in health and disease should be viewed with caution.

Diet during treatment for cancer. Weight loss resulting from loss of appetite results not only from cancer itself but also from the effects of cancer treatment. These symptoms are common even in patients with no cancer involvement of the gastrointestinal tract itself. No research suggests that diet or nutrition cures any type of cancer, but therapists have found that a well-nourished patient has fewer side effects from chemotherapy and radiation therapy and has faster recovery from surgery. A sound nutritional status gives a patient a reserve to carry him through periods of stress when food may be intolerable.

Cancer patients need to realize that eating nutritious meals and snacks daily is essential to survival. For convenience during times of aversion to food, concentrated portions can be made by adding dry instant meal mixes in only half the recommended liquid, which may be tart orange juice instead of milk if preferred. Chemotherapy requires large amounts of liquids to assure kidney and bladder functions without complications. These liquids can also be carriers of essential nutrients, namely, protein and calories, since minerals and vitamins can be furnished in a capsule or pill. The role that informed family and friends can play is obvious and highly essential to help patients maintain body weight.

The success of an effective dietary regime during cancer treatment depends on the initiation of a specified eating program at the beginning of the therapy. This program, like that of early detection of cancer itself, assures greater success of survival. However, eating problems should not become a source of contention or hostility since forced eating can be frustrating. A recommended schedule to follow includes a good breakfast about two hours prior to radiation or chemotherapy. After treatment anti-nausea drugs should be used along with ample rest. Even though liquids of various types are usually recommended, patients have found that dry, crisp foods containing protein settled a squeamish stomach better. In nausea the stomach undergoes muscle contractions and spasms that are eased by small amounts of bland, protein-rich food, such as toasted bread, small pieces of lean beef (broiled or roasted) at room temperature, or similar items that appeal to the patient. Naturally, the specific foods used as carriers of nutrients for the nauseous patient must be items that he likes and can accept.

Liquids are important to the nauseous patient if actual vomiting has occurred. Such loss of liquid from the body can complicate the kidneys' ultimate excretion of the drugs used in chemotherapy and can contribute to both kidney and bladder irritation from crystals or stones formed. All drugs must eventually be excreted via kidney and bladder, which requires several quarts of fluid intake daily. The required liquid intake should provide at least part of the daily supply of nutrients.

—Mina W. Lamb

Information sciences

Efforts to improve the capabilities and effectiveness of computers, especially in regard to their software, dominated the year in the information sciences. Among other developments, a new series of U.S. weather satellites, TIROS-N, was put into orbit.

Computer science

The difficulty in the development of software, that is, the programs that run on a computer, is the most important factor preventing the growth of computer applications from being even more rapid than it is. For example, the lack of appropriate software is one of the major barriers to the spread of home computers. The following discussion deals with some recent and promising approaches to overcoming this problem.

The roots of computer science lie mainly in two disciplines, mathematics and electrical engineering. Because most early computer scientists were more interested in what computers could do and in their theoretical aspects than in how to build them, computer science as a discipline has had much closer ties to mathematics. This led to a widespread belief that computer science was really a branch of mathematics like, for example, mathematical statistics.

But computer science is not mathematics. Its values and its foci are quite different. Mathematics values elegance, while computer scientists tend to be pragmatists, interested in results rather than the beauty of their presentation. Perhaps most important, computer science focuses far more on process than does mathematics. For example, a central theme in computer science is the construction and analysis of algorithms (step-by-step procedures for solving problems); this subject has been, at most, a side issue in classical mathematics.

So it is not surprising that computer science has, as a discipline, grown steadily away from mathematics during recent years. Ironically, however, this has been just the period when the need for more mathematics in computer science, particularly in its core software area, has become increasingly clear. Although this need has been recognized by some for a number of years, it is only recently that real progress has been made in applying the tools and techniques of mathematics to the problems of software design and development. Thus,

1977 may well have been the year in which major progress was made for the first time toward the mathematization of computer science.

Program specification. The object of applying mathematics to the software process is to be able to treat programs as mathematical objects and, thereby, to be able to prove things about programs. The starting point for such an aim must be to specify formally the purpose of a program.

As an example let us consider the following problem:

Write a program that will accept as input a nonnegative integer *a* and a positive integer *d* and that will produce as output the remainder *r* when *a* is divided by *d*. (The positive integers do not include zero, while the nonnegative integers do.)

This informal description of a program to find the remainder when one integer is divided by another is ideally suited to communication between humans but is not formal enough to provide a basis for mathematical analysis. It is, therefore, useful to replace it with the following:

Formal Specification of Remainder Program
Name of program, type of input and output quantities:
REM (integer,integer) RETURNS integer
Behavior:

$$\underbrace{a \geqslant 0,\ d > 0}_{P}\ \ \underbrace{[REM(a,d)]}_{Q}\ \ \overbrace{\left[\begin{array}{l} 0 \leqslant REM(a,d) < d \\ \textbf{and}\ Divides\ [d,a-REM(a,d)] \end{array}\right]}^{R}$$

where

Divides $(x,y) = \exists$ i: integer $\ni$ y=x $*$ i

Notes:
1. In the statement of the behavior note the P{Q}R notation where
   P: $a \geqslant 0,\ d > 0$ is the *precondition*, which states the condition on the input variables. ($\geqslant$ means greater than or equal to; $>$ means greater than.)
   Q: REM(a,d) is an abbreviation for the program that must be written.
   R: $0 \leqslant REM\ (a,d) < d$ **and** Divides [d,a−REM(a,d)] is the *postcondition*. It states the conditions on the result, namely that the remainder is nonnegative and less than the divisor *and* that the divisor must divide exactly *a* minus the remainder. ($\leqslant$ means less than or equal to; $<$ means less than.)
2. The description of Divides states that Divides is true if there exists ($\exists$) an integer *i* such that ($\ni$) the first argument (*x*) is a multiple of the second (*i*).

All definitions in the above specification are formal mathematical statements with precise definitions. Therefore, they can be processed by a computer to, for example, detect inconsistencies and incompleteness in the specification and to test the correctness of a program written to implement REM (a,d) against these specifications.

Formal specification of programs is an active area of research that is just beginning to produce applicable results. For large, complex tasks such specifications may be very difficult to generate. However, the attempt to generate them may itself provide insights into the development of a program to meet the specifications.

Formal derivation of programs. Programming has long been an art form more than a science. The methodology by which programmers produce programs is informal, personal, and not usually the result of the application of well-defined techniques. Can this be changed? Is it possible to derive a program using a formally described set of rules? Recent developments suggest that the answer is yes. But it should be understood that the application of rules to the formal derivation of programs will not remove the creativity from the programming process. What it will do is provide the programmer with a set of formal tools to apply in the programming process. The answer to the question of which tools to use and in what sequence will continue to require creativity and insight just as, for example, the integral calculus provides many tools but the calculation of a particular integral is often a difficult intellectual problem.

First fully operational magnetic bubble lattice device features storage area (parallelogram in center, 1/64 inch long on actual device) that contains 1,024 information-bearing bubbles in a lattice arrangement. Each stores data at a density of more than five million bits per square inch.

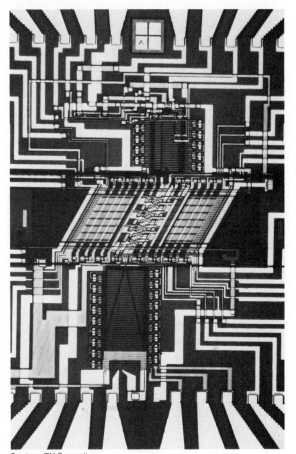

Courtesy, IBM Corporation

IBM engineer takes measurements on model of the firm's new 3032 Processor, which features 32,000 characters of high-speed buffer storage, integrated channels, and up to six million characters of main storage.

Some insight into the meaning of the formal derivation of programs can be achieved by considering the remainder problem discussed above. A basic assumption is that the computer cannot perform division directly, because otherwise the program would be trivial. The following reasoning then takes place:

(1) Since division is a process of successive subtraction, the program can be expected to involve a sequence of subtractions from the dividend a. Such a sequence of identical operations in a computer program is almost always embodied in a loop, probably the most basic and important structure in computer programming. (2) All loops have two properties. One is a condition P, called the loop invariant, which is true before entry to the loop and which remains true during execution of the loop. The other is a condition B, which is true upon entry to the loop but whose change from truth to falsity determines the end of the loop. B is called the loop termination condition. (3) The condition to be satisfied at the end of the loop, the postcondition, is, therefore, [P **and** (**not** B)]. (4) For the remainder problem the postcondition R is $0 \leq \mathrm{REM}(a,d) < d$ **and** Divides $[d, a - \mathrm{REM}(a,d)]$.

Since R = [P **and** (**not** B)] and since the successive

subtraction process should be continued while the remainder $r \geq d$, it is natural to choose

P: $0 \leq r$ **and** Divides $(d, a - r)$

B: $r \geq d$

since then P **and** (**not** B) is precisely R in the previous paragraph if r is replaced by $\mathrm{REM}(a,d)$.

This suggests the program loop

while $r \geq d$ **do**

  $r \leftarrow r - d$ \qquad (1)

repeat

where the arrow ($\leftarrow$) indicates replacement of the left part (r) by the right part ($r-d$) because, if d divides $a - r$ on entry to the loop, d will divide $a - r$ after every execution of (1). Thus P will remain satisfied. The condition P also suggests setting r to a initially. Then, invoking the precondition to assure that the input data is valid, one arrives at the following program:

Remainder Program
if $a \geq 0$ **and** $d > 0$ **then**
  $r \leftarrow a$
  while $r \geq d$ **do**
    $r \leftarrow r - d$
  repeat
  print (r)
            else
  print ("invalid data")
Example: $a = 35$, $d = 4$
  The successive values of r are
    35, 31, 27, 23, 19, 15, 11, 7, 3
  and 3 is printed.

Two further comments about this program are in order: (1) Because of the way this program has been formally derived, the proof that it is correct is inherent in the derivation. That is, the derivation of the program assures that, after execution of the loop, the desired postcondition is satisfied. Discussed below is a second approach to proving programs correct. (2) The derivation does not imply that the program is best in any sense, only that it is correct. The techniques that have been described briefly here may, indeed, also be used to derive more efficient programs.

It should be asked whether these techniques can be used to derive large programs, the area in which software problems are the most difficult. The answer is not yet clear, but because large programs are composed of smaller modules, it is certainly not hopeless to try to apply these techniques. In any case, the patterns of thought embodied in the formal derivation of programs seem certain to be useful to all programmers.

Program verification. In the area of program verification, computer scientists are concerned with generating a formal mathematical proof that a program derived by any technique, formal or informal, does indeed satisfy its specifications. Among the various approaches to this problem, the most characteristic is depicted in the figure. The flow chart corresponds precisely to the remainder program derived in the preceding section. Associated with each branch of the flow

318

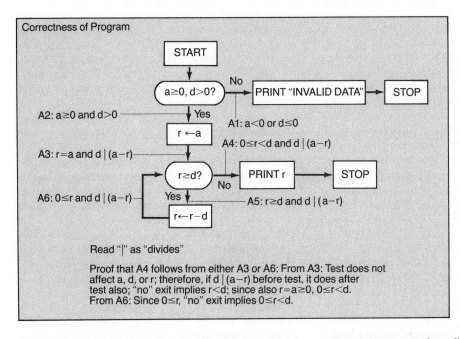

Correctness of Program

START

a≥0, d>0? —No→ PRINT "INVALID DATA" → STOP

A2: a≥0 and d>0 ——— Yes

A1: a<0 or d≤0

r ←a

A3: r=a and d | (a−r) ———

A4: 0≤r<d and d | (a−r)

r≥d? —No→ PRINT r → STOP

A6: 0≤r and d | (a−r) ——— Yes

A5: r≥d and d | (a−r)

r←r−d

Read "|" as "divides"

Proof that A4 follows from either A3 or A6: From A3: Test does not affect a, d, or r; therefore, if d | (a−r) before test, it does after test also; "no" exit implies r<d; since also r=a≥0, 0≤r<d. From A6: Since 0≤r, "no" exit implies 0≤r<d.

chart is an *assertion* about the state of the program variables in the flow chart. A proof of the correctness of the program consists in showing that the postcondition assertion A4 is a consequence of the precondition assertion A2. Such a proof involves showing that

> A2→A3→A4 if the "no" exit is taken the first time through the r≤d? box

or   A2→A3→A5→A6→A4.

One part of the proof is shown in the figure.

A complete verification of the correctness of this program also requires a proof that the program actually terminates, that is, that the "no" exit is really taken at some point. But this can be demonstrated because r is initially set equal to a ≥ 0 and each traversal of the loop decreases r by d>0 so that eventually r must get smaller than any positive d.

As with the formal derivations of programs, proofs of this kind can only be applied to quite simple programs. The ultimate goal of such research is an automatic program verifier, which, given a program and its specifications, would determine whether the program implemented its specifications. Though such an instrument probably is not attainable, research along these lines is nevertheless important because it provides insights into programming design.

The areas of formal specification of programs, formal derivation of programs, and program verification all require the use of standard mathematical techniques to enhance the quality and accuracy of the programming process. In 1977 the recognition of the value of such techniques began to be widely realized for the first time. But the application of mathematics to the programming process is not limited to the areas discussed above. There is at least one more area where mathematical techniques are beginning to be applied.

Program comprehensibility. The quality of a program is closely related to its readability. This is true because significant programs generally have one writer but many readers, for whom comprehensibility is clearly vital. But can comprehensibility be measured and, if so, how? During recent months researchers began to develop mathematical systems to measure program readability. Success in those efforts may be expected to provide additional insights into good programming practice and the design of programming languages.

One of the most interesting aspects of the areas of research described in this article is that, while they provide different perspectives on programs and programming, these perspectives seem to be leading to similar conclusions as to what constitutes good programming languages and good programming practices. This probably should be no surprise because the application of formal mathematical techniques might be expected, whatever the perspective, to lead to similar conclusions. In any case, it would be hard to overemphasize the importance of the increasing use of mathematical techniques in developing software.

—Anthony Ralston

Communications systems

Three recent developments seemed likely to have a long-term impact on communications systems. Many major computer and terminal manufacturers, responding to the increased demand for remote computing capability, established "architectures" and standards to achieve compatibility among their products and also with the telecommunications networks and services. Most nations planned to upgrade their existing switching and transmission capabilities substantially. And, finally, many governments were attempting to formulate long-range national goals for their telephone systems and for the networks that transmit computer data.

Architectures and standards. A terminal does not simply "plug into" a remote computing system via a communications line and then operate smoothly. Many other factors are involved. Some of these concern relationships between the terminal and the communication service; examples include physical plug arrangements, electrical characteristics of the signals to be sent, and the means for initiating or receiving dial digits for a switched network connection. In addition, the transmitted data must be understood by both the terminal and the host system; considerations in this regard include the alphabet or code structure to be used, control commands that may be issued and allowable responses to them, and signals for acknowledging receipt of a message. Other standards are required to deal with, for example, error-recovery techniques and the synchronization of data-base files.

Under the guidance of the UN-sponsored International Organization for Standardization (ISO) and the International Telegraph and Telephone Consultative Committee (CCITT, a worldwide organization of com-

Scientist Anthony Dewey holds in tweezers a solid-state laser that "writes" information in a liquid crystal material. Housing on the right contains devices to operate the laser and control its temperature.

Courtesy, IBM Corporation

munications companies), most of the electrical and physical attachments of terminals to communication facilities have been standardized. These standards allow manufacturers to make equipment with the assurance that it can be attached to similar facilities throughout the world.

In regard to the interpretation of the transmitted data, there is little or no international standardization. Nonetheless, such standards are required for system operation. The codification of these rules and procedures for a particular data processing manufacturer is called a "communications system architecture." Between 1974 and 1977, several major data processing companies (among them IBM Corp., Digital Equipment Corp., Sperry Univac, Fujitsu, and Hitachi) announced that they would make their future products to conform to their respective architectures, thus ensuring compatibility within each firm's own products. Prior to the commitment to adhere to such internal standards, telecommunications products built by one manufacturer often used different rules and procedures from similar equipment offered by the same firm. These dissimilarities caused inefficient network operation.

Even though these corporate architectures differ from one another in detail, they represent a significant advance in communications systems. This is true not only because they will perhaps lead to some international standardization but more importantly because they give the purchaser of a distributed processing system a basis on which he can plan the growth of a terminal system with assurance that reprogramming will not be required with every technological change in either the communications or computer industries. This should spur even more growth in an industry in which in 1977 the revenue for communications services exceeded $1 billion.

New data networks. As of 1978 the large majority (probably greater than 95%) of data traffic was carried on facilities designed for voice communication service. In almost every major country, however, there were plans for improving communications services for data transmission. Some of these would upgrade the quality and quantity of voicelike facilities that would then be used for data communication; others would be new networks designed exclusively for data transmission.

Canada, Japan, and the U.S. are among the nations that have specialized digital data transmission networks in operation. Because digital transmission characteristics are more like the digital data signals generated by computers and terminals than the signals of voice communication, these data networks promise improved speed, fewer errors, and cost benefits to the computer-communication system user. A recent study in the U.S. projected that by 1985 there would be five million terminal attachments to communications common carrier networks, about half of them to the new digital services. Another study, conducted for the major

European telephone companies and administrations, projected that in 1980 approximately one-third of all data traffic would be on leased, private, voice-grade lines; another one-third would be on the public switched voice telephone network; and the remaining third on new public data networks.

As was noted above, international standards have been applied to electrical and physical interfaces between terminals and communications lines. With the goal of achieving higher levels of compatibility, a new standard called X.25 was recommended by the CCITT in 1976. To conform with this standard a terminal must group the characters of its message into a block (or "packet") of 512, 1,024, or 2,048 bits and append information that controls the routing of the packets to their desired destination and that aids in error recovery should transmission noise or other network disturbances interfere. Interfaces between the terminal and the common carrier network prior to X.25 did not require such "packeting"; dialing information for routing was passed in a way similar to the push-button telephone, and the terminal and receiving computer grouped the message characters in ways convenient to them. Packet networks using interfaces based on X.25 began operation in Canada and the U.S. in 1977 and were planned in France and Japan in 1978–79. Networks for other countries were planned for the 1980s.

A unique characteristic of packet networks is that, in addition to a fixed monthly access charge, the user pays for the service on the basis of the actual number of packets transmitted. Fees for most conventional switched communication services are based primarily on distance, duration, and time of day. Leased-line rates are primarily based on distance alone. Charging on the basis of volume promised to be attractive to users with light traffic loads.

Regulatory studies. In most countries the national telephone system is owned and administered by the government, often allied with both postal and telegraphic services. In countries where the telephone system is provided by a corporation independent of the government, as in Canada, a monopoly is usually granted that company. This avoids costly duplication of national resources and ensures coverage for the entire population.

The U.S. differs from this pattern. The American Telephone and Telegraph Co. is privately owned and is the dominant supplier of telephone services (about 80%). In addition, however, there are about 1,600 other independent telephone companies. Altogether, they provide service to the 150 million telephone subscribers in the U.S.

In addition to the Federal Communications Commission (FCC), which was created by the U.S. Congress in 1934 to oversee common carriers, such as the telephone companies, on national interstate matters, each state has a public utility commission to regulate the intrastate activities of the carriers. These commissions grant and enforce monopoly rights as appropriate and regulate the prices charged for services so as to allow carriers a fair rate of return on their investment. They also protect the public from excessive charges.

Since the late 1960s, the FCC has been encouraging

On a page of the London telephone directory is magnetic tape containing entries compiled in alphabetical order by computer. This tape is used to produce a second tape with typographical instructions added, from which a telephone directory is automatically produced by photocomposition. This method has cut in half the time needed to produce British phone books; the system was recently purchased by the New Zealand Post Office.

Courtesy, Post Office, U.K.

Final check before it goes into operation is given to Northern Telecom SP-1, a Canadian-produced electronic telephone switching system. Sales and orders of the system total more than $700 million.

processing equipment might play in communications. A 1971 FCC inquiry concluded that there was no need to regulate data processing services and that competition in the data processing industry was its most effective form of regulation; that communications services were properly offered only by carriers regulated by the FCC; and that there was a middle ground that could be called "hybrid service."

A hybrid communications service permitted regulated carriers to engage in data processing if it was incidental to their principal purpose of communications offerings, and also permitted data processing companies to engage in non-regulated communications if they were incidental to their major service. A simple example is a computer time-sharing company that allows many customers to run programs on its computer facilities and to gain access to this service by terminals connected to the computer by communication lines. In this case, communications is incidental and none of the service is regulated.

The rapid advances of technology which enabled a terminal to include a small computer as an integral part; the increasing computer industry trend toward widely distributed data processing by means of mini- and microcomputers; the computer-aided enhancement of communications services; and new carrier offerings such as packet networks soon caused the FCC concern that its 1971 conclusions might be already obsolete. Thus, in 1976 the commission began a second computer-communications inquiry to establish in which competitive data processing activities carriers would be allowed to participate under regulation.

Among the primary issues were the use of computers in areas of network control and routing (such as message switching, speed and code conversion, transmission error detection and correction, and analog/digital conversion); and the entrance of carriers into the areas of input/output processing, such as the manufacture of processing equipment designed to make information compatible between differing terminal types, and of terminal manufacture and sales. A concern of the unregulated data processing manufacturers was that telephone companies might subsidize their terminals and related equipment with revenues generated by conventional voice telephone services, thereby gaining a significant cost advantage. Of concern to the regulated carriers was that they might be unfairly prohibited from competing in a vigorous industry.

Although the inquiry was not expected to be complete until late 1978 or 1979, its outcome could significantly alter the relationship between the two industries. Regardless of the outcome, however, new terminal products, new communications services, and new applications of computer-communications services are expected to grow at an accelerating rate throughout the world.

—Edward H. Sussenguth

competition in the area of interstate data transmission. A landmark decision of the FCC in 1968 was the Carterfone case, which permitted direct attachment of equipment not supplied by the telephone company to the public switched network; prior to that decision only the monopoly carriers were allowed such attachments. Other decisions allowed non-monopoly carriers to construct and offer terrestrial transmission services (Specialized Common Carriers, 1971) and permitted the launching of communication satellites by new common carriers that could compete directly with terrestrial communication systems (Open Skies Decision, 1971).

There is a strong and close relationship between the data processing and communications industries. As remote data processing grew in volume and the users became more dependent on the two industries, it became clear that there was no benchmark to determine what role, if any, the regulated common carriers might play in data processing and what role providers of data processing services and manufacturers of data

Satellite systems

Earth-orbiting satellites that utilize their vantage points in space for economic and military purposes are called applications satellites. There are three major classifications of such satellite systems: communications, Earth observation, and navigation. Though just 20 years have passed since the first primitive satellites were orbited, by 1978 a large number of such craft were in use throughout the world. Users were countries (for domestic and military purposes), groups of nations, and private industrial enterprises.

The U.S. and the Soviet Union continued to dominate such activities because of their large booster rockets, which they also used to launch satellites for other nations. However, the European Space Agency (ESA), Japan, and China were all developing increased launch capabilities. A major effort of ESA was the development of the Ariane booster, with test launches scheduled to begin in 1978. The Ariane had a planned capability of placing 1,700 kg in Earth orbit and 970 kg (1 kg = 2.2 lb) in geostationary orbit, and with it ESA hoped to capture a portion of the market now shared by the U.S. and the U.S.S.R.

Communications satellites. The International Telecommunications Satellite Organization (Intelsat), a consortium of more than 100 nations, continued to grow in size and capability. Intelsat 4 and 4A satellites were located in geostationary orbit over the Atlantic, Pacific, and Indian oceans. These satellites provided global transmission of telephone, television, facsimile, and digital data. (A geostationary, or geosynchronous, orbit is at 35,900 km altitude above the Equator. At that altitude a satellite travels at the same angular velocity as the Earth's surface, and thus remains at a constant point above the Earth. Three such satellites can provide global coverage except at the highest latitudes.)

The Communications Satellite Corporation (Comsat) is the U.S. member of Intelsat and manages its development and satellite operations. Founded 15 years ago, Comsat launched the first commercial satellite, Early Bird, in 1965. It had a capacity of 240 simultaneous telephone calls. In 1978 each Intelsat 4A satellite could handle 6,000 simultaneous telephone calls plus television. Although additional ocean cables have been laid in recent years, about one-half of all transatlantic telephone calls in 1977 were made via satellite. The charge for a call from New York to London, $12 before Early Bird, had fallen to about $5.

In 1977 three domestic U.S. communications satellite systems were operational. Two Westar satellites, owned by Western Union, were used to transmit telegrams, mailgrams, Telex, and high-speed facsimile data. The Mutual Broadcasting System and Public Broadcasting Service (PBS) entered into agreements to use Westars for their radio programs in the near future. RCA Corp. used its Satcom 1 and 2 satellites for commercial leased-line service and transmission to more than 100 small, receive-only, Earth stations to distribute pay television by cable. Comsat General Corp., a

Intelsat 4A communications satellite is checked out at the Kennedy Space Center before its launch on May 26, 1977. Weighing 1,360 kilograms (2,992 pounds) in orbit, the spacecraft can relay more than 6,000 simultaneous telephone calls and two television programs.

Courtesy, NASA

subsidiary of Comsat, leased the Comstar satellite to national telephone service companies.

A fourth domestic service, Satellite Business Systems (SBS), was authorized to provide voice, data, and facsimile service. SBS planned to utilize a new higher transmission frequency (12–14 GHz) rather than the 4–6 GHz bands that are used by other communications satellites.

The Communications Technology Satellite (CTS), which the U.S. National Aeronautics and Space Administration (NASA) shared with the Canadian Department of Communications (DOC), continued its pioneering methods of providing communications services in the fields of medicine, education, community interaction, data collection, and broadcasting. One cooperative experiment between NASA and DOC was enabling engineering students at Stanford University in California to take courses televised by Canada's Carleton University in Ottawa, Ont., some 2,500 mi away. CTS also proved its versatility during the Johnstown, Pa., flood in July 1977 when it was teamed with a Comsat-developed transportable Earth terminal to provide communications. For two days this combination handled the only messages received by the community.

The three Marisat marine communications satellites launched by Comsat General in 1976 proved successful. In use by the U.S. Navy and a number of maritime fleets, they provided high-fidelity voice, data, Telex, and facsimile service. By 1978 almost 100 ships were equipped with Marisat antennas. Agreement was reached between Comsat and a Japanese communications carrier to build a shore station to provide communications service to commercial shipping in the Indian Ocean. This service would make commercial maritime satellite communications available throughout the world for the first time.

The second Palapa satellite was launched as part of a system to link 130 million Indonesians with modern communications. Each Palapa provides a capacity for 5,000 two-way telephone circuits or 12 television channels, or combinations of telephone, television, radio, telegraph, and data services. Forty ground stations were located along the archipelago, linking each of the 26 provincial capitals.

The Soviet Union announced plans to launch five different systems of geostationary Comsats during 1978–81. According to the U.S.S.R. application to the International Telecommunications Union, seven Statsionar satellites would be used for non-military communications; others would provide maritime and aeronautical services, and still others military communications. One series, Loutch P, would operate in the high transmission frequencies of 11–14 GHz.

During 1977 NASA successfully launched experimental communications satellites for Italy, Japan, and ESA. Using its own launch vehicle, Japan also placed a satellite in geostationary orbit. India announced plans for a direct television broadcast satellite with point-to-point communications capability as well as weather observation. Geostationary communications satellite systems were being planned by China and a consortium of Arab nations.

Earth observation satellites. This category of applications satellites has three major types: weather, Earth resources, and military reconnaissance.

Weather satellites. Meteorological satellites view the Earth's weather in darkness and in daylight. This is done by measuring the temperature difference between the tops of clouds and the surface of the seas and the land. Until recently such satellites were launched into nearly circular polar orbits at altitudes of 1,500 km (900 mi). But in 1978 a new series of U.S.

Qualification model of the Orbital Test Satellite, the first telecommunications satellite of the European Space Agency, is checked out in the laboratory of the Centre National d'Études Spatiales, Toulouse, France.

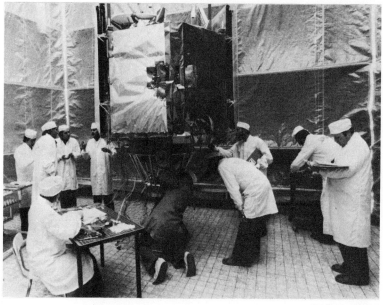

Engineer tests weather satellite sensor that will return imagery with a near constant one-third-mile resolution across the entire width of the sensor scan during daylight and twilight conditions. This is the best resolution yet achieved in a satellite.

satellites, TIROS-N, was put into orbit at altitudes of 870 km (540 mi) and 830 km (515 mi). These satellites were designed to collect transmitted data from remote, untended platforms and buoys, as well as to monitor solar X-rays and variations in the Earth's magnetic field.

In 1974–77 the U.S. placed four weather satellites in geostationary orbit, two of which were operational and two in standby status. From longitudes 75° W and 135° W the two operating satellites provided images of weather and cloud movement over the U.S. every half hour. During 1977 Japan launched its Geostationary Meteorological Satellite and the ESA put into orbit its Meteosat, at longitudes 141° E and 0°, respectively.

A fifth satellite, to be launched by the U.S.S.R. (possibly in 1979), would complete the system of continuous global weather coverage with the exception of the high latitudes. These areas are covered by polar-orbiting satellites. The most spectacular immediate benefit of such coverage was expected to be the hourly tracking of hurricanes, typhoons, blizzards, and other severe storms. The early storm warnings that such a system would provide could lead to incalculable poten-

tial savings in human lives and property. In addition, improvement in both short- and long-term weather forecasting was expected.

In the U.S. the National Oceanic and Atmospheric Administration (NOAA) is responsible for the collection and distribution of weather data. In recent years infrared imagery from NOAA satellites has been used to pinpoint the location of upwellings of cold ocean water, which bring plankton and other nutrients to the surface and thus attract food fish such as tuna and salmon. Maps of such upwellings were supplied by NOAA to more than 1,000 fishing boats, saving fuel used normally to search for fish and also increasing the size of the catch. In a recent experiment by NOAA and the Exxon Corp., NOAA provided satellite data showing ocean current flow and eddy circulation patterns in sea lanes. By steering into favorable currents and avoiding contrary ones, half the Exxon fleet of tankers (15) saved $400,000 in fuel bills in one year compared with the ships that were not provided such data.

Citrus growers in Florida were also benefiting from weather satellites. The satellites monitored continuously the location and movement of the frost line in the U.S., providing advance warning of danger to farmers.

Earth resources satellites. This type of satellite observes the Earth in a manner similar to weather satellites but with multispectral cameras. The most advanced of such craft is the U.S. Landsat. In 1978 two of these were operational in polar orbit, transmitting images in four wavelengths: blue, green, and two bands of infrared. They covered each area of the Earth every nine days at the same hour, so that the angle of the Sun was consistent. Increasingly sophisticated imaging devices on the satellites studied the radiation associated with land, water, ice, minerals, vegetation, and man-made structures on the Earth's surface. Minor variations in radiation were enhanced, providing such data as the extent of crop growth and the presence of blight. The U.S. Department of Agriculture, after joint investigation with NASA and NOAA, began expanding its program of large-crop inventory, aimed at knowledge of the world's total grain production. Also, the potential for accurate forecast of the success of future harvests appeared to be great. The Soviet Union, Eastern Europe, Australia, and other nations showed keen interest in this work.

During 1977 NASA used Landsat data as the basis for a number of programs. A high-quality geological map of Minnesota was made, of direct value to regional planners, environmentalists, foresters, soil scientists, agronomists, and hydrologists. The 84,000-sq-mi area was mapped at less than 1% of the cost required by previous methods. NASA also started a project to determine the technical feasibility of monitoring 1.7 million ac of timberland in the southeastern U.S. for the St. Regis Paper Co. The objectives were to identify kinds of trees, timber volume and productivity, and the health

Courtesy, RCA Corporation

Artist's concept of the Satcom 2 communications satellite shows it in orbit over the Earth. The two extended panels contain 75 square feet of silicon solar cells, which produce sufficient power to drive the operating functions of the spacecraft. RCA Corporation uses the satellite for commercial service.

and growth of forests. Other ways in which Landsat data were being used included detection of oil slicks and industrial pollution, the monitoring of strip mining, the locating of potential earthquake zones, and the mapping of snow cover in order to anticipate spring run-off volume.

Military reconnaissance satellites. The U.S. and the U.S.S.R. began using military reconnaissance satellites for photographic and electronic monitoring about 1960. No information about such activities is made public by either country, but it was known that the cameras on reconnaissance satellites had much greater resolution than those producing the Landsat imagery. Whereas current Landsats could identify objects about 270 ft across, military satellites were said to be able to read the markings on ships.

Navigation satellites. The U.S. Navy Transit navigational satellite system was first deployed for use by Navy vessels in 1964 and made available to commercial shipping three years later. A shipboard computer is used to measure the Doppler shift of the satellite's signal. By 1978 more than 1,000 sets were in operation, providing accurate position data, day or night, in any weather.

A new generation of improved navigation satellites was under development during the year. Called Navstar/Global Positioning System, such satellites would carry an extremely stable atomic clock. Twenty-four of these satellites would provide global coverage for the U.S. land, sea, and air forces, as well as for commercial vessels. By listening to four satellites, the

user can in about 30 seconds determine his surface or altitude position within about 30 ft and his velocity to better than 0.6 ft per second.

—F. C. Durant III

Information systems and services

Information science seeks to improve the organization, processing, and dissemination of information. Research in the field has led to the creation of information systems (data bases and information centers) in which information on specialized topics is coded for storage, processing, and retrieval by computers. In 1978 the first information systems, in the fields of medicine, science, and technology, continued to expand, while new systems were being created for areas in which the public had special interest or which required special attention from policymakers.

International information systems. The problems inherent in science and technology policymaking are complex. Difficulties stem from the fact that information needed for effective policymaking is often highly technical, is spread over numerous disciplines, and is disseminated in a wide range of documents originating in countries having different economic, political, and social structures. When faced with a crisis in the field of science and technology, policymakers generally conduct ad hoc studies and searches. Obviously, under these circumstances, the information gathered may be far from complete. Policy decisions based on such data are likely to be inadequate.

Computer-driven wall map informs dispatcher of the exact location of each bus along selected scheduled routes in the Cincinnati area. The map was developed by the Urban Transportation Laboratory (UTL), a joint project of the city of Cincinnati and the Transportation Systems Division of General Motors Corporation.

Recognizing the importance of the problem, a steering committee of UNESCO appointed a group of 16 international experts, who submitted a report proposing an international system for the exchange of information on science and technology policymaking, management, and development. The system, called SPINES, would establish a decentralized international information exchange between UNESCO member states. Each participating country would be responsible for collecting, processing, and disseminating basic bibliographical and numerical data on science and technology generated by its own citizens, with particular emphasis on all aspects of the application of science and technology to development. All countries would share in the information data base, and less developed countries would receive special assistance in selecting those scientific advances and technologies most suited to their specific needs. Much of the preparatory work in establishing such a system had been accomplished by early 1978, and the remaining years up to 1982 were to be devoted to the implementation of a prototype program limited to volunteer countries and international and national organizations.

UNESCO also established a Computerized Documentation System (CDS) to maintain bibliographic control over its own documents and publications and to provide information to member states and participating organizations of the UN system. Additionally, CDS was used in preparing indexes to UN publications.

Many individual countries developed specialized data bases for their own use and for sharing with infor-

mation seekers in other nations. The Stellar Data Center, located at the Strasbourg Observatory in France, contained star catalogs and computer-readable files of astrometric, photometric, and spectroscopic data on stars. The center critically evaluated these data and made them available to astronomers in 16 countries. One of the special services provided by the center was its star index, which listed the bibliographic references to relevant literature for the period 1950–75. The index contains more than 6,000 references to 56,000 stars.

The Scientific Documentation Centre in the United Kingdom offered a number of services on energy, including utilization, distribution, and conservation of non-conventional energy sources such as wind, tides, Sun, and waste products. Information was also available on combustion chemistry and oil prospecting and drilling. This data bank contained more than one million classified references.

Demands for a coordinated information service by broadcasting corporations, newspaper publishers, and researchers in the Scandinavian countries led to the establishment of the Nordic Documentation Center for Mass Communication Research with headquarters in Denmark. The center coordinated the work of national documentation agencies in Norway, Sweden, Denmark, and Finland, but it was hoped that eventually a worldwide network of regional documentation centers on mass communications would be established.

In order to make scientific and technical information accessible in many locations and as rapidly and cheaply as possible, the Commission of European Communities established a European Data Processing Network (Euronet). The pilot network, already in operation, consisted of four switching centers located in London, Paris, Frankfurt, and Rome; the Euronet data processing facilities were situated in Luxembourg. The computer, in addition to providing rapid and reliable information services, kept accounting records and monitored the performance of the network. The data bases covered a wide range of subjects and science disciplines, including metallurgy, food and agriculture, education, environmental protection, and energy.

Directing information users in Europe to the more than 500 available machine-readable data bases was the function of the European Scientific Referral Network (Eusiref). Headquartered in Stockholm, it had affiliate information dissemination centers throughout Europe. Should an inquiry be directed to a center that did not have the appropriate computer-based service, it could be redirected to another center at which the desired information was available.

U.S. developments. As an aid to members of the U.S. Congress and of congressional committees, a House Information System provided reports on the status of bills and other legislative data such as presidential messages, treaties, nominations, and petitions. The Bill Status Office estimated that approximately 25,-000 pieces of legislation are introduced during an average congressional session. Information concerning the status of any piece of legislation could be requested by telephone, mail, or in person; responses were by phone or by printed report. It was anticipated that status data would soon be accessible by computer terminals located in legislative offices, as a service provided by the Member Information Network.

The safety of energy systems received special attention, and an Information Center for Energy Safety was established at the Oak Ridge (Tenn.) National Laboratory. The center collected, analyzed, and disseminated information related to the safety of various non-nuclear forms of energy. Indexes and abstracts were prepared, and these became part of the computerized data base and network maintained by the U.S. Department of Energy. Staff scientists prepared reviews concerning safety aspects of various energy systems and safety standards to be used in the design, construction, and operation of energy support facilities.

In response to a variety of national needs, a number of new information services were created. The National Driver Registration Center stored, in a computer-readable file, the records of drivers whose licenses had been denied, suspended, or revoked. The National Highway Traffic Safety Administration recommended that this system be upgraded in order to allow for computer processing of requests from state motor vehicle bureaus.

The Radcliffe Data Resource and Research Center collected and maintained data relevant to the economic, social, and psychological aspects of societal changes that have affected women. The records contained a wide range of information on the life-styles of educated women, including their work, marriage, and family patterns. Research based on these files was providing improved understanding of important aspects of the lives of educated women in contemporary society.

The U.S. Committee for UNICEF operated an Information Center on Children's Cultures to disseminate information about the social and cultural activities of chil-

The Kurzweil Reading Machine for the blind converts ordinary printed material into English spoken at a normal speed. The system can read type of several hundred different styles and most sizes.

dren throughout the world. The New York City center maintained a comprehensive collection of books and pamphlets, photographs, color transparencies, films, paintings, games, and toys. This center was unique in that it responded to questions from children, parents, and teachers as well as to more scholarly requests from researchers. Among the typical requests were to find a Pen Pal, instructions for playing outdoor and indoor games from different countries, and lists of books on a given topic.

Research and future developments. Experiments were continuing to provide blind people with access to information contained in conventionally printed materials. Computers with special output devices can be used to print in Braille; however, the words must first be encoded into machine-readable form, a process that is expensive and time-consuming. To improve the situation an experimental Kurzweil Reading Machine was being tested at the Library of Congress, Division of the Blind and Physically Handicapped. The machine, which is both a scanning device and a computer, reads the printed words on a page and produces synthesized speech and Braille code.

News editing procedures were being revolutionized as the *New York Times* converted the production of the newspaper into an electronic computer-based information system. News stories were prepared on typewriter keyboards with video terminals connected to a minicomputer. In typing a report, the electronically coded words appeared on the screen and could be easily corrected or changed. When a reporter was satisfied with the story, a "send" command transmitted the copy to the editor's terminal. The copy could then be held in temporary storage until the editor was ready to view it on the editing screen. Changes made at the editor's terminal were displayed on the screen in a distinctive type style so that the editing could be reviewed by the desk chief. Eventually all news, even that submitted by reporters in the field and by news services, was expected to be prepared in machine-readable form and transmitted to the computer-based information system for storage, editing, and cold-type composition.

During 1978, each of the 56 states and territories of the U.S. planned to hold conferences on how to improve library and information services. All of these separate recommendations were to be coordinated and provide a basis for discussion at the White House Conference on Library and Information Services, scheduled to take place in the fall of 1979. Information specialists, educators, librarians, publishers, and state and local officials from all parts of the country were to attend the meeting. They would seek ways of encouraging more effective use of libraries by the public and of improving the nation's libraries and information centers through the development of a balanced system of services and support from local, state, and fed-

eral sources. In addition to, and in conjunction with, the conference, it was proposed that a Library and Information Services Fair be held. It would incorporate exhibits and demonstrations of equipment and services already available and of those anticipated in the future.

—Harold Borko

Life sciences

One of the most significant discoveries of recent years in the life sciences took place in 1977 when scientists announced that their studies indicated that methanogens constitute a third class of life. Other developments included the beginning of programs to produce more hydrocarbons from plants and continued research on recombinant DNA.

Botany

Among the many interesting advances in botany during the year was the serious initiation of programs to produce more hydrocarbon products from plants. Further information became available on the regulation of algal blooms, flowering inhibitors, plant senescence, and uptake of heavy metals from sludge. A possible case of imminent plant extinction was traced to the extinction of a bird 300 years ago.

Plants and resources. Anticipating a shortage of natural and synthetic rubber, the National Academy of Sciences suggested a return to the cultivation of guayule (*Parthenium argentatum*) and other sources of natural rubber. Those studying the situation estimated that demand for natural rubber, now secured mostly from *Hevea brasiliensis* trees in Malaysia and Indonesia, would be triple the supply within the next decade. In addition, about 70% of all rubber used is derived from petroleum products.

Guayule, a shrub that grows on the arid plateaus of Mexico and the southwestern U.S., was cultivated extensively in Mexico and California earlier in the 20th century, when about half of the rubber used in the U.S. came from this source. Wartime demands in the early 1940s were met partially under the Emergency Rubber Project, which placed 32,000 ac of guayule into production. After the war, however, improved synthetic rubber, renewed availability of Asian rubber, the difficulty of processing guayule rubber, and other factors diminished interest in guayule. Mexico began to reemphasize research on guayule in the early 1970s with the aim of improving techniques for processing wild plants. Legislation introduced in the U.S. Congress would authorize $60 million for five years of guayule research, but even with this aid it was estimated that ten years would be needed to improve guayule plants and another ten to achieve profitable rubber production.

Meanwhile, research was continuing to determine

Guayule, a source of natural rubber that has attracted renewed attention in recent years, is tended in California (top). Below is the crude form of the rubber.

the feasibility of using plants as sources of fuel and other hydrocarbon materials as well as rubber. For example, workers from the Agricultural Research Service of the U.S. Department of Agriculture found that guayule plants treated with 2-(3, 4-dichlorophenoxy)-triethylamine produce more rubber than untreated plants. Workers from the University of California at Berkeley reported the initiation of a program of chemical analysis of a large group of plants to determine their appropriateness for "petrochemical plantations." Among these plants are one or more species of *Achras* (sapodilla), *Asclepias* (milkweed), *Cryptostegia, Euphorbia* (spurge), *Monadenium, Pedilanthus, Sarcostemma,* and *Synadenium* in addition to *Hevea brasiliensis.* Up to 10% of the dry weight of these plants can be extracted as rubber, wax, glycer-

ides, and other organic compounds. The researchers suggested that the cost per barrel of these products would compare favorably with the current cost of petroleum. The first plant to be cultivated on a large scale would probably be jojoba (*Simmondsia chinensis*), the seeds of which contain a liquid wax that is very similar to sperm whale oil. (See 1977 *Yearbook of Science and the Future* Feature Article: THE JOJOBA: CINDERELLA CROP FOR THE '70s?)

Many foresters believed that increasing concern over nonrenewable fuels would lead to a new emphasis on forests as a renewable fuel resource. In some cases this would mean the careful harvesting of existing forests, but there was a growing feeling that the most practical technique would utilize plantations. Suitable tree species for this purpose should be easy to propagate and plant, grow rapidly with a minimum of care, and, ideally, would thrive on lands not presently employed in intensive agriculture, such as stripmined wastelands or eroded soils in the East and Midwest. A promising possibility might be hybrid poplars, which have been known to grow 40 or more feet high and 11 or more inches in diameter in ten years on spoil banks in Pennsylvania. They are readily rooted from cuttings, and old plantings regenerate quickly by root sprouting, so that harvesting is followed by reforestation. It was expected that poplars planted 6 by 6 ft apart would yield 10 cords of pulpwood or fuel at 6–10 years, 30 more cords at 15 years, and saw logs at 25–30 years. Some researchers believed that frequent harvests of smaller, more closely spaced trees would be the most efficient way to manage the crop. In research based on this method at Pennsylvania State University, one of the unsolved problems was finding an efficient method of mass harvest on hilly land.

Animals and plant extinction. Plant-animal relationships may be mutualistic; that is, two or more species may benefit from certain characteristics of the relationship. Many examples exist, but perhaps one of the most widespread is the relationship between some frugivorous (fruit-eating) birds and the plants that produce the fruit; the birds have a food supply and the plants have a method of seed dispersal. Apparently many plants have developed fruits and seeds adapted to this method of dispersal; *e.g.*, fruits have become attractive so birds will eat them, but the seeds inside have tough, thick seed coats so the embryo within will not be subjected to digestion. The bird's digestive system wears down the seed coat so that germination can occur following excretion.

While mutualism appears to favor survival, it may also work against it if one partner becomes scarce or unavailable. Elimination of plant species has been known to lead to the demise of animal species, but the opposite has rarely been suggested, largely because plants may depend on more than one animal species for the same function. However, a University of Wis-

Because wood is a renewable resource, tree plantations such as the one of loblolly pines in Mississippi (above) are attracting interest.

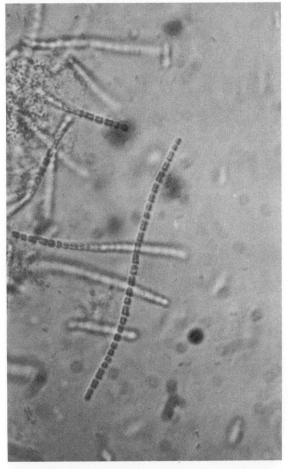

Photomicrograph shows Pseudanabaena galeata, *blue-green algae that cause pollution and obnoxious odors in lakes that have an excess of nutrients.*

consin researcher, Stanley Temple, may have found a case where a plant is nearly extinct because a bird upon which it depended is extinct.

Temple presented evidence that a tree (*Calvaria major*) on Mauritius depended completely on the dodo bird (*Raphus cucullatus*) for reproduction. Apparently the large (50-mm) fruit was swallowed whole by the dodo, the fleshy part was digested away, and the remaining, very thick seed coat was worn down so the seed could germinate later. Without such treatment the thick seed coat inhibits germination. The dodo was probably the only bird large enough to eat the fruits and with a gizzard powerful enough to abrade the seed coats. Even though the remaining 13 *Calvaria* trees on Mauritius produce seed, there is evidence that no reproduction has occurred for 300 years—almost exactly the length of time since the dodo became extinct (1681). Some *Calvaria* seeds can be made to germinate by force-feeding them to turkeys, and artificial reduction of seed-coat thickness may make it possible to produce new plants and thus save the species.

Allelopathy and algal blooms. Algal blooms are commonly observed, especially in summer, when a pond or other body of water has an excess of nutrients. Thus algal blooms are often associated with water pollution, and the algae, in turn, produce such undesired results as obnoxious odors, distasteful drinking water, oxygen depletion upon death and decay, and disrupted food chains. Attempts to solve the problem of blooms by controlling excess nutrients have been only partially successful.

As in the case of many ecological problems, biological control may be the answer. In her research on the relationships of several species of blue-green algae inhabiting a pond at North Branford, Conn., Kathleen Keating of Rutgers University produced evidence that blooms occur in a sequence, each stage of which is dominated by one or a few species. She also showed that this is due in part to the ability of the dominant organisms to control others by producing toxic substances. This relationship, called allelopathy, is known to be responsible for many phenomena in nature. If the

331

allelopathic substances could be identified, produced, and applied in a carefully regulated manner, it might be possible to use them in lake management to control blooms, although techniques for doing this had yet to be worked out.

Flowering switches in plants. Plants may be classified on the basis of how they flower with respect to the length of day or photoperiod. Short-day plants will flower when days are short (set at 8 hours for experimental purposes), long-day plants will flower when days are long (set at 16–20 hours), and day-neutral plants flower independently of day length. It is well established that flowering is directly controlled by a hormone, "florigen," which is produced by the leaves, and thus it is the leaves that are sensitive to day length. It has not been so well accepted that there is also an inhibitor produced by leaves that will keep the plant from flowering during an unsuitable photoperiod. Some researchers have produced evidence against the presence of inhibitors; however, A. Lang of Michigan State University and his associates from the K. A. Timiryazev

Graft of Nicotiana silvestris *is placed on* Nicotiana tabacum Trapezond *stock so that both the graft and the stock produce shoots. (See* text.)

From A. Lang, M. Kh. Chailakhyan, and I. A. Frolova, *Proceedings* of the National Academy of Sciences of the U.S., Vol. 74, No. 6, June 1977, pp. 2412–16

Institute of Plant Physiology in Moscow have provided evidence that inhibitors do exist in some plants, specifically, of the genus *Nicotiana*.

Lang used a technique of grafting short-day shoots of *Nicotiana tabacum* cultivar Maryland Mammoth or long-day shoots of *Nicotiana silvestris* on stocks of day-neutral *N. tabacum* cultivar Trapezond. The graft was arranged so that a shoot of the stock would grow from a bud above the shoot of the introduced plant. The result was a plant having two shoots, one from each of two flowering types. Lang supported the findings of others by noting that flowering in the day-neutral shoot can be controlled by regulating the photoperiod of the grafted short-day or long-day shoot. Thus a Maryland Mammoth shoot kept under short days will accelerate flowering in a Trapezond stock to which it is grafted, as will a *N. silvestris* graft kept under long days. It was concluded that a flower-promoting substance is transmitted from the graft to the stock under appropriate day-length conditions.

Plants were also observed under conditions where the photoperiod was reversed; *i.e.*, short-day grafts (Maryland Mammoth on Trapezond) were subjected to long days, and long-day grafts (*N. silvestris* on Trapezond) were subjected to short days. The latter showed definite inhibition, not only of flowering in Trapezond but also of growth. This indicates that flower-inhibitory material(s) was produced in the long-day plant when it was grown under short-day conditions, and that inhibition was transmitted to the usually day-neutral plant. The graft of Maryland Mammoth did not show the same effect, *viz.*, inhibition of flowering and growth in Trapezond stock when Maryland Mammoth was kept in long days, indicating that *N. tabacum*, unlike *N. silvestris*, does not produce flower and growth inhibitor.

Plant senescence. Plant senescence is the series of events leading to death of the plant, such as depletion of chlorophyll, breakdown of protein, and increase in membrane permeability. Though a wide variety of plant systems has been studied, the mechanism leading to the onset of senescence is unknown. It has been difficult to separate the causes of senescence from the effects that accompany and are characteristic of it. Most current studies involve annual plants, usually food crops such as oats, wheat, or soybeans, that have a single fruiting phase and then die (monocarpy). Some procedures involve placing the plants in darkness for various periods of time to determine how long it takes to induce senescence, what factors may be involved in reversing it, and therefore what factors may be instrumental in delaying it. The depletion of one or more of these factors in nature might be the "senescence signal." Some workers, *e.g.*, Vernon A. Wittenbach of E. I. du Pont de Nemours and Co., have contended that chlorophyll loss is dependent upon protein loss or degradation. Such loss is delayed by a group of hormones called cytokinins.

Another interesting aspect of senescence in the soybean was reported by S. J. Lindoo and L. D. Nooden of the University of Michigan. In the soybean plant, senescence of leaves follows the period when pods are rapidly filled by seed growth. It was shown that careful surgical removal of seeds before a certain degree of maturity was realized would delay senescence. Thus the senescence signal is probably produced by the developing seeds. Lindoo and Nooden also demonstrated that, unlike the flowering signal, the senescence signal does not travel very far in the plant. Seeds allowed to mature on only one side of a Y-shaped plant, or even on one side of a single stalk, produced very little senescence in the remaining parts of the experimental plants.

Plants and heavy metals. The relationships between the growth of plants and harmful substances in their immediate environment were being explored, with some interesting results. Heavy metals are of particular concern because they tend to accumulate in soil and lake-bottom deposits where they are available to plants. Robert Dowdy of the Agricultural Research Service measured zinc, copper, and cadmium uptake by beans grown in plots to which varying amounts of anaerobically digested sludge were applied. He noted that zinc content increased up to 58 parts per million (ppm), copper up to 10 ppm, and cadmium hardly at all. None of these levels was considered high enough to affect human nutrition.

Nevertheless, these plants were concentrating the metals, because the level of metals in the soil was lower than that in the plants. That plants have considerable variability in tolerance was shown by M. R. Macnair of the University of Liverpool, England, who found that levels as low as 0.5 ppm of copper inhibited root production in *Mimulus guttatus* (yellow monkey flower). Perhaps more alarming was the finding that this plant produces copper-tolerant races that apparently can bind the copper within the plant, thus nullifying the negative effect of the metal on plant growth and also concentrating it in the plant. Macnair produced evidence that such tolerance may be controlled by only two gene pairs, indicating that the genetic basis of tolerance may be changed more easily than had been thought.

—Albert J. Smith

Microbiology

An exciting discovery was announced during the past year at the University of Illinois by scientists who had been studying a group of poorly known microorganisms called methanogens. Until then only two classes of life had been recognized: procaryotes, which include most microorganisms, and eucaryotes, the higher animals and plants. The studies proved that methanogens are different in many fundamental ways from all other organisms, and offered strong evidence that they actu-

Sludge is sprayed on crops from device designed to handle agricultural wastes containing up to 10% solid matter. Tests with the sludge revealed that it produced better yields of corn and reed canarygrass than did commercial fertilizer. Some plants treated with sludge, however, reveal increased content of potentially harmful heavy metals.

Agricultural Research

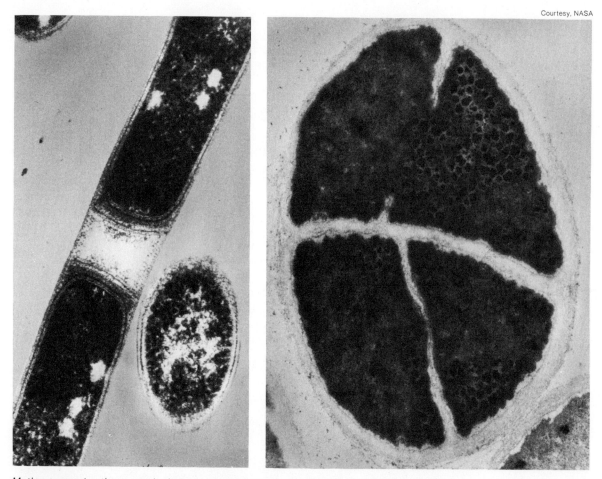

Courtesy, NASA

Methanogens (methane-producing organisms) are revealed in photomicrographs magnified 30,000–50,000 times. At the left is a chain of two and a cross-section of one; a methanogen about to undergo cell division is at the right.

ally constitute a third class of life. In the fitting together of the story of evolution through scientific study of the fossil record and living cells, such a reclassification would clarify several puzzling aspects of the chemical origin of life on Earth. The Illinois group proposed that, because of the apparent antiquity of the methanogens, they be named archaebacteria.

The methanogens are morphologically diverse; that is, there are many kinds. The most striking property they share is that they grow anaerobically, or without the need for oxygen. Instead, they convert carbon dioxide and hydrogen into waste methane (giving them their name), a reaction that allows them to produce essential cellular compounds. In a parallel though dissimilar process, plants combine carbon dioxide and water into sugar, from which starches and cellulose are then manufactured with the release of oxygen as waste. Organic matter decays by means of a complicated pattern of attacks by bacteria, oxygen, and other chemicals. Once-living matter is degraded finally to water, carbon dioxide, hydrogen, and a few other

compounds, thus providing the methanogens with their food. These organisms were thought to be just another category of bacteria.

As long ago as 1950, however, Horace Barker of the University of California proposed that the methanogens represent a radically different class. Several lines of evidence now indicate that they are as unrelated to bacteria as bacteria are to higher organisms: (1) Methanogens have RNA base sequences (part of the protein-synthesis machinery of the cell) that are markedly different from those in bacteria and higher organisms. (2) Methanogens contain unusual coenzymes (the nonprotein components of enzymes), some of which are apparently unique to these organisms. Other coenzymes found in most bacteria have not been detected in methanogens. (3) The cell walls of methanogens lack peptidoglycan, a compound that is found in cell walls of all bacteria except the extreme halophilic bacteria. The latter, which also need much further study, live in environments of high salt concentration. (This and other evidence indicate that the extreme halophiles may also belong to the same third class of life as the methanogens.) (4) Scientists have been unable to demonstrate the way that methanogens convert, or "fix," carbon dioxide into cellular organic compounds. Thus, the carbon dioxide fixation pathways shared by other organisms apparently are not used by the methanogens. (5) The cellular lipids (fatty organic compounds) of the methanogens also appear to be unique.

The Illinois scientists suggested that the methanogens might have evolved at a time when an anaerobic atmosphere rich in hydrogen and carbon dioxide enveloped the Earth, and thus could have played a pivotal role in the Earth's physical evolution. Moreover, they believed that the methanogens share a common ancestor with procaryotes and eucaryotes but branched off as an independent line of descent about the same time that the other two diverged.

Applied and environmental microbiology. Bacteria of the genus *Rhizobium* cause nodules and fix atmospheric nitrogen (make it available) in the roots of legumes. Before nodulation begins, the root becomes covered with large numbers of bacteria. Recently, scientists at Montana State University reported that a glycoprotein compound is produced and extruded from the root and serves to attract several strains of *Rhizobium*. The name chemotactin was proposed for this glycoprotein. Chemotactic attraction of rhizobia toward the legume root surface may be the first step in the complex interaction that leads to nodule formation and nitrogen fixation.

Other investigators found that lectins of legumes play a role in the highly specific recognition process between the roots and *Rhizobium* species; each species of legume can be infected by one species of *Rhizobium*. Lectins are a class of plant proteins that recognize and chemically bind specific sugars. In this instance they are thought to recognize and bind specific sugars in the complex carbohydrate-containing materials found on the surface of species of *Rhizobium*. In this manner the lectins would provide a bridge for the preferential adsorption of infective *Rhizobium* species.

Lectins were also thought to play a role in plant defense mechanisms against microorganisms. Recent evidence indicates that a lectin found in the leaves of the red kidney bean plays such a role. Specifically, the lectin causes initial attachment of bacteria to the leaves, after which the bacteria are immobilized and encapsulated and thereby apparently prevented from multiplying.

Scientists at the University of Wisconsin succeeded in transferring genes from *Rhizobium* to *Azotobacter*, a free-living, nitrogen-fixing bacterium. The genes are responsible for a surface substance that binds specifically to a protein from the legume. This transfer of genes between *Rhizobium* and *Azotobacter* may prove useful in detailed laboratory studies of *Rhizobi-*

um because these bacteria fix nitrogen only in root nodules but not in the test tube.

In 1976 scientists in New Zealand reported that they had "forced" cells of the nitrogen-fixing bacterium *Azotobacter vinelandii* into cells of a fungus that grows in and around the roots of a species of pine tree and in a symbiotic relationship helps the tree absorb nutrients from the soil. It was hoped that the altered fungus could reduce atmospheric nitrogen to a form that the tree could assimilate. In subsequent tests with pine tree seedlings, four of five modified fungal strains formed associations with most of the seedlings and fixed nitrogen. Thus, this portion of the experiment must be considered a success.

Ten seedlings inoculated with one modified strain, however, died within a month. Kenneth Giles, the scientist heading the project, destroyed all preparations of that strain because containment facilities at his disposal were inadequate for the study of a possible new disease-causing fungus. Opponents of "genetic engineering" seized upon this as an example of how scientists may create lethal organisms foreign to the environment. It was accorded sensational treatment in New Zealand, though there was no proof that the modified fungal strain was actually pathogenic.

Some bacterial species can reduce nitrate compounds to nitrous oxide (N_2O), a gas that rises in the atmosphere, while other bacteria can oxidize ammonia to nitrous oxide. Although the theory is controversial, nitrous oxide is thought to be a potential threat to the Earth's layer of stratospheric ozone that filters out harmful ultraviolet radiation from the Sun. Some researchers believed that synthetic nitrogen fertilizers, which contain nitrogen chiefly in the form of ammonia, are an important source of atmospheric nitrous oxide owing to bacterial oxidation of the ammonia. (*See* Feature Articles: STRATOSPHERIC OZONE: EARTH'S FRAGILE SHIELD; FOOD, FAMINE, AND NITROGEN FIXATION.)

Various hydrocarbons seep through the soil around many oil deposits. Such hydrocarbon gases as methane, ethane, and propane can migrate from great depths toward the surface. The gases collect in small quantities above oil-bearing regions in soil where their presence over long periods of time has allowed the evolution of bacteria able to live on them. These bacteria have identifiable growth characteristics, and it was proposed that their presence could aid in locating oil deposits.

Living microorganisms were discovered thriving inside semitranslucent rock from dry, snowless Antarctic valleys that previously had been thought utterly sterile because of their harsh conditions. Fracturing the rocks revealed the organisms as a greenish layer several millimeters deep that represented assemblages of bacteria, algae, and fungi which had colonized the sheltered spaces between mineral grains. The discoverers, a team from Florida State University, suggested using their find as a model for evaluating likely locations in which to search for life in the hostile environment of Mars.

Medical microbiology. Chemotactic attraction of microorganisms to specific tissues is thought to play a role in certain diseases. Studies have shown that the ability to colonize the surface of the intestines is an important factor in the capacity of some microorganisms to cause disease. There was growing evidence that chemotactic behavior influences the ability of such microorganisms to be attracted to, and subsequently colonize, the intestinal surface. Thus, this behavior would be significant in the onset of the disease process. Otherwise, the microorganisms would be rapidly propelled along the intestines with fecal matter and eliminated from the body.

Microbiologists recently demonstrated that the yeast *Candida albicans*, which causes a type of vaginitis, rapidly adheres to vaginal epithelial cells. The question has not been satisfactorily answered, however, how this yeast overcomes the body's natural protective barriers, especially the vaginal mucosal secretions that constantly bathe and wash away invading microorganisms. Chemotactic attraction is a step toward an answer because it indicates that *C. albicans* is specifically attracted to some component in vaginal epithelial cells. After the various chemotactic substances from tissue cells have been identified, it is possible that they could be used as a prophylactic against disease-causing microorganisms and in the treatment of diseases.

Scientists at the Center for Disease Control in Atlanta, Ga., isolated a bacterium that was considered to be the causative agent of Legionnaires' disease, a mysterious respiratory illness that killed 29 people in Pennsylvania during the summer of 1976. The identity of the bacterium remained unknown and its mode of transmission likewise was obscure. (*See* Feature Article: LEGIONNAIRES' DISEASE: STALKING A KILLER EPIDEMIC.)

New disease-causing bacteria continued to be discovered. During the past year a species of *Spiroplasma* was described that could be cultivated at body temperature and that caused cataracts and other disease symptoms in mice. It was isolated from rabbit ticks. *Spiroplasma* belongs to the mycoplasma group of bacteria that lack cell walls, and until now the species were regarded as plant and insect parasites. Whether *Spiroplasma* species play a role in human diseases was still unknown.

Experiments with animal model systems provided additional evidence to implicate viruses in diabetes. A variant of a virus that infects the brain and heart muscle was found to produce a diabetes-like disease in mice by attacking pancreatic beta cells, the source of insulin. It was thought probable that a similar role may be played by viruses in at least some cases of human diabetes.

There was increasing evidence of involvement of viruses in multiple sclerosis, an often paralytic disease of the brain and spinal cord. Whereas the measles virus was a prime suspect, there was evidence that at least two additional viruses may also be involved. Multiple sclerosis apparently is a "slow-virus" disease; *i.e.*, the onset of symptoms occurs months or years after initial contact with the virus. The classical animal model of a slow-virus disease is scrapie in sheep; it was shown recently that inoculation of the scrapie virus into newborn mice caused no immediate disease and no virus replication until at least one year had passed. During the interval, the virus was in a latent state.

Chlamydia, mycoplasma, and rickettsia microorgan-

Dark line about one-fortieth inch beneath the surface of sandstone found in a snowless valley of Antarctica (arrow) is the part of the rock found to be teeming with microbes, algae, and fungi. Whitish area below contains fungus filaments. No life was expected to be found in such rock because of the harsh Antarctic climate. Photo is magnified about ten times.

Courtesy, Center for Disease Control

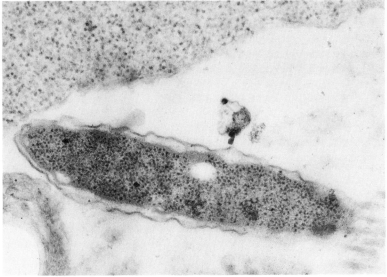

Bacterium held to be responsible for the deaths of 29 present at an American Legion convention in July 1976 was isolated by scientists at the U.S. Center for Disease Control after months of investigation.

isms were detected in clams and oysters in Chesapeake Bay. Serious diseases of humans and animals are caused by representative species in all three groups. It was not determined whether the recently detected ones were disease-producing, but the findings had economic and public health significance since clams and oysters are often consumed raw.

When mice were inoculated with the virus responsible for a type of inflammation of the membranes covering the brain, they exhibited long-lasting behavioral abnormalities. The finding suggested that infectious agents cause some types of human behavioral disorders and psychoses. Moreover, the experiment augmented already existing evidence that some cases of human slow-virus encephalitis (inflammation of the brain) result in psychotic symptoms.

A strain of Hong Kong influenza virus that had not been found in humans for several years was recently isolated from pigs. This was added evidence that pigs can serve as a reservoir of influenza virus variants.

An experimental vaccine was prepared to rid mice of "cold sores" that are caused by herpes simplex viruses. The vaccine was prepared from viruses with their DNA removed. This achievement was important because, although not conclusively proven, herpes simplex viruses have been implicated in human cancer, and even inactivated viral DNA has been shown to cause cancer in laboratory animals.

In 1976 scientists reported that they could grow one of the human malarial parasites in a continuous culture system containing human red blood cells. Recently this technique was used to obtain potent vaccine material

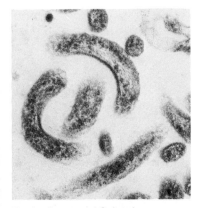

Newly discovered Spiroplasma *bacteria (above) attacks cell walls and causes cataracts (left) in mice.*

(Left) H. F. Clark; (right) D. L. Williamson and J. G. Tully

for immunization experiments in monkeys, and for the first time monkeys were successfully immunized against a human malaria parasite.

Drug resistance in *Neisseria gonorrhoeae*, the causative agent of gonorrhea, was shown to be transmitted from one bacterial cell to another via conjugal (sexual) mating. It was not yet determined whether conjugal transfer of drug resistance could be carried out between *Neisseria* and other bacterial genera, but this was a distinct possibility. (*See* Feature Article: THE MICROBES FIGHT BACK.)

A new synthetic drug, arabinosyladenine (ara-A), was used successfully to treat herpes encephalitis in humans. This was one of the few instances where a viral disease responded well to antiviral drug treatment.
—Robert G. Eagon

Molecular biology

Recombinant DNA experiments provided much of the excitement in molecular biology during the past year. In some cases public attention was drawn to the spectacular results of the experiments themselves; in others it focused on government hearings in the U.S. and the political repercussions of the experiments.

Recombinant DNA methods were developed principally to provide a convenient system for purifying and amplifying genetic material from complex organisms. The common bacterium *Escherichia coli* contains about 10,000 genes arrayed on a single circular DNA molecule, or chromosome. As a bacterium grows, its chromosome is duplicated so that each daughter cell, following cell division, can receive a complete set of genes identical to those of its parent. In addition to the single major chromosome, some bacterial strains harbor smaller circular DNA molecules called plasmids. These are replicated independently of the chromosome; they may contain as few as three or four genes or as many as a hundred. Replication of some plasmids is tightly regulated so that each cell contains no more than a few copies of it; others have a more relaxed control system, replicate abundantly, and populate the cell with between tens and thousands of copies.

The latter plasmids provide the "vectors," or carrier agents, for recombinant DNA. Plasmid DNA can be introduced into *E. coli* by a process similar to transformation, a natural mode of genetic recombination in which free molecules of DNA are absorbed by the recipient cell from the surrounding medium. Cells that have acquired plasmid DNA can be recognized easily because the plasmids that are used carry genes for resistance to several antibiotics. To construct recombinant DNA molecules, the purified plasmid DNA vector is cut with a restriction endonuclease, an enzyme that recognizes particular sequences of nucleotides, the molecular building blocks of DNA. A very large number of restriction endonucleases is now available from a wide variety of microorganisms. In some cases the nucleotide sequence that must be present for the molecule to be cut by a particular restriction endonuclease contains a nucleotide combination found so rarely by chance that the cutting site occurs only once in the plasmid DNA. Moreover, some restriction endonucleases cut one of the paired strands of DNA at a point several nucleotides removed from the cut on the other strand. This "staggered" cut produces a linear molecule with short "sticky" ends bearing complementary nucleotide sequences. (The nucleotide bases in DNA comprise four kinds: adenine, abbreviated A; guanine, or G; cytosine, or C, and thymine, or T. Adenine and thymine are complementary structures, as are guanine and cytosine; *i.e.*, oppositely located nucleotides in paired strands of DNA always link up in these combinations.) These ends can be reconnected, or annealed, in vitro to reform the original circular plasmid of DNA.

Alternatively (and this is how recombinant DNA is made) any fragment of DNA from any source, bearing the same sticky ends produced by the same restriction endonuclease, can be annealed to the plasmid DNA prior to its return to circular form. The chimeric plasmid made by circularizing that molecule, which essentially consists of the original plasmid with a piece of foreign DNA inserted into it, can be introduced into *E. coli* by transformation. When the plasmid replicates in *E. coli*, so does its DNA passenger. This general procedure of insertion and replication is often called gene cloning.

The above description covers just one of the ways of joining DNA fragments to a plasmid vector. Many are in use and more are continually being developed for specific purposes. For example, if a gene that is to be attached to a plasmid contains many cutting sites itself, use of restriction nucleases would carve it into two or more fragments, destroying its integrity. In such cases the DNA to be joined is not cut but instead has attached onto one end of each strand a segment of polydeoxyadenylic acid (polydA). The plasmid vector, cut only once, is similarly "tailed" with polydeoxythymidylic acid (polydT). Being complementary and thus sticky, the dA and dT tails can then be annealed together to form the chimeric plasmid.

A few simple figures demonstrate why these techniques have been adopted so rapidly in molecular biology laboratories. *E. coli* contains 10,000 genes. If one gene is transferred from the *E. coli* chromosome to a plasmid and the new plasmid allowed to multiply to a level of 1,000 copies per cell, then the gene in question has been increased from 0.01% of the cell's DNA to nearly 10%; moreover, it is in a form (part of a small circle) that can be separated conveniently from all the rest of the cellular DNA. Cells from more complex organisms, such as corn, rats, fruit flies, or man, contain many more genes than *E. coli*. Moving a gene from the rat into *E. coli* provides a purification (away from other rat genes) and an amplification in the millions.

Courtesy, National Institutes of Health, National Institute of Allergy and Infectious Diseases

Technician adjusts microscope and views closed-circuit television screen in laboratory shakedown procedure before U.S. National Institutes of Health scientists begin recombinant DNA "risk-assessment" experiments. The laboratory, at Fort Detrick in Frederick, Maryland, is the first U.S. "maximum physical containment," or P-4, facility for recombinant DNA experiments.

Forming a recombinant DNA molecule containing both plasmid vector and the piece of DNA to be cloned is only half the job. The recombinant plasmid must be introduced into *E. coli*, and the *E. coli* cells carrying the desired plasmid must be identified. Most often the identification is done by a miniature DNA-RNA hybridization test performed on individual bacterial colonies. This procedure requires preparation of radioactive RNA molecules constructed of nucleotide sequences complementary to that of the DNA being cloned. Small amounts of each bacterial colony to be tested are transferred to filter paper, the cells are opened, and the DNA in them is denatured chemically (*i.e.*, broken into short single-stranded fragments) and then dried onto the paper. Hundreds of colonies can be transferred and their DNA denatured in a single operation. This genetic material is then mixed with radioactive RNA, which will associate only with material from those colonies whose DNA contains sequences complementary to the RNA. These associations can be located by virtue of their radioactive RNA components through a photographic detection technique known as autoradiography. The appropriate colonies can then be selected and grown in quantity to provide the DNA desired.

Because recombinant DNA molecules are formed in the test tube, there are no technical or practical limits to the source of DNA chosen to be cloned. It may come from plants, animals, viruses, or other bacteria. Soon after these cloning techniques were developed, their awesome versatility gave concern to both scientists and nonscientists about the possibility of creating bacteria with properties that could be hazardous to man or the environment. After many symposia and conferences involving experts in infectious disease and epidemiology, scientists agreed almost unanimously that it is not possible for *E. coli* to be converted accidentally into an infectious disease agent in the course of recombinant DNA experiments. Nevertheless, in 1978 such experiments in the U.S. were still governed by guidelines, promulgated by the National Institutes of Health, which classify recombinant DNA experiments according to hypothetical risk and which prescribe levels of physical containment for the laboratories involved. In the first four years during which recombinant DNA experiments were done (two years prior to the introduction of the guidelines and two years following), there was noted not a single instance of disease caused by bacteria containing recombinant DNA or of escape from a laboratory of such bacteria.

In spite of such difficulties and restrictions, several

spectacular results were achieved in the past year. The first of these to be published was the construction of recombinant DNA plasmids containing large fragments of the sequences constituting the gene that codes for (contains instructions for the synthesis of) insulin from the rat. The hormone insulin contains two short polypeptides (chains of amino acids), called A and B, which are linked by sulfur-sulfur bonds. In 1967 Donald Steiner and co-workers at the University of Chicago discovered that the mature insulin molecule is made by removal of a short peptide (the C-peptide) from the middle of a single-chain precursor of insulin called proinsulin. More recently Steiner and his students found that proinsulin is in turn made from another precursor called preproinsulin, which contains a "leader" peptide at one end. The leader, or prepeptide, is also removed during construction of the hormone.

The beta cells in the islands of Langerhans of the pancreas, which produce insulin, contain messenger RNA (mRNA) whose nucleotide sequence carries instructions for preproinsulin synthesis that have been copied, or transcribed, from the gene for preproinsulin in the nuclear chromosomes. In the living beta cell the instructions so transcribed are normally transported via this mRNA to the cell's protein-synthesis machinery, where preproinsulin is assembled. In the laboratory this mRNA can be isolated and, through the use of special enzymes, be made to serve as a pattern to reconstruct

a copy of the original gene away from the remainder of the cell's genetic content. Cloning of fragments of most of this reconstructed gene in a bacterial plasmid was announced during the year by a team consisting of A. Ullrich, J. Shine, J. Chirgwin, R. Pictet, E. Tischer, W. J. Rutter and H. Goodman at the University of California, San Francisco.

Production of this cloned DNA was an experimental tour de force involving a number of interesting tricks. The plasmid chosen as vector is called pMB9 and carries a gene for resistance to tetracycline. The nucleotide sequence AAGCTT, paired with TTCGAA, occurs only once in pMB9. That sequence is recognized by the restriction endonuclease called HindIII, which cuts between the two A's on each DNA strand. The action of HindIII on circular pMB9 DNA thus creates a linear molecule with complementary AGCT sequences unpaired at each end. Stretches of DNA containing insulin-gene sequences and the same sticky AGCT ends were prepared as follows. Total RNA was extracted from islands of Langerhans that were in rat pancreas. Because insulin is the major protein manufactured by these differentiated cells, it was hoped that insulin mRNA would be the most abundant of the messages; that turned out to be true. The nucleotide sequence of all RNA was copied into single-stranded DNA by the enzyme reverse transcriptase. The mRNA was next removed by alkaline digestion, and reverse transcrip-

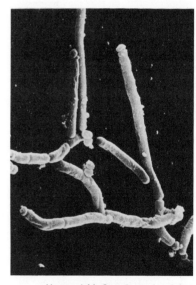

Howard M. Goodman explains diagram of the rat insulin molecule and the gene that codes for it. Above is a strain of the bacterium Escherichia coli *into which the gene was transferred.*

Adapted from Axel Ullrich, *et al., Science,* Vol. 196, pp. 1313–19, fig. 1, June 17, 1977, © AAAS

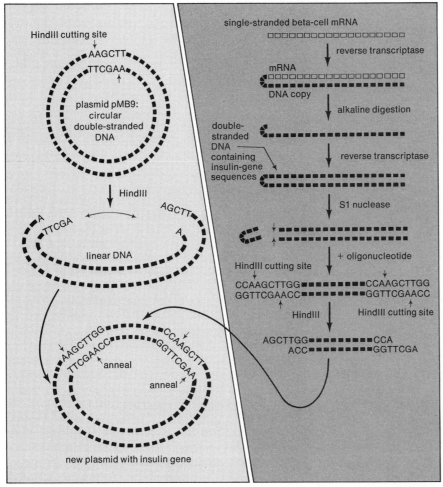

Schematic diagram illustrates the method by which rat insulin genes were prepared enzymatically from pancreatic islands of Langerhans and then inserted into bacterial plasmids. (See text.)

tase was used again, this time to convert single-stranded DNA into double-stranded DNA. The double-stranded product was then trimmed with S1 nuclease, an enzyme that has the property of digesting single-stranded loops and tails of DNA.

Next, a chemically synthesized short nucleotide chain (oligonucleotide) with the sequence CCAAGCTTGG, paired with GGTTCGAACC, was joined to each end of the double-stranded, insulin-gene-containing DNA using an enzyme called T4 DNA ligase. Finally, that product was cut by HindIII. The oligonucleotide contains the site cut by HindIII, so that the last cut created a DNA fragment containing insulin-gene sequences flanked by AGCT sticky ends. Again using T4 DNA ligase, this fragment was annealed to the linear pMB9 and then circularized, creating a new plasmid with insulin-gene sequences inserted into pMB9. The new plasmid was introduced into *E. coli,* where it replicated efficiently. The entire scheme is illustrated in the figure above.

Creation of a double-stranded DNA copy of a mRNA sequence requires two successive transcriptions starting from opposite ends of the sequence. If either tran-

scription is terminated prematurely, the final product will be truncated. The San Francisco group characterized four independent, truncated gene inserts in pMB9. One contains the entire proinsulin sequence; one contains the preproinsulin sequence up to the middle of the C-peptide; another contains the remainder of the preproinsulin sequence; and the fourth contains a short fragment corresponding to a portion of the A chain. The DNA sequence confirmed the published amino-acid sequence of rat proinsulin and allowed prediction of the sequence of the prepeptide, which was only partially known before. The rat insulin genes do not direct the manufacture of parts of the insulin molecule in *E. coli,* however, presumably because they lack a promoter sequence required by the cellular machinery to begin the process of transcription.

In order to construct an *E. coli* strain that can produce reasonable quantities of a mammalian polypeptide hormone, another group in California went to even greater lengths of genetic manipulation. K. Itakura, T. Hirose, R. Crea, and A. D. Riggs of the City of Hope National Medical Center, Duarte, Calif., collaborated with H. L. Heyneker, F. Bolivar, and H. W. Boyer of the

341

University of California, San Francisco, to synthesize chemically a fragment of DNA containing a sequence that codes for the hormone somatostatin. This hormone contains only 14 amino acids, is made in tiny amounts in the brain of animals, and has as yet poorly understood action on the secretion of other hormones.

The basic manipulation required was to fuse the chemically synthesized gene for somatostatin into a plasmid that contained the control region of the bacterial gene for β-galactosidase, an enzyme made abundantly in E. coli. The protein product of the fused gene contains β-galactosidase at one end and somatostatin at the other. The gene was so constructed as to endow its product with a sensitivity to specific chemical attack at the connection between its two disparate parts. Treatment of the chimeric protein with cyanogen bromide cut intact somatostatin from the protein in a biologically active form. The new plasmids were not very stable and appeared to lose the gene control region rapidly during growth of the bacteria. In some cases the chimeric protein seemed to be destroyed by enzymes in E. coli before it could be extracted. Nevertheless the general procedure of chemical synthesis of a gene followed by fusion to a good bacterial promoter was established.

The two examples just described have as their goal the production of useful materials in bacteria. Other research illustrates the power of recombinant DNA techniques to explore the structure of the genes themselves in new ways. In bacteria, it has been shown that the nucleotide sequence of the gene is completely transcribed into RNA, which in turn is completely translated into protein except for the leader sequence, which precedes instructions specifying the first amino acid, and the few nucleotides that may follow the translation termination signal. Thus, considerable surprise attended the recent discoveries that several cloned genes from higher organisms contain nucleotide sequences in the interior of the gene that are not represented by amino acids in the finished protein.

Philip Leder and his colleagues at the National Institute for Child Health and Human Development, Washington, D.C., prepared recombinant DNA containing the mouse genes for β-globin, a part of the hemoglobin molecule. The cloned DNA was taken directly from chromosomes, not copied from mRNA. The astonishing find was that the cloned DNA contains an intervening sequence of 550 nucleotides not present in mature globin RNA and certainly not present as amino acids in the globin protein. In addition, Susumu Tonegawa and his colleagues at the Basel Institute for Immunology in Switzerland, in collaboration with Walter Gilbert and Allan Maxam at Harvard University, found that several such intervening sequences (called introns by Gilbert) are present in the mouse genes for immunoglobulins.

It appears that the initial transcript of the gene in the cell nucleus is an RNA molecule that contains all the nucleotides of the gene. The extra nucleotides are removed during maturation of mRNA somewhere between the nucleus and the cytoplasmic ribosomes, the sites of protein synthesis. This extra bit of RNA processing further increases the distinction between bacteria and cells with nuclei and reduces the hazard of recombinant DNA experiments, since many genes whose products are to be manufactured by recombinant DNA techniques cannot be expressed accidentally in bacteria.

—Robert Haselkorn

Zoology

Recent developments relating to animals include the discovery of spacer or intervening sequences of unknown function in eucaryotic DNA genes; identification of a specific human chromosome as an SV40 cancer virus integration site; further refinement of tests for carcinogens; new interest in the rat, both in the laboratory and in the field; and continuing pressure on the survival of several animal species, including giraffes, elephants, crocodiles, and wolves. The fossil record of Precambrian life forms became more complete.

Cellular zoology. One of the surprising events of the year was the discovery by several investigators that the arrangement and expression of genetic information in eucaryotic (animal and higher plant) cells differ significantly from what had been expected based on knowledge of bacterial (procaryotic) systems. In the latter, the DNA code is "read" by an RNA polymerase enzyme, forming a complementary strand of messenger RNA (mRNA). The ribosomes, the cellular bodies that are the sites of protein synthesis, immediately attach to this strand and begin the process of assembling a linear sequence of amino acids. All this is neat and orderly, and eucaryotes seemed to have the same master plan. The molecular biologists worked out techniques to trick the bacterium Escherichia coli into making copies of foreign DNA, and some said the manufacture of hormones and antibodies for humans was imminent.

The problem just being discovered is that some eucaryotic genes have a "spacer sequence" or "intervening sequence," often in the interior of the DNA molecule. The function of these intervening sequences is not known. So far they have been found in genes that code for the β-globin chain of the hemoglobin molecule, in ovalbumin and immunoglobulin genes, and in ribosomal and transfer RNA's. (See Molecular biology, above.)

The picture that emerges from this and from work with the fruit fly Drosophila and with yeast is that the spacer sequence apparently can be excised enzymatically out of the mRNA sequence, with what must be great precision, and later the mRNA ends can be joined together to make a single, complete polypeptide chain.

As Jean Marx, writing in the magazine Science, con-

Courtesy, Lindesay Harkness, Massachusetts Institute of Technology

Chameleon wears glasses positioned so that it must look through them when taking aim with its tongue at an insect. Chameleon eyes normally move independently, but when aiming at an insect both eyes focus directly on the target to calculate the distance of the prey.

cludes, these results are significant with respect to genetic engineering and recombinant DNA techniques. They suggest that large-scale syntheses by bacteria of proteinlike hormones and antibodies will prove more difficult than had been thought (or perhaps impossible), because procaryotes almost certainly do not have the requisite eucaryotic type of excision enzymes. Thus the potential danger that some pathogen might be transferred across the barrier between the taxonomic kingdoms (bacteria to man) by way of an "engineered" *E. coli* seemed less likely.

Cancer in animals apparently can begin as a single mutation in almost any cell and can be caused by many different kinds of mutagens. Yet if one examines the chemical structure of a variety of known carcinogens, there appears to be little similarity among them. James A. Miller and Elizabeth C. Miller have proposed that one general feature these compounds share is their net positive charge; stated another way, they are electrophiles, or substances with a strong affinity for electrons. The important informational molecules DNA. RNA, and protein, have abundant electrons, and therefore associations between these electron-donors and the electron-acceptor carcinogens are likely.

A majority of investigators believe that carcinogens cause cancer by acting directly on the DNA. In the bac-

terial test system developed by Bruce Ames and other researchers, about 90% of the known carcinogens, as established by animal studies, give positive tests for mutagenicity in bacteria. This finding argues strongly for a direct effect on DNA by the carcinogen, one that results in a permanent, heritable change in cell characteristics.

Other investigators, however, including I. Bernard Weinstein of Columbia University, believe that the effects of carcinogens on the control of gene expression may be more important than the mutagenic effects. They hold that carcinogen-induced changes in the cell RNA or proteins are the basis for a cell becoming cancerous; proponents of this view cite recent discoveries of conditions under which tumor cells appear to revert to the normal state. Since there are more than 100 clinically distinct types of human cancer, and many more in other animals, there is no reason to exclude either carcinogenic process; each may be operative in different cases.

Recently it has become possible to identify a specific chromosome, in this case a human chromosome, as the one involved in the transformation of a normal cell into a tumorous one. Carlo Croce and Hilary Koprowski reviewed the evidence for the assignment of human chromosome 7 as the target site for the tumor-inducing

343

Courtesy, Marc Bekoff, University of Colorado

Dropping down on its forelegs and leaving its rear end high in the air is the signal that a dog wants to play. Known as the bow, this crouch is also seen in wolves and coyotes.

virus designated SV40 (simian virus 40). In a cell originally derived from a human/mouse cell fusion, long subculturing eliminated all the human chromosomes except number 7. SV40 virus was then used to transform cells in culture. The transformed cells showed the characteristic T antigen in their nuclei, diagnostic for tumor-producing capability, when the human chromosome 7 was present but not when it was absent. The presence of other human chromosomes along with the mouse chromosomes generally did not allow the active expression of T antigen. The exception to this situation appeared to be chromosome 17, which allowed expression and thus also appeared susceptible to SV40 virus infection.

Testing of carcinogens. Cancer investigations have broad implications for zoology, in part because of the intensity and amount of effort being applied to cancer research. The heated discussion about wheth-

er or not the artificial sweetener saccharin is a carcinogen finally translates into the question of how close is the relationship between man and rat (or mouse). Taxonomy based primarily on morphology places both man and rat in the infraclass Eutheria (placental mammals) but separates them into different orders, Primates and Rodentia. Thus one might expect that the monkey virus SV40 would be more likely to integrate with a human chromosome than with a mouse chromosome, and this was nicely illustrated for human chromosome 7 in the case just considered. Clearly it would have been better to use monkeys for the saccharin tests, but hundreds of expensive and hard-to-get monkeys would have been required. In one of the Canadian tests of saccharin, which used 100 rats, 8.9% of the animals exposed to saccharin at 5% of their diet developed tumors. The much cited human equivalent of 800 cans of diet soda per day is inaccu-

In its aggressive stance an African weaver ant opens its mouth parts and raises its abdomen. Such ants are successful in defending their home territories because a chemical deposited by their nest mates causes them to act confidently and recruit fellow fighters quickly.

B. Holldobler and E. O. Wilson, *Proceedings* of the National Academy of Sciences of the U.S., Vol. 74, 1977, pp. 2072–75; photo by Turid Holldobler

rate, according to consumer advocate Ralph Nader, who told a congressional press briefing that, because of the rats' higher metabolic rate and shorter lifespan, the proper human equivalent (of 5% of the rat's diet) is about two cans per day.

In the case of bacterial testing, the taxonomic distance is about as far as one can get, and the dosage problem is even more acute. Earlier experiments by Edith Yamasaki, Joyce McCann, and Bruce Ames at the University of California at Berkeley detected no genetic changes in bacteria due to saccharin. However, a recent report by Robert Batzinger, Suh-Yun L. Ou, and Ernest Bueding at Johns Hopkins University showed that mutagenicity could be detected in bacterial tests depending upon the method of administration. The authors concluded that a major portion of the mutagenic capability of commercial preparations of saccharin resides in the impurities they contain, but that a small amount of activity remains in the purest preparation. This could be due to a residual contaminant or a metabolite of saccharin itself. In this same study, no mutagenic activity was detected for two other sweeteners, neohesperidin dihydrochalcone (NHDC) and xylitol.

A major zoological/physiological question is whether carcinogens, like many poisons, exhibit threshold levels below which no toxicity occurs; i.e., a small dose of the anticoagulant heparin may be beneficial to a patient, whereas a large dose would be fatal. After reviewing the data from 151 experiments, Paul Craig and Gene Miller of the Franklin Institute in Philadelphia found no evidence that there was a threshold dose below which a carcinogen would not cause cancer.

They concluded that chemical carcinogens induce responses in a manner analagous to radiation, in which the probability of a normal cell becoming transformed into a cancer cell is directly proportional to the dosage. Thus, the likelihood of leukemia in a given animal depends upon the amount of radiation received. Similarly, the likelihood of lung cancer is proportional to the number of cigarettes smoked. Of course, there may be individual genetic differences of response and ability to recover. Nevertheless, the evidence strongly suggests that animal and bacterial tests both detect mutagens which affect a common genetic message system, the DNA, and thus appear to have good predictive value for cancer in man.

Zoology of the rat. *Homo sapiens* has become the dominant species on Earth, and his activities play an increasingly major role in biological relationships. It seems reasonable to ask what animal ranks second in terms of general biological success, usually defined in terms of such factors as number of animals, range of habitats, and adaptability to new environments. The answer is, second place probably goes to the rat.

The rat is a generalized animal, omnivorous and innovative, extremely adaptable, and with awesome reproductive capacity. Theoretically, a single pair of rats can have 15,000 descendants in one year. An average rat can wriggle through a hole the size of a quarter, scale a brick wall, swim half a mile and tread water for three days, gnaw through lead pipes and cinder blocks with chisel teeth that can exert 24,000 lb of pressure per square inch, and fall five stories to the ground without apparent injury. Of the more than 400 species of *Rattus*, four are most successful, and these are also

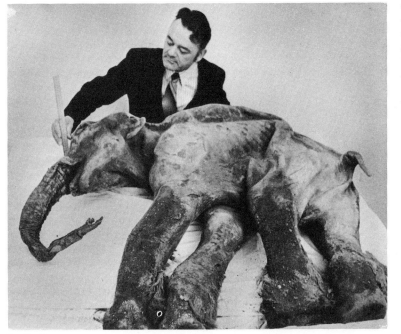

Soviet scientist views the body of a six-month-old baby mammoth. Until its discovery in 1977 it had been preserved in the permafrost of eastern Siberia for 10,000–15,000 years. The two "fingers" at the end of the trunk were depicted in Stone Age cave paintings of mammoths.

Tass/Sovfoto

Norway rat, one of the four most successful species of Rattus, *was the subject of several studies during the year. One experiment showed that under field conditions an alien rat may be attacked by an established group; however, the fight usually does not result in serious injury because the alien rat runs away.*

the most nearly competitive with man. They are the Norway rat (*Rattus norvegicus*), the roof rat (*R. rattus*), the Polynesian rat (*R. exulans*), and the lesser bandicoot (*Bandicota bengalensis*), which has become the predominant species in India. Rats consume approximately one-fifth of the world's crops annually and destroy a billion dollars worth of property. They and their parasites spread at least 20 kinds of disease, including typhus, trichinosis, Lassa fever, and plague. They survived the atomic blasts on Eniwetok atoll, and some strains have acquired a genetic resistance to anticoagulant poisons so that they can withstand a dosage one hundred times the normal lethal amount.

Richard Lore and Kevin Flannelly of Rutgers University, reviewing work on the social behavior of *Rattus norvegicus*, discussed the question of how much of this behavior is instinctive and how much is learned, and whether behavioral traits are a predominant force in the success of the species. For example, rats have a reputation for unbridled aggressiveness. In his book *On Aggression*, Konrad Lorenz suggested that rat and man were uniquely similar in their propensity to attack and kill their own kind. However, these studies were based on captured wild rats kept in small enclosures, circumstances that may have contributed to these behavioral patterns. More recent work suggests that under field conditions an alien rat may be attacked by an established group, but the fight seldom lasts long enough to permit serious injury because the alien rat runs away.

In experiments by Lore, Flannelly, and Philip Farina, an intruder rat, when placed in a cage for the first time with an established resident rat, was usually attacked by the resident rat, and both rats lost weight during a 24-hour test. However, when the same intruder was placed in a cage with another resident rat one week later, the resident seemed to accept the intruder peacefully and both animals maintained their body weight. The most pronounced difference in the behavior of the intruder in this second encounter was the increased tendency to emit long sequences of ultrasonic cries with frequencies of about 22 kHz. The cries, which appeared to inhibit attacks by the resident rat, were produced much earlier during the second test, especially during the initial 30 minutes. While the production of ultrasonic cries was probably an unlearned response to stress, nevertheless this very effective submission signal proved to be readily conditionable. In this case the particular stimulus that evoked the response was determined by previous experience.

Another misconception relates to the prevalent idea that adult male rats readily kill infant and juvenile rats. In fact, when breeding pairs were kept together during lactation, if the female was removed the male behaved quite maternally toward the pups. If an alien male was placed in the cage with the mother and her litter, the female's threats kept the male away from the litter for the first hour or so. But even when this protective behavior diminished, no pups were killed by any of the males in several tests. In field conditions it appears that rats tend to live in burrows in rather small, separate social units, but if conditions are favorable and numbers increase, the units are built closer together. Thus, within a colony, rats might come to know each other as individuals rather than simply as colony members recognizable by a common colony odor. Under these conditions rats probably accept alien members quite readily.

One remarkable trait of rats is their development of

admirably efficient feeding strategies that allow them to avoid poisoned foods and to adjust to rapid changes in food supply. In general, rats tend to avoid any contact with novel objects in the environment; they will ignore new food for several days, and if the nutritional supply is adequate they may never sample it at all. Eventually small, sublethal quantities may be eaten, but if some animals get sick, the entire colony thereafter avoids this food. Such a response, called conditioned food aversion, is especially interesting to psychologists. It may take many trials to teach a hungry rat to press a bar to receive a food reward (and then the food must be presented immediately or the trick is never learned). Yet a rat learns to avoid poisoned food in only one trial, even though he may not get sick for six hours or more. Apparently the mother's diet influences the odor and taste of her milk; the offspring are sensitive to these clues and later tend to select foods with the same taste and odor. It is clear that pups carefully follow the feeding preferences of the adults.

Experiments also seem to show that when food is scarce, behavioral patterns allow some individuals a higher percentage of food, and that about 60% of these are females. Thus, male dominance behavior such as is found in lion prides, in which females eat only after adult males have fed, seems absent in rats. The overall impression is that rat social structure is largely cooperative and characterized by an easy exchange of sex-associated roles when such an exchange is beneficial to both sexes and to survival as a whole.

The threat of extinction. The success of the rat is in sharp contrast to the decline of many other animal species. While the worldwide list of endangered species continues to grow, the African plains animals are under particularly severe pressure. One example is the giraffe, which is represented by only nine subspecies, all restricted (except for zoos) to Africa. The giraffe is a remarkable animal with many highly evolved features besides the obvious one of height. For example, it has control valves in the jugular veins and a unique network of blood vessels in the head, called the "wonder net of the carotids" (rete mirabile caroticum), which help maintain constant blood pressure in the brain as the animal raises and lowers its head. The large surface area of the giraffe apparently facilitates cooling in the hot environment that sends the rhinoceros, hippopotamus, and elephant to a frequent dip in a pool or mud bank. To utilize its favorite food, the whistling-thorn acacia tree, the giraffe has tough, long, hairy lips and an 18-in tongue that can extract the leaves and twig tips from among the thorns. Giraffes normally obtain sufficient water from acacia leaves and tips and rarely need to drink.

Compared with the giraffe population, which numbers only in the thousands, the African elephant population, estimated to be at least a million, is large. How-

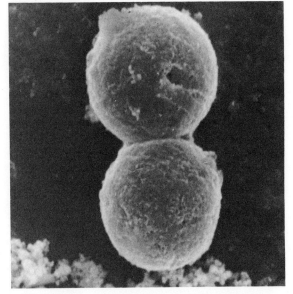

Courtesy, J. William Schopf, University of California, Los Angeles

Microfossil from the Precambrian era, more than 600 million years ago, is part of a growing body of evidence that primitive organisms existed at that time. The fossil is magnified 1,700 times in the photo.

ever, the rise in the world price of ivory has led to dramatically increased rates of poaching. In 1974 the total official export of ivory to Hong Kong from all of East Africa was 107 tons, while the Hong Kong import figure was 461 tons, suggesting that much of it was acquired illegally. Furthermore, elephants are being driven from their native habitats into national parks, and in some areas overcrowding has resulted in large numbers of deaths by starvation. The overcrowded herds need to be culled, but this places conservation experts in the difficult position of telling some governments that more protection is required while at the same time telling others that more elephants need to be killed intentionally.

While the giraffe and elephant have long been viewed with something approaching affection, animals like crocodiles and wolves are a different matter. The crocodilians, survivors of the dinosaur age, are divided into three families based on dentition, scales, and skull morphology. Alligators and caimans, which form one family, have broad snouts for crushing and eating small fish, birds, and mammals. Except for the Chinese alligator, all are found in North and South America. Of these, 19 species and subspecies are classed as endangered and one as declining; only the American alligator is safe. Of the true crocodiles, distinguished by the exposed lower teeth when the jaws are closed, only a few American forms are left in Florida and, possibly, in the Zapata Swamp in Cuba; the rest are in Africa and Asia. All three African crocodiles are endangered, and in Asia only the New Guinea and Johnson's crocodiles are safe. The sole survivor of the third family, the long-

Stalklike tube worms and many other marine animals cluster in dense colonies around vents of warm water percolating upward from below the ocean floor. The photograph was taken at a depth of about 9,000 feet from the research submersible "Alvin."

nosed gavial or gharial, is highly evolved as a fish catcher with long, narrow jaws and many small teeth. For a time it was thought to be extinct, but it is now known that about 60 survive in India and perhaps 40 in Nepal.

Except for the gavial, all the crocodilians are potentially dangerous to man and seemingly unpredictable. Some injuries and deaths from alligator attacks have been reported. In the U.S. careful regulation of the number of alligators that can be killed each year and of sales of alligator leather goods has resulted in a strong recovery in the alligator population, especially in Louisiana.

Wolves have a reputation almost as bad as that of crocodiles. Their attacks are legendary, especially those on sheep and, by inference, on all somewhat helpless creatures. It is true that they tend to run in packs and to attack the young, the lame, and the weaker members of a group. There is a report, apparently documented, of wolves attacking more than a hundred persons, killing many and eating parts of many, in the Gévaudan region in southern France between 1764 and 1767. The attacks stopped after two huge wolflike animals were killed. After studying the records of these mysterious beasts, C. H. D. Clarke of Ontario concluded that they were "unique in the history of their kind—natural first-generation dogwolf crosses with hybrid vigor." Certainly crosses between wolves and dogs are compatible, and the results are highly unpredictable. In general, however, attacks on humans by nonrabid wolves are extremely rare.

The main problem is that of attacks on sheep and other livestock. If the wolf is allowed to remain in wilderness areas, where he "falls on" only natural prey,

there is a potential biological benefit. The weak will be culled out and the survival of others encouraged, thus helping to preserve the "balance of nature." But man continually presses forward into wilderness areas and disturbs this balance, sometimes in subtle ways, though the wolf is legally protected throughout the U.S. and in Canadian national parks. Meanwhile, research continues in an effort to provide better understanding of this enigmatic animal and to help guide authorities in management programs.

Evolution. Paralleling man's search for evidence of other biological creatures somewhere in space has been the search for early forms of life on Earth. During the year the Alan T. Waterman Award was given by the National Science Foundation to J. William Schopf of UCLA for "Outstanding capability and exceptional promise for significant future achievement." Schopf's contributions involved discoveries of fossil records of the earliest, most primitive organisms known to have lived on Earth, dating back to the Precambrian era, prior to 600 million years ago. The fossil record of these organisms is more complete than was previously believed and shows that some biological systems were in existence more than three billion years ago.

A unique underwater biological phenomenon associated with active hydrothermal vents in the deep sea was explored by a group led by John B. Corliss and sponsored by the National Science Foundation as part of the International Decade of Ocean Exploration. The special biology, discovered in waters off the Galápagos Islands, results from the conversion, by high pressure and heat, of sulfate in seawater to hydrogen sulfide, a process known as chemosynthesis. Energy is obtained by certain bacteria that metabolize the hydrogen sulfide, and these bacteria in turn serve as the basis of a food chain that includes filter feeders and larger organisms. The size of the clams and the tube worms (pogonophorans) was described as impressive. The temperature in this underwater oasis was 17° C (63° F), while that of the surrounding waters was almost freezing. (*See* Feature Article: RESEARCH SUBMERSIBLES: EXPLORERS OF THE OCEAN DEPTHS.)

—Darryll Outka

Materials sciences

Efforts to conserve energy in the production of ceramics and to improve resistance to corrosion of metals were among the highlights of the past year in the materials sciences.

Ceramics

Many ceramic products are essential for the efficient generation, use, and conservation of energy, but the ceramic industry itself is also a major energy consumer. A U.S. Federal Energy Administration study showed that in 1975 ten major industries used over 90% of the energy consumed in manufacturing, and that the stone, clay, and glass industry was the fifth largest energy user among them. Because of the emphasis on energy conservation, the ceramic industry seemed certain to receive close scrutiny in the future. Fortunately, a recent study by Battelle Laboratories (Columbus, Ohio) showed that significant energy savings are possible, as much as 16% by 1980. For example, a highly efficient kiln could produce building brick with less than half the energy currently required.

Since virtually all ceramics are fired to high temperatures to develop their hardness, strength, chemical durability, and other desirable properties, attention focused on the kilns and furnaces used. Motivated by rising costs and potential shortages of fuel, many companies modified existing kilns by adding insulation and installing more efficient burners; they also shortened firing schedules wherever possible. Some brick and cement producers considered conversion to powdered coal or even sawdust, while others considered conversion from scarce natural gas to more plentiful fuel oils.

The ceramic industry also looked carefully at ways of altering traditional fabrication processes to reduce energy consumption. For example, organic finishes often have replaced more durable ceramic enamels on appliances because of the costs of the ceramic enamel coating and firing processes. The Ferro Corp., however, recently showed that those costs can be reduced considerably by a new electrostatic process for spraying powdered enamels. Dry enamel powder is transported in an airstream past an electrode system where it becomes electrically charged by ion bombardment.

The charged powder is then electrostatically attracted to and retained on the oppositely charged metallic part to be coated. Almost none of the powder is lost, and several energy-consuming steps involved in conventional wet spraying techniques are eliminated.

Ceramic electrodes and insulators for magnetohydrodynamic (MHD) generators, which extract electricity from an intensely hot ionized gas stream, were also investigated. A U.S.-U.S.S.R. program tested the ability of ceramics to withstand the extremely corrosive MHD environment in a combined MHD-steam turbine power plant in Moscow. Doped zirconium oxide, silicon carbide, and various spinels were tested with modest success in limited-duration runs.

Nuclear fusion is a promising solution to long-range energy needs. Since any apparatus containing a fusion reaction must withstand very-high-energy charged-particle impacts and intense neutron fluxes, the selection of material for an inner wall is a critical problem. Recent research by the General Atomic Co. showed that carbon and silicon carbide may be candidates. Ceramics may also play a role in the difficult problem of generating the extremely high temperatures and pressures required to initiate the fusion reaction. One of the most

Washing machine top receives ceramic enamel coating when it is sprayed with an inorganic powder in an energy-saving electrostatic process (see text).

promising approaches focuses high-power laser beams on a mixture of deuterium and tritium frozen into small hollow glass spheres. The sudden implosion within the sphere produces the conditions needed for the thermonuclear reaction. Unfortunately, an economically practical fusion reactor would require lasers about ten times as powerful as the best now available. Owens-Illinois Inc. scientists studied fluorophosphate glasses, and Corning Glass Works scientists investigated beryllium fluoride glasses and other fluoride-containing glasses in a search for materials capable of operation at much higher power levels with less beam distortion and energy dissipation.

In the effort to conserve petroleum there was continued emphasis on the use of ceramic materials to increase engine operating efficiencies. Experimenting with gas turbines, the Ford Motor Co. passed a major milestone by successfully operating an uncooled, aerodynamically loaded ceramic turbine rotor at 2,500° F for more than 1.5 hours. Ford's all-ceramic rotor (consisting of a reaction-bonded silicon nitride blade ring pressure-bonded to a dense, hot-pressed silicon nitride disk) was undertaken to meet the economic goal of a mass produced, relatively low-cost engine. The reaction-bonded blade ring is injection molded to its finished shape to avoid costly machining, and the much stronger hot-pressed material is used only in the central portion of the rotor where the stresses are highest. Pratt and Whitney Aircraft and Garrett AiResearch Co. scientists made similar advances in the fabrication and testing of hybrid turbine rotors consisting of ceramic blades retained by carefully designed attachment surfaces in metal disks. While much remained to be done before a small, reliable automotive ceramic tur-

bine can be produced commercially, the payoff in lower production costs and fuel savings will be tremendous. Ford estimated that U.S. fuel import savings could be as high as $7 billion a year. Substantial strides toward the development of ceramic turbines were also made in West Germany.

Although the use of ceramic gas turbines in automobiles did not seem likely before the late 1980s or early 1990s, there may well be earlier military applications. These might include naval propulsion or auxiliary power units where metallic engines are subjected to extremely corrosive conditions, and cruise missile engines where the ceramics might offer considerable performance and cost advantages. Ceramics may also soon find applications in more conventional automotive engines. Many companies were looking at the possibility of ceramic pistons or piston caps, cylinder liners, precombustion chambers, and valve train components for diesel engines, and some predicted that they would be in use by the early 1980s. There was also considerable study of high-temperature, very-high-speed ceramic turbocharger rotors to increase the efficiency of diesel engines.

Two major developments in silicon nitride and silicon carbide ceramics involved methods for their fabrication into useful components. The Swedish ASEA Co., which pioneered hot isostatic pressing (HIP) of ceramics, announced that it had successfully used the process to produce silicon nitride that had a much lower content of yttrium oxide than required for silicon nitride densification by hot pressing. For example, at a pressure of 35,000 psi and at 1,750° C the Swedish firm achieved full densification with only 0.5% yttrium oxide. This reduction of yttrium oxide should significantly improve

Ceramic turbine rotor, consisting of a reaction-bonded silicon nitride blade ring that is pressure-bonded to a dense, hot-pressed silicon nitride disk, was developed to increase engine operating efficiencies. If perfected, it could save the U.S. about $7 billion per year in fuel imports, according to the Ford Motor Co.

Courtesy, Bell Telephone Laboratories

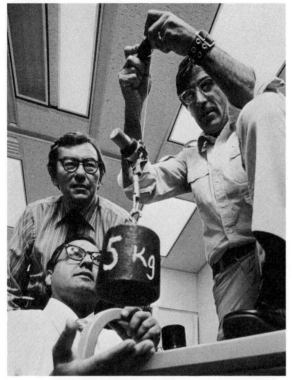

Hair-thin glass fiber is strong enough to hold a 5-kg (11-lb) weight and withstand pulling forces of more than 600,000 psi. An organic resin coating makes such strength possible.

the strength and durability of silicon nitride at high temperatures. ASEA's results have already indicated much lower creep rates and much less scatter in high-temperature strength for HIP-processed specimens. Their results suggest the exciting possibility of low-cost, high-quality silicon nitride blades and integral rotors.

Semiconducting amorphous (non-crystalline) chalcogenide glasses, largely ignored until recently, appeared highly promising for many microprocessor and energy-conversion applications. Stanford Ovshinsky of Energy Conversion Devices Inc. advocated their use instead of crystalline silicon and germanium in electronic switching and memory devices. Great progress was made in recent months toward the use of these glasses in electrically alterable memory devices that can retain information indefinitely, in amorphous microfilm, and in low-cost energy-conversion devices.

Optical waveguides, which can carry enormous volumes of information in small-diameter glass fiber cables, also came closer to commercial realization during the year. One problem had been the difficulty of producing long lengths of strong fibers. Bell Laboratories scientists, however, recently announced a protective resin coating that allows thin fibers to retain strengths as high as 600,000 psi for many years. In the U.K., large numbers of cable television subscribers watched programs transmitted through low-loss optical waveguides. An experimental program to evaluate their use in such cable TV applications as banking and shopping was initiated in Japan. In Italy, an optical waveguide carried messages experimentally for more than five miles without intermediate amplification.

Graphite fibers, used primarily to reinforce composite materials in military and sporting equipment, seemed likely to gain the expanding market needed for a substantial reduction in their cost. Faced with the need for lighter cars that can meet projected fuel economy standards, the auto industry investigated the use of graphite- and glass-reinforced composites for a variety of body and engine parts. For example, Ford studies indicated that composites reinforced with graphite fiber could cut weights of automobile parts by as much as 70%. If these applications reach the millions-of-pounds-per-year level anticipated, the cost of high-quality polyacrylonitride-derived graphite fibers could decline from about $32 per lb ($70 per kg) to about $10 per lb ($22 per kg).

—Norman M. Tallan

Metallurgy

During the past year there was a significant increase in interest in the mechanical properties of thick films deposited from a vapor phase onto substrate materials. Interest in these films, the thicknesses of which can range from 10^{-3} to 2 mm, arises from their potential use as corrosion-resistant or wear-resistant coatings and from the application of the deposition techniques to fabrication of self-supporting shapes such as sheets, foils, and tubes.

Depending on the conditions under which the films are grown, they can produce unusual microstructures that give rise to a range of interesting mechanical properties. The structures of the growing films are determined principally by atomic diffusion processes occurring either on the surfaces of the films or within the bulk of the deposited material. Because the processes of surface and bulk diffusion are thermally activated, they have associated with them activation energies, the magnitudes of which are determined by the melting temperature of the material. Consequently, the major variables in determining the microstructures of deposited films are the melting temperature of the material being deposited, T_m, and the temperature of the substrate onto which deposition is being made, T. Attempts to understand the microstructures and, therefore, the properties of the films have resulted in models that predict the microstructures of films grown within certain limits of the ratio T/T_m.

When T/T_m is less than 0.1, film growth is determined primarily by the degree of roughness of the surface of the substrate. The temperature of the substrate is too low to permit diffusion of the deposited atoms

Courtesy, R. F. Bunshah, University of California, Los Angeles

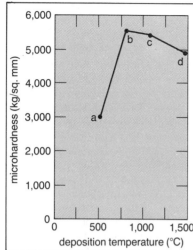

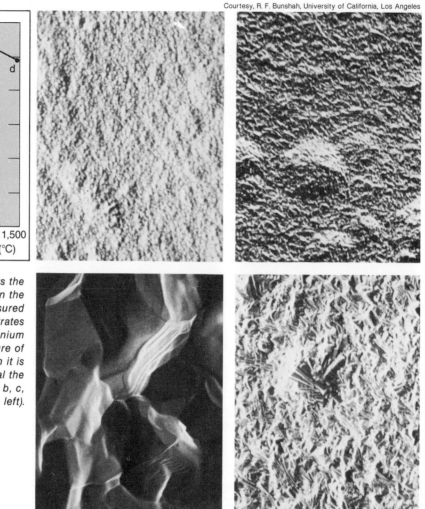

Graph (above) shows the relationship between the microhardness (hardness measured by an indenter that penetrates microscopic areas) of titanium carbide film and the temperature of the substrate on which it is deposited. Micrographs reveal the deposit surfaces of samples a, b, c, and d (clockwise from top left).

over the surface, and deposited atoms therefore tend to remain at the site of their collision with the surface. The "hillsides" on the rough surface receive a greater flux of atoms than do the "valleys" lying in the shadows of these "hills" and therefore grow more rapidly than do the valleys. The structures thus tend to be highly disordered, with open boundaries between the individual grains (crystals). The actual structure depends on the temperature and surface roughness of the substrate and on the chemical composition of the film being deposited. Researchers have found that, even at liquid-helium temperatures ($-269°$ C), pure metals have sufficient atomic mobility to condense in crystalline states, whereas alloys and compounds condense in an amorphous state.

When T/T_m exceeds 0.1, sufficient thermal energy is available for activation of surface diffusion. Atoms arriving on the surface transfer their kinetic energy to the crystal lattice and become loosely bonded adsorbed atoms that diffuse over the surface until they are either trapped at low-energy sites or desorb from the surface.

Within the T/T_m range of 0.1–0.3, the films grow as assemblages of dome-topped tapered crystals with high densities of dislocations (defects occurring along certain lines in a crystal structure, the movements of which allow plastic deformation).

As a result of the high dislocation densities, films of pure metals such as nickel, titanium, tungsten, niobium, vanadium, and molybdenum, and of single-phase alloys, such as nickel-20% chromium, have hardnesses two to three times greater than they would in the annealed (heated and then cooled) state. (A phase is a constituent of an alloy that is physically distinct and homogeneous in chemical composition.) The actual structures still depend on the temperature and roughness of the substrate, but for any degree of roughness a temperature is reached at which a limiting form of the structures of deposited compounds and complex alloys occurs. This form comprises tightly packed fibrous grains of poorly defined structure with weak grain boundaries (interfacial surfaces between individual crystals).

With T/T_m in the range 0.3–0.5, the thermal energy is sufficiently high that the enhanced surface diffusion facilitates a decrease in the density of adsorbed atoms on the surface and film growth is dominated by surface recrystallization. Nucleation of new crystals is inhibited, and existing crystallites (rudimentary crystals) grow as columnar grains separated by distinct dense intercrystalline boundaries in which are located the majority of the dislocations.

Increasing T/T_m in the above range increases the average grain size and the ductility of the film and decreases its strength and hardness. Thus, desirable combinations of mechanical properties can be obtained by suitable manipulation of T/T_m. Of particular interest are the mechanical properties of dispersion-strengthened alloy films that are produced by co-deposition of the carbides of niobium or titanium or the oxides of zirconium or aluminum with metals such as iron, nickel, or iron-nickel alloys. The yield strengths (stresses above which materials exhibit permanent deformations) of such films increase with increasing volume fraction and particle size of the dispersed carbide or oxide phases, and decrease with increasing temperature of deposition. (The "volume fraction" of the dispersed carbide is that fraction of the volume of the material which is occupied by the carbide phase.) Niobium carbide increases the strength of iron at 25° C and at 700° C, and alloying with nickel gives additional strength at both temperatures; the latter demonstrates the possibility of combining solid-solution hardening with dispersion-hardening in deposited films.

Because of their resistance to wear, deposits of such refractory compounds as oxides, nitrides, and carbides are of particular industrial importance. Strongly dependent on the deposition process, the properties of deposited compounds are quite different from those of metals. In contrast with the properties of metal films, the hardnesses of ceramic films of alumina, zirconia, and yttria are very low, in the T/T_m range of 0.1–0.3. This is presumed to be due to the high concentration of growth defects, which cause structural imperfections in the films. However, deposition in the range 0.3–0.5 occurs with less structural imperfection, and the hardnesses of the films are therefore increased. This increase in hardness is also aided by sintering within the films. Titanium carbide deposited in this range is second in hardness only to diamond, and such coatings on cutting tools give a 3–8-times improvement in service life over normal carbide and high-speed tool steels.

With T/T_m in excess of 0.5, bulk diffusion becomes the dominant influence on the final structure of metallic coatings. This structure is characterized by grains of equal dimensions in all directions. Produced by recovery and recrystallization, they occur at points of high lattice strain. In this range of temperature the properties of metallic films vary from those typical of bulk cast

and wrought structures to those typical of the fully annealed state. The dense deposits obtained at high values of T/T_m provide effective barrier-layer coatings.

In addition to being affected by T/T_m and the roughness of the surface of the substrate, the structures of deposited complex alloys and compounds often depend on the technique by which deposition is achieved and the rate at which the material is deposited. The vapor from which deposition occurs is produced by direct or electron-beam evaporation, which generates vaporized atoms of relatively low energy, or by ion bombardment, which produces atoms of high energy. Difficulty is often encountered in electron-beam evaporation of alloys or compounds, the elemental components of which have widely varying vapor pressures, and in direct evaporation, which frequently produces films that are deficient in the non-metallic elements. These difficulties are overcome by using either the sputtering process, involving ion bombardment, in which material is transferred to the vapor phase without a significant alteration in its chemical composition, or by using reactive evaporation. In this latter technique metal atoms are evaporated from a thermally heated source into a chamber containing a reactive gas, and

Carl Cline of Lawrence Livermore Laboratory holds rod made of fused metallic glasses. Because of their random atomic structures such glasses are much stronger than crystalline metals and have greater resistance to corrosion than the corresponding crystalline alloy.

Courtesy, Lawrence Livermore Laboratory

the pressures are kept low enough that reaction between the evaporated metal atoms and the reactive gas occurs only on the substrate. In this manner alumina deposits have been formed by reaction between evaporated aluminum atoms and oxygen gas. An improvement on this technique, called activated reactive evaporation, involves activating and/or ionizing both the metal and gas species in the reaction zone. Titanium carbide deposits have been produced using this method to effect reaction between titanium metal vapor and acetylene gas.

Although almost all simple metal and single-phase alloy films conform with the foregoing scheme, the low diffusion rates and the dominance of surface diffusion can produce unusual combinations of phases in complex alloys. Scientists have found that sputtered films of chromium-nickel alloys, deposited at both high and low temperatures, can contain phases not present in the equilibrium phase diagram (the graphic representation of the phase-stability relationships in an alloy system as a function of temperature). Also, alloys or intermetallic compounds that exhibit polymorphism, the ability to exist in two or more crystal forms, can be deposited as non-equilibrium phases. For example, sputtered titanium deposited at liquid nitrogen temperatures ($-196°$ C) has the high-temperature crystal structure, which under equilibrium conditions does not exist below $882°$ C, whereas deposition at room temperature produces the equilibrium low-temperature structure. Sputtered complex cobalt-samarium alloys form amorphous deposits at $20°$ C, which, on annealing, transform to the high-temperature equilibrium phase at $500°$ C and then revert to the low-temperature equilibrium phase on heating to $800°$ C. This deposition of non-equilibrium phases, followed by annealing at higher temperatures, is a potential method for varying the structures of the phases present and the distributions of those phases.

Combining the properties of their individual phases makes laminated composites attractive as engineering materials. Vapor deposition techniques are thus well suited to the production of such composites, particularly if, in order to improve the strength and toughness of the composite, the layers are required to be very thin. Researchers have found that iron-copper and nickel-silica laminated composites formed by vapor deposition are stronger than those fabricated by conventional techniques.

—David R. Gaskell

Mathematics

Several issues made mathematical news in 1977. U.S. high school students achieved a singular distinction in international mathematics competition; mathematical researchers solved a major conjecture that had sty-

mied experts for nearly a quarter of a century; and computer scientists found an ingenious way to employ some elementary mathematics to create foolproof codes that require no key and cannot be cracked. Each of these developments is discussed below.

International Mathematical Olympiad. Every summer teams of high school mathematics students from various nations convene for an intensive competition in which they attempt to solve challenging problems in elementary mathematics. This international competition was established in the late 1950s in Europe, and has been dominated since then by Hungary, the U.S.S.R., and East Germany. The United States entered the competition in 1974, and since then has finished in second or third place each year.

In 1977, for the first time, the U.S. team took first place in the Olympiad, held on July 5–6 in Belgrade, Yugos. The eight-man U.S. team achieved a total of

---

1977 International Mathematical Olympiad

1. Equilateral triangles *ABK, BCL, CDM, DAN* are constructed inside the square *ABCD*. Prove that the midpoints of the four segments *KL, LM, MN, NK* and the midpoints of the eight segments *AK, BK, BL, CL, CM, DM, DN, AN* are the 12 vertices of a regular dodecagon.
(The Netherlands)

2. In a finite sequence of real numbers the sum of any 7 successive terms is negative and the sum of any 11 successive terms is positive. Determine the maximum number of terms in the sequence.
(Vietnam)

3. Let *n* be a given integer > 2, and let V_n be the set of integers $1 + kn$, where $k = 1, 2, \ldots$. A number $m \in V_n$ is called *indecomposable in* V_n if there do not exist numbers $p, q \in V_n$ such that $pq = m$. Prove that there exists a number $r \in V_n$ that can be expressed as the product of elements indecomposable in V_n in more than one way. (Expressions which differ only in the order of the elements of V_n will be considered the same.)
(The Netherlands)

4. *a, b, A, B* are given constant real numbers and $f(\theta) = 1 - a \cos \theta - b \sin \theta - A \cos 2\theta - B \sin 2\theta$. Prove that if $f(\theta) \geq 0$ for all real θ, then $a^2 + b^2 \leq 2$ and $A^2 + B^2 \leq 1$.
(Great Britain)

5. Let *a* and *b* be positive integers. When $a^2 + b^2$ is divided by $a + b$, the quotient is *q* and the remainder is *r*. Find all pairs (*a,b*), given that $q^2 + r = 1977$.
(West Germany)

6. Let *f(n)* be a function defined on the set of all positive integers and taking on all its values in the same set. Prove that if $f(n + 1) > f(f(n))$ for each positive integer *n*, then $f(n) = n$ for each *n*.
(Bulgaria)

202 points, including two perfect papers by Randall Dougherty of Fairfax, Va., and Michael Larsen of Lexington, Mass. The second-place team prize went to the U.S.S.R. with 192 points. Great Britain and Hungary tied for third with scores of 190.

First-place individual prizes were awarded to Dougherty and Larsen. Three members of the U.S. team achieved second-place prizes (Mark Kleiman, Victor Milenkovic, and Peter Shor), and one (James Propp) received a third-place prize. The U.S. team was selected by means of a two-step national competition that began in the early spring of 1977 with more than 340,000 contestants and culminated on May 3 when about 100 students who achieved top scores in the first round won the U.S.A. Mathematical Olympiad. The top eight winners of the U.S.A. Olympiad were invited to form the U.S. team for the international competition.

The International Olympiad comprised six problems (displayed in the accompanying box) that were solved in two four-hour sessions. These problems were selected by a committee of judges from proposals submitted by the competing nations, and then translated into the dozens of different languages of the contestants. Each of these problems involves only the elementary (pre-calculus level) mathematics that is common to the secondary school curricula throughout the world. Their solution depends on ingenuity, inventiveness, and insight, rather than on specific formulas or esoteric theorems. The International Mathematical Olympiad provides a worldwide standard by which various nations and schools within those nations can judge the effectiveness of their high school mathematics programs.

The Calabi Conjecture. As every schoolchild learns, area and volume measurements are based on the more primitive concept of length. Mathematicians call a measure of length (or distance) a metric and frequently derive from it the higher dimensional measures of area and volume. The relation between distance and volume (or, in technical terms, between metrics and measures) is of crucial importance in differential geometry, that part of geometry that is concerned with the properties of curved, higher dimensional spaces. (Because of their unconventional, "non-Euclidean" structure, these spaces frequently serve as models for research in cosmology and relativistic physics.)

In the early 1950s Eugenio Calabi hypothesized that not only do distances determine the way volume is measured but also that the measure of volume frequently determines how distance must be measured. Specifically, he provided a compelling (but logically incomplete) argument that the natural measure of volume on certain "complex manifolds"—curved spaces whose coordinates are complex numbers—determines a unique metric, called a Kähler metric, that is intrinsically related to the geometry of the manifold.

(A complex number is any number of the form $a + bi$, where a and b are real numbers and $i^2 = -1$.)

During 1977 the final link in Calabi's chain of reasoning was closed by Shing-Tung Yau of Stanford University. Yau did so by solving a complicated system of nonlinear partial differential equations, the hardest kind of equations in mathematics. Differential equations are used widely in the physical sciences because they serve to define unknown functions by relating together—in a "differential equation"—the rates at which functions change. Partial differential equations (PDE's) involve several simultaneous rates of change. Nonlinear PDE's contain products of the changing rates of the unknown functions; these products cause interaction between the variables that makes it difficult to find solutions to the equations.

Yau solved the set of equations required for Calabi's conjecture by first finding a solution to a simpler, related set of equations, and then carefully changing the equations (and their solutions) from the simple to the more complex version. Doing this took several years of calculation guided by tremendous insight into the interplay between the geometric and analytic behavior of the partial differential equations.

Yau's accomplishment not only confirmed the Calabi conjecture, but also yielded considerable new information about the relationship between PDE's and the geometry of surfaces. Yau and others used these methods to resolve other conjectures related to Calabi's original problem, proving, for instance, that certain measurements of distance on abstract spaces are unique. Results of this sort, which say that the examples already known are the only possible kinds, are of tremendous use in mathematical research, for they not only provide a definitive explanation for observed structure but also indicate fruitful directions for future investigation.

Trapdoor codes. During recent months a virtual revolution has occurred in the age-old problem of coding secret messages. Based on a strikingly simple application of elementary mathematics, this new type of cryptography is having an enormous effect on the way secret codes are used in business and in government. It is now possible to create simple codes that are completely unbreakable except by the person for whom they are intended.

Top-security messages used in military or business situations have always been sent in some sort of code. But in order for the intended recipient to be able to read (or decipher) the coded message, he must have been given a key to the code in advance. These keys must be changed regularly, at great expense, because a computer search of patterns in coded messages will always enable an intelligent and interested eavesdropper to crack the code.

So it was with both a sense of excitement and fear that computer experts learned a year ago of the con-

"Putting a box around it, I'm afraid, does not make it a unified theory."

ceptual breakthrough achieved by Whitfield Diffie and Martin Hellman of Stanford University. They devised a way to send and receive messages in complete security without the need for any special keys. Their work also made possible forgery-proof computer signatures, so that one could be completely sure the message received really did come from the person whose name was signed to it.

This near miracle was made possible by exploiting special mathematical functions termed "trapdoor" or one-way functions. These functions change one positive integer into another in such a way that one can reverse the computation only by knowing certain special information. They serve as trapdoors in the processing of information: once one has fallen through one of them, there is no way to get back without special help.

Here is how a trapdoor function can provide the basis for a foolproof exchange of secret messages. Each person in a communication group adopts a particular trapdoor function as his signature or coding function. A list of these functions is published in a master directory, so that everyone knows everyone else's trapdoor function. (However, no one but the individual who created it knows the clue to inverting any particular trapdoor function.) To send a message to another person, it must first be changed into a large number by using a standard code (for example, A = 1, . . . Z = 26); then the sender applies the receiver's published coding function to it. The receiver of the message simply

applies his secret decoding algorithm to recover the original message. (An algorithm is a set of well-defined rules for the solution of a problem in a finite number of steps.)

To make sure that the receiver knows who sent the message, the sender could first transform the message in reverse through his own secret code and then translate that message into the receiver's language by using the latter's published function. The receiver untransforms it by using his secret algorithm, and then applies the sender's public function to the answer to recover the original message. If at that point a meaningful message is obtained, the receiver will know who sent it, for no one else could have originally translated it with that particular decoding formula.

The specific implementation of this scheme depended on the development of simple, useful trapdoor functions. One scheme, proposed by Ronald Rivest, Adi Shamir, and Leonard Adleman of the Massachusetts Institute of Technology (MIT), is based on the special properties of prime numbers. Prime numbers are those (like 7, 13, 37) that cannot be factored into the product of two smaller numbers. Numbers that are not prime are called composite; they can always be factored into the product of primes (for example, $35 = 5 \cdot 7$, and $50 = 2 \cdot 5 \cdot 5$).

The important fact about primes and composites that is relevant to cryptography is that computers can rather easily find large primes and verify that a specific number indeed is prime, but they are impossibly slow at trying to find factors of large numbers that are not prime. For example, to test a 130-digit number to determine if it is prime will take only a matter of minutes, while to factor such a number (when it is composite) would take billions of years. Multiplying two large numbers is very simple (for a computer), as is dividing one large number by another. But searching for factors when none is known is essentially impossible.

This situation provides a clue to the strategy behind the trapdoor codes. The MIT researchers proposed a simple coding function using "modular" or "clock" arithmetic based on a very large (130-digit or so) number that is the product of two large prime numbers selected at random. The product of these numbers would be published in the directory of coding functions, but only the creator of the number would know the two factors from which it was created and only he could decode messages sent with that particular trapdoor code.

Other trapdoor codes were also being studied; one involves, for instance, the task of choosing at random a dozen or more 20-digit numbers from a published list of 200 possible numbers and then adding them up. Doing that is easy, but it is a hidden trapdoor; all the computer power on earth could not discover *which* dozen numbers were added up if all one knew was the total.

356

Each trapdoor function depends on the computational intractability of certain inverse problems. Although theoretically each trapdoor code can be broken, none can be carried out in reasonable time even on the fastest computer. The security of the trapdoor is guaranteed by the fact that the inverse problems belong to the class of problems (called NP-complete) whose solution algorithms grow exponentially as the size of the numbers increases. Each of these problems quickly outstrips the power of any computer to search for a solution.

As a result of the trapdoor codes, cryptography will never again be the same. Those who are trying to find a strategy to beat the next guy's code are now faced with the hard rock of mathematical certainty: trapdoor codes are hard to break not just because no one knows how but because mathematically they have been shown to be intractable.

—Lynn Arthur Steen

Mechanical engineering

Automated typing machines that can produce 1,000 words per minute, and the use of alcohols to replace petroleum for energy needs were among the year's leading developments in mechanical engineering.

Typewriters. As the nations of the world become more interdependent, it is conceivable that the UN might want a complete listing of all the citizens of the world. If this list were to be handwritten by one person at the rate of five names per minute during a 40-hour workweek, it would require about 6,000 years to write the four billion names. Alternatively, to accomplish the task in one year in handwritten form would require 6,000 people and could result in a nonuniform end product.

Mechanical writing machines—typewriters—were invented approximately 250 years ago to produce written material faster and of a more uniform quality than could handwriting. However, at the typical mechanical typing speed of 60 words per minute and averaging three words per name, it would still take a single typist about 1,500 years or 1,500 typists one year to create the list of names. One problem that the typing machine created, noise, would be incessant in a room where 1,500 typists are working.

It is apparent that quiet writing machines are needed that can read or be supplied with information and reconstitute it at very high speeds relative to handwriting. For the typing of the world list of names, high speed would represent creation of the list in a month's time. This would require a rate of 100,000 names per minute, 24 hours per day.

Several serious problems are encountered in trying to automate a typewriter to approach such speeds. Electric typewriters have incorporated some improve-

ments relative to the older mechanical instruments to achieve greater speed. For example, in many machines the typewriter carriage no longer moves because its mass offered too much inertia (resistance to changes in motion). The signals from the typist operating the keys or the signals from an automatic reading device such as a scanner are transmitted electrically to the writing element, which selects the correct character and impresses it through a printing-sensitive material onto the paper. The elimination of mechanical linkages between the letter key and the writing element further reduced inertia. Higher typing speeds and a more uniform product are the results. However, the inertia of the writing element in positioning the character and in advancing along the writing line limits such a machine to a maximum of about 180 words per minute, and the noise from the machine is significant. This machine combined with an automated reader would still require 125 years to type the names of all the people in the world.

To break free of the inertia limitation and noise prob-

Letter is formed when tiny ink droplets, 117,000 per second, are directed electrostatically at paper. The machine can print up to 92 characters per second.

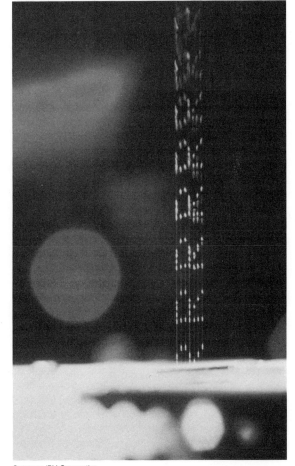

lem, engineers from IBM Corp. developed an entirely different method of writing. It is known as ink-jet printing. Ink is literally sprayed on the paper. The example in the illustration on the preceding page shows a letter being formed by an ink-jet typewriter. While a single ink-jet printer cannot yet create the list of world citizens in one month, by 1978 it was already six times faster than the automated electromechanical typewriter.

An ink-jet creates a character such as a letter of the alphabet by putting an electrical conducting ink under pressure and vibrating the pressure container as the ink is sprayed from a nozzle attached to the container. The pressure in the container produces the ink-jet, and the high-frequency vibration causes the jet to break up into tiny droplets that follow each other toward the paper. Each droplet is selectively charged electrically as it travels past an electrode. It then can be selectively deflected by passing it through an electrostatic field. By proper preprogramming of these fields, the correct letter is formed in a stream of ink drops when a key is pressed on the typewriter.

On an average it takes 1,000 drops to create every letter shown in the example. But because droplets are formed at the rate of 117,000 every second, 92 letters can be formed in that period of time. This results in a writing speed of about 1,000 words per minute, which is eight to ten times faster than what a typist can produce on an electric machine. The ink-jet machines are appearing where high speed or automated typing is required. Because they are quiet, it is conceivable that they may also become popular as office typewriters.

At writing speeds of ten times that of the electric typewriter, the ink-jet machine can reduce the time to produce the four billion names from 6,000 years for the handwritten copy to 12.5 years. This does not meet the goal of one month, but it has moved much closer to it.

Alcohols for energy. The need to find energy alternatives to natural gas and liquid petroleum products is pressing ever harder on the world's population. The most optimistic evaluators of world petroleum resources estimate that there is an adequate supply for 50 years, while the more pessimistic reduce the time period to 25 years.

The possible utilization of alcohols in energy systems that now use liquid and gaseous petroleum products is attracting increased interest for several reasons. During recent months automobiles, gas turbines, steam power plants, and diesel engines have all been operated experimentally with alcohol fuel with reasonable success. In general, success means that the systems develop as much or more power, are equal or better in efficiency, and produce exhaust pollutants in equal or less quantities than when these same systems are operating on petroleum. The technology exists to make alcohols from coal and natural gas and by processing plant life. This latter avenue is particularly true of sugarcane.

Brazil for many years has used alcohol manufactured as a by-product from the sugarcane industry as a blending agent with gasoline to extend its petroleum supply. Recently the nation embarked on a major expansion of its sugarcane supply, to provide marketing flexibility. Thus, if prices are low for sugar, the cane can be processed into alcohol. The increased production of alcohol can also reduce the cost of importing petroleum. (*See* Year in Review: FOOD AND AGRICULTURE: *Agriculture*.)

—Richard K. Pefley

Medical sciences

Major developments during recent months in the medical sciences included new findings in regard to laetrile as a treatment for cancer, the rapid spread among young people of a new strain of influenza, increased understanding of the relationship between the body's immune system and allergic reactions, and the outbreak of an infection in horses that greatly reduces the breeding efficiency of mares.

General medicine

Cancer was the target of considerable research and experimentation by medical scientists during the past year as they sought to develop more effective methods of diagnosis, prevention, and treatment. Other important developments included the outbreak of a new strain of influenza, the successful testing of a vaccine against streptococcal pneumonia, and the first effective drug therapy for a life-threatening viral disease.

Cancer research. For physicians and public alike the year 1977 seemed for, of, and about cancer. The magnitude of the problem was shown when an estimated 700,000 new cases of cancer were predicted in 1978 for the United States alone. Physicians were deluged by new diagnostic techniques, new treatments, and an almost endless (and confusing) array of chemotherapeutic agents. The specialty of oncology, embracing those physicians who treat only cancer, was not only well-established and increasing in size but most importantly was proving that its approach of treating malignancies with surgery, radiation, and chemotherapy—singly or in various combinations—could effectively increase the survival rate for many patients.

The psychosocial and the nutritional aspects of cancer received new and appropriate study and emphasis. Research efforts by universities and institutes continued relentlessly in an attempt to understand better the basic structure and biochemistry of the disease. Gradually, as awareness developed that more emphasis should be placed on the prevention of cancer rather than on its diagnosis and treatment, many funding agencies redirected their allocations accordingly.

In general, the overall incidence of cancer has decreased slightly in the past 25 years. Its incidence has decreased substantially for malignancies of the stomach, uterus, rectum, and esophagus. Between the ages of 20 and 40 cancer is three times as common in women as men, but between 60 and 80 years more men are afflicted. The death rate from cancer in males rose during the period, chiefly because of lung cancer. In 1950 there were 18 deaths per 100,000 from lung cancer in men; by 1975 this figure had risen to 53 deaths per 100,000. In women the death rate declined by 8% for blacks and 10% for whites. This was due mainly to a considerable decline in deaths from cancer of the uterus, attributed to the increased use of Pap tests and regular examinations. However, the lung cancer rate for women more than tripled, from 4 per 100,000 in 1950 to 13 in 1975.

In comparison with other countries, the U.S. in 1972–73 ranked 22nd in incidence of male cancer and 21st for female cancer. Scotland ranked first for male cancer with 205 deaths per 100,000; The Netherlands was first for female cancer with 160 deaths per 100,000.

Among the major developments during the past year were the continuing controversy concerning the drug laetrile; a general consensus about the use of mammography; the increasing efficacy of chemotherapy for some tumors; and the rapidly increasing importance of the U.S. Food and Drug Administration (FDA) in regulating drugs, food additives, and medical devices.

Laetrile. To its more than 75,000 American users in 1977 laetrile, an extract from apricot pits, offered hope for the improvement or cure of their cancer. The term laetrile may be confusing because it refers to a specific chemical compound but is also used interchangeably with amygdalin, nitriloside, and vitamin B-17. Although all these can be extracted from the seeds and kernels of most fruits, biochemically important differences are present and should be noted.

Research scientist sits in 1.5-ton magnet that is part of a fonar, a device designed to detect cancer cells because they emit radio signals different from those emitted by healthy cells.

Laboratory worker in Tijuana, Mexico, extracts amber-colored laetrile from apricot pits. Each year thousands of Americans with cancer cross the border into Tijuana for injections of laetrile.

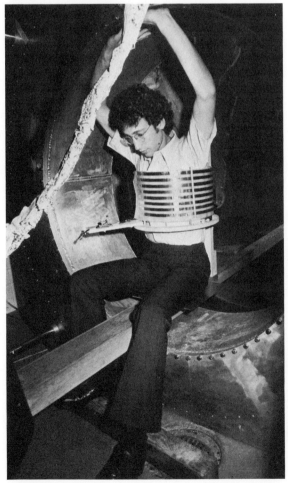

Wide World

Lester Sloan—*Newsweek*

Amygdalin was first isolated in 1830 from bitter almonds, the name being derived from amygdala, the Greek word for almonds. Amygdalin occurs naturally in several thousand plants, particularly in the seeds of apricots, peaches, cranberries, gooseberries, lima beans, cherries, and nectarines, and in such grasses as corn, sorghum, and millet. Chemically it is composed of two glucose molecules and one molecule of mandelonitrile, a chemical in which hydrogen cyanide is combined with benzaldehyde. The naturally occurring combinations of cyanide and glucose that form compounds are termed cyanogenetic glucosides (also called cyanophoric glucosides).

Vitamin B-17 is defined as a group of water-soluble, sugary compounds found in many plants. They generally are cyanogenetic glucosides but may not be pure amygdalin or laetrile. Sometimes, vitamin B-17 is used synonymously for laetrile. Nitriloside is a term proposed by Ernst T. Krebs, Jr., for all cyanogenetic glucosides of dietary significance. Laetrile, which was isolated, named, and described by Krebs in 1952, has only one glucose molecule attached to the mandelonitrile radical. It is obtained by the hydrolysis and oxidation of amygdalin.

In all these substances (amygdalin, laetrile, nitriloside, and vitamin B-17) the common and significant reaction is their breakdown into glucose, benzaldehyde, and hydrogen cyanide. According to the proponents of laetrile for cancer treatment, it is the release of hydrogen cyanide that selectively kills tumor cells.

The therapeutic benefits of laetrile for cancer were first advanced by Ernst T. Krebs, Sr., a California physi-

cian, and his son, Ernst T. Krebs, Jr., a biochemist. According to the Krebses' theory, laetrile is effective against the more than 150 different types of cancer because of the unitarian theory of cancer etiology. This thesis, proposed by John Beard (1902), states that all cancer cells are derived from a particular cell, the trophoblast, normally found during embryonic and fetal development. Trophoblastic multiplication beyond fetal life is stopped by the enzyme chymotrypsin, which normally occurs in the pancreas. According to Beard, the growth of a trophoblast except during pregnancy is cancer. If there is an adequate amount of chymotrypsin, the trophoblast will be destroyed and no cancer will result. If there is a deficiency of chymotrypsin, cancer occurs. This unconventional theory of cancer is supported by few, if any, other biologists.

According to the Krebses, laetrile is split by an en-

Supporters of laetrile (right) pack Indiana statehouse during vote by the legislature to legalize use of the substance. Press conference at Memorial Sloan-Kettering Cancer Center (below) revealed that tests had proven laetrile ineffective as a tumor treatment.

(Top) Rob Lewis; (bottom) courtesy, Memorial Sloan-Kettering Cancer Center and *The Sciences*, Jan. 1978

zyme, beta-glucosidase, into glucose and mandeloni-trile. The latter molecule then decomposes into benz-aldehyde and hydrogen cyanide. The released cyanide kills the cancer cells but does not destroy normal tissue because in the latter there is another enzyme, rhoda-nese, which converts cyanide into a less toxic sub-stance, thiocyanate. The Krebses presumed that can-cer tissue is rich in beta-glucosidase and that cyanide is selectively released into the cancer cells.

Several flaws exist in this hypothesis, according to many biochemists. Numerous investigations have failed to show any increased amount of beta-glucosi-dase in tumor tissues compared with other organs such as the liver and kidney; and no evidence exists that rhodanese is present in appreciably greater amounts in normal than in tumor tissues.

When these and other biochemical objections to the hypothesis of laetrile action were raised, the Krebses proposed a new theory, namely that laetrile is a vitamin and its deficiency can cause cancer. Thus, the ab-sence of vitamin B-17 would allow the trophoblastic cells to grow, and only by taking extra amounts of vitamin B-17 could cancer be prevented. Biologically, a vitamin is defined as a nutritional component of or-ganic composition required in small amounts for the health and well-being of the organism. A vitamin is not utilized primarily to supply energy or as a source of structural tissue, but it is required for necessary physio-logical processes within the organism. The vitamin cannot be synthesized by the organism and must be supplied from an external source. When the deficiency of a vitamin exists, certain well-defined diseases occur. These include scurvy, beriberi, pellagra, and rickets. They are cured by the addition of the appropriate vita-min.

Laetrile, amygdalin, nitriloside, and vitamin B-17 do not satisfy any of the above criteria for vitamins. How-ever, labeling the extract of apricot pits as vitamin B-17 or simply BEE-17 did occasion the selling of these substances in many health food stores.

The early use of laetrile has a confusing history, but as early as 1932 Krebs, Sr., had made amygdalin avail-able to researchers and physicians in the U.S. and elsewhere as a treatment for malignant tumors. Subse-quently he wrote that his apricot extract was so toxic that he and his colleagues who were experimenting with him were reluctant to continue its use, except in dire circumstances. It was this toxicity problem that prompted Krebs, Jr., to seek to improve his father's work. In 1952 he claimed to have purified laetrile so that it was sufficiently safe for parenteral use. In a pamphlet in 1965 it was stated that "laetrile does not palliate, it acts chemically to kill the cancer cell selec-tively . . . ."

The proponents of laetrile have relied heavily on popular journalism, radio, television, health organiza-tions, and word-of-mouth to spread their claims that laetrile is a safe and effective anti-cancer drug. There is no doubt about the honesty and sincerity of those patients and relatives testifying for laetrile, but many of the positive experiences they have reported can be accounted for by explanations other than the claimed effectiveness of the drug. Undoubtedly many beneficial responses are due to the placebo effect of any medica-tion given to a patient desperately seeking relief or cure; also, based on a scrutiny of their records, some of the patients never had cancers, and in others the vagaries of cancer itself may have caused a temporary or even permanent cure. Finally, it must be remem-bered that in many cases laetrile had no effect; the patient worsened and died.

Considerable controversy has occurred as to wheth-er laetrile is a "new drug" in the legal sense. If so, it is subject to certain legal requirements before its sale, distribution, and general usage. If not, then it must be generally recognized by qualified experts as an estab-lished safe and effective (cancer) drug. For this, two criteria must be satisfied: (1) controlled clinical investi-gations should exist showing the safety and efficacy by published reports in the scientific literature; (2) recog-nized experts should agree that it is safe and effective. As of early 1978, no adequate or well-controlled stud-ies had been published about the clinical investigation of laetrile.

Chemical diagrams represent (top) amygdalin and (bottom) laetrile.

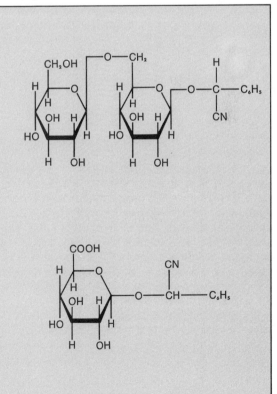

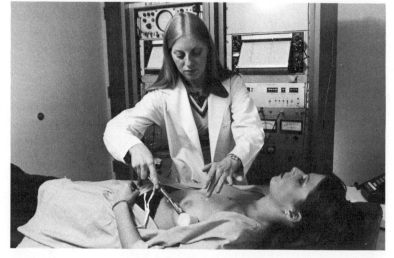

Woman is examined for breast cancer with microwave detector. Because of its fast rate of growth and increased blood supply a tumor is hotter than normal tissue and thus emits more radiant energy, including microwaves. Sensitive antennas on the device are able to detect the location of a tumor emitting microwaves up to 10 cm (4 in) below the skin's surface.

The safety of any "new drug" must have ". . . adequate tests by all methods reasonably applicable." Previous tests for the safety of laetrile failed to show that amygdalin was non-toxic, particularly when given orally. When any of the cyanogenic glucosides are taken by mouth, the release of hydrogen cyanide occurs in the intestine. Cyanide is extremely poisonous and may be fatal. Cases of cyanide poisoning and death in humans from eating apricot pits and taking laetrile are well documented.

There have been many controlled and extensive animal test studies to evaluate laetrile at various research centers. The tests were done on a variety of both induced and spontaneously occurring tumors, this being the scientifically accepted way to test anti-cancer properties of drugs. Among those conducting such studies have been the U.S. National Cancer Institute, Memorial Sloan-Kettering Cancer Center, the Catholic Medical Center, and Arthur D. Little, Inc. In none of these was there acceptable evidence that growth of the primary tumor or metastatic spread of the malignancy to other parts of the body was appreciably affected by the administration of laetrile.

Laetrile's proponents have sought to give the impression that it is used throughout the world but that in the U.S. there are overly restrictive drug laws that prevent it from being marketed. There is no evidence of such international recognition for the use of the drug. It has been banned in Mexico, where most of it is being produced. Similarly its use for cancer patients is not approved in Switzerland, the United Kingdom, Belgium, Italy, West Germany, France, Korea, the Philippines, Japan, South Africa, Taiwan, Hong Kong, India, and many other countries. Because of public demand, however, 14 states in the U.S. legalized the sale and use of laetrile despite the lack of any scientific evidence regarding its scientific benefits. It was legalized for cancer patients at their request after they signed written informed consents.

A careful and extensive hearing was held by the U.S. Department of Health, Education, and Welfare (HEW), in Kansas City, Mo., in May 1977. The FDA commissioner, Donald Kennedy, concluded that: (1) Neither laetrile nor any other drug called by its various interchangeable terms is recognized to be safe and effective for any therapeutic use. (2) Animal studies conducted to date have failed to demonstrate any anticancer activity by these substances. (3) Laetrile is not in general use as cancer therapy anywhere in the world. (4) There is no evidence that B-17 is a vitamin.

But the laetrile cult persists. At the year's end U.S. Federal District Court Judge Luther Bohanon issued a permanent injunction lifting all federal restrictions against the use and importation of laetrile by cancer patients. This was the result of a much-publicized and emotional court struggle initiated by Glen Rutherford, who believed that laetrile had helped him in his 1971 battle with rectal cancer. Also HEW began a nationwide study to obtain a statistical analysis of those who had received laetrile.

Mammography. For many years the early and accurate diagnosis of breast tumors has been of utmost importance. Breast cancer is the most common malignancy in women. About 7%, or 1 of every 13 women, will develop it. In 1978 in the U.S. there will be 91,000 (estimated) new cases of breast cancer with approximately 34,000 deaths.

If the malignancy is detected at an early stage, there is an excellent chance to achieve a full cure. The ten-year survival rate for cancer of the breast treated surgically when the lesion is less than 1 cm is 97.1%. When the tumor becomes palpable but lymph nodes are not involved, the ten-year survival rate is 70.2%, and when metastasis (spread) to the lymph nodes is present the ten-year survival rate is 38.4%.

The time-honored method for the diagnosis of breast tumors has been by history and physical diagnosis—inspection of the breast, its careful palpation, and, oc-

362

casionally, transillumination if the breast mass feels cystic. Recently many different and new approaches have been utilized, chief among which are breast X-rays (mammography or xerography) and thermography. The latter method is neither as fully developed nor as accurate for small lesions as mammography. In addition, thermography does not localize breast tumors for biopsy, and there are appreciable numbers of patients diagnosed incorrectly. However, when thermography indicates an abnormal condition, it is at least 15 times more likely that a breast cancer is present than if there were no such indication. Its main advantages are as a screening method because it does not expose a patient to potentially harmful X-rays.

In 1926, at Rochester (N.Y.) Memorial Hospital, Stafford L. Warren was attempting to standardize X-ray techniques for study of the thoracic aorta. In oblique views he noticed that the breast was silhouetted. During examination with a fluoroscope he found that by putting the patient's arm over her head he could obtain a view that showed the entire breast and the axillary contents. Warren subsequently made further studies using a variety of radiographic techniques and compared these with examination of specimens from operating rooms and the anatomy laboratories. He then could correlate documented pathological changes in the breast with the X-ray appearance.

Warren's early efforts were not taken seriously by his colleagues until from his radiographs he made several diagnoses of very small tumors not detected by physical examination. His activities were supported by numerous patient referrals from George Pack of Memorial Hospital in New York.

Although Warren's work stimulated interest in breast radiography during the 1920s and 1930s, interest in mammography then gradually diminished. This was due to erratic results because of the inferior quality of the radiographs. The subject was attacked with renewed vigor in the 1950s and 1960s. Gradually an awareness developed of the importance of high-quality, technically accurate radiographs to visualize the various anatomic features of the breast: the fat, the lymphatic vessels, the glandular tissue, and the ductal system. After much trial and experimentation a method of soft-tissue radiography was developed using high-milliamperage and low-kilovoltage techniques.

Most radiologists produce mammograms by xeroradiography. This is a process in which X-rays form an electrostatic image on a photoconductive insulating medium; the charged image areas attract and hold a fine powder, and this powder image is transferred to paper and fused there by heat. This technique provides high resolution and permits identification of small structures. All structures of the breast can be recorded

Patient prepares to immerse hands in ice water (left), a first step in detecting breast cancer without undergoing the radiation exposure of mammography. Afterward, a probe scans the patient's breasts (right) for spots that remain hotter than other tissue; these are possible sites of malignancies.

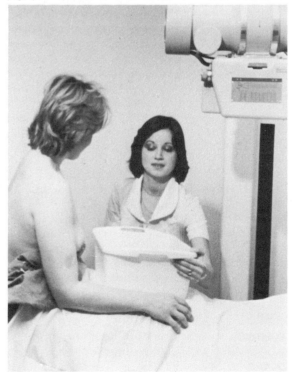
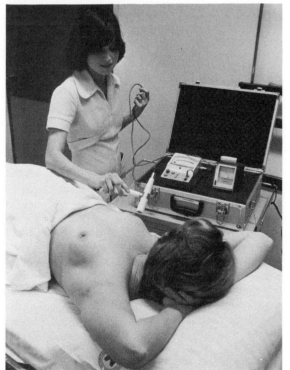

Courtesy, Memorial Sloan-Kettering Cancer Center

Guy Gillette

in good detail on one image as compared with conventional film mammography, where proper exposure of the subareolar area exempts visualization of the deeper structures. Finally, xeroradiograms are more easily inspected without the requirement of special viewing equipment.

After it was recognized that mammography was a reliable method for diagnosing the presence of breast tumors, the possibility that it might cause harmful radiation exposure demanded further study. John C. Bailar III, editor of the *Journal* of the National Cancer Institute, wrote, "I am very concerned by the fact that the radiation required by mammography will eventually cause many deaths from breast cancer—the very disease we want to detect and treat."

The radiation exposure problem of mammography arose chiefly from a 1972 National Academy of Sciences report. It concluded that for each rad (R) delivered to the breast there was a risk of inducing six new breast cancers per million women after a ten-year latency period. (1R=100 ergs absorbed per gram of body tissue.) Several years ago the median X-ray dosage given at various institutions during a mammogram was 2.7 R. The surface exposure per image has since been decreased to a median of 1.2 R. It is hoped that with further development the amount of radiation needed will continue to decrease.

Most of the problems about mammography were resolved in 1977 after a study by the National Breast Cancer Detection Demonstration Project, a commission of the National Cancer Institute. Twenty-seven research centers found more than 2,500 patients with unsuspected breast cancer in the 280,000 women receiving mammograms. About 45% were found by this procedure alone, and 30% were in women under 50. The overwhelming majority were in the early, highly curable stages. According to James T. DeLuca, chief of radiology at Community Hospital, Glen Cove, N.Y.: "There are no other reliable tests that will permit so much information at so high an accuracy rate (90%) or allow detection of cancer in its infancy state."

As a result of its screening program the National Cancer Institute recommended that for women showing no evidence of breast cancer (1) mammography should be used to screen those aged 50 and over for breast cancer; (2) mammography should be used for those aged 40–49 only if they have had previous breast cancer or if they have a mother or sister who has had cancer; and (3) mammography at an earlier age (35–39) should be restricted to those with a history of breast cancer.

Chemotherapy for testicular tumors. Although chemotherapy, treatment with drugs, may be thought of as a relatively new and undeveloped mode in treating cancer, particularly in comparison with surgery and radiation, its value has been established with several tumors. Prior to chemotherapy the overall mortality of

Hodgkin's disease, a type of lymphoma, was approximately 90% when involvement of more than one part of the body had occurred. At the present time, chemotherapy has proven so successful that complete remission for more than ten years can be obtained in about 40% of the patients.

Similar results have also been shown for a type of lymphoma known as histiocytic lymphoma. Using a combination of four or more chemotherapeutic agents, physicians have increased the five-year survival rate of patients with this malignancy from essentially zero to approximately 35%.

In 1977 a dramatic breakthrough was announced in the treatment of testicular tumors using a combination of chemotherapeutic agents and various other treatment. Testicular tumors are relatively rare, accounting for only 0.5–1% of all malignancies in men. However, in the 15–34 age group they are comparatively common, exceeded only by leukemia, Hodgkin's disease, and brain tumors, and 40% of them are fatal. There are several histological types of testicular tumors, the most prevalent being the seminoma, with others including the teratocarcinoma, the embryonal cell, the choriocarcinoma, and mixtures of these.

As described by Robert B. Goldey, chief of the Solid Tumor Service at Memorial Hospital for Cancer and Allied Diseases in New York City, the new treatment involved the use of three chemotherapeutic agents, vincristine sulfate, actinomycin D, and bleomycin. In all instances, the men had been castrated and had disseminated disease. The chemotherapeutic agents caused frequent complications, including transient weight loss, loss of hair, sores in the mouth, rashes, and slight kidney damage. In another treatment program three drugs were used, but cisplatinum diamminedichloride was added. This last drug causes damage to the kidneys, and therefore, additional fluid replacement and the giving of a diuretic (Mannitol) were utilized during its administration. Other drugs were subsequently added (cyclophosphamide and doxorubicin hydrochloride) with variations also in dosage and scheduling. By early 1978 physicians estimated that between 90% and 100% of those with nonseminomatous tumors of the testicle had responded to one or more of these chemotherapeutic regimens with occasional side effects as noted.

A similar study by Lawrence H. Einhorn at the Indiana University Medical Center reported similar encouraging results in the treatment of 47 patients. According to Einhorn, his chemotherapy regimen requires at least two years. The common side effects are loss of hair, sores in the mouth, decline in weight, muscle aches, lowering of the white blood cell counts, and reversible damage to the kidney. However, after several courses of chemotherapy, all the patients regained their hair and their weight and were back in school or at work full time.

Liver tumors and oral contraceptives. Tumors of the liver are rare. During the past decade, however, there has been a definite increase in the incidence of benign liver tumors (adenomas). Most of these have appeared in women of child-bearing age who have taken oral contraceptives. Thus, a relationship between such contraceptives and the development of these tumors is strongly suggested. In a national survey initiated by the National Cancer Advisory Board such an association was noted, and tumors were found to have occurred in an estimated 1,000 women. No such increase in tumors was found in males.

Most often these tumors were an incidental finding at the time of an abdominal operation for other reasons, but some tumors bled spontaneously and required surgical intervention. In many instances the tumors were multiple.

Although the explanation for the tumor growth was not established as of early 1978, it was known that oral contraceptives contain steroid sex hormones (progesterone and estrogen) that can produce functional and structural changes in liver cells. According to Stanley Goldfarb, a pathologist at the University of Wisconsin Medical School, "Especially noteworthy in this regard is the observation that steroid sex hormones induce high levels of enzymes in the liver that alter the chemical structure of drugs. They reduce the efficiency of biliary excretion of certain drugs. . . . This combination of effects could conceivably induce the formation and retention of compounds, derived from the sex steroids themselves or from some other drug, that might cause the development of liver tumors."

Infectious diseases. A new strain of influenza, termed Russian flu because it was first detected in the Soviet Union, reached near-epidemic proportions in some parts of the U.S. early in 1978. It closely resembled the strain that had been prevalent throughout the world from 1947 to 1957, and, therefore, most people older than their early 20s had at least a partial immunity to it. It did, however affect many young people and virtually shut down several college campuses for brief periods. The disease was relatively mild, and many of those afflicted with it recovered in about four days. At the same time, the more severe A/Texas and A/Victoria influenzas affected many people of all ages during the winter of 1977–78.

Results of a vaccine test on 77 children and young adults, administered by medical scientists at the University of California at San Francisco, were revealed in 1977. All of the test subjects had nonfunctioning spleens. This made them particularly vulnerable to streptococcal pneumonia, a disease that kills about 25,000 persons in the U.S. each year. Over a period of about two years none of the 77 contracted pneumonia, compared with 8 from a closely matched control group of 106 who did.

The study added further support to earlier tests that had revealed vaccines to be 80% effective on 14,900 U.S. and 12,000 South American adults. It also was the first to show that such vaccines are safe for children over two years of age.

The vaccines contain molecules of polysaccharides, complex sugars which are found on the outer membranes of pneumococcus bacteria. The polysaccharides are later "remembered" by the body's immune system if introduced with bacteria, enabling the body to fight off the microbes. The success of the vaccines is particularly significant because bacteria have recently

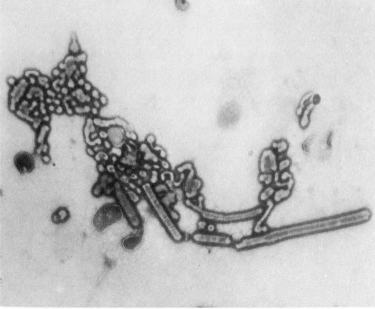

Electron micrograph magnified 65,800 times reveals influenza virus designated A/USSR/77 because it first appeared in the Soviet Union. Similar to the virus that was dominant throughout the world from 1947 to 1957, the relatively mild strain mostly affected young people.

Courtesy, Tommie Sue Tralka, National Cancer Institute, National Institutes of Health

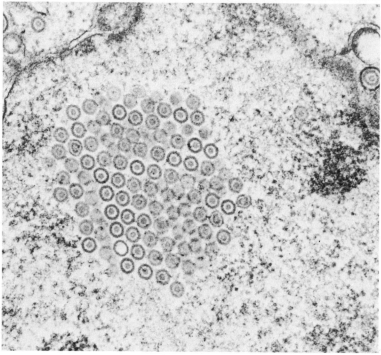

Herpes Type II virus, which causes the usually fatal herpes encephalitis, can be seen as a cluster of circles in photo-micrograph magnified 73,200 times. During the year researchers announced that they had developed a drug that could combat the virus; this was the first successful chemical therapy of a life-threatening viral disease.

been evolving strains that are resistant to antibiotics. (*See* Feature Article: THE MICROBES FIGHT BACK.)

In August a team of investigators headed by Charles A. Alford and Richard J. Whitby of the University of Alabama Medical Center announced the first successful drug therapy of a life-threatening viral disease. According to their test results as many as 90% of patients with the usually fatal disease herpes encephalitis can be cured with the drug arabinosyladenine, also called adenine arabinoside (ara-A) and given the trade name Vira-A by its manufacturer.

In the tests the investigators identified 28 patients with herpes encephalitis, an infection characterized by severe inflammation of the brain and for which there had been no effective treatment. Eighteen received ara-A and ten a placebo. Of the latter ten, seven (70%) died, while there were only five deaths (28%) among the 18 taking the drug. Furthermore, only one of the ten who took the drug before lapsing into a coma died.

Ara-A had previously been demonstrated to be effective against two other herpes virus diseases, chicken pox and herpes zoster (shingles). Its success gave support to the controversial concept that drug therapy can be effective against viruses without killing an unacceptably large number of host cells. As of early 1978, however, ara-A remained limited in its applicability because it must be given intravenously continuously.

Early in 1977 two microbiologists at the U.S. Center for Disease Control announced that they had isolated the bacterium responsible for the July 1976 outbreak of Legionnaires' Disease in Philadelphia. Further study revealed that the microbe had been involved in several earlier outbreaks, among them a pneumonia epidemic at St. Elizabeths Hospital in Washington, D.C., in 1965. There were also cases of the disease reported from various parts of the U.S. in 1977. Although studies continued, researchers as of early 1978 had not yet been able to determine precisely the habits of the bacterium or the conditions under which it strikes. (*See* Feature Article: LEGIONNAIRES' DISEASE: STALKING A KILLER EPIDEMIC.)

In December 1977 the World Health Organization announced that variola major, the most virulent form of smallpox, had been eradicated throughout the world. The last known case of the disease had occurred in October 1975 in Bangladesh. The virus also has not been detected in any animals. Variola minor, a less severe form of the disease, still officially exists, but the last reported case was in October 1977 in Somalia.

Education. A noteworthy development was the increasing enrollment in U.S. medical schools. The total in 1976–77 was 58,266 compared with 33,423 in 1966–67. Of the students 22.4% were women, an increase of 2% from a year earlier. Minority groups increased their representation from 4,595 in 1975–76 to 4,841 in 1976–77, of whom 3,570 were blacks.

Continuing medical education courses increased in number as more and more states and medical societies required physicians to attend them in order to gain renewals of their licenses and memberships. In 1975–76 the number of such courses offered in the U.S. was 4,862; in 1976–77 it was 5,800, and the estimate for 1977–78 was 7,330.

—C. Frederick Kittle

Adapted from *American Scientist*, Vol. 64, p. 158, March–April, 1976, © by Sigma Xi, The Scientific Research Society of North America

Allergy research

After many years of case-by-case diagnoses and treatment of allergic diseases, the science of allergy was given gigantic impetus in 1967 by the identification of a protein in blood serum, immunoglobulin E (IgE), as the substance responsible for the allergic reaction in man. Since then literally thousands of scientific articles have appeared, leading to a clearer understanding of the chemical and molecular biologic reactions of allergy, reactions previously believed to be due to emotional or other vague causes. As a result, scientists now can ascribe allergic reactions such as hay fever, asthma, eczema, hives, and allergic shock (anaphylaxis) to the same fundamental mechanism, the immunologic release of histamine.

Characteristics of an allergic reaction. The sequence of events in the induction of an allergic reaction is as follows. In a genetically susceptible individual, exposure (by ingestion, injection, inhalation, or contact) to a sensitizing allergen (such as pollens, dust, molds, insects, chemicals, etc.) results in the production of specific antibodies of the IgE class that are able to react with some part of the allergen. Unlike other antibodies, IgE does not protect man from infection. (However, the author and others have suggested that IgE does play a protective role against parasites such as worms and insects. The evidence for this idea is more convincing in animal studies than in man.)

One of the hallmarks of an allergic reaction is its rapidity. The time between inhaling some pollen granules and sneezing is only a few seconds. The reason the reaction is so rapid is that the pollen allergen does not have to seek out its specific IgE antibody in the bloodstream. That antibody is already sitting on the mast cell surface in the mucous membrane in the nose waiting for the next encounter with the pollen. When

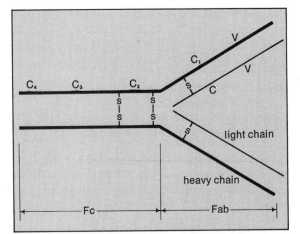

Figure 1. Schematic structure of a molecule of immunoglobulin E, the protein in the blood serum that causes the allergic reaction in man. When a allergen touches nasal mucus, one or more proteins are dissolved off the allergen surface and bind to the Fab ends of IgE molecules, causing a rapid allergic reaction. Other biologic functions are performed by the Fc end. V and C represent, respectively, variable and constant domains of the heavy chain. s–s indicates sulfhydryl bonds linking the chains.

the pollen granule touches the nasal mucus, one or more proteins are dissolved off the pollen surface and bind to the Fab ends (the antibody fractions) of IgE molecules (Fig. 1). This triggers the release of histamine, which is stored in granules in the mast cells in the tissues and in the basophil leukocytes (colorless nucleated cells) in the bloodstream (Fig. 2). The histamine reacts predominantly on smooth muscle and capillaries, producing dilation of blood vessels and the leakage of fluid into the tissues—the characteristic redness and swelling of the allergic reaction.

Figure 2. When allergen proteins bind to the Fab ends of IgE molecules (Figure 1), this causes the release of histamine stored in granules in mast cells and in leukocytes in the bloodstream. The effect of the histamine on smooth muscle and capillaries produces the allergic reaction.

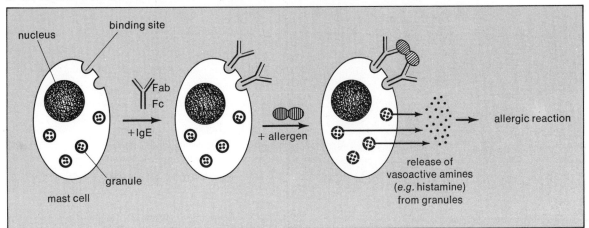

Adapted from *American Scientist*, Vol. 64, p. 159, March –April, 1976, © by Sigma Xi, The Scientific Research Society of North America

If a little histamine is injected into the skin, it will duplicate the natural local allergic reaction, which looks just like a mosquito bite. In fact, it itches just like a mosquito bite, and that is another characteristic of most allergic reactions. The mosquito bite response is also a reaction mediated by IgE.

Antihistamines relieve allergy symptoms but not because they prevent the allergic reaction or the release of histamine. All of the reactions described above occur even if one has taken an adequate dose of an antihistamine. Instead, the antihistamine works by competing with histamine at the binding site. Antihistamines prevent some of the released histamine from getting to the vascular, bronchiole, and smooth muscle sites where the reactions are set off.

Although histamine was identified as the primary "mediator" of the allergic reaction, other symptoms, especially less rapid responses, could not be explained by histamine alone. As a result, researchers isolated and described several other mediators that participate in certain aspects of allergic reactions. For example, SRS-A is a slow-reacting substance that is associated with anaphylaxis and also contributes to a longer lasting bronchospasm in asthma; and kinins (polypeptides that cause contraction of isolated smooth muscles and increased permeability of capillaries) are released in acute allergic reactions.

Physician uses seven-applicator device to put antigens on a patient's arm before pricking it during a skin test for allergies.

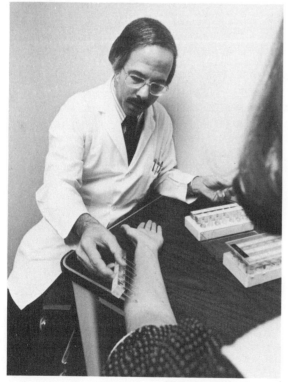

All individuals produce some IgE, but only those who spontaneously become sensitized to ubiquitous substances in minute amounts are classified as allergics. In childhood almost 20% of the population is found to be allergic, whereas in adults the incidence of allergy is less than 10%.

A technique to measure accurately the minute amounts of IgE in blood serum has permitted the developmental and genetic studies discussed below. Recently, a new and simpler method reported from Sweden can allow almost any laboratory to provide accurate assessments of the quantities of IgE in serum. The measurement of specific antibody IgE against various allergens was being improved and may one day replace skin testing. In 1978 it was being used to standardize allergen extracts for use in the treatment of allergy.

Genetic and environmental influences. While the observation that allergy is inherited was made as early as 1872, the number of variables contributing to its expression made it virtually impossible to discern the mode of inheritance. Quantitative analysis of individual aspects of allergy such as serum IgE levels, number of basophil or eosinophil blood cells, or the capacity to respond vigorously to certain allergens, called "Immune response" or "Ir genes," contributed to further understanding. The inheritance of any one of the allergic diseases thus appears to be dependent upon many different genes and is therefore termed polygenic.

Childhood developmental patterns of IgE reveal that, in general, serum IgE levels are higher in allergic individuals and that allergic people are characterized by the ability to react to very small amounts of antigens (substances that stimulate the production of antibodies) and, once having responded, to persist or maintain that ability for prolonged periods. During recent months linkages or genetic connections to other characteristics have been sought by researchers in several laboratories, especially at Stanford and Harvard universities.

With the publication of the amino-acid sequence of the heavy chain of IgE, the basic structure of IgE could be compared with those of other globulins, and the various functions of the IgE molecule could be located on the chain. This led to new and productive studies of small peptides, which are discussed below.

In the late 1930s it was stated that environmental modifications could alter the expected incidence of allergic diseases in highly allergic families. This became a hotly debated topic since opinions were based solely on clinical observations. However, a recently completed study confirmed that environmental controls such as strict breast feeding with reduced intake of cow's milk by the mother, and diet and living areas with low tendencies to induce allergic reactions did indeed result in a lower incidence of allergic symptoms in a baby during the first two years of life. They did not, however, significantly lower the baby's serum IgE levels (genetically controlled) compared with those of the control group. The use of various kinds of filters for cleaning the air of dust, mold spores, and pollen did not prove as useful in preventing allergic reactions as was expected.

The immune system. Until recently it was thought that there were two separate parts to the immune system, the humoral and the cellular. The humoral immune system consisted of five different immunoglobulins, each responsible for some aspect of immunity to bacterial infections. The cellular immune system was known to be composed of three kinds of cells: those that processed antigens, those that produced (humoral) antibodies called plasma cells, and those responsible for viral immunity and graft rejection. But through the work of numerous investigators, scientists were beginning to understand that there was a single but much more complex immune system, with the cellular and humoral components completely interwoven with thymus-derived T cells.

The understanding of this integrated, single immune system brought about an awareness of new relationships between very different immune diseases. Thus, the allergic diseases seem to be related to immunodeficiency diseases, such as Bruton's agammaglobulinemia, DiGeorge's syndrome or thymic hypoplasia, and the Wiskott-Aldrich syndrome. An approach to therapy of both the allergic and immunodeficiency diseases may well derive from awareness of the newly described T cells, which can act as suppressors. Viewed in this new way, one might describe the development of an allergy as a failure of the activation of the appropriate suppressor cell (the cell that would tell a B, bone-marrow-derived cell not to make any more IgE). The immunodeficiency disorder, Bruton's agammaglobulinemia, instead of being the absence of certain immunoglobulin-producing cells, is now believed to be a failure to turn on or activate cells that are, in fact, present in the patient.

Treatment. The awareness of the various cells involved in the immune system suggests completely new approaches to the therapy of allergy. The present injection therapy utilizes fluid extracts of the whole pollen to which the patient is allergic. After six months to two years of injections of this fluid once or twice a week there may be some symptomatic improvement. Reexamining injection therapy in the light of new knowledge suggests that the allergen extracts exert their effects through cell receptors and thereby modulate the IgE and other immune responses. This idea produced a variety of research approaches such as fractionation of the components of extracts, a search for haptenes (small parts of the allergens), and synthesis of "active" sites of allergens. These and other efforts are designed to inhibit the specific IgE response to each natural allergen, thus preventing the allergic disease.

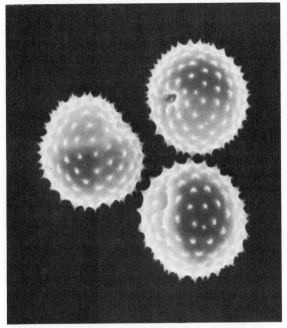

Pollen of western ragweed, magnified 1,000 times in the photomicrograph, is among the most common causes of allergic reactions.

In the realm of drug treatment, to the old standbys of ephedrine, epinephrine, theophylline, and antihistamines have been added, for severe asthma, inhaled cromolyn and an inhaled steroid that is remarkably effective in the lungs without any of the undesirable side effects of injected or oral steroids. (Mild side effects include weight gain, acne, and emotional changes. More severe side effects, after more prolonged usage, include steroid diabetes, eye damage, depressed resistance to infection, gastric ulcers, and osteoporosis. In children steroids can cause severe growth retardation.) In addition, a series of new orally effective drugs derived from isoproterenol recently became available, and newer, even more effective ones were under development. With the large number and variety of medications from which to select it is, therefore, the rare patient who cannot be given significant relief today.

All of the above medications treat the symptoms rather than the underlying allergic disease. But as the immunology of allergy has become understood new research approaches to therapy have been opened. For example, a scientist in Birmingham, England, in an effort to find a general therapy, was searching for a small peptide that would block the "trigger site" so that the message to release histamine would effectively be blocked irrespective of the offending allergen. In an analogous approach the author reported that a synthetic peptide composed of five amino acids had the ability to inhibit a passively transferred allergic reaction in the human skin. This pentapeptide was undergoing extensive animal and tissue culture cell studies prior to

369

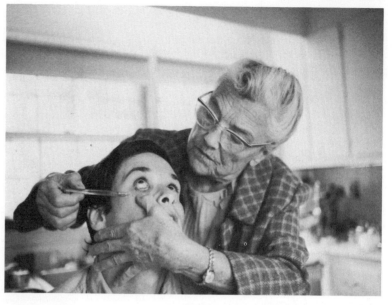

Physician puts a drop of diluted pollen extract into a patient's eye every five minutes, doubling the strength until the first signs of redness and itchiness appear. In this way she determines the correct dosage for the patient.

human trials. Its mechanism of action is not fully understood, but it has a measurable affinity for the same binding site on the mast cell and basophil as does IgE. This observation provides a research approach to the treatment of allergic diseases, which, if successful, would eliminate the need for desensitizing each individual sensitivity.

Even more esoteric ideas were being examined, in the area of what could be termed "genetic engineering." An example of these would be the insertion of a gene or genes that control total IgE production so that a person who produces large amounts of IgE would no longer do so.

—Robert N. Hamburger

Dentistry

During the year the dental profession in the U.S. continued its strong opposition to attempts by so-called denturists (dental laboratory personnel who make dentures for patients without the supervision of a dentist) to legalize their activities. At its annual session in October 1977 at Miami Beach, Fla., the American Dental Association (ADA) reaffirmed its position that denture treatment is and should be provided only by licensed dentists. "Only an individual with the education and experience of a licensed dentist is qualified to accept this responsibility," the ADA statement said. "In the complex area of denture treatment, an important facet of comprehensive oral health care, there are too many risks to oral and general health to allow persons of lesser training to assume patient responsibility."

At the same meeting, the ADA altered long-standing policy and called for the inclusion of comprehensive dental benefits, including denture care, under Medicare. The ADA also planned to seek federal legislation

requiring the inclusion of dental care in benefits for all persons eligible under Medicaid.

The ADA challenged a Kellogg Co. advertising campaign suggesting that sugary foods, such as presweetened cereals, do not contribute substantially to dental decay. In its statement, the ADA declared that such claims are seriously misleading. "Sugar is a primary causative factor in the decay process," the ADA said, "and frequent consumption of sweets, particularly those that lend themselves to snacking, should be discouraged. The advertising campaign, by Kellogg Company, tends to obscure the essential truth that children consume far too much sugar." The ADA indicated that "presweetened cereals are eaten not simply at breakfast but also as snacks. Nutritionists raise serious questions about the nutritional value of foods, such as presweetened cereals, which may be as much as 50 per cent sugar. Sweet snacks pose a special danger to dental health, particularly in children." The ADA joined other groups in calling for substitution of nutritious foods for sugar-rich snacks in school vending machines and for the elimination of advertising of sugar-rich products from children's television programs.

Speaking at the 55th general session of the International Association for Dental Research in Copenhagen, Den., Danny H. Lewis of the Southern Research Institute in Birmingham, Ala., suggested that a controlled-release process to provide continuous topical fluoride application to the teeth might become a new adjunct in fighting tooth decay. The key to the idea is the slow, precisely controlled release of fluoride from a three-layer plastic container placed within the mouth. The benefits of water fluoridation in lessening the incidence of tooth decay have been well established in numerous studies, Lewis pointed out. Other methods of fluoride therapy include tablets, table salt, mouthwashes, and toothpastes, as well as topical fluoride application administered by dentists.

Water fluoridation received a strong endorsement from U.S. Pres. Jimmy Carter in October 1977 when, in a telegram to the ADA's annual session, he declared that the dental profession for more than a quarter of a century has "carried the banner for fluoridation of our municipal water supplies." Recalling that, as governor of Georgia, he had signed a mandatory fluoridation bill, the president went on to state, "I believe now, as I believed then, that fluoridation is safe and that it is the most effective public health measure available to improve the nation's dental health and reduce unnecessary dental health expenditures."

New orthodontic procedures using brackets directly bonded to teeth instead of braces do not reduce the vulnerability of the teeth to cavities, according to A. John Gwinnett of the State University of New York at Stony Brook. In a pilot study it was found that, after orthodontic brackets were bonded to newly cleaned teeth, plaque was rapidly reestablished in exactly the same sites where it had been identified previously. Plaque is a sticky, colorless film constantly forming on teeth and considered to be a major factor in the development of tooth decay and periodontal disease. The plaque determinations were made using a new ultraviolet dental camera which "sees" plaque deposits before they are visible to the eye in ordinary light. By photographing the teeth of volunteer subjects over a specific period of time, Gwinnett was able to examine the pattern and distribution of plaque associated with the orthodontic brackets.

The use of relaxation techniques, including biofeedback and viewing videotapes of dental scenes, can help patients overcome deep-seated apprehension of dental treatment, according to Sven Carlsson, a behavioral scientist at the University of Göteborg, Sweden. Dental phobia in its graver forms is a handicapping affliction, not only because its victims avoid dental care, resulting in a miserable dental status, but also because of psychological and social complications. Most cases of dental phobia can be traced to some unpleasant early dental experience. In his studies of patients suffering from dental phobia, Carlsson found that desensitization therapy was highly effective. He defined such therapy as "a procedure where you gradually learn to perceive an initially feared phenomenon without experiencing anxiety." Through biofeedback, the patient's ability to relax is measured by monitoring his muscle responses with electromyograph equipment. As his tension control ability increases, he is shown videotaped scenes of different types of dental treatment. The tape is stopped if the patient shows any signs of anxiety and then resumed later until the patient no longer becomes tense when viewing dental scenes.

Reporting on a study of children suffering from dentofacial disorders, Bruce S. Fieldman and M. Michael Cohen of Children's Hospital in Boston pointed out

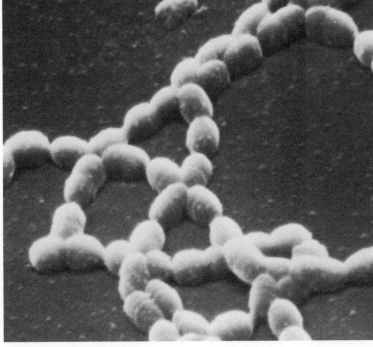

Streptococcus mutans *bacteria, arranged in a necklace form, cause dental caries (cavities). A sugar-rich diet generally leads to a greater incidence of cavities because these bacteria form a sort of glue out of sucrose that enables them to stick onto tooth enamel and use the tooth as a nutrient.*

Naval Dental Research Institute, Great Lakes, Illinois

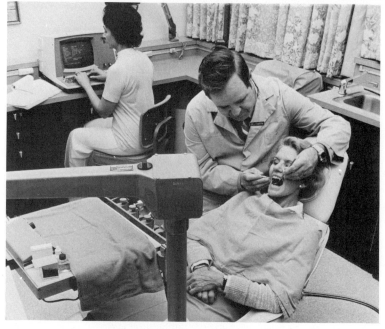

Joseph P. Moffa, U.S. Public Health Service Hospital, San Francisco

New patient is examined at U.S. Public Health Service Hospital in San Francisco, while dental assistant at a computer terminal enters information requested by the computer on a typewriter keyboard. The computer-augmented facility was established primarily to assess the efficacy and durability of dental fillings.

that, although it is impossible to conduct controlled experimental studies of growing children, much information can be gained from observations of children who have conditions that adversely affect development of the face, teeth, and jaws. Their study involved eight young males with Duchenne muscular dystrophy, a hereditary neuromuscular disease characterized by progressive weakness and disability. This condition leads to destruction of the muscle tissues of the jaws, which are gradually replaced by fatty tissue. All eight patients developed deformities of the jaw and grossly enlarged tongues. The two researchers felt that by learning how and why such changes take place, dentists may be able to detect such conditions in the early stages and to take preventive measures.

A new technique for saving decayed teeth with diseased pulp or nerves by chemically inducing hard tissue to form a natural seal within the root canal was successfully tested in young rhesus monkeys, according to Alan J. Nevins of the University of Connecticut. First, the pulp was removed from both the central chamber and the root canals of the upper and lower front teeth of the animals, following the same procedures used by dentists to clean and shape human root canals. Before sealing the crowns, the researchers filled the root canals of most of the front teeth with a gel of tropocollagen to which several salts were added. In the control teeth new tissue developed within the root canals, but in the canals of the experimental teeth new tissue resembling cementum and bone replaced the gel. If the treatment proved effective in humans, it could, in some cases, replace the current endodontic therapy utilizing cements and solid filling materials.

Research designed to determine how long dental fillings will last and what can be done to avoid the need for periodic replacement was being carried on at the Public Health Service Hospital in San Francisco, where the first completely computer-augmented dental treatment facility had been developed. According to Joseph P. Moffa, dental director of the hospital, the computer can rapidly and efficiently analyze the multitude of complex factors relating to the safety, efficacy, and performance of dental restorative materials and procedures. The patient's demographic background, medical history, dental care needs, and the specifics of the care provided are fed into the computer, which recalls patients on an annual basis. Fillings previously placed under known controlled conditions are then reevaluated independently by two different dentists. The television screen displays for each dentist the identity of the teeth he must examine and records his ratings of performance parameters. The system utilizes an in-house minicomputer that directs the clinical data onto a magnetic disk. One disk has the capability of storing the records of more than 6,000 patients over a five-year recall period.

—Lou Joseph

Veterinary medicine

Of major concern to the veterinary profession and livestock industry of the United States during 1977 was the proposal by the Food and Drug Administration (FDA) to ban the use of certain antibiotics at subtherapeutic levels in animal feeds. If implemented, this would remove penicillin and two forms of tetracycline from the feeds, where they have been used to promote growth and prevent disease of livestock. The efficacy of these compounds is apparent from the great increase in their use during the past 25 years; in 1975, 48.6% of the total production of antibiotics in the U.S. was for nonmedical uses, mainly as feed additives. Although other compounds, including various antibiotics, have been used similarly, penicillin and the tetracyclines proved to be the most effective and least expensive. As of 1978 they were estimated to be used in feed for all turkeys, 30% of chickens, 80% of swine and veal calves, and 60% of cattle raised for food in the U.S.

According to the FDA, the basis for its proposal was that questions regarding the safety of penicillin and the tetracyclines as used in feed had not been answered satisfactorily. In 1972 a task force composed of scientists from government, universities, and industry reported that continuous low-level feeding to livestock of some antibiotics could increase the numbers of antibiotic-resistant intestinal bacteria in these animals. Because food animals constitute a major reservoir of certain bacteria pathogenic to man, such as those causing salmonellosis, there was concern that transfer of this resistance to bacteria in human beings would make these drugs ineffective in combating bacterial infections in people. Thus, the proposed ban reflected the belief that the potential human health hazard of such use outweighed the benefits for livestock producers.

The terms of the ban would effectively eliminate any use of penicillin in animal feed. Use of the tetracyclines as feed additives for disease prevention would be allowed if no adequate substitute were available, specific exceptions being control of infectious synovitis in poultry, anaplasmosis in beef cattle, and vibrionic abortion in sheep. Any feed use of tetracycline would require a written prescription by a veterinarian. Both penicillin and the tetracyclines could be used by veterinarians in treatment of animal disease. Although the American Veterinary Medical Association had not endorsed the proposal, its president, William L. Anderson, said, "The AVMA will do all that it can to assure the cooperation and effective action of veterinarians in the matter [and] there are adequate numbers of veterinarians distributed throughout the country to carry out the proposed program."

Many scientists, veterinarians, and livestock producers, however, opposed the proposal, and the AVMA passed a resolution urging the FDA not to take action on the basis of currently available evidence. Great Britain had implemented such a ban in 1971 for similar reasons, but according to the British livestock nutritionist Raphael Braude these restrictions had little effect. Although an immediate result was a 50% reduction in the amount of antibiotics being fed to animals, by 1976 the level had returned to the peak it had reached before the ban. Braude also said that there was "no evidence of any obvious effect on human health resulting from reductions in drug-resistant bacteria [and] the only possible achievement of the Swann report was that it relieved the public anxiety originally created by a few individuals about the use of antibiotics as growth promotants."

Officials of the antibiotic industry believed the action to be without justification, and said that it would penalize farmers and the public because of its economic implications. They pointed to an FDA study that indicated that such a ban would increase the price of pork by 15 cents per pound and that of beef by 7 cents, causing consumer food bills to rise about $2 billion annually. Also, they pointed out that there have been no documented instances where the use of antibiotics in feed has led to epidemics of untreatable disease due to

Grant Heilman

Feed for approximately 80% of the hogs raised for human consumption in the United States in 1978 contained penicillin and two forms of tetracycline. The U.S. Food and Drug Administration proposed that these antibiotics be banned from livestock feed because they might eventually increase the levels of antibiotic-resistant bacteria in both the animals and man.

antibiotic-resistant bacteria in man. Canadian health protection officials announced that Canada would not follow the U.S. or British examples because evidence of a health hazard did not exist. (*See* Feature Article: THE MICROBES FIGHT BACK.)

An unusual genital infection designated as contagious equine metritis appeared among mares in the Newmarket area of England in May 1977, causing breeding operations to be suspended on many farms. Though it was at first believed to be a new disease, an investigation revealed that mares in France had been affected as early as 1975 and that from there it apparently spread to Ireland, where it appeared on ten stud farms during the 1976 breeding season. After the British outbreak, imports of mares and stallions from those countries were prohibited by the U.S. Department of Agriculture, and the ban was later extended to include Australia. Nonetheless, the disease broke out in the U.S. early in 1978.

Although relatively mild in its effects on mares, the disease is highly contagious, and it greatly reduces breeding efficiency on farms where it appears. Many mares fail to conceive, and others abort their foals. The disease is caused by a bacillus that is transferred from infected to clean mares by stallions during breeding and by contaminated instruments or hands of personnel during examination of mares. Penicillin appears to be effective in treating it, but it is difficult to know when a cure has been achieved.

During the past several years pseudorabies (Aujeszky's disease, "mad itch") increased in prevalence in the U.S. to the point where it became a serious threat to the swine industry; some herds were wiped out. It was estimated that the disease cost swine producers approximately $3 million in 1977 and that without an adequate control program this figure would increase to more than $180 million in 1979. The disease was difficult to diagnose because the virus produces signs like those of some other diseases; available blood tests are time-consuming and expensive, and under certain conditions they are unreliable. As of 1978 there was no effective treatment, and, once infected, swine remain carriers of the virus for life. The virus can be transmitted to many other species of mammals and birds, in which the disease is usually fatal, but as of early 1978 no cases had been reported in man.

A commercial vaccine that minimizes losses in infected herds and may protect swine on adjacent premises was marketed in 1977, but it had the disadvantage of producing the carrier state in vaccinated animals. In part because it was believed that eradication of the disease might not be feasible, no federal money was appropriated for that purpose; instead, the limited funds available were being used to survey the extent of the disease and determine the most effective control methods. Adequate control was believed possible if shipment of infected swine could be prevented and that of other swine held to a minimum.

During an outbreak of canine rabies in Laredo, Texas, beginning in November 1976 and lasting through July 1977, 55 rabid dogs were captured and 59 persons exposed to them underwent antirabies treatment; no human cases were reported. The outbreak was controlled by a program that involved the roundup of more

Horses in France, the U.K., Ireland (right), and the U.S. suffered from an outbreak of contagious equine metritis, a venereal disease that often causes sterility and abortions in mares.

than 1,700 stray dogs and vaccination of some 13,000 of the estimated 20,000 dogs in the city. During a concurrent outbreak across the Rio Grande in Nuevo Laredo, Mexico, 25 animal cases of rabies were reported, 1,146 stray dogs were destroyed, and more than 15,-000 of the estimated population of 45,000 dogs were vaccinated. Before the outbreak no rabies cases had been reported in Laredo for 29 years. Nuevo Laredo had reported one canine case per year during 1971–74 and none in 1975–76.

During the fall of 1977 many pet owners became alarmed when a New Jersey physician claimed to have found a possible link between household pets and multiple sclerosis. As reported in a letter to the editor of the *Journal of the American Medical Association* and a news release from the AMA calling attention to the letter, however, the data related to only 50 multiple sclerosis patients, 46 of whom had had close contact with a house pet; serving as a control group were 50 patients with other diseases, 24 of whom had house pets. The National Multiple Sclerosis Society and the AVMA quickly pointed out that this did not establish a causal relationship, proof of which would require a very large number of multiple sclerosis patients and of control groups in diverse geographic areas. Because certain diseases can be transmitted from domestic animals to persons in contact with them, however, the AVMA used this report to emphasize the desirability of keeping pet animals healthy.

In the field of veterinary education, a continuing demand for increased student enrollment was reflected by the opening of new schools at Louisiana State University (1974), the University of Florida (1976), the University of Tennessee (1976), and Mississippi State University (1977). Additional schools were expected to open during 1979–81 at Oregon State University, North Carolina State University, and Tufts University (regional school for the New England states). In 1973–74 the 18 veterinary colleges in the U.S. had 5,720 students; by 1976–77 this had increased to 6,571 students in 21 schools, and a further increase to more than 8,000 was anticipated by 1981–82. The number of women students increased from fewer than 100 in 1960 to more than 2,000 in 1977, at which time they comprised 28% of the total enrollment.

—J. F. Smithcors

Optical engineering

During the past year a number of advances took place in optical engineering. James Merz and Ralph Logan of Bell Telephone Laboratories reported success in fabricating the first complete integrated optical circuit. The circuit, on a gallium arsenide (GaAs) chip, consists of a laser source, waveguide, and detector and has an overall length of about 1 mm. The impetus for the development of integrated optics to replace conventional electrical cables is the urgent need for a compact communications system. Such systems show great promise for increasing the capacity of presently clogged telephone lines in central urban areas. Illinois Bell Telephone Co. began field testing miniature lasers and fiber optics for telephone communications under real operating conditions. These might one day provide fast and efficient telephone service at low cost. The most exciting developments, however, were in the use of lasers to produce energy from nuclear fusion. This work was underway primarily in the United States and the Soviet Union.

Nuclear fusion reactions are the prime source of the Sun's energy, and fusion is what sets off the hydrogen, or thermonuclear, bomb. Because the reactants required for fusion are plentiful and cheap and because essentially no radioactive wastes are produced, the search for a technology of controlled fusion has been going on intensively. The major engineering problem concerns the containment of the reactant nuclei at temperatures high enough to bring about their interaction. No known substance can withstand the millions of degrees of heat required in this process. Therefore, the major thrust of the experimental technology has been with various devices that have, instead of actual walls, enormously powerful magnetic fields focused so that they trap and contain the charged particles being energized to fusion.

In the last decade an alternative technology has resulted in a different approach. Minute quantities of the reactants are used instead of large volumes of gaseous plasma, and laser beams are used to attain the required temperatures instead of massive electrodynamic speeding up of the particles. In October 1977, at the University of California's Lawrence Livermore Laboratory, the world's most powerful laser system, Shiva, was ready for its first test in a long series of experiments to achieve a controlled production of energy from fusion.

In the Shiva system, the goal is to aim a focused laser beam at a minute pellet containing atoms of deuterium and tritium, two isotopes of the element hydrogen, and thereby make them fuse into atoms of helium in a microscopic thermonuclear explosion. Ultimately, after scientific feasibility has been demonstrated, the goal is to build a system that would release more energy than the amount needed to generate the laser beams. An almost unlimited quantity of deuterium exists in molecules of heavy water, which can be readily and inexpensively separated from ordinary water. The world's oceans contain enough to meet present rates of power consumption for at least 100 billion years. Tritium is easily manufactured in a well-known nuclear technology in which neutrons are made to react with lithium.

The pellet of deuterium and tritium is less than a

Photos, courtesy, Lawrence Livermore Laboratory

Shiva laser system is designed to produce energy from nuclear fusion by aiming a focused laser beam at atoms of two isotopes of hydrogen and thereby making them fuse into helium atoms in a miniature thermonuclear explosion. The system contains 20 laser chains mounted in an open grid structure (right). Amplifiers in the chains contain glass disks (below), within which light pulses trigger additional waves that are then joined to the original bundle.

millimeter in diameter. The laser beam must heat it to 100 million degrees Celsius and compress it to nearly 10,000 times its normal liquid density. A relatively low temperature—though still in the millions of degrees—would only boil away the electrons around the nuclei of the deuterium and tritium atoms, leaving them positively charged ions, or naked nuclei. A far higher temperature is required to provide the particles with sufficient energy of motion to overcome the electrical repulsion and smash them together. When the nuclei are almost touching, a nuclear force of attraction, far more powerful than the electrical force but effective only over such short distances, fuses the nuclei into a nucleus of a helium atom. Huge quantities of energy and fast neutrons are liberated. It is the rocket-like blowoff on the hot surface of the pellet that produces the compression needed for efficient conversion of deuterium and tritium into helium.

But heat and pressure are not the only requirements for fusion. The laser beam is generated in pulses, and the pulse must deliver its energy fast enough to achieve appreciable conversion before the hot plasma has time to disperse. The method is called inertial confinement. To obtain as much energy from thermonuclear fusion in the pellet as is needed for heating it, 100 trillion watts of light power in a pulse lasting less than a billionth of a second are required. This is the goal planned for the $25 million Shiva system, scheduled

for completion in the early 1980s. The objective for 1978 is significant thermonuclear burn during experiments, and this can be met with a fusion energy output greater than 1% of the laser energy required.

In the first Shiva test, one of 20 beams was fired. It delivered 526 joules of energy in a billionth of a second. A month later, in November 1977, all 20 beams were simultaneously fired, producing more than 10,000 joules in a pulse lasting less than a billionth of a second. This pulse amounts to a power output of more than ten trillion watts, ten times the entire generating capacity of all the power plants in the United States, even though it is of extremely short duration.

The 20 laser chains of the system, consisting of more than 600 amplifiers, polarizers, mirrors, and other major optical components, are mounted in an open grid structure that forms an enormous optical bench. The frame for the laser system itself is about 40 yd long and stands 4 stories high; the target section is approximately 15 × 15 × 15 yd. The grid of 6 × 6 in-square steel tubing with 4 × 4-in diagonals provides the exceptional rigidity required to focus 20 separate beams that travel about 100 yd and make them converge simultaneously on a microscopic pellet. The frame twists no more than a few ten-thousandths of a degree between any two points during a time span of 100 seconds. This twist tolerance if extended 25 mi would vary from the true direction by the diameter of a basketball. Air temperature at any point is so well controlled that it varies less than 0.5° C in 15 minutes, which causes the steel temperature to vary less than 0.01° C.

The system starts with a master laser oscillator that generates a one million-watt initial pulse of light. The pulse can be tailored to any shape desired. Proper pulse shape is important to obtain maximum compression of the pellet. The ideal shape is like a staircase, with the first steps low and wide and successive steps ever higher and narrower. This is necessary to achieve steady compression when the pulse strikes the pellet because, as the pellet is compressed and its density increases, more pressure is required to achieve further compression. The initial pulse is shaped by splitting it into a number of smaller pulses, amplifying each smaller pulse as required, and recombining the separate pulses so that their amplitudes add together in such a way as to obtain the desired shape. The shaped pulse is then split into 20 separate beams that are guided along separate paths of laser chains. Each beam is repeatedly amplified as it passes first through a rod amplifier and then a series of disk amplifiers of increasing diameter. The separate beams finally impinge simultaneously on the target pellet.

Glass disks in the amplifiers are the heart of the chain. It is in them that the pulse triggers additional waves which are carried along joined to the original bundle. Containing neodymium atoms to absorb ultraviolet light, the disks are first excited by xenon-filled flash lamps. About 8% of their flash is absorbed by the neodymium and 15% of this absorbed light is extracted by the pulse by means of stimulated emission as it passes through, increasing the power of the pulse by

Holographic image of a telephone, in correct and normal proportions, is illuminated by sodium light. Improvements in emulsions allow light sources other than lasers to be used.

Theo Bergström, *Light Fantastic*, Bergström and Boyle Books Ltd.

about 200 billion watts in each of the last few stages of amplification.

The first few disks are 1 cm in diameter, but the last is 20 cm. The beam is therefore widened as it approaches the target, although in the final step all 20 beams have to be focused on the pellet. The reason is the extremely high intensity of the light and the nonlinear refractive index of the glass. The refractive index is a comparison of the velocity of light in a medium, such as glass, to its velocity in a vacuum, and it states the degree to which the light is bent when passing from one to the other. The angle is determined by the atomic structure of the medium. Ordinarily, a high-purity glass affects all parts of a monochromatic light beam uniformly; however, the electronic structure of the bonds that hold atoms together is modified slightly by intense electric fields in such a way that the refractive index is changed very slightly. At high intensities, tens of billions of watts per square centimeter, even minute deviations from uniformity in the glass can have disastrous effects. Phase shifts in the light wave resulting from different velocities in different parts of the beam can cause it to split into fragments that prevent focusing on the target. More than that, self-focusing of the beam within the glass, resulting from the nonlinear refractive index, can be destructive. At high intensity the electric field of the light wave can accelerate free electrons to break chemical bonds and knock other electrons free. These, in turn, are accelerated and set still more electrons free in a process known as electron-avalanche breakdown. The process produces a local electron plasma that can absorb enough laser light energy to damage the glass. To prevent these disastrous effects, the beam is allowed to diverge somewhat as it progresses through the laser chain before it is finally focused onto the target.

Between the amplifiers in the laser chains are spatial filters that consist of a lens to focus the beam on a pinhole and a second lens to collimate (make parallel) the diverging beam on the exit side of the pinhole. That part of the beam that is uniform can be focused to pass through the pinhole; however, diffraction effects prevent small spatial variations in the beam from passing through the pinhole. Because of the high quality of the optical components and the resulting highly uniform beam, only a small fraction of the beam energy is removed in the filtering process.

Other optical components in the laser chain are polarizers and Faraday rotators for rotating the polarization 45°. These devices ensure that light, reflected from the target or other optical components in the chain, does not propagate back into the amplifier system. Light reflected from the target could be as much as 50% of the incident beam and could do considerable damage if reflected back.

The Shiva system is controlled by a network of minicomputers and microprocessors. Electrical storage banks, which must provide a peak discharge current of 4,000 amp for each of 1,000 flash lamps, are computer-controlled. The laser beam input to each laser chain and its output on the target are automatically aligned by means of mirrors mounted on gimbals driven by stepping motors and controlled by optical sensors.

—Frederick Wooten

Physics

In any field of human thought, opinions of the most knowledgeable people evolve continually, so that the exact time at which a new concept becomes accepted doctrine of the discipline is hard to define. Correspondingly, accepted doctrine is not certain truth; too often in the history of science new data have effected revolutions in established theories and have changed man's concept of nature. Nevertheless, it is possible to interpret 1977 as the year in which the quark model of elementary particles matured to general acceptance, its utility and predictive power quite firmly established.

Developments in nuclear physics during the year also continued to effect quiet revolutions of their own; particularly exciting was the accumulation of new evidence suggesting the existence of superheavy elements. And three solid-state theorists who contributed importantly to the current scientific and technological revolution in electronics were recipients of the 1977 Nobel Prize for Physics.

High-energy physics

Since 1964 physicists have discussed the "quark model" as a conceptual and mathematical tool to interrelate the properties and interactions of an ever expanding collection of observed subatomic particles called hadrons. Hadrons are distinguished from other particles by their ability to undergo strong interactions (*e.g.*, in energetic collisions between hadrons) during which there exist high probabilities of other hadrons being created and of transforming the character of the original particles. Two classes of hadrons are recognized: the baryons, which consist of the proton, neutron, and other hadrons that can transform into protons and neutrons; and the mesons, which may decay spontaneously into photons, electrons, and neutrinos. During the past 25 years, discoveries have increased the number of these so-called elementary particles to more than 200, each distinguished by some values of quantum properties such as electric charge and intrinsic angular momentum (spin). It became burdensome to accept that all of these particles might be really fundamental entities.

In its early versions quark theory postulated that all hadrons were composed of combinations of only three kinds of truly fundamental particles (and associated antiparticles) called quarks, which are usually labeled u, d, and s ($\bar{u}$, $\bar{d}$, and $\bar{s}$ for antiparticles). Later, both theory and experimental evidence required the addition of a fourth entity called a charmed or c quark.

Tank 20 feet in diameter and 48 feet long is located 4,900 feet underground as part of an experiment to detect solar neutrinos. Neutrinos from the Sun's interior are the only particles that penetrate through the ground and into the tank, where they are captured by an isotope of chlorine to form the radioisotope argon-37. The argon-37 is subsequently removed from the tank and conveyed to an instrument that counts the trapped neutrinos.

Courtesy, Brookhaven National Laboratory

Spark chambers are used by physicists to detect the paths of interacting high-energy particles. They consist of a series of charged metal plates separated by a gas in which observable electric discharges follow the path of the particle. At the left, the particle interactions are taking place at the center of the concentric cylinders.

Other considerations led physicists to the belief that these basic types of quarks are subdivided still further by a quantum property called color, and again for each quark of each color there exists a corresponding antiquark.

Within this scheme, each kind of baryon is conceived to be made up of a unique combination of three quarks or antiquarks, whereas each meson is made up of a quark-antiquark pair. One rule that must be followed, however, in constructing hadrons in this fashion is that quarks be combined in such a way that the resulting object is "colorless"; *i.e.*, that the quantum properties of color cancel out. For example, protons (composed of quarks *uud*) and neutrons (*udd*) each contain three differently colored quarks, conventionally termed red, blue, and green, which are assumed to cancel so that these baryons exhibit no net color. Mesons, formed of quark-antiquark pairs of the same basic color, are also colorless, because each color and its "anticolor" cancel. The selection rules that govern the combination of quarks to form hadrons, including those related to the color quantum number, are incorporated into a current, comprehensive theory called quantum chromodynamics (in analogy with the quantized electromagnetic theory of quantum electrodynamics). Some physicists believe that "free color" may not be observable; if so, this would preclude the existence of uncombined quarks. (For a detailed discussion of elementary particles, see *1977 Yearbook of Science and the Future* Feature Article: PARTICLE PHYSICS: A REALM OF CHARM, STRANGENESS, AND SYMMETRY.)

Charm and charmonium. Much of the enthusiasm for the quark model has come from a remarkable unfolding of experiments in the U.S. and West Germany, in particular with respect to mesons containing *c* quarks. Following upon the discovery in 1974 of the psi (ψ) or J meson, with a mass (rest energy) of 3.1 billion electron volts (GeV), detailed studies of meson states with masses from about 2.5 to 4 GeV were carried out; what emerged was a rich spectrum of ψ-like meson states. Soon after its discovery, the ψ/J meson was interpreted as a state composed of a charmed quark (*c*) and a charmed antiquark ($\bar{c}$), and in this it resembled positronium, a short-lived "atom" composed of an electron and a positron, or anti-electron. Theoretically, such a particle-antiparticle system should exhibit a spectrum of quantized energy levels, analogous to the energy levels of the hydrogen atom, which are functions of the relative energy states of its proton and electron. Just as transitions from higher energy levels to lower ones in hydrogen correspond to radiation of light, so the transitions among energy states of the ψ/J system should be revealed through characteristic gamma rays.

Indeed, these spectral states and transitions were observed. In the cases of the hydrogen atom and positronium, which consist of bound systems of particles with opposite charge, the electromagnetic force operating within the constraints of quantum mechanics determines the spacing, or magnitude of the transition, between energy levels. In the case of the $c\bar{c}$ system, referred to as charmonium, for which the force law that

Physics

governs quark-antiquark binding was unknown, the spacing of the observed energy states of charmonium was used to deduce the properties of the force law.

Although there are still many uncertainties, a self-consistent force law was derived that for small separation distances between quarks resembled the electromagnetic force, whose strength drops off in proportion to the square of the separation distance between particles. Yet at large distances the strength of the force between quarks rises, rather than approaching zero as in electromagnetic interaction. Hence, the force between a quark and an antiquark remains strong as they are separated, so that it may be impossible to completely separate them given any amount of energy.

The upsilon particle. Without doubt the most exciting experiment of 1977 was carried out at the Fermi National Accelerator Laboratory (Fermilab) near Batavia, Ill., by Leon Lederman of Columbia University and his collaborators, who bombarded a metal target with protons and employed two magnetic spectrometers to detect pairs of μ mesons (muons) produced in the collisions. This experiment was a higher-energy version of the kind done by Samuel C. C. Ting at Brookhaven (N.Y.) National Laboratory, which resulted in the discovery of the ψ/J particle. Whereas Ting used a proton beam of 30 GeV, detected electron-positron pairs, and discovered the ψ/J at a mass 3.1 GeV, Lederman used a proton beam of 400 GeV, detected pairs of oppositely charged muons ($\mu^+\mu^-$), and discovered a new particle with a mass of 9.4 GeV. In both cases, the momenta and angles of the electron pairs or muon pairs may be interpreted to result from the decay of a short-lived particle state of a particular mass. When the observed pairs were analyzed in this way, a continuum of "masses" was seen, and superimposed on this background appeared a sharp bump or resonance, indicative of an especially well-defined mass.

Lederman dubbed this new object the upsilon (Υ) particle, and careful analysis of his data indicated that there are at least two and possibly three such states between 9 and 10.5 GeV. Because of the obvious analogy with charmonium and its charmed quark, theoretical physicists interpreted the upsilon as an "-onium" state of some new fifth quark. In a search for a name for the unique quantum property of this quark, "beauty" and "bottom" were suggested, so that the upsilon may be a state composed of a beauty and an antibeauty quark ($b\bar{b}$).

A difficulty is that the four-quark set is quite self-consistent, and indeed comfortably fits the phenomenology of hadronic physics without need for, or indeed room for, a new quark. It is possible that the new quark embodied in the upsilon is only the lowest-mass member of yet a new quartet of quarks that may relate little or not at all to the u-d-s-c quark quartet. It is also possible that the upsilon is some other, new manifestation of known quarks. In any case, it has sharply whet-

Adapted from *CERN Courier*, Vol. 17, No. 10, October 1977, p. 319

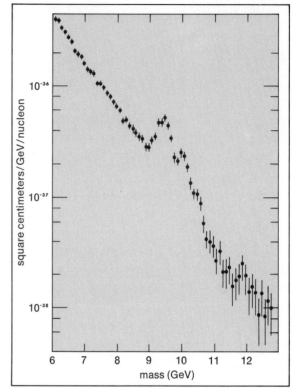

Collision experiments at Fermilab using high-energy protons yielded an enhancement of muon-pair ($\mu^+\mu^-$) production at a combined mass of 9.4 GeV, a second at 10 GeV, and a possible third at 10.4 GeV—evidence that well-defined particles (called upsilons) which decayed into muons existed briefly at those masses.

ted the appetites of physicists for experiments at even higher energies.

New heavy leptons. Physicists had been happy with the fourfold symmetry of both hadrons and another system of elementary particles called leptons: the u-d-s-c quark quartet for hadrons, and the electron, muon, electron-neutrino, muon-neutrino quartet for leptons (e-μ-ν_e-ν_μ). Whereas the discovery of the upsilon seemed to have shattered the neat symmetry of the hadronic quarks, there was also good evidence that a new, heavy lepton, the tau (τ), correspondingly disrupts the fourfold symmetry of the leptonic system. A group led by Martin Perl of Stanford University, working at the Stanford positron-electron storage ring, first saw evidence of this new particle over two years earlier, and in 1977 storage-ring experiments at Deutsches Elektronen-Synchrotron (DESY) in Hamburg, West Germany, confirmed Perl's observations.

The Stanford experiment studied the distribution of electron-muon pairs, unaccompanied by other charged particles or photons that emerged from the collisions of electrons and positrons. It is highly improbable that such pair production would result from known processes, but when the electron-positron collision energy exceeded about 3.8 GeV, electron-muon pairs were detected. Perl's group interpreted this phenomenon as the production of a pair of new oppositely charged particles, the taus (τ^+ and τ^-), followed by the decay of each into a known lepton (muon or electron) and neutrinos. (It was known that a conventional muon decays spontaneously into an electron and two neutrinos.) The energies and angles of the observed leptons matched the prediction of this model; the neutrinos were not and should not have been observed. The mass of the tau was set at about 1.8–1.9 GeV, almost 20 times the mass of the muon.

Such evidence has made it embarrassingly clear that the stable of leptons must accommodate the new τ, its antiparticle, and almost certainly a corresponding neutrino and antineutrino. Thus apparently there are not four leptons (and their antiparticles) but at least six. As with quarks, physicists' horizons have been forcibly broadened to contemplate a complexity in nature that many theorists at least would have preferred to do without.

Free quarks. In the decade following the first proposal that quarks are the constituents of hadrons, there was an intense search among cosmic rays, at particle accelerators, and in stable matter for free particles carrying an electric charge of $\frac{1}{3}$ or $\frac{2}{3}$, which are

First observation of four muons emerging from a neutrino interaction was made at the European Organization for Nuclear Research (CERN) in Switzerland. Images are reconstructions of the muon tracks from detected signals.

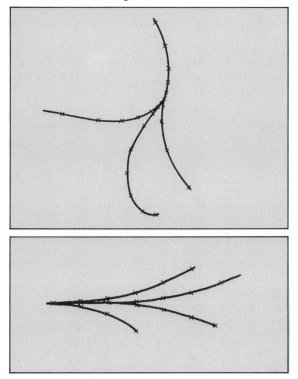

Adapted from *CERN Courier*, Vol. 17, No. 12, December 1977, cover and p. 408

postulated properties of quarks in order to explain the observed charges of hadrons. In spite of a few transient flurries of excitement, however, no free quarks were found by convincing, reproducible experiments. As was discussed above, if quantum chromodynamic theory describes reality, then observable matter must be "colorless" and free quarks are forbidden to exist.

Early in 1977, William Fairbank and colleagues, working in low-temperature physics at Stanford University, announced that they had isolated two microscopic pellets of superconducting niobium metal each with a net electric charge of $\frac{1}{3}$ that of the electron. Their interpretation of these results—that a free quark had somehow been deposited on these samples of material—caused considerable excitement in the physics community, as well as some skepticism. First, such evidence seemed hard to reconcile with worldwide negative evidence for the presence of quarks in cosmic rays. Second, a research group under the direction of Giacomo Morpurgo in Genoa, Italy, conducted an independent, somewhat more sensitive low-temperature search with negative results. Morpurgo also criticized Fairbank on technical grounds, and a lively debate ensued. Third, recent theoretical arguments suggested that in rare instances an uncombined quark might be bound in a nucleus, even though it might not be found as a free particle. In this way it could be possible to reconcile Fairbank's result with the dominant, if not perfect, confinement of quarks in colorless hadrons.

There has been no subsequent confirmation of Fairbank's data, and one senses a general ambivalence over its validity among the particle-physics community. Whether it proves true or false, the report of a free quark has generated less excitement than might have been expected. Yet this line of research seeks to answer a very fundamental question, and a variety of serious experiments were under way in order to verify or disprove the Fairbank result.

—Lawrence W. Jones

Nuclear physics

Important developments in nuclear science in recent months centered on the continued search for atomic nuclei much heavier than presently known, the phenomena surrounding accelerator-produced nuclear collisions, and the giant resonances in which nuclear protons and neutrons participate collectively.

Superheavy nuclei. Intensive search continued for superheavy nuclei, much more massive than any presently known to exist in nature. Theoretical understanding of such heavy nuclei as lead (proton number $Z = 82$) and uranium ($Z = 92$) predicts that superheavy species with about 114 or 126 protons in their nuclei might have long lifetimes, once produced. Thus far, attempts to create such species directly, by fusing two lighter species in an accelerator-produced nuclear collision, were unsuccessful, but improved facilities for such work neared completion at Dubna in the Soviet Union, GSI in Darmstadt, West Germany, the University of California at Berkeley, and Caen in France.

In 1976 Robert Gentry and his collaborators from Oak Ridge (Tenn.) National Laboratory, Florida State University, and the University of California at Davis had announced exciting evidence for the presence of naturally occurring element 126 in certain rare samples of Madagascan mica. Unfortunately, subsequent work showed that this identification was faulty. During 1977, however, Soviet physicist Georgi N. Flerov and his associates at the Joint Institute for Nuclear Research in Dubna presented evidence for superheavy species in samples of the Allende meteorite that fell in northern Mexico in 1969. In a very elaborate process, the group isolated a meteorite fraction that showed an anomalously high probability for fissioning spontaneously— and an anomalously high number of neutrons associated with each of these spontaneous fission events. Both of these are expected signatures for superheavy nuclei. Flerov and his associates also were completing construction of a high-resolution cyclotron that should be of use in identifying the precise number of protons in the fissioning species.

In parallel with this work, a group from the University of Chicago used geochemical techniques on other samples of the Allende meteorite. From the abundance of certain rare isotopes of xenon in their samples, Edward Anders and his associates were able to suggest the presence of as many as 55 billion atoms of superheavy elements (with Z near 114) per gram of sample.

Superheavy atoms. Since the turn of the century the structure of the atom has been seen as a tiny, heavy nucleus surrounded by a cloud of electrons equal in number to the nuclear protons. Electron cloud dimensions, however, are typically 100,000 times larger than those of the nucleus.

Several years ago, Walter Greiner and his collaborators at the University of Frankfurt, West Germany, noted that the characteristic speeds of the remote electrons in their clouds were vastly greater than the speeds of heavy nuclei colliding with one another. They suggested that, if scientists could not produce stable superheavy nuclei, perhaps they could produce ones that lived long enough to assemble their characteristic electron clouds to form transient superheavy atoms for study. For example, the cloud electrons should find it essentially impossible to distinguish between two colliding lead nuclei with 82 protons each and one superheavy nucleus having 164 protons. In 1976 Jack Greenberg and his collaborators at Yale University

Nucleus of iron-56 accelerated to an energy level of 1.9 GeV leaves fragments trailing through an emulsion of silver bromide in an experiment at the Lawrence Berkeley Laboratory.

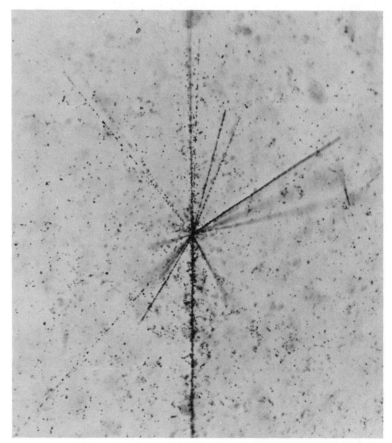

showed conclusively that this suggestion was valid by studying the X-rays emitted from two colliding nickel (Z = 28) and two colliding niobium (Z = 41) systems and by showing that this radiation came from restructuring of the electron cloud about effective nuclei having Z = 56 (barium) and Z = 82 (lead).

As the number of nuclear protons increases, the electric field around the nucleus becomes more intense and the electrons become bound more tightly to the nucleus. Indeed, Greiner originally calculated that when the number of protons reached about 170 the inner cloud electrons would be pulled down into the sea of negative-energy electrons described by the very fundamental Dirac equation of quantum electrodynamics. According to this view, empty space can be imagined to be permeated by a vast indeterminate number, or sea, of physically undetectable electrons in a state of "negative energy." Adding energy in excess of twice the equivalent of the electron's mass can pry loose a particle of "positive energy" from this sea in the form of a conventional, detectable, negatively charged electron. Left behind is a "hole," or an absence of a negative-energy electron. This negative-of-a-negative quality can be considered a state of positive energy in the same sense as a conventional electron, and thus the hole is also physically manifested as a particle, one equivalent in mass to an electron. Because a hole represents the subtraction of a negatively charged particle from "neutral" or uncharged space, it appears as a positively charged electron; *i.e.*, an anti-electron or positron. Such a description is equivalent to pair production, or the materialization of a particle and its antiparticle from a quantity of energy.

On an atomic level, when electrons are missing from inner cloud orbits, electrons normally fill the vacancies by cascading down from outer orbits, emitting characteristic X-rays in the process. But if such vacancies exist when the orbits reach the Dirac sea, they can be filled by negative-energy electrons from the sea. In the process, holes would be left behind, and single unaccompanied positrons therefore would be expected to appear.

Based on his earlier work at Yale that showed the possibility of creating transient heavier nuclei in collisions, Greenberg joined forces with Paul Kienle of the University of Munich, Egbert Kankeleit of the University of Darmstadt, and others to use the newly available facilities of GSI. Lead (Z = 82) and uranium (Z = 92) beams were made to collide with lead and uranium targets to produce effective transient nuclei having 164 and 184 protons respectively. Following a series of very difficult experiments, this group announced observation of what appear to be the predicted positrons. This was an important new test for the validity of quantum electrodynamics, which in this case predicted the dominant effect rather than a tiny correction to other effects, as had been the case to date. A great many new experiments were expected to be triggered by this apparent success.

Deep inelastic scattering. Until a few years ago, all nuclear interactions fell into two broad classes, compound and direct. In the former the projectile and target fused, losing all detailed information concerning the formation mechanisms; subsequently, the compound system disposed of its excess energy through emission of particles or radiation. In the latter the projectile left the target largely undisturbed, exchanging only a small number of particles or a small amount of energy with it in passing.

A totally new mechanism, called deep inelastic scattering, was discovered almost simultaneously by A. J. Artukh and his collaborators at Dubna and by John Huizenga of the University of Rochester, N.Y., and his collaborators using the Berkeley super-HILAC accelerator. Briefly, in these new interactions the energy of relative motion is very largely converted into internal excitation, or heating, of the two interacting species but with only limited exchange of particles; afterward the species separate very much like fission fragments in that they appear to be driven almost entirely by their mutual electrostatic repulsion. The mechanism that mediates the energy transfer from external (motion) to internal (excitation) energy remained a major mystery. Recently, Ricardo Broglia and others from the State University of New York at Stony Brook calculated that nuclear giant resonances possibly could function as "doorways" through which this energy transfer could occur.

In the giant resonances all neutrons and protons of the nucleus participate together in rather well-defined collective motions. In the monopole resonance they all move radially as the overall nucleus expands and contracts; in the dipole resonance all the neutrons oscillate against all the protons; in the quadrupole the nuclear shape oscillates between football and doorknob configurations; and in the octupole the nucleus has a pear shape and oscillates by sloshing matter from one end of the pear to the other. Broglia's suggestion was that, if these collective oscillations—particularly the quadrupole for detailed reasons—could be set in motion during the initial stages of the interaction, they could absorb the large amount of kinetic energy required and subsequently—over a more leisurely time scale—disperse it into much more complex internal modes of neutron and proton motion.

Working with light nuclei, specifically carbon and aluminum, which were chosen to increase the probability of observing the interaction products while one of them was still in the doorway state, Russell Betts and his collaborators at Yale recently showed that in this case the giant quadrupole (and to a lesser extent the giant octupole) resonances, indeed, do appear to play the suggested doorway role. Work was begun to extend this new insight to much heavier systems.

Cockcroft-Walton injector room at the Los Alamos (New Mexico) Meson Physics Facility, five stories high, is where a beam of protons begins its journey down a half-mile-long accelerator. The facility is designed to provide proton beams at energies up to 800 MeV in order to investigate the atomic structures of materials.

Monopole, or breathing, resonances. Until 1977 monopole giant resonances, wherein the nucleus alternately expands and contracts—or breathes—had never actually been seen, although all theories predicted that they should be present in nuclei. D. H. Youngblood and his associates at Texas A & M University succeeded for the first time in observing this breathing resonance in the scattering of helium nuclei (alpha particles) from such rare earth nuclei as samarium and neodymium and from lead.

From measurements on these new breathing resonances, the researchers were able to extract new measurement of the compressibility of nuclear matter, a constant of fundamental importance both in nuclear physics and in nuclear astrophysics, where it is crucial to the understanding of neutron stars. They derived values of 200 million and 175 million electron volts (MeV) for lead and for samarium, respectively, very close to the value obtained some ten years earlier from Yale data of James Maher and others on collisions between oxygen nuclei. This apparent constancy of compressibility across the periodic table, as well as the value obtained, makes it possible to rule out an entire class of postulated density-dependent nuclear forces that had been widely considered in both nuclear physics and nuclear astrophysics (these would predict a value of 300 MeV for this constant).

—D. Allan Bromley

Solid-state physics

The Nobel Prize for Physics in 1977 was awarded to three men who made major contributions to solid-state theory. It was an unusual award in two ways. First,

though many of their achievements dated back 40 or more years, exciting physics continued to come from these men. Second, the prize was given for a series of achievements that has had a tremendous effect not only on physics but also on chemistry, metallurgy, and, through practical applications, the world we live in. This article will concentrate on the achievements of these men because they illustrate well the long-term impact of knowledge of the solid state.

The winners of the prize were John H. Van Vleck (Harvard University), Nevill F. Mott (University of Cambridge), and Philip W. Anderson (Bell Telephone Laboratories and Princeton University). Van Vleck and Mott were among the handful of outstanding young physicists in the 1920s and 1930s who recognized and made use of quantum theory as the key to understanding the electrical and magnetic properties of solids. They published books in the 1930s that are still useful today and that laid the foundation for much of the scientific and technological revolution of the last two or three decades. This revolution created the modern electronics industry, which in turn was combined with other disciplines to develop such diverse products as computers and space satellites. Less well recognized is the deep effect of quantum theory on such diverse areas as chemistry and metallurgy.

Van Vleck, Anderson, and magnetism. The principal work of Van Vleck and the early work of Anderson were aimed at the understanding of magnetism. About a decade after the establishment of the modern quantum theory, Van Vleck published a book, *The Theory of Electric and Magnetic Susceptibilities* (1932). It laid the foundation for the understanding of the electrical and magnetic responses of solids (and gases) to external electric or magnetic fields. New concepts that have had wide applications were introduced.

A contribution of Van Vleck was the elaboration of the concepts of the crystal field and the ligand field, developed to understand the magnetism associated with foreign atoms in a crystal. Briefly, these concepts explain how a given atom or ion in a solid is affected by the atoms or ions surrounding it in a crystal lattice. For example, if a foreign atom or ion is placed in two different crystals, crystal or ligand theory explains how its magnetic, electric, and optical properties are modified by the surrounding ions of the host lattice. This understanding played a major role in the development of the first laser, which utilized the energy levels of a chromium ion as modified by an aluminum oxide (Al_2O_3) crystal in which it was placed.

Crystal field theory is most applicable to ionic crystals, an example of which is sodium chloride (NaCl). In such crystals, electrons are removed from one component (for example Na) and placed on the other (Cl), producing a crystal made up of ions with opposite charge. It is the attraction between these charges that holds the crystal together.

Ligand field theory can be thought of as taking into account a more subtle type of bonding. This is the bonding due not to movement of electrons completely from one atom to another (as in ionic bonding) but to the sharing of electrons by adjacent atoms. Such bonding is often called "covalent." It is important in a wide variety of materials, ranging from the semiconductors from which transistors are made to the huge and complex organic molecules of which the human body is formed. Applications of ligand field theory were also found in such diverse fields as molecular biology, medicine, and geology. Thus, concepts and analytical methods that Van Vleck developed to explain the response of matter to external electric and magnetic fields have had much broader application than anyone could have foreseen almost 50 years ago when they were first articulated.

Before modern quantum theory was fully developed, it was recognized that ferromagnetism (the spontaneous appearance of a magnetic field in a solid) must be associated with the interactions between many very small "minimagnets," which were similar to atoms in size. Van Vleck, using quantum theory, first discovered that the interactions between electrons on a given atom could lead to such localized magnets. He pointed out the so-called correlation effects by which electrons in partially filled atomic orbits arrange themselves so as to minimize their interaction. Further, the very electron orbits which minimize that interaction maximize the magnetic field produced by each atom. The spontaneous alignment of these atomic magnets creates permanent magnets.

The work of Van Vleck and the other pioneers left much of the details of magnetism unresolved. For example, what were the detailed interactions that aligned

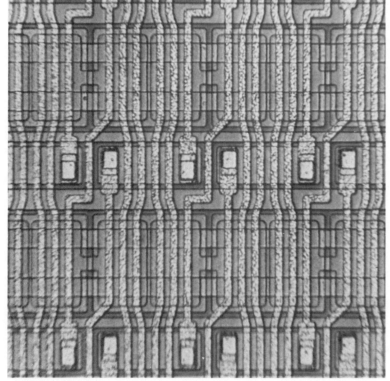

Photomicrograph reveals 16 memory cells in the experimental Josephson memory chip, a device used to test the elements of a prototype Josephson 16,000-bit main memory chip.

adjacent atomic "magnets" in a solid so as to create the long-range magnetic order and, thus, spontaneous magnetization? If one places a magnetic impurity into a metal that does not exhibit spontaneous magnetization, what new states will result? These were some of the many questions that could be asked. The answers are important not only to magnetism but also to a large range of other fields extending from the mechanical and electronic properties of alloys to catalysis.

It was natural that Philip Anderson, who started his scientific career by studying under Van Vleck at Harvard University, should address himself to the questions mentioned above. In a paper published in 1961, Anderson was able to give a critical theoretical description of a magnetic atom placed as an impurity in a metal. (Van Vleck's theories were only applicable to impurities in nonmetals.) Anderson's theory explained such complex behavior as the abrupt change in the strength of the magnetic field associated with a given atom or groups of atoms as a result of variations of only a few percent in the impurity content. It also explained why iron, for example, retained its atomic magnetic field when dissolved in copper, whereas other metals did not.

Anderson's work also included a consideration of the interactions giving rise to the long-range magnetic order. Perhaps one of his greatest accomplishments in this area was his explanation in 1963 of the mechanism by which magnetic alignment is achieved by magnetic atoms in, for example, oxides, where the magnetic (metallic) ions are separated by an oxygen (nonmetallic) atom. This mechanism is called superexchange. Anderson's explanations of superexchange, which involved coupling through the nonmetallic ions, provided a quantitative basis for all subsequent explanations of this phenomenon.

Some of Anderson's most recent work has centered on the electrical and magnetic properties of disordered solids, attempting to determine what happens to these properties when one destroys the long-range crystalline order with which solid-state physics usually deals. In this area the work of Mott and Anderson was strongly intertwined. A discussion of their contributions follows a summary of Mott's earlier work.

Nevill Mott and the electrical and magnetic properties of solids. In the 1930s Mott played a role similar to that of Van Vleck with the difference that he applied quantum theory to a wide range of solid-state physics rather than concentrating principally on magnetic phenomena. Mott focused his attention on metals and alloys. One of his first contributions was in recognizing that two groups of electrons could be important in metals. All metals contained the first of these groups, which acted in many ways like electrons in free space and moved relatively freely through solids. The second group, which were contained by only certain metals (called the transition metals and including iron,

nickel, and platinum), also carried current but acted much more sluggishly than the first group, as though they had much greater mass. This second group of electrons gave the transition metals special properties. It is these electrons that can spontaneously produce a magnetic field, and they also greatly enhance the structural strength of metals.

Before and just after World War II Mott made an impressive and diverse series of contributions to solid-state physics. These included advances in the understanding of a number of processes. One was the rectification process, in which electrons move easily through a solid in a given direction but not in the opposite direction. This understanding led to the development of the solid-state rectifier, one of the first important solid-state electronic devices.

Mott also made important contributions to the understanding of the photographic process, showing that it depended on the motion of electrons followed by a motion of silver ions. Similarly, he helped advance the understanding of electrolytic conduction, which is conduction resulting from the motion of ions rather than of electrons.

Could quantum theory also aid in the understanding of the strength of materials and the theory of the detailed mechanism by which they grow? Mott showed that this was possible. His contributions to the understanding of oxide growth played an important role in the development of techniques for the growth of silicon dioxide on silicon. This growth is essential for the production of integrated circuits, which have made modern computers and communications possible.

Developments in amorphous materials. In recent years Mott and Anderson played increasingly central roles in developing an understanding of amorphous solids. The atoms in crystalline materials demonstrate long-range order, simplifying greatly their theoretical treatment; however, there is no such order in amorphous materials, making their theoretical treatment much more difficult.

One of the characteristics first identified with amorphous materials was their tendency to be much more electrically resistive than those crystalline materials with identical chemical compositions. For example, crystalline silicon with a small amount (approximately one part per million) of phosphorus impurity was quite conductive, whereas the same material in the amorphous form had a conductivity many orders of magnitude lower. For many years most solid-state physicists believed that this behavior (as well as other properties of amorphous materials) resulted from the lack of long-range order. As more experimental and theoretical work was done, however, it became increasingly clear that the dominant effects were due not to the lack of long-range order but rather to the unsatisfied chemical bonds that may accompany that disorder. Recent work in the U.K., at Harvard, at RCA laboratories, and elsewhere showed that if the energy levels due to unsatisfied bonds are removed the conductivity can be increased. Furthermore, it was found that impurities can be added to the amorphous material so as to change its conductivity in a controlled manner.

Workers at RCA, using amorphous silicon and satisfying its dangling bonds by attaching hydrogen to them, were able at low cost to make solar cells with efficiencies of conversion above 5%. This has important potential implications for conversion of solar energy to electrical energy because of the relatively small projected expense of mass producing such solar cells. If the efficiency of conversion can be increased to approximately 10%, it appears that this may be an economically viable system.

One large unsolved problem in amorphous materials containing unsatisfied bonds was the lack of magnetic response that should have been associated with electrons in the dangling-bond states. A resolution of this was provided by Anderson, who showed theoretically that it was energetically favorable for electrons in these states to pair up and thus cancel each other's magnetic field. Anderson's theory showed that there were complex quantum-mechanical forces which would overcome the natural repulsion between two electrons in order to pair them up. Mott further refined this work by suggesting detailed interactions that would lead to this pairing in various classes of materials.

—William E. Spicer

Psychology

During the year the 48,000-member American Psychological Association (APA) showed increasingly clear signs of a functional cleavage into three more or less sharply differentiated power structures: academic/scientific, with a focus on research and teaching; clinical/professional (applied); and social/public interest.

Historically, since its inception in 1892 by a small group of university professors, the APA had been dominated by the academic group. After World War II, when

Infants as young as 12 days can imitate facial gestures of adults. This new discovery will require child psychologists to reconsider their theories of cognitive learning.

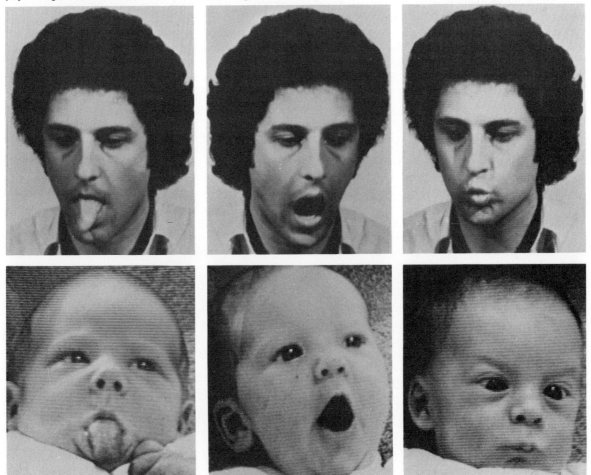

Courtesy, Andrew N. Meltzoff, Child Development and Mental Retardation Center

modern clinical psychology began to develop, its practitioners became increasingly vocal. Complaints about the dominance in the APA of academic and scientific interests—with regard to the holding of major offices, such as the presidency, for example—bore fruit within recent years as the sheer numbers of clinicians and other practitioners grew far beyond the relatively constant numbers of academic persons, and as political leverage was exercised (formally, from 1972). Practitioner presidents and an increasing concern with such bread-and-butter issues as the inclusion of professional psychologists within the framework of the impending national health insurance program provided clear evidence of this shift in power.

The diminishing effectiveness of professors within the APA reflected the markedly reduced number of appointments to academic positions and the consequent radical reduction in acceptances of new graduate students in the major nonapplied graduate training programs. Training departments could not continue to produce doctoral candidates in experimental psychology in numbers that so greatly exceeded the available employment opportunities. Meanwhile, growth of the public interest and social activism movement within psychology had been stimulated by the various forces pushing for minority rights, most notably by the women's rights movement.

Scientific psychology. Despite the reductions in graduate training programs, experimental psychologists continued to perform and report research at what seemed to be a pell-mell pace. This was particularly true of certain focal areas, such as information processing in human learning and memory and attribution of responsibility in social psychology.

Among the more promising and interesting contributions, an important paper on "hidden preattentive processes" was published by British psychologist Donald Broadbent, one of the pioneers in the information-processing field. Broadbent had been examining the sources of decision making, long a relatively neglected research topic considering its great significance. He was concerned with "the causes of . . . strange selections and jumps of topic, which do not themselves appear in consciousness." Having reviewed the role of what he earlier identified as "filtering" and "pigeonholing" mechanisms, he concluded that there is some evidence "for at least two stages of perceptual selection . . . [an] early global . . . stage [which] packages information from the environment into different segments . . . [and] a later inquiry, or verification, stage [which] works with more detailed information from the original packages or segments and is perhaps more affected by semantic context, by the pleasantness of a word, and by co-occurrence probability of detailed features such as the sequential probability of letters in words." He found this view "an enormous advance over positions current even 15 years ago." (*American Psychologist*, 32:109–118, 1977.)

Sleep continued to be an actively researched phenomenon with large numbers of ramifications, behavioral as well as neurophysiological. A research group at the University of Colorado reported that sleep following

Early childhood education programs such as Project Head Start help disadvantaged children substantially, according to recent studies. The boy at the right is using an audio device in a class in California.

David Strick—The New York Times

study, even after several hours, has a strong beneficial effect on memory; sleep preceding study does not show this effect on memory (although it may, of course, have other beneficial effects).

This research was the latest confirmation of the beneficial effect of sleep on memory, initially demonstrated by psychologists as long ago as 1924 on both human and animal (cockroach) subjects. The original research was interpreted as demonstrating the interfering effects of activity on memory, but some modification of that conclusion was now needed because the subjects who stayed awake seven hours after learning in the Colorado study did as well as those that slept immediately after learning, and both did better than those kept awake for all 14 hours before retention was tested.

In a separate University of Colorado (Medical Center) study, the role of the so-called twilight zone in learning was investigated. A special role for stimulating creativity has often been attributed to this transitional period when one is neither wide awake nor clearly asleep. By utilizing biofeedback techniques to induce continued relaxation of forehead muscles, the Colorado researchers trained subjects in the laboratory to maintain the twilight state (marked by slow, small-amplitude theta brain waves). The group developed the so-called Twilight Learner, a device that turns on a cassette tape recorder, thereby providing the subject with auditory information *only* when the theta waves are maintained. If the subject moves toward deeper sleep, as indicated by increasing amplitude or decreasing frequency of the theta waves, the Twilight Learner increases the volume of the taped message. Preliminary results with this device in treating a variety of cases involving emotional blocks in learning were reported as extremely promising.

In the area of comparative psychology, an interesting technique for testing self-recognition in higher organisms was described. The subjects were given extended exposure to mirrors and then tested for self-recognition (utilizing special facial marks not visually evident without a mirror). Clear evidence of self-recognition was obtained in chimpanzees and orangutans after two or three days. These results are important because previous efforts to demonstrate self-recognition in species other than man have been negative and because they have implications for the analysis of consciousness, which has recently become a popular theoretical problem after decades of neglect during the heyday of behaviorism.

The most actively discussed theoretical problem of the year was Julian Jaynes' intriguing theory of the origin of consciousness, fully described in his book *The Origin of Consciousness in the Breakdown of the Bicameral Mind*. Basically, he analyzed the functions of three types of human awareness: the bicameral early mind (two separate functions, associated with the two cerebral hemispheres), modern consciousness, and schizophrenia, which he interprets as a kind of regression to ancient mental functioning in that external voices are heard and responded to, but now in a socially unacceptable context. This fascinating theory was discussed in an interview with Jaynes that appeared in the November 1977 issue of *Psychology Today*. Nothing that had appeared on this problem within recent years had stirred so much argumentation and critical discussion.

Professional and applied psychology. Perhaps the most disappointing large-scale enterprise with which psychologists were involved over the past decade or so was the Head Start program designed to provide educational and cultural enrichment for "culturally deprived" preschool children. Despite much fanfare and high hopes for compensatory education, as represented by the massive effort expended in Head Start, little in the way of significant improvement was reported. Even many of the erstwhile strong supporters of early intervention expressed their disappointment. Recent research, however, provided new hope for the supporters of early intervention. In an American Association for the Advancement of Science symposium on the subject, psychologist Francis Palmer reviewed the results of ten studies of compensatory education in which longitudinal data had been collected. Previously only the immediate test results had been reported and interpreted, but in these studies more than 2,000 schoolchildren, in a variety of experimental and control groups, were studied from prekindergarten through the third grade and beyond.

The following generalizations were offered: (1) There was a consistent advantage in IQ scores for children who had had some form of compensatory education (mean scores of approximately 100 for treated versus 90 for untreated subjects), even though the treatment had taken place several years earlier. (2) A durable increment in reading ability was found for treated subjects. (3) Treated subjects were less likely to fail and be set back a year in school grade. (4) Programs that had involved parental teaching of children were more effective in these respects than those that did not involve the parents. (5) The earlier the treatment started and the longer it was continued, the better were the results.

Although far more definitive data will be required before unequivocal conclusions can be drawn on this crucial problem, these new data may be expected to breathe new life into compensatory education as an early intervention technique and to justify its continued support by federal agencies.

Certain new forms of applied activities by psychologists emerged during the year. For example, strictly behavioral research programs were funded within the U.S. Energy Research and Development Administration (later absorbed into the Department of Energy).

The practical problem relates to energy conservation and how homeowners in particular and consumers in general can be encouraged to change their life-styles (and not simply their verbal expressions) so as to lower energy consumption.

Another relatively new enterprise in which psychologists were becoming increasingly involved was that of evaluation of ongoing social programs or industrial practices. With the shrinking academic job market an unpleasant fact of professional life for many recently trained Ph.D.'s, this kind of activity offered a reasonable occupational alternative. Unfortunately, doctoral candidates in the U.S. were not yet receiving training appropriate to this activity, because most graduate training followed either the research or the clinical model. Some remedying of this deficiency could be expected in the near future.

An especially promising research program with tremendous applied potential was that of psychologist Tom Bower of the University of Edinburgh. Providing very young blind babies with appropriate auditory information, Bower was able to teach them to "see." Only a very small proportion of blind adults had been able to learn to utilize auditory information effectively, as in echolocation, but Bower believed this was due to their years of "faulty" learning. He concluded that the baby's more plastic perceptual system can respond to energy changes through any modality, and that if proper cross-modality channeling is arranged, a blind child can be trained to "see," as evidenced by successful locomotion. Bower reported one strikingly successful case of such training in an infant.

For many years, ever since the emergence of clinical psychology as a separate professional category, there had been a problem in reconciling the psychologist (Ph.D. and more recently Psy.D.) and the psychiatrist (M.D.). Despite occasional expressions of mutual goodwill by the two APA's, no durable accommodation had been achieved. By 1978 the issue promised to come to a head because of the imminence of a national health insurance program. In 1977 Charles Kiesler, executive officer of the American Psychological Association, took issue with the president of the American Psychiatric Association, who had testified before Congress that reimbursement by the government should be made only to psychiatrists. In an editorial in the February issue of *American Psychologist*, Kiesler reviewed the comparative training data for the two professions, pointing out that "Psychiatrists receive standard medical training, little formal training in the study of human behavior, and practically no experience in research. Clinical psychologists, on the other hand, receive very little training in medicine (although many have strong backgrounds in neuroscience), rather standardized and extensive sets of experience research, and are engaged for five or more years in a broad study of human behavior."

He concluded that if drugs are needed a client should go to a psychiatrist (legally authorized to prescribe medicines because of his M.D.), but that a psychologist might be preferable for other purposes because of his more extensive human behavioral background and research-generated skepticism and open-mindedness. This latter characteristic is especially important because of the danger that clients may succumb to one or another of the current fads.

Social affairs, public interest. The most dramatic involvement of psychologists in social activism during 1977 was the cancellation by the APA Council of Representatives of convention contracts with three cities in states that had not passed the proposed Equal Rights Amendment to the U.S. Constitution (Atlanta, Ga., Las Vegas, Nev., and New Orleans, La.). Although this action was stimulated primarily by activist women's organizations (women constituted 27% of the total APA members), it was overwhelmingly supported by the council. The action was taken despite warnings by APA attorneys that the organization would be liable for up to $21 million in breach of contract lawsuits if the cities decided to sue.

Another cancellation by the APA council was that of the tentative new popular journal *Psychology*, which had a trial run as a slick quarterly and was aimed at lay as well as professional readers. It was believed that the venture was too risky financially because there had been insufficient positive response to the pilot issue and because the organization did not appear to have sufficient expertise in this field to ensure success.

Human rights in one form or another continued to change the ground rules for a variety of activities in which psychologists were involved. For example, late in 1977 a federal judge in Pennsylvania declared that the constitutional rights of retarded persons, guaranteed under the Equal Protection Clause of the Fourteenth Amendment, are violated when such persons are kept segregated in institutions. The judge's decision was based on the premise that retarded persons maintained in isolation from other segments of society are not receiving "minimally adequate habilitation," defined as the education and care required by such people to achieve their maximum development. At the end of 1977 it was unclear how the ruling would be implemented, but it might well produce significant changes in the treatment of retarded persons.

—Melvin H. Marx

Space exploration

The first test flights of the shuttle orbiter "Enterprise," a new record for continuous time spent in space, and the launching of two probes to Jupiter and Saturn were outstanding developments of recent months in space exploration.

Manned space flight

A delegation from the U.S. National Aeronautics and Space Administration (NASA) met Nov. 14–17, 1977, in Moscow with counterparts from the Soviet Academy of Sciences Intercosmos Council. The meetings covered potential scientific areas in which joint missions involving the U.S. space shuttle and the U.S.S.R. Salyut space stations would be of value.

Space shuttle. Rising 60 ft above the Joshua trees and other flora of southern California's Mojave Desert, the vertical tail of the shuttle orbiter "Enterprise" seemed incongruous in the chill January morning. The orbiter was being moved at 3 mph on a "strongback" transporter 36 mi overland from the assembly plant in Palmdale, Calif., to NASA's Dryden Flight Research Center, Edwards Air Force Base.

At the Dryden Center, "Enterprise" was readied for a series of test flights from atop a modified Boeing 747 carrier aircraft to simulate the final five minutes of return from orbit when it will briefly become an airplane or, more correctly, a glider. Taxi tests and flights with no crew aboard "Enterprise" determined that the "world's largest biplane" was airworthy.

Two teams of NASA test pilots then alternately piloted "Enterprise" in the approach and landing tests at Dryden. Fred W. Haise, Jr., and Charles G. Fullerton comprised one team, and Joseph Engle and Richard H. Truly the other. Three mated flights, with "Enterprise" remaining attached to the carrier aircraft, measured aerodynamic loads and verified the capabilities of the electrical fuel cell, hydraulic, and control systems.

Haise and Fullerton piloted the first of five free flights on August 12 when frangible attach bolts were detonated to release "Enterprise" from the 747 at an altitude of 24,000 ft. Slightly more than five minutes later, the orbiter touched down on the dry lake runway at 220 mph, and the "Enterprise" had passed a critical milestone in its test program. Two additional free flights were flown with the tailcone covering the orbiter's main engines. The tailcone was designed to reduce drag and buffeting between the orbiter and the carrier aircraft during ferry flights between landing sites and the Kennedy Space Center launch complex in Florida.

Without the tailcone the orbiter's glide angle steepens from 11° to 22°, closer to what the actual glide angle will be on an orbiter returning from space. The fourth and fifth "Enterprise" free flights were without the tailcone, and the final landing was on the 15,000-ft main runway. Flight time from release to touchdown without tailcone for the fourth flight was 2½ minutes and for the fifth about 2 minutes.

The second shuttle orbiter was under construction during the year at Palmdale and was to be the first orbiter to go into space. With approach and landing test flights complete, preparations were begun to ferry "Enterprise" from Dryden to NASA's Marshall Space Flight Center in Alabama for vibration and acoustics tests in a vertical test stand during 1978.

In other space shuttle developments during 1977, the first test firing was made in July of the strap-on, solid-rocket, recoverable booster at the manufacturer's plant in Utah. Three more firings were scheduled during 1978.

Worker stands inside one of the fuel tanks being constructed for the space shuttle. Each tank will hold more than 1,000,000 pounds of propellant to boost the shuttle into Earth orbit.

Wide World

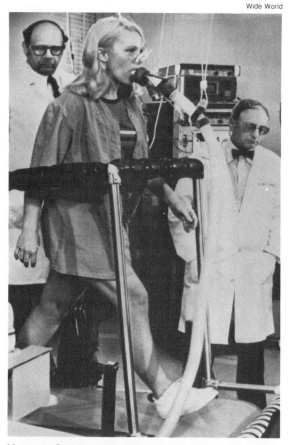

Margaret Seddon, one of six women applicants who were selected as space shuttle astronauts, takes a test on a treadmill at NASA's Johnson Space Center in Houston, Texas.

Test versions of the shuttle orbiter's main engine had accumulated burning time equivalent to 27 launches by the year's end at the NASA National Space Technology Laboratories in Mississippi. The first external fuel and oxidizer tank for the orbiter's main engines was completed in September, and it was scheduled to be used in combined testing with a trio of main engines during 1978 at the laboratories.

By early 1978 extensive planning was underway for operation of the Space Transportation System, for which the shuttle will serve as the vehicle. Policies for accepting commercial, military, and civil government payloads and for pricing orbiter cargo-bay space were taking shape. Several firm payload commitments were reflected in cargo manifests for shuttle flights in 1980 and 1981.

The European Space Agency (ESA) began construction in 1977 on the first flight version of Spacelab, a scientific space station to be carried in the shuttle orbiter's cargo bay. The first Spacelab mission, with a mixed U.S. and European crew, was scheduled for the eleventh operational shuttle flight in December 1980.

With the pool of active astronauts at NASA's Johnson Space Center, Houston, Texas, down to 27, applications for space shuttle pilot astronaut and mission specialist candidates were open for the year ending June 30, 1977. A total of 8,079 applications were received, and from these 208 were selected for week-long interviews and medical exams at the Center. In January 1978 NASA chose 35 final candidates. Among them were six women, the first ever chosen for U.S. space flights.

Soyuz 24/Salyut 5. The Soviet spacecraft Soyuz 24, manned by Col. Viktor Gorbatko and Lieut. Col. Yury Glazkov, lifted off from the Tyuratam Cosmodrome on Feb. 7, 1977. It rendezvoused with the Salyut 5 space station after 12 orbits and then docked with the Salyut the following day. Salyut 5, launched June 22, 1976, was in an orbit with an apogee of 177 mi, a perigee of 135 mi, and an inclination to the Equator of 51.6°.

Gorbatko and Glazkov activated the space station and began 18 days of experiments in life sciences, chemistry, and Earth observation. Investigations into the cosmonauts' cardiovascular and vestibular (inner-ear) functions, including electrocardiograms, and a study of weightlessness effects upon seed germination were included in the life sciences group. Basic studies were made in fluid behavior, surface tension, and crystal growth. Experiments concerning the diffusion of dibenzyl and tolane under weightless conditions—with an eye toward improving the manufacture of semiconductors—were also run. The Soyuz 24 crew measured the transparency of the Earth's atmosphere in the infrared region of the spectrum and made Earth surface observations in infrared for agricultural purposes.

After leaving Salyut 5 in automatic mode, the Soyuz 24 crew undocked from the space station on February 25 for reentry and landing. The spacecraft's descent module landed near Arkalyk in Kazakhstan during a blowing snowstorm.

Four days prior to the Soyuz 24 launch, the Salyut 4 space station was maneuvered by Soviet ground control to reenter the atmosphere and be destroyed over the Pacific after more than 12,000 Earth orbits. Salyut 4 had been manned for a total of 93 days by two cosmonaut crews, Soyuz 21 and 22. On Aug. 8, 1977, Salyut 5 was also deorbited and destroyed during atmospheric reentry.

Soyuz 25/Salyut 6. Soyuz 25 was launched on October 9 from Tyuratam to dock with the Salyut 6 space station. Attempts by cosmonauts Lieut. Col. Vladimir Kovalenok and Valery Ryumin to carry out a hard docking with Salyut 6 were fruitless, and the Soyuz was brought down northwest of Tselinograd on October 11. Salyut 6 had been launched on September 29 into an initial orbit with a perigee of 136 mi, an apogee of 171 mi, and an inclination of 51.6°. Two days before the Soyuz 25 launch, the Soviet control center maneu-

Soviet cosmonauts Yury Romanenko and Georgy Grechko train underwater in order to experience conditions similar to those they would encounter on a spacewalk. Subsequently, Grechko made an 88-minute spacewalk while the Soyuz 26 that he and Romanenko had taken into orbit was docked with the Salyut 6 space station.

vered Salyut 6 into a near-circular orbit with perigee/apogee of 209/219 mi.

It is unclear as to whether the difficulty was mechanical or procedural, but the failure of the Soyuz 25 to dock with the space station was the second within a year in the Soyuz/Salyut series. It was also the fifth Soyuz mission failure attributable to docking problems and the eighth failure in the Soviet Union's previous 13 attempts to carry out various space-station missions.

Soyuz 26–28/Salyut 6. Lieut. Col. Yury Romanenko and civilian flight engineer Georgy Grechko were launched December 10 from the Tyuratam Cosmodrome aboard Soyuz 26 to dock with Salyut 6. Soyuz 26 docked at the port opposite the one attempted by Soyuz 25. In explaining this, Soviet space scientist Konstantin Feoktistov said, "The first docking device was found to be suspicious and the decision was made to dock at the other end."

Grechko made an 88-minute spacewalk on December 20 wearing a newly designed "semirigid" spacesuit with an integral life-support backpack that eliminated the umbilicals used on previous walks. He inspected the primary docking port and reported that the mechanism was "brand new as though just taken off a machine tool. There are no scratches or dents on it. All of the docking equipment . . . is in fine order."

Grechko's spacewalk was the first from a Salyut space station and was made from an airlock near the primary docking port. Romanenko was also suited and passed tools, a television camera, and lights through the open hatch to Grechko. Inspection of the primary docking port left the way open for a continuously manned space station by means of future visits to Salyut 6 by relief crews or by unmanned resupply spacecraft.

Progress 1, the first unmanned space supply mission, is photographed just before it docked with the Soviet space station Salyut 6. The spacecraft took fuel and scientific equipment to Soviet cosmonauts Yury Romanenko and Georgy Grechko, enabling them to remain in space a record 96 days.

On Jan. 10, 1978, Lieut. Col. Vladimir Dzhanibekov and flight engineer Oleg Makarov were launched from Tyuratam in Soyuz 27 to join Romanenko and Grechko in Salyut 6. After a successful docking with the space station, Dzhanibekov and Makarov brought fresh supplies to the two earlier cosmonauts and remained with them in the Salyut until January 16. They then returned to the Earth in Soyuz 26, leaving their spacecraft for Romanenko and Grechko.

The first unmanned space supply mission took place on January 20 when the Soviets launched the Progress 1 capsule to Salyut 6. It provided Romanenko and Grechko with additional supplies of food, fuel, and scientific equipment.

The first man to enter space from a country other than the U.S. or the Soviet Union was Capt. Vladimir Remek of Czechoslovakia. He and the Soviet crew commander, Col. Aleksey Gubarev, were launched from Tyuratam on March 2 in the Soyuz 28. The next day they docked with Salyut 6 and joined Romanenko and Grechko, who on that date broke the record for continuous time in space, 84 days, set by the crew of the U.S. Skylab 4 in 1973–74.

—Terry White

Space probes

Continued monitoring of the Viking spacecraft on Mars and the launching of Voyagers 1 and 2 to Jupiter, Saturn, and, perhaps, beyond were among the highlights of the past year. In addition, the U.S. launched

its largest and most elaborate scientific probe.

Viking mission to Mars. During 1977 Mars continued to receive the attention of Vikings 1 and 2. On January 28 the Viking lander failed to respond to command signals from Madrid, Spain, and four days later it similarly ignored signals from Goldstone, Calif. Such failures caused alarm among mission controllers since the malfunction was in the probe's only remaining radio receiver. On February 2, however, controllers managed to reestablish contact. The failure was probably caused by temperatures in the receiver that were lower than anticipated. The Viking landers had been programmed to perform an automatic mission in case of failures, transmitting engineering and weather data as well as one color picture every five days. Following the failure in Lander 1, ground controllers rewrote the automatic mission program to include more data and sent it to both landers.

As February ended, the orbit of the Viking 1 orbiter had been changed so that the probe would approach within 70 km (1 km = 0.62 mi) of the Martian satellite Phobos, which was under ideal lighting conditions to be photographed. Instruments aboard the orbiter also measured the satellite's temperature and gravitational field.

Cameras aboard both landers continued to see haze in the Martian atmosphere almost everywhere they were pointed. Scientists theorized that it was probably a combination of crystals of water and carbon dioxide in the thin planetary air. The cameras also kept a close watch on the sky so that they could record how the light

Phobos, the inner satellite of Mars, is revealed in a photomosaic taken by the Viking 1 orbiter at an altitude of 300 miles. As seen here, the satellite is approximately 75% illuminated and measures about 13 miles across and 11.8 miles from top to bottom.

appeared to fade with the onset of autumn on Mars. Similarly, they examined the surface for evidence of the movement of dust that would be expected as the planet neared its closest approach to the Sun. Data from the seismometer on the Viking 2 lander indicated that the planetary crust in the region of Utopia Planitaria is approximately 15 km thick.

On March 12 commands were sent to the Viking 1 lander to turn off the gas chromatograph mass spectrometer, which had searched for organic compounds in the soil. The instrument had an electrical short circuit that rendered it inoperative. Because the spectrometer had completed its assigned tasks, its loss was not a major one to the scientific mission of the lander. Before the malfunction the spectrometer had established that there were no organic compounds on the surface of Mars at the lander's location and had discovered isotopes of argon in the atmosphere. On March 14 the lander signaled mission controllers on the Earth that the instrument had been turned off.

An ambitious attempt to build a stockpile of small Martian rocks for use in the inorganic soil analysis experiment of Lander 2 was frustrated on March 22 when the soil sampler arm of the lander failed to obey an order to scratch the surface for such pebbles. All attempts to find bacterial forms of life in the Martian soil ended in May. The biology instrument aboard Lander 2 was turned off on May 28 and that on Lander 1 two days later. Lander 1's experiment had begun on July 28, 1976, and that of Lander 2 on Sept. 11, 1976. Both instruments had operated continuously and were decommissioned only after their supplies of helium gas, nutrients, and other consumables had been exhausted. All planned tests were completed.

Based upon the findings of the landers, biologists were unable definitely to confirm or deny the presence of some form of life on Mars. Though no proof of life was found, scientists were unable to determine what caused the strong reactions when Martian soil was analyzed. In summing up, Carl Sagan, director of the Laboratory for Planetary Studies at Cornell University, said, "We have gone to Mars with three Viking biology experiments and two of them have turned up data which nobody understands, data which certainly have left the biological hypothesis open."

In June consideration was given to increasing the already extended Viking mission by an additional eight months. Funds permitting, both landers and orbiters would transmit scientific and engineering data through early 1979.

On October 15 the Viking 2 orbiter dipped within 23 km of the surface of Deimos and photographed the crater-pocked, dusty surface of that Martian satellite. Measurements made of the perturbations of the probe's trajectory as it passed Deimos indicated that the density of the satellite was approximately 2 grams per cubic centimeter.

As the year ended, mission controllers were attempting to stretch the lives of the two Viking orbiters by transferring helium from their propulsion systems to their attitude-control systems. The successful transfer of the gas would enable the attitude-control systems of the probes to function through the end of 1978. The helium would replace nitrogen, which was exhausted early in 1978.

Voyagers 1 and 2. During 1977 two probes departed on an ambitious journey to the outer giants of the solar system. On August 20, Voyager 2 was launched from Cape Canaveral in Florida on a trajectory that would take it on a flyby of Jupiter in July 1979 and then to a meeting with Saturn in August 1981. If everything goes well, the probe could also visit Uranus and Neptune later in the century.

About an hour after lift-off, telemetry from Voyager 2 indicated that its science boom, a 7.5-ft arm holding scientific instruments, had not deployed as had been programmed. Mission controllers were puzzled because the signals could be interpreted in two ways: the boom had actually deployed but one of its switches had failed, or the boom had not deployed to its full extent. The fact that the magnetometer and radioisotope thermoelectric generator booms and other antennas had deployed added to their concern. Later events, however, proved that the boom was deployed enough to accomplish its task. Early in the journey the probe's on-board computer switched gyroscopes within the guidance unit, perhaps because of higher vibration levels than usual during launch. This, however, did not seriously jeopardize the mission.

Voyager 1 was launched September 5 and experienced few of the problems of its sister craft. Its science boom had been modified to assure that it would function properly. On September 11 and 13 trajectory maneuvers were made by firing thrusters. During the procedure mission controllers noticed that exhaust plumes were probably impinging on the spacecraft structure and thus requiring more fuel than anticipated. The same problem arose during course-correction maneuvers of Voyager 2.

Both probes carried a phonograph recording and a cartridge and needle to play it. On the copper record were greetings in many languages; music of various cultures and periods; natural Earth sounds of animals, ocean, and weather; and digital information by which intelligent beings elsewhere in space could decipher the record and learn from where it came. The record also carried signals convertible to pictures, which included 115 photographs of the solar system and of the Earth and man's activities on it.

As 1977 ended, Voyager 1 had overtaken its sister probe and was 164,829,170 km (102,420,100 mi) from the Earth. Voyager 2 at the time was 162,708,660 km (101,102,480 mi) from the Earth. The date of the closest approach to Jupiter for Voyager 1 was then estimated to be March 5, 1979, and for Voyager 2 the date was to be July 9, 1979. By the year's end, mission controllers had abandoned plans to observe Comet Kohler with the two probes because of possible damage to optical systems since the cameras would have to be pointed for long times in the direction of the Sun.

Jupiter also received a visit from another probe. On June 10 Pioneer 11 for the second time crossed the orbit of that planet on its way to a rendezvous with Saturn in September 1979. The probe was programmed to fly just outside the rings of Saturn and within 15,000 mi of the planet's surface, performing a scouting mission for the two Voyagers. If it does not survive the outer fringes of the rings, then the Voyager 2 mission to Uranus would have to be abandoned.

Mysteries from deep space. On November 29 NASA held a news conference to discuss the findings of the largest and most elaborate scientific probe ever launched by the United States. Sensors aboard the High Energy Astronomy Observatory (HEAO) revealed

what been recorded during the first 100 days of the probe's estimated lifetime of 15–18 months. HEAO was designed to collect data on the theoretical black holes, survey the entire sky in the X-ray region of the spectrum, and gather information on gamma-ray activity in deep space.

X-ray instruments aboard the satellite detected emissions that seemed to be two superimposed frequencies coming from the constellation Circinus, deep in the southern sky. While some astrophysicists believed the source of the emissions to be a black hole, others were skeptical. The probe also recorded a gamma-ray flash on October 20 that was simultaneously recorded by two other satellites. Scientists hoped that the probe would settle conclusively the question of whether or not black holes exist.

HEAO-B, a follow-up probe, was scheduled for launch in October 1978. It is programmed to maneuver and to lock on for long periods of time to X-ray sources identified by HEAO and other X-ray probes and satellites.

Titan IIIe rocket (left) launches Voyager 1 on its journey to Jupiter and Saturn on Sept. 5, 1977. When it was 7,250,000 miles from the Earth, Voyager 1 returned the first photo ever taken by a spacecraft of the crescent Earth (right bottom) and crescent Moon.

(Left) UPI Compix; (right) Courtesy, NASA

Future probes. Plans for the Pioneer mission to Venus remained on schedule. On May 19 the atmospheric entry body of the probe passed a crucial test when it was dropped from a balloon at an altitude of 10 mi above the U.S. Army's White Sands (New Mexico) Missile Range. Its parachute deployed as planned after a nine-minute drop through a simulated Venusian atmosphere. Pioneer Venus A, scheduled for launch on May 22, 1978, was designed to orbit the planet and study its upper atmosphere. Its Pioneer Venus B companion, scheduled for launch on Aug. 11, 1978, was to release probes into the Venusian atmosphere.

An even more sophisticated future experiment for analyzing the Venusian atmosphere is that of the joint French-Soviet mission to the planet scheduled for 1983. The U.S.S.R. planned to launch a Venus orbiter that would carry a French 9-m-diameter balloon filled with helium. The balloon would be ejected into the Venusian atmosphere and drift above the surface of the planet at an altitude of 55 km with a gondola weighing 150 kg (330 lb) hanging beneath it. Within the gondola would be about 30 kg (65 lb) of scientific instruments. In commenting on the joint mission, Jacques Blamont, chief scientist of the French Centre National d'Études Spatiales, said, "We want to play the game by their rules." Thus, he clearly indicated that the Soviets were in charge of the project.

West Germany entered into an agreement with the U.S. to participate in NASA's proposed Jupiter orbiter probe, scheduled for launch in early 1982. The interplanetary spacecraft would be the first to be launched by the space shuttle and was designed to perform the most detailed scientific investigation of that planet yet undertaken. It consisted of an orbiter that would circle Venus for at least 20 months and a probe that would plunge deeply into the planet's atmosphere. The West Germans were to provide the retropropulsion module for injecting the probe into orbit around Venus and also scientific experiments.

NASA also was planning another cooperative venture with European space scientists. The U.S. space agency proposed launching two probes to investigate the Sun from positions outside the plane of the ecliptic, the plane of the Earth's orbit extended to meet the celestial sphere. In effect, the two probes would be sent into polar orbits of the Sun. One probe would be built by NASA, and the other would be provided by the European Space Agency. The two craft would be launched by the space shuttle to orbit the Sun in 1986 at a distance of some 70 million mi, as close as they could approach because of the intense heat.

—Mitchell R. Sharpe

NASA's High Energy Astronomy Observatory (HEAO) is tested prior to its launch in August 1977. The probe was designed to survey the entire sky in the X-ray region of the spectrum, and scientists hoped that it would determine whether black holes exist.

Courtesy, NASA

Transportation

No major breakthroughs in transport technology were announced during 1977, as inflation continued to have an adverse effect on research and development. The objectives of such R&D also continued to change because of the ever increasing governmental regulations and standards in the environmental and safety areas.

The major stimulant to research in transportation technology in recent months was the growing threat of severe petroleum shortages in the near future, along with expected oil price rises. Without oil, transportation as it presently exists in the developed nations would virtually cease. For example, in the United States transportation accounts for more than 50% of total U.S. oil consumption, and there is no practical alternate fuel—at least in the short run—for most of the transport equipment now in use. As a result, there has been a steady stream of innovations that seek greater efficiency in the use of petroleum fuels. This common feature recurs throughout the following discussion.

The McDonnell Douglas Super 80, carrying 155 passengers in a 147.8-foot fuselage, is a stretched version of the original DC-9, which had a length of 104.4 feet and held 80 passengers.

Air transport. Faced with insufficient R&D funds for new air transport development, estimated at $1.5 billion or more, the major U.S. commercial aircraft manufacturers evaluated other ways of filling the growing demand for commercial aircraft during the 1980s. The Boeing Co. announced that it was dropping its plans to build a new-generation 7N7 or 7X7 design and would instead concentrate on a variation of existing models for its next aircraft line. This plane would offer 180–200 seats and two- and three-engine versions at $20 million–$25 million each.

Even this change could be threatened by action taken by the McDonnell Douglas Corp., which for the fourth time was stretching the fuselage of its two-engine DC-9 from its original 80-passenger, 104.4-ft version in 1965 to a 155-passenger, 147.8-ft version for use in the 1980s. Called the Super 80, the new aircraft was designed to have a range of 2,000 mi, one-third greater than its predecessor. It was to use a modified Pratt & Whitney JT8D-209 engine that could operate on 20% less fuel per seat-mile as well as produce only half the noise of currently flying narrow-body jets. McDonnell Douglas reported that it had received $400 million in orders for 27 Super 80s from Swissair, Southern Airways, and Austrian Airlines.

The new, quiet Pratt & Whitney engine to be used in the Super 80 could discourage new transport purchases if airlines decided to use it as a replacement for noisy, fuel-thirsty engines on their still operational but technically obsolete DC-8s and B-707s. For the airlines, buying new engines would be less costly in the short run than buying new planes, and they would still be able to comply with tough new aircraft noise standards recently established by the U.S. Federal Aviation Administration (FAA).

Aircraft builders were also considering stretched fuselages as a means of increasing the capacity of their new widebody jumbo jets for use on high-density, short-to-medium-distance routes. For example, Lockheed Aircraft Corp. proposed a double-deck, 456-passenger version of its L-1011 with a 20-ft-longer fuselage. McDonnell Douglas would add about 22 ft to its DC-10 to provide 20% greater passenger capacity along with an 18% reduction in fuel and other operating costs on a per-passenger basis.

Boeing reported studies for building a 600-seat version of its B-747 jumbo jet, a capacity boost of 150 passengers, although it said this would require engines with thrusts exceeding 60,000 lb. Boeing subsequently reported an order from All Nippon Airways for three 500-seat, short-haul B-747s, with options for eight more. Another version of this aircraft, the B-747SP (special performance), was used by Pan American World Airways to celebrate its 50th anniversary with a record-breaking round-the-world flight of 26,706 mi in 54 hours—48 in the air—at an average speed of 494 mph. The flight began and ended in San Francisco and included passage over both the North and South poles.

The British-French Concorde supersonic transport was finally given permission to operate out of New York's Kennedy Airport, which its owners regarded as an important step to help hold down the soaring costs of the aircraft. Latest estimates showed that $4,280,-000,000 had been spent for R&D and production of 16 Concordes, two of which were prototypes flown only for test purposes. By early 1978 only nine had been sold, at a reported price of $80 million apiece; the price for the remaining five was $92 million each. While the U.K. and France continued to predict breakeven or profitable operations, on a direct cost basis, for their North Atlantic Concorde routes, the overall direct operating losses of the fleet were estimated at $78 million in 1977.

The Soviet Union's Tu-144 SST completed its first scheduled passenger flight from Moscow to Alma-Ata, a distance of approximately 2,000 mi, at speeds of more than 1,250 mph. Its schedules were frequently delayed, however, because of problems with excessive noise, vibration, and high fuel consumption.

The Langley Research Center, Hampton, Va., announced a major milestone in aircraft propellants by burning, for the first time, hydrogen in a scale model of an air-breathing, supersonic, combustion ramjet engine that could be the forerunner of engines for hypersonic aircraft. This was part of a joint $80 million–$100 million R&D program being funded by the U.S. National Aeronautics and Space Administration (NASA) and the U.S. Air Force, aimed at eventual development of a Mach 6–8 hypersonic transport with a 5,000-mi range and 200-passenger capacity.

The use of new technology to assure safer aircraft landings continued to increase, as the FAA reported that all 63 major U.S. airports had installed Minimum Safe Altitude Warning Systems to alert controllers both aurally and visually when a plane on their radar was too low. Houston's commercial airport became the first to begin operating an automated collision alert system, which gives air controllers visual and aural signals when planes are on conflicting courses. The other 62 airports planned to obtain this new system.

The ambitious and promising program to develop an advanced-technology STOL (short-takeoff-and-landing) aircraft for the U.S. Air Force took a turn for the worse, as the Office of Management and Budget moved to cut the program from the U.S. budget despite the fact that prototypes built by competing Boeing and McDonnell Douglas were already flying under Air Force contracts worth $200 million. Such a move could jeopardize a huge potential commercial market for the two aircraft manufacturers.

Highway transport. Faced with highway size and weight limits, truck manufacturers continued to seek ways to increase truck capacity. Strick Corp., a trailer manufacturer, entered the tractor market with its new

Two prototypes of the Sikorsky S-76 helicopter are joined by an S-70 Black Hawk (foreground) in a test flight over West Palm Beach, Florida. Capable of accommodating up to 12 passengers and of attaining a speed of 180 mph, the S-76 is designed for business and industrial uses. The Black Hawk, with a passenger capacity of 11, is to be used by the U.S. Army as a utility transport.

"Cab-Under," a 26-ft-long, two-axle vehicle that carries the first of a twin-trailer combination clamped on its back. Strick tested its two prototypes over 20,000 mi of durability runs. The tractor is only 49 in high, yet ground clearance is 8¼ in, or about the same as conventional rigs. The one-man cab is at the front left, and the radiator is at the front right. To engage the first trailer, the tractor moves under it and then secures it tightly. The second trailer is then hitched, making a total combined length of 55 ft. Payload space is increased by 600 cu ft, about 20% more than conventional 55-ft combinations. Strick planned to build 50 units at a cost 10% above that of conventional 55-ft combinations. Another prototype, with two front steering axles and longer trailers, was intended for western truck operations.

Innovations to help save fuel in over-the-road truck use were reported as successful, according to a survey by the U.S. Department of Transportation. The survey showed that 1976-model trucks with such fuel-economy devices as advanced engines, special fan clutches, radial tires, and aerodynamic shields to reduce wind resistance saved truck operators 155 million gallons of fuel in 1976. Detroit Diesel Allison introduced two new diesel engines that can be easily adjusted to provide a variety of performances as the buyer desires; for example, a governor adjustment can upgrade a 365-hp engine at 1,950 rpm to a 430-hp engine at 2,100 rpm, or the number of transmission speeds can be altered to match the engines for maximum fuel economy.

U.S. tire manufacturers started testing new high-pressure radial tires, inflated about 50% above regular radials, which they claimed would boost car mileage 3–10%. A major drawback, however, especially for the tire replacement market, was the need for larger wheels to handle the different configuration of the tire. The Firestone Tire & Rubber Co. subsequently announced that it was introducing a version of such a tire that would go on standard auto wheels and would result in fuel savings of 9–12% over belted-bias tires and 3–4% over conventional radials.

The Goodyear Tire & Rubber Co. started marketing a steel-belted, all-weather radial tire designed for year-round use. The firm claimed that its new tread design provides traction on ice and snow that is nearly as good as its winter radial. The new tire was not expected to have as long a lifetime as the standard radial, but would exceed it in fuel economy, high-speed handling, and traction on dry pavement.

Other fuel-saving innovations for automobiles were reported under way, with mixed results. Eaton Corp. unveiled a computerized Valve Selector System for shutting off half an engine's cylinders when full power is not needed, with predicted fuel savings of 30% on the highway and 10–15% overall. The innovation is a renewal of a similar system used 60 years ago but discontinued. Ford Motor Co. reported similar efforts on its "3 by 6"-cylinder engine, but later announced

Courtesy, General Motors Corporation

The 512E is an experimental electric car designed by General Motors Corporation for urban use. The batteries of this two-passenger model are located beneath the seat.

that it was discontinuing its plans to sell the new engine in 1978-model light trucks because 18 months of testing showed that the engine was only 6% more fuel-efficient than normal six-cylinder engines (compared with an expected 10–15% gain) and that it did not perform as well as expected on the road. Another research program setback was announced when General Motors Corp. discontinued its efforts on the rotary engine because extensive tests failed to demonstrate its potential for meeting required low-emission and fuel-economy standards.

Several promising developments concerning electric cars were announced. General Motors said that its research was progressing rapidly and that it could foresee large-scale production in four to seven years. Based on its research in this field during the past five years, GM was aiming at the following specifications: weight, 1,700–1,800 lb; wheelbase, 90 in; length, 150 in; top speed, 55 mph; range, 100–150 mi per day with nightly recharge; load, two passengers plus groceries; and price, $5,500-$6,000. GM said that the electric car should be an ideal second family car for strictly city driving. The major problems remained the cost, weight, and inadequate power of existing batteries. Though the common lead-acid battery was being improved, the breakthrough was expected in other types. For example, the zinc-nickel type takes only 25% of a car's gross weight, has a 60–120-mi range, and can be 80% recharged in one hour at special recharging stations. GM was also exploring the lithium-iron sulfide type, with a potential power six times that of lead-acid types.

General Electric Co. and the AiResearch division of

Garrett Corp. were selected by the Energy Research and Development Administration (ERDA), later absorbed into the U.S. Department of Energy, to produce test models of a practical electric car. Specifications required a car for "stop and go" commuting and urban driving, with a range of 75 mi and top speed of 55 mph. Test models had to be developed within two years and technology advanced so that mass production was feasible by 1982. The program, funded by recent legislation, called for building 2,500 electric autos within two years and, if possible, an additional 5,000 more advanced models during the following four years. The total costs could reach $160 million.

The U.S. Department of Transportation received on contract from Volkswagen an experimental auto that stressed fuel savings, passenger safety, and emission reductions. A two-door hatchback, it weighed 2,072 lb, had a turbocharged four-cylinder diesel engine, and seated four. The most outstanding feature was its fuel economy, 55 mpg for city and 69 mpg for rural driving. Safety features included automatic shoulder belts, a pretensioning device that tightens the belt against the chest in an accident, and an energy-absorbing device that reduces the high acceleration forces on the occupant. Emissions in all categories—hydrocarbons, carbon monoxide, and oxides of nitrogen—were about 50% less than the standards set by the U.S. Environmental Protection Agency for gasoline engines.

Pipelines. The 800-mi, 48-in-diameter trans-Alaska pipeline was completed in 1977 and started moving crude oil at an initial rate of 600,000 bbl a day, to be increased to 1.2 million by early 1978 and to 2 million eventually. The crude oil was then transshipped at Valdez, Alaska, via tankers directly to U.S. West Coast refineries and storage facilities, and to the Gulf and East coasts via the Panama Canal. A more economical way to haul it across the U.S. would be by pipeline to refineries in the Middle West, but government environmental and safety regulations were delaying several planned projects. The plan receiving most attention, because it could be built the fastest, was one proposed by the Standard Oil Co. of Ohio, which would convert an existing 669-mi natural-gas pipeline into part of a 1,000-mi crude-oil line from Long Beach, Calif., to Midland, Texas. Once the remaining approvals were obtained, construction of the line plus a tanker terminal was expected to take about two years.

Exploration for offshore oil sources, plus construction of large offshore oil ports, stimulated innovations in installing submarine pipelines. For example, R. J. Brown and Associates reported the third successful use of a new method that it designed and developed. The latest involved the movement of a 7,050-ft section of 36-in pipeline across 244 mi of the North Sea at a depth of 1,260 ft. Seven pipe strings were assembled side by side along a special launchway. As each string was pulled into the water by a 22,000-hp oceangoing

tug, the next string was moved into place and welded into a single line. The entire line was then pressurized to 300 psi with air. It required 40 hours to move the bottom tow over the 244 mi because of poor weather conditions on the surface, with waves up to 13 ft. At the destination, a newly developed underwater plow, about 36 ft long and weighing 50 tons, was pulled by the same tug to dig a trench for final positioning of the pipeline. Inspection showed a clean, steep-side trench with no damage to the plow, and revealed that the pipeline itself remained within tolerance limits.

The construction of several long-distance coal slurry pipelines continued to be delayed because of the refusal of railroads to permit them to cross their rights-of-way and the inability of the pipelines' backers to obtain rights of eminent domain from a number of states. The congressional Office of Technology Assessment (OTA) concluded an 18-month analysis of coal slurry pipelines and found them to be technically feasible and more economical than rail unit trains for high-distance routes close to both mines and markets. OTA also found that rail coal-carrying capacity could be increased more quickly than coal production and that some states' resistance to release of their scarce water supplies remained a major stumbling block for the slurry lines. The issue thus centered on whether Congress would approve pending legislation giving such pipelines federal eminent domain rights because of their interstate nature.

Samarco Mineração, a South American firm, reported completion of what it called the "world's largest iron-ore pipeline," a 250-mi, 20-in, welded-steel line with a maximum design capacity of 12 million metric tons per year. The line was to transport hematite ore, another first, since other such lines transported only magnetite, which is only half as corrosive and abrasive. The ore-water mix was expected to vary from 66 to 70% solids, increasing at the second pump station. The new pipeline extended from the deposit, 484 mi north of Rio de Janeiro, to Ponta Ubu, an Atlantic port, and it crossed two mountain ranges with a maximum elevation of 3,878 ft before dropping to sea level. At no point, however, did the gradient exceed 15%.

Rail transport. Railroad electrification in the U.S., little used because of the efficiency of the diesel locomotive, took a major step forward when the U.S. Department of Transportation approved a $256 million plan to complete electrification of the Northeast Corridor (Washington, D.C., to Boston) and to upgrade the corridor's old system (300 of 456 mi were electrified) to permit high-speed passenger-train operations up to 120 mph. The department awarded International Engineering Co. a $441,733 contract to design an experimental high-voltage electrification system for 20 mi of test track in Pueblo, Colo. To be completed by March 1979, it was intended for application to the Northeast Corridor electrification program.

The ''Six Pack,'' a piggyback car designed by the Santa Fe Railway, costs less to build and weighs 35% less than conventional railroad flatcars of equal capacity. The lighter weight results in a considerable saving of fuel.

Two subway cars with energy-storing flywheels achieved energy savings of 20–40% in nine months of revenue testing on New York Metropolitan Transportation Authority lines. As the cars brake, the traction motors convert energy that would normally be dissipated as heat into electricity to drive motors that speed up the flywheels. When energy for acceleration is needed, flywheel motion is converted back into electricity to power the traction motors. The AiResearch division of Garrett Corp., which built the cars with a $1,260,000 grant from the Urban Mass Transportation Administration (UMTA), predicted annual savings of $19 million if 200 cars were equipped with the device. The flywheel innovation was also being applied in the UMTA-backed program to develop an Advanced Concept Train for urban rail transit.

Despite a ten-year effort and an estimated $150 million investment the U.S. railroad industry voted to discontinue its Automatic Car Identification (ACI) system, designed for greater utilization of freight cars. ACI required labeling of all cars and installation of roadside scanners that read the labels and fed data into a central computer, which in turn provided carriers with up-to-the-minute car locations. Problems with the labeling, the cost of the scanners, and the preference of many railroads for their own computerized car-control systems resulted in performance of ACI far below goals.

The Union Pacific Railroad announced successful tests of a new device which it believed could cut fuel consumption by trains as much as 12%. Installed on the locomotive, the device enables the engineer of multi-locomotive trains to cut the power of one or more units when not needed, with the remaining units handling the load. The amount of savings depends largely on the skill of the engineer. Union Pacific foresaw possible savings in diesel fuel of approximately eight million gallons a year.

Sizable fuel savings were also promised by another rail innovation. The Santa Fe Railway announced its new ''Six Pack,'' a lightweight piggyback car that consists of little more than a center sill with a fixed hitch at one end and aprons for trailer wheels or container bolsters at the other end. The six single-trailer/container skeleton-type cars, semipermanently connected by articulated couplings, are less expensive to build and weigh 35% less than conventional railroad flatcars of equal capacity. The lower weight translates into an estimated savings of 5,200 gallons of diesel fuel in a round-trip load of 100 trailers between Chicago and Los Angeles.

Another announced fuel saver for rail piggyback traffic, but one which would require a major shift in rail operations, was the ''Road-Railer'' concept being promoted jointly by the North American Car Corp. and the Bi-Model Corp. Reintroducing an innovation tried on a limited basis some time ago, the combination highway-railway trailers contain a unique rear-axle suspension and transfer mechanism that allows them to be pulled by a standard truck tractor for highway operations, and to be coupled directly together for rail piggyback operations. By eliminating piggyback flatcars, rail operators hoped to achieve weight savings as high as 67% along with 28% lower equipment costs. In addition, there was a potential saving of 50% in costs of fuel compared with normal operations because only half the locomotive power is required. The first prototype 45-ft Road-Railer van was scheduled for tests during 1978, and 20-ft, 27-ft, and 40-ft units were also to be built.

Increased freight-car utilization by railroads serving paper companies was promised by Pullman-Standard, which demonstrated its new "Blue Ox" car to shippers. The car can unload chips, short logs, or long logs in less than three seconds. The builder claimed that it would eliminate the need for the following types of cars: woodchip hopper, woodrack flatcar for short logs, and side-stake flatcar for long logs.

Reduced empty-car mileage was the objective of tests of unusual hopper-bottom boxcars designed to haul grain in bulk one direction and packaged or palletized freight or lumber in the other direction. The two test cars, built by National Steel Car Corp. and leased from the British Columbia Railway, had top hatches and hopper bottoms for loading and unloading grain, as well as conventional side doors for loading and unloading the packaged or palletized cargo or lumber. A grid-type floor prevented interference with the grain flow for unloading, yet supported the non-bulk cargo.

Water transport. Communications and navigation utilizing new technology moved ahead rapidly in the water transport field. The U.S. National Aeronautics and Space Administration and the U.S. Army Corps of Engineers began monitoring the Mississippi River from St. Louis to the Gulf of Mexico via a satellite 22,800 mi out in space. The satellite relayed data on water level, rainfall, and water quality received from water data transmitters at strategic locations along the river to a central receiving station and control point at Vicksburg, Miss., for storage in a computer and display on a map. Data were used for computer models of river regulation schemes and to help in response to floods, low water, and environmental emergencies. Such information should help to prevent damage to ships and structures. The system began operation with 20 monitoring stations and was expected to expand to 80.

The U.S. Coast Guard announced its schedule for completion of installation of LORAN-C radio navigation service in U.S. coastal waters: Gulf Coast by July 1978; East Coast by July 1979; and Great Lakes by February 1980. Alaska and the West Coast already had LORAN-C, which replaces the less exact LORAN-A used since World War II. The new system allows a ship to fix its location to within one-fourth of a nautical mile and has a range of 1,500 nautical miles, more than twice that of LORAN-A.

After a year of introductory service to ocean shipping, the Communications Satellite Corp. and its RCA

"El Paso Southern" undergoes sea trials in April 1978. The 948½-foot-long tanker is designed to carry about 163,750 cubic yards of liquefied natural gas, enough to service a town of 34,000 for a year.

Courtesy, Newport News Shipbuilding and Dry Dock Company

Courtesy, Halter Marine Services, Inc.

Tug-supply ship "Padre Island" was developed for use in the offshore oil and gas industry. Among its duties are towing drilling rigs and delivering cargo to offshore installations.

Corp., ITT Corp., and Western Union International partners began marketing the first commercial maritime communications satellite service via the Marisat system of three geostationary satellites located 22,300 mi above the Atlantic, Pacific, and Indian oceans. Marisat provided instantaneous radio communications for ships by relaying messages to and from shore stations. Operating 24 hours a day, the system could provide ships with the latest navigation and weather data for schedule and route changes if needed, and advise of port delays and fuel and repair facilities. A complete shipboard unit sold for about $55,000.

Port navigation improved with the start of operations by MarineSafety International of a computerized simulator to train ships' officers. Located in LaGuardia Airport's Marine Terminal, the simulator—first of its kind—has an exact replica of a ship's bridge and a panoramic screen showing port conditions and the bow of the ship as they would actually appear. Movement of the ship, with accurate changes in course and speed, is simulated on the screen by projections of photographs of the port taken by moving television cameras that respond to commands from the bridge. Different photographs and charts are used to simulate actual ports. Various harbor traffic and weather conditions, such as fog, wind, and current, and their effects on an actual vessel can be duplicated. Instruments on the bridge, such as the fathometer, radar, and radio direction finder, also behave exactly as they would for a given position.

Two innovative offshore tug-supply vessels with advanced propulsion systems were being built by Halter Marine Service for delivery to Acadian Marine Service in mid-1978. The 216-ft vessels, costing more than $3 million each, were designed primarily to supply offshore oil projects, but could carry 180 20-ft containers when drilling activity is slack. They were the first offshore supply vessels to feature electric diesel engines

regulated by silicon-controlled rectifier systems; these rectifier systems pool power from the five diesel-driven electric generators, allowing any number of them to be idled when less than full power is needed. Direct control of the electric power eliminates the need for gears and clutches and allows placement of engines so as to maximize cargo capacity.

A study by the U.S. Maritime Administration in conjunction with a maritime industry team (Newport News Shipbuilding & Dry Dock Co., Bechtel Inc., Mobil Shipping and Transportation Co., and the Oceanic Division of Westinghouse Electric Corp.) resulted in a proposal to use nuclear submarine tankers to deliver crude oil from Arctic areas. Newport News Shipbuilding, developer of the design, claimed that the technology already exists to build the ships, which could operate under the polar ice cap continuously. Long-range sonar would warn of icebergs and other submarines, and loading/unloading would take place underwater at terminals with sealed cavities to prevent leaks. The likelihood of spills would be greatly reduced because the submerged vessels would not be subject to the surface perils of heavy seas and rough weather.

—Frank A. Smith

U.S. science policy

When Jimmy Carter, trained in nuclear engineering by the U.S. Navy, was inaugurated as president of the United States on Jan. 20, 1977, the leadership of the U.S. scientific community looked forward to his term of office with high expectations. The "blank check" decade, which had begun with the launching of the first Soviet sputnik in 1957, had been marked by extraordinary generosity on the part of the federal government. In the face of an implied threat of Soviet technological supremacy, established research groups had only to ask in order to receive, and newcomers found little difficulty in attracting public funds to establish new "centers of excellence." But, as in the biblical story of Joseph, the fat years had been followed by lean ones. In terms of constant, uninflated dollars, there was less federal money available for basic research in 1978 than there had been in 1968. Older scientists had to scratch for funding, younger researchers turned to other fields, and major scientific projects had to be shut down for lack of money. For research and development (R and D), the decline in federal funding was even more precipitous.

The new science adviser. It was against this dismal background that Jimmy Carter came to power, the first technically trained president since Herbert Hoover. The initial indication of Carter's attitude toward science came with his announcement that Frank Press, an internationally renowned geophysicist at the Massachusetts Institute of Technology, would be both his science adviser and director of the Office of Science and Technology Policy.

Press was highly regarded by his scientific colleagues, but it was also noted that this appointment had come rather late and that the White House seemed to be in no hurry to obtain Senate confirmation. Although President Carter had made most of his major appointments before his inauguration, he did not tap Press until February 1977, and Press was not confirmed until April.

The science adviser's first year was something of a rollercoaster ride. No sooner had he been nominated than journalists pointed out that two earlier appointees, White House energy chief James Schlesinger and Defense Secretary Harold Brown, were also familiar with R and D matters, were closer to the president, and were favored with far larger staffs. But then Jimmy Carter put his arm around Press's shoulders and told friends that this was the man who would be by his side when he made important decisions on R and D funding. Later, in midsummer, the White House announced that Carter would carry out a campaign promise by making sharp cuts in the staff of the Executive Office. For a period of weeks it was feared that the new Office of Science and Technology Policy would be reorganized out of existence, but when Reorganization Plan Number One was announced on July 15, OST was still there, somewhat pared down from its original size but in business nevertheless.

At the end of his first year, Press found himself in calmer waters. His original staff of 32 had been reduced by about a third, but he had drawn in supporting help from other agencies on temporary loan. Although the President's Committee on Science and Technology, a group of distinguished individuals who were to have provided independent judgments on science-policy issues, had been eliminated in the reorganization, Press had formed a number of ad hoc groups to offer guidance in specific areas. Unlike his predecessors George Kistiakowsky and Jerome Wiesner, he was not called upon to participate in significant defense policy decisions. In other areas, however, he still had the ear of the president when he needed it.

Basic versus applied research. One matter of critical concern to the scientific community was the attitude of the new administration toward basic as opposed to applied research in the allocation of budgetary resources. Carter had inherited from previous administrations a growing bias in favor of applied research. Lyndon Johnson, during a visit to the National Institutes of Health, had complained about research that was not immediately useful in fighting disease. The National Science Foundation had found that budgetary increases could be obtained only through development of an ambitious program known as Research Applied to National Needs. Even in private industry, research groups had been forced by economy-minded manage-

Courtesy, NASA

The U.S. Senate Subcommittee on Science, Technology, and Space holds videoconference hearings in Washington, D.C., while the witnesses testify from Springfield, Illinois. The hearings concerned a proposed new national weather and climate program.

ments to shift their resources away from basic research into applied areas.

This trend caused apprehension among all manner of research institutions. According to William Hittinger of RCA Corp., "There is no question today that research funds from the government are directed much more than they had been before, and I think this is a dangerous trend." In a discussion on public television, Wiesner, now president of MIT, pointed out that "Even in the big prestigious institutions we're finding pressures that drive us more to applied things rather than to basic research. . . .There is a growing awareness of the fact that basic research, while very healthy today, is in very serious trouble in the universities. . . . I don't think the audience should be left with the impression that we're talking about a problem that's going to hit us twenty or thirty years from now. . . . In my impression, I would say that we could be in very serious trouble in five or ten years; it could get increasingly worse. . . ."

While the scientific community anxiously awaited Carter's 1978 budget message as the first public test of the relationship between Press and the president, a promising indication surfaced on the occasion of the National Medal of Science awards in November 1977. In his address, Carter said: "As President, I now have the responsibility to prepare the national budget presentation to Congress, after consultation with Frank Press. . . . We were impressed with some of the problems that we have. The quality of scientific equipment, the number of top-ranked research centers and the percentage of faculty members who are scientists and who are also young have been falling off rapidly in recent years. In 1968, about 45% of the faculty members were young men and women. Now that has dropped off to about only 25%—which shows that in the future we have a problem on our hands, unless we take strong action to correct these trends.

"I am assessing each individual agency's budget these days. . . . In many instances the heads of those agencies, the cabinet members and others, have relegated research and development to a fairly low position of priority. But I directed the Office of Management and Budget to boost those research and development items much higher, and they will be funded accordingly.

"Finally I would like to say that we want to make sure that the climate for research and development in our country is enhanced with my own imprimatur of approval and interest. . . ."

Carter made good on his promise in his state of the union message: "The health of American science and technology and the creation of new knowledge is important to our economic well-being, to our national security, to our ability to help solve pressing national problems in such areas as energy, environment, health, natural resources. I am recommending a program of real growth of scientific research and other steps that will strengthen the Nation's research cen-

Sidney Harris

"Now, if we run our picture of the universe backwards several billion years, we get an object resembling Donald Duck. There is obviously a fallacy here. . ."

ters and encourage a new surge of technological innovation by American industry. The budget increase of 11% for basic research will lead to improved opportunities for young scientists and engineers, and upgraded scientific equipment in the Nation's research centers. I am determined to maintain our Nation's leadership role in science and technology."

In the budget, Press pointed out to reporters, attention was focused on R and D support as a distinct consideration. While the budget was in the process of being prepared, the president had asked his Cabinet members to submit a list of important research questions. Press had also joined with Vice-Pres. Walter Mondale and a high official in the Office of Management and Budget to consider the state of U.S. science. They met with the heads of government agencies, industrial leaders, and university presidents and pored over numerous reports from science-policy analysts in and out of government. Their principal findings were that there were inadequate research opportunities for young Ph.D.s, that deficiencies in scientific instrumentation were beginning to extract a heavy toll, and that the quality of academic science had begun to fall off.

Two major sources of data supported the findings. One was a study published in June 1977 by two political scientists, Bruce L. R. Smith of Columbia University and Joseph J. Karlesky of Franklin and Marshall College in Lancaster, Pa. Their report, *The State of Academic Science*, received considerable favorable publicity when it was issued. It warned that the nation should be concerned about the mounting deterioration of much of the scientific support system. The evidence for this was found to be "extensive." In addition, research and laboratory facilities were becoming outdated, general support funds for such facilities had grown increasingly scarce, and long-term funding for basic research was far less certain. There had been a noticeable shift away from basic to applied and mission-oriented research and from risk-taking to relatively safe and predictable lines of inquiry. The less prestigious universities and departments were being neglected, and the number of top-ranked research centers was declining.

Confirmation of this diagnosis could be found in a mountain of data entitled *Science Indicators 1976*, issued by the National Science Board of the National Science Foundation in February 1978. Like *The State of Academic Science*, it found that the continuing success of U.S. scientific research served to conceal long-term problems beneath the surface. Once more attention was called to the decline in federal support of R and D in constant dollars. In 1964 federal and private support of R and D in the U.S. totaled 2.9% of the gross national product. In 1974 the figure had fallen to 2.29% and in 1976, to 2.25%.

The confidence crisis. Dependent as it is on public support, the U.S. scientific community, over the years, has become inordinately sensitive to public attitudes toward science. Many perceived (perhaps incorrectly) a relationship between public confidence in science and the generosity of federal funding. It was certainly true that the drop in funding that began in the late 1960s was accompanied by a decline in public confidence in science as measured by national public-opinion polls. Whereas 56% of those polled had a high level of trust in scientific research in 1966, later surveys registered a drop to 32% in 1971 and a slow recovery to 41% in 1977.

The sudden drop-off could probably be traced to two unrelated factors. The first was the historic circumstance of the Moon shots; it could hardly be expected that the extraordinary public exhilaration engendered by those triumphs could be sustained indefinitely. The second was the pervasive impact of the troubled '60s on all institutions. According to a Harris Poll, public confidence in religion, higher education, government, industry, and the media all declined sharply after 1966.

Surveys sponsored by the National Science Foundation indicated that confidence in science actually rose and fell with the tide, with scientists consistently remaining just behind physicians on the scale of public trust. Other polls indicated that 70% of the public, despite an awareness of the occasionally adverse effects of science-based technology, continued to look on science and technology as having done more good than harm. Another Harris Poll placed "scientific research" at the top of a list of major factors that would be more important in the next 25 years than in the past;

91% held this to be true. Similarly, 78% of the respondents saw "technological genius" as a key to future national greatness. A 1977 survey of European opinion produced similar results: 69% saw science as "one of the most important factors in the improvement of our daily life" and 89% believed that even more auspicious discoveries were yet to come.

Policy evaluation. It would be a mistake, however, to assume that the public viewed science only in its role of benefactor. Science in the 1970s has another function—that of evaluating in advance the relative risks as well as the benefits of new technologies. And it was that role that often led into the boggy ground of uncertainty or, worse, the minefields of public acrimony.

Some of the questions that policymakers brought to scientific judgment in 1977 were familiar, but cast in new and more complex configurations. The risk/benefit calculus of nuclear energy, the subject of bitter partisan debate within the scientific community for more than a decade, had broadened to encompass new and more frightening possibilities. The old specter of reactor meltdown and the subsequent release of radiation to the environment paled almost into insignificance before the new threat of nuclear proliferation, the possible result of widespread use of fast breeder reactors. The fast breeder reactor manufactures its own fuel in the form of plutonium, and in the process produces more plutonium than it can utilize. Some argued that the plutonium, an ingredient of nuclear weapons, could be stolen by terrorist groups or misused by irresponsible nations.

Prominent among the scientific considerations involved in this policy issue was the availability of uranium to fuel conventional nuclear plants. A plentiful supply of uranium, it was argued, would make it unnecessary to rush into development of the breeder reactor. Economists argued that uranium, like most natural resources, would be discovered and extracted in response to demand. In other words, as the supply dwindled, prices would rise, more money would be available for prospecting and development, and thus more uranium would come on the market. Such, generally, was the view of a blue-ribbon panel organized by the Mitre Corp. and funded by the Ford Foundation.

Not so, said the Uranium Resources Group, a panel organized by the National Research Council as part of its study of nuclear and alternative energy sources. Its members, primarily Earth scientists, argued that even though the hoped-for reserves might exist, it would not be possible—under any imaginable economic scenario—to locate and exploit them in time to meet the anticipated demand for nuclear power during the next decades. There the matter stood, agonizingly undecided, in the spring of 1978.

Other scientific concerns also became political issues. Was the artificial sweetener saccharin a potential carcinogen? What dangers were presented by the presence of organic pollutants in drinking water? What would be the environmental impact of a vast underground antenna the U.S. Navy proposed to construct in Upper Michigan? If nuclear reactors were a potential threat to life, what about the long-term effects of stack gases from coal-burning power plants? And even if these were not immediately life-threatening, would the increased burden of carbon dioxide that they added to the atmosphere raise global temperatures to an intolerable degree a century hence?

The process by which scientific authority was brought to bear on these perplexing, often frightening issues had become something of an issue in itself. One viewpoint was expressed by William M. McGill, the president of Columbia University, to a group of Roman Catholic lawyers in New York: "We are weakening America's scientific leadership by unwittingly establishing the principle that the conflicting advocacy of the legislature or the courtroom is the best way to develop sound public policy in science and technology. . . . The adversary method for arriving at truth on which our legal procedures are based is, in simple language, not appropriate for arriving at sound public policy on scientific matters. Scientific questions simply cannot be set-

Researcher examines rat being used in tests of various food substances. The U.S. Food and Drug Administration banned saccharin because, when given in large doses, it caused cancer in rats.

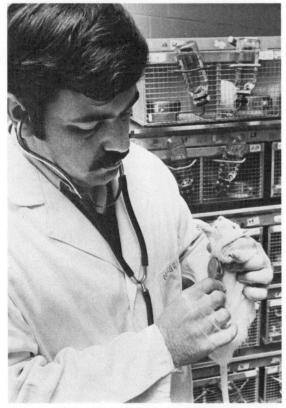

tled by persuasive argument. The only effective method for resolving safety questions in nuclear or biological research is the objective analysis of experimental results by our best scientific minds. . . . What I am saying, in unvarnished simplicity, is that the use of the adversary legal process to control scientific research is likely to lead to serious scientific errors and to badly thought-out policy."

Yet some of the leading spokesmen of science were forced, in all candor, to question whether "objective analysis" was indeed the crucial point. In an address to members of the American Association for the Advancement of Science in February 1978, Philip Handler, president of the National Academy of Sciences, admitted that such analysis is not always possible. Costs, he pointed out, are reckoned in dollars, benefits in esthetic or material values, and risks in terms of human lives. "Formal risk/benefit analysis may inform the decision maker, but decision necessarily continues to turn on value judgments; the acceptability of a given level of risk remains a political, not a scientific question. Hence, essentially political beliefs easily becloud seemingly scientific debate when scientists fail to recognize these boundaries."

The DNA controversy. There was no better illustration of this dilemma than the dispute over recombinant DNA. Ever since the revolutionary technique for rearranging genetic information in the laboratory was announced in 1974, the public had been fascinated by its awesome potential. But while its practitioners held out the promise of great forward leaps in medicine and agriculture, others raised terrifying possibilities of test-tube monsters, unstoppable plagues, and rampant cancer viruses.

Although the scientists themselves agreed first to a moratorium on certain forms of recombinant DNA research and then to a set of guidelines for the conduct of such research, several members of the U.S. Congress saw the need for legislation. For one thing, the guidelines had been promulgated by the National Institutes of Health and therefore applied only to research funded by that organization. Industrial research was not affected, except through voluntary action. A second concern was whether there should be a single national set of regulations or whether any community should be free to issue its own.

A dozen bills were presented to Congress early in 1977. Although a few scientists who were implacably opposed to all recombinant DNA research believed that the bills were not strong enough, the weight of the scientific community was on the side of legislative forbearance. Outweighing the fear of laboratory-created horrors was the specter of a sudden appetite within the federal government for political control of the search for knowledge.

What ensued was almost unprecedented for the U.S. scientific community—an effective lobby. Scientists had lobbied publicly in the past, but always on behalf of some great public issue, such as civilian control of atomic energy in the late 1940s. In 1977, however, the publicity triumphs being scored by groups opposed to recombinant DNA research, which were clearly having a dramatic impact on Congress, had the additional unplanned effect of generating a counterattack from the center. According to *Science*, the weekly journal of the American Association for the Advancement of Science, the lobby was fathered by Harlyn O. Halvorson, an officer of the American Society for Microbiology. Angered because he had been unable to present his organization's views to congressional groups, he decided to see what he could do through organized effort.

With the advice of lobbying experts, he created a coalition of scientific organizations opposed to federal regulation of research in recombinant DNA. Rather than attacking all legislation, Halvorson and his colleagues decided to support the most acceptable bill then available, which had been introduced in the House of Representatives by Paul Rogers (Dem., Fla.). On the Senate side, the lobby—which had grown to include some 20 scientific societies—became even more adventurous. Offended by provisions in a bill offered by Sen. Edward M. Kennedy (Dem., Mass.), the coalition helped persuade Sen. Gaylord Nelson (Dem., Wis.) to introduce a less restrictive substitute measure.

Some unexpected help came from the laboratory. Roy Curtiss III of the University of Alabama, whose early work had suggested that the threat of adverse consequences from DNA research was real indeed, was persuaded otherwise by his own findings. In a letter to the director of the National Institutes of Health, he wrote that "the introduction of foreign DNA sequences into EK1 and EK2 host-vectors offers no danger whatsoever to any human being." Later in the year Stanley Cohen, another pioneer in the field, made available the results of research indicating that DNA recombination occurs routinely in nature, so that laboratory experiments pose no radically new threat to existence.

By the end of the year the move to push restrictive legislation through Congress seemed to have lost almost all its momentum. Senator Kennedy had withdrawn support from his own bill, and the House bills were being rewritten. As of early 1978 it appeared that the most likely outcome on the House side would be the introduction of a co-sponsored bill extending the NIH guidelines to industrial research for a period of two years and mandating a study of the long-term problems of "genetic manipulation."

Sociobiology. In large measure, the DNA controversy aroused public attention because of the grave reservations announced by a few scientists who were perceived by the public as both concerned and informed. A second scientific controversy that arose during the year also was inflamed by the contentious statements of scientific authorities. The debate was a delayed response to a book published by the Harvard University Press in 1975, *Sociobiology: The New Synthesis*. Its author, a distinguished biologist named Edward O. Wilson, proposed that enough was now known about the role of genetic factors in controlling or influencing the behavior of the lower animals—from slime molds to nonhuman primates—to suggest that the field had ripened into a full-fledged discipline worthy of a higher level of effort.

If he had ventured no further, it is doubtful that Professor Wilson would have had a pitcher of water poured over his head at the 1978 meeting of the American Association for the Advancement of Science. But in his book he indicated that "the discipline [of sociobiology] is also concerned with the social behavior of early man and the adaptive features of organization in the most primitive contemporary human societies." Indeed, he implied, it would be only a matter of decades before the new field would be part of the foundation of the social sciences: "It is hoped that knowledge of the subject will assist in identifying the origin and meaning of human values, from which all ethical pronouncements and much of political practice flow."

The prospect that observations of animal behavior would be extended to form the basis for understanding the social behavior of humans was highly alarming to a small group of biologists and social scientists—notably Richard C. Lewontin and Stephen Jay Gould. Even more frightening, to a political action group called Science for the People, was the suggestion that research in this area might well provide guidelines for public policy. Therefore, in mid-February the group issued a statement that concluded, "We believe that sociobiology can tell us nothing about the suitability and consequences of the social life we experience or which we may wish to bring into being. We oppose efforts to invoke the biological sciences outside the areas of their applicability and beyond the powers of their methodology."

Although the session on sociobiology at the AAAS meeting excited a great deal of controversy, the tactics of the group that tried to prove Wilson was "all wet" appeared to be counterproductive. Gould, who identified himself as a member of Science for the People, disclaimed any responsibility on the part of that organization and blamed the disruptive tactics on a group formed to combat racism in science. In any event, the reaction of the packed auditorium was to give Wilson a standing ovation by way of apology.

But in a later press interview, one AAAS observer seemed almost nostalgic. "The good old days are gone," he was quoted as saying. "There's none of the fire we used to have around here." For those who saw science as a source of light rather than of heat, it was not a cause for regret.

—Howard J. Lewis

Scientists
of the Year

Honors and awards

The following is a selective list of recent awards and prizes in the areas of science and technology.

Architecture and civil engineering

AIA Gold Medal. The American Institute of Architects named Philip C. Johnson recipient of its 1978 Gold Medal. The prestigious award, first given in 1907, acknowledges "most distinguished service to the profession of architecture or to the Institute." Outstanding examples of Johnson's work include his Glass House (1949) in New Canaan, Conn.; New York City's Seagram Building (1958), done in collaboration with Ludwig Mies van der Rohe; the Munson-Williams-Proctor Institute (1960) in Utica, N.Y.; and the New York State Theatre (1964) at Lincoln Center, New York City.

Franklin Medal. The 1978 Franklin Medal was presented to Cyril M. Harris, professor of electrical engineering and architecture at Columbia University in New York City. The Franklin Institute of Philadelphia cited Harris' many contributions to acoustical science and engineering and his design of numerous concert halls of superlative acoustical quality. His credits include the Metropolitan Opera House and the remodeled Avery Fisher Hall, both in New York City, and the Kennedy Center for the Performing Arts in Washington, D.C.

Astronomy

Bruce Medal. Bart J. Bok, professor emeritus at the University of Arizona, was selected by the Astronomical Society of the Pacific to receive its Catherine Wolfe Bruce Award for 1977. Bok long studied the structures and evolution of galaxies and gave his name to very small dark nebulae ("Bok Globules") that may be sites of stellar birth.

Draper Medal. Since 1886 the National Academy of Sciences in Washington, D.C., has periodically presented its Henry Draper Medal to scientists who have distinguished themselves in the field of astronomical physics. Arno Penzias and Robert W. Wilson, both employed by Bell Laboratories in Holmdel, N.J., received 1976 Draper medals for their roles in discovering cosmic microwave radiation and interstellar molecules.

NASA Medal. For "outstanding contributions to space science, particularly in the field of planetary astronomy," James Elliot of Cornell University was awarded the 1977 NASA Medal for Exceptional Scientif-ic Achievement. During occultation experiments undertaken aboard the Kuiper Airborne Observatory (a converted C-141 transport aircraft), Elliot discovered the rings of Uranus.

Pierce Prize. The American Astronomical Society presented its 1977 Newton Lacy Pierce Prize to Donald N. B. Hall of Kitt Peak National Observatory in Arizona. Hall developed an infrared grating spectrometer and used infrared detectors to produce a spectra atlas of the solar photosphere and sunspot umbrae covering wavelengths between 11,900 and 25,000 angstroms. In addition, his work on Fourier-transform spectrometers made it possible to obtain very-high-resolution spectra of late-type stars.

Plyler Prize. The American Physical Society presented its first Earle K. Plyler Prize to Charles H. Townes of the University of California at Berkeley. Among other reasons, Townes was chosen for "his part in the initiation of microwave interstellar molecular spectroscopy and for his participation in the first detection of the spectral lines of ammonia and water molecules in outer space."

RAS Medal. John Bolton, employed by the Commonwealth Scientific and Industrial Research Organization as a research scientist in the Australian National Radio Astronomy Observatory at Parkes, New South Wales, Australia, was awarded the Gold Medal of the Royal Astronomical Society, London. Bolton, who is credited with outstanding contributions to both radio and optical astronomy, was cited for his studies of radio sources in space.

Rumford Prize. The 1976 Rumford Prize of the American Academy of Arts and Sciences was given to

Donald Hall

410

Frank Shu

Bruno B. Rossi of the Massachusetts Institute of Technology. Rossi's abiding interest in celestial sources of X-rays sparked the development of a rocket-borne detector that in 1962 discovered X-rays emitted from Scorpius X-1. Previously only the Sun was definitely known to emit such radiation. Rossi, who with colleagues first detected gamma rays from deep space, also helped to develop grazing-incidence telescopes that can take X-ray photographs of the Sun.

Warner Prize. Frank Hsia-san Shu, an astrophysicist at the University of California, Berkeley, was selected by the American Astronomical Society to receive the 1977 Helen B. Warner Prize. After working on the theory of spiral density waves in galaxies, Shu undertook research on the dynamics and evolution of disk-shaped galaxies. His recent studies have focused on contact binary stars and the exchange of matter in close binary systems.

Chemistry

AIC Medal. Max Tishler, emeritus professor of sciences at Wesleyan University in Connecticut and long-time research scientist at Merck & Co., Inc., was awarded the 1977 Gold Medal of the American Institute of Chemists. Tishler was involved in the discovery of many new drugs, including antibiotics and sulfonamides, and in the development of practical processes for manufacturing them on a large scale.

CIC Medal. The Chemical Institute of Canada Medal for 1977 was awarded to Ronald J. Gillespie of McMaster University in Hamilton, Ont. Gillespie was cited for his many contributions to inorganic chemical research.

Cope Award. Every second year the American Chemical Society presents its Arthur C. Cope Award to an outstanding organic chemist. In addition to a gold medal and an honorarium of $10,000, the award includes a $10,000 grant for research at an institution of the recipient's choice. Orville L. Chapman of the University of California at Los Angeles was honored in 1978 for his contributions in synthesizing and determining the properties of many organic compounds that previously were thought incapable of existence and for his identification of chemical compounds by which flying insects communicate with each other.

Garvan Medal. Madeleine M. Joullié of the University of Pennsylvania was named recipient of the 1978 Garvan Medal by the American Chemical Society. Joullié, who specializes in medicinal and heterocyclic chemistry and in mechanisms of organic reaction, helped evolve two new simple methods to synthesize a compound that has proved to be an orally active antiviral agent in mice.

Gibbs Medal. The Willard Gibbs Medal, awarded by the Chicago Section of the American Chemical Society, was given in 1977 to Melvin Calvin, director of the Chemical Biodynamics Laboratory at the University of California at Berkeley. The award committee noted especially Calvin's "discoveries on the complex chemistry of photosynthesis, for which he received the Nobel Prize in 1961, and . . . his work on nuclear applications in chemistry, in radioactive isotopes, and in chemical evolution."

Houdry Award. The biennial Eugene J. Houdry Award in Applied Catalysis was presented in 1977 to Vladimir Haensel, a vice-president at UOP, Inc., in Des Plaines, Ill. The Catalysis Society of North America cited Haensel's pioneering research and development of duo-functional catalysts. Haensel wrote the feature article "The Catalysis of Chemical Reactions" in the 1978 *Yearbook of Science and the Future.*

Langmuir Award. The Irving Langmuir Award in Chemical Physics is awarded in even-numbered years by the American Chemical Society and in odd-numbered years by the American Physical Society. The 1978 award, together with a $5,000 honorarium sponsored by the General Electric Foundation, was given to Rudolph A. Marcus of the University of Illinois at Urbana-Champaign. Marcus was honored for his work in theoretical chemical kinetics and chemical dynamics, including his theory of electron transfer reactions in solution.

Nobel Prize. The Royal Swedish Academy of Sciences named Ilya Prigogine recipient of the 1977 Nobel Prize for Chemistry. He is both professor of physical chemistry and theoretical physics at the Free University of Brussels and director of the Center for Statistical Mechanics and Thermodynamics at the University of Texas at Austin. Prigogine, who was born in Moscow in 1917 and settled in Belgium in 1929, was honored for his work in thermodynamics. Scientists had long known a fundamental law of thermodynamics;

Ilya Prigogine

namely, that physical systems tend to run down. Prigogine was the first to explain how some systems defy this tendency and increase the degree of their internal organization.

Perkin Medal. Paul J. Flory of Stanford University was named recipient of the 1977 Perkin Medal. The award, jointly sponsored by six American and European scientific organizations, honors Flory for his overall contributions to chemistry. He has received numerous other awards for specific accomplishments, notably for his studies of macromolecules, which have been one of his special interests.

Priestley Medal. The 1978 Priestley Medal of the American Chemical Society was awarded to Melvin Calvin. His two major interests are to promote the development of a screening test for carcinogens (cancer-producing substances) and to design a synthetic device to capture solar energy by imitating the light-dependent steps of photosynthesis in green plants.

Washington Academy Award. Lin Ming-chang; head of the chemical section of the Naval Research Laboratory in Washington, D.C., received the 1976 Washington Academy of Sciences Award. The citation described Lin as one of the first scientists to recognize the potential of lasers in synthetic chemistry.

Earth sciences

AAAS-Rosenstiel Award. The $5,000 American Association for the Advancement of Science-Rosenstiel Award in Oceanographic Science was given to Henry M. Stommel of the Massachusetts Institute of Technology in 1977. His research encompassed currents, tides, eddies, oceanic turbulence, and circulation.

Abbe Award. Horace R. Byers, professor emeritus at Texas A & M University, was given the 1978 Cleveland Abbe Award for Distinguished Service to Atmospheric Sciences by an Individual. The American Meteorological Society called attention to the many contributions Byers has made both as a teacher and as a research scientist. His studies on thunderstorms and cloud physics are especially well known.

Chree Award. The Institute of Physics in London announced that its biennial Charles Chree Medal and Prize had been awarded to two geophysicists in 1977. Drummond H. Matthews of Cambridge University and Frederick J. Vine of the University of East Anglia were honored for expanding scientific knowledge of seafloor spreading.

Day Medal. Since 1948 the Geological Society of America has annually awarded the Arthur L. Day Medal to individuals whose scientific achievements involved the application of physics and chemistry to the solution of geological problems. The 1977 Day Medal was presented to Akiho Miyashiro of the State University of New York at Albany, whose most recent work has included "incisive investigations of the mineralogy, geochemistry, and origin of abyssal tholeiites, serpentinized ultramafic suites, continental margin and island arc volcanics, and the contrasting chemical and physical environments of oceanic versus circumoceanic lavas."

Meisinger Award. The 1978 Meisinger Award of the American Meteorological Society was given to Alan K. Betts of Colorado State University "for his theoretical and observational studies of cumulus convection, in particular his work on non-precipitating cumulus convection and its parameterization and his application of data from the Venezuela International Meteorological and Hydrological Experiment to the investigation of the behavior of mesoscale convective systems."

Penrose Medal. The Geological Society of America's Penrose Medal, first given in 1927, was awarded in 1977 to Robert P. Sharp of the California Institute of Technology. Sharp has had an enduring interest in planetary surfaces, especially those of the Earth and Mars. His research has included studies of basin-range structures, the mechanism of glacier flow, landslide and mudflow processes, pediment formation, the mechanics of dune formation, Precambrian erosion surfaces of the Grand Canyon, Pleistocene glaciation in the U.S., and Martian ice and channels.

Rossby Medal. The most prestigious award of the American Meteorological Society is its gold Carl-Gustaf Rossby Research Medal given "for outstanding contributions to man's understanding of the structure and behavior of the atmosphere." The 1978 medal was awarded to James W. Deardorff of Oregon State University "for his imaginative research on the structure of the convective atmospheric boundary layer and its applications to prediction models and diffusion."

412

Second Half Century Award. Joost A. Businger of the University of Washington was named 1978 recipient of the American Meteorological Society's Second Half Century Award. The citation noted "his definitive analysis of atmospheric surface layer properties and his leadership in the field of boundary layer research."

Sverdrup Medal. "For his pioneering measurements of low-frequency variability in the oceans and for his development of a new class of oceanographic instruments," John C. Swallow was given the 1978 Sverdrup Gold Medal by the American Meteorological Society. Swallow is a physical oceanographer with the Institute of Oceanographic Sciences in Surrey, England.

Vetlesen Prize. The $50,000 Vetlesen Prize, administered by Columbia University in New York, was awarded in 1978 to J. Tuzo Wilson, director general of the Ontario Science Centre in Toronto. Wilson was among the first to accept the theory of plate tectonics as a highly probable explanation of earthquakes and other geological phenomena.

Energy

Jacob Award. The Max Jacob Memorial Award, sponsored jointly by the American Society of Mechanical Engineers and the American Institute of Chemical Engineers, is presented annually for work in the area of heat transfer. The 1976 award was bestowed on Robert G. Deissler of the NASA Lewis Research Center in Ohio for his contributions to the theory of turbulence and turbulent transfer.

Environment

Browning Award. Each year the New York Community Trust requests the Smithsonian Institution in Washington, D.C., to select a nominee for the Edward W. Browning Conserving the Environment Award. When the selection is approved, the Smithsonian makes the presentation. The 1977 recipient of the $5,000 honorarium was Charles Elton of Great Britain. In his book *Animal Ecology* (1927) Elton established the basic principles of modern ecology while elucidating such subjects as the balance of nature and the food cycle of animals.

Institute of Life Prize. A Japanese research team headed by Makio Ushida shared the Institute of Life Prize with Swedish chemist Sören Jensen. The honorarium, amounting to approximately $65,000, was sponsored by Electricité de France. The Japanese were honored for their studies on the toxicity of methylmercury, which causes Minamata disease. Jensen was selected for his research on polychlorobiphenyls (PCB's). These organic derivatives, used in paints, lubricants, rubbers, and so forth, are suspected to be carcinogenic agents.

Tyler Award. Eugene Odum of the University of Georgia was named 1977 recipient of the $150,000 John and Alice Tyler Ecology Award. Pepperdine University in Malibu, Calif., which administers the unusually large award, selected Odum for his contributions to basic and applied ecology. He was a pioneer in the field of radiation ecology and has written extensively on the use of radionuclide tracers in the study of ecological processes.

Wildlife Conservation Prize. The third recipient of the annual $50,000 J. Paul Getty Wildlife Conservation Prize was Ian Robert Grimwood, a British conservationist. The choice of Grimwood as the 1977 winner was based on his lifelong efforts to save endangered species of animals in many parts of the world. Notable successes were achieved in Kenya, Ethiopia, Saudi Arabia, and Peru. The prize is administered by the World Wildlife Fund—U.S.

Food and agriculture

Actonian Prize. The Royal Institution of Great Britain named R. L. Wain of the University of London recipient of the Actonian Prize for his work on the chemical control of plant growth and on the chemical basis of disease resistance in plants.

AIBS Award. The American Institute of Biological Sciences named Elvin C. Stakman, Paul J. Kramer, and William C. Steere recipients of its 1977 Distinguished Service Award. Stakman was honored as longtime head of a team of plant pathologists at the University of Minnesota, whose work led to the control of such devastating diseases as smut and rust in cereal grains. Kramer, long associated with Duke University in North Carolina, pioneered studies in water-plant relationships and was the motive force behind the establishment of several research facilities with controlled environments. Steere, an expert in the study of mosses and liverworts and president emeritus of the New York Botanical Garden, was lauded as a teacher, a research scientist, and as a founder of the Council of Biology Editors.

Babcock-Hart Award. The 1977 Babcock-Hart Award, funded by the Nutrition Foundation, was presented to David B. Hand by the Institute of Food Technologists. The retired head of the Department of Food Science and Technology at Cornell University received a $1,000 honorarium in recognition of his worldwide contributions to improved public health through the use of more nutritious food.

Borden Award. The American Institute of Nutrition selected Milton L. Scott of Cornell University as recipient of the 1977 Borden Award in Nutrition. Scott was cited for a series of studies on poultry that focused on the interrelationships between vitamin E and selenium. Scott showed that selenium is an essential nutrient for poultry apart from its relationship to vitamin E, and he described in detail the lesions of vitamin E and selenium deficiency in poultry, and their pathologies. The award includes a $1,000 honorarium.

Elvehjem Award. The American Institute of Nutrition named Philip L. White recipient of the 1977 Conrad A. Elvehjem Award for Public Service in Nutrition. White, associated with the Department of Foods and Nutrition of the American Medical Association, was cited for promoting improved nutrition education for both medical students and the general public. He also conceived and implemented the Western Hemisphere Nutrition Congresses. The $1,000 honorarium that accompanies the award was supplied by WARF Foundation.

Goldberger Award. The Goldberger Award in clinical nutrition was given to George F. Cahill, Jr., of the Harvard University Medical School in Boston. The Department of Foods and Nutrition of the American Medical Association cited Cahill for exceptional research in endocrinology and metabolism and for his clinical management of patients critically ill from starvation and carbohydrate deprivation.

Humboldt Award. The Alexander von Humboldt Foundation Award, which includes a $10,000 honorarium sponsored by the Alfred Toepfer Co. of West Germany, was shared in 1977 by Wendell Roelofs of Cornell University's Agricultural Experiment Station and Harry H. Shorey of the University of California at Riverside. The two were chosen for applying their research on insect sex pheromones to reduce the need for chemical pesticides on crops.

Johnson Award. Anthony W. Norman of the University of California at Riverside received the 1977 Mead Johnson Award for Research in Nutrition from the American Institute of Nutrition. Norman, who received a $1,000 honorarium, was cited for furthering understanding "of the metabolism of vitamin D and of the endocrine system which is responsible for the biological actions of vitamin D through production of the metabolite, 1,25-dihydroxy-vitamin D_3."

Lindbergh Award. Administrators of the newly established Charles A. Lindbergh Fund presented the first Lindbergh Award in 1978. Robert O. Anderson, chairman and chief executive officer of the Atlantic Richfield Co., was named recipient for contributing "most to achieving a balance between technology and the environment throughout his lifetime."

Osborne and Mendel Award. The 1977 annual Osborne and Mendel Award of the American Institute of Nutrition was presented to George Wolf of the Massachusetts Institute of Technology. Wolf, who received a $1,000 honorarium supplied by the Nutrition Foundation, presented evidence that vitamin A both participates in and helps control the biosynthesis of specific glycoproteins in intestinal, tracheal, and corneal tissues.

Stone Award. The Carolina-Piedmont Section of the American Chemical Society presented its 1977 Charles H. Stone Award to John D. Hatfield, a senior project leader with the Tennessee Valley Authority in Muscle Shoals, Ala. Hatfield was cited for many accomplishments, including his research on the physicochemical aspects of nitrogen, phosphorus, and potassium fertilizers.

Thom Award. Robert H. Burris of the University of Wisconsin at Madison was named recipient of the Charles Thom Award by the Society for Industrial Microbiology. Burris was honored for furthering understanding of nitrogen fixation.

Information sciences

ACM Award. The Association for Computing Machinery named Thomas B. Steel, Jr., recipient of its 1977 Distinguished Service Award. He was specifically honored for two decades of work on computer standards with diverse organizations. This work involved the collection through research and the dissemination of all fundamentally sound data-processing principles and methods.

Ballantine Medal. The Franklin Institute of Philadelphia named Charles Kuen Kao of the Electro-Optical Products Division of ITT in Roanoke, Va., and Stewart E. Miller of the Guided Wave Research Laboratory of Bell Laboratories in Holmdel, N.J., joint recipients of its 1977 Stuart Ballantine Medal. Both were honored for their contributions to light-guide and lightwave communications technology.

Fahrney Medal. The Delmer S. Fahrney Medal of the Franklin Institute was given to William Oliver Baker, president of Bell Laboratories, for his inspiring leadership in research in telecommunications, which led to "important and innovative technology for industry."

Goode Award. The American Federation of Information Processing Societies presented the 1977 Harry Goode Memorial Award to Jay W. Forrester of the Alfred P. Sloan School of Management at the Massachusetts Institute of Technology. Forrester's many contributions include computer modeling and simulation techniques, which have been used to examine the forces underlying inflation, unemployment, energy shortages, foreign exchange rates, the mobility of people, and tax policy.

Pioneer Award. Robert M. Page, retired director of research at the Naval Research Laboratory, was given the 1977 Pioneer Award of the Aerospace and Electronic Systems Society for his development of radar systems and techniques.

Turing Award. The 1977 Turing Award of the Association for Computing Machinery was presented, together with a $2,000 honorarium, to John Backus of the IBM Research Center in San Jose, Calif. Backus was cited for "profound, influential, and lasting contributions to the design of practical high-level programming systems, notably through his work on Fortran, and for seminal publication of formal procedures for the specification of programming languages."

Life sciences

Bailey Medal. Richard A. Howard, director of the Arnold Arboretum of Harvard University, was awarded the Liberty Hyde Bailey Medal by the American Horticultural Society. During his explorations in South America, the Caribbean, the Soviet Union, Austria, Turkey, and Pakistan, he gathered an impressive collection of plant specimens.

BSA Awards. Three persons were named by the Botanical Society of America as recipients of its 1977 Merit Awards. Sherwin Carlquist of Rancho Santa Ana Botanic Garden and Pomona College was honored for studies that advanced knowledge of xylem (tissue in the vascular system of higher plants), the evolution of plants on islands, and plant dispersal. Rogers McVaugh of the University of Michigan was cited for his systematic studies of New World plants. Peter H. Raven of the Missouri Botanical Garden was selected for his contributions to angiosperm biogeography and the systematics and general biology of onagraceae.

Ehrlich Award. Ludwik Gross, chief of the cancer research unit at the Bronx Veterans Administration Hospital, and Werner Schäfer, of the Max Planck Institute for Virus Research in Tübingen, West Germany, shared the 1978 Paul Ehrlich and Ludwig Darmstaedter Prize. Each received a gold medal and a $10,000 honorarium from the government of West Germany.

FASEB Award. The Federation of American Societies for Experimental Biology named Ronald W. Estabrook of the University of Texas Health Science Center recipient of the second FASEB Award for Research in the Life Sciences. The award, valued at more than $15,000, was established to reward research that has significantly contributed to the health and welfare of mankind. Estabrook's work has contributed to an understanding of how the body processes, responds to, and transforms a wide variety of chemicals, including drugs, hormones, pesticides, and agents with cancer-causing potential.

Horwitz Prize. The annual $25,000 Louisa Gross Horwitz Prize was jointly awarded to three scientists in 1977, each of whom made significant contributions in the field of human immunology. Michael Heidelberger, professor emeritus at Columbia University and adjunct professor of pathology at the New York University School of Medicine, is regarded as the father of modern immunology for discovering that antibodies are proteins. Elvin A. Kabat of Columbia University was honored for vastly extending knowledge of antibodies through research into their chemical composition and activity, including their role as a gamma globulin component. Henry G. Kunkel of Rockefeller University helped develop a classification of these antibodies in

the blood, thereby deepening understanding of the process of disease and cure.

Lilly Award. Charles R. Cantor of Columbia University was named recipient of the 1978 Eli Lilly Award in Biological Chemistry. Among other scientific contributions, Cantor detected the locations of biologically important sites in bacterial ribosomes, including the identification of the proteins on the 50S ribosomal subunit at the peptidyl-RNA binding site.

Pfizer Award. The 1978 Pfizer Award in Enzyme Chemistry was presented to Paul R. Schimmel of the Massachusetts Institute of Technology. He and his colleagues thoroughly studied a little-recognized deacylation activity possessed by aminoacyl-tRNA synthetases. Particularly significant was their observation that an amino acid covalently attached to a wrong tRNA can be deacylated much more rapidly than the correctly formed complex. This suggests that the deacylation activity is an important component of the cell's regulatory mechanism, and ensures the accuracy of translation of genetic information during protein synthesis.

Rosenstiel Award. Peter Dennis Mitchell, director of the Glynn Research Laboratories in Cornwall, England, was presented with the sixth annual Lewis Rosenstiel Award for Distinguished Work in Basic Medical Research. Mitchell received a $5,000 honorarium from Brandeis University for his research on "the conservation and movement of energy across the mitochondria membrane in animal cells, the chloroplast membrane in plants, and across the outer membrane in bacteria."

Materials sciences

Acheson Medal. N. Bruce Hannay, vice-president of research and patents at Bell Laboratories in New Jersey, was awarded the 1976 Edward Goodrich Acheson Medal of the Electrochemical Society for contributions to the society and electronic-materials science.

Acta Metallurgica Medal. The annual Acta Metallurgica Gold Medal, sponsored by Pergamon Press, was presented in 1977 to John W. Cahn of the Massachusetts Institute of Technology. The citation acknowledged his pioneering work in the fields of thermodynamics, quantitative metallography, and spinodal decomposition.

Clamer Medal. The 1978 Francis J. Clamer Medal of the Franklin Institute went to William A. Krivsky, the inventor of the argon-oxygen-decarburization process that revolutionized the manufacture of stainless steel.

Welch Award. Leslie Holland of the University of Sussex, England, was the seventh recipient of the Medard W. Welch Award given by the American Vacuum Society. The 1976 award included a $1,000 honorarium and a citation that noted his significant contributions to surface science and to vacuum and thin-film technology. During World War II he designed aircraft instruments and high-vacuum process systems.

Mathematics

NAS Mathematics Award. The National Academy of Sciences presented the 1976 and the 1977 NAS Award in Applied Mathematics and Numerical Analysis during its 114th annual meeting. Lin Chia-chiao of the Massachusetts Institute of Technology received the 1976 award and an honorarium of $5,000 "for his fundamental contributions to fluid mechanics, especially for his path-breaking work on stability of fluid flows." The 1977 award went to George B. Dantzig of Stanford University "for pioneering and fundamental work in the theory and application of linear programming, operations research, and in mathematical modeling of economic systems."

Medical sciences

Baekeland Award. Angelo A. Lamola of Bell Laboratories in Murray Hill, N.J., was given the 1977 Leo Hendrik Baekeland Award of the North Jersey Section of the American Chemical Society. During the presentation he was cited "for fundamental contributions to photochemistry, for pioneering studies of electronically excited biological molecules, and for the creative use of fluorescence to diagnose human diseases, particularly in young children."

Ciba-Geigy Drew Award. Robert C. Gallo, head of the Laboratory of Tumor Cell Biology at the National Cancer Institute, and Fred Rapp, professor and chairman of the Department of Microbiology at the Milton S. Hershey Medical Center, Pennsylvania State University, shared the first Ciba-Geigy Drew Award in Biomedical Research. Gallo has been studying retroviruses, which appear to be mainly responsible for leukemia and sarcoma induced in laboratory animals. After characterizing the properties of these viruses, Gallo hopes to apply his findings to human leukemia. Rapp's research has centered on the cancer properties of human herpesviruses, especially herpes simplex and cytomegaloviruses. These viruses have shown the capacity to transform normal cells in culture into cells with malignant properties and to stimulate cellular DNA synthesis, which seems to be a prerequisite for conversion of normal cells into cancer cells. These studies support previous suspicions that these viruses may play a role in human cancer, especially cancer of the cervix, prostate, and perhaps also the bladder. The award, administered by Drew University in New Jersey, included a $2,000 honorarium for each recipient.

Coolidge Award. The American Association of Physicists in Medicine named Edith Quimby recipient of its 1977 William D. Coolidge Award. Quimby, professor emeritus at Columbia University's College of Physicians and Surgeons, was cited for her work in nuclear medicine, radiation therapy, diagnostic radiology, and radiation protection.

Gairdner Awards. Each year since 1958 the Gairdner Foundation in Ontario, Canada, has given Gairdner International Awards for outstanding contributions to medical science. In 1977 five winners were announced, each of whom received a $10,000 honorarium. K. Frank Austen of Harvard Medical School was chosen "for his contributions to our understanding of the factors involved in the initiation, amplification and control of the inflammatory response." Sir Cyril A. Clarke of the Nuffield Unit of Medical Genetics in England was cited for "his original and far-reaching contribution to the prevention of haemolytic disease of the newborn." Jean Dausset of the Institut de Recherches sur les Maladies du Sang in Paris was honored for studies "of the effects of histocompatibility antigens in humans, and his continuing leadership in the application of this knowledge to such diverse fields as transplantation immunology and the study of genetically determined diseases." Henry G. Friesen of the University of Manitoba received his award for "contributions to the understanding of the biochemistry, physiology and pathophysiology of lactogenic hormones, and in particular, for the identification of human prolactin." Victor A. McKusick of the Johns Hopkins University School of Medicine was selected for "his many contributions to the development of the field of clinical genetics and his role in placing human genetics in the mainstream of clinical medicine."

Hufeland Prize. Kurt Biener of the University of Zürich Institute for Social and Preventive Medicine received the 1977 Hufeland Prize for his studies of drug use among Swiss youths. The annual award, which includes a grant of DM10,000 (about $4,000), recognized the importance of Biener's research and the value of his recommendations for improving public health. These included dissemination of scientific information on drug abuse to parents and teachers; less sensational publicity about drug use; greater efforts to control illegal use of drugs; and the establishment of information and counseling centers for youth.

Lasker Awards. The Albert and Mary Lasker Foundation named five medical scientists as recipients of its 1977 awards. The $15,000 Albert Lasker Clinical Medical Research Award was shared by Inge G. Edler, long associated with University Hospital in Lund, Sweden, and C. Hellmuth Hertz of the Lund Institute of Technology. Edler received the award for pioneering the clinical application of ultrasound in the medical diagnosis of heart abnormalities. Hertz was cited for developing the ultrasonic technology that led to a non-invasive method of diagnosing heart ailments and other diseases related to the reproductive, neurological, and excretory systems.

The $15,000 Albert Lasker Basic Medical Research Award was given jointly to K. Sune D. Bergström, chairman of the World Health Organization Advisory Council on Medical Research, Bengt Samuelsson of the

Rosalyn Yalow

Roger Guillemin

Andrew Schally

Karolinska Institutet in Stockholm, and John R. Vane of the Wellcome Research Laboratories in England. Bergström was credited with classic achievements in isolating prostaglandins and elucidating the chemical structures of the types designated as E and F. Samuelsson elucidated the mechanism of the biosynthesis of prostaglandins, analyzed their metabolism, and developed new methods for their measurement. Vane received the award for discovering prostaglandin X (re-named prostacyclin), which prevents blood clots that may lead to heart attacks and strokes.

Nobel Prize. The 1977 Nobel Prize for Physiology or Medicine was shared by three U.S. scientists. Rosalyn Sussman Yalow, who is affiliated with the Bronx Veterans Administration Hospital and with the Mount Sinai School of Medicine in New York City, received half of the $145,000 prize for her role in developing the radioimmunoassay. The technique is now widely used for measuring biologically active substances, many of which are present in the body in such small amounts that they are practically undetectable by other means.

The second half of the prize was shared equally by Roger Guillemin of the Salk Institute for Biological Studies in San Diego, Calif., and Andrew Schally, a staff member of the New Orleans VA Hospital and Tulane University of Louisiana. Working together and later separately, the two isolated and identified TRH, the hormone that causes the pituitary to produce the hormone TSH, which then stimulates the thyroid to produce still other hormones that in turn influence the metabolic rate throughout the body. The relatively simple TRH compound is now used to treat certain conditions related to deficiencies in pituitary hormone secretion.

Potts Medal. The 1977 Howard N. Potts Medal of the Franklin Institute was awarded to Godfrey N. Hounsfield, senior staff scientist at EMI Central Research Laboratory in England. The award acknowledged the importance of Hounsfield's invention of the computerized axial tomography diagnostic system, widely considered to be the most significant contribution to radiology since the discovery of X-rays.

Wyeth Award. Erwin Neter of the State University of New York at Buffalo received the Wyeth Award from the American Society for Microbiology. His main research has been the etiology and diagnosis of disease, the chemotherapy of infections, and the characterization of endotoxins.

Optical engineering

Ives Medal. Emil Wolf of the University of Rochester, New York, was given the 1977 Frederic Ives Medal by the Optical Society of America. The silver medal recognizes overall distinction in the field of optics. Wolf's research has been mainly in electromagnetic theory and physical optics, especially diffraction and the theory of partial coherence.

Mees Medal. The 1977 C. E. K. Mees Medal of the Optical Society of America was awarded to André Maréchal, director of the Institut d'Optique Théorique et Appliquée in Paris. His major contributions include the application of his theory of diffraction to optical-imaging systems.

Meggers Award. Mark S. Fred and Frank S. Tomkins, both associated with the Argonne National Laboratory in Illinois, were named joint recipients of the

417

1977 William F. Meggers Award. The Optical Society of America cited the two for their contributions to spectroscopy and to the design of spectroscopic measuring instruments.

Michelson Medal. The Franklin Institute of Philadelphia bestowed its 1977 Albert A. Michelson Medal on Albert V. Crewe of the University of Chicago. Crewe invented the scanning transmission electron microscope, a device that enabled scientists to obtain both the first still photographs and the first motion pictures of isolated atoms.

Richardson Medal. The 1977 David Richardson Medal of the Optical Society of America was given to Walter P. Siegmund of the American Optical Corp. for his contributions to applied optics. One of his major interests has been fiber optics.

Young Award. The Institute of Physics in London named R. Clark Jones recipient of its 1977 Thomas Young Medal and Prize. Jones, who works for the Polaroid Corp. in Massachusetts, was cited for his contributions to the theory of optics.

Physics

ASA Medals. The biennial Gold Medal of the Acoustical Society of America was presented in 1977 to Raymond W. B. Stephens, long associated with the Imperial College of Science and Technology in London. Stephens was lauded for his numerous contributions to acoustics, but "above all as a research supervisor who has taught and inspired a generation of acoustics students." Martin Greenspan, consultant to the National Bureau of Standards, was given the Silver Medal for his theoretical and experimental work in physical acoustics, particularly in the area of propagation of sound in gases and liquids.

Bingham Medal. Arthur B. Metzner of the University of Delaware received the 1977 Bingham Medal from the Society of Rheology. His early work on generalizing the traditional friction factors and Reynolds numbers of fluid mechanics to allow for non-Newtonian behavior was followed by generalizations in the areas of heat transfer and mixing. Recently his research has centered on measurement of normal stresses and the development of ways of dealing with relationships between stress and strain.

Boltzmann Medal. The 1977 Boltzmann Medal of the International Union of Pure and Applied Physics went to Ryogo Kubo of the University of Tokyo. The triennial medal was awarded to Kubo by the Union's Commission on Thermodynamics and Statistical Mechanics for his work on the theory of nonequilibrium statistical mechanics and on the theory of fluctuating phenomena.

Bonner Prize. Stuart T. Butler and G. Raymond Satchler were named recipients of the 1977 Tom W. Bonner Prize in Nuclear Physics by the American

Physical Society. The two were cited "for their discovery that direct nuclear reactions can be used to determine angular moments of discrete nuclear states and for their systematic exploitation of this discovery permitting the determination of spins, parities and quantitative properties of nuclear wave functions." Butler is on the faculty of the University of Sydney; Satchler is a physicist at the Oak Ridge National Laboratory.

Born Award. The annual Max Born Medal and Prize, jointly sponsored by the German Physical Society and Britain's Institute of Physics, was awarded in 1977 to Walter E. Spear of the University of Dundee, Scotland, for work on the transport of electric charge in noncrystalline (amorphous) semiconductors.

Boys Prize. John Clarke of the University of California at Berkeley was awarded the 1977 Charles Vernon Boys Prize by the Institute of Physics, London. He was cited for developing a device called SLUG (superconducting low-inductance undulatory galvanometer), which measures extremely small voltages, and for finding uses for the instrument in studying a wide variety of physical problems.

Davisson-Germer Prize. "For their contributions to the understanding of the inhomogeneous interacting electron gas and of its application to electronic phenomena at surfaces," Walter Kohn of the University of California at San Diego and Norton Lang of the IBM Thomas J. Watson Research Center in New York were awarded the 1977 Davisson-Germer Prize by the American Physical Society.

Duddell Award. The 1977 Duddell Medal and Prize of the Institute of Physics in London was presented to Ronald F. Pearson of the Mullard Research Laboratories in England. He was specifically honored for contributing to an understanding of crystal anisotropy and other single-crystal properties of substituted ferrimagnetic substances.

Europhysics Prize. Walter E. Spear of the University of Dundee, Scotland, was named recipient of the 1977 Hewlett-Packard Europhysics Prize by the European Physical Society. He received the award, which includes an honorarium of 20,000 Swiss francs (about $8,000), for outstanding achievements in the field of solid-state physics. Spear and his colleagues systematically altered the electronic properties of the amorphous semiconductors silicon and germanium by means of substitutional doping.

Faraday Medal. The Institution of Electrical Engineers in London named John B. Adams recipient of its 1977 Faraday Medal. Adams, the executive director general of the CERN Laboratories in Geneva, was selected for his contributions to the design and construction of high-energy particle accelerators.

Holweck Award. Maurice Goldman of the Center for Nuclear Studies in Saclay, France, received the 1977 Holweck Medal and Prize, which is jointly sponsored by the French Physical Society and the Institute of Phys-

Philip Anderson *Sir Nevill Mott* *John Van Vleck*

ics in London. Goldman's research centered on nuclear magnetism, with special emphasis on nuclear magnetic resonance in solids and spin temperature theory.

Maxwell Prize. The annual James Clerk Maxwell Prize of the American Physical Society was given in 1977 to John M. Dawson, a member of the faculty of the University of California at Los Angeles. The award, which includes a $3,500 honorarium, acknowledged Dawson's "contributions to plasma physics and controlled fusion as both an innovative theorist and a prolific inventor, whose ideas have provided the basis for several fusion configurations."

Nobel Prize. The 1977 Nobel Prize for Physics was shared by John H. Van Vleck of Harvard University, Sir Nevill F. Mott of Cambridge University, and Philip W. Anderson of Bell Laboratories and Princeton University. All three were honored for their contributions to an understanding of the behavior of electrons in magnetic, noncrystalline solid materials. Their discoveries were essential to the development of such devices as tape recorders, office copying machines, lasers, high-speed computers, and solar-energy converters. Van Vleck undertook extensive research on the magnetic properties of individual atoms in a long series of chemical elements. The ligand theory that he formulated has been one of the chemist's most useful tools in understanding the patterns of chemical bonds present in complex compounds. The focus of Mott's research changed from nuclear physics to metals, semiconductors, and photographic emulsions, and then to electrical conduction in noncrystalline solids. He is credited with formulas that describe the scattering of a beam of particles by particles of atomic nuclei and the transitions of certain substances between electrically conductive (metallic) states and insulating (nonmetallic) states. Anderson's contributions include methods of deducing details of molecular interactions from the

shapes of spectral peaks; theories that account for the effects of impurities on the properties of superconductors and established correlations between superconductivity, superfluidity, and laser action; and explanations of the interatomic effects that underlie the magnetic properties of individual metals and alloys. He also studied the semiconducting properties of disordered solid materials.

Oppenheimer Prize. Feza Gursey of Yale University and Sheldon Glashow of Harvard University shared the 1977 J. Robert Oppenheimer Memorial Prize, which is given annually by the Center for Theoretical Studies at the University of Miami. Each received a gold medal and an honorarium for theoretical elementary-particle physics. Gursey has also done considerable research on the chiral symmetry and spin independence of strong interactions. Glashow's special interests extend to strong, weak, and electromagnetic interactions and to the fundamental constituents of matter.

Planck Medal. For outstanding contributions in the fields of relativistic quantum theory and elementary-particle physics, Walter Thirring of the CERN Laboratory in Geneva was awarded the 1977 Max Planck Medal by the German Physical Society. His most recent interests have centered on problems combining quantum mechanics and thermodynamics, such as the stability of systems composed of charged particles.

Ricard Award. The French Society of Physics presented its 1977 Jean Ricard Physics Award to Roger Balian of the Center for Nuclear Studies in Saclay, France. Balian, who specializes in many-particle systems and has done research on subjects ranging from nuclear physics to the physics of condensed matter, is also known for his studies on wave behavior and on the isotope helium-3.

Schottky Prize. The annual Walter Schottky Prize of the German Physical Society was awarded in 1977 to

419

Siegfried Hunklinger of the Max Planck Institute for Solid-State Research in West Germany. Hunklinger received the DM 5,000 (about $2,000) honorarium supplied by the Siemens Corp. for his research in the area of acoustical and dielectric anomalies discovered in amorphous solids at low temperatures.

Psychology

Applications in Psychology Award. Starke R. Hathaway, who retired in 1970 after a long career at the University of Minnesota, received the 1977 Distinguished Contribution for Applications in Psychology Award from the American Psychological Association (APA). His contributions to clinical psychology include helping to organize the University of Minnesota Hospitals Psychopathic Unit and developing the Minnesota Multiphasic Personality Inventory, one of the most widely used structured personality tests.

ASA Medal. Lloyd A. Jeffress, who served on the faculty of the University of Texas for more than 50 years, received a 1977 Silver Medal of the Acoustical Society of America for his work in such fields as psychoacoustics and binaural hearing. He received his Ph.D. in psychology from the University of California at Berkeley and joined the Acoustical Society in 1939.

Professional Contribution Award. George Katona, long associated with the Institute for Social Research at the University of Michigan, received the 1977 Distinguished Professional Contribution Award from the APA. Katona's citation read in part: "His great methodological innovation in behavioral economics was to explain changes in the economic system by analyzing actions and predispositions to action on the individual level and applying micro-data to macro-economic analysis and prediction."

Scientific Contribution Award. Three psychologists were named joint recipients of the 1977 Distinguished Scientific Contribution Award by the APA. Richard C. Atkinson, director of the National Science Foundation, was cited "for combining classical methods of mathematics with emerging techniques of computer science, the best traditions of experimental psychology with new concepts of information processing, in the advancement of psychological theory and its applications." Russell L. De Valois of the University of California at Berkeley was honored for his "pioneering studies of color and pattern discrimination in primates." His studies "revealed the near identity of monkey and human visual systems." Edward E. Jones, who recently transferred to Princeton University after many years at Duke University, was selected for contributing "to basic knowledge of the processes by which the individual understands the social environment and acts upon it." His studies focused on social behavior designed to elicit desired responses and on processes by which individuals analyze the behavior of others.

Space exploration

NASA Award. Carl Sagan, David Duncan professor of astronomy and space sciences at Cornell University, was named recipient of the 1977 NASA Medal for Distinguished Public Service for "his outstanding contributions to NASA's scientific achievements and the distinguished service he has rendered the Nation in communicating to the public the value and significance of space science." Sagan played a leading role in the Mariner, Viking, and Voyager missions to the planets. He wrote a feature article on extraterrestrial life for the *1978 Yearbook of Science and the Future.*

Waterman Award. The second annual $150,000 Alan T. Waterman Award, authorized by the U.S. Congress and administered by the National Science Foundation, was presented in 1977 to J. William Schopf, professor of geology and geophysics at the University of California at Los Angeles. NASA called upon Schopf to examine the lunar materials returned by Apollos 11 and 12 for evidence of past or present life on the Moon. He later advised NASA on future explorations of terrestrial planets and satellites.

Transportation

AIAA Award. The American Institute of Aeronautics and Astronautics presented its 1977 Fluid and Plasmadynamics Award to Harvard Lomax of the NASA Ames Research Center in California. He was chosen for "contributions to the theoretical analysis of supersonic aerodynamics by small perturbation theory."

Collier Trophy. The U.S. National Aeronautic Association designated Gen. David C. Jones, chief of staff of the U.S. Air Force, and Robert Anderson, president and chief executive officer of Rockwell International Corp., recipients of its 1976 Collier Trophy. The two men represented "the USAF/Industry Team that successfully produced and demonstrated the B-1 Strategic Aircraft System."

Kremer Prize. A standing offer of £ 50,000 (about $86,000) for the first manpowered flight over a figure-eight course was finally awarded in 1977 to Paul MacCready, an aeronautical engineer and glider expert from California. The Royal Aeronautical Society, which administered the award in London, agreed that MacCready's 77-lb "Gossamer Condor," piloted by Bryan Allen, had met all requirements.

Science journalism

AAAS-Westinghouse Awards. Each year the American Association for the Advancement of Science administers journalism awards sponsored by the Westinghouse Electric Corp. A $1,000 prize is assigned to each of three categories: articles appearing in U.S. newspapers having a daily circulation exceeding

100,000; articles appearing in newspapers having a more limited circulation; and articles appearing in magazines intended for the general public. The first of the 1977 awards went to Robert C. Cowen for a series of four articles, "Coping with Nature's Forces," which appeared in the *Christian Science Monitor* (June 20–23, 1977). Lee Hotz and Lee Bowman, writing for the *News-Virginian* of Waynesboro, Va., were selected for a series of five articles, "Profile of a Stream" (Sept. 13–17, 1977). The magazine award was given to William Bennett and Joel Gurin for the article "Science That Frightens Scientists: The Great Debate Over DNA," which was published in the *Atlantic Monthly* (February 1977).

AIP-U.S. Steel Award. Steven Weinberg, senior scientist at the Smithsonian Astrophysical Observatory in Cambridge, Mass., and professor at Harvard University, was named winner of the American Institute of Physics-U.S. Steel Foundation Science-Writing Award for 1977. Weinberg was honored for his book *The First Three Minutes: A Modern View of the Origin of the Universe* (1977), in which he relates the theory of elementary particles to problems associated with the beginning of the universe.

Grady Award. The annual James T. Grady Award for Interpreting Chemistry for the Public was given in 1977 to Michael Woods, senior editor of the *Blade* in Toledo, Ohio. The American Chemical Society selected Woods for his more than 300 articles, many of which were drawn from primary scientific sources. His writing, often on complex topics, has been admired by scientists as well as by the general public.

Miscellaneous

Kalinga Prize. Each year since 1952 the Kalinga Prize for the Popularization of Science has been awarded to individuals for distinguished careers of public service that involved interpreting science as writers, editors, speakers, or radio program directors. UNESCO selected two recipients for the 1976 award: Aleksandr Oparin, a Soviet biochemist, and George Porter, a British chemist. The recipients are expected to spend a month or more in India studying its life and culture. The £1,000 honorarium is supplied by an Indian industrialist.

Longstreth Medal. The Franklin Institute of Philadelphia named Norris Fitz Dow, chairman of N. F. Doweave, Inc., in Pennsylvania, as recipient of its 1977 Longstreth Medal. Dow invented an exceptionally strong triaxial fabric, which has been described as the most important invention of its kind in modern history.

Science Talent Awards. The 37th annual Science Talent Search, sponsored by the Westinghouse Educational Foundation and administered by Science Service, produced the following winners in 1978. The first-place award, a $10,000 scholarship, was given to Michael S. Briggs of High Point High School in Beltsville, Md. For his project in the field of game theory, he devised a method for approximating the value (the least chance of winning) of infinite games. The second-place $8,000 scholarship went to Joseph P. Tanzi of Cranston High School East in Rhode Island for designing and building a computer with two memories. Winner of the third-place $8,000 scholarship was Philip G. King of Rumson-Fair Haven Regional High School in New Jersey, whose project involved an eight-error corrector for a digital transmission system. Three other winners each received a $6,000 scholarship: Samuel A. Weinberger of New Rochelle, N.Y.; Judith L. Bender of Honolulu, Hawaii; and Michael P. Mattis of Scarsdale, N.Y. Four others received scholarships worth $4,000: Lawrence R. Bergman of Bayside, N.Y.; Daniel S. Rokhsar of Staten Island, N.Y.; Ann Piening of Bethalto, Ill.; and Jay B. Stallman of Forest Hills, N.Y.

Michael Briggs

Joseph Tanzi

Philip King

Photos, courtesy, Westinghouse Electric Corp.

National Medal of Science. The U.S. government's highest scientific award, the National Medal of Science, is presented annually by the president of the U.S. to persons who have done outstanding work in the physical, biological, mathematical, or engineering sciences. The 1976 gold medalists were: Morris Cohen of the Massachusetts Institute of Technology, for research in metallurgy; Kurt O. Friedrichs of New York University, for mathematical research contributing to the theory of flight; Peter C. Goldmark of Goldmark Communication Corp. in Connecticut, for contributions to communications sciences; Samuel A. Goudsmit of the University of Nevada, for co-discovery of electron spin as the source of a new quantum number; Roger Guillemin of the Salk Institute for Biological Studies, for demonstrating the presence of a new class of brain hormones; Herbert S. Gutowsky of the University of Illinois, for pioneering studies in nuclear magnetic resonance spectroscopy; Erwin W. Mueller of Pennsylvania State University, for invention of the field-emission, field-ion, and atom-probe microscopes; Keith R. Porter of the University of Colorado, for electron microscopy; Efraim Racker of Cornell University, for work on oxidative and photosynthetic energy in living cells; Frederick D. Rossini of Rice University, for research in chemical thermodynamics; Verner E. Suomi of the University of Wisconsin, for research in meteorology; Henry Taube of Stanford University, for contributions to the understanding of reaction mechanisms in inorganic chemistry and nitrogen fixation; George E. Uhlenbeck of Rockefeller University, for co-discovery of electron spin as the source of a new quantum number; Hassler Whitney of the Institute for Advanced Studies in New Jersey, for founding the discipline of differential topology; and Edward O. Wilson of Harvard University for studies of insect societies.

Presidential Awards. Each year the Republic of Korea's Ministry of Science and Technology honors a scientist, an engineer, and a technician for scientific achievements during the preceding ten years. Recipients of the 1977 Presidential Awards, each of whom received an honorarium worth about $4,000, were scientist Jhon Mu-Shik, engineer Kim Do-Sim, and technician Yun Byung-Hack. Jhon, professor of chemistry at the Korea Advanced Institute of Science, has done research on the structure and properties of water and has applied his theory of significant liquid structure to high polymers, phase separation, hydrocarbon solution, physical absorption, and liquid crystals. Kim, director of the Korea Plastic Industry Corp., manufactured the first Korean high-pressure reactor and introduced numerous technological improvements that hastened the country's commercial development. Yun, who works at the Pohang Iron & Steel Co., is credited with inventing or designing new tools, devices, dies, and equipment that increased production and improved manufacturing techniques.

Obituaries

The following persons, all of whom died in recent months, were widely recognized for their scientific accomplishments.

Adrian, Edgar Douglas Adrian, 1st Baron, of Cambridge (Nov. 30, 1889—Aug. 4, 1977), British electrophysiologist, shared the Nobel Prize for Physiology or Medicine (1932) with Sir Charles Sherrington for discoveries relating to the nerve cell (neuron) and its processes. Adrian graduated (1915) from Trinity College, Cambridge, where he spent a major portion of his professional career conducting research on nerve impulses that led to a better understanding of the physical basis of sensation and the mechanism of muscular control. His studies (1934) on the electrical activity of the brain opened new fields of investigation in epilepsy and in the location of cerebral lesions. Adrian was awarded the Order of Merit in 1942. He subsequently served as president of the Royal Society (1950–55) and was created a baron in 1955. His writings include *The Basis of Sensation* (1928) and *The Physical Background of Perception* (1947).

Barach, Alvan Leroy (Feb. 22, 1895—Dec. 13, 1977), U.S. physician, was a specialist in respiratory therapy who devised the first practical ventilated oxygen tent (1920s), and later discovered that helium-pressure breathing and the immobilizing lung chamber effectively aided persons afflicted with asthma and other lung disorders. He also initiated the development of a mechanical coughing device which relieved patients of life-endangering secretions accumulated in the lungs and bronchial tubes. After receiving his medical degree from Columbia University's College of Physicians and Surgeons, Barach began studying respiratory physiology at Harvard Medical School and Massachusetts General Hospital (1920–21). He continued his research at Presbyterian Hospital in New York and was associate professor of clinical medicine at Columbia.

Barbour, George Brown (Aug. 22, 1890—July 11, 1977), British-born geologist, made important geological expeditions in China where he was involved in the discovery of Peking man, whose remains were found (1920s) in a cave at Chou-k'ou-tien. This discovery established that Peking man, now classified as *Homo erectus*, flourished about 500,000 years ago, and was the last link in the evolution of *Homo sapiens* (modern man). Barbour's worldwide travels also took him to South Africa where he sought to determine the geological setting in which prehistoric man roamed the Transvaal veld more than one million years ago. Barbour obtained his Ph.D. from Columbia University (1929) and served as dean (1938–58) and professor of geology (1938–60) at the University of Cincinnati. His 20-year friendship with Pierre Teilhard de Chardin, French paleontologist and philosopher, was highlighted in *In the Field with Teilhard de Chardin* (1965).

Beams, Jesse Wakefield (Dec. 25, 1898—July 23, 1977), U.S. physicist, developed (1934) an air-driven, vacuum-enclosed ultracentrifuge, which produced centrifugal forces millions of times greater than that of gravity and enabled him to obtain the first separation of isotopes by centrifuging (1935). Several years later Beams achieved the successful separation of the fissionable isotope ^{235}U from naturally occurring uranium. Following World War II he invented a much improved ultracentrifuge that was levitated and spun magnetically; this device soon became a basic tool in research laboratories and allowed the purification and characterization of many substances of high molecular weight, including proteins and heavy viruses. He also devised the magnetic densitometer, which determined the partial specific volume of a molecule, a necessary step in determining the absolute value of its weight by centrifugation. After receiving his Ph.D. from the University of Virginia in 1925, he returned there in 1928 as associate professor of physics and served as chairman of the department from 1948 to 1962. Although Beams retired from teaching in 1969, he continued to make significant contributions to physics and biophysics and invented a method for measuring the constant of universal gravitation.

Bramlette, Milton Nunn (Feb. 4, 1896—March 31, 1977), U.S. geologist, conducted an investigation (1930s) of the transatlantic series of Piggott cores, a study of deep-sea stratigraphy that led to the first transoceanic correlation of glacial deposits. He also made petrological studies in California, where he tried to determine the genesis of the extensively bedded cherts of the Monterey Formation. In his classic paper on this formation he suggested a polygenetic mode of origin of cherts. A forerunner in the field of Earth history, he also studied the fossil coccoliths, tiny organisms that sink so slowly into the sea that they are distributed by currents worldwide. Bramlett's research of these marine sediments was the prelude to a geologic history connecting the entire Earth. In 1936, 15 years after graduating from the University of Wisconsin, Bramlette obtained his Ph.D. from Yale University. He was a member of the U.S. Geological Survey (1921–24 and 1931–41), and a geologist for the Gulf Oil Corp. (1925–29) before moving to the University of California at Los Angeles (1941–51). He then transferred to San Diego, Calif., where he became professor at the Scripps Institution of Oceanography.

Brauer, Richard Dagobert (Feb. 10, 1901—April 17, 1977), German-born mathematician, collaborated (1934–35) with Hermann Weyl on a classical exposition of spinors, and thus provided the mathematical background used by Nobel laureate Paul Dirac for his theory of the spinning electron. Brauer then became interested in the mathematical work of Ferdinand Frobenius, who introduced group characters in 1896. Brauer carried forward Frobenius' work and developed a theory of modular characters that gave new insights into the study of group characters and advanced the development of algebra. In the late 1950s he began formulating a method for classifying finite simple groups, a task that absorbed his attention for the rest of his life. Brauer studied in Berlin under the renowned algebraist Issai Schur, and taught at Königsberg until 1933. In 1935 he accepted a position at the University of Toronto but moved to the U.S. in 1948, where he became a member of the faculties at the University of Michigan (1948–52) and Harvard University (1952–71).

Braun, Wernher von (March 23, 1912—June 16, 1977), German-born space scientist, was already fascinated with space travel when he began building rockets at age 12, and by age 18 was one of a dedicated group of amateurs and engineers experimenting with rockets. After Braun received a Ph.D. in engineering physics (1934) from the University of Berlin, he was employed by the German Army and directed a research team that produced a series of liquid-propellant rockets, notably the V-2 that devastated London in 1944–45. At the end of World War II, Braun and his team of scientists and engineers surrendered to the U.S. and accepted positions with the U.S. Army Ordnance Corps to do research at Ft. Bliss, Texas, and later at Huntsville, Ala. In 1950 he became a U.S. citizen. In 1960 Braun and his team were transferred from the U.S. Army Ballistic Missile Agency to the newly formed National Aeronautics and Space Administra-

Wernher von Braun

Courtesy, NASA

tion (NASA) George C. Marshall Space Flight Center, with Braun serving as its director. The Braun NASA team launched the first U.S. satellite, Explorer 1, on Jan. 31, 1958, and on July 16, 1969, Apollo 11, powered by the Saturn V rocket developed and designed by Braun, carried the first astronauts to land on the Moon. The same rocket was also used to launch the first U.S. space station (Skylab) into orbit on May 14, 1973. He retired from NASA in 1972 to become vice-president of Fairchild Industries, Inc., in Germantown, Md. Braun wrote hundreds of articles and several books, including, with others, *Across the Space Frontier* (1952), *History of Rocketry and Space Travel* (1966), and *The Rocket's Red Glare* (1976).

Budker, Gersh Itskovich (May 1, 1918—July 1977), Soviet physicist, was an innovative designer of accelerators who devised a series of storage rings, the first operating in 1963. His second (1967) was an electron positron device, VEPP-2 of 2 × 700 MeV, and the third (1972), VEPP-3 of 2 × 2.2 GeV, was used for synchrotron radiation research. The fourth, VEPP-4 of 2 × 7 GeV, was still under construction at the time of Budker's death. Besides developing a process by which a beam of electrons collides with a beam of positrons, Budker inaugurated an electron cooling method for narrowing the beams of protons and antiprotons. After graduating (1941) from Moscow State University he joined (1946) Igor V. Kurchatov at the Institute of Atomic Energy of the U.S.S.R. Academy of Sciences, where the first Soviet atomic bomb was produced (1949). In 1957 he was appointed director of the Nuclear Physics Institute of the Siberian branch of the Soviet Academy of Sciences, a position he held until his death.

Chick, Dame Harriette (Jan. 6, 1875—July 9, 1977), British nutritionist, carried forward the study of nutrition for over 50 years. After graduating from University College in London, she worked at the Hygienic Institutes of Vienna and Munich under Max Gruber. In 1904 she was made a doctor of science for her work on the function of green algae in polluted waters. In 1905 Chick went to the Lister Institute, where she examined disinfectants, blood proteins, and antitoxins. In 1914 she turned from bacteriology to nutrition and recommended that Allied soldiers serving in Egypt and Palestine during World War I supplement their diets with dried eggs and dried yeast to combat a nutritional disorder resembling beriberi. In 1919 she jointly led a team to study nutrition and rickets in postwar Vienna and proved that rickets could be treated, cured, and prevented with cod liver oil and exposure to ultraviolet light. Returning to London in 1922, Chick continued her research on proteins and vitamins, particularly vitamin B and cereal protein (which produced Britain's World War II "national loaf" in 1940). She retired in 1946, but at the age of 100 attended the annual general meeting of the Lister Institute. Chick was made a dame of the British Empire in 1949.

Cohen of Birkenhead, Henry Cohen, 1st Baron (b. Feb. 21, 1900—d. Aug. 7, 1977), British physician, was highly regarded both for his expertise in clinical medicine and for his administrative ability within the British National Health Service (NHS). After graduating with honors in medicine from the University of Liverpool (1924), Cohen was appointed an assistant physician to the Royal Infirmary. In 1934 he returned to his alma mater, where he spent the greater part (1934–65) of his professional career as professor of medicine. His acute memory and speaking ability served him well when he was called upon to assist in establishing the NHS. He became first vice-chairman of the Central Health Services Council in 1949 and chairman in 1957. Cohen also served as president of both the British Medical Association (1951) and the General Medical Council (1961). He was knighted in 1949 and raised to the peerage in 1956.

Cotzias, George Constantin (June 16, 1918—June 13, 1977), Greek-born neurologist, was a research scientist whose systematic and persistent investigations into the metabolism of the brain proved that Levodihydroxyphenylalanine (L-dopa) could reverse most or all major manifestations of Parkinson's disease, a chronic malady affecting the central nervous system. His revolutionary therapeutic agent remedied the deficiency of dopamine in the brain, thereby eliminating the need for brain surgery. L-dopa, which was introduced into the practice of medicine in the 1970s, proved effective against brain damage from manganese poisoning, and remained the preferred treatment for patients afflicted with Parkinson's disease, despite its sometimes toxic side effects. Cotzias, who graduated (1943) from Harvard Medical School, was associated with Rockefeller Institute (1947–52) but spent the major portion of his career (1953–75) as the head of the Physiology Division of the Medical Research Center at Brookhaven National Laboratory in New York.

Eiseley, Loren Corey (Sept. 3, 1907—July 7, 1977), U.S. anthropologist, eloquently expounded his theories on the mysteries of man and nature in a poetic style that bridged the gap between art and science. Eiseley perhaps best expressed the motivation for his career as writer, scientist, and educator in the essay "The Enchanted Glass," which concerns the role of the contemplative naturalist in a technological world. He recalled in his autobiography, *All the Strange Hours* (1975), that his interest in anthropology had been kindled under the influence of William Duncan Strong, who discovered (1946) the ten-century-old tomb of the Peruvian warrior god, Ai apaec. Eiseley graduated (1937) from the University of Pennsylvania, where he later taught for some 30 years. His national reputation was established through such books as *The Immense Journey* (1957), *Darwin's Century* (1958), *The Mind as Nature* (1962), *The Invisible Pyramid* (1970), and *The Night Country* (1971).

Loren Eiseley

Falconer, Murray Alexander (b. May 15, 1910—d. Aug. 11, 1977), New Zealand neurosurgeon, gained international renown for his contributions to psychosurgery and the surgical treatment of epilepsy. He was graduated in medicine from Otago University in Dunedin, and then became a fellow of the Royal College of Surgeons of England in 1935 and a master in surgery in 1938. He was a fellow of the Mayo Clinic in Minnesota, was Nuffield Dominions fellow in surgery at Oxford University, and served in the Royal Army Medical Corps in World War II until he was appointed associate professor of neurosurgery at Otago University in 1943. In 1950 he returned to England to direct the neurosurgical units of Guy's, Maudsley, and King's College hospitals before retiring in 1975.

Fieser, Louis Frederick (April 7, 1899—July 25, 1977), U.S. chemist, developed a synthesis for vitamin K, a naphthoquinone compound present in the green leaves of plants and a substance vital in the complicated process involved in blood-clotting. He has also been credited with helping to develop processes used in preparing cortisone from abundant raw materials. Fieser's research led to the invention of napalm, a jelly-like gasoline mixture first used as an incendiary in flamethrowers and fire bombs during World War II. He also did considerable research on carcinogens, attempting to understand the cancer-producing roles of certain chemicals. Fieser graduated from Harvard University (1924), where he became (1930) a professor of organic chemistry. Besides some 300 research papers, Fieser wrote *Organic Chemistry, Style Guide for Chemists,* and *Reagents for Organic Synthesis.*

Goldblatt, Harry (March 14, 1891—Jan. 6, 1977), U.S. pathologist, conducted experiments in hypertension that established a direct relationship between high blood pressure in humans and the amount of blood supplied to the kidneys. Later he established a new international standard (Goldblatt unit) for measuring human renin, an enzyme produced in the kidney that raises blood pressure by breaking down a protein present in the blood plasma. Goldblatt's research interests also focused on the development of such diseases as rickets, cancer, and peritonitis. After earning his M.D. (1916) from McGill University in Montreal, Goldblatt became assistant professor of pathology (1924) at Western Reserve University School of Medicine in Cleveland, Ohio, and director (1953–75) in Cleveland of the Louis D. Beaumont Memorial Research Laboratories.

Goldmark, Peter Carl (Dec. 2, 1906—Dec. 7, 1977), Hungarian-born engineer, developed the first color television system used in commercial broadcasts (1940) and the 33⅓-rpm long-playing (LP) phonograph record (1948), both while working for the Columbia Broadcasting System Laboratories from 1936 to 1971. The LP, which permitted the equivalent of six 78-rpm records to be compressed into one 33⅓-rpm disk, was a major innovation in the recording industry. Goldmark, who became a vice-president of CBS in 1950 and president of CBS Laboratories in 1954, was also credited with the development of an electronic video recording (EVR) system which recorded television images on unperforated plastic film stored in cartridges for viewing through any standard television receiver (black and white or color). He also invented a scanning system that allowed spacecraft to relay photographs 238,000 mi from the Moon to Earth. Two weeks before his death, Goldmark was awarded the National Medal

Peter Goldmark

of Science by Pres. Jimmy Carter for his contributions to communications, education, and culture.

Green, George Kenneth (Nov. 3, 1911—Aug. 15, 1977), U.S. physicist, designed and supervised the construction of atomic particle accelerators, notably the first proton synchrotron to exceed one billion electron volts and the alternating gradient synchrotron at Brookhaven National Laboratory in New York. Using these facilities, scientists made important fundamental discoveries about the particles that constitute the nucleus of an atom. Green, who earned his Ph.D. in physics from the University of Illinois, entered the U.S. Army Signal Corps (1942), where he helped invent the proximity fuse, a triggering mechanism for firing artillery and rockets. He joined Brookhaven in 1947 as a senior scientist and soon established himself as one of the world's finest particle accelerator designers. One of his last major contributions was the designing of a synchrotron radiation facility to be called the National Synchrotron Light Source.

Haagen-Smit, Arie Jan (Dec. 22, 1900—March 17, 1977), Dutch-born biochemist, conducted ozone experiments that dramatically demonstrated the then little-understood dangers of air pollution. As a result of Haagen-Smit's work, pollution of the air was viewed for the first time as a serious and urgent problem. Almost single-handedly Haagen-Smit battled oil and auto industries which were blamed for the chemical pollutants emanating from petroleum facilities and auto exhausts. These industries not only refused to accept Haagen-Smit's findings but engaged scientists to disprove his claims. The accuracy of his theory was confirmed by these studies with only minor modifications. An outstanding teacher and research scientist at the California Institute of Technology (1937–71), Haagen-Smit received such honors as the Hodgkins Medal of the Smithsonian Institution, the National Medal of Science, and the $150,000 John and Alice Tyler Ecology Award.

Heezen, Bruce Charles (April 11, 1924—June 21, 1977), U.S. oceanographer, confirmed through his maps and expeditions with Maurice Ewing that the several great sections of the known active oceanic ridges and rifts form a continuous 45,000-mi network. Heezen, whose findings constituted a landmark in geology and lent credence to the theory of plate tectonics, also discovered the role of underwater flows of suspended sediments, called turbidity currents, in shaping the contours of the seafloor. He obtained his Ph.D. (1957) from Columbia University and was associated with the Lamont-Doherty Geological Observatory in New York since its founding in 1949. Heezen used deep-diving submarines to explore seafloor features, and at the time of his death was aboard the navy research submarine NR-1 en route to submerged mid-Atlantic mountains off the coast of Iceland.

Helpern, Milton (April 17, 1902—April 22, 1977), U.S. forensic pathologist, was widely regarded as one

of the most erudite and skillful medical examiners in the history of New York City, where he served for more than 40 years (1931–74). Though Helpern had an extensive knowledge of anatomy, toxicology, and related fields, it was his uncanny ability to utilize this knowledge to uncover and interpret evidence that made him

UPI Compix

Milton Helpern

so successful. As a consequence, he was repeatedly called upon to play the role of key witness in murder trials and often gave testimony that proved decisive when juries deliberated. Helpern received his medical degree (1926) from Cornell University Medical College and became interested in forensic pathology while completing his internship at Bellevue Hospital, New York City. He also contributed to *Legal Medicine: Pathology and Toxicology*, a 1,350-page work that became a classic in its field.

Hill, Archibald Vivian (Sept. 26, 1886—June 3, 1977), British physiologist, shared the Nobel Prize for Physiology or Medicine in 1922 for discoveries relating to heat production in muscles that helped establish the fact that muscular force originates in the breakdown of carbohydrates with the formation of lactic acid in the absence of oxygen. Hill studied the sartorius muscle (a straplike thigh muscle) of the frog and determined that oxygen is required only for the recovery, not the contractile, phase of muscular activity. This research led to the discovery of the series of biochemical reactions that take place when muscles contract. Hill, who began his physiological studies at the University of Cambridge in 1911, shared the Nobel Prize with German biochemist Otto Meyerhof. Hill was the Royal Society's Foulerton research professor from 1926 to 1951, and from 1940 until 1945 was an Independent Conservative member of Parliament for the University of Cambridge. After World War II he reestablished his laboratory for biophysical research at University College, London. His writings include *Muscular Activity* (1926), *Living Machinery* (1927), and *Muscular Movement in Man* (1927).

Hobbs, Leonard Sinclair (Dec. 20, 1896—Nov. 1, 1977), U.S. engineer, was chief engineer (1927–58) of Pratt & Whitney Aircraft (now United Technologies Corp.) when he developed the engines that powered the first U.S. jetliners and B-52 intercontinental bombers. When Hobbs's J-57 engine was installed in the F-100 Super Sabre fighter, the airplane attained a speed exceeding 750 mph and was the most powerful aircraft engine in the world, producing a thrust equivalent to 40,000 hp. This engine was also commercially adapted to power the Boeing 707, served as a model for succeeding engines, including those for Boeing 747 jumbo jets, and initiated the airline industry's transition from propeller to jet airplanes. Early in his career, Hobbs designed the carburetor for the "Spirit of St. Louis," which Charles Lindbergh flew on his historic trip from New York to Paris in May 1927. Hobbs retired in 1958 and served on United's board of directors until 1968.

Ilyushin, Sergey Vladimirovich (March 30 [March 18, old style], 1894—Feb. 9, 1977), Soviet aircraft designer, established his reputation with his heavily

Sergey V. Ilyushin

Wide World

armored attack airplane, the Il-2 Stormovik, used by the Soviet Union during World War II. The Soviets called it "the flying tank," but German troops dubbed the dive bomber "black death" because of its devastating power. Ilyushin designed approximately 50 airplanes, including the Il-18 Moskva four-engine turboprop transport (1957) used extensively throughout Eastern Europe and China, and the Il-28, the Soviet Union's first jet bomber (1948). Among his other notable accomplishments were the Il-62 turbojet transport (1962) used for flights between Moscow and New York beginning in 1968, and the Il-86 four-engine, 350-seat airbus, which made its first flight in 1976. Before qualifying as a pilot in 1917, Ilyushin served as a mechanic in the Russian Imperial Army's air arm. He subsequently entered the Zhukovsky Air Force Engineering Academy in Moscow, graduating from there in 1926. He became a lieutenant general in the Engineering and Technical Service and professor at the Zhukovsky Academy. Ilyushin was awarded the Order of Lenin several times.

Keenan, Joseph Henry (Aug. 24, 1900—July 17, 1977), U.S. engineer, was an expert on engineering thermodynamics whose studies and writings on the properties of steam revolutionized teaching throughout the world. His *Steam Tables* (1930, 1936, and 1969) became basic tools for generations of students and engineers as were the *Air Tables* and *Gas Tables* of which he was co-author. In recent years, his adaptation of Josiah Willard Gibbs's thermodynamic concepts to steady-flow engineering processes influenced the formulation of U.S. energy policy. Two of his major works are *Thermodynamics* (1941), which remains a standard reference, and *Principles of General Thermodynamics* (1965), which clarifies conceptual difficulties encountered in the study of thermodynamics. After graduating (1922) from the Massachusetts Institute of Technology, he became a steam-turbine engineer with General Electric Co. In 1928 he became assistant professor of mechanical engineering at Stevens Institute of Technology in New Jersey, but returned (1934) to MIT where he became professor and head of the department of mechanical engineering (1958–61).

Kleinschmidt, Edward E. (Sept. 9, 1875—Aug. 9, 1977), German-born inventor, created and introduced (1914) the Teletype machine, which doubled the existing Morse code reception rate of 30 words a minute and represented a major breakthrough in communications. Though Kleinschmidt was a tinkerer by nature and had little formal education, he held over 100 patents and became a multimillionaire for his many inventions, which included the high-speed stock market ticker, an automatic fishing reel, various railway signaling devices, and a police radio-teleprinter. His company, which after merging with its only competitor became successively known as Morkun-Kleinschmidt and then Teletype Corp., was acquired in 1930 by the American

Edward Kleinschmidt

Telephone and Telegraph Co. in exchange for 150,000 shares of AT&T stock. The teletype stock was then turned over to Western Electric Co.

Kompfner, Rudolf (May 16, 1901—Dec. 3, 1977), Austrian-born physicist, invented the traveling-wave tube, a device used to generate microwave frequency radiation or to amplify ultrahigh frequency (UHF) waves. This electron tube, improved and refined, has been used in telecommunications, defense, and space guidance systems because it can produce high-powered amplification of microwave energy. After graduating from the Technical University of Vienna, where he studied architecture, Kompfner developed a fascination for microwave electronics, radio engineering, and physics. At the University of Oxford he earned a Ph.D. in the sciences, and collected more than 50 patents for inventions in radio and electronics. He undertook research for the British Royal Naval Science Service (1944–51) before joining Bell Laboratories in New Jersey as director of electronics and radio research, later serving as associate executive director of research and communication sciences (1962–73).

Lee, Benjamin W. (Lɪ Hᴜɪ Sᴏ) (Jan. 1, 1935—June 16, 1977), Korean-born physicist, was a leading theorist in the field of particle physics and a principal investigator of gauge theories, which use concepts of symmetry to better understand the four forces known to operate in nature, particularly the way they govern the interaction of elementary particles in such phenomena as nuclear binding, radioactive decay, and

behavior during high-energy collisions. Lee took special interest in applying gauge theories in a scheme to show that the widely differing properties of the electromagnetic force, which is responsible for all electric and magnetic phenomena, and the weak force, which governs certain decay processes, derive from a common fundamental origin. Lee taught (1960–66) at the University of Pennsylvania, his alma mater, and at the State University of New York at Stony Brook (1966–73) before joining (1973) the Fermi National Accelerator Laboratory in Batavia, Ill., the site of the world's largest proton synchrotron. Lee also found time to teach at the University of Chicago Enrico Fermi Institute.

Levy, David Mordecai (April 27, 1892—March 2, 1977), U.S. psychiatrist, introduced (1926) the Rorschach test in the U.S., a method of psychological testing in which a trained professional interprets a subject's description of what he sees in a series of inkblots. Levy, an innovator in child therapy, was credited with coining the phrase "sibling rivalry" and originating "activity-play therapy," which proved to be a useful method of evaluating a child's emotions. He received his medical degree (1918) from the University of Chicago. While in Chicago, he organized a mental-hygiene clinic for children at Michael Reese Hospital. Levy was later associated with numerous New York institutions, notably the Psychoanalytic Clinic for Training Research, Henry Ittleson Center for Child Research, and New York State Psychiatric Institute.

Lilly, Eli (April 1, 1885—Jan. 24, 1977), U.S. pharmaceutical chemist, played a leading role in shaping modern pharmacology while serving as president (1932–48) and chairman (1948–61, 1966–69) of the

Eli Lilly

428

company founded by his grandfather. Eli Lilly & Co. developed such drugs as insulin for diabetes and liver extract for pernicious anemia (1920s), barbiturates (1930s), penicillins and Salk polio vaccine (1940–50s), and new agricultural compounds used for weed control and animal health (1960–70s). Lilly began to work in the family business when he was ten years old and in 1907 received his degree as a pharmaceutical chemist from the Philadelphia College of Pharmacy and Science. After being named superintendent of the company's manufacturing division in 1909, he quickly gained an edge on competitors by being the first to make efficiency in the manufacturing of products one of his top priorities.

Littlewood, John Edensor (June 9, 1885—Sept. 6, 1977), British mathematician, was a theoretician whose work, particularly during a 35-year period of collaboration with Godfrey H. Hardy, led to impressive discoveries in the theory of series, the Riemann zeta function, inequalities, and theory of functions. Their series of papers entitled "Partitio numerorum" utilized the new Hardy-Ramanujan-Littlewood analytical method. Littlewood was a scholar of Trinity College, Cambridge, where he became a life fellow, and Rouse Ball professor of mathematics. At 30 he was elected a fellow of the Royal Society and later received its Royal (1929), Sylvester (1943), and Copley (1958) medals.

Luria, Aleksandr Romanovich (July 16 [July 3, old style], 1902—Aug. 14, 1977), Soviet neuropsychologist, specialized in research that led to an understanding of brain functions and to the treatment of persons afflicted with brain damage. He headed the Moscow Institute of Defectology and Budenko Institute of Neurosurgery, Moscow. His pioneering work with L. S. Vygotskiy in Moscow on the structure of thought, speech, nervous activities, and play in children, particularly abnormal children, proved valuable during World War II when he undertook the rehabilitation of soldiers who had sustained head wounds. He also worked in the area of child development and suggested that retarded children be placed in special schools according to their individual handicaps. Two of his major works were *The Nature of Human Conflicts* (1932) and *Higher Cortical Functions in Man*, which was published in English in 1966. Luria received his education at Kazan V. I. Lenin State University and at the Moscow Medical Institute.

Mueller, Erwin Wilhelm (June 13, 1911—May 17, 1977), German-born physicist, devised the field ion microscope (1955), which has a magnification of one million times. Using this instrument, he became the first person to observe visually the images of single atoms located on a metal surface and the atomic structures and atomic processes that occur on such a surface. Mueller, who also invented the field emission microscope and the atom probe, graduated from the Technical University of Berlin, where he studied under Nobel laureate Gustav Hertz. Before migrating to the U.S. in 1952, Mueller taught physics at the Kaiser Wilhelm Institute for Physical Chemistry from 1947 to 1952. He joined the faculty of Pennsylvania State University in 1952, where he remained until his retirement in 1976.

Muschenheim, Carl (Feb. 4, 1905—April 27, 1977), U.S. physician, revolutionized the treatment of tuberculosis by introducing the use of isonicotinic hydrazide, a drug that reduced the death rate from tuberculosis in the U.S. by some 70%. Having been afflicted with tuberculosis as a resident physician in the early 1930s, Muschenheim turned to research and became one of the country's leading authorities on diseases of the lung and an ardent advocate of better health care, especially for the Eskimos and American Indians. After graduating from Columbia College and Columbia University's College of Physicians and Surgeons, he served on the staffs of Bellevue Hospital and New York Hospital before joining (1946) the faculty of Cornell University Medical College. In 1955 his contributions to medical science were given special recognition when he received an Albert Lasker medical research award.

Pitts, Robert Franklin (Oct. 24, 1908—June 6, 1977), U.S. physiologist, was a medical research scientist whose studies of kidney functions and the nervous system led to an understanding of diuretic drugs used to eliminate excess water in the kidneys of persons afflicted with heart disease and hypertension. Pitts discovered that the manner in which the kidney excretes acidic wastes governs the body's delicate biochemical balance between acidic and alkaline states. These findings prompted Pitts to feed salt water and intravenous fluids to patients after surgery, a procedure that gradually became routine therapy. A graduate of New York University, where he earned his medical degree (1938), he was chairman of the department of physiology of Cornell University Medical College (1950–74) and a research professor at the University of Florida in Gainesville. His books include *The Physiological Basis of Diuretic Therapy* (1959) and *Physiology of the Kidney and Body Fluids* (1963).

Reid, Donald Darnley (May 6, 1914—March 26, 1977), British epidemiologist, specialized in respiratory and cardiovascular diseases and was especially noted for his work on the etiology of bronchitis. Through his research on bronchitis, he became an acknowledged expert on the health hazards associated with air pollutants and cigarette smoke. Reid was able to distinguish genetic from environmental influences on health by comparing the incidence of disease among migrants in Britain, Britons themselves, and persons in the migrants' home countries. He graduated from the University of Aberdeen in Scotland (1946) and spent a major portion of his career as professor of epidemiology at the London School of Hygiene and Tropical Medicine, University of London, and as the director of the Department of Medical Statistics and Epidemiology.

Jean Rostand

Rostand, Jean (Oct. 30, 1894—Sept. 3, 1977), French biologist, was known to the scientific world for his research on genes and chromosomes and for his experiments in parthenogenesis. The general public, however, knew him better as an outspoken advocate of peace and abortion and as the author of satirical and moral writings. He was, for example, a vociferous opponent of France's Pacific Ocean nuclear tests in 1970. In such books as *Can Man Be Modified?, Thoughts of a Biologist,* and *Misgivings of a Biologist*, Rostand simultaneously popularized biology and his own philosophical views, which were couched in such phrases as "science has made gods of us before we were ever worthy of being men." He was elected to the French Academy in 1959.

Thornton, Sir (Henry) Gerard (Jan. 22, 1892—Feb. 6, 1977), was a forerunner in the study of soil bacteriology whose research on biological nitrogen fixation in root-nodulated leguminous plants established the bacteroid (an irregularly shaped bacterium) as the nitrogen-fixing site in the nodule. He also outlined the role of ineffective, non-fixing nodules. Thornton, who began his work when the study of soil microbiology was in primitive stages, devised techniques for isolating, identifying, and counting bacteria in the soil, and became one of the first to use statistics for enumerating bacteria. His investigations regarding the effects of competing strains in soil led to the development of inoculants for leguminous crops. An enthusiastic amateur

archaeologist, Thornton discovered a new species of plesiosaur, which is housed in the British Museum (Natural History). After graduating from the University of Oxford, he joined (1919) the Department of Soil Microbiology at Rothamsted Experimental Station outside London, and headed the department from 1940 to 1957.

Tréfouël, Jacques (Nov. 9, 1897—July 11, 1977), French chemist, discovered (1936) the chemotherapeutic properties of sulfanilamide and its effectiveness in fighting bacterial infections. His success sparked a revolution in therapeutic medicine. Tréfouël and his wife synthesized over 100 derivatives of sulfanilamide (first synthesized in 1908), and extracted the sulfones that later proved to be effective in chemotherapeutic treatment of leprosy. The protracted use of sulfone drugs is now standard treatment in combating this disease. Tréfouël, who studied under the French chemotherapist Ernest Fourneau, resumed the work of Nobel laureate Paul Ehrlich, the first to discover a cure for syphilis. Tréfouël's entire career (1921–65) was spent at the Pasteur Institute in Paris, where he was named director-general in 1940.

Trueta, Joseph (Oct. 27, 1897—Jan. 19, 1977), Spanish surgeon, developed such effective new techniques for the treatment of war wounds that doctors were able to avoid amputating many badly damaged limbs. Educated at the University of Barcelona, Trueta specialized in accident surgery and became an assistant professor at the University of Barcelona and director of surgery at the General Hospital of Catalonia. He moved to England before Barcelona fell to the Nationalists (1939) and was in charge of the accident service at the Radcliffe Infirmary, Oxford (1942–44). Trueta was later appointed Nuffield professor of orthopedic surgery at the University of Oxford (1949–68). His textbooks published in English include *Treatment of War Wounds and Fractures* (1939) and *An Atlas of Traumatic Surgery* (1949).

Vickers, Harry Franklin (Oct. 10, 1898—Jan. 12, 1977), U.S. hydraulic engineer, shortly after World War I established his own company where he developed the balanced vane pump which is especially important in the oil industry, the first practical power steering for heavy vehicles, naval and aircraft hydraulic power systems, and power brakes. Vickers' company, which became a subsidiary of Sperry Corp. during World War II, produced hydraulic power systems for airplanes, tanks, ships, and guns. In 1952 he became president of Sperry Corp., which merged (1955) with Remington Rand Inc. to become Sperry Rand Corp. Its electronic data processing division eventually made large profits with Univac, the first commercial computer to handle numerical and alphabetical information with equal ease. Vickers, who acquired some 95 patents, retired as chairman of the board and chief executive officer of Sperry Rand Corp. in 1967.

Index

Index entries to feature and review articles in this and previous editions of the *Yearbook of Science and the Future* are set in boldface type, *e.g.,* **Astronomy.** Entries to other subjects are set in lightface type, *e.g.,* Radiation. Additional information on any of these subjects is identified with a subheading and indented under the entry heading. The numbers following headings and subheadings indicate the year (boldface) of the edition and the page number (lightface) on which the information appears.

All entry headings, whether consisting of a single word or more, are treated for the purpose of alphabetization as single complete headings and are alphabetized letter by letter up to the punctuation. The abbreviation "il." indicates an illustration.

Acknowledgments

6   Photos by (top left and bottom left) William S. Weems—Woodfin Camp; (top right) Chuck Nicklin; (center left) Joy Spurr—Bruce Coleman, Inc.; (bottom right) Riccardo Levi-Setti, University of Chicago. Illustration by (center right) John Youssi

12–13   Illustration by John Craig

72   (Detail) adapted from G. D. Sales and J. D. Pye, *Ultrasonic Communication by Animals*, p. 63, Chapman and Hall Ltd., London, 1974

73   (Detail) adapted from Robert Burton, *The Life and Death of Whales*, p. 42, Universe Books, New York, 1973

82   Adapted from *Popular Science*, March 1976, p. 75, with permission © 1976 Times Mirror Magazines, Inc.

91   Adapted from information obtained from Sandia Laboratories

100   Adapted from information obtained from Lockheed Missiles and Space Company

104, 110, 111   Illustrations by John Draves

136   Adapted from *New England Journal of Medicine*, Dec. 1, 1977, p. 1193

153   Illustration by John Youssi

157, 158   Illustrations by John Youssi, adapted from *National Geographic*, November 1976, pp. 584–585

174   Illustration by Dave Beckes

177, 181   Illustrations by Eraldo Carugati

196, 197   Illustrations by Dave Beckes